CW01620019

ART IN FLORENCE

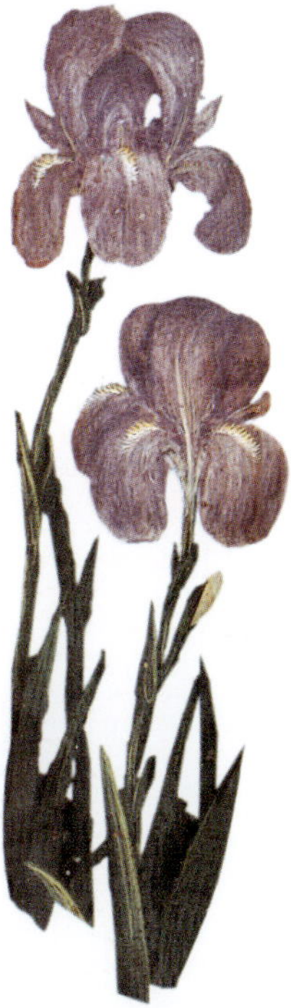

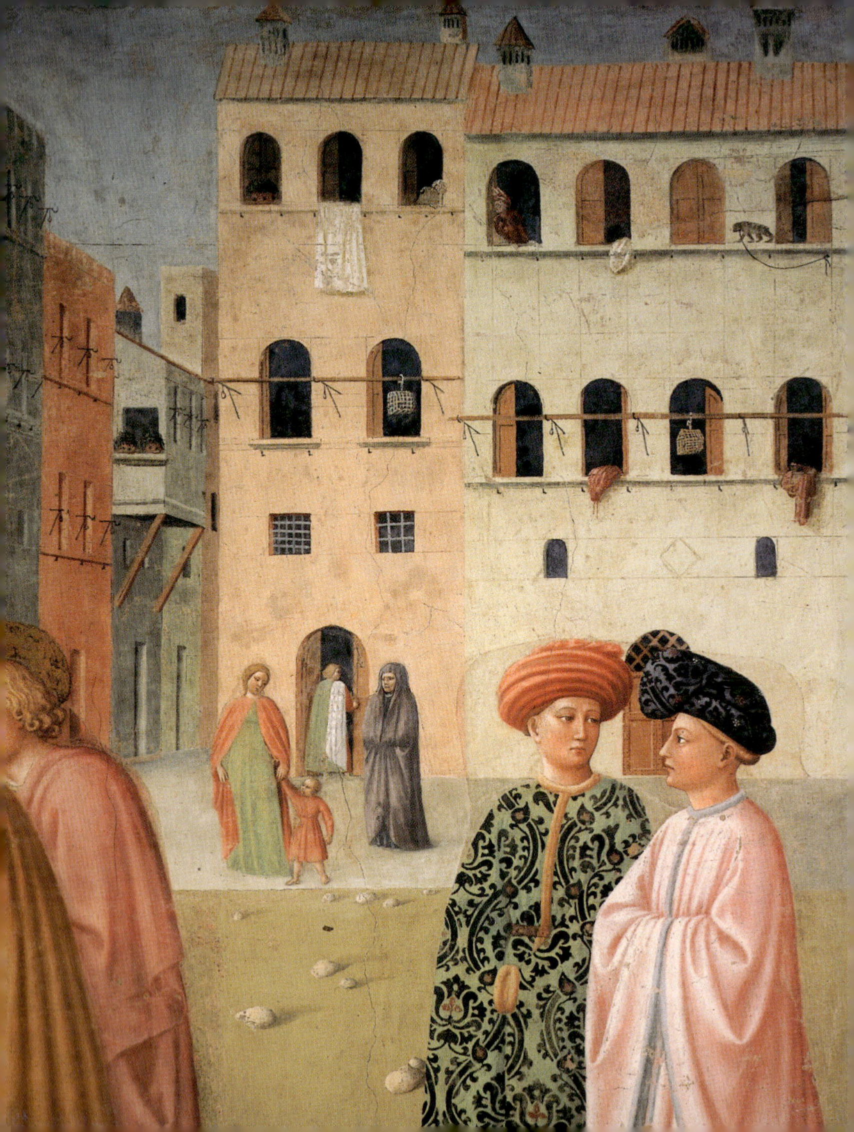

GLORIA FOSSI

ART IN FLORENCE

GIUNTI

To Matteo

Editorial project, texts and selection of pictures:
Gloria Fossi
Translation:
Catherine Frost
Graphics and page format:
Cristina Baruffi

Iconographic research:
Cristina Reggioli
Editorial assistance:
Giovanni Bartoli

www. giunti.it

© 2006 Giunti Editore S.p.A.
Via Bolognese 165 - 50139 Florence, Italy
Via Dante 4 - 20121 Milan, Italy
First edition: July 2006

Reproduction by any means is prohibited.

As regards reproduction rights, the publisher is willing to settle any royalties that may be due for the publication of pictures from unascertained sources.

Reprints	Year
5 4 3 2 1 0	2009 2008 2007 2006

Printed by Giunti Industrie Grafiche S.p.A. - Prato

TABLE OF CONTENTS

ILLUSTRATIONS OUTSIDE OF TEXT:
- page 1: Gentile da Fabriano, *Iris of Florence*, detail from a pilaster of the *Adoration of the Magi*, 1423, tempera on wood. Florence, Uffizi.
- page 2: Masolino, *Daily life in Florence*, detail from the *Healing of the Lame Man and Resurrection of Tabita*, c. 1425, fresco. Florence, Santa Maria del Carmine, Brancacci Chapel.
- pages 8-9: Francesco Botticini, *View of Florence*, detail from the *Assumption of the Virgin*, c. 1475-1477, oil on wood. London, National Gallery.
- pages 18-19: Raffaellino del Garbo (attr.), *Allegory with View of Florence*, c. 1490, oil on wood. Uffizi, Storage.
- page 20: Anonymous, *Scene of Florentine Life*, mid-16th century, oil on wood. Amsterdam, Rijksmuseum.
- page 534: Filippino Lippi, *Porta San Frediano*, detail from the *Virgin and Child with Saints*, 1494, tempera on wood. Florence, Santo Spirito, Nerli Chapel.
- page 624: Aerial view of the Medicean Villa of Careggi.

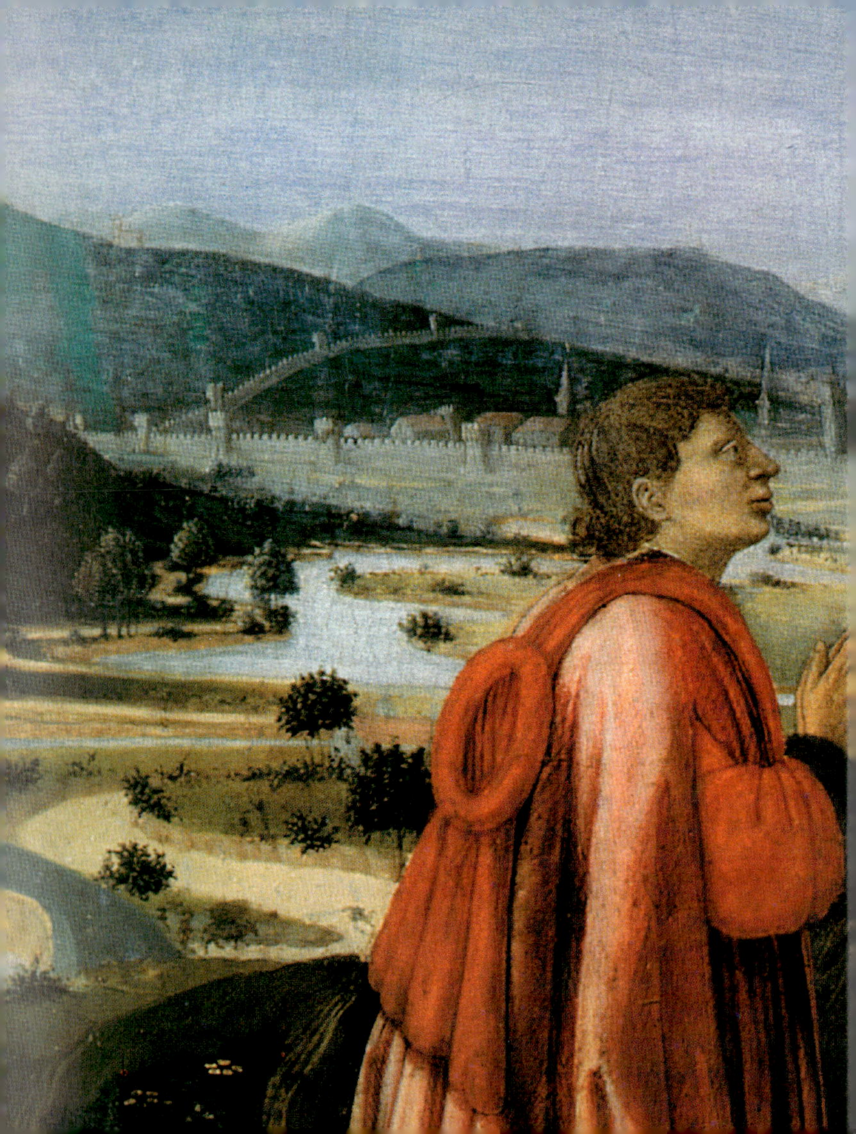

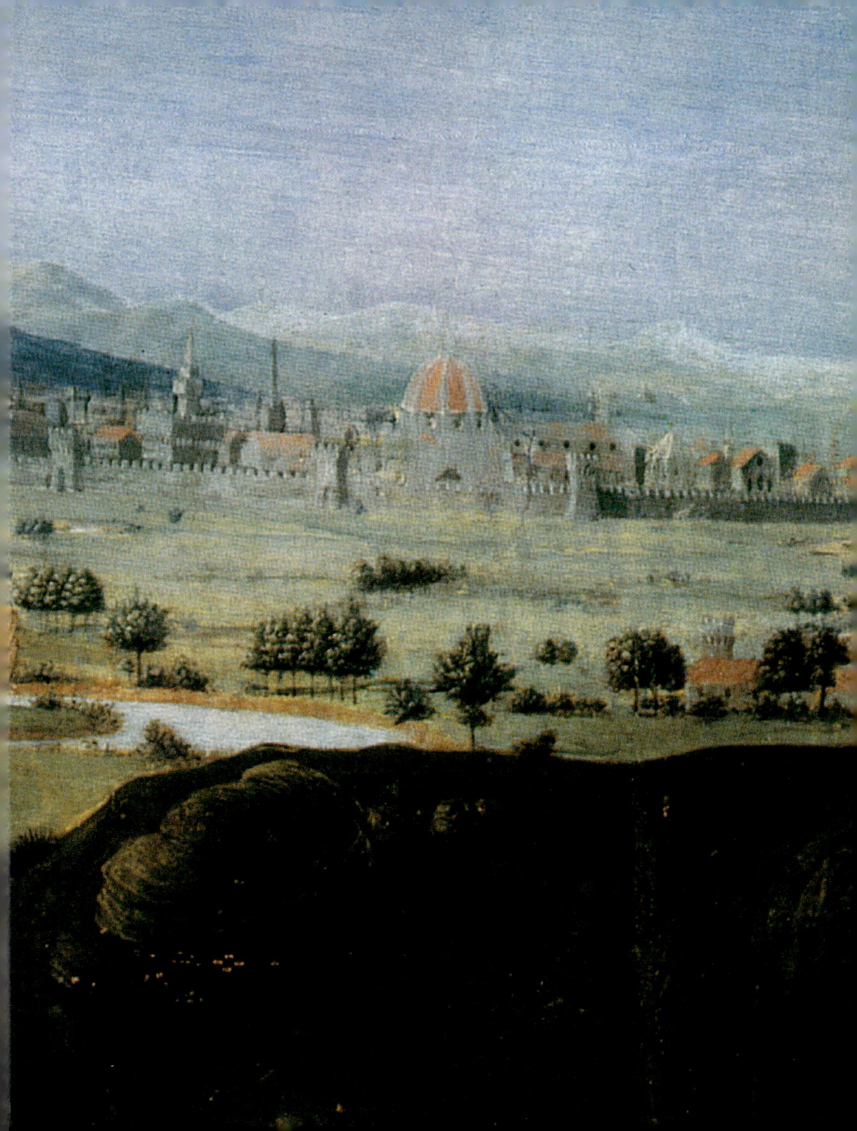

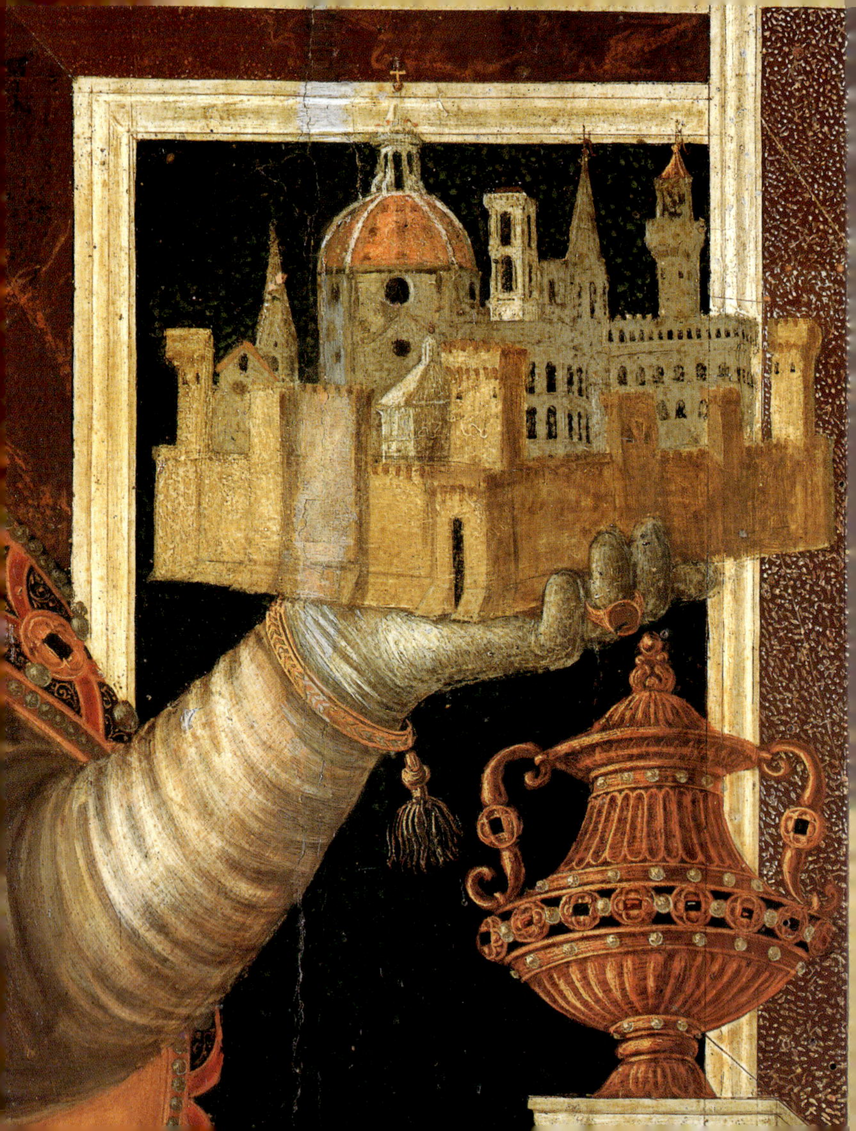

Florence, its Legend, its Image

Florence originated and developed as a microcosm. Any 'città d'arte' may claim in some way to be a world unto itself. But of this autonomy, this capacity to enclose within its walls everything necessary, every kind of knowledge, every beauty, Florence has been the supreme master – despite an unfavorable site, narrowed in by hills on either side of the Arno, with an unpleasant climate, cold in winter, hot and humid in summer; of this even a painter such as Filippo Lippi had complained in the 15th century, imploring his patron Cosimo the Elder to send him to stay in the country, since it was so hot in the city that he was unable to work. "Florentia bella" possesses seven things, the most important that a city should have, proudly wrote, near the end of the 15th century, the merchant Benedetto Dei, a diplomat for the Signoria who had seen many other worlds. Florence has "whole freedom", and "a great number of rich, well-dressed people" and "a river of sweet water" and "the lordship of castles and lands and peoples" and still more, it has the "Studio" where "Greek and the abacus" and "every art whole and perfect" are taught, and then the "banks". Florence was thus a microcosm, which could however, when the occasion arose, open out to the whole world, and summon from other cities the finest experts in every discipline; and this was its true greatness. With its soaring

Opposite page:
Andrea Verrocchio and Assistants, *The Patron Saint Zanobius holding up the model of Florence,* detail from the *Madonna and Child with Saints*, 1472, oil on wood. Bagno a Ripoli (Florence), San Martino a Strada.

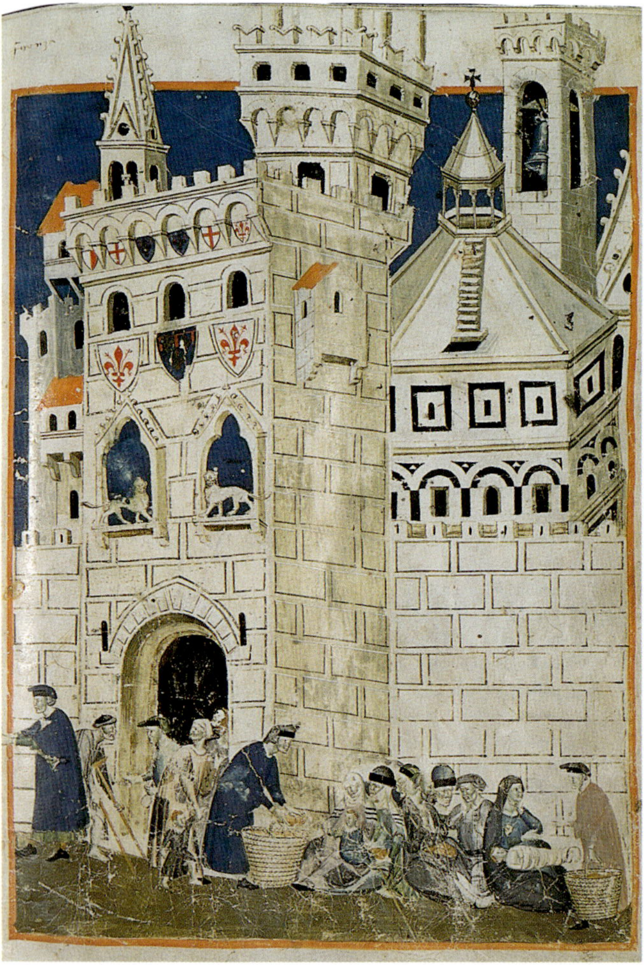

towers, Florence could be likened to Manhattan (to paraphrase a recent metaphor on San Gimignano). In the early 14th century there were some 150 towers, each 120 "braccia" (seventy meters) high, and for this the city "appeared on its little site from outside, from far away and nearby, the most beautiful and flourishing land that could ever be found." The Guelph Lapo da Castiglionchio told this to his son, already regretfully, when towards the end of the century, after the conflict between Guelphs and Ghibellines had come to an end, half of the towers had been torn down and the others "scapitozzate" (decapitated). In the 15th century artists such as Verrocchio portrayed Florence still enclosed within its walls, renewing pride in those symbols for which it was admired throughout the known world: Palazzo dei Priori with its tower crenellated like a fortess; the Badia bell tower, that tolled "the sixth and ninth hours" and marked the working hours of the citizens, as Dante says; and Orsanmichele, the unique monument where a single building contained the most important economic, civil and spiritual activities of the city's life – a grain market, pantheon of the city's guilds and place of worship dedicated to Saint Anne (the saint portrayed in 1343 offering arms to the citizens in revolt against the tyranny of the Duke of Athens); and still more, "bel San Giovanni", the beloved Baptistery ever-present in the city's early iconography. Lastly, and above all, the dome over the Cathedral: so enormous, so perfect,

Opposite page:
Maestro del Biadaiolo, *The Florentines welcome the Sienese driven out of their City by Famine*, c. 1328-1330, Florence, Biblioteca Medicea Laurenziana, Laur. Tempi 3, c. 58r.

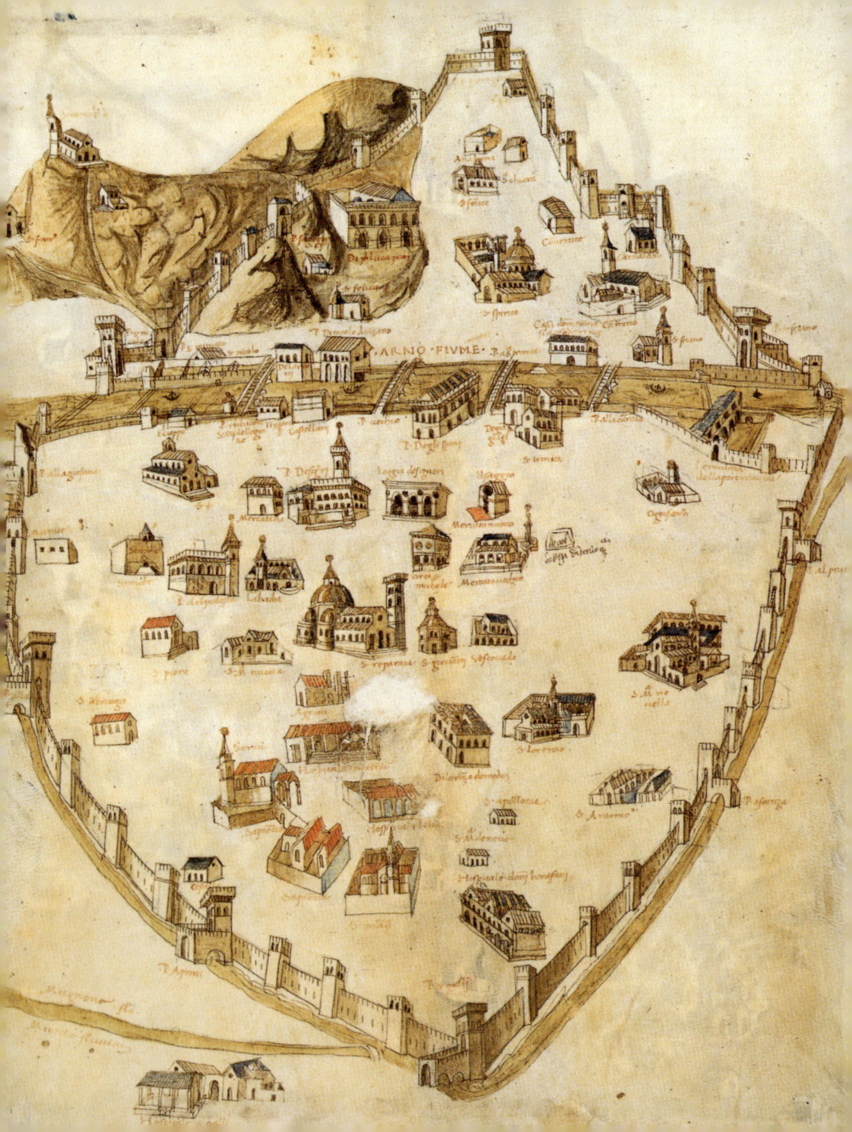
ARNO FIUME

"raised against the sky, to cover the people of all Tuscany", as declared Leon Battista Alberti, and yet as welcomiing and maternal as the embrace of a loving mother. The shape of the dome, according to Roberto Longhi, was echoed by Masaccio in a veiled, occult manner in a famous painting now in the Uffizi, in which Saint Anne's embrace opens wide to protect, like a sheltering dome, her daughter Mary with her Child in her lap. Seen like this, all enclosed in the model held up by its Patron Saint Zanobius, Florence looks almost like a dollhouse. And this was how it appeared to an illustrious foreigner in the 16th century, when he caught sight of it from the hilltops as he arrived. Still today, looking down on it from the height of the hills, Florence appears almost the same as then. Viewed from above, far from its hectic pace of life, its traffic and its smog, Florence evokes the proud words of its ancient chronical writers, evokes a microcosm. If we then go down into the city and wander through its squares, amid statues and fountains, if we enter its churches and museums, we realize that each of these splendid monuments is, in turn, a microcosm. For this reason too, I have tried here to briefly review the history of Florence and its art by "fragments", through the description of each of these little worlds, separate but often correlated with one another. The happenings of squares, churches, palaces, and museums can narrate the history of a city. So that

Opposite page:
Piero di Jacopo del Massaio, *Florentia*, 1469, from Ptolemy's *Cosmography*. Biblioteca Apostolica Vaticana, Vat. Lat. 5699, c. 126v.

the concept of microcosm, which has been the strength and greatness of Florence, will not fossilize to become only an arrogant barrier, an insurmountable limit to its potential capacity for renewal.

g.f.

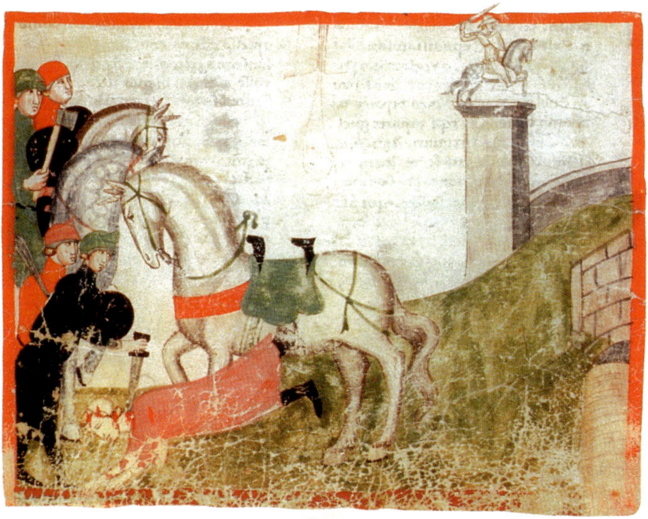

Above:
Bottega di Pacino, *The Assassination of Buondelmonte at the end of Ponte Vecchio*, from the "*Cronaca" by* Giovanni Villani, mid-14th century. Biblioteca Apostolica Vaticana, Codice Chigiano, L.VIII. 296.

Opposite page:
Andrea Orcagna, *Eclipse*, c. 1345, fragmentary fresco. Museo dell'Opera di Santa Croce (from a lost cycle in the church).

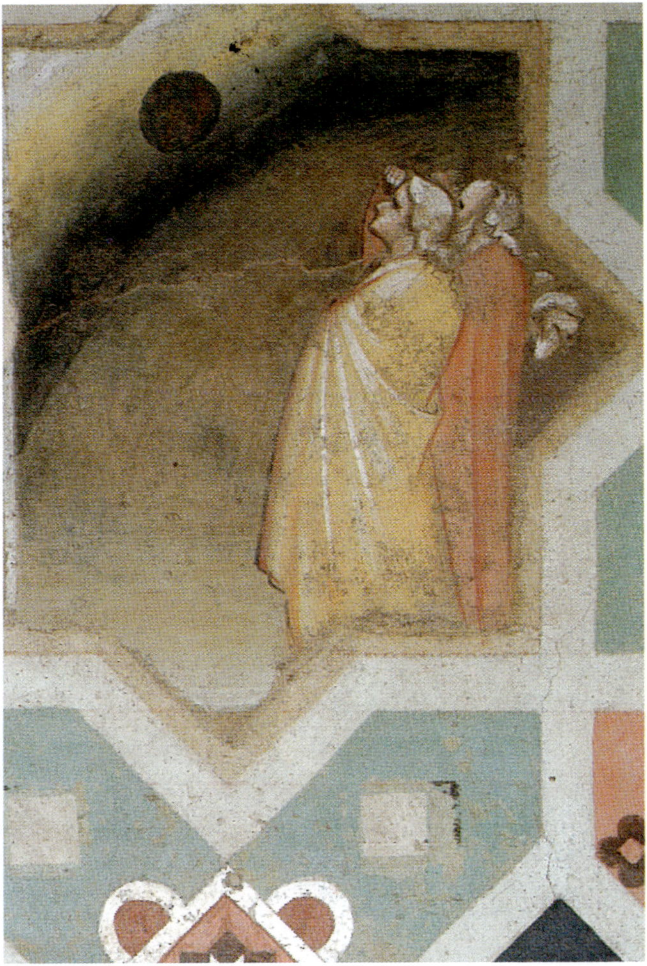

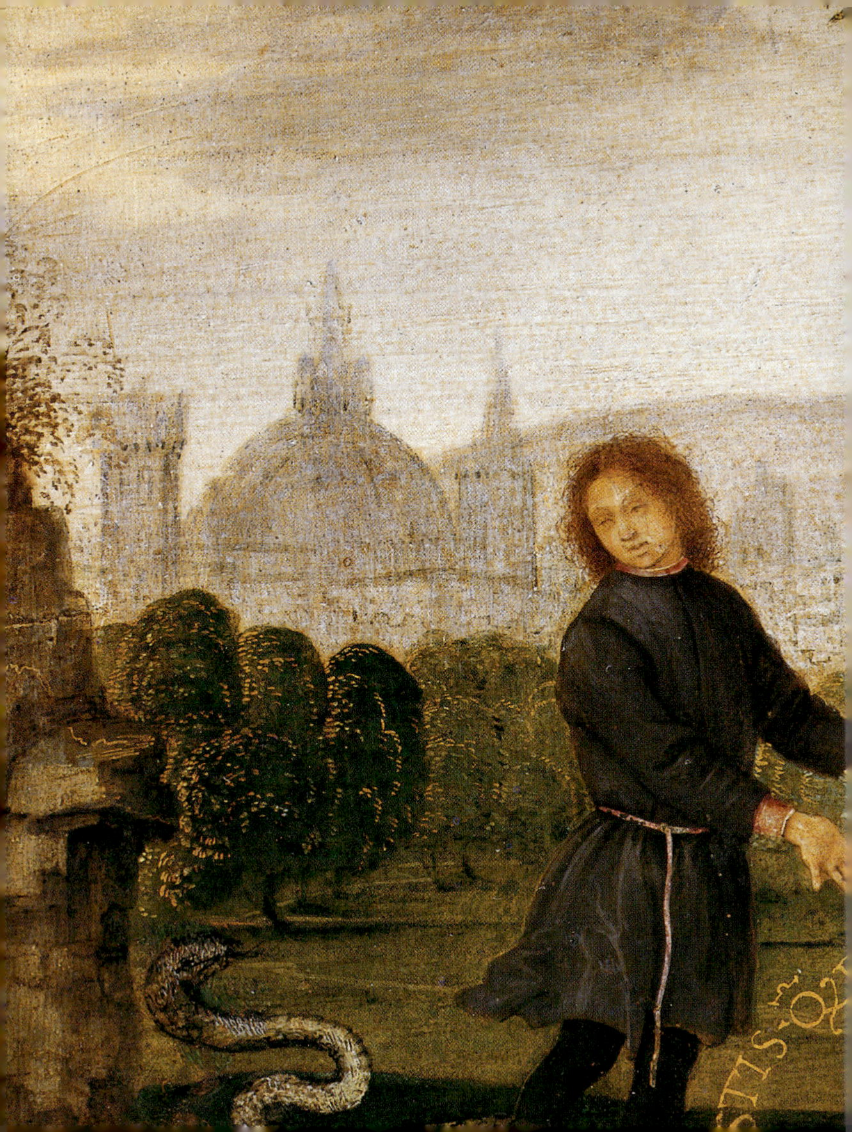

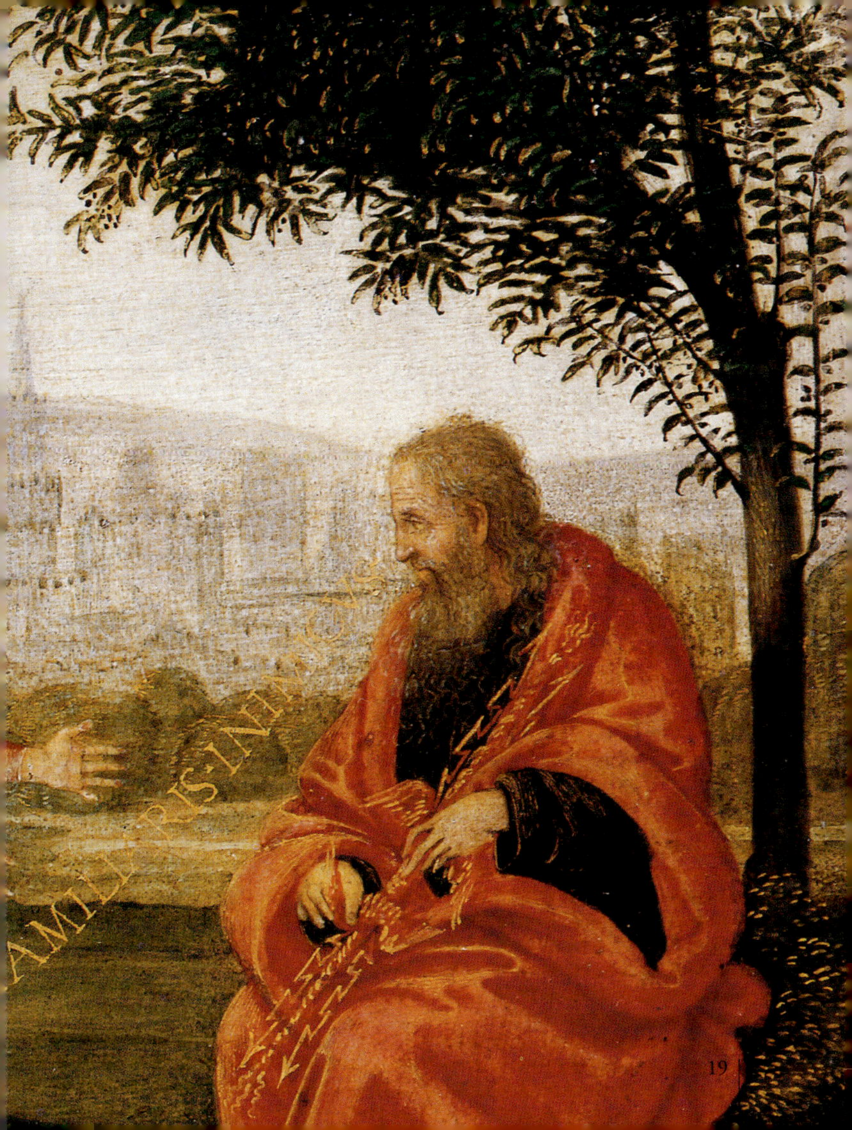

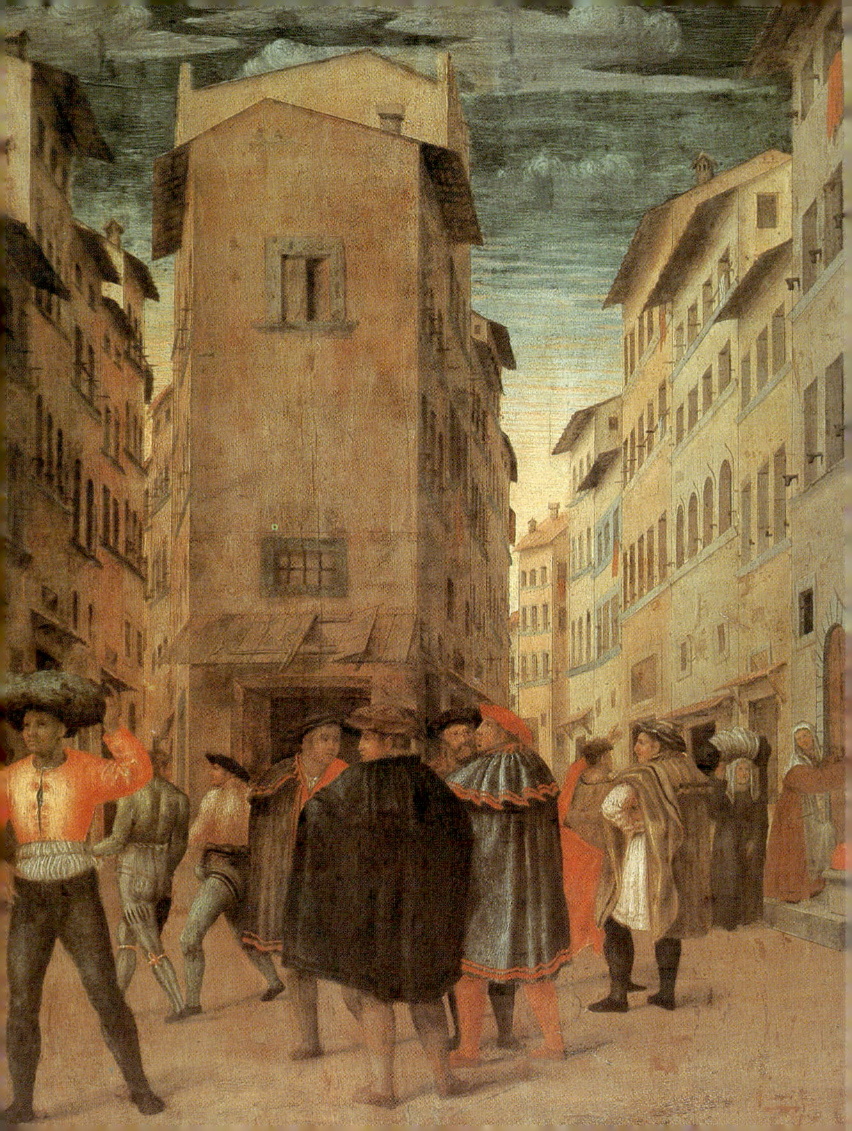

ON THIS SIDE OF THE ARNO

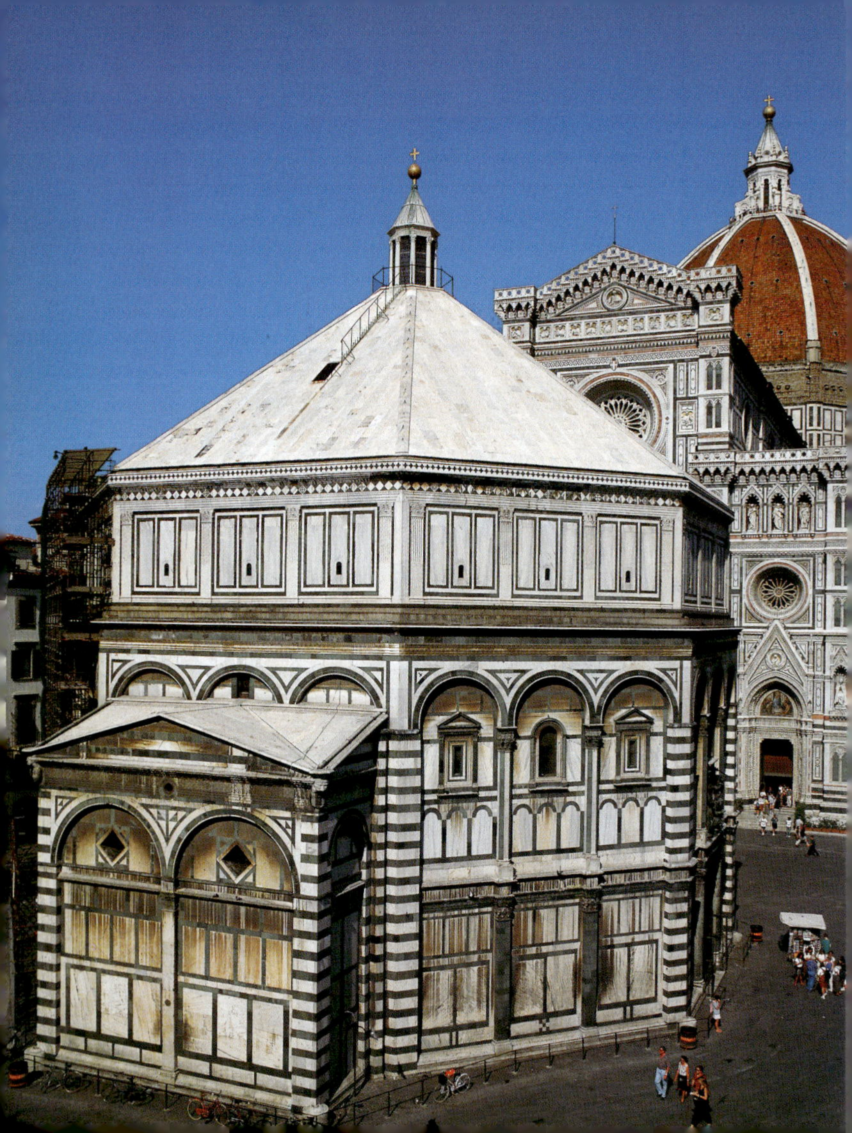

Piazza del Duomo

The Duomo, the Baptistery, the Bell Tower, the Bigallo Loggia

The heart of Florentine religious life, Piazza del Duomo, with the adjoining Piazza San Giovanni, is dominated by the city's most emblematic religious monuments: the Cathedral of Santa Maria del Fiore (the name also alludes to the city, *Fiorenza*), with Brunelleschi's grandiose dome and Giotto's soaring bell tower, and the baptistery dedicated to the Patron Saint of Florence ("beautiful San Giovanni", as Dante called it in the *Paradise*). The history of the monuments in this extraordinary religious complex followed the progressive economic and cultural flowering of the city and the construction of other illustrious buildings, according to an urban development scheme that did not unfold at random. Piazza del Duomo and Piazza San Giovanni constitute in fact the fulcrum of the thoroughfares that from the Annunziata and San Marco continue straight on, crossing the Arno, up to Palazzo Pitti and Santo Spirito. The Cathedral and the Baptistery, the latter once surrounded by a tiered base, were in the past connected by a portico, called the "Paradiso". The harmonious effect of the whole depends on precise geometric similarities: both buildings stand parallel to the section of the ancient walls that bounded the northern perimeter of the Roman *Florentia* (entered through the gate *contra Aquilonem*, later

Opposite page:
Piazza del Duomo and Piazza San Giovanni: this view highlights the west side of the scarsella on the Baptistery, part of the Cathedral's 19th century façade, and Brunelleschi's dome.

called the Porta del Vescovo, or Bishop's Gate, where today's Borgo san Lorenzo opens onto the square); both lie on the same axis, and their apses are built to the same proportions. Since medieval times, moreover, the space between the Baptistery and the Duomo has been an extraordinary outdoor theater, the scenic site of processions and liturgical ceremonies held on major feast days, such as Easter (with the "Scoppio del Carro"), and the Festival of Saint John the Baptist on June 24 (with the "Palio dei Ceri"). The Baptistery was also, up to nearly the end of the 19th century, the place where all babies born in Florence were baptized. The Duomo and the Baptistery also played an important civic role during the period of the medieval Communes. Not only did bishops and cardinals send their messages to the peo-

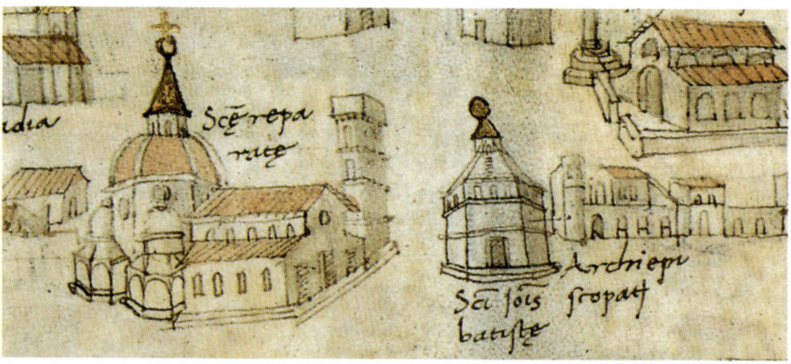

Above: The Cathedral of Santa Maria del Fiore, the Baptistery and the Bishop's Palace, detail of *Florentia*, 1469, illuminated page from Ptolemy's *Cosmography*. Biblioteca Apostolica Vaticana, Urb. Lat. 277, c. 130v.

Opposite page:
Workshop of Bernardo Daddi, *Representation of the city of Florence* within its walls, detail of the *Madonna della Misericordia*, c. 1342, fresco. Museo del Bigallo.

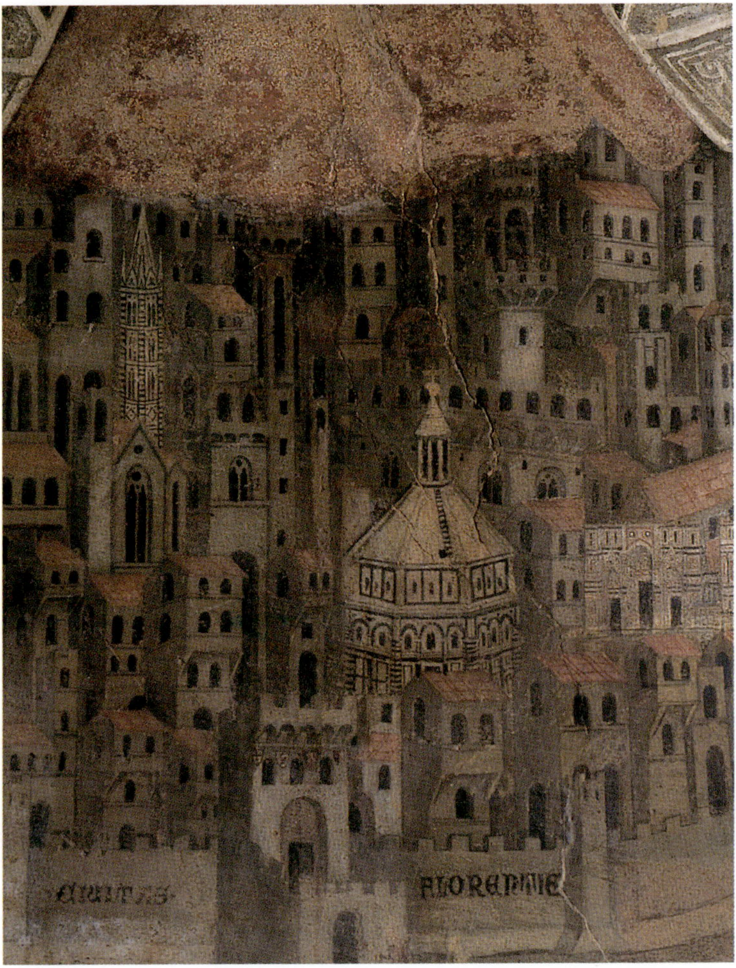

ple from here, but it was also the place where knights were appointed, prisoners of war were consecrated to St. John the Baptist, and meetings of Parliament were held. In front of the south side of the baptistery – in which the "carroccio" and military trophies were also kept – was a municipal cage of lions, symbol of the Republic, which was moved to Piazza dei Priori in 1319 and later to the back of Piazza Signoria. And in 1479 the Cathedral, which had housed the Council of 1439, was the site of the Pazzi Conspiracy, in which Giuliano de' Medici was assassinated and his brother, Lorenzo the Magnificent, narrowly escaped death by fleeing from the sacristy.
In Medicean and Lorraine times the Baptistery and the Duomo were splendidly decorated, often with radical initiatives, on the occasion of illustrious christenings or weddings. For the christening of Prince Filippo, son of Francesco I de' Medici, in "bel San Giovanni" sumptuous decorative sets were designed by Buontalenti and the vast octagonal enclosure mentioned also by Dante was demolished (some fragments are now in the Museo dell'Opera (Museum of Cathedral Works), while in the Duomo, for the wedding of Violante di Baviera and Ferdinando, son of Cosimo III, the two choirstalls by Donatello and by Luca della Robbia were dismantled (they too were then moved to the Museo dell'Opera).
Between the Duomo and the Baptistery remain two more significant landmarks in the city's history. On either side of the

Opposite page:
Monte di Giovanni, *St. Zanobius bestowing blessings and view of the city of Florence within its walls*, 1505, mosaic.
Museo dell'Opera del Duomo.

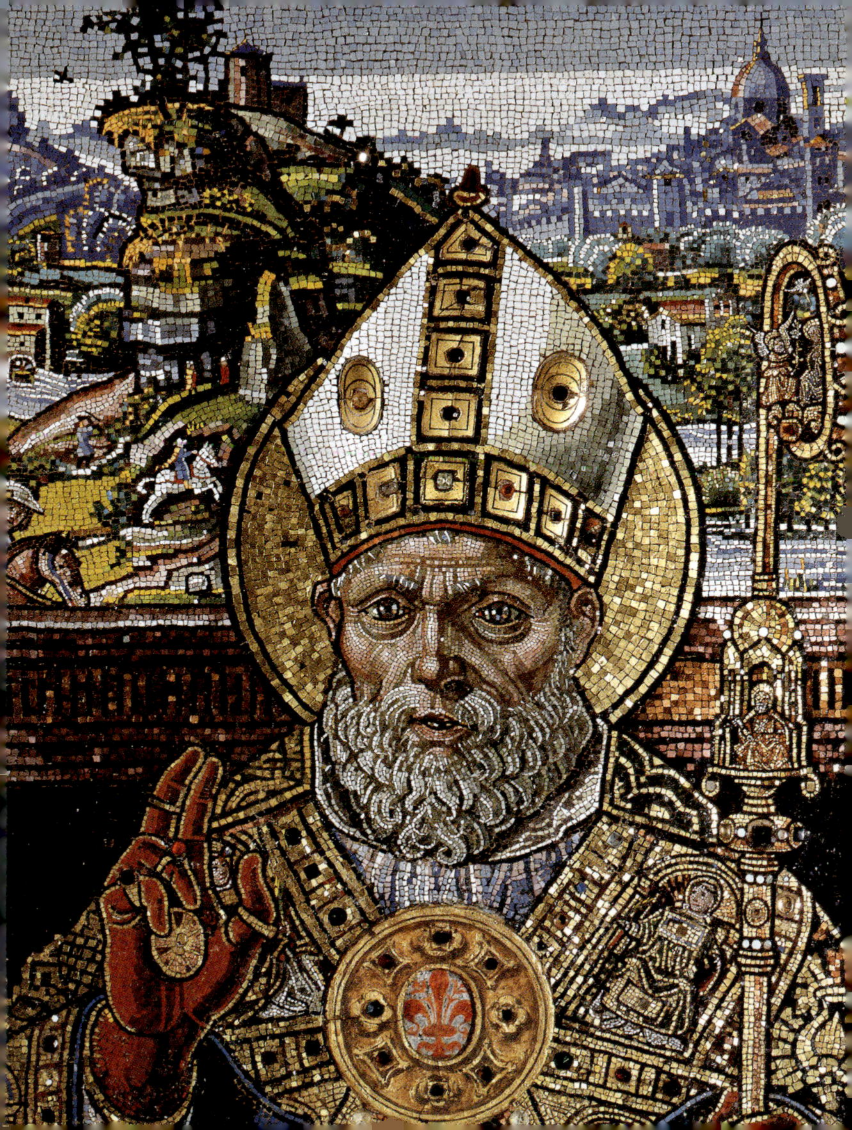

Baptistery's east door stand the porphyry columns donated in 1171 by the Pisans to the Florentines in gratitude for their help in the war of the Balearic Islands. Standing before the north side, a column recalls the miracle of the dead elm tree that, according to legend, sprouted green leaves as the body of Saint Zanobius passed by. The translation of the bishop's body from the former Cathedral of San Lorenzo to the new one of Santa Reparata is still recalled today in a solemn ceremony held on May 25, the presumed date of death of the saint, who lived in the 4th-5th century and is venerated as one of the earliest patron saints of Florence.

THE BAPTISTERY

The most ancient monument in the square, whose origins are however still debated, is the beautiful, refined Baptistery with its octagonal plan, surmounted by a cupola "*a tenda castrense*". Probably founded even before Saint Ambrose's visit to Florence in 394, mentioned in a document from the year 897, it was reconsecrated in 1059 (or 1061) by Pope Nicholas II. From the middle of the 11th century up to 1128 the Baptistery, it seems, played the role of cathedral while the Church of Santa Reparata was undergoing reconstruction (the latter was then demolished in 1375 to be replaced by the new building of Santa Maria del

Opposite page:
The south side of the Baptistery, with the door by Andrea Pisano (1330), formerly on the east side, where it was replaced by Ghiberti's Door of Paradise.

Above the medieval door is the 16th century sculptural group representing the *Beheading of the Baptist by* Vincenzo Danti, an artist from Perugia.

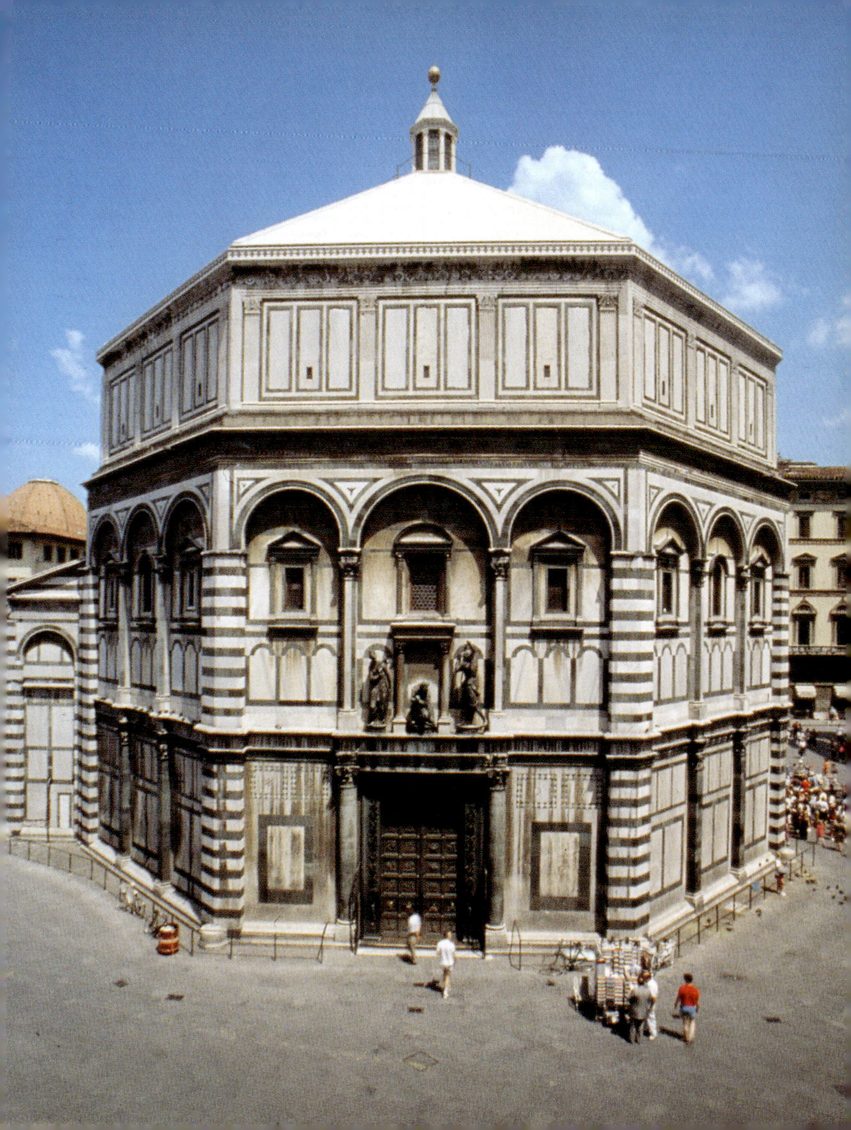

Fiore). From 1078, the year in which the city was divided into four districts, the Baptistery gave its name to the San Giovanni quarter, bounded to the northwest by the Porta del Vescovo, to the east by today's Via del Proconsolo, and to the south by the area once occupied by the ancient Forum (now Piazza della Repubblica), at the center of the *castrum* of the Roman *Florentia* (now Piazza della Repubblica). With the division of the city into six zones, in 1172, the Sestiere (district) of San Giovanni incorporated the Basilica of San Lorenzo, formerly outside the walls, and stretched as far as the crossroads beween today's Via de' Pucci and Via dei Servi, being bounded to the east by the Porta degli Albertinelli (where the Arch of San Piero now stands).
The elegant, refined geometric decoration of "*bel San Giovanni*", in white Luni marble and green Prato marble, is thought to date from the 11th and 12th centuries, while the cupola was finished by a lantern presumably in 1150, the year in which the patronage of the monument was assigned to the Merchants' Guild of Calimala. Dating from the early 13th century is the addition, on the western side, of a rectangular tribune (called "scarsella"), decorated inside with figures from the zodiac. The splendid marble floor made of white, green and red tesserae, with plant, animal and geometric designs, like a precious carpet, dates from this time. The master mosaicists who

Opposite page:
Anonymous mosaicist, *Capital with inscription*, detail of the mosaics in the scarsella, c. 1225. Baptistery.

Following pages: View of the interior of the Baptistery looking toward the scarsella. On the right can be seen the funerary monument to the anti-pope John XXIII.

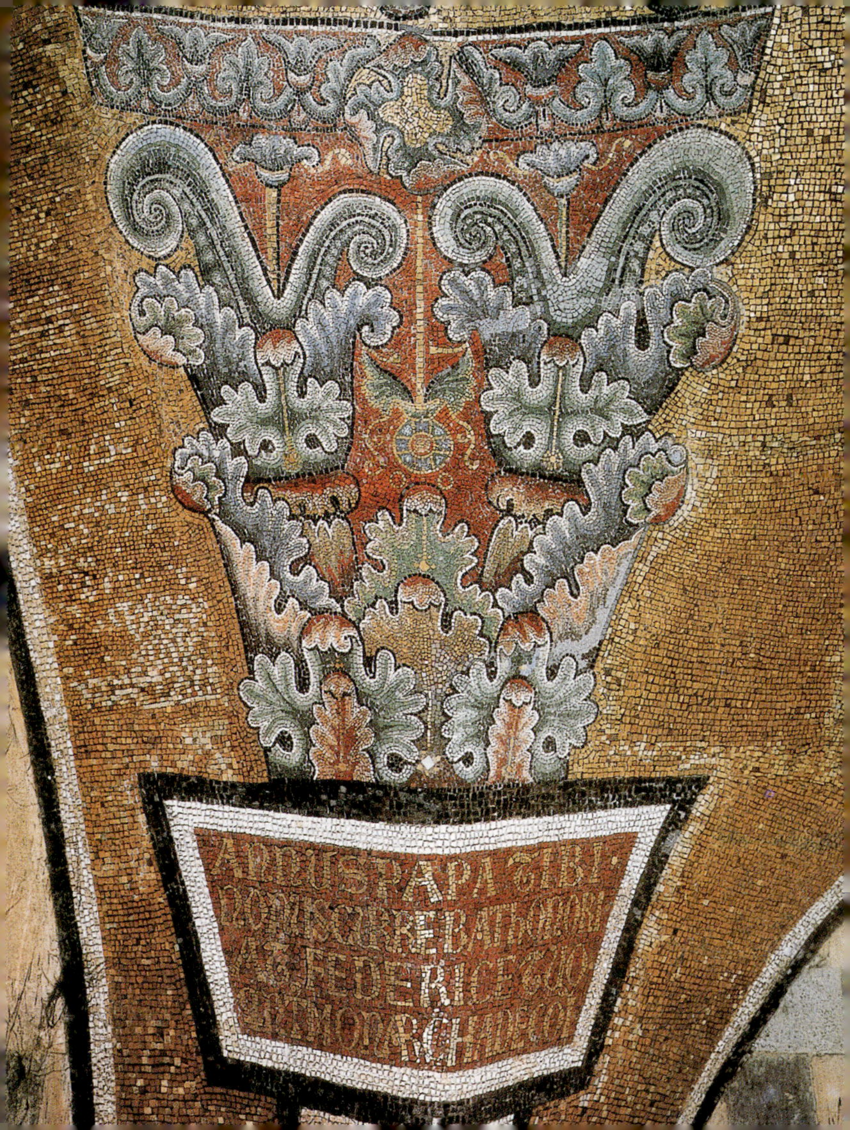

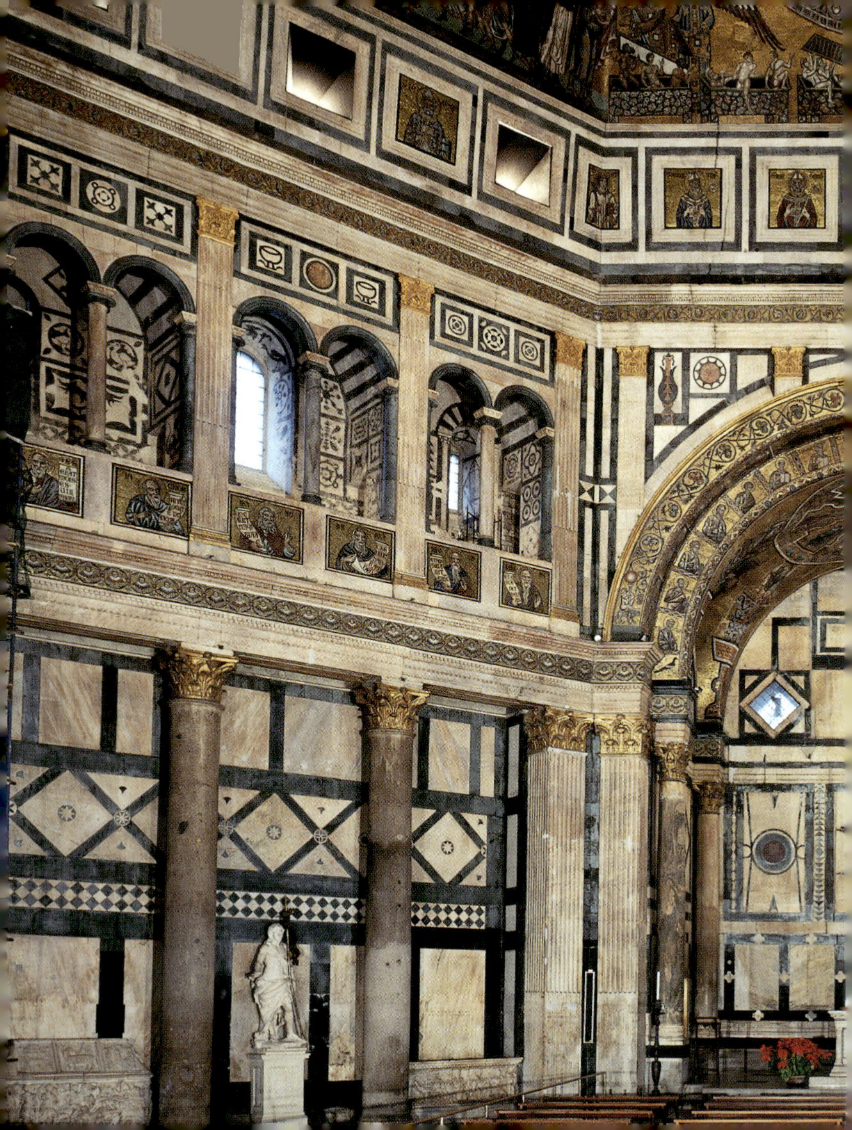

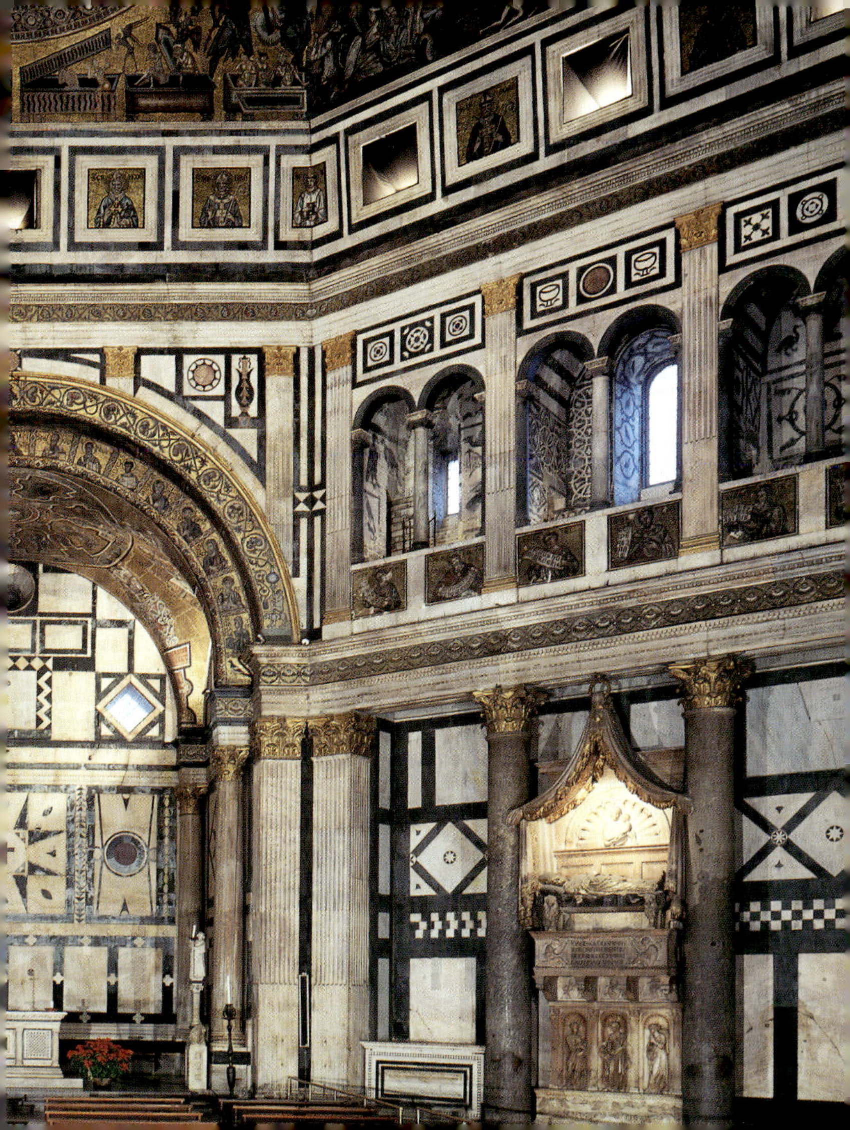

worked on the grandiose iniative of the cupola (1225-early 14th century) have not yet been precisely identified, although it seems that, at a certain stage, Florentine artists such as Cimabue, Coppo di Marcovaldo, Meliore, the Master of the Magdalene and Gaddo Gaddi participated. Perhaps begun in 1225 by a monk known as "Jacopo francescano" who signed the mosaics on the ceiling of the *scarsella*, work continued in the great octagonal cupola for nearly a century. In the earliest stages the so-called "Greek masters" must have been involved, perhaps Venetians trained by Byzantine or Sicilian artists, by whom Cimabue too may have been influenced. Their style, in fact, played a significant role in the development of Florentine painting in the late 13th century.

Moreover, the refined use of materials and the sober play of polychrome marbles on both the exterior and the interior of the Baptistery evoke a classical-style *esprit de géometrie* typical of Florentine Romanesque architecture (San Miniato al Monte in particular). This supremely elegant, abstractly geometric style was to exert its influence over architects and theorists of the humanist age such as Leon Battista Alberti. The exterior marble revetment of the Baptistry was in any case finished by the end of the 13th century, and the square was paved in brick at that time.

Opposite page:
Anonymous mosaicist,
Christ the Judge, c. 1260-1270,
mosaic. Baptistery, large vault.

Following page, from top:
Giovanni di ser Giovanni, known as Scheggia, *The Adimari Chest,*
c. 1450, tempera on wood.
Galleria dell'Accademia.

Giovanni Toscani, The *Palio of St. John,* before 1429, chest. Museo Nazionale del Bargello.

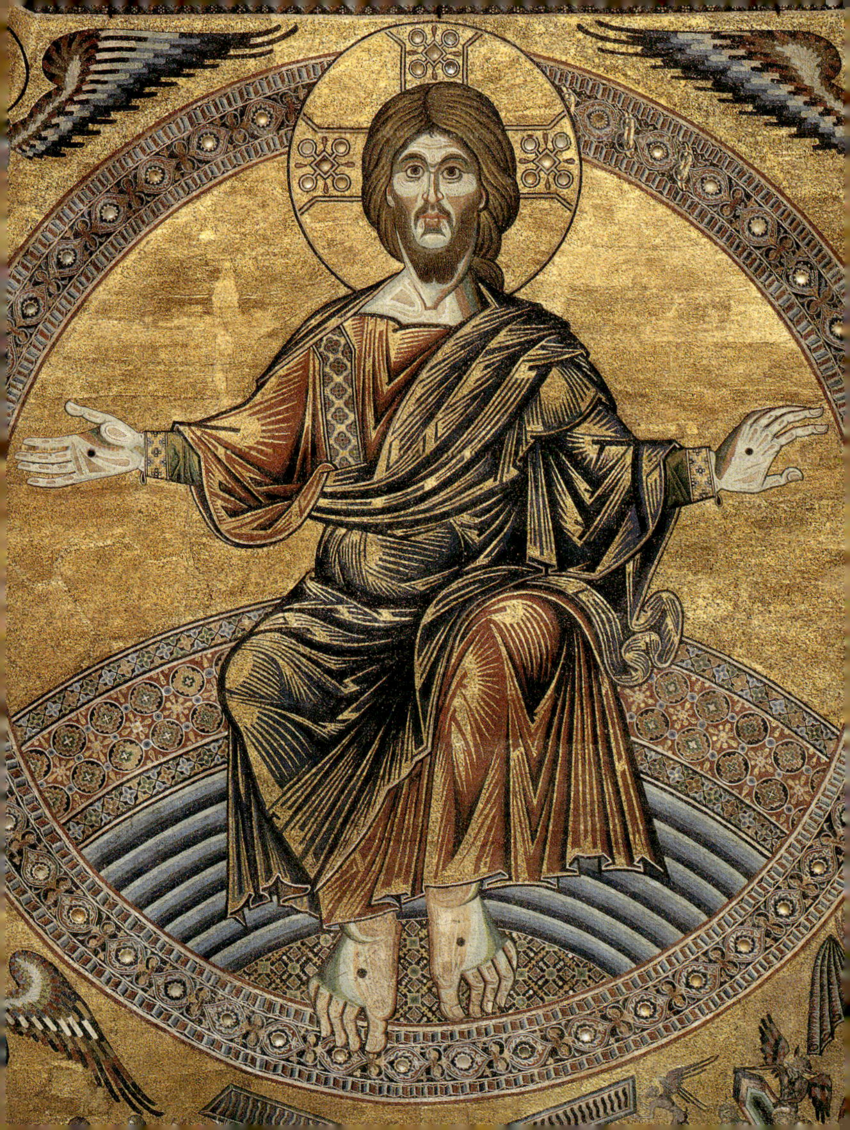

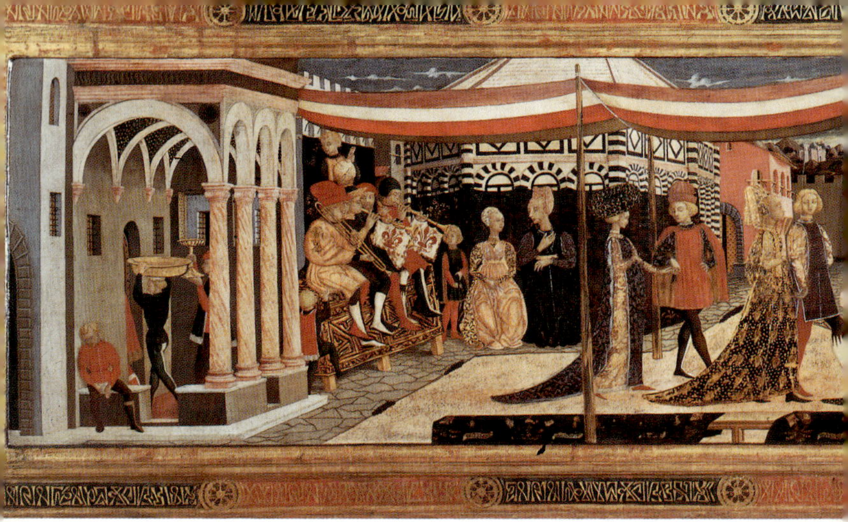

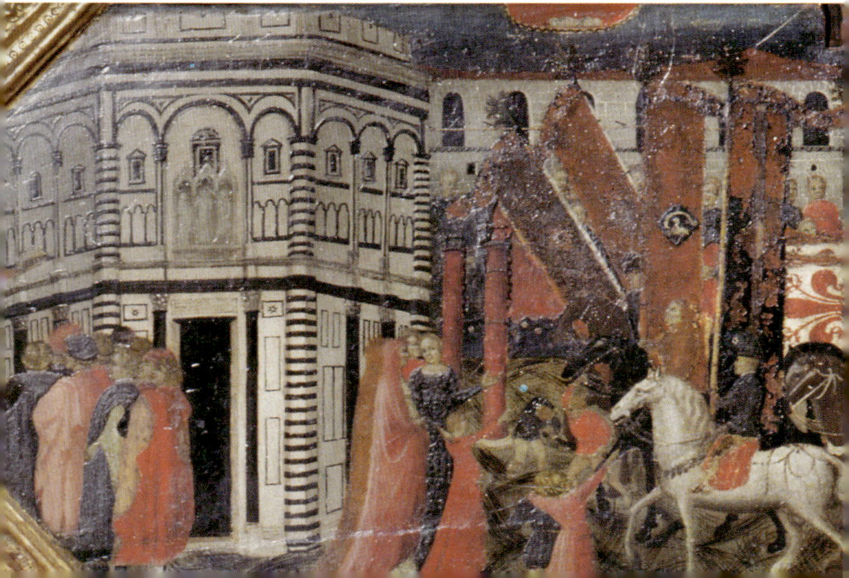

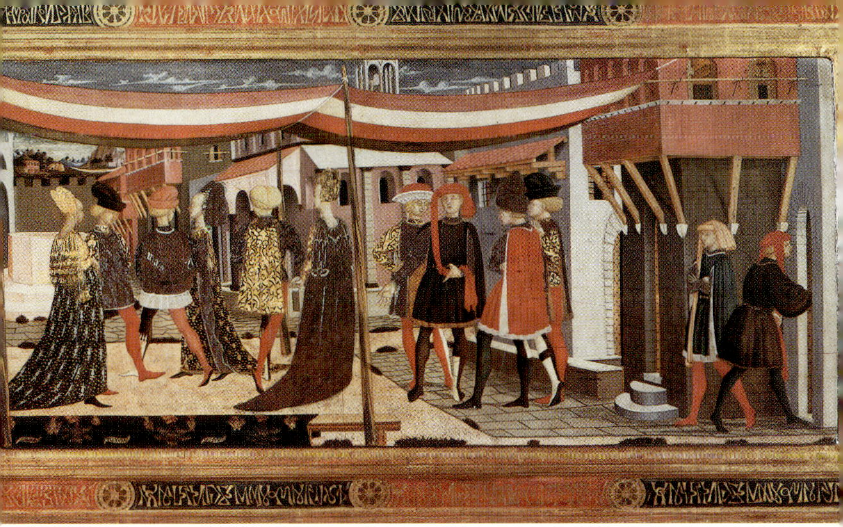

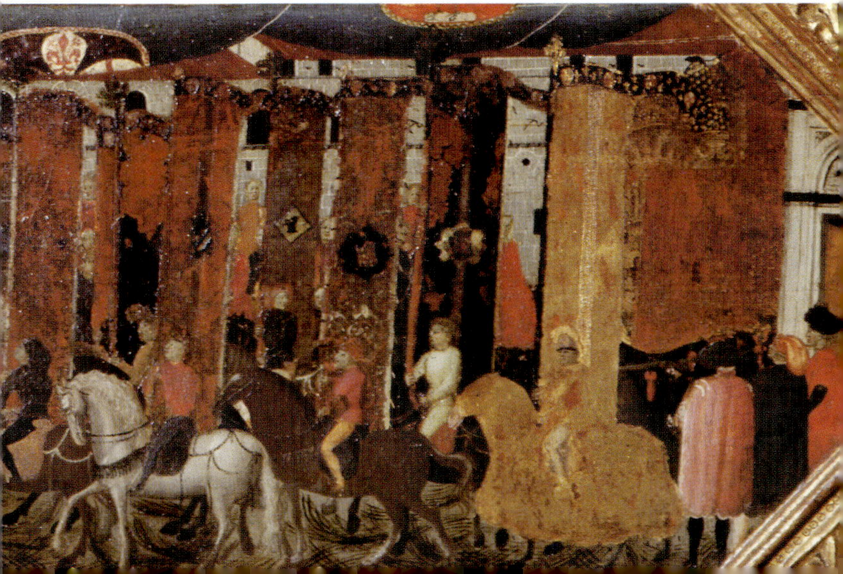

THE CATHEDRAL AND THE BELL TOWER

In 1293 the republican government decided to build the new Cathedral of Santa Maria del Fiore, and all Florentines were ordered to contribute to the expense by bequeathing some of their property to the Opera del Duomo, instituted to superintend the project. Under the guidance of Arnolfo di Cambio, on September 8, 1296, the first stone was laid. The work, interrupted by the death of the great architect (1302), was resumed in 1330, under the control of the Wool Merchants Guild. From 1334 to 1337 the direction of the worksite for the Duomo and the Bell Tower (84 meters high, 14 wide) was entrusted to Giotto, and after his death (1337) to Andrea Pisano (up to 1348) and then to Francesco Talenti (1349-1359). Santa Maria del Fiore was one of the most brilliant and revolutionary achievements of the western world in the late Middle Ages, almost a first foretaste of the Renaissance, and is the fourth largest church in the world (at the time it was designed it was the very largest, later to be exceeded only by the Basilica of St. Peter's in Rome and then by Saint Paul's in London). It is a classical-style basilica, with three broad naves and a choir surrounded by the trefoil tribune, onto which is grafted Brunelleschi's dome, of gigantic size:

Opposite page:
View of the interior of the Duomo looking toward the inner façade.

Following pages:
View of Giotto's Bell Tower from the southwest side of the Duomo.

Florentine Manufactury, *The Cathedral of Santa Maria del Fiore, Giotto's Bell Tower and the dome, detail from the Ex Voto of Cosimo II*, "commesso in pietre dure", enamel, diamonds. Palazzo Pitti, Museo degli Argenti.

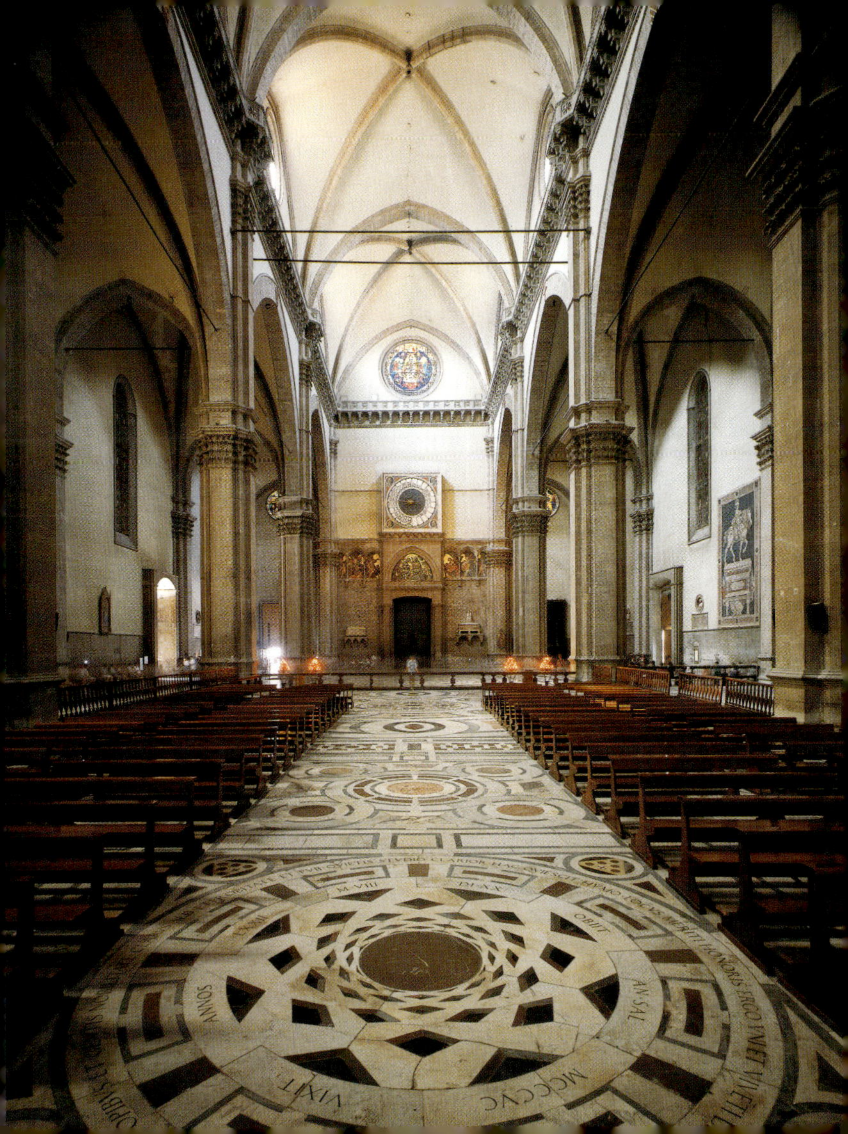
ANNOS
VIXIT
MCCCXC
AN SAL
OBIIT

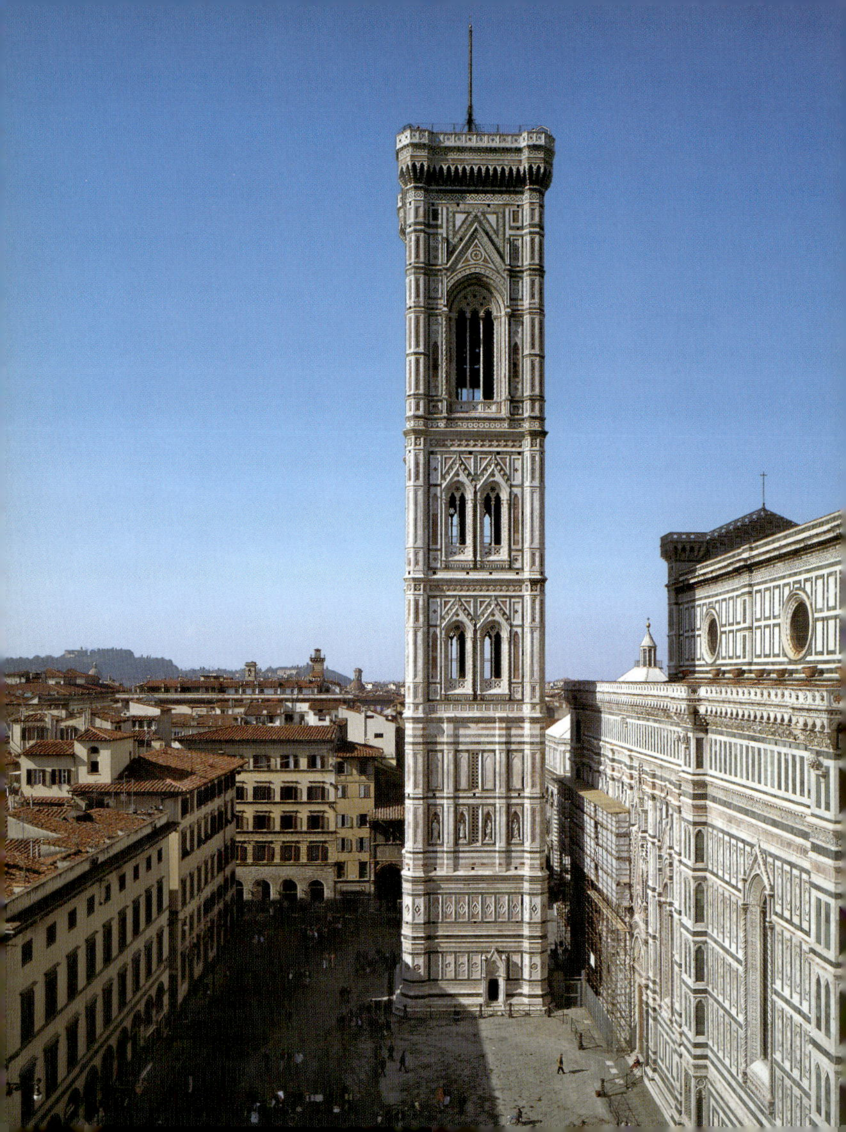

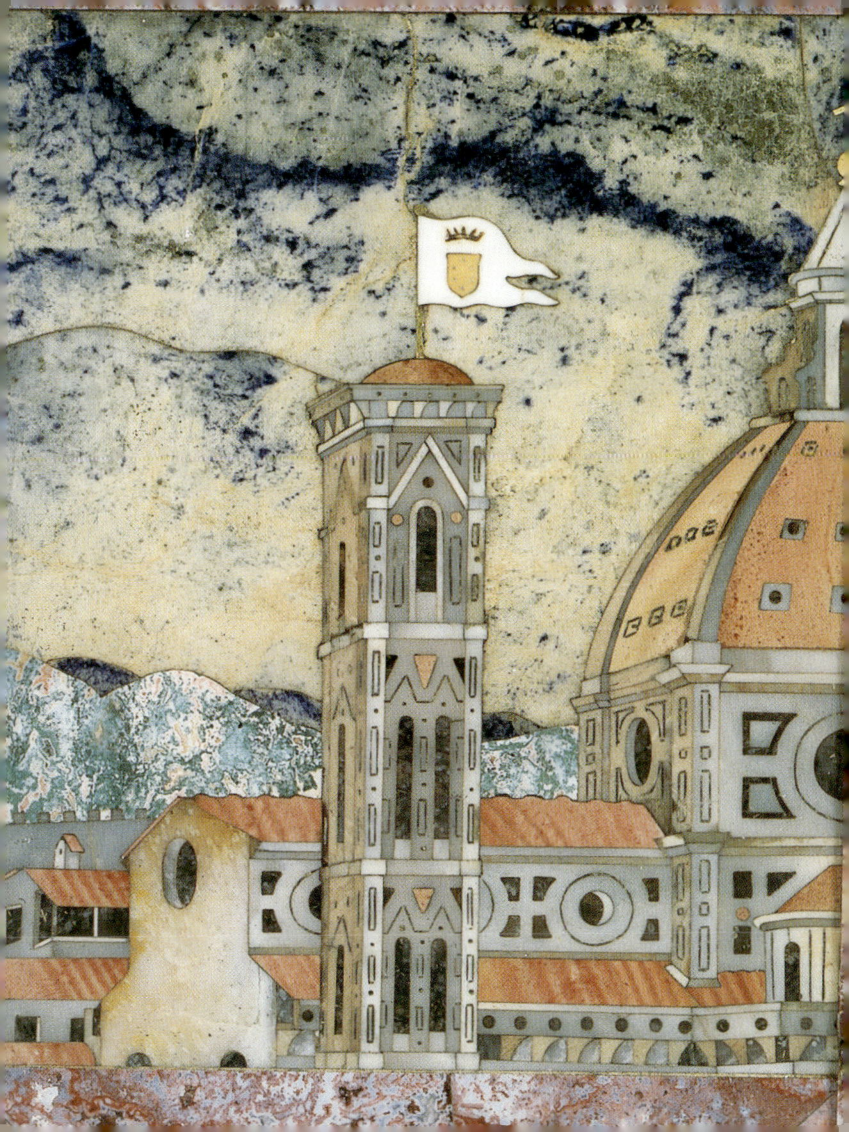

45.5 meters in diameter, with proportions identical to those of the Baptistery. It should be recalled that already in Arnolfo's plan, provisions had been made for a cupola over the apse, as shown by the fresco in Santa Maria Novella by Andrea Bonaiuti, who had been a member of the commission that supervised the building of the Duomo.

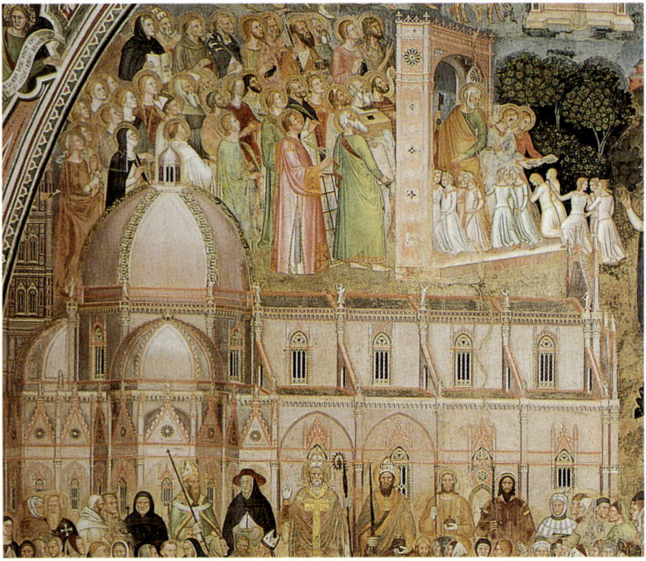

Andrea Bonaiuti, *Allegory of the Church*, c. 1365, idealized detail of the Duomo. Florence, Santa Maria Novella, Chapel of the Spagnoli.

Opposite page:
View of the cupola over the Duomo with the *Last Judgment* frescoed by Giorgio Vasari and Taddeo Zuccari between 1572 and 1579.

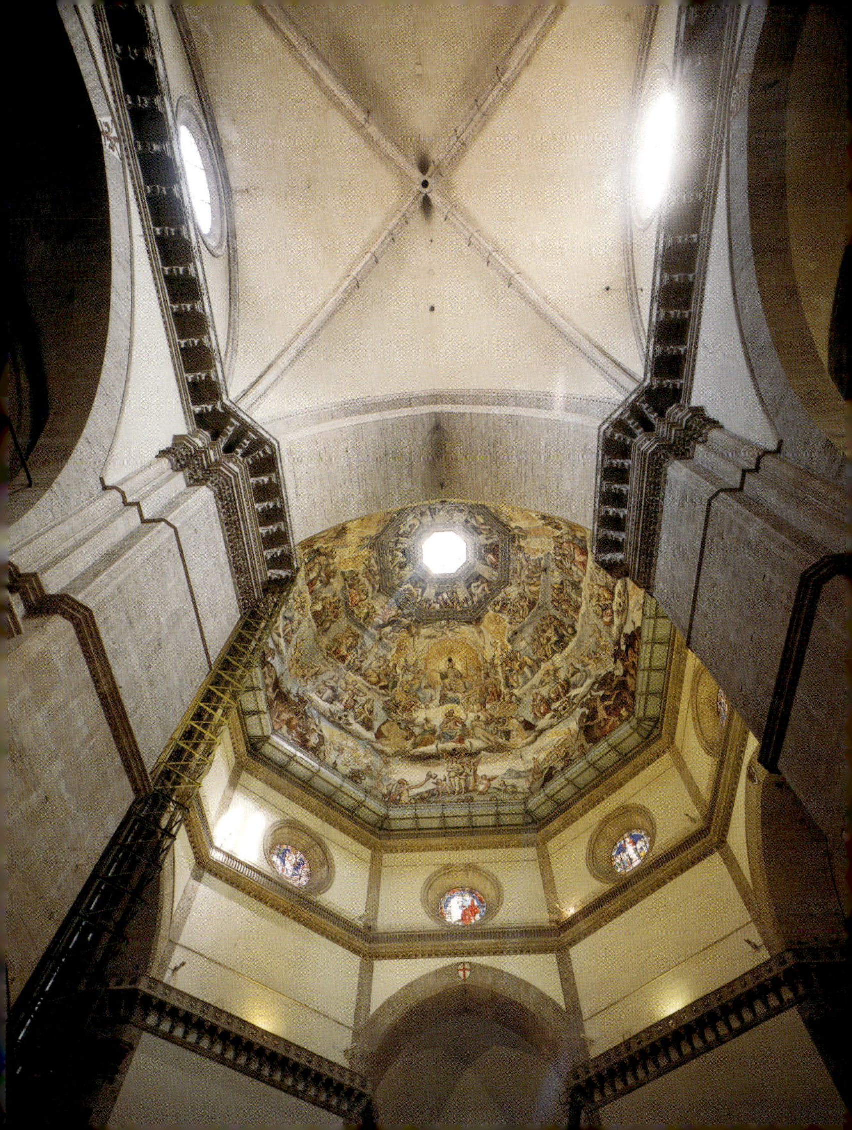

THE DOORS OF THE BAPTISTERY AND THE BIGALLO

Meanwhile, in 1338 there was placed, on the east side of the Baptistery, facing the Duomo, the bronze door by Andrea Pisano, later moved to the south to be replaced by Lorenzo Ghiberti's *Porta del Paradiso*. In 1339, for the purpose of displaying more emphatically this exceptional group of religious buildings, the streets that led into the square from the south were lowered, and this may also have been the occasion of the demolishing of the tiered steps around San Giovanni, which had been surrounded by a vast cemetery. In those years the Florentine Comune promulgated a number of decisions to ensure the "decorum" of the square, prohibiting overly bright colors on the facades as well as "*sporti*" (those wooden superstructures that projected from the houses and frequently appear in paintings of the time). To expose orphans put up for adoption the Confraternita della Misericordia, still today an efficient organization providing assistance to the ill, commissioned Alberto Arnoldi to design the loggia (1352-1358) facing the south side of the Baptistery, where the houses of the powerful Adimari family stood. In 1425 the Compagnia del Bigallo was annexed to the Confraternita della Misericordia; still today, it gives its name to the Loggia and the Museum, rich in works of art linked to the Compagnia's history.

Opposite page:
Emilio Burci, *Corso degli Adimari, on which stood the Loggia del Bigallo before its 19th century destruction, 19th century*, drawing on paper.
Gabinetto Disegni e Stampe degli Uffizi, inv. no. 1103.

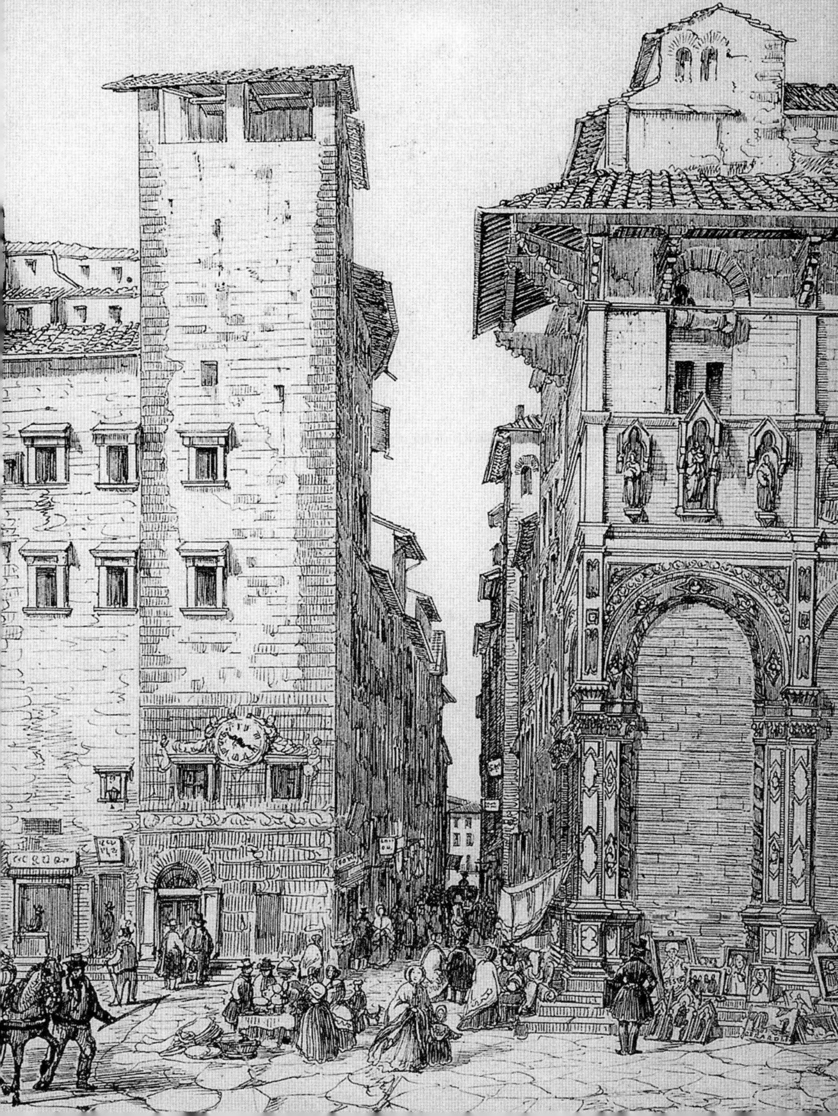

BRUNELLESCHI'S DOME

Dating from those years (1420-1434) is Brunelleschi's extraordinary project for the gigantic cupola over the Duomo, which was immediately to become the city's fundamental urban and symbolic reference point, and was to be topped after the master's death, in 1461, by a lantern surmounted by an immense bronze ball fabricated in Verrocchio's workshop. The competition for the model of the dome, whose first projects date from a century earlier, had been announced in 1418, but the prize had remained unawarded. Brunelleschi, who had already been to Rome with his friend Donatello to study the ancient monuments, had intensified his journeys in search of a solution that would allow him to "vault" without external reinforcement a dome of great size, to be adapted to such an immense structure as the Florentine Duomo, which is, as has been seen, one of the biggest cathedrals in the western world. Appointed co-superintendent with his rival Ghiberti in 1420, but by now the master of incomparable knowledge, Brunelleschi continued the undertaking alone, adopting a herring-bone system, partially inspired by Roman building techniques, that allowed the dome to support itself progressively, as it was constructed, through the counterthrust of the ribs. The cupola, 91 meters high (with the addition of the lantern it now arrives at the height of 114.5 meters)

Opposite page:
Brunelleschi's dome
in a view from above.

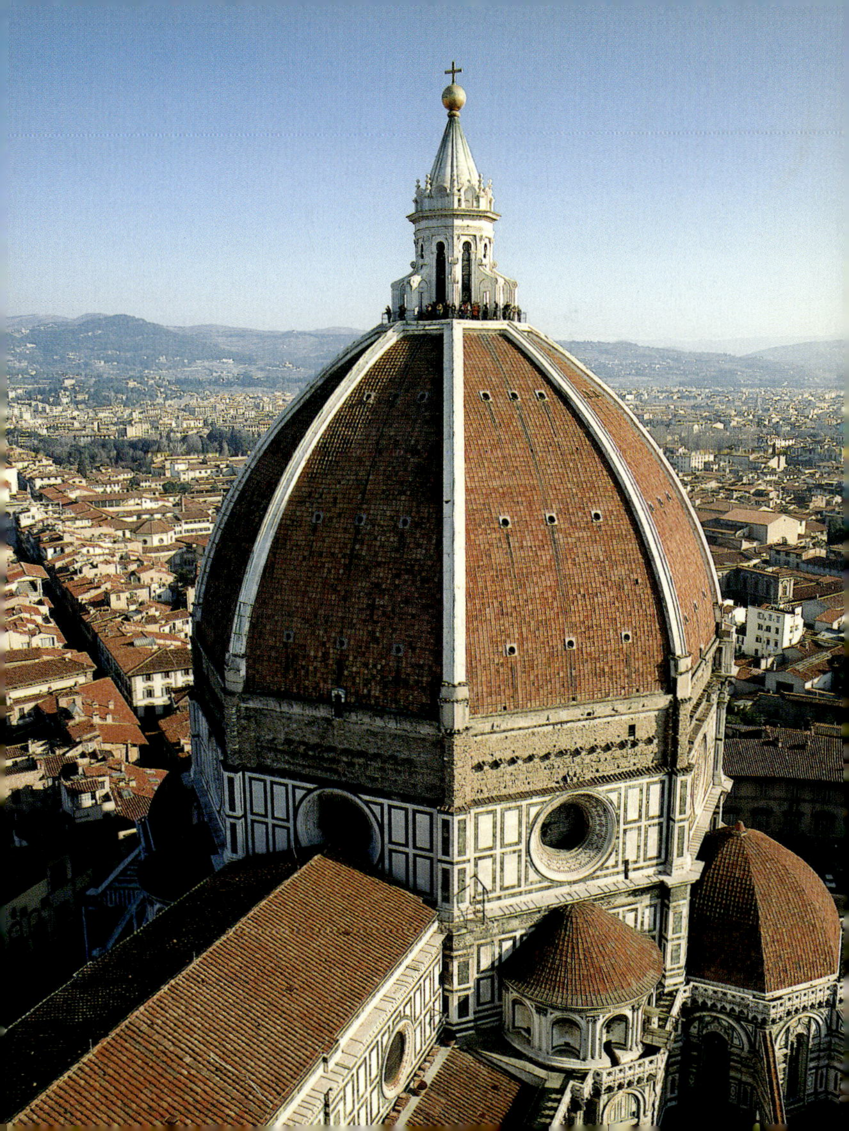

was finished in 1434. Despite the humiliation he had suffered in relation to the great architect, Ghiberti was finally able to show his genius, consecrating his fame through an achievement that was also immortal: the Porta del Paradiso, placed opposite the façade of the Duomo in 1452.

For centuries the Baptistry and the Duomo were enriched by works of art and new decorations, some still in their original places, which will be discussed below, others now in the Museo dell'Opera del Duomo, founded in the late 19th century, as will be seen, to house the dismantled choir stalls of Donatello and Luca della Robbia. It should also be noted that the original unfinished façade of Santa Maria del Fiore, a sort of sculptured jewel casket "embroidered"with sculptures, with a gallery embellished by tracery and three portals, designed by Arnolfo di Cambio, was demolished in 1587 by Grand Duke Ferdinando I de' Medici to replace it with a new one. However, it was only between 1876 and 1887 that the present-day façade was built. Tourists often mistake it for the original (as is also the case with the façade of Santa Croce) while it was instead designed, much later, in neo-Gothic style, by Emilio de Fabris (the surviving medieval scuptures are in the Museo dell'Opera del Duomo).

Following pages:
Florentine painter, *The Baptistery and Arnolfo's facade for the Duomo, detail from the Arrival of the Minorites,* late 14th century, detached fresco. Museo dell'Opera di Santa Croce.

Opposite page:
Alessandro Nani (by Bernardino Poccetti), Arnolfo's facade for the Duomo before it was demolished in 1587, 17th century, drawing in ink, black pencil and water color. Archivio dell'Opera del Duomo.

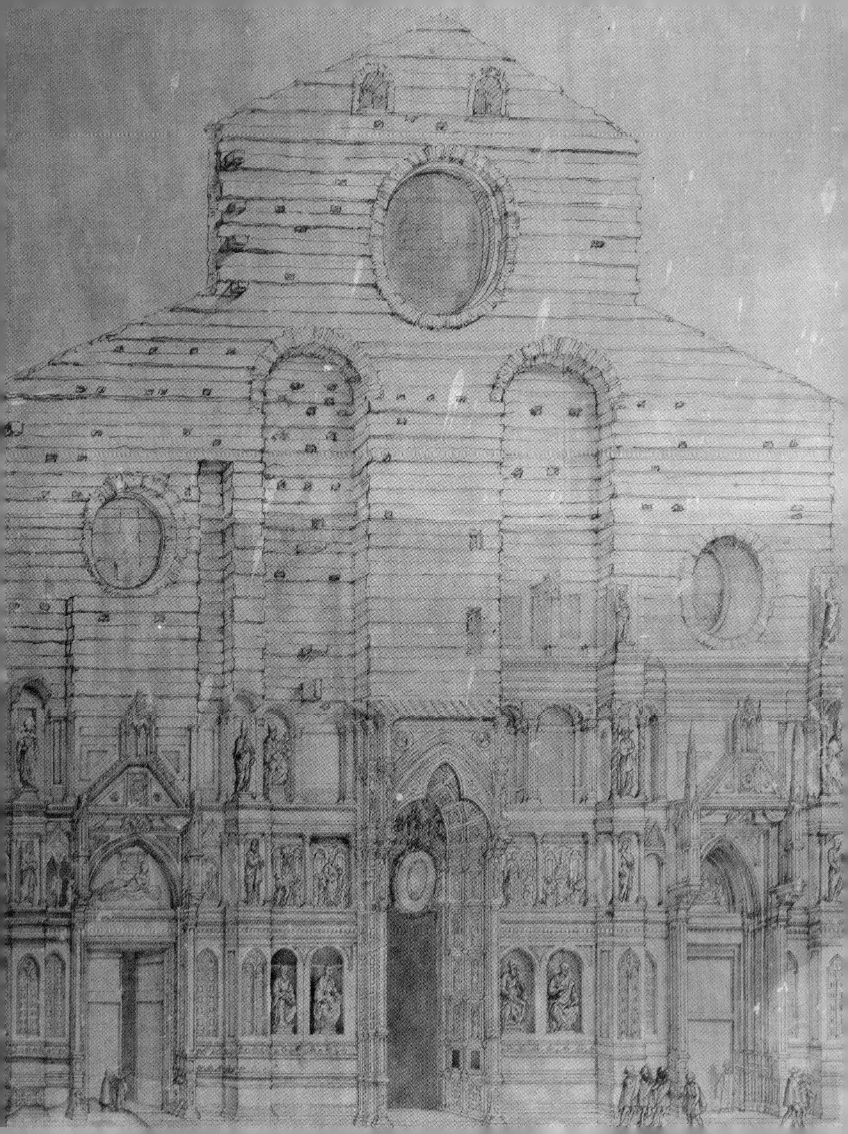

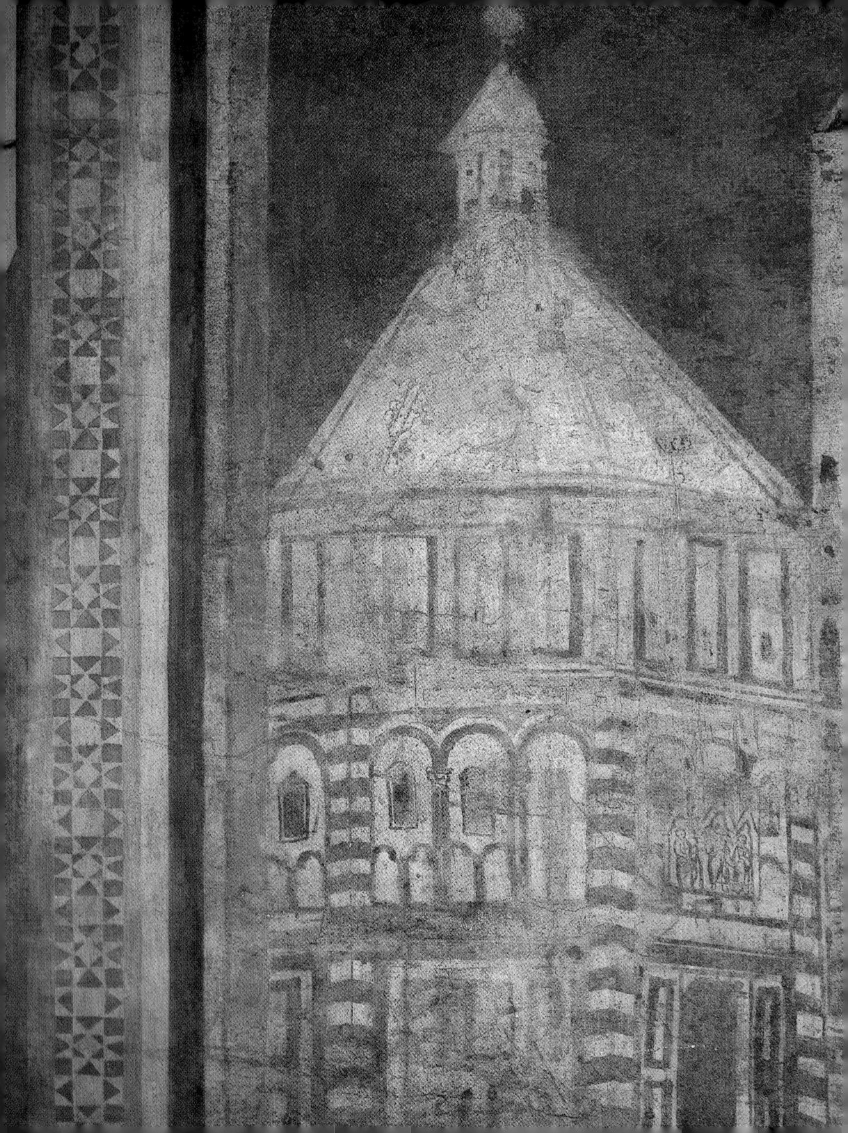

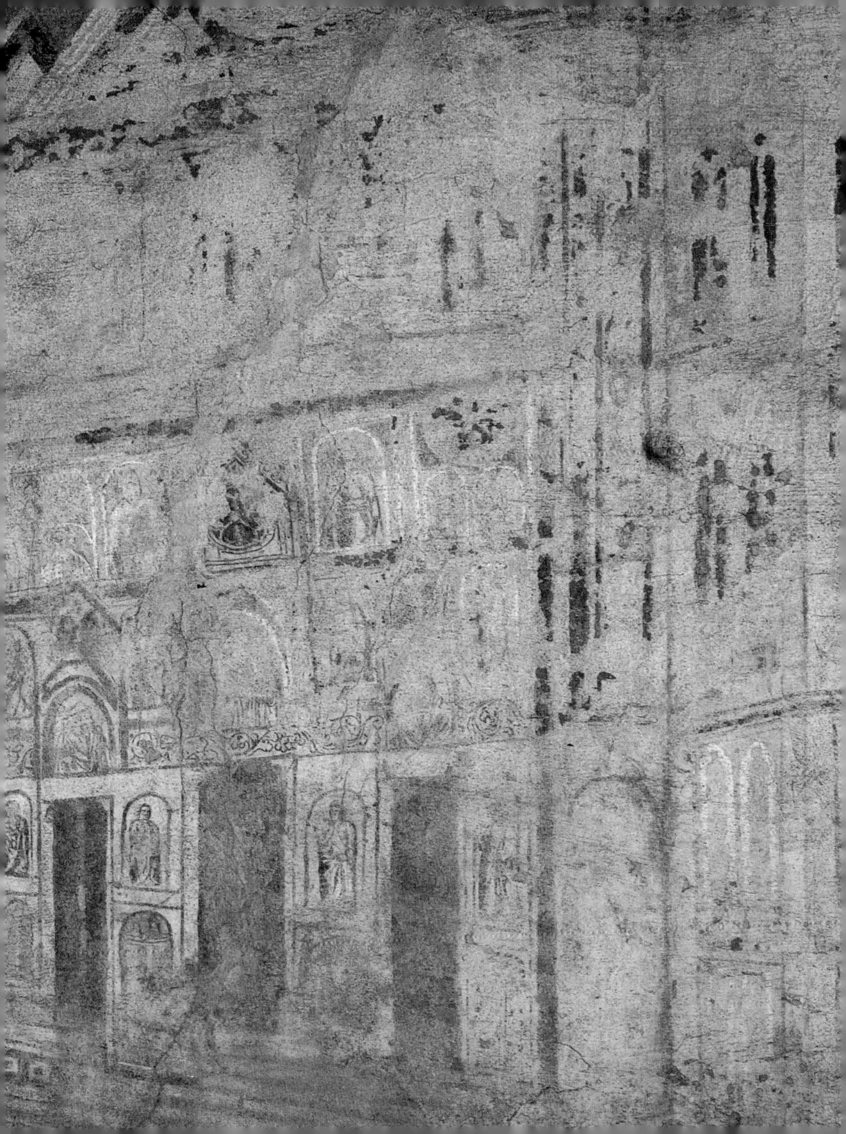

VISITORS' ITINERARY AND WORKS OF ART

- ON THE OUTSIDE OF THE BAPTISTERY
  - the three doors; the South Door by Andrea Pisano (1330), with *Stories of the Baptist, Theological and Cardinal Virtues*, framed by a decoration of plants, animals, and figures by Vittore Ghiberti (1452-1462); the North Door by Lorenzo Ghiberti, with *Episodes from the New Testament, Evangelists and Doctors of the Church* (1); The Porta del Paradiso, with *Episodes from the Bible* (some of the panels are in the Museo dell'Opera del Duomo).
- INSIDE THE BAPTISTERY
  - in addition to the mosaics and the inlaid marble floor, the *Tomb of the Anti-Pope John XXIII* (the former Baldassarre Coscia, c. 1427) by Donatello and Michelozzo.
- ONTHE OUTSIDE OF THE DUOMO, NORTH SIDE
  - the Porta della Mandorla, whose tympanum with *Our Lady of the Assumption in a Mandorla* by Nanni di Banco (1414-1421), decorated with a pattern of oil lamps inlaid in marble, evokes the sacred representations that were held in Florence with intricate lighting mechanisms and suspended cables, experimented one of the first times by Brunelleschi for the festivities of San Felice in Piazza and those of the Carmine.

Opposite page:
Lorenzo Ghiberti,
Jesus walking on the waters and saving Peter,
detail of the North Door,
c. 1403-1424. Baptistery.

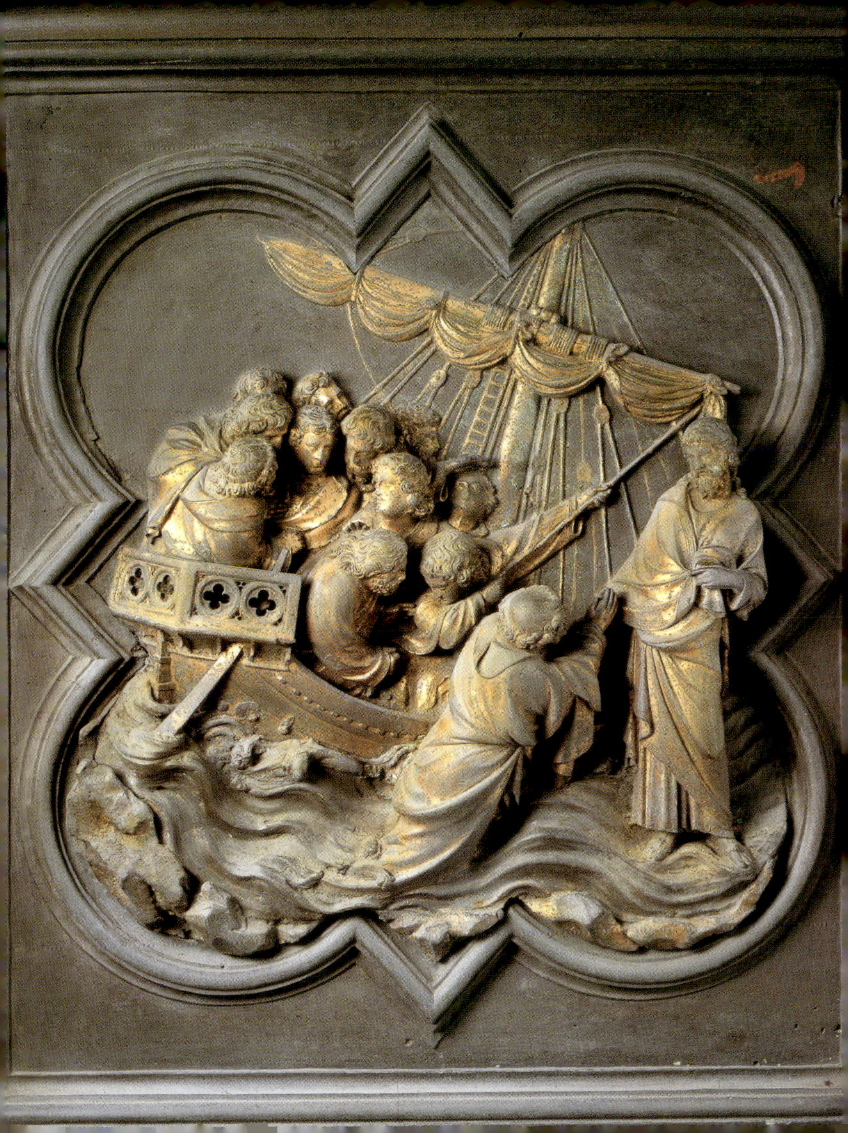

• INSIDE THE DUOMO

- the *Tomb of Bishop Orso* (died 1321) by Tino di Camaino.
- the *Clock with Prophet's Heads* (1443) frescoed on the inner façade by Paolo Uccello, and by the same artist the equestrian monument to *Giovanni Acuto* (1436), which serves as companion piece to that of *Niccolò da Tolentino* frescoed by Andrea del Castagno in 1456.
- the *Bronze Door* (1445-1469) by Luca della Robbia, for the New Sacristy, fabricated with the assistance of Michelozzo and Maso di Bartolomeo.
- *the Sacristy of the Mass*, decorated with perspective inlaid work during the course of the 15th century.
- the numerous stained-glass windows, designed by, among others, Donatello, Ghiberti, Andrea del Castagno, and Paolo Uccello.
- on the lower level, the remains of the ancient cathedral, dedicated to one of the most ancient Florentine patron saints, the Palestinian martyr *Saint Reparata*. The dimensions of this first building were much smaller than those of Santa Maria del Fiore, and the church was adorned by an elegant mosaic floor with geometric patterns that rested on the ruins of ancient Roman houses.

Opposite page:
Lorenzo Ghiberti, *Stories of Joseph*, detail of a panel from the Porta del Paradiso (after restoration), 1425-1452, gilded bronze. Museo dell'Opera del Duomo.

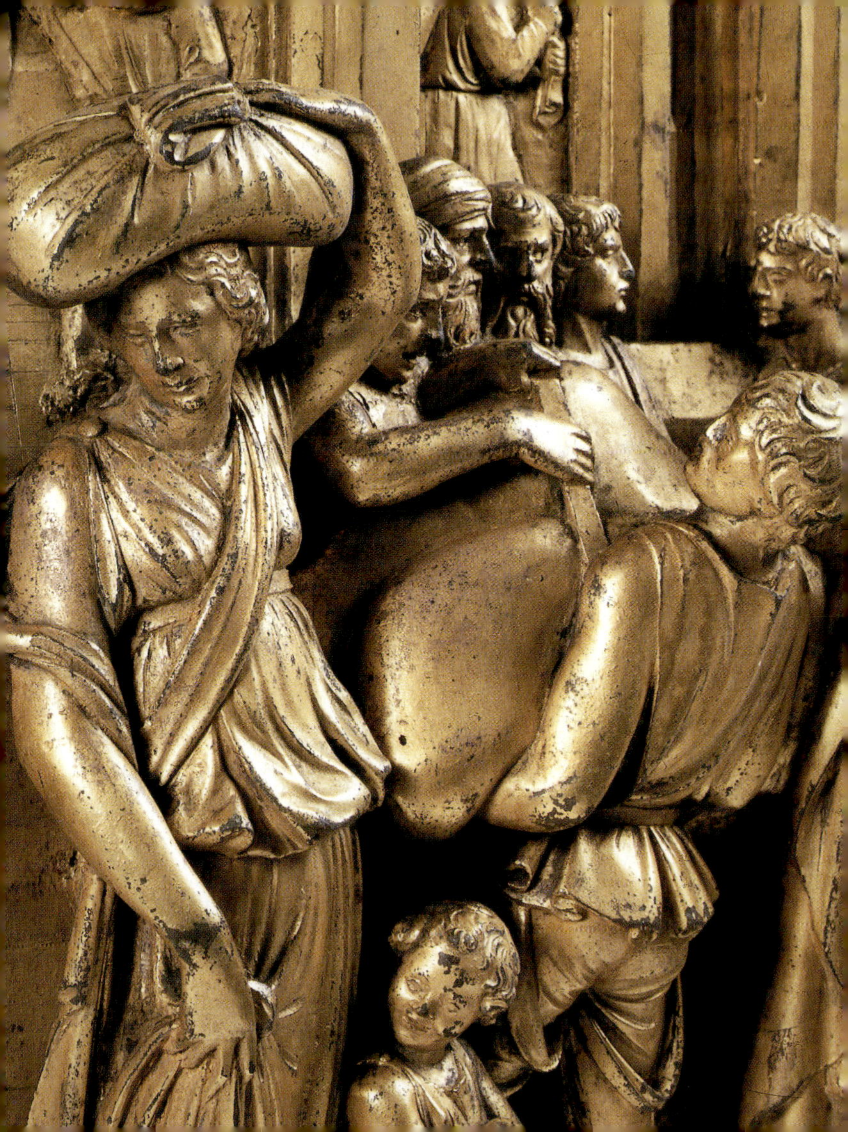

Below:
The elegant inlaid marble and tracery decoration of the Porta della Balla on the south side of the Duomo.

Opposite page:
The Porta della Mandorla, on the north side of the Cathedral of Santa Maria del Fiore, on which numerous artists collaborated in the early decades of the 15th century, among them Donatello, Nanni di Banco, and Jacopo della Quercia.

Following pages:
Michelozzo and Donatello, *Tomb of the anti-Pope John XXIII, the former Baldassarre Coscia*, detail, 1427. Baptistery.

Tino di Camaino, *Funerary monument to Bishop Antonio degli Orsi*, partially dismantled (other parts are in the Museo Nazionale del Bargello and in foreign museums and collections), 1321, marble. Duomo.

Luca della Robbia: *Head of a man*, full-round sculpture, detail from the bronze door, c. 1445-1474. Duomo, New Sacristy (or Sacristy of the Mass).

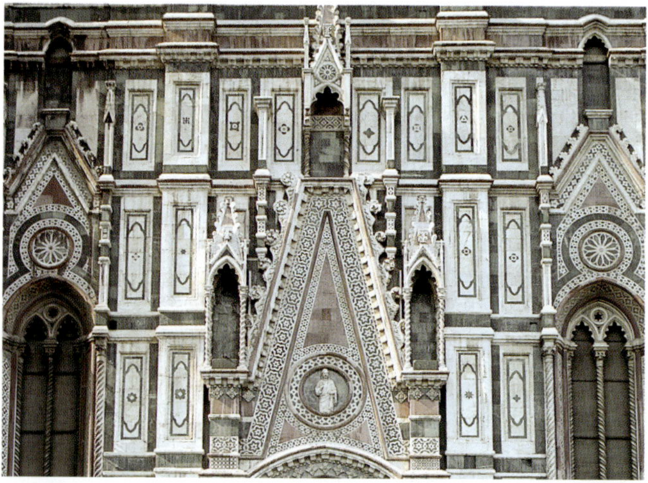

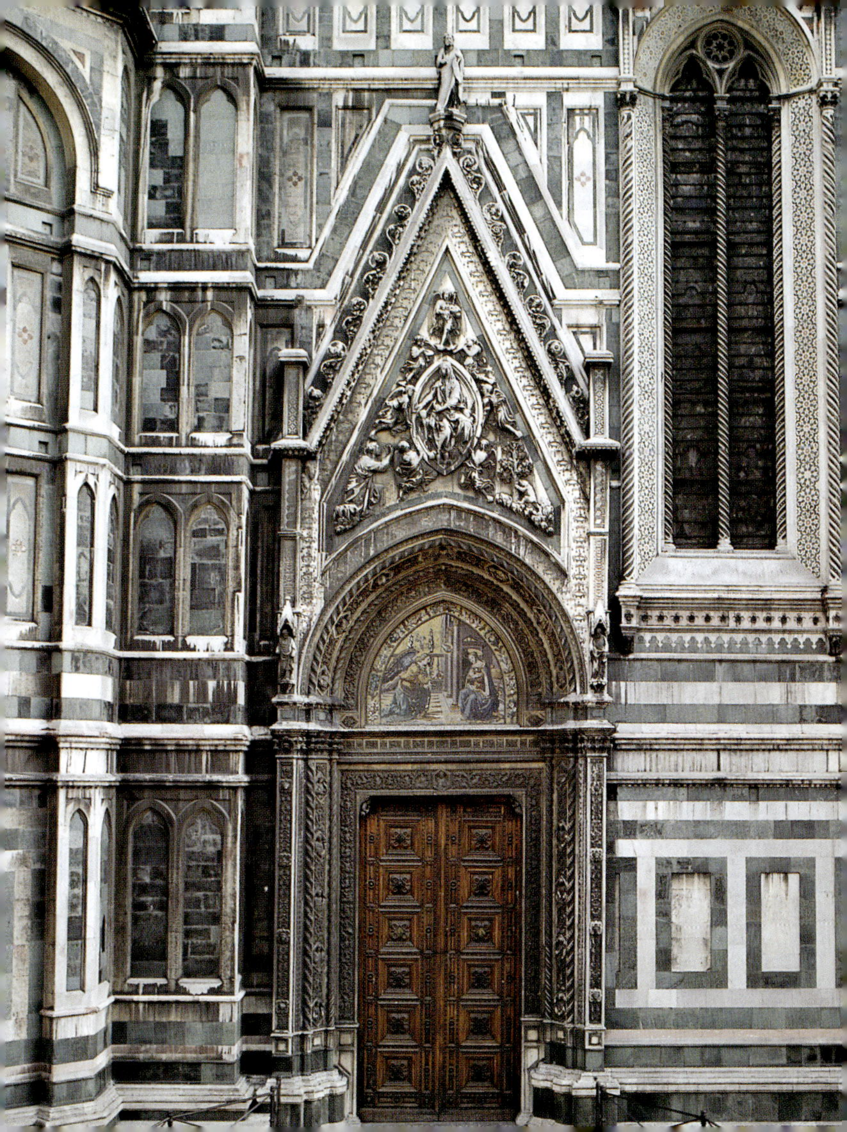

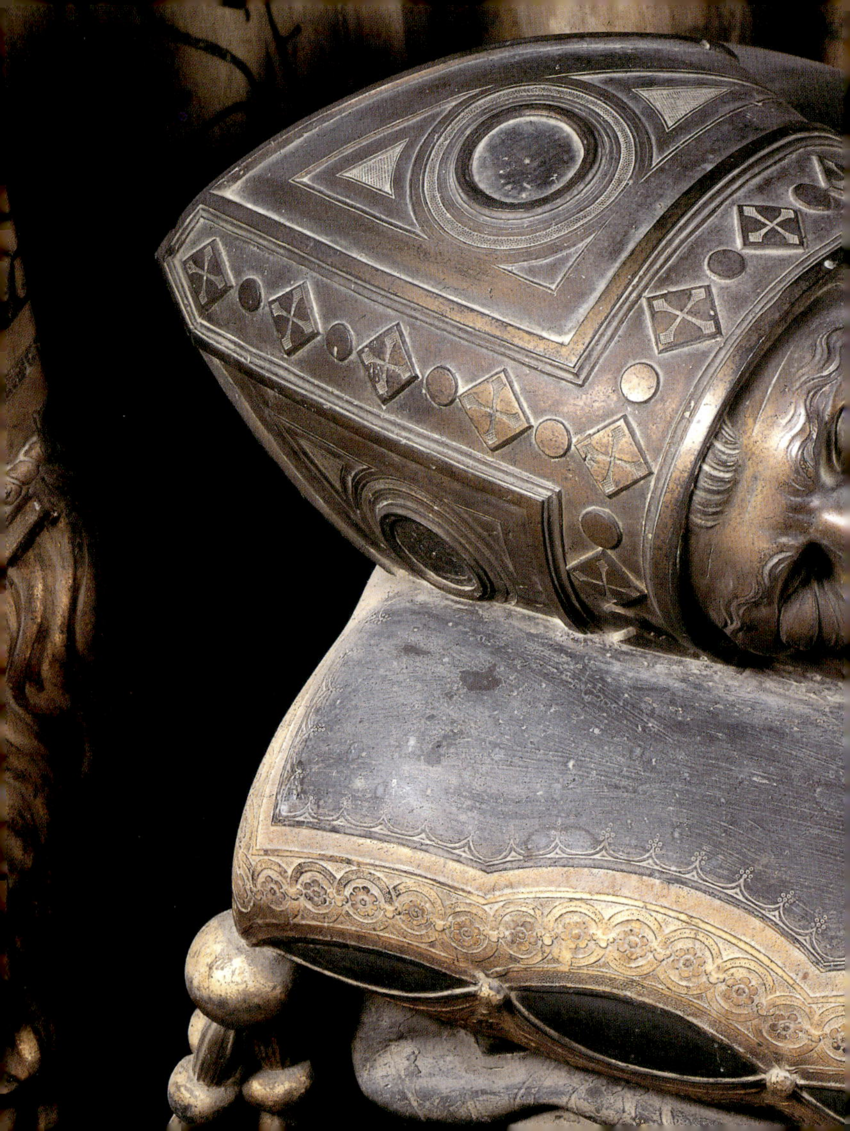

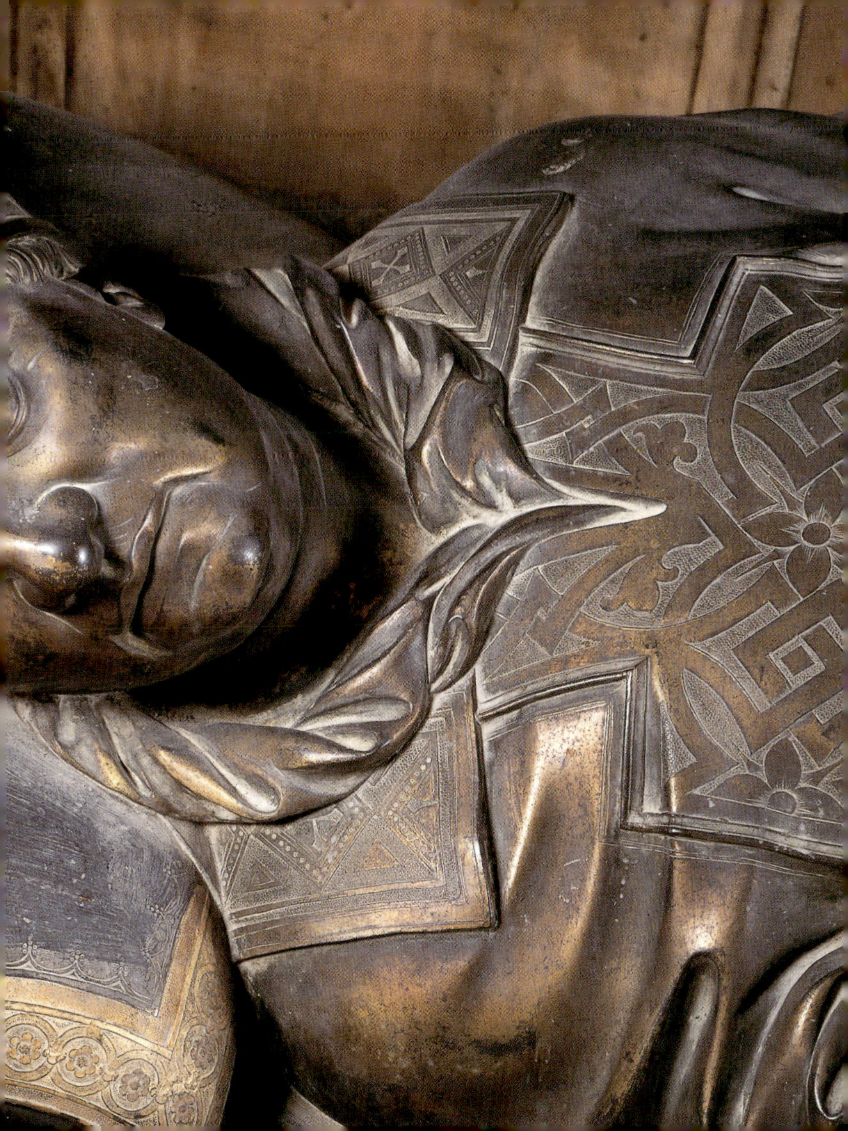

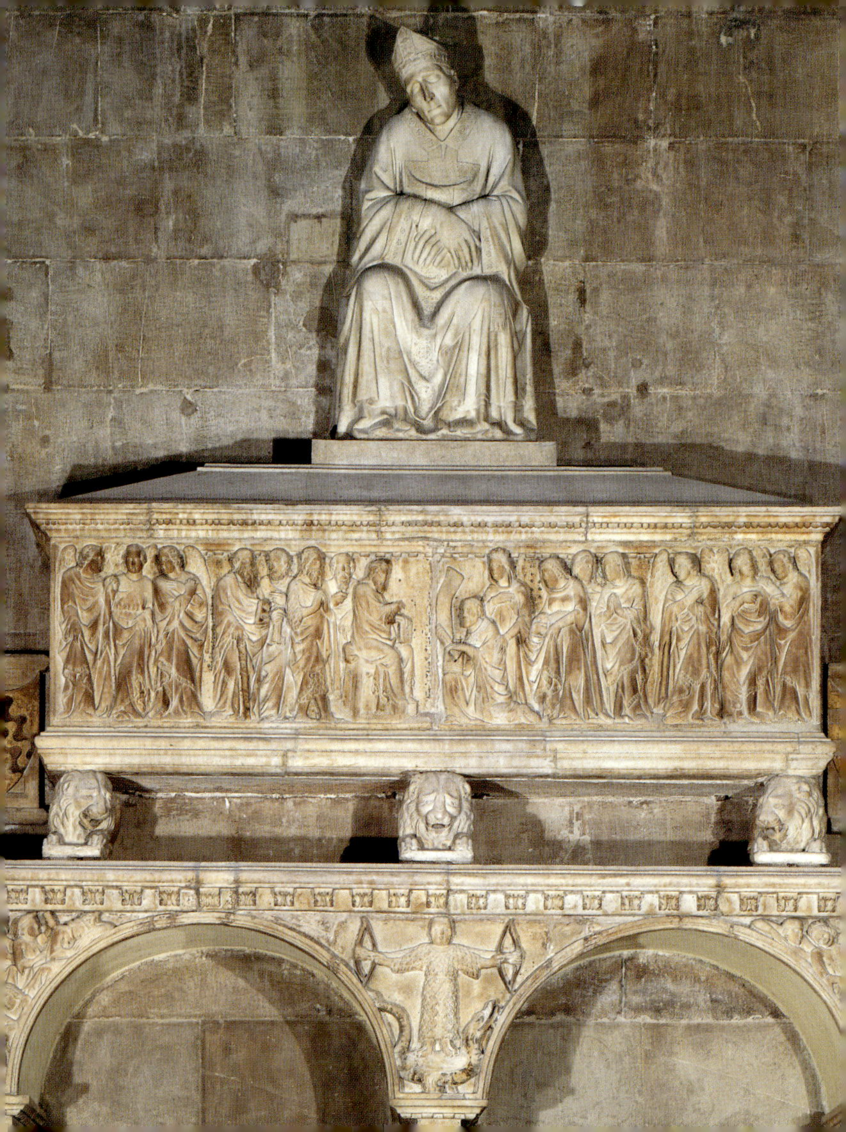

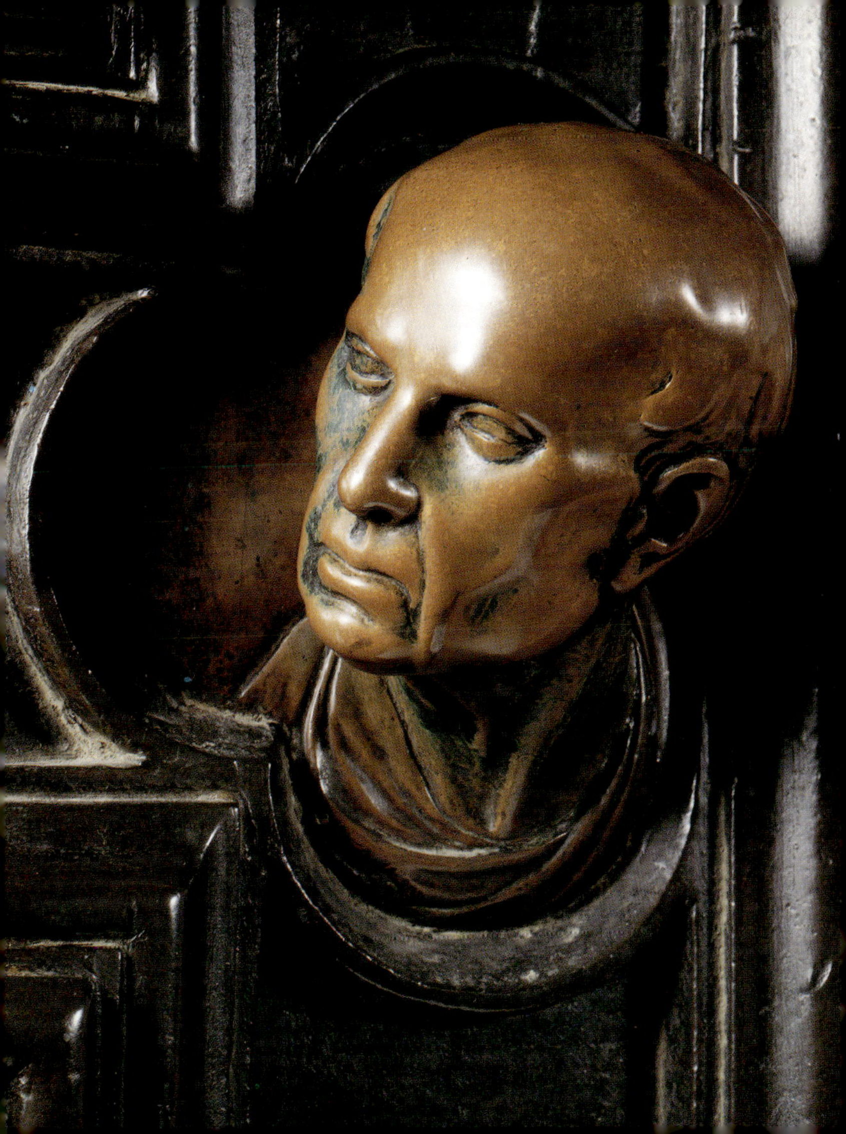

Opposite page:
Paolo Uccello, *Clock with prophets' heads*, 1443, fresco. Duomo, inner façade.
This is one of the rare surviving mechanical clocks of the age, which marks the time in the ancient way, measuring it from one sunset to another.

Following pages:
Paolo Uccello, *False equestrian monument to Giovanni Acuto*, 1436, fresco. Duomo, left nave.
"Giovanni Acuto", as the English "Capitano di Ventura" John Hawkwood was called, was a brave condottiero of the Florentine army from 1377 to the year of his death, 1394.

Andrea del Castagno, *False equestrian monument to Niccolò da Tolentino*, 1456, fresco. Duomo, left nave.
Niccolò da Tolentino was an outstanding figure in the military history of the Florentine Republic; it was he who led the Florentines to victory in the Battle of San Romano in 1432. He was buried in the Duomo in 1435.

Luca della Robbia, *Resurrection of Christ*, detail of the lunette over the portal of the New Sacristy (or Sacristy of the Mass), 1442-1444, glazed terracotta. Duomo.

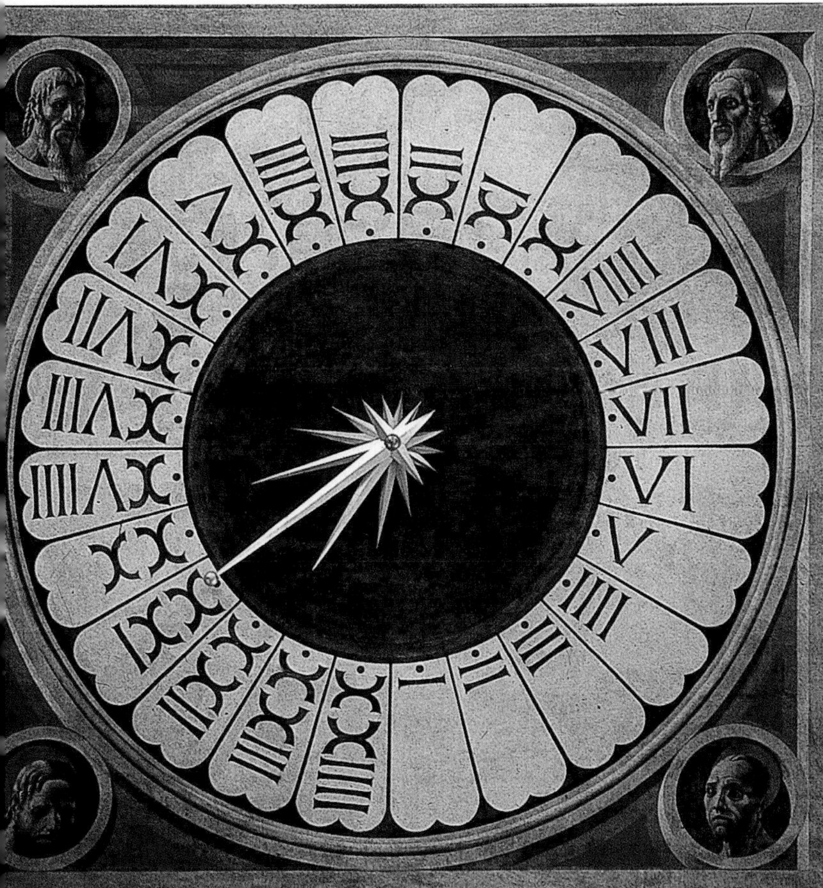

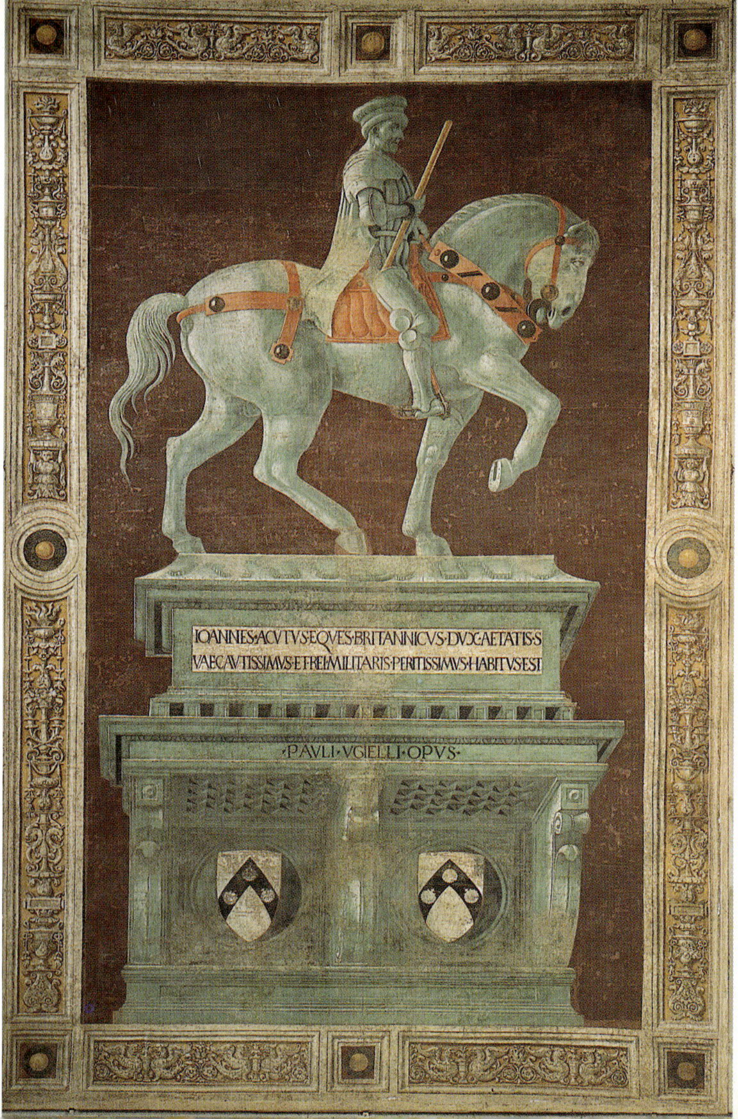
IOANNES·ACVTVS·EQVES·BRITANNICVS·DVX·AETATIS·S
VAE·CAVTISSIMVS·ET·REI·MILITARIS·PERITISSIMVS·HABITVS·EST
·PAVLI·VGIELLI·OPVS·

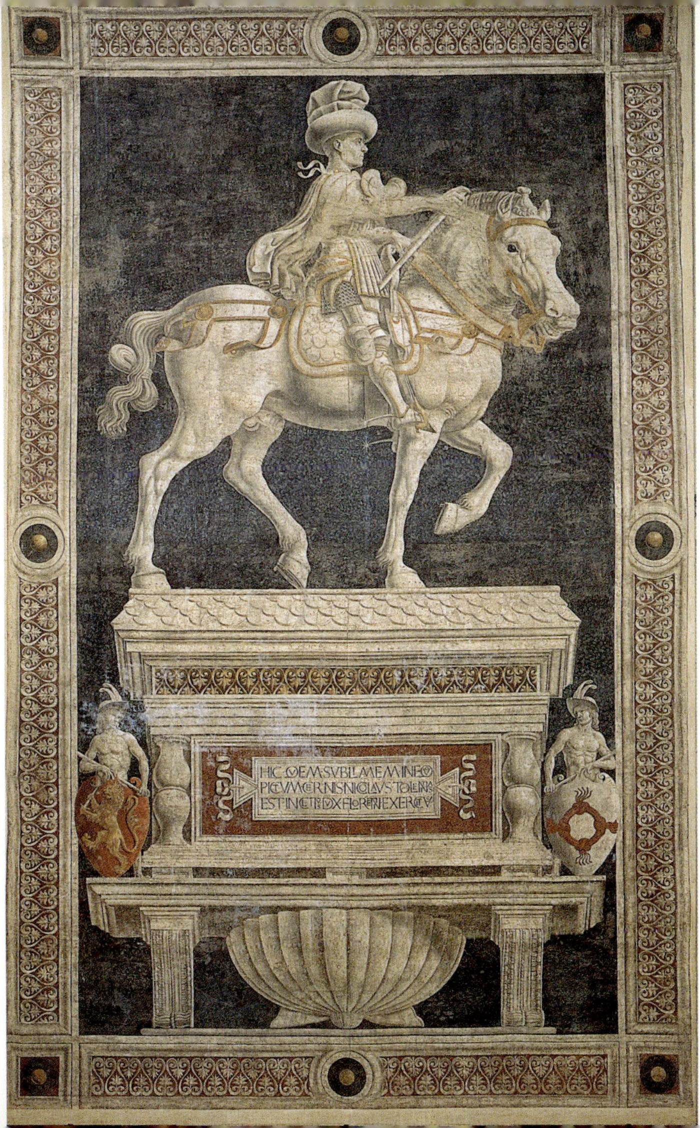
HIC QVEM SVBLIMEM IN EQVO
PICTVM CERNIS NICOLAVS TOLENTINAS
EST INCLITVS DVX FLORENTINI EXERCITVS

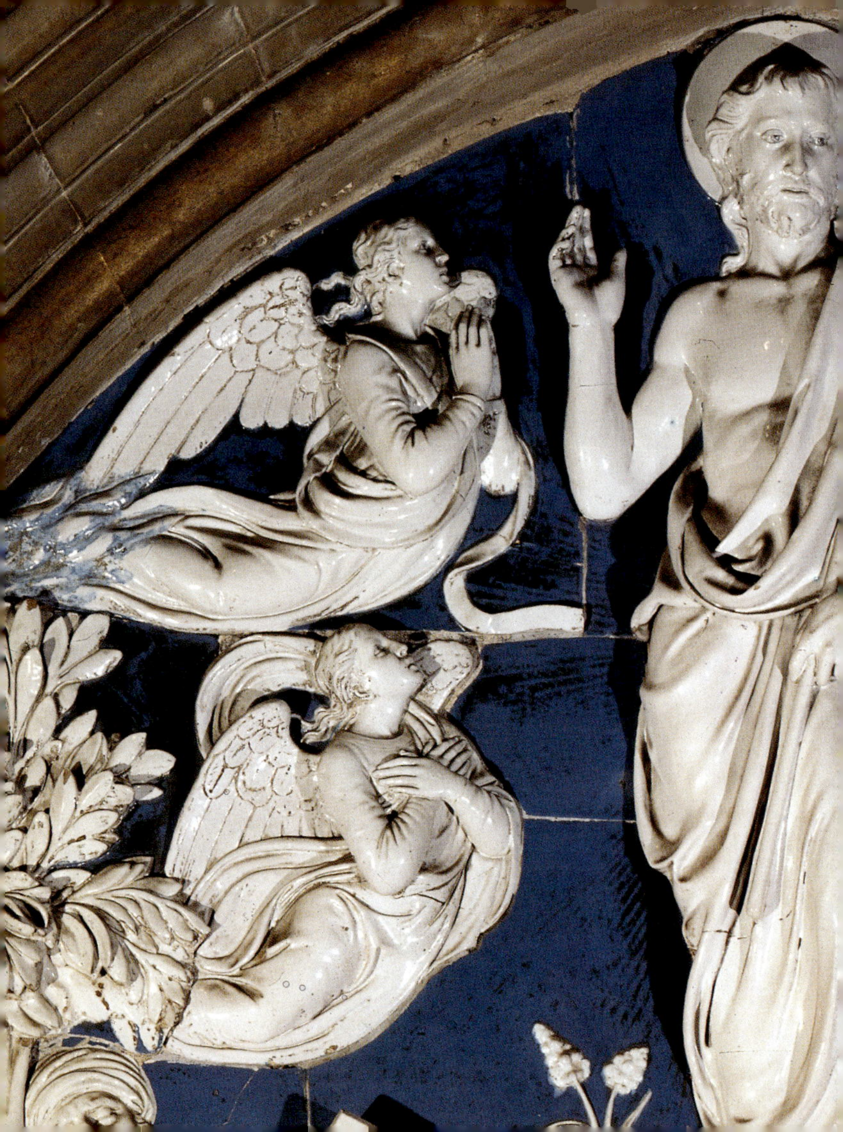

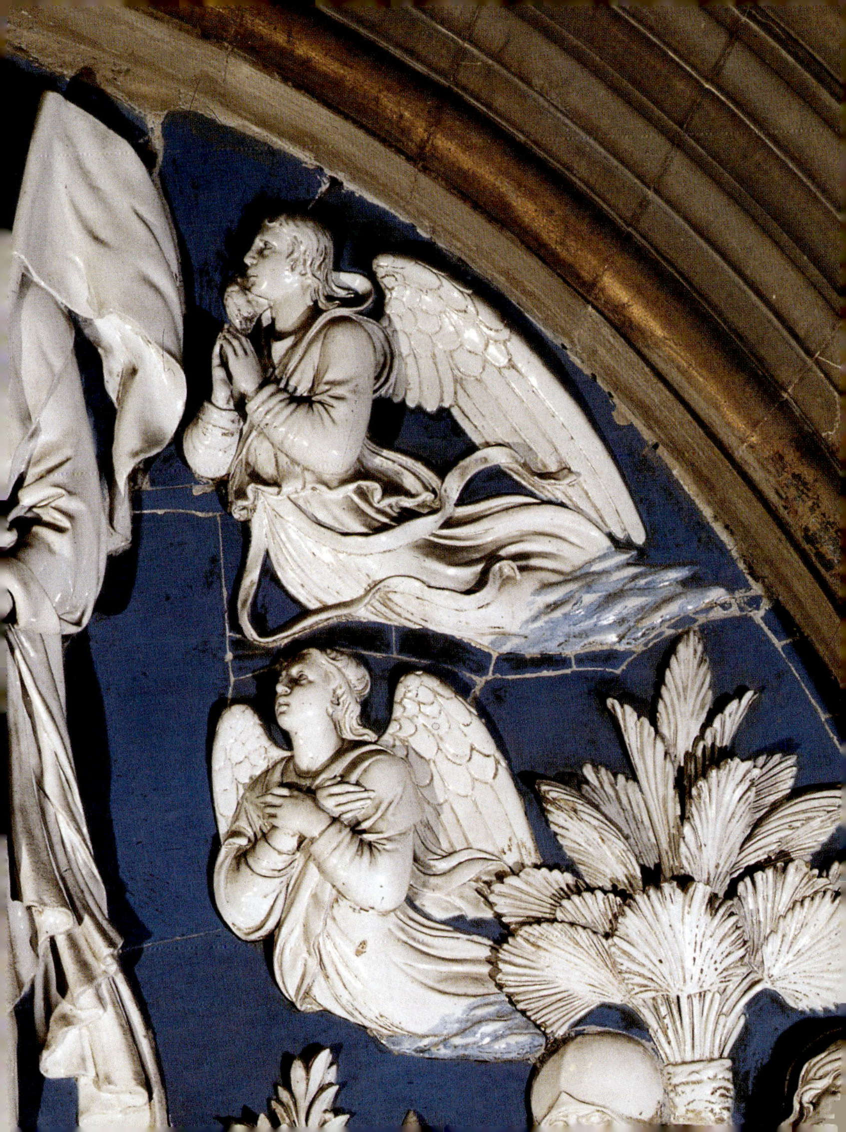

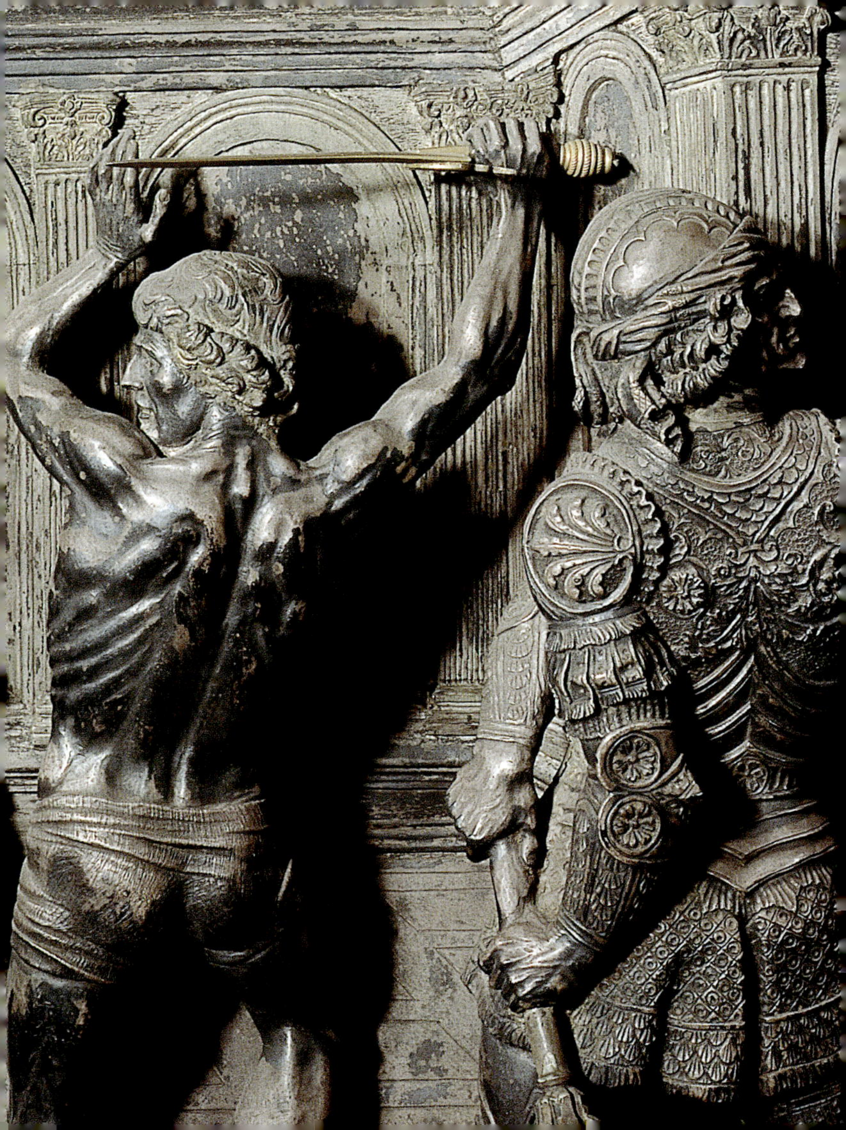

Museo dell'Opera del Duomo

The Museo dell'Opera di Santa Maria del Fiore (better known as the Museo dell'Opera del Duomo), is located at the back of Santa Maria del Fiore, in a palace remodeled by Brunelleschi, which since the beginning of the 15th century has housed the administration of the Opera, or Cathedral works. The museum is, in fact, a direct descendent of the institution founded in the late 13th century to superintend the construction site of the new cathedral, and which is still today responsible for the cathedral's maintenance. Instituted as a museum in 1891, it contains a great number of masterpieces coming from the Baptistery and the Cathedral of Santa Maria del Fiore, moved here at various times for reasons of conservation. It also displays the surviving sculpures and decorations from the original façade of the Duomo, designed by Arnolfo di Cambio, as well as sumptuous illuminated manuscripts, refined works of embroidery, altar frontals, various liturgical objects, busts, tombstones, sarcophaguses, ancient fragments, wooden models of various projects for the façade of the Duomo, and original tools used in the construction site. Over the course of time, materials and art objects from other religious buildings in the city have also been brought to the museum, recently remodeled in keeping with the most modern canons of museum design.

Opposite page:
Andrea Verrocchio, *Beheading of St. John the Baptist*, detail from the *Altar frontal of St. John*, 1477-1480, embossed silver.
Museo dell'Opera del Duomo.

Noteworthy among the works displayed are:

- fragments of marble slabs from the Baptismal Font and the presbytery enclosure of the Baptistery, with beautiful tracery in inlaid black marble (13th century).
- the statues of Arnolfo di Cambio coming from the central portal of the Cathedral of Santa Reparata: the *Virgin and Child bestowing Blessings*, of majestic beauty and humanity, with the eyes made even more lifelike by the use of blue glass, the *St. Reparata* and the *St. Zanobius* (c. 1300-1302).
- other statues by Arnolfo di Cambio and his assistants, among them the *Boniface VIII*, which must also have been placed on the façade, near the reclining figure of the *Virgin of the Nativity*.
- fragments of the 14th century sculptures that were placed on the south door of the Baptistery, among them the *Christ bestowing Blessings* and the *Head of St. John the Baptist* by Tino di Camaino.
- the marble hexagonal panels, carved in bas-relief, which decorated Giotto's Bell Tower until 1967, now replaced by copies made of concrete. The iconographic program was inspired by the arts, the sciences and the trades, the planets, the virtues, and the liberal arts. Twenty-one of them are by Andrea Pisano

Opposite page:
Arnolfo di Cambio and Assistants, *Boniface VIII*, c. 1297-1298, marble. Museo dell'Opera del Duomo.

Following pages:
Arnolfo di Cambio, *Reclining figure of the Nativity*, and *Virgin and Child*, details, 1296, marble. Museo dell'Opera del Duomo.

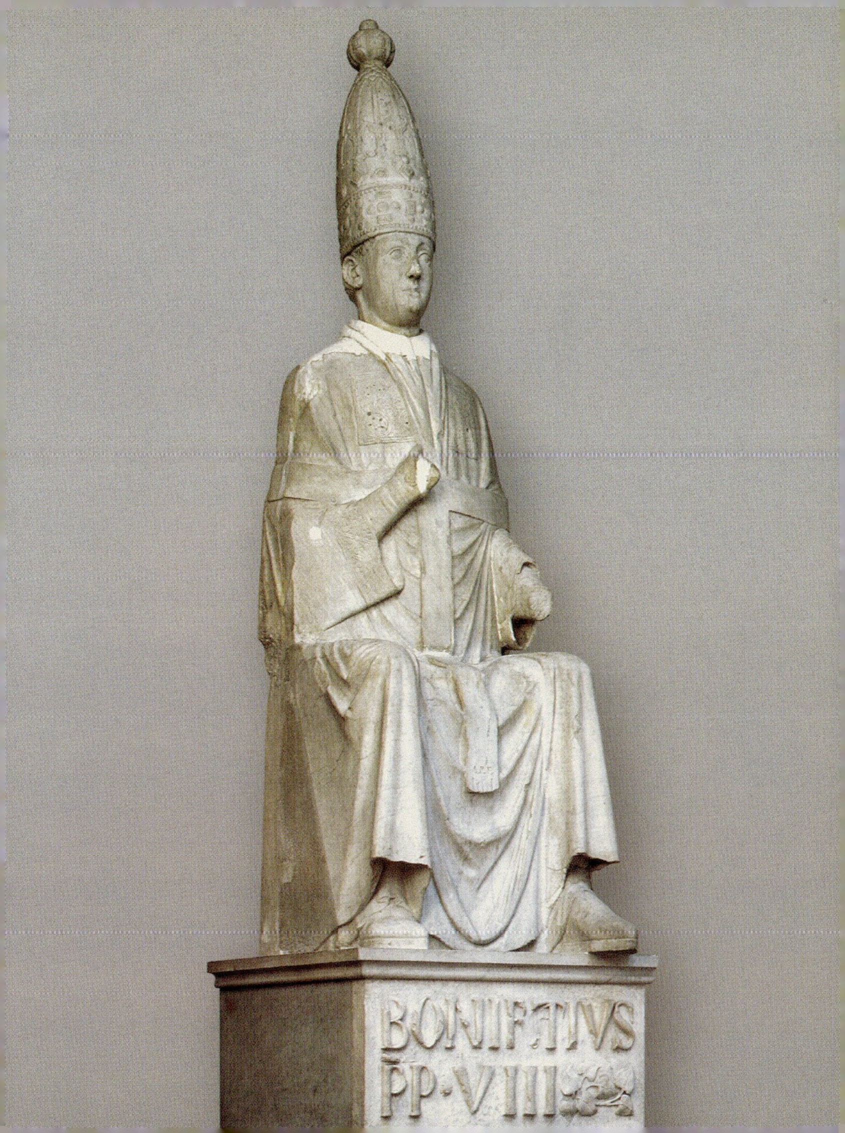
BONIFATIUS
PP·VIII

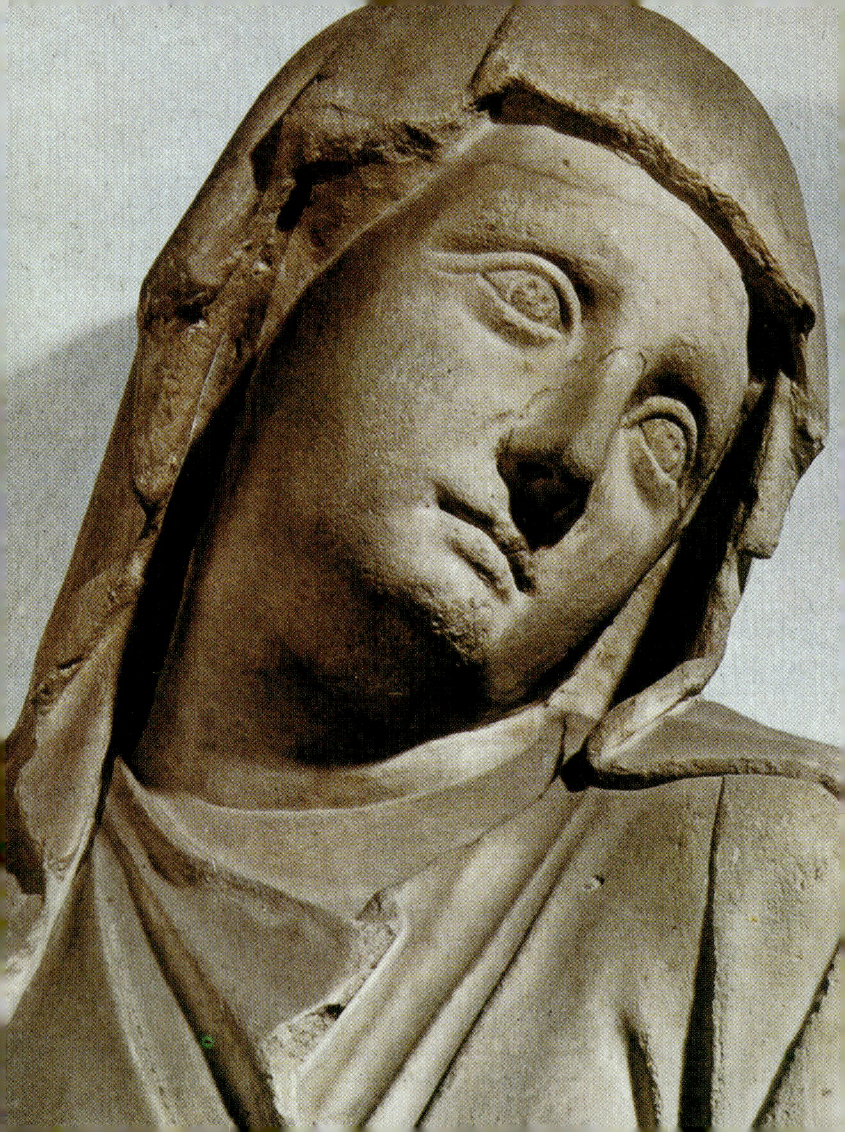

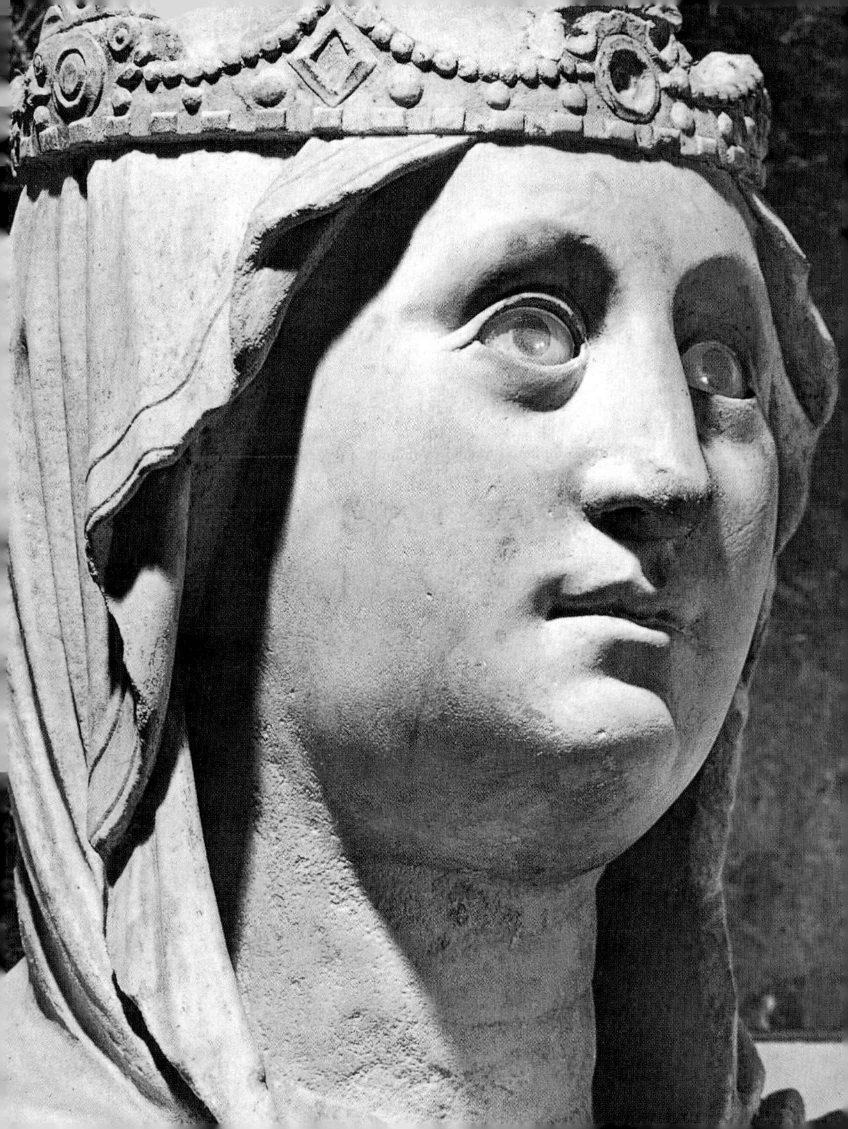

(1334-1336), while the five illustrating the liberal arts are by Luca della Robbia (1437-1439).

- the 15th century sculptures for the ancient façade designed by Arnolfo, among them the *St. Luke* (1408-1414) by Nanni di Banco and the *St. John the Evangelist* (1408-1415) by Donatello.
- the statues of *Jeremiah* and *Abacuc* (1426-1432) by Donatello, remarkably expressive, forming part of the

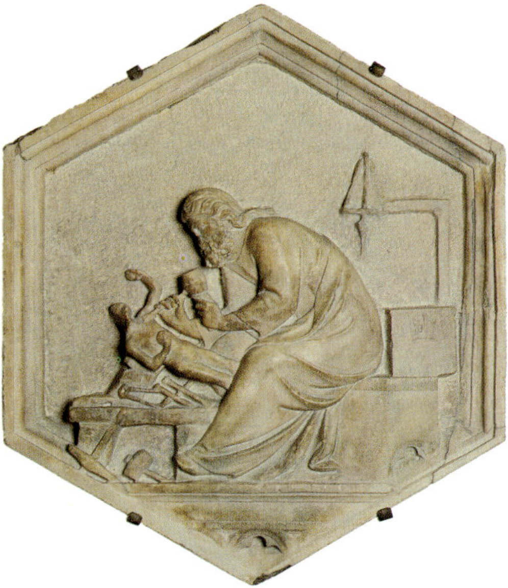

Andrea Pisano, *Sculpture,* 1334-1336, marble, panel from Giotto's Bell Tower. Museo dell'Opera del Duomo.

Opposite page: Donatello, *Abacuc,* 1426-1432, marble. Museo dell'Opera del Duomo.

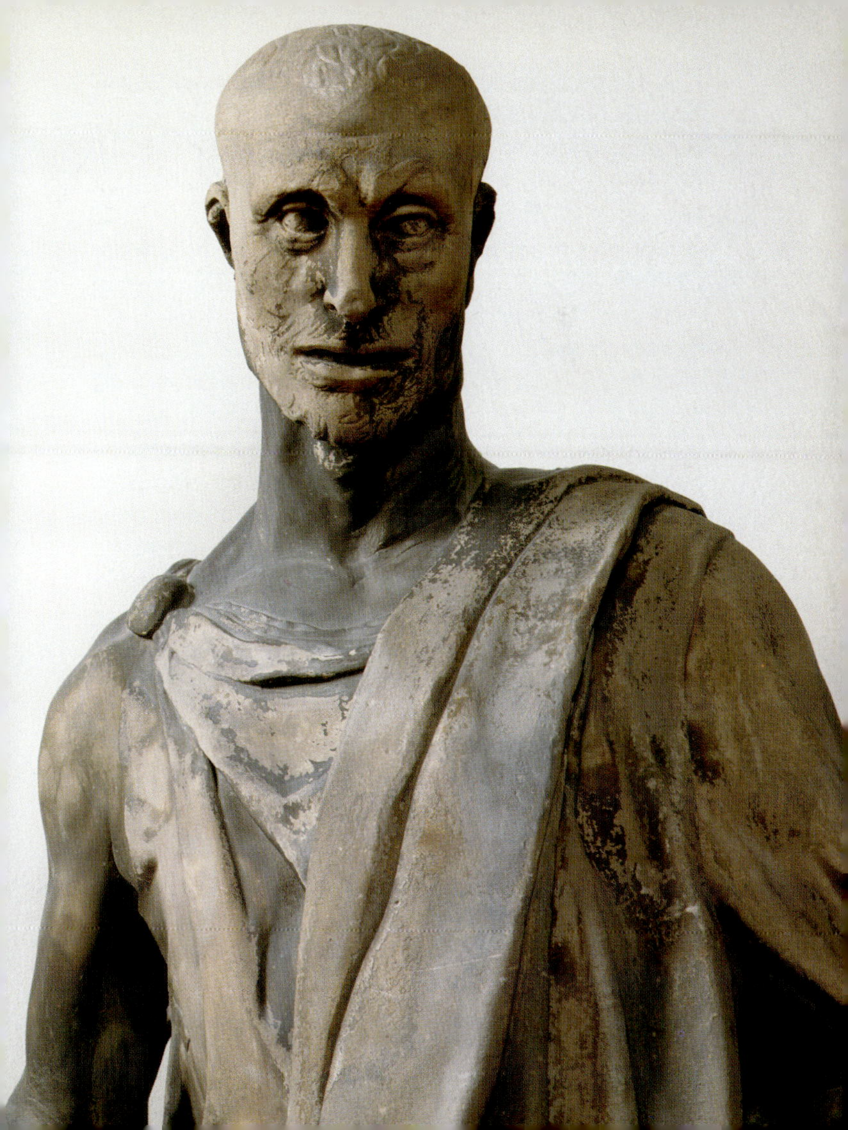

group of 16 scultures for the niches in the Bell Tower (sculpted also by Andrea Pisano and Nanni di Bartolo).

- the *Magdalene* by Donatello (1455), formerly in the Baptistery, portrayed with the emaciated face of an old woman.
- four original panels from the Porta del Paradiso by Lorenzo Ghiberti (1425-1452), in gilded bronze, replaced by copies on the door of the Baptistery.
- the *Altar frontal of St. John the Baptist*, in gilded and embossed silver, which served as altar for the Baptistery, on which worked the greatest Florentine artists (among them Verrocchio and Michelozzo) from 1366 to the end of the 15th century. The pinnacles and the niches on the slender pilasters are inspired by the decorations on the Bell Tower and the south door of the Duomo. The base of the *Silver Cross of St. John* (1457-1459), exhibited on the Patron Saint's feast day, shows how Pollaiolo drew inspiration from the shape of the lantern on Brunelleschi's dome.
- the *Cantoria* (1431-1438) by Luca della Robbia, formerly above the portal of the Sacristy of the Mass in the Duomo, where the new organ was placed, in a position symmetric to the *Cantoria* by Donatello (1433-1439), which over the portal of the Sacristy of the Canons housed the old restored organ.
- the *Pietà* by Michelangelo (1549-1553), where the hooded face of Nicodemus represents that of the artist. This work, intended by the sculptor for his own tomb in Santa Maria

Opposite page:
Michelozzo, *St. John the Baptist*, 1452, detail from the *Altar frontal of St. John*, silver and enamel.
Museo dell'Opera del Duomo.

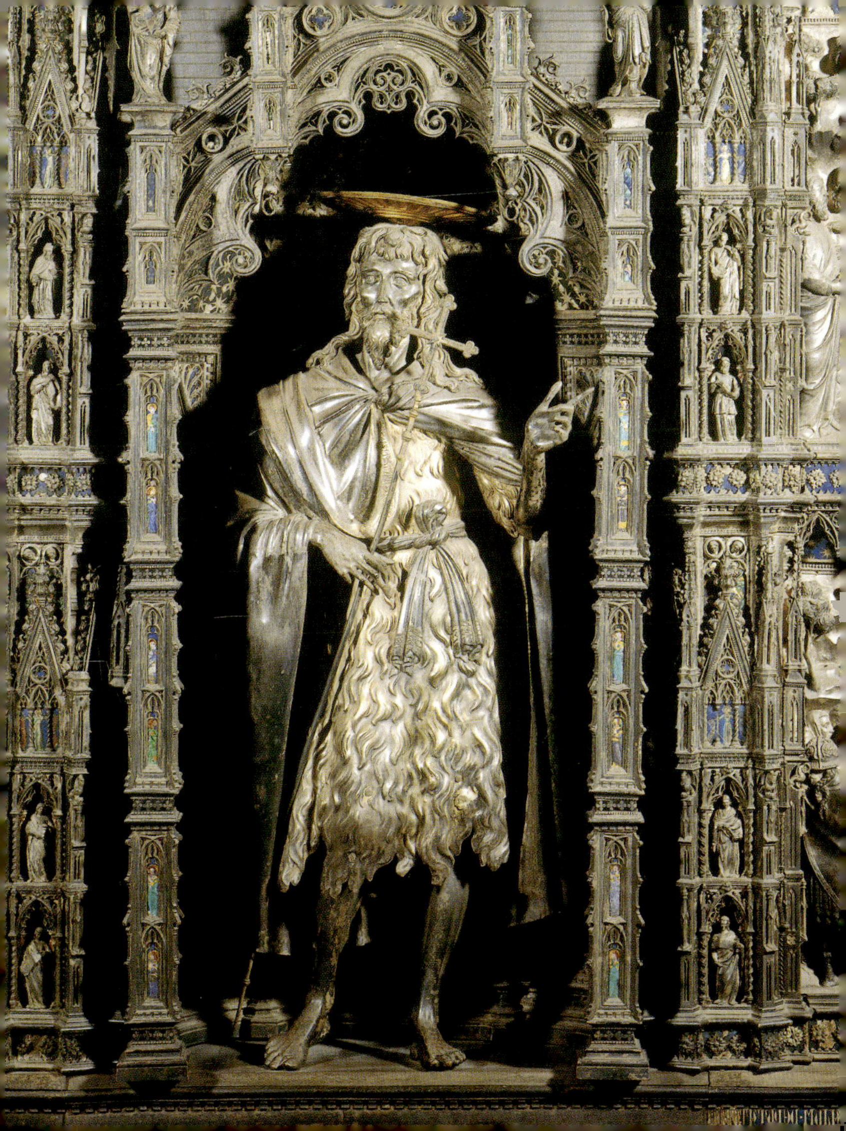

Maggiore, Rome, was purchased by Cosimo III dei Medici and arrived in Florence in 1674.

- the *Tapestry of St. John* (1466-1488), designed by Antonio Pollaiolo, an exquisitely fine work of embroidery in silk and gold.
- wooden models of Brunelleschi's dome.

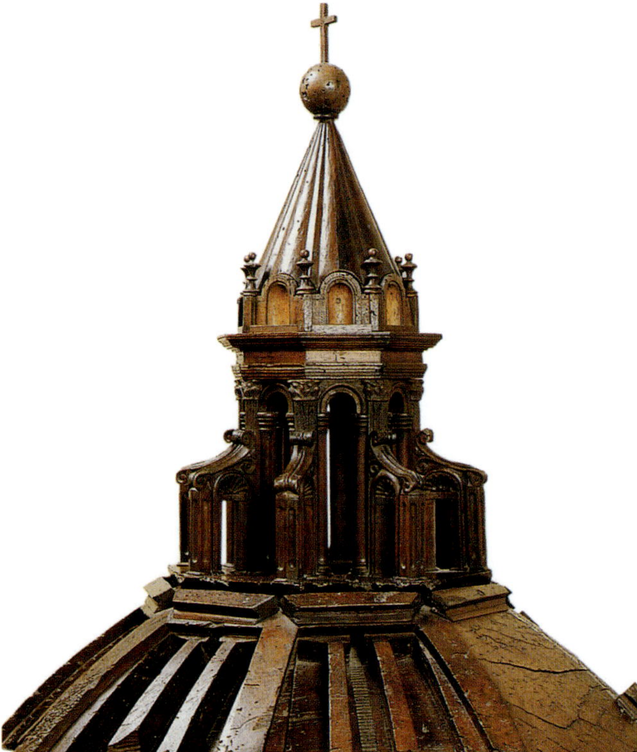

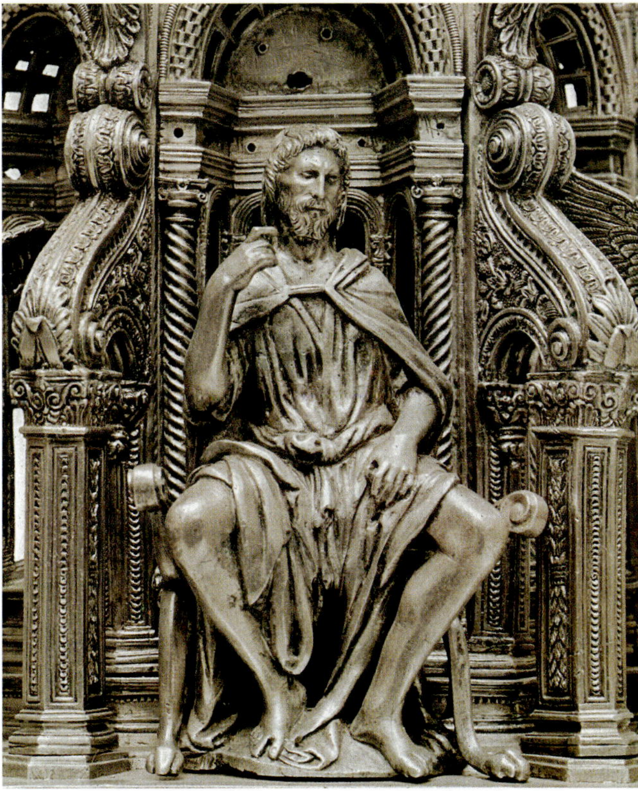

Opposite page:
From Filippo Brunelleschi,
Model of the lantern over the dome,
1679 (?), carved wood.
Museo dell'Opera del Duomo.

Above:
Antonio Pollaiolo,
Cross of St. John, detail, 1457-1459,
embossed silver leaf. Museo
dell'Opera del Duomo.

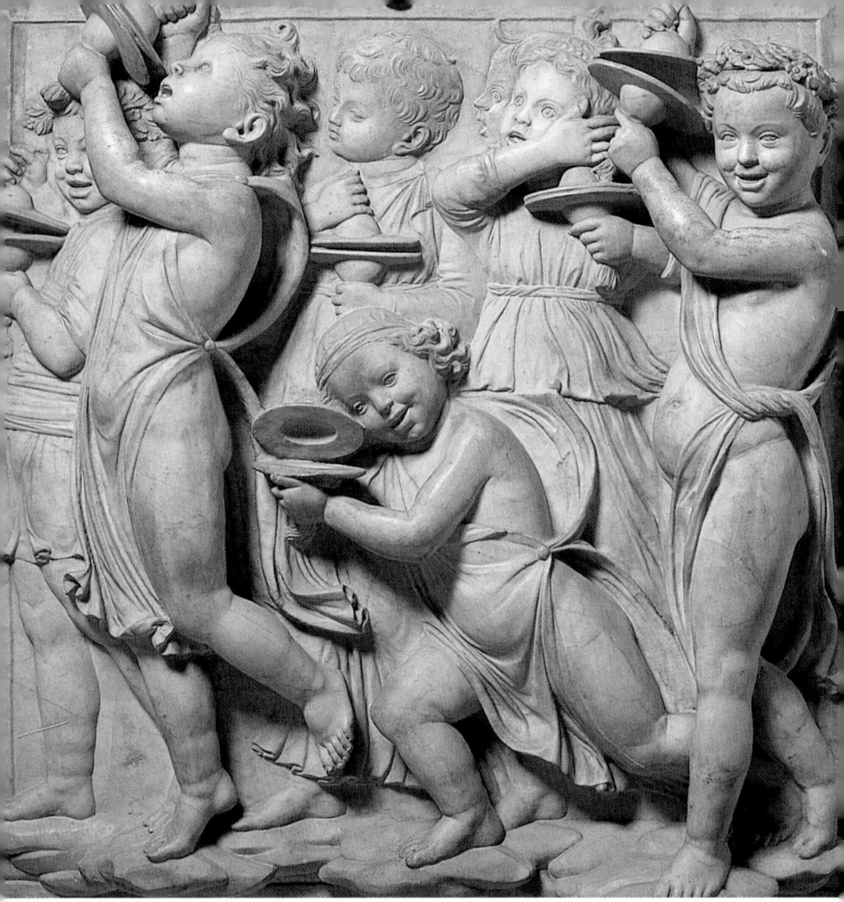

Above:
Luca della Robbia, *Putti,* detail from the *Cantoria,* 1431-1438, marble. Museo dell'Opera del Duomo.

Opposite page:
Donatello, *Cantoria,* 1433-1439, marble. Museo dell'Opera del Duomo.

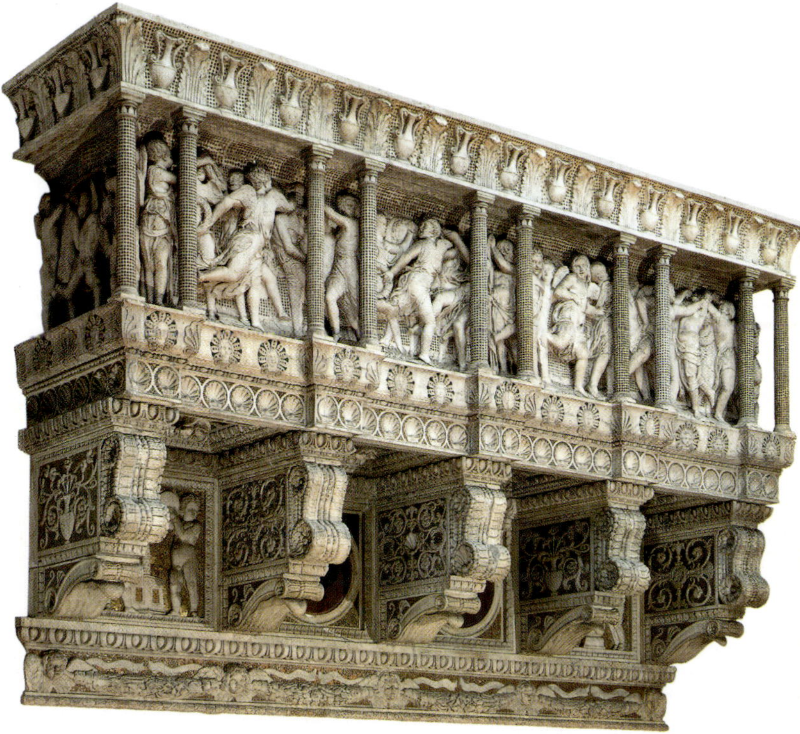

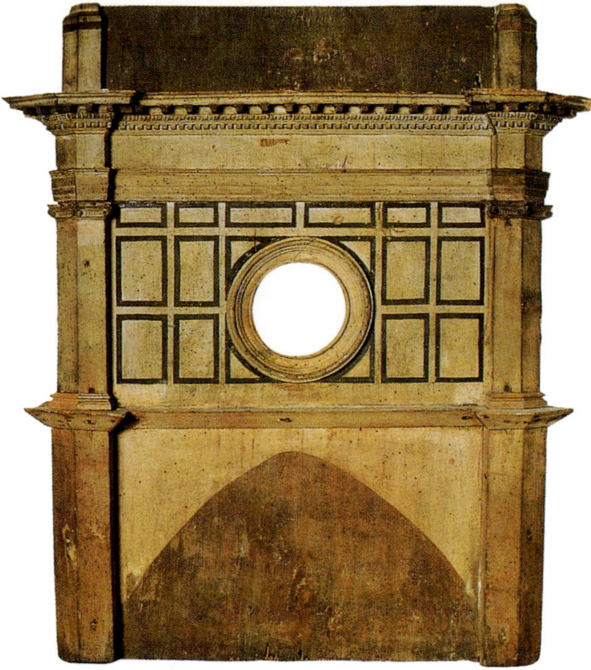

Above:
Michelangelo Buonarroti (attr.), *Model of the tambour and the gallery on the Duomo,* after 1516 (?), carved wood.
Museo dell'Opera del Duomo.

Opposite page:
Filippo Brunelleschi (attr.), *Model of the dome and the apse section of the Duomo*, 1429 (?), carved wood.
Museo dell'Opera del Duomo.

Following pages:
Paolo di Giovanni Sogliani, *Reliquiary of the Libretto*, 1501, gold, silver and enamel. Museo dell'Opera del Duomo.

Michelangelo Buonarroti, *Pietà*, 1549-1553, marble.
Museo dell'Opera del Duomo.

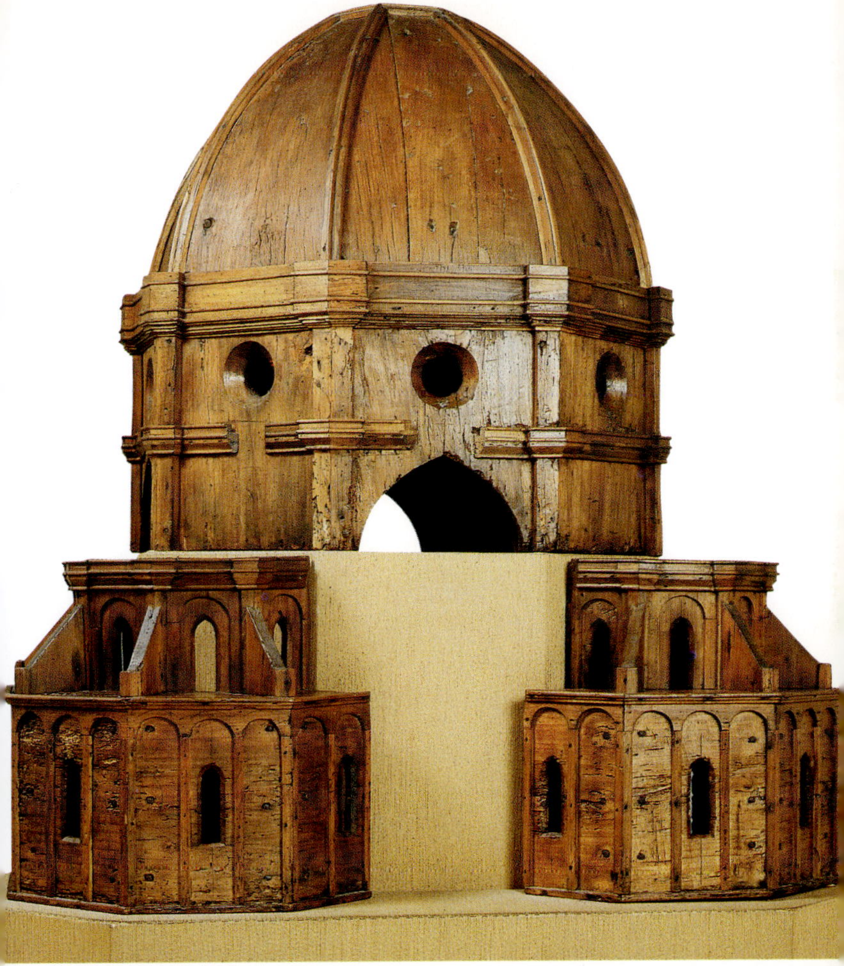

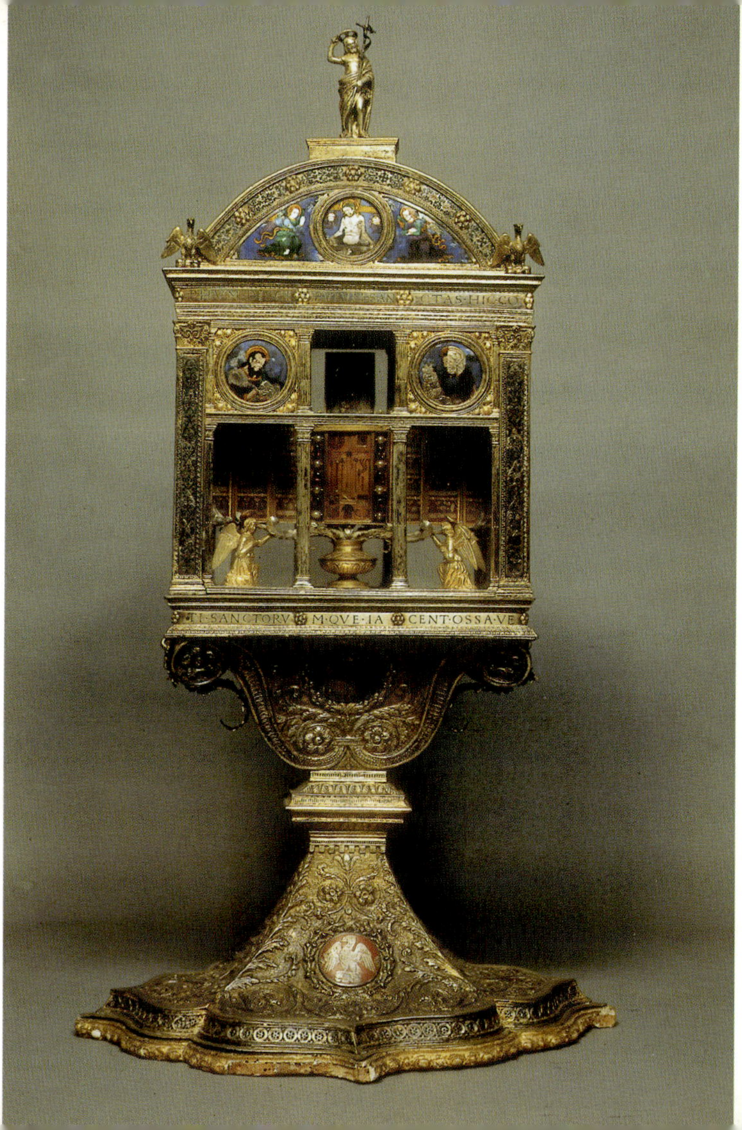
TI·SANCTORV M·QVE·IA CENT·OSSA·VE

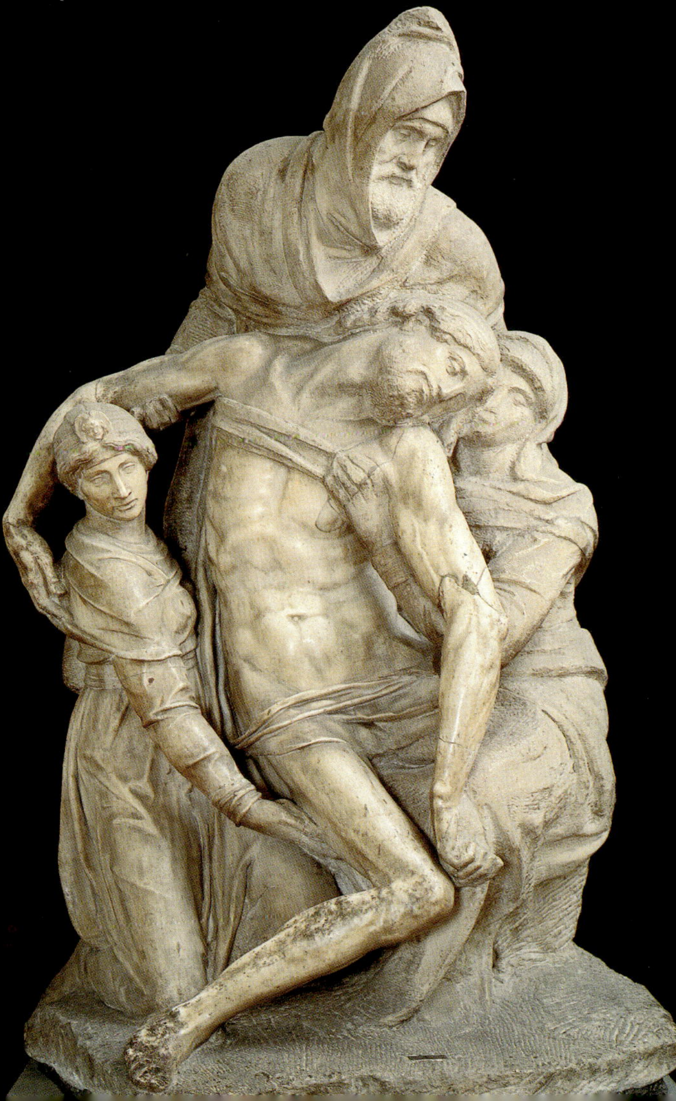

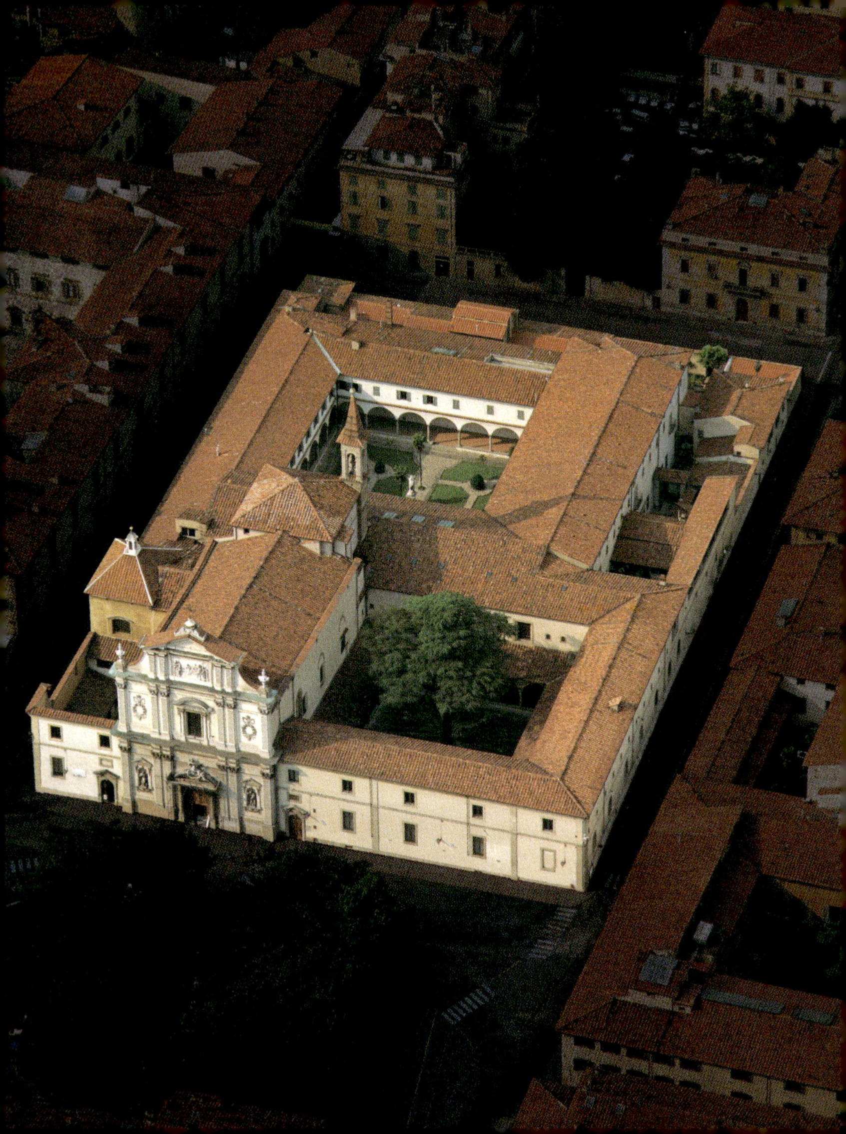

Piazza San Marco

The Church, the Monastery and the Museum

Still today a lively meeting place, in the vicinity of university buildings, academies and museums, Piazza San Marco represented, in the 15th century, a fundamental pole for the interests of the early Medicis, and was for years a place of great importance for the city's political and religious life at the time of Savonarola. Its monastery, frequented by Cosimo the Elder, by other humanists, and by artists such as Fra Angelico, was lastly to be the theater of Savonarola's republic. The vast complex consisting of the Dominican monastery and church stands, not by accident, on a straight line leading directly to the Medici palace in Via Larga (today's Via Cavour) and then on to the Duomo. In the time of Lorenzo the Magnificent, moreover, the garden of San Marco, on the corner of today's Via degli Arazzieri, played a primary role in the artistic research carried out in those years. Here Lorenzo had gathered an extraordinary collection of ancient sculptures that young artists, first among them Michelangelo, frequented "for delight, for study and for pleasure". Later Francesco I was to commission Bernardo Buontalenti to design the Casino destined to his scientific research of all kinds, in the fields of porcelain, semiprecious stones and crystal.

Opposite page:
Aerial view of the San Marco building complex with the church and the monastery.

HISTORY

The work of renovating the church and monastery of San Marco had been financed by the grandfather of Lorenzo the Magnificent, Cosimo the Elder. Since the 13th century, San Marco had belonged to the Silvestrine monks, and in 1436 it had been assigned by Pope Eugene IV, after many troubled years, to the reformed Dominicans of San Domenico di Fiesole. The Domenican monks were at the time guided by an outstanding personage in Florentine history, the vicar-general Antonino Pierozzi, who became prior of the monastery during the course of its reconstruction (in 1446 he was to be appointed Archbishop of Florence). At that time Cosimo the Elder, a wealthy banker, had only recently returned from exile, and in 1435 had been appointed Gonfalonier of Florence. The architect chosen for the work (1437-1452) was Michelozzo, who was soon to design the new family palace in Via Larga and other works sponsored by the Medici, such as the marble tempietti at the Annunziata and at San Miniato al Monte. The new church of San Marco, renovated mainly in the sacristy and the apse, was consecrated by the pope in 1443 (the interior was to be remodeled in 1678, in Baroque style, by Pier Francesco Silvani, while the present façade, dating from 1780, was designed by G. Pronti from Rimini).

Opposite page:
The San Marco building complex, from the *Codice* by Francesco di Bartolomeo Rustici, 1447. Biblioteca del Seminario Maggiore.

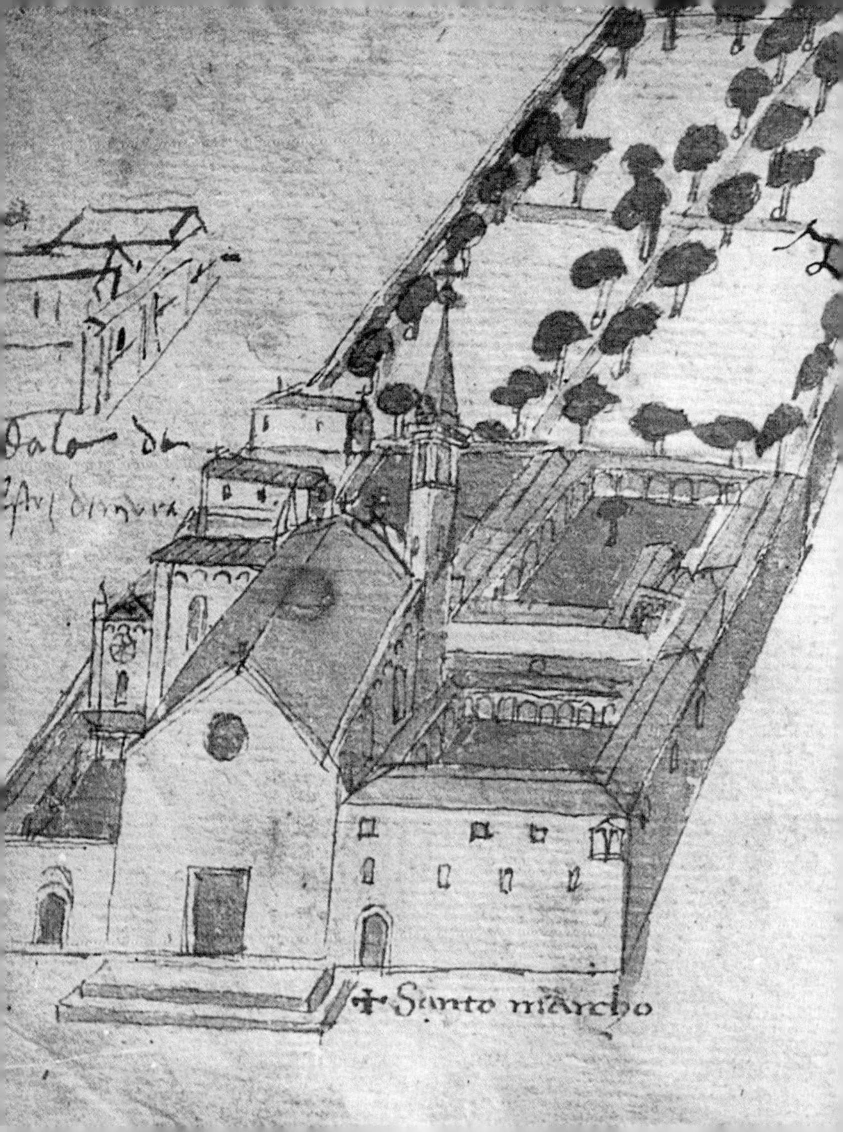
Santo marcho

The work on the monastery, supervised by Michelozzo, continued for some years, and in 1444 the famous humanist library was grafted onto the northern wing of the monastery. Some ancient buildings were included in the new complex, raised above their former level. In Michelozzo's project, the buildings on the first floor were skillfully harmonized around a cloister and the levels of the existing ones were raised, providing substantially greater space for the monks. The cells were frescoed by Giovanni da Fiesole, he too a Dominican monk. One of the most esteemed painters of the time, *pictor angelicus* as he was called by his contemporaries, the monk who became known as Beato Angelico, or Fra Angelico, had moved temporarily from the monastery of San Domenico to San Marco for the decoration of the cells, concluded around 1445. The iconographic program of the frescoes in the cloister and the cells is of high spiritual value, clearly inspired by the principles of the Dominican Order: education to prayer, incitement to charity and humility. It should also be recalled that one cell in the northern dormitory toward the second cloister had been reserved for Cosimo the Elder, who sometimes withdrew here in meditation; and it seems that Pope Eugene IV stayed here for some days in 1443, on the occasion of the consecration of the complex.

In addition to following the artistic itinerary of the cells and monastery, a visit to the museum, housed in the oldest part of

Opposite page:
Michelozzo, *Library*, 1444.
Monastery of San Marco.

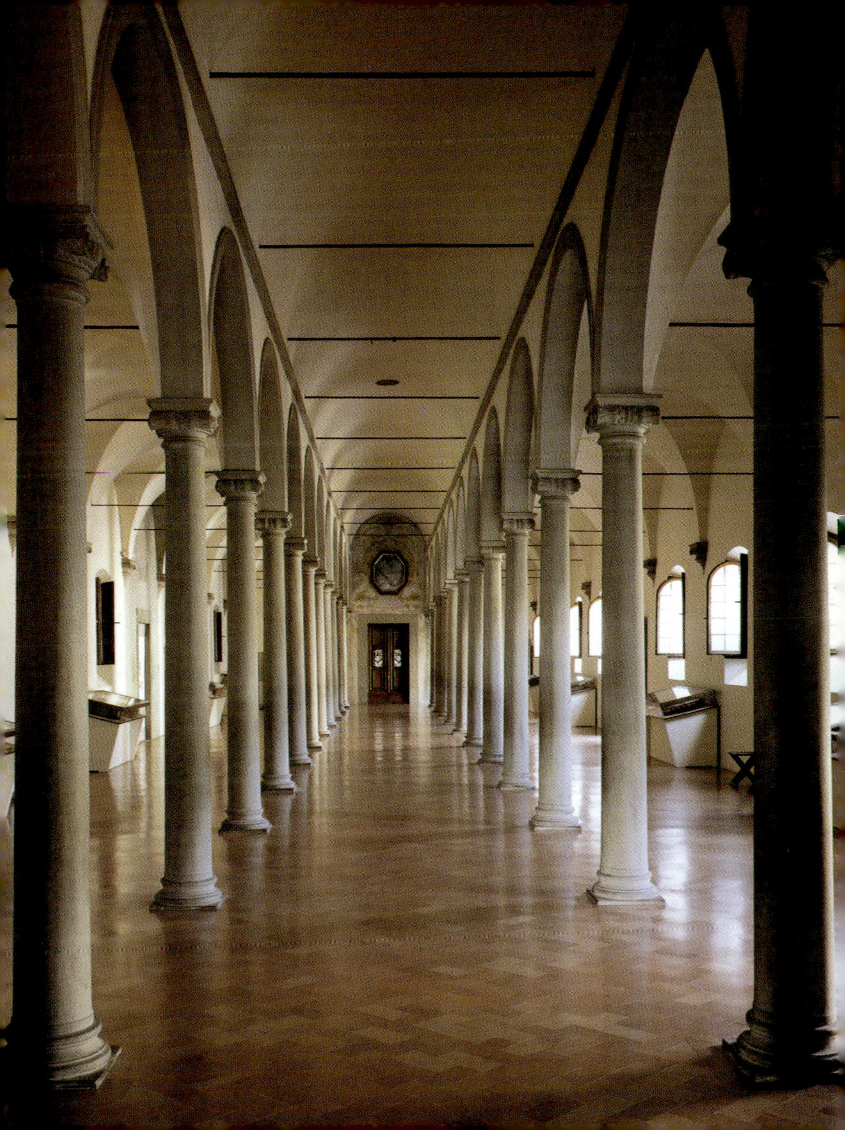

the monastery (still partly inhabited by monks) allows us to admire in the vast hall of the former pilgrims' hospice a conspicuous collection of panel paintings by Fra Angelico coming from Florentine churches and monsteries.

VISITORS' ITINERARY AND WORKS OF ART

Noteworthy among the works displayed are:

• IN THE CHURCH
- the sacristy (1437-1443) designed by Michelozzo.
- the Salviati chapel, built at the order of Averardo and Antonio Salviati in 1579 to honor the Florentine Bishop Saint, whose body was translated here in 1589, on the occasion of the wedding of Ferdinando I de' Medici and Cristina di Lorena. Designed by Giambologna, it was decorated with frescoes and piantings by Bronzino (1588).
- the marble door (early 17th century) by Cigoli.

• IN THE SANT'ANTONINO CLOISTER
- *St. Dominic worships the Crucifix* (c. 1442), fresco by Fra Angelico, and the 17th century cycle, financed by Florentine families, with *Scenes from the life of Sant'Antonino* frescoed in the lunettes by artists such as Bernardino Poccetti and Alessandro Tiarini.

Opposite page: View of the Salviati (or Sant'Antonino) Chapel in the church of San Marco. Above the altar, the altarpiece representing the *Descent into Limbo* by Bronzino (c. 1588).

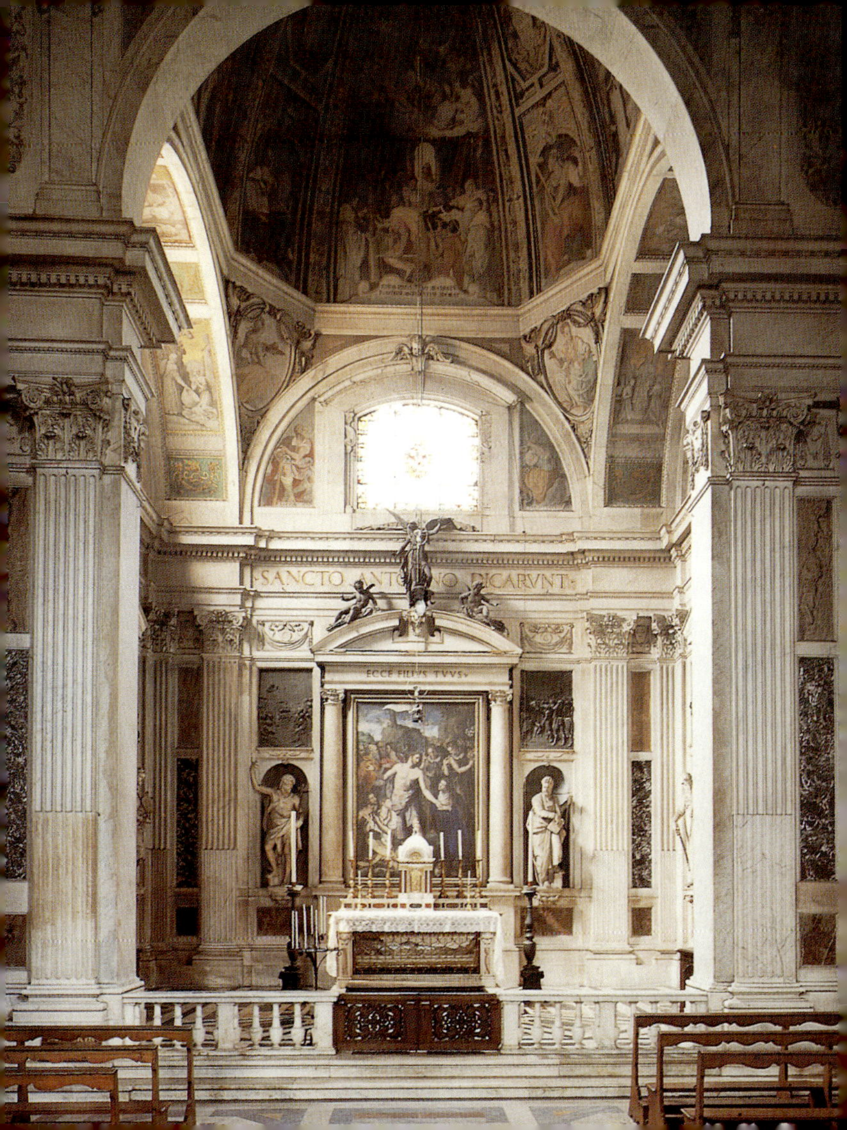

·SANCTO ANTONINO DICARUNT·
ECCE FILIUS TUUS·

• IN THE HOSPICE

- Panel paintings by Fra Angelico, among them the *Deposition* (1431-1432), with a predella by Lorenzo Monaco (1422-1425), commisssioned by the banker Palla Strozzi for the sacristy of Santa Trinita. In addition: the *Last Judgment* (c. 1425), by Santa Maria degli Angeli.
- the doors of the *Silver Cabinet* (1448-1453), executed by Fra Angelico in collaboration with others, among them Alesso Baldovinetti. The painted doors originally served to close off an area in the church of the Santissima Annunziata where the liturgical silverware was kept; they were commissioned by Piero di Cosimo de' Medici.
- the great *Tabernacle of the Linen-drapers* (1433-1436), commissioned by the Linen-drapers Guild for its own headquarters, demolished in the late 19th century.
- the *San Marco Altarpiece* (1438-1443), one of Fra Angelico's finest works, formerly placed over the high altar of the church of San Marco, in which are portrayed, among others, the Medicean clients, Cosimo and Lorenzo, in the guise of Saints Cosmos and Damian, and which shows refined inventions such as the false tabernacle in the foreground, above a Persian carpet.

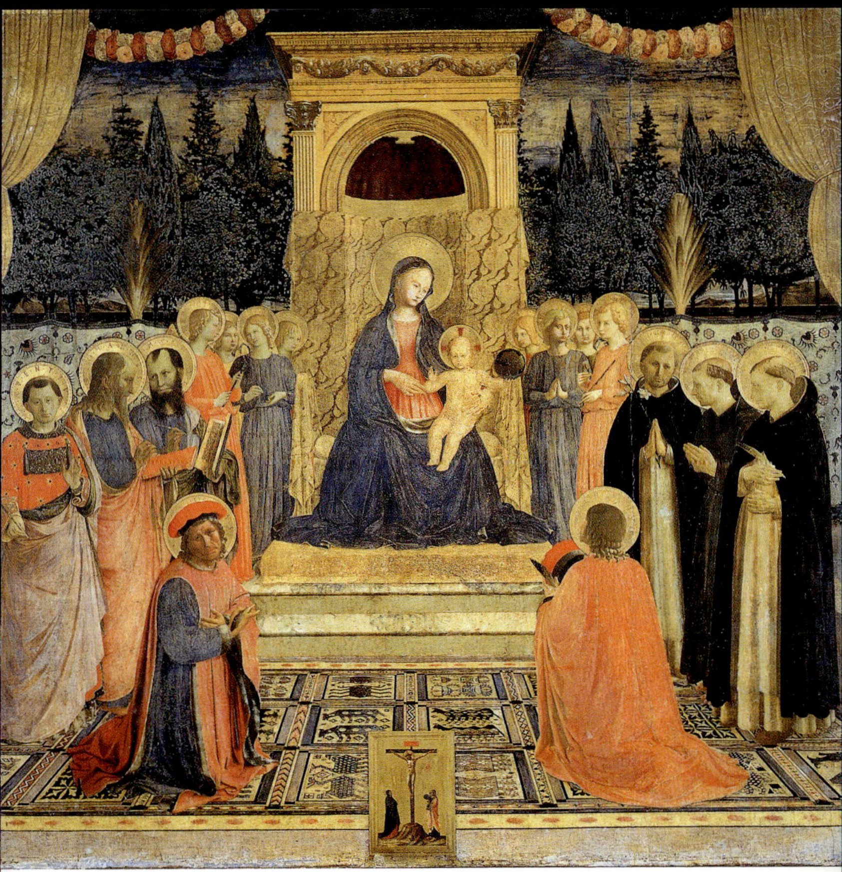

Fra Angelico,
San Marco Altarpiece,
1438-1442, tempera on wood.
Museo di San Marco.

• IN THE "LAVABO" ROOM

- the *Enthroned Virgin and Child* (1450-1460), an all-round sculpture in glazed terracotta by Luca della Robbia.
- the *Last Judgment* (1499-1501), a detached fresco by Fra Bartolomeo and Mariotto Albertinelli.

• IN THE FRA BARTOLOMEO ROOM

- several works by this follower of Savonarola, who had a painter's workshop in San Marco from 1500 to 1517, the year of his death.

• IN THE CHAPTERHOUSE

- the great fresco depicting the *Crucifixion and Saints* (1442) by Fra Angelico, in a poor state of conservation especially as concerns the background of the sky, where the blue pigment has been lost.
- the bronze bell known as the *Piagnona* (c. 1445), attribuited to Michelozzo, commissioned by the Medici for the bell tower of San Marco, and so called for having rung the tocsin, on April 8, 1498, for the followers of Savonarola, who were captured in the Monastery of San Marco on that day.

• IN THE SMALL REFECTORY

- the great fresco of *The Last Supper* (1479-1480) by Domenico Ghirlandaio, dating from slightly earlier than its twin painted by the same artist for the church of Ognissanti.

Opposite page:
The Sant'Antonino Cloister, encountered immediately upon entering the Museum, was designed by Michelozzo around 1440 with an elegant loggia having five columns per side, surmounted by Ionic capitals.
In the early 17th century the lunettes were frescoed with a cycle dedicated to Sant'Antonino.

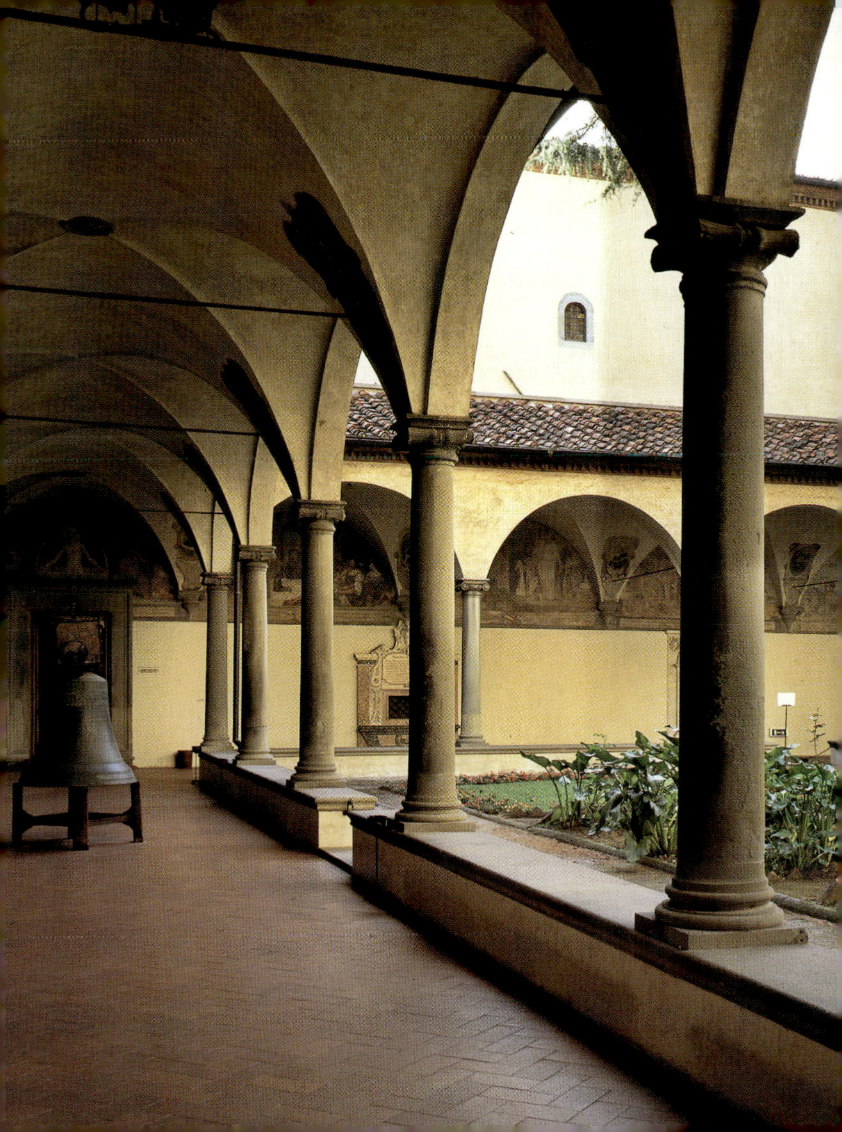

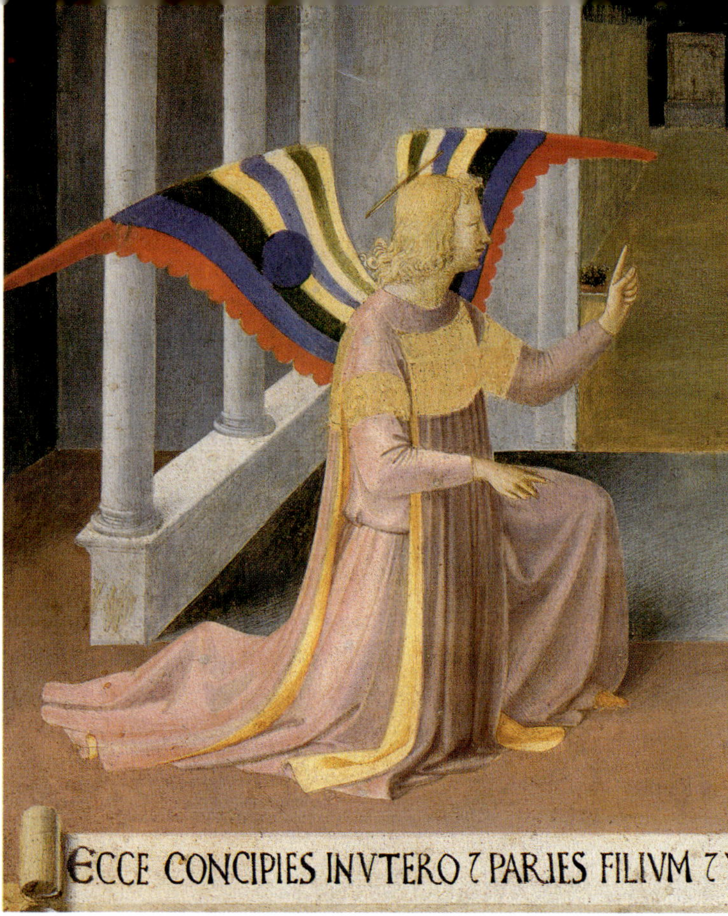

Fra Angelico and Assistants, *Announcing Angel,* detail from the *Silver Cabinet,* 1452, tempera on wood.

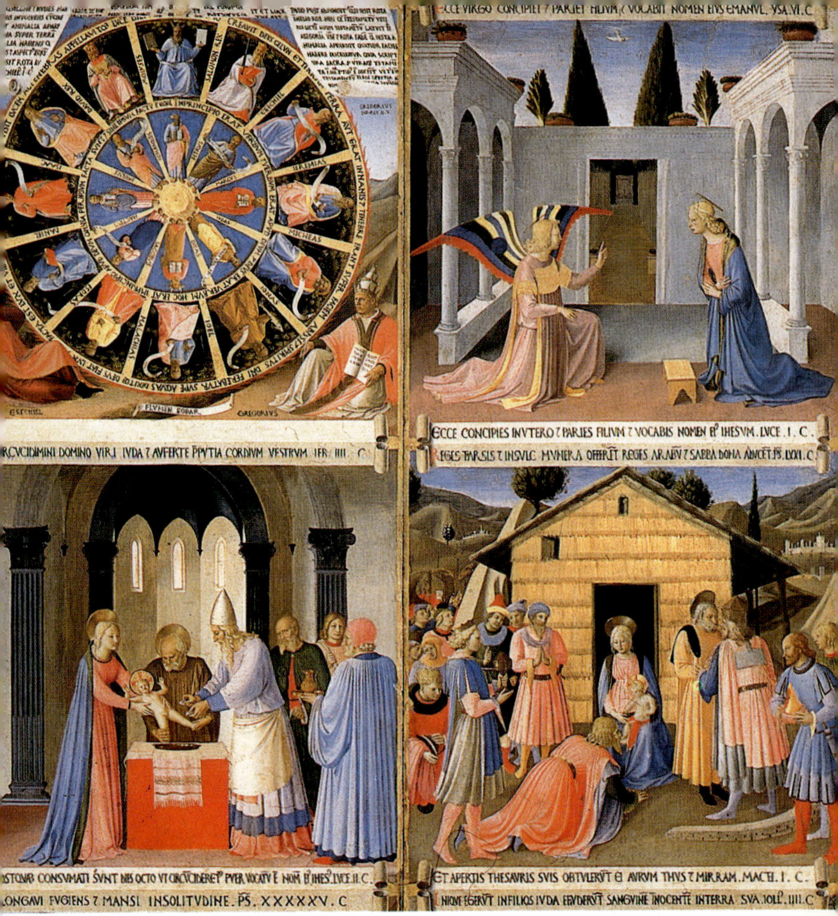

Fra Angelico, *Silver Cabinet*, detail, 1448-1453, tempera on wood. Museo di San Marco.

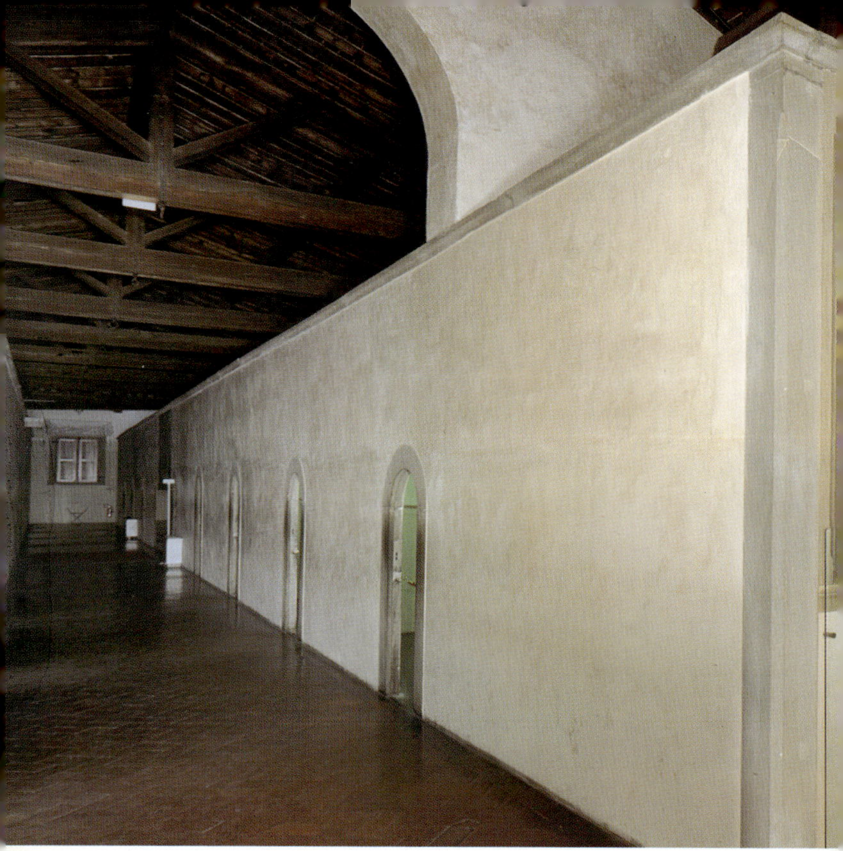

Above: View of the East Corridor, known also as the Corridor of the Altar Boys, and of the corner toward the Lay Brothers' Corridor. On the wall, the fresco by Fra Angelico of the *Annunciation*, c. 1442, illustrated on the following page.

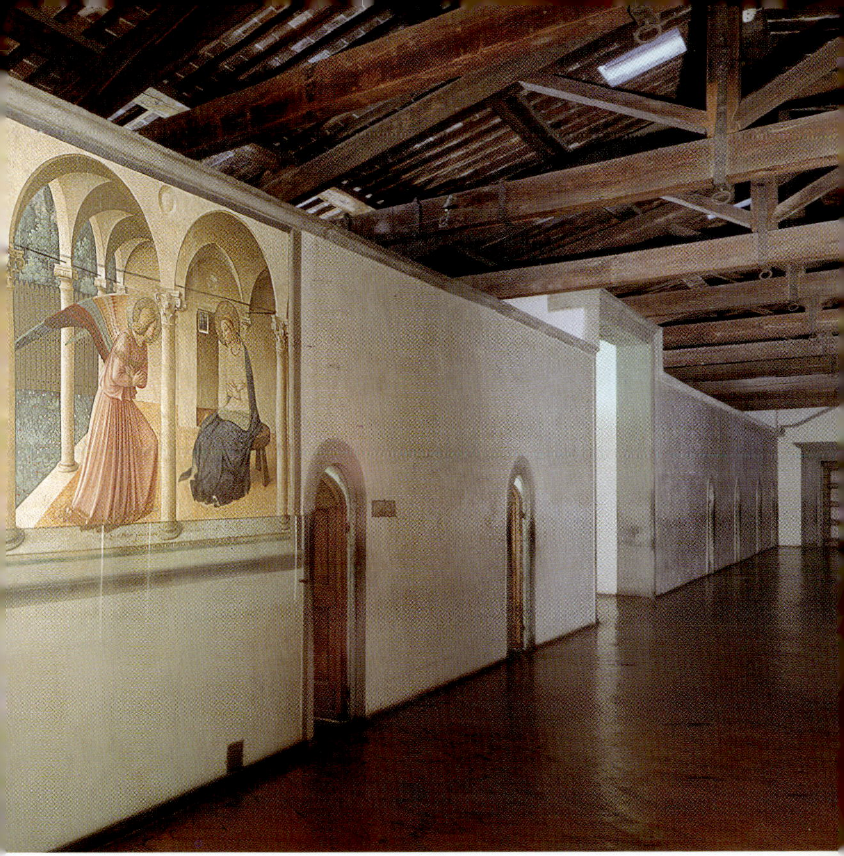

Following pages:
Fra Angelico, *Annunciation,*
c.1442, fresco. Monastery of
San Marco, Lay Brothers Corridor.

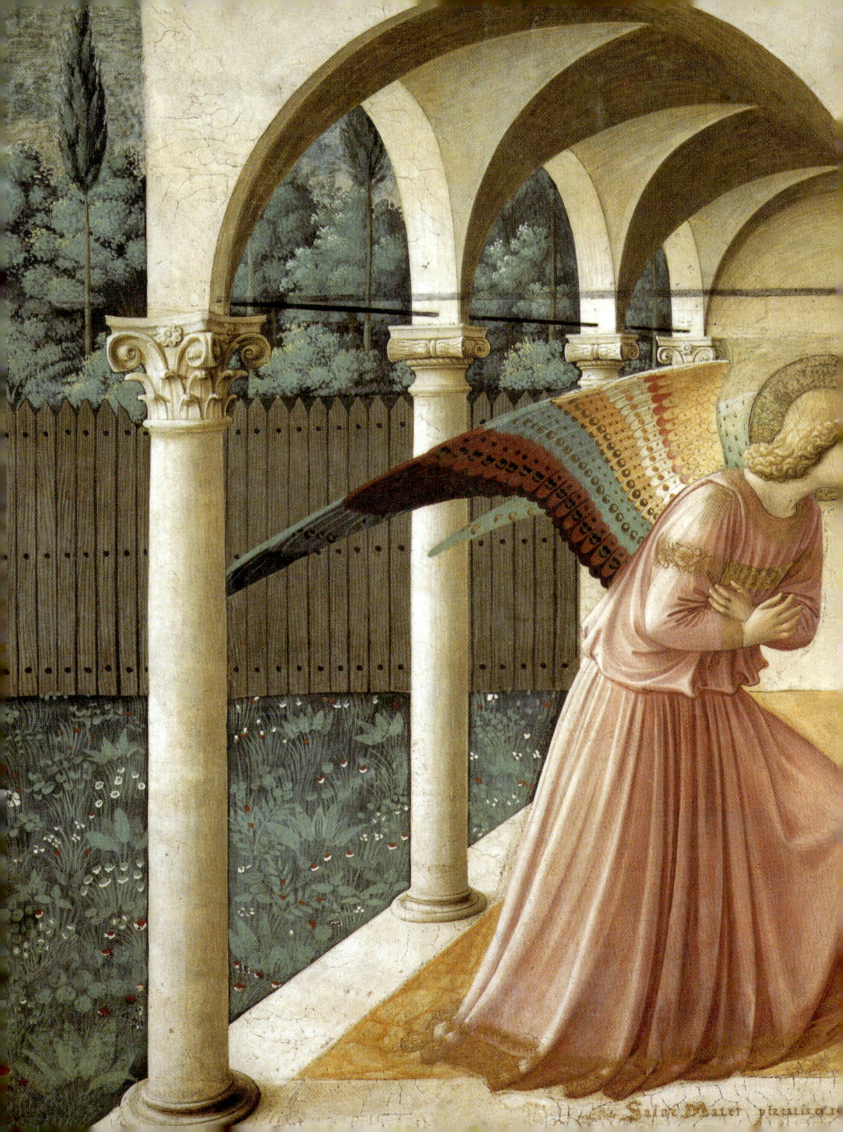
Salve Mater

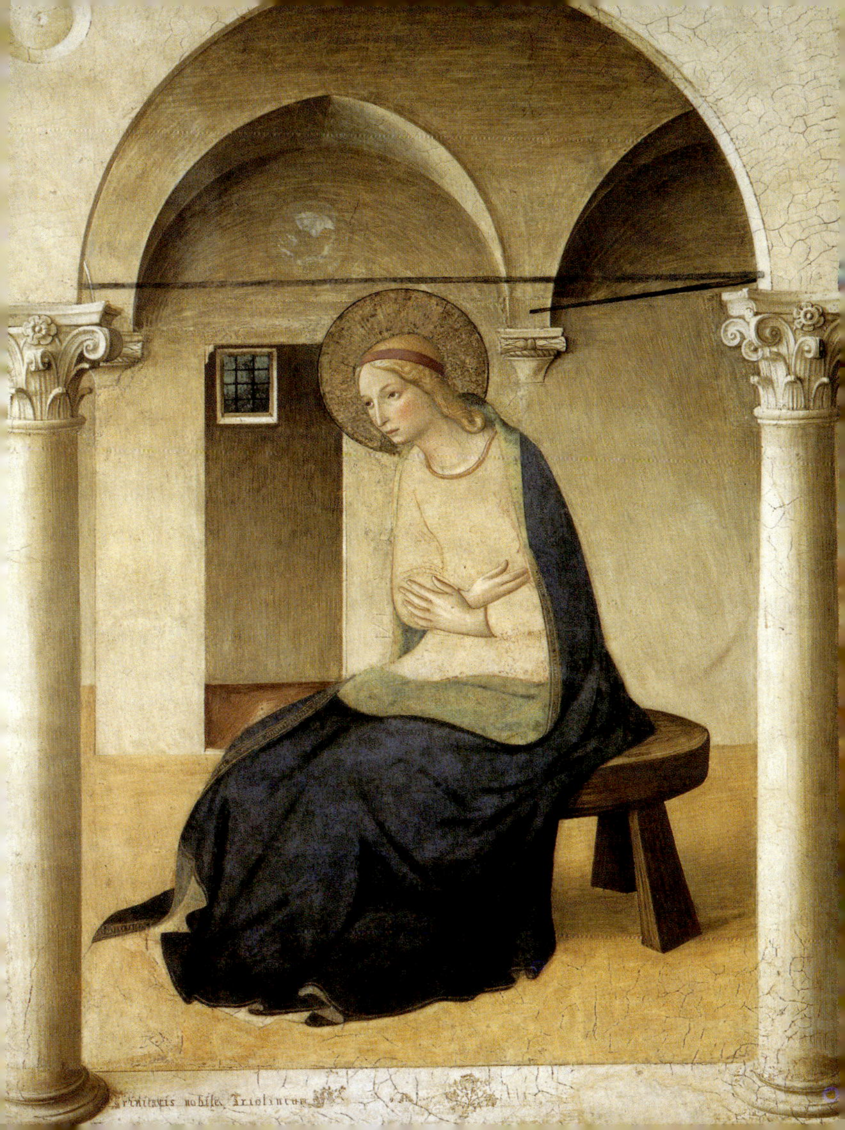

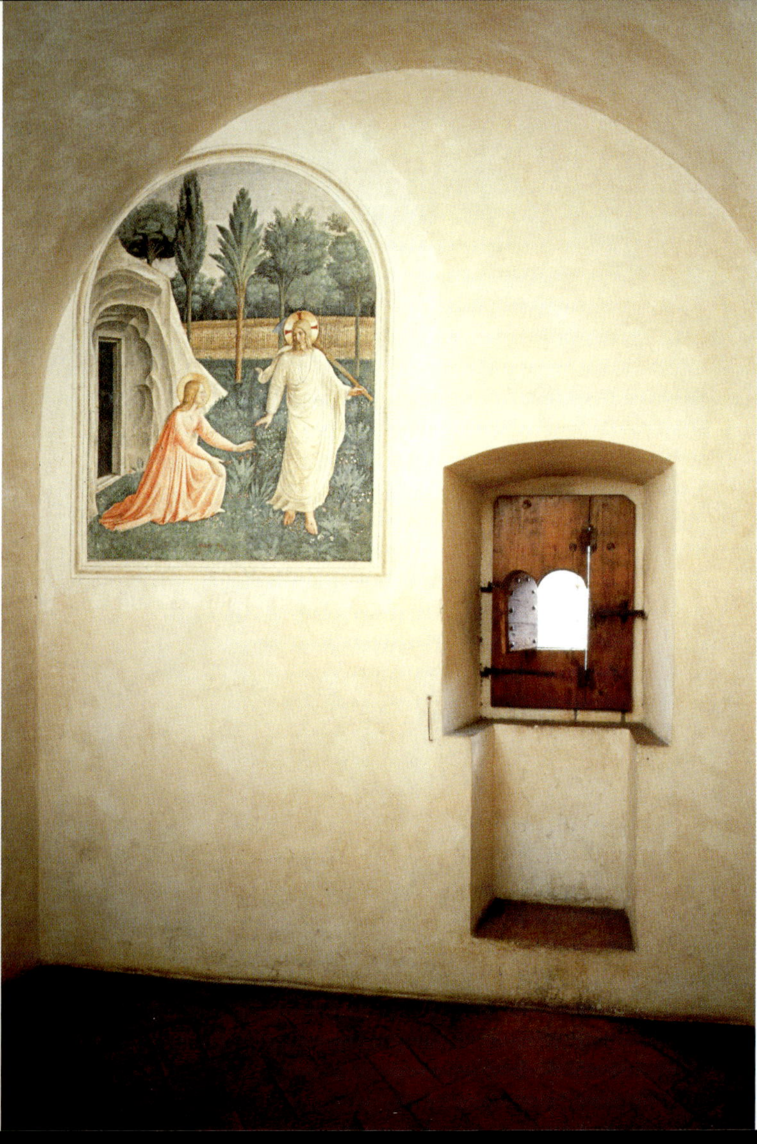

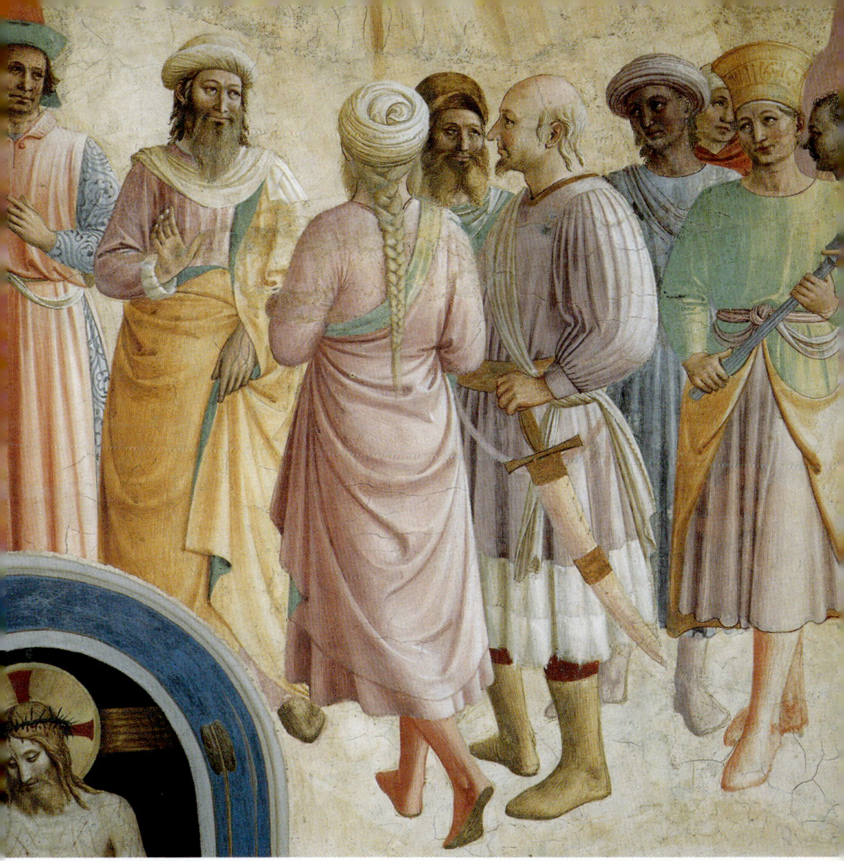

Opposite page:
View of cell no. 1 in the East Corridor, with the fresco by Fra Angelico *Noli me tangere*, 1438-1443.

Above:
Fra Angelico, *Adoration of the Magi,* detail of the procession of the Wise Men, 1440-1443, lunette in cell 39, North Corridor.

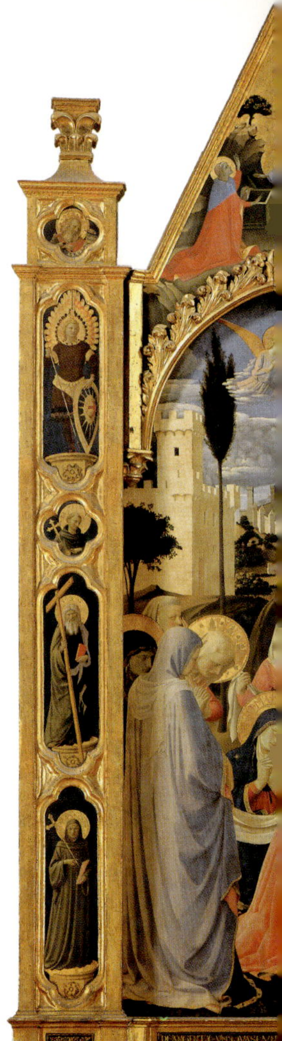

This page:
Fra Angelico,
Deposition from the Cross,
1431-1432, tempera on wood,
(cusps and predella, not illustrated here, by Lorenzo Monaco).
Museo di San Marco.
The altarpiece was begun by Lorenzo Monaco for the altar in the funerary chapel of the Strozzi family in Santa Trinita, and probably remained unfinished at the painter's death in 1425. The central part and the pilasters were painted by Fra Angelico, who has immortalized here one of his masterpieces.

Following pages:
Fra Angelico,
Tabernacle of the Linaioli,
1433-1436,
tempera on wood.

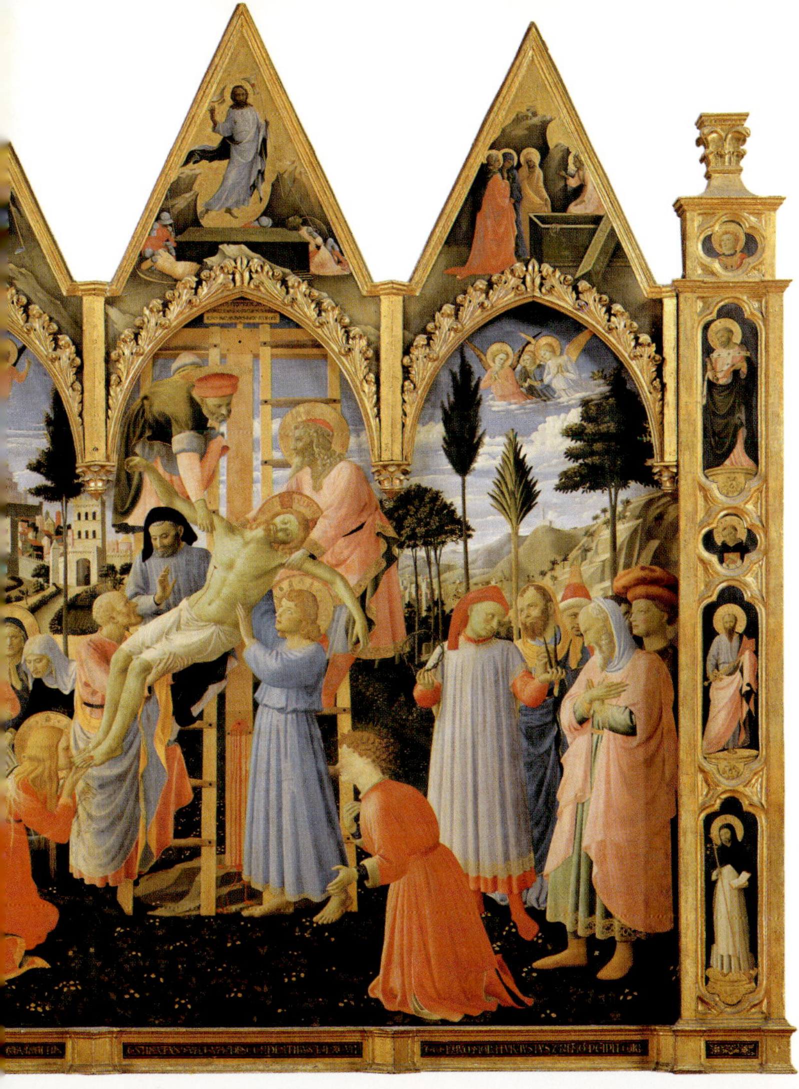

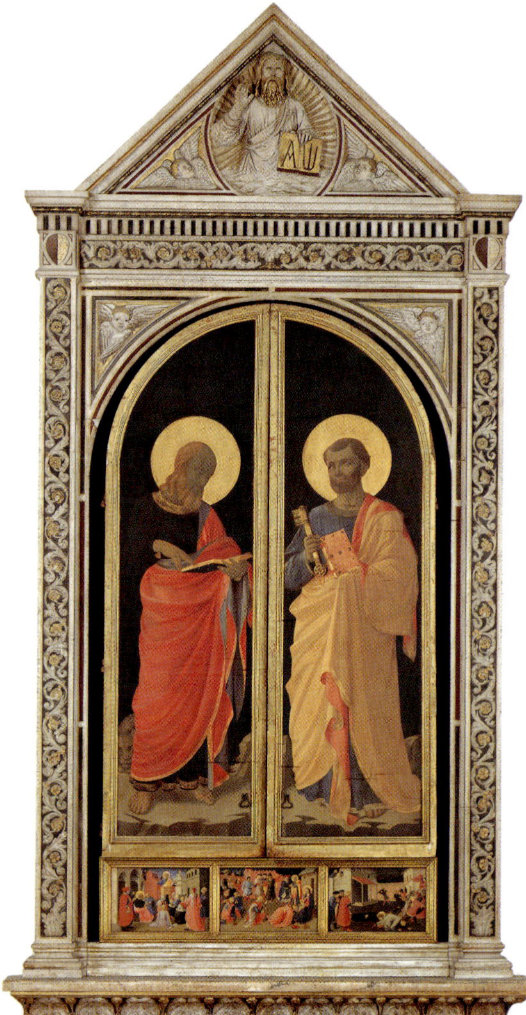

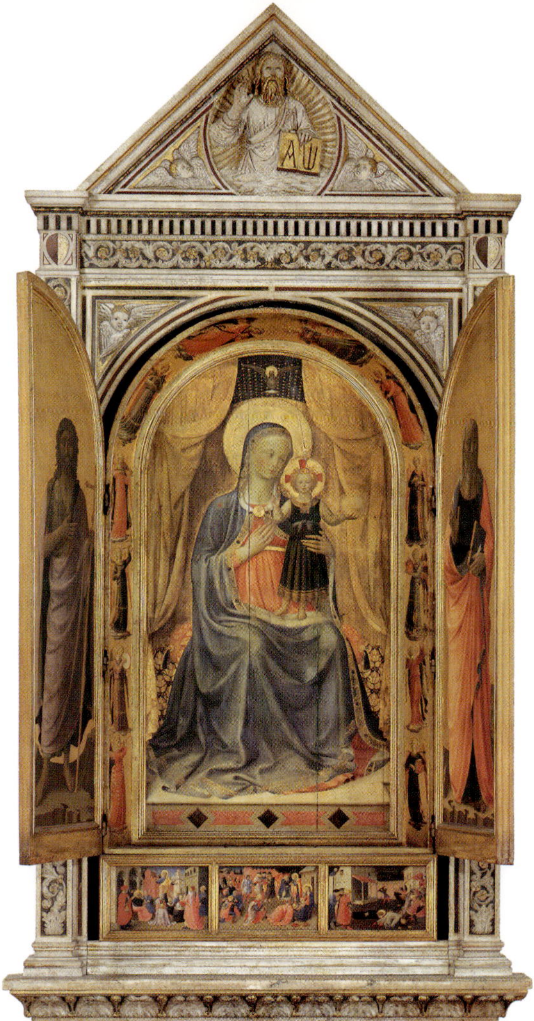

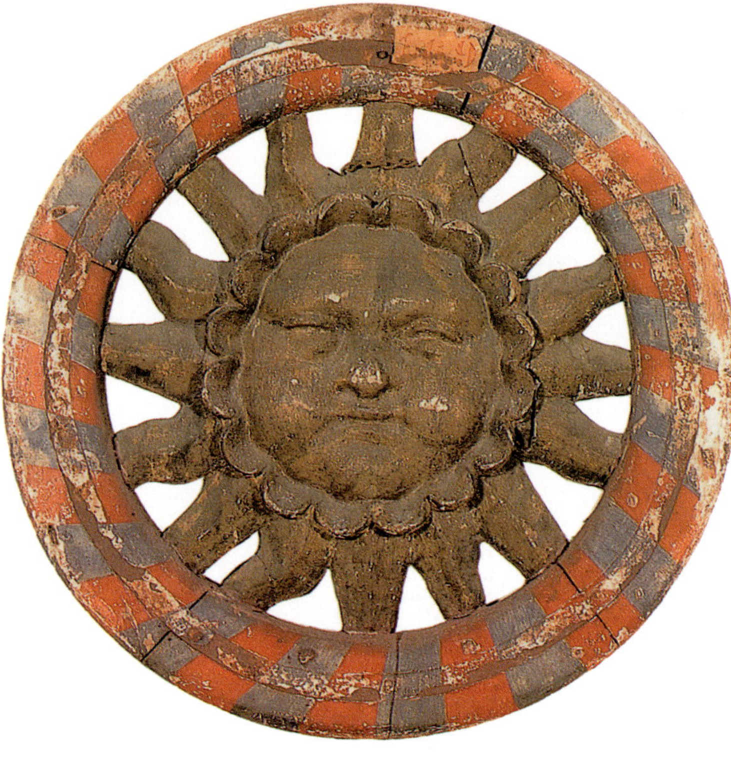

Florentine Manufactury,
Wooden shop's sign painted with the emblem of the Santa Maria Novella quarter, 15th century.
Museo di San Marco.

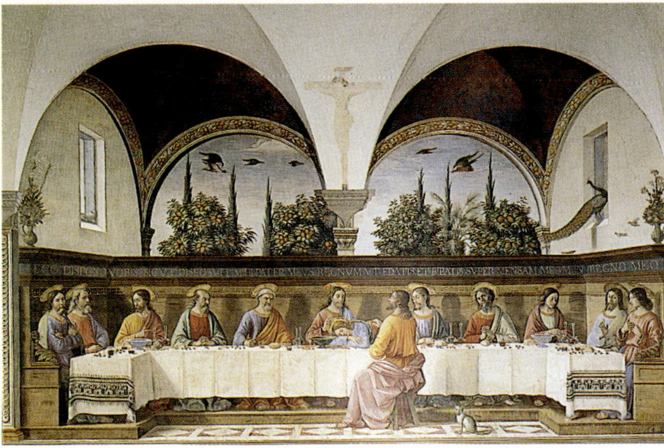

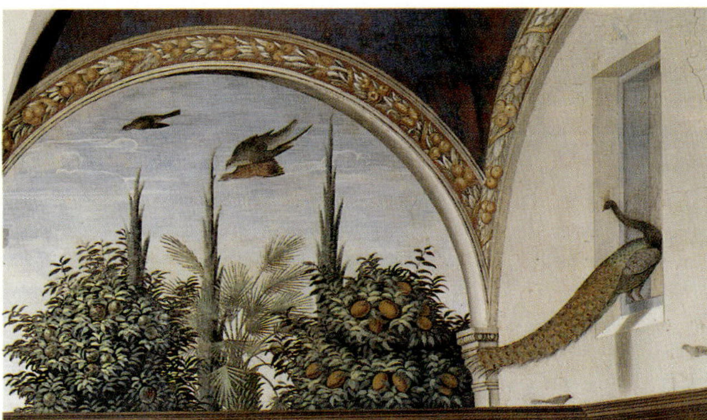

Above:
Domenico Ghirlandaio, *Last Supper,* whole and detail, c. 1480, fresco. Monastery of San Marco, small Refectory.

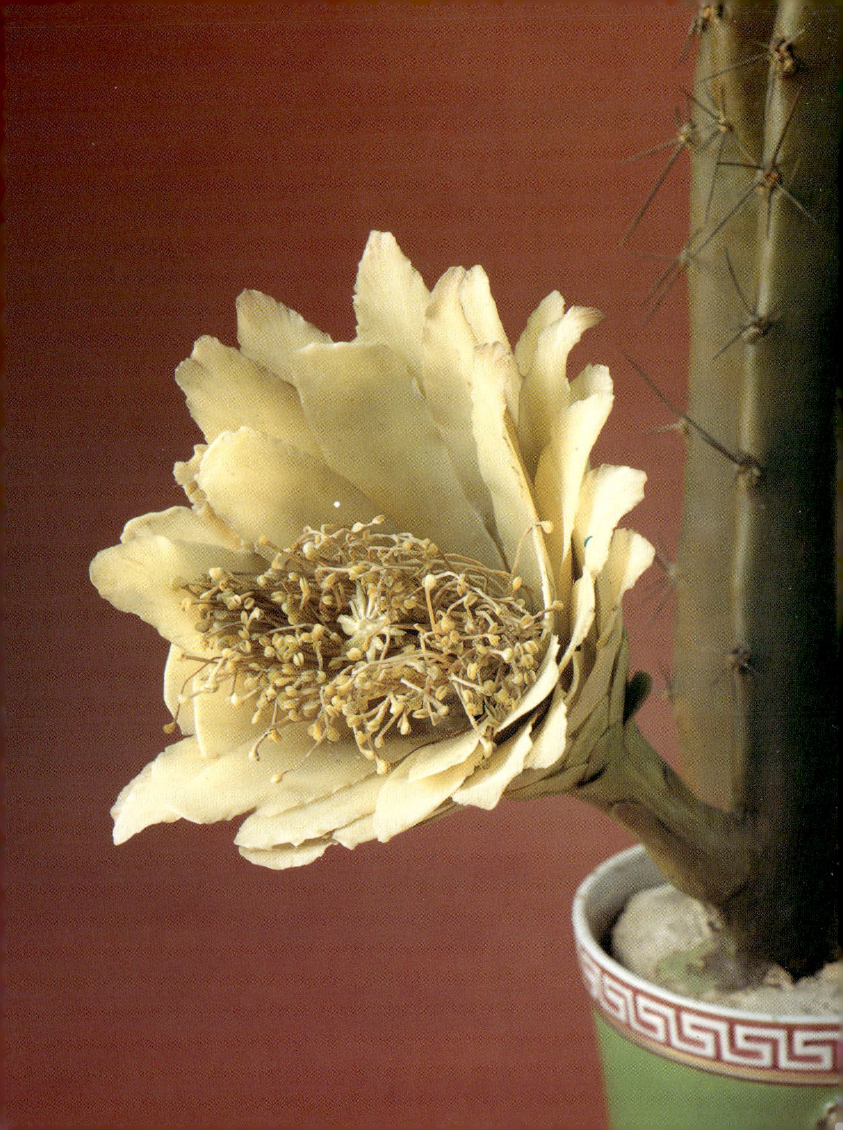

The Botanical Garden and the Scientific Museums

The Florence Botanical Garden, to which are now annexed the university's natural science institutes, was originally called the "Giardino dei Semplici", that is, the garden of medicinal herbs. Situated on a spacious lot between San Marco and the Annunziata, bounded by today's Via Micheli, Via La Pira amd Via Giusti, the garden was founded by Cosimo I in 1545 on land rented from the nuns of San Domenico. The Duke was not concerned with his own pleasure alone, but also and above all with having exotic botanical specimens collected, to be used for the instruction of medical students. The project for the garden was drawn up by Tribolo, sculptor and architect, who created other splendid Medicean gardens during those same years. The cultivations were incremented by Francesco I, who brought to the garden "the first orange trees from China", the "pilgrim jasmin" and other rarities. The Serraglio of Piazza Signoria was also moved to another location nearby. Here the Duke instituted a riding stable (the "cavallerizza"), and kept rare animals brought from Africa and America. The collections, further enriched under the Lorraines, now occupy in part areas annexed to the Institutes of Geology, Paleontology, Mineralogy and Botany.

Opposite page:
Clemente Susini, *Cactus Heptagonus (Cereus Heptagonus)*, a wax plant in a porcelain vase from the Manifattura di Doccia, detail, c. 1792. University of Florence Museum of Natural History, "F. Parlatore" Botany Section.

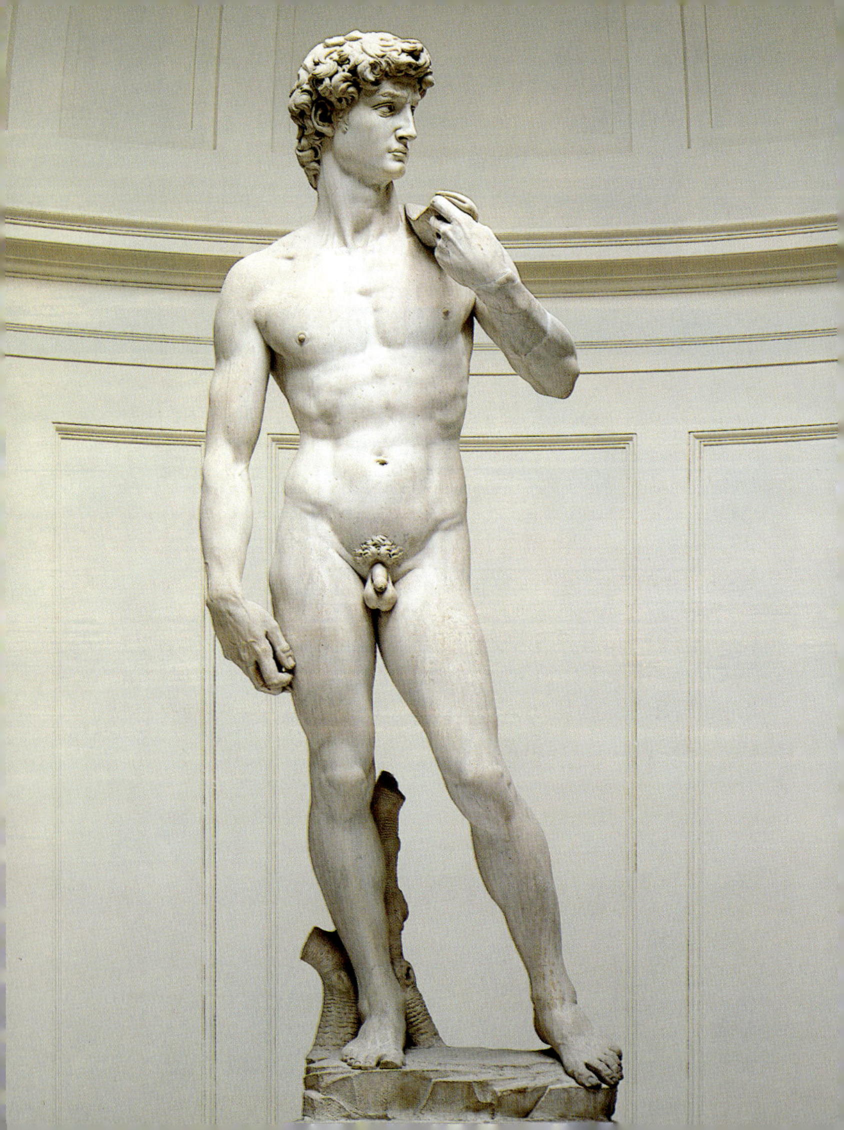

Galleria dell'Accademia

One of the most important Florentine museums, boasting over a million visitors a year, the Accademia Gallery is known above all for Michelangelo's *David.* But in fact, this fascinating museum where the tourists swarm to admire one of the most mythicized "icons" of art of all times, also contains a precious collection of works dating from the Medieval period to the 19th century. The collections of the museum, which occupies the site of two ancient buildings, the Spedale di San Matteo, which faced on Piazza San Marco, and the Monastery of San Niccolò di Cafaggio, originated as the art collection of the Accademia del Disegno (founded in 1563 by Cosimo I de' Medici) and then of the Accademia di Belle Arti, the art school instituted in 1784 by Pietro Leopoldo di Lorena. The works collected here were thus intended to serve as masterpieces from the past for the instruction of young artists. The pinacoteca also contains a conspicuous number of paintings of religious subject, brought here after the suppression of the monasteries (1785-1808); others were brought from the Uffizi and the Pitti Palace. The *David*, instead, originally placed in Piazza Signoria in front of Palazzo Vecchio, was brought here in 1873, while in 1909 there arrived other famous sculptures by Michelangelo, the *Slaves* and the *St.*

Opposite page:
Michelangelo, *David*,
1501-1504, marble.
Galleria dell'Accademia.

Matthew, and in 1939 the *Pietà di Palestrina*. The paintings of Fra Angelico formerly kept here have instead been moved to the San Marco Museum, while other masterpieces were transferred to the Uffizi during the course of the last century. The Galleria, having undergone major renovation in the last decades, also contains, on the ground floor, the gallery of plaster casts by Lorenzo Bartolini and Luigi Pampaloni, 19th century sculptors, and on the first floor an important collection of Florentine Late Gothic painting and a group of Russian icons collected by the Lorraines. Since 2001 the collection of musical instruments owned by the Medici and Lorraine Grand Dukes, unique of its kind the world over, belonging to the adjacent Luigi Cherubini State Music Conservatory, has also been been annexed to the Galleria.

VISITORS' ITINERARY AND WORKS OF ART:

Noteworthy among the works exibited are:

- the collection of Florentine gold leaf paintings, which ranges from the end of the 13th century to the first years of the 15th (from the work of Giotto and his followers to the time of Masaccio), is exhibited on the ground floor, in the rooms adjacent to the left wing of the Tribuna of *David*, and in four rooms on the first floor. Among the artists represented are Taddeo Gaddi, Bernardo Daddi, the Orcagnas, Giovanni da Milano, and Lorenzo Monaco: artists who, from the revolu-

Opposite page:
Giovanni da Milano, *Christ as the Man of Sorrows*, 1365, tempera on wood. Galleria dell'Accademia.

FIRENZE
MVSEI

Giardino di Boboli
IL GIARDINO ANTICO
DA BABILONIA A ROMA

Museo degli Argenti
Galleria del Costume
Museo delle Porcellane
Giardino Bardini

Serie N.

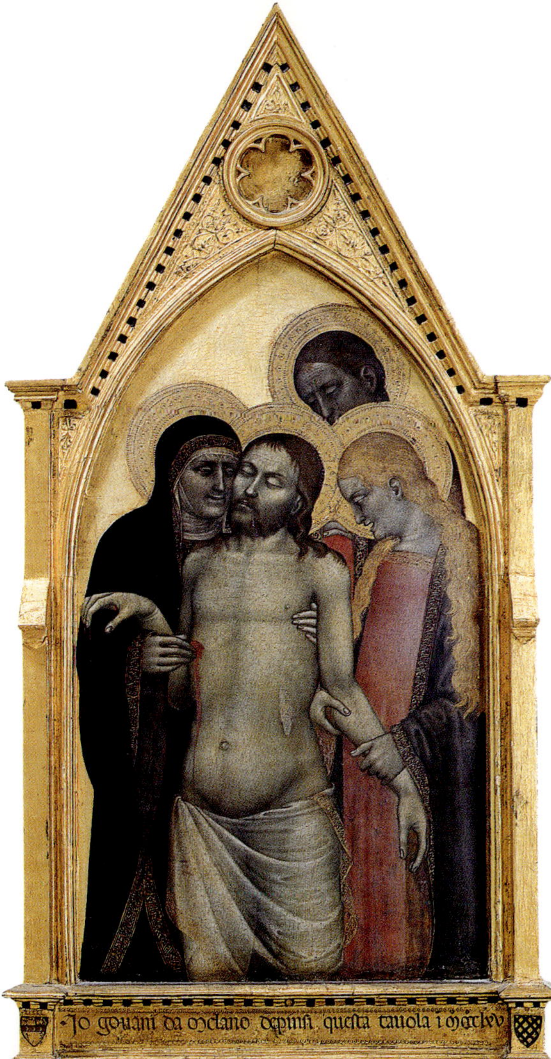
Io govanni da milano depinsi questa tavola i mccclxv

tionary lesson taught by Giotto, developed highly expressive figurative languages.

- the collection of 15th and 16th century paintings, exhibited in the Hall of the Colossus, the Gallery of the Slaves and the Tribuna of David. Among the masters represented are Paolo Uccello, Ghirlandaio, Botticelli, Filippino Lippi, Perugino, Granacci, Ridolfo del Ghirlandaio, Andrea Del Sarto, and Fra Bartolomeo. In the two wings of the Tribuna, as fitting accompaniment to the *David*, hang paintings by artists from the Mannerist period such as Salviati and from that of the Counter-Reformation such as Bronzino, Allori, and Santi di Tito.
- the masterpieces of Michelangelo: in a spectacular scenario the *David* dominates the center of the Tribuna designed by Emilio de Fabris between 1872 and 1882. Commissioned by the Opera del Duomo in 1501 of the thirty-year-old sculptor now famous for his work exhibited in the Cathedral, the giant *David* carved of Carrara marble, finished in slightly over two years, was placed in 1504, at the decision of a commission whose members included, among others, Leonardo and Botticelli, on the "aringhiera" of Palazzo della Signoria, in the place of Donatello's *Judith*, moved to a niche in the courtyard and then under the loggia on one side of the piazza. Having thus become the symbol of the values of republi-

Opposite page:
Michelangelo, *David*, 1501-1503, detail, marble.
Galleria dell'Accademia.

Following pages:
Attr. to Michelangelo, *Pietà di Palestrina*, 1547-1559, detail, marble.

Michelangelo, *Slaves*, c. 1530, marble.
Galleria dell'Accademia.

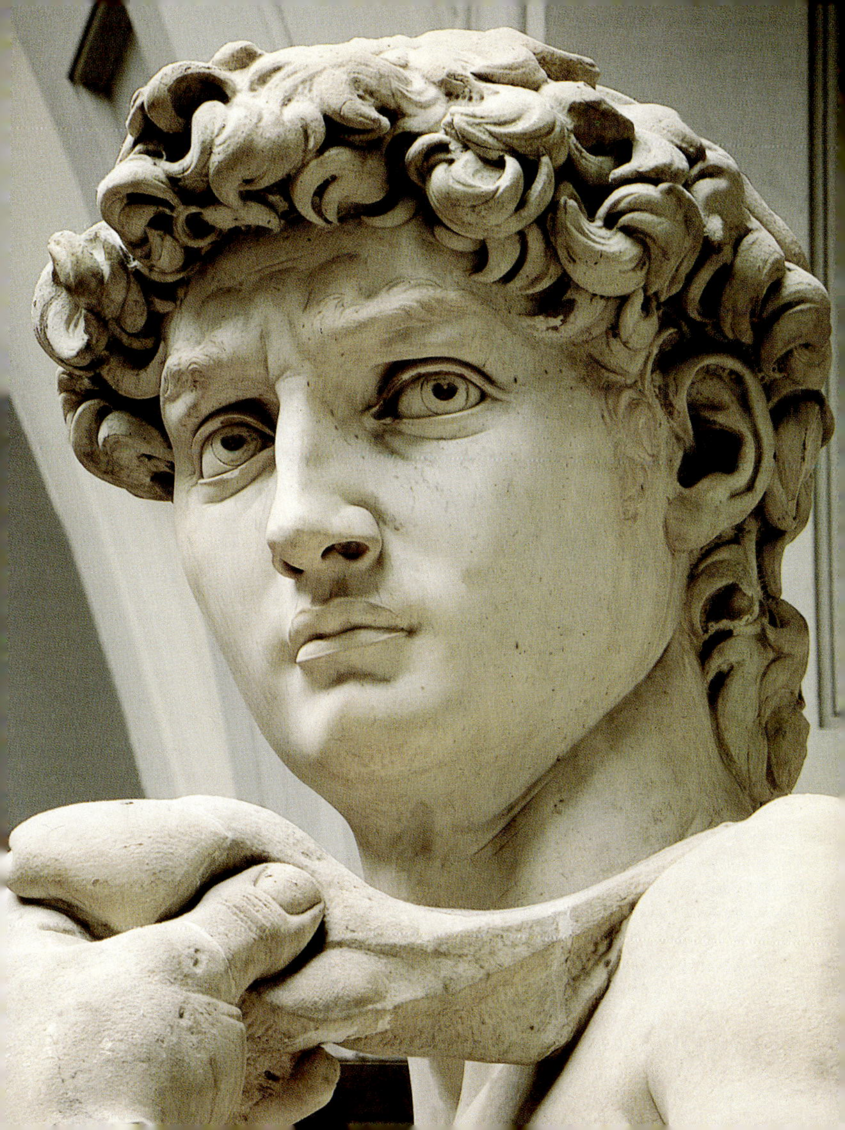

can freedom, Michelangelo's "Giant", as it was immediately called, was moved to the Accademia in 1873 to ensure its conservation, transported within a complicated cagework of supporting structures.

- In addition to the *David*, the famous *Slaves* or *Captives*, originally intended to decorate the tomb of Pope Julius II in Rome, are exhibited in the Galleria. The sculptures, still in the "*non finito*" state, remained however in the sculptor's Florentine workshop until the time of his death in Rome. Only then were the Slaves donated by Michelangelo's nephew to Duke Cosimo. These scuptures in the rough state, subject to endless debate on whether or not they should be considered finished statues, were then placed in Buontalenti's grotto in the Boboli Gardens, as they appeared fully consonant with the typically Mannerist program of "naturalist caprice" distinctive of the grotto.
- Since 1939 the Galleria has also exhibited the *Pietà di Palestrina*, whose attribution to Michelangelo is now considered highly debatable.

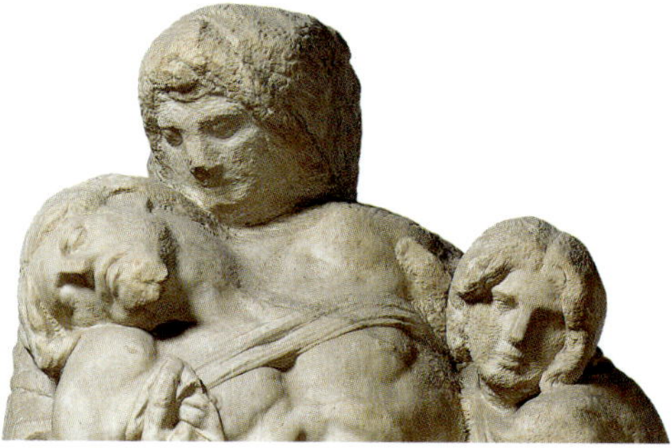

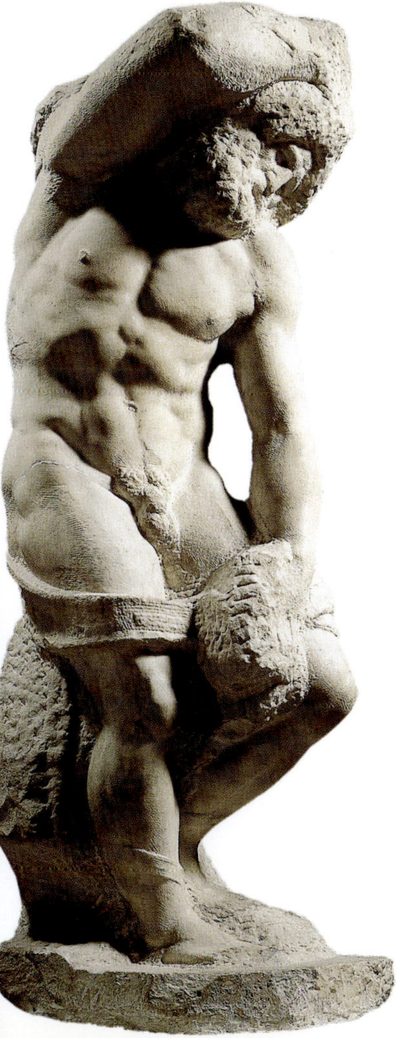
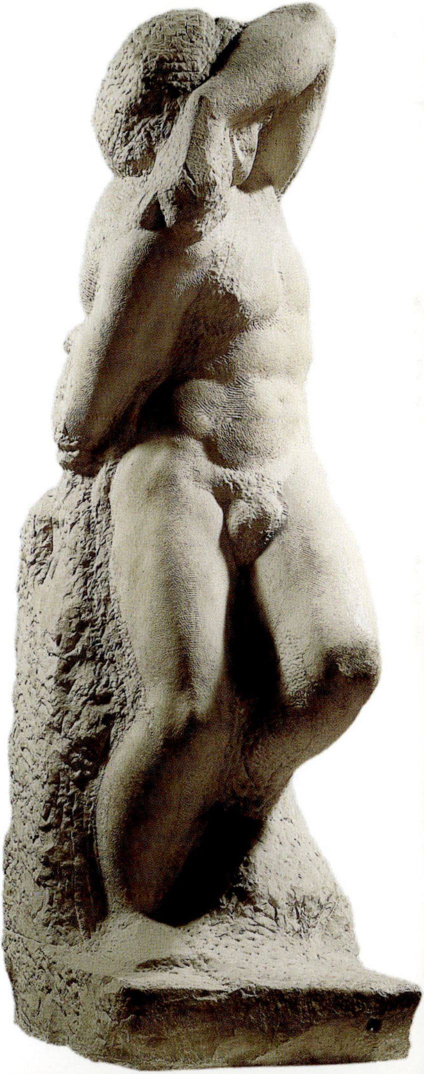

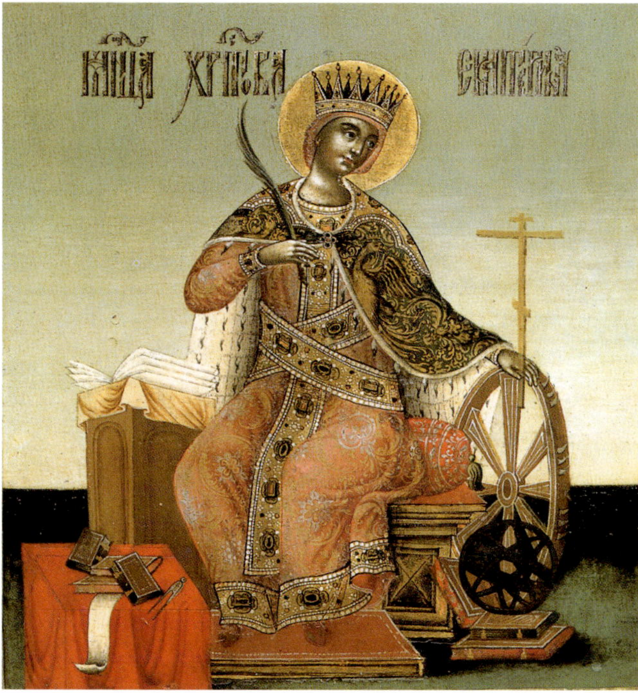

Above:
Russian School, *Saint Catherine*, 18th century, tempera on wood. Galleria dell'Accademia.

Opposite page:
Maestro della Maddalena, *St. Mary Magdalene and Episodes from her Life*, c. 1280-1285, tempera on wood. Galleria dell'Accademia.

Following pages:
Bernardo Daddi, *Crucifixion with the Virgin and St. John*, c. 1348 tempera on wood. Galleria dell'Accademia.

Lorenzo Monaco, *Prayer in the Garden*, c. 1395-1400, tempera on wood. Galleria dell'Accademia.

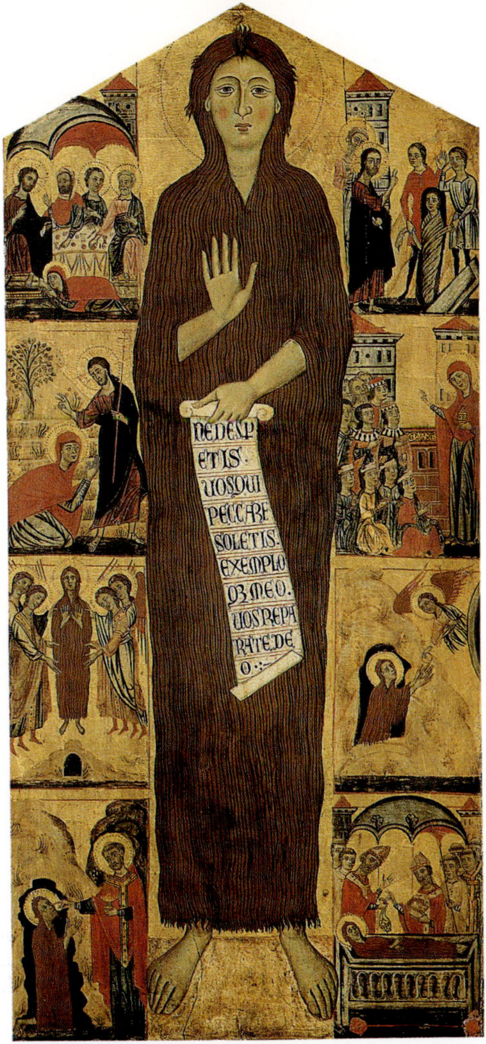
NEDESP
ETIS·
UOSQUI
PECCARE
SOLETIS:
EXEMPLO
QZMEO.
UOSREPA
RATE.DE
O.:-

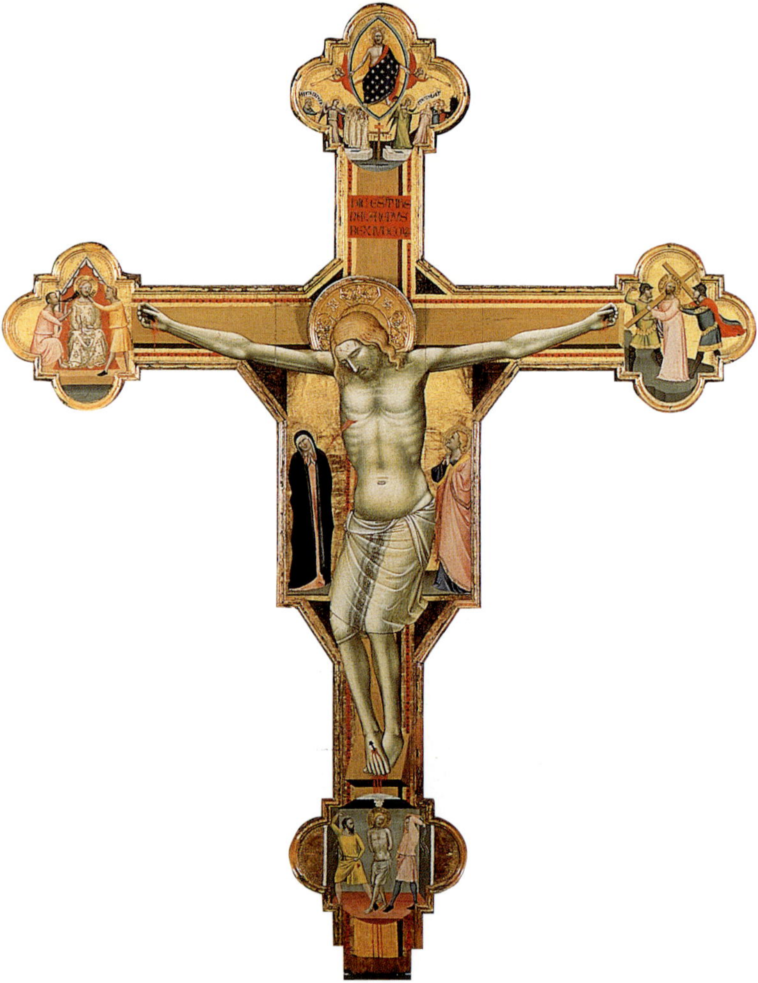

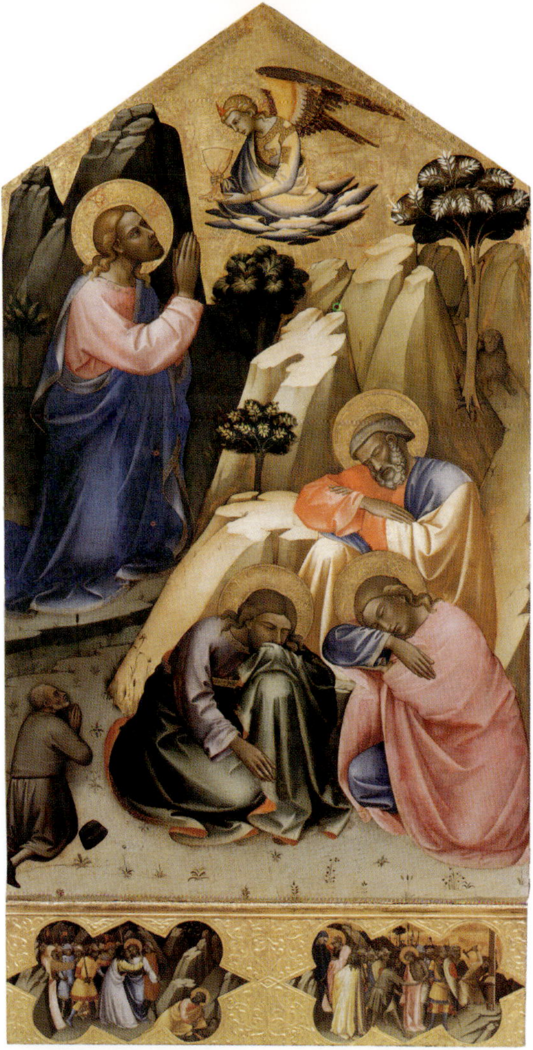

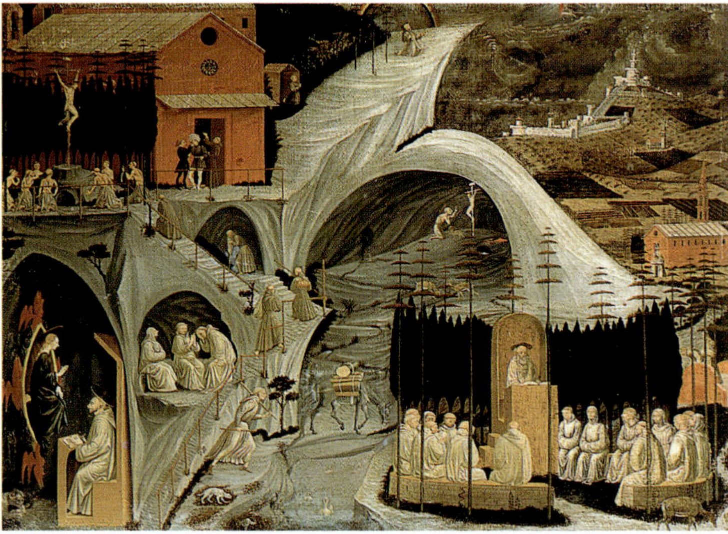

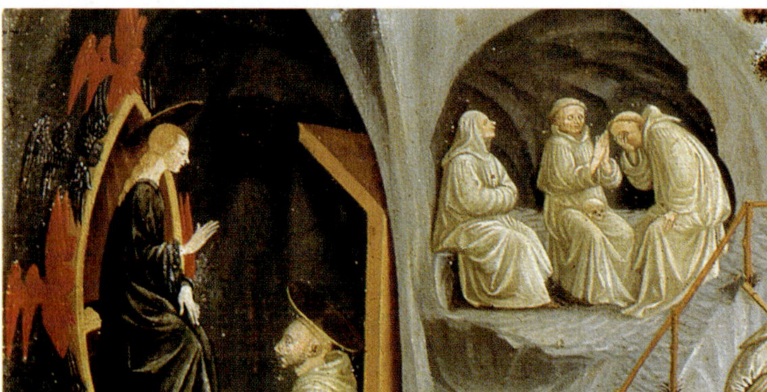

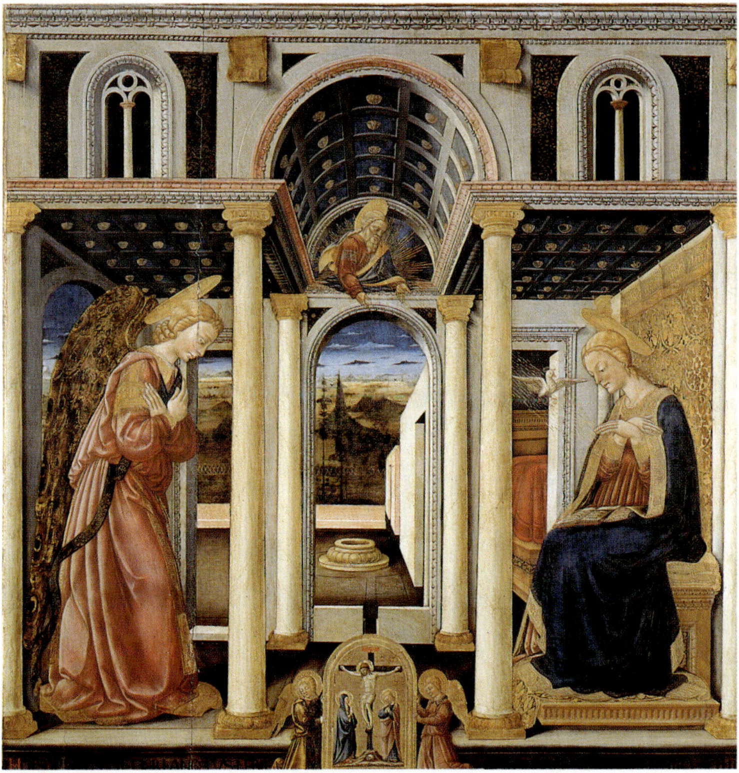

Opposite page:
Paolo Uccello, *Scenes of the Hermit's Life or Thebaide*, c. 1460, whole and detail, tempera on canvas. Galleria dell'Accademia.

Above:
Neri di Bicci, *Annunciation*, c. 1464, tempera on wood. Galleria dell'Accademia.

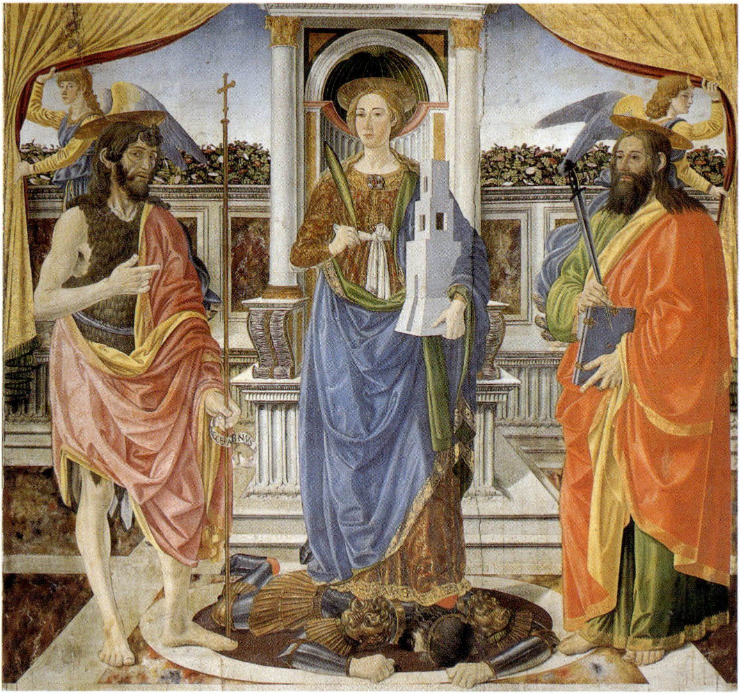

Above:
Cosimo Rosselli, *Saint Barbara with St. John the Baptist and St. Matthew, c.* 1470, tempera on wood. Galleria dell'Accademia.

Opposite page: Sandro Botticelli, *Virgin and Child with the Infant St. John and Two Angels, c.* 1468, tempera on wood.

Following pages:
Sandro Botticelli and Assistants, *Our Lady of the Sea*, 1475-1480, oil on wood. Galleria dell'Accademia.

Filippino Lippi and Pietro Perugino, *Deposition,* oil on wood, 1504 and 1507. Galleria dell'Accademia.

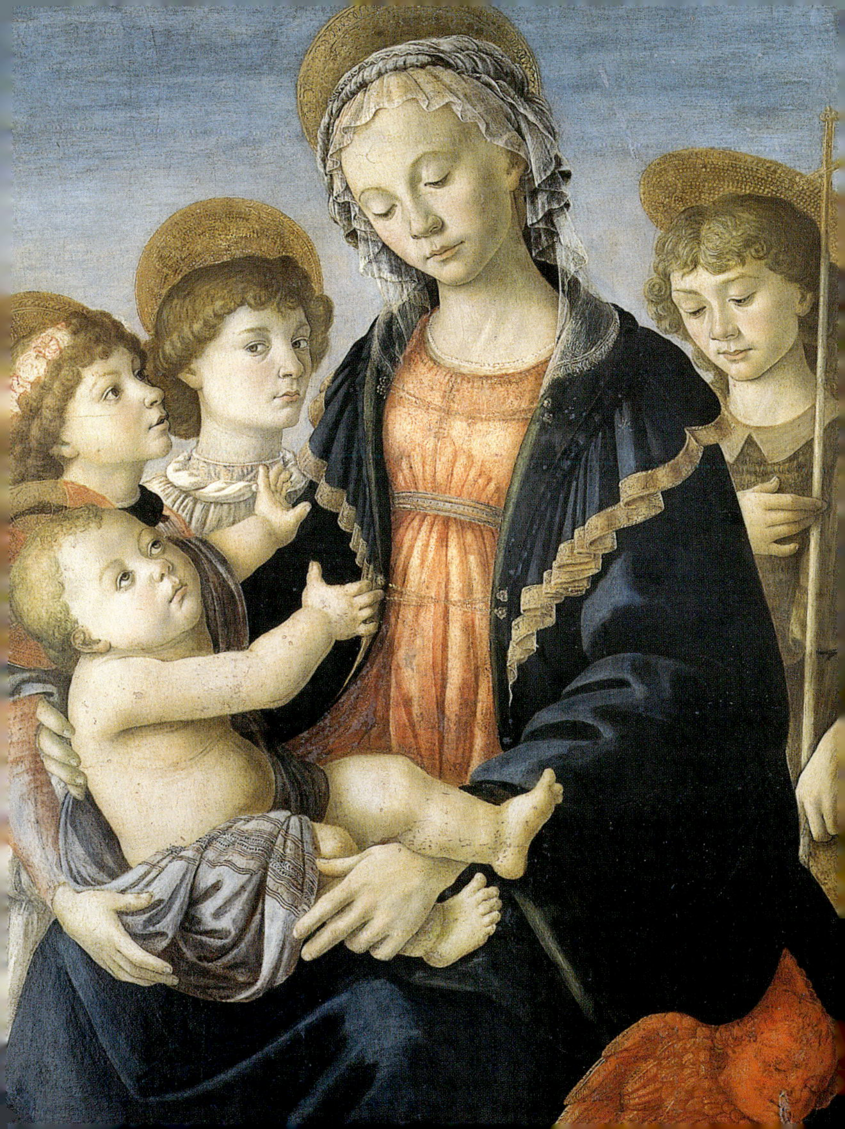

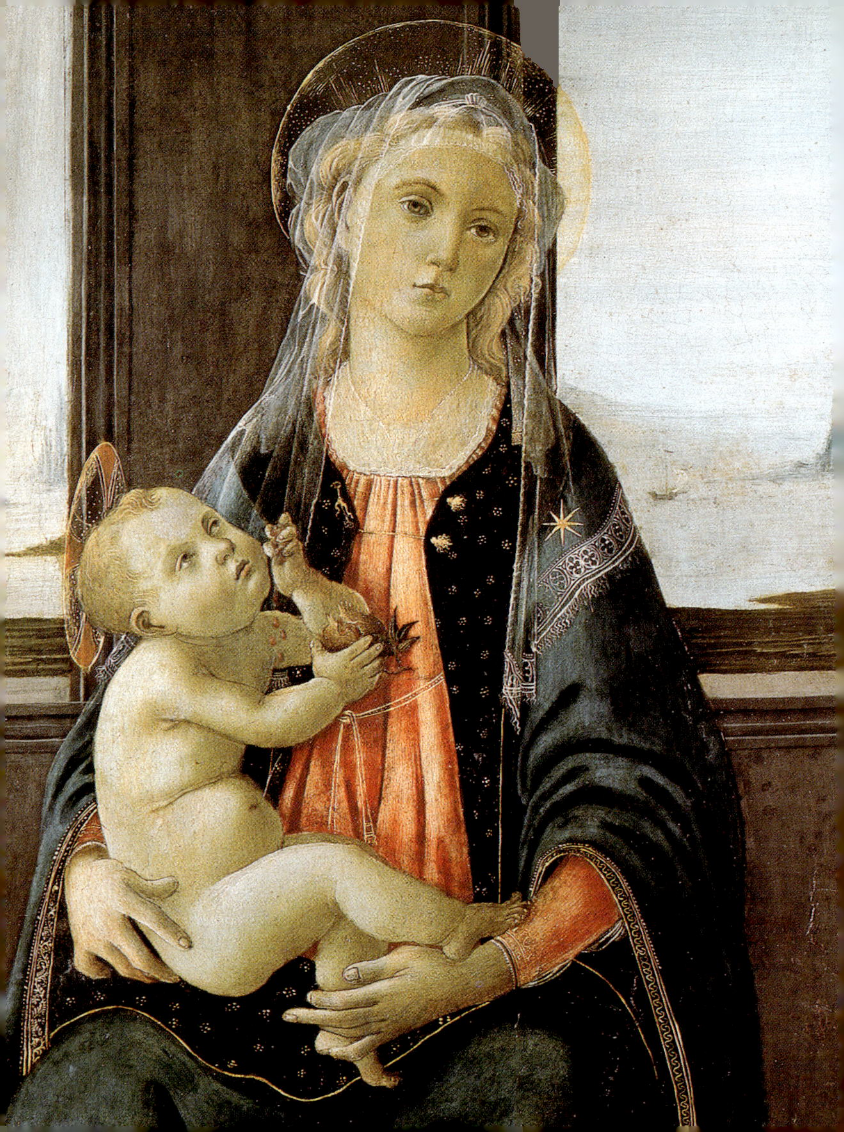

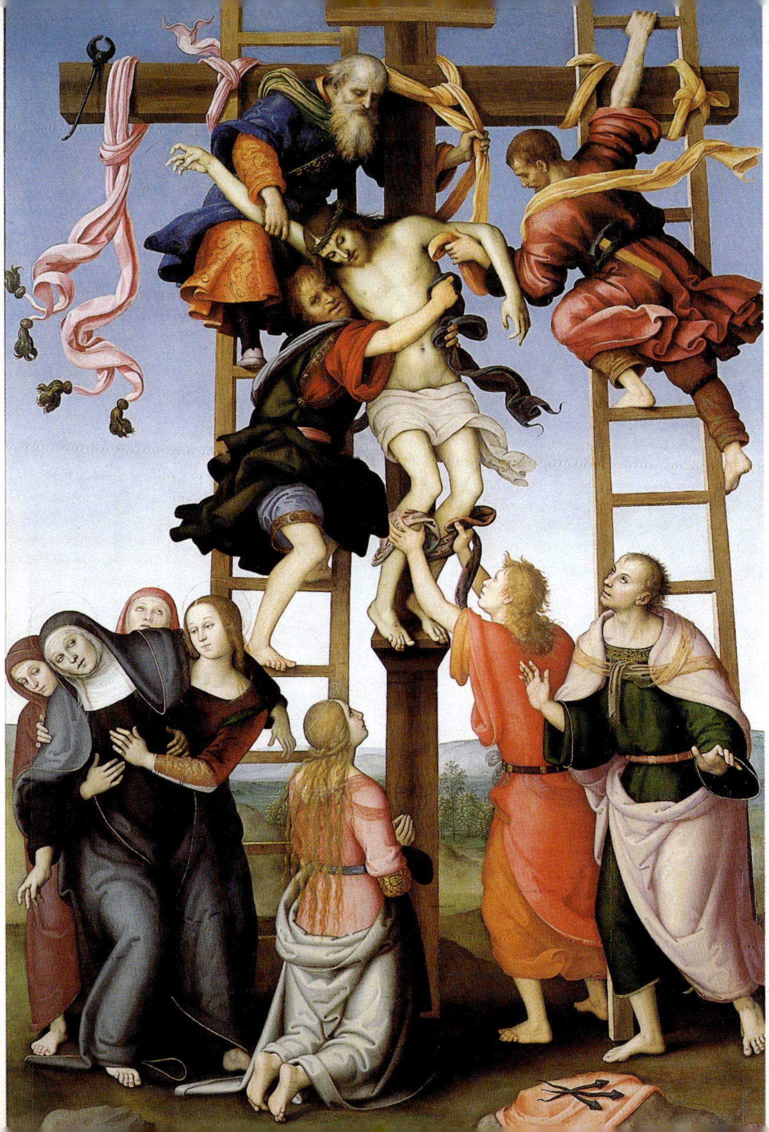

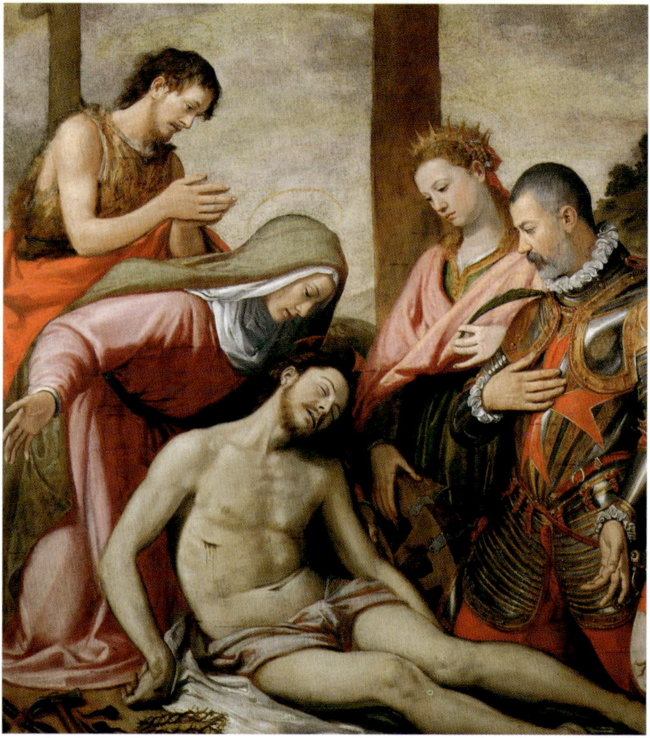

Above.
Santi di Tito, *Christ's Deposition from the Cross with the Virgin, St. John the Baptist, Saint Catherine of Alexandria and the Patron*
c. 1590, oil on wood.
Galleria dell'Accademia.

Opposite page:
Fra Bartolomeo, *The Prophet Job*, c. 1514-1516, oil on wood.
Galleria dell'Accademia.

Following pages: Pontormo, *Venus and Cupid, c.* 1535, oil on wood. Galleria dell'Accademia.

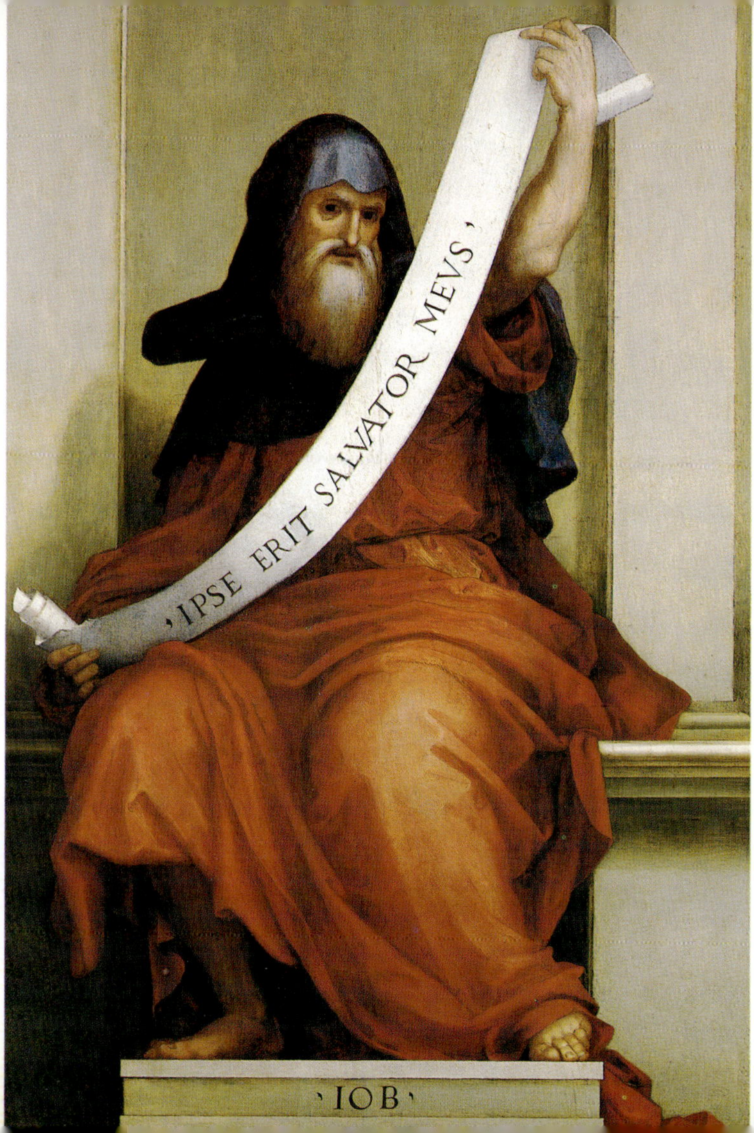
IPSE ERIT SALVATOR MEVS
IOB

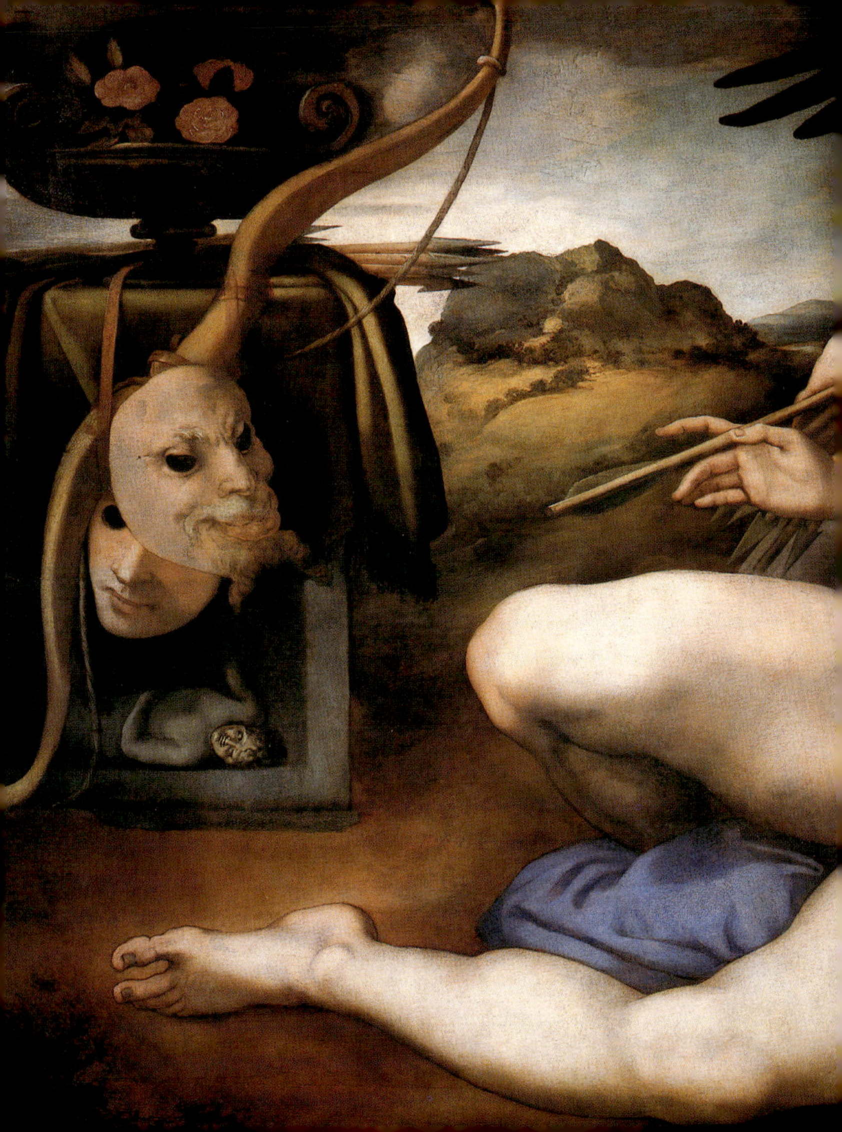

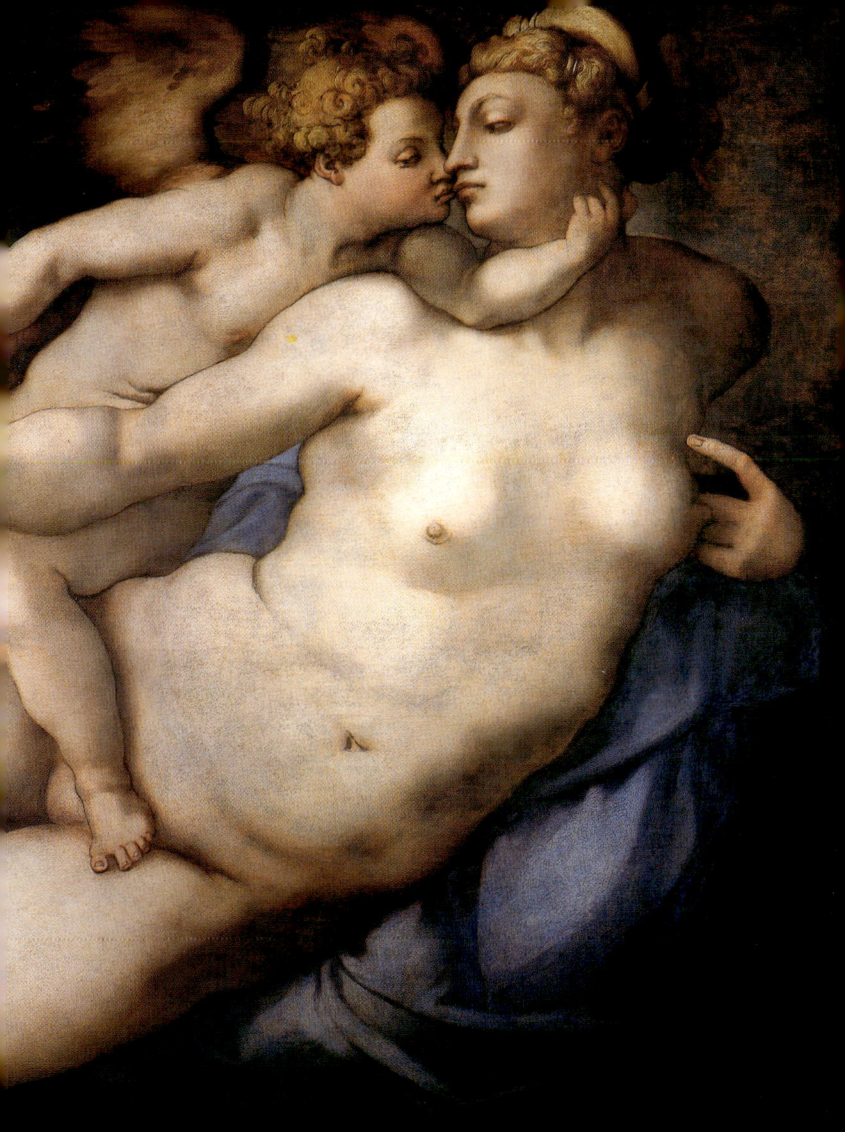

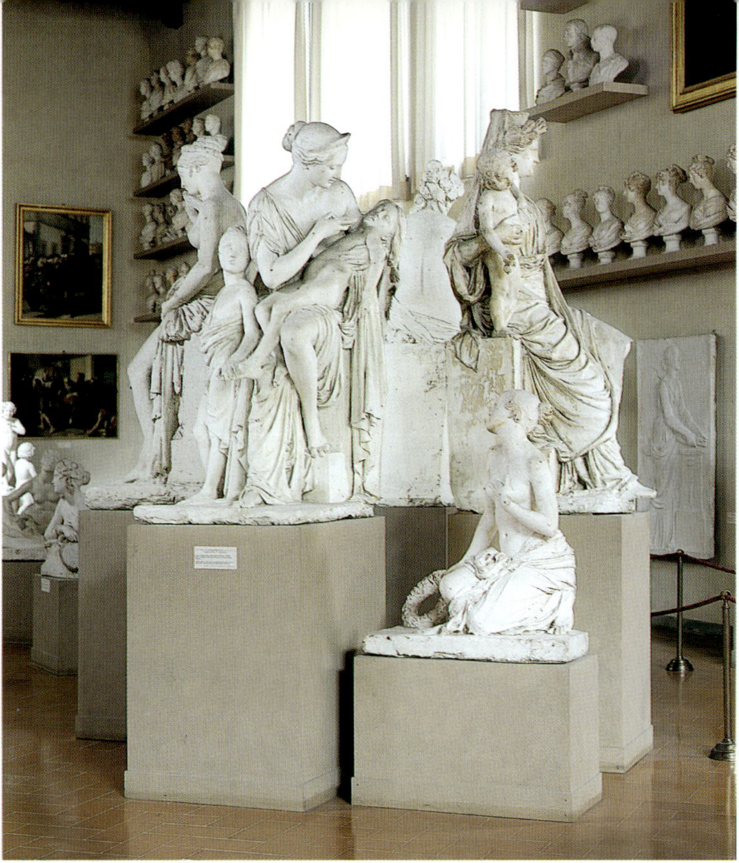

Above:
The 19th Century Room, with plaster casts by Lorenzo Bartolini and Luigi Pampaloni and paintings by 19th century Tuscan artists.

Opposite page:
Luigi Mussini,
Sacred Music,
1841, oil on canvas.
Galleria dell'Accademia.

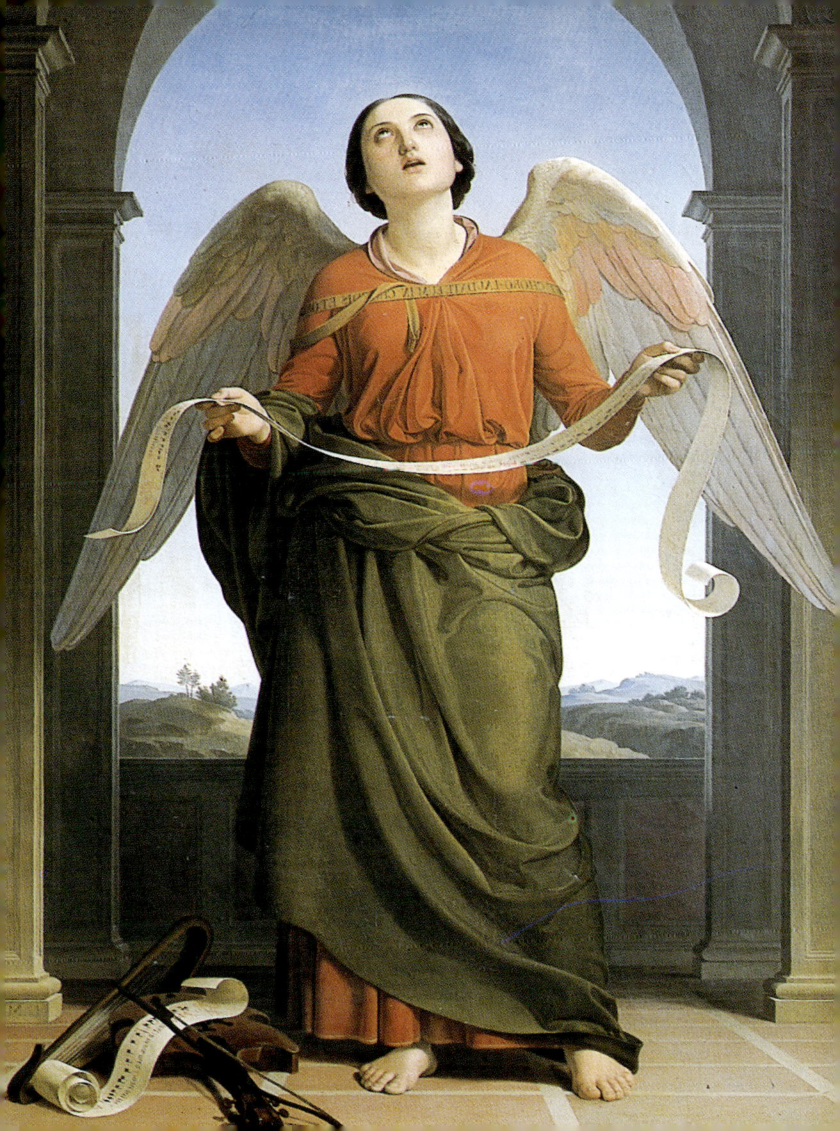

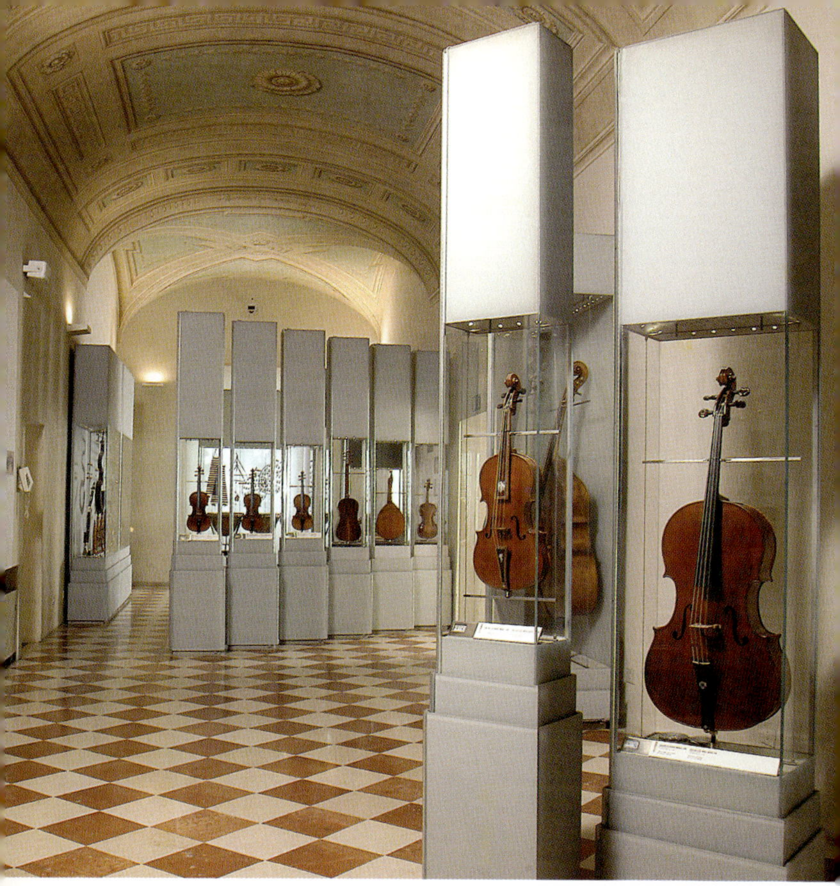

Above:
One of the rooms in the Museum of Musical Instruments, inaugurated in 2001 at the Galleria dell'Accademia.

Opposite page:
Nicolò Amati, *Violoncello*, c. 1650, spruce and oak wood.
Galleria dell'Accademia, Museum of Musical Instruments.

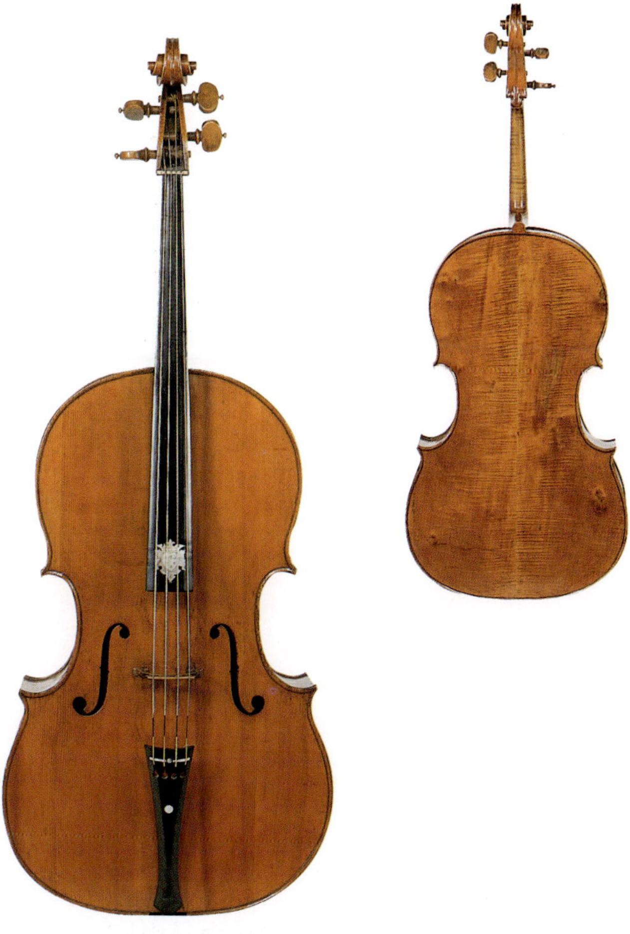

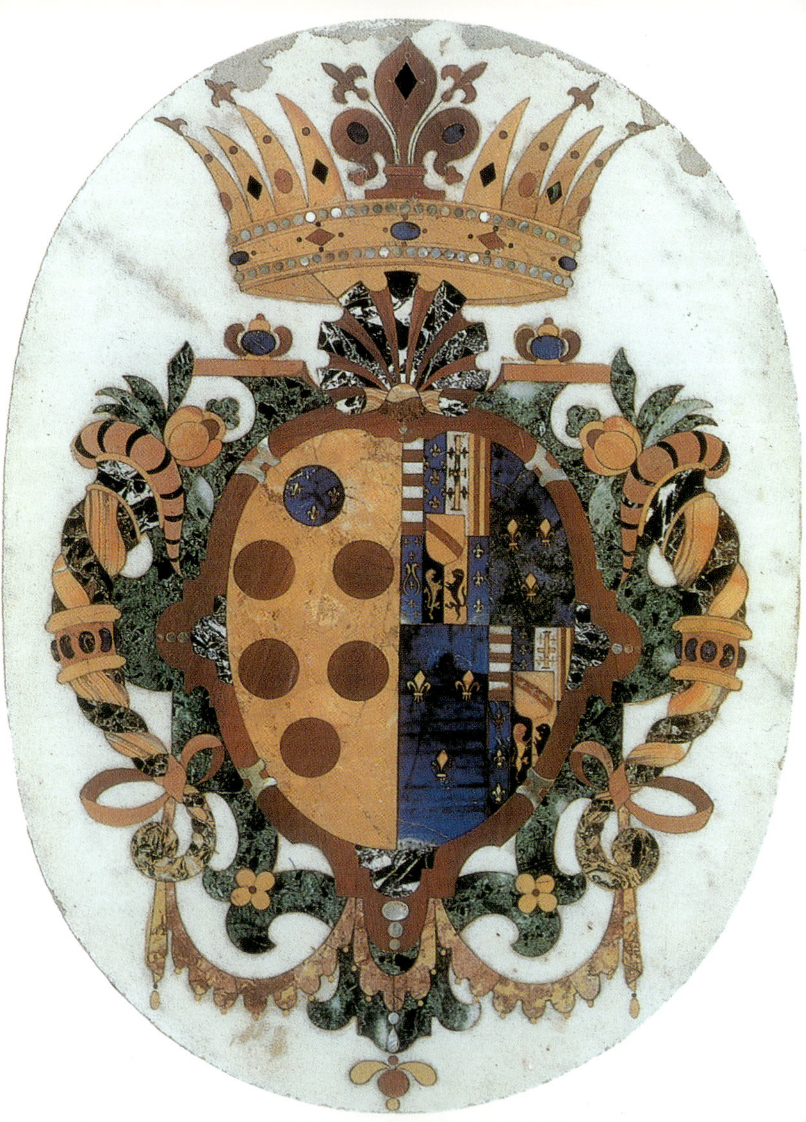

Museo dell'Opificio delle Pietre Dure

Situated in Via degli Alfani, in the building that once housed the Monastery of San Niccolò di Cafaggio, the museum is annexed to the Opificio delle Pietre Dure, founded in 1588 by Ferdinando I de' Medici under the name "Galleria dei Lavori". Originally located on the first floor of the Uffizi, the Manufactury was dedicated to fabricating furniture and other objects with semi-precious stones, through the technique known as "commesso" (or Florentine mosaic), which already by the end of the 16th century had made the Florentine craftsmen famous throughout Europe. The semiprecious stones (jasper, granite, chalcedony, porphyry and lapis lazuli) were cut into thin pieces of different shapes and put together with almost invisible joins. The Opificio, which has for years now been transformed into the world's most efficient laboratory and school of restoration for stone materials, has occupied its present site since 1796, where it continued to produce objects made of semi-precious stone up to the end of the 19th century. The museum was established at that time, and was rearranged and remodeled in 1995. In it are displayed important examples of various objects in "commesso di pietre dure" and scagliola, another traditional product of Florentine craftsmen starting from the 18th century. The long history of the Chapel of the Princes in San Lorenzo, the most grandiose work in semiprecious stone ever created in Florence, is also documented here.

Galleria dei Lavori, *Medici-Lorena coat of arms*, late 16th century, inlaid hard and soft stones on Carrara marble. Museo dell'Opificio delle Pietre Dure.

The objects displayed include:

- tools used for working semiprecious stone and scagliola, as well as objects made of porphyry, figured panels, painted models for mosaics, documenting more than three centuries of activity of the Florentine manufactury and other centers.

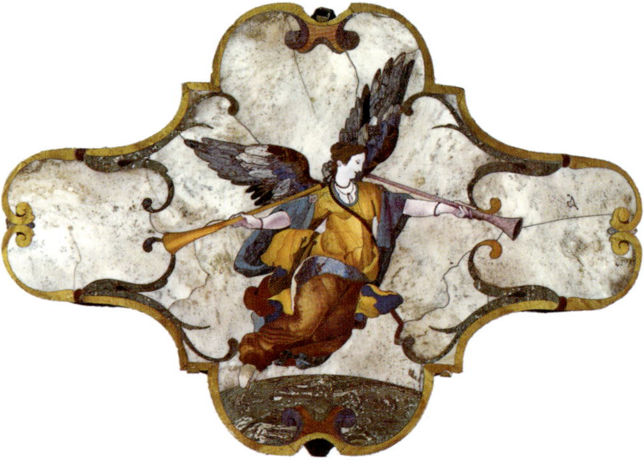

Above:
Prague Manufactury, *Fame,* 1600-1630, "commesso in pietre dure" on background of chalcedony and jasper. Museo dell'Opificio delle Pietre Dure.

Opposite page:
Florentine Manufactury, *Table top, detail,* 1816, porphyry with inlaid semiprecious stones. Museo dell'Opificio delle Pietre Dure.

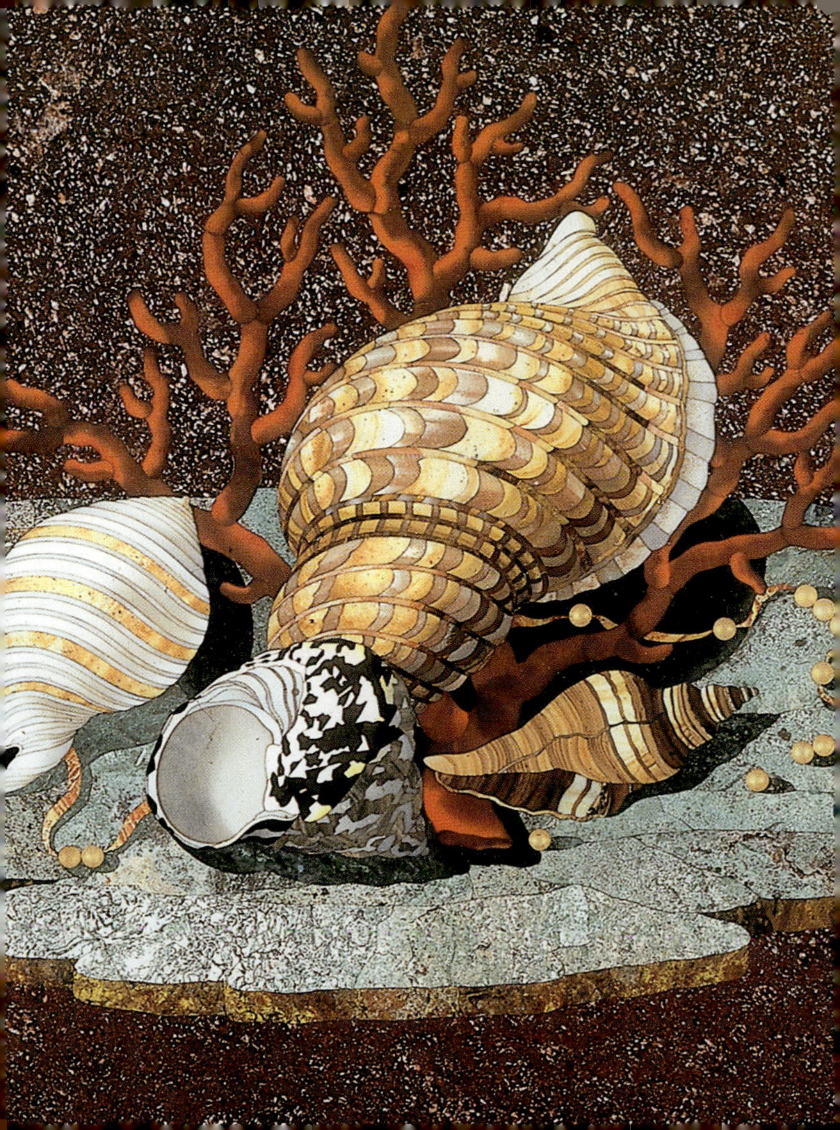

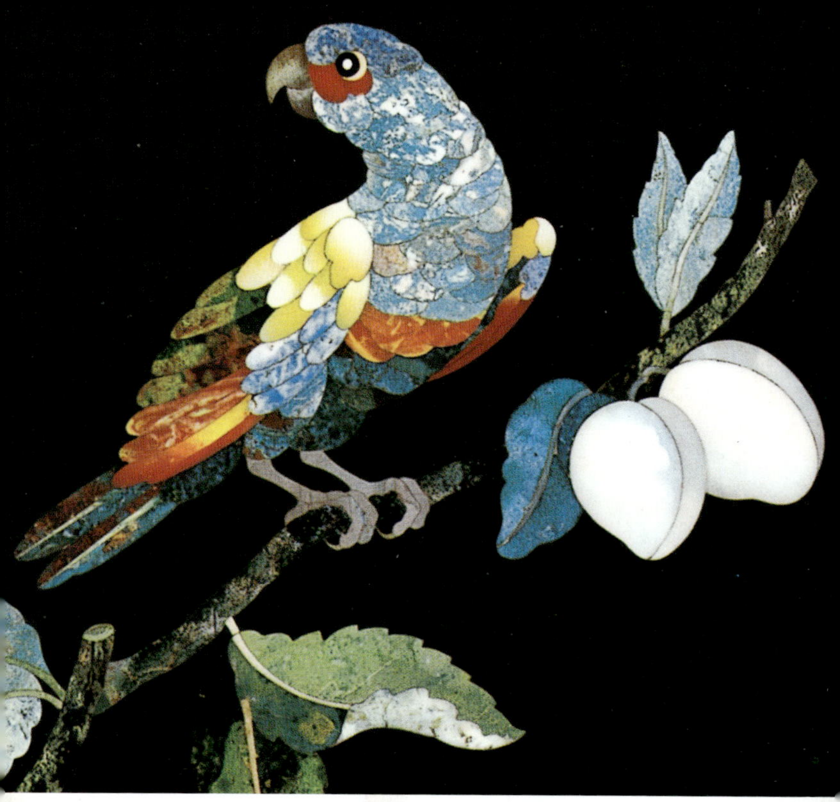

Above:
Galleria dei Lavori, *Parrot on a plum tree branch,* detail, 17th century, polychrome scagliola. Museo dell'Opificio delle Pietre Dure.

Opposite page:
Galleria dei Lavori, *Vase of flowers,* 1690, inlaid hard and soft stones on black marble. Museo dell'Opificio delle Pietre Dure.

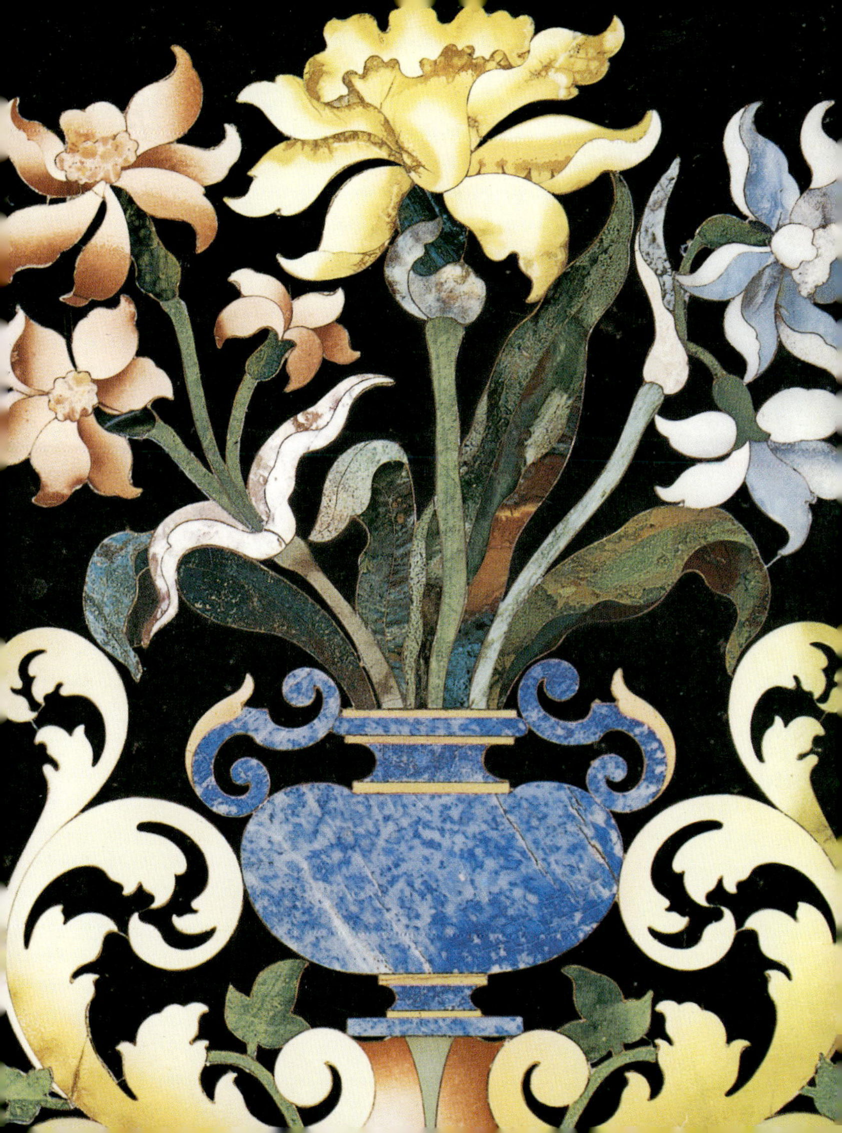

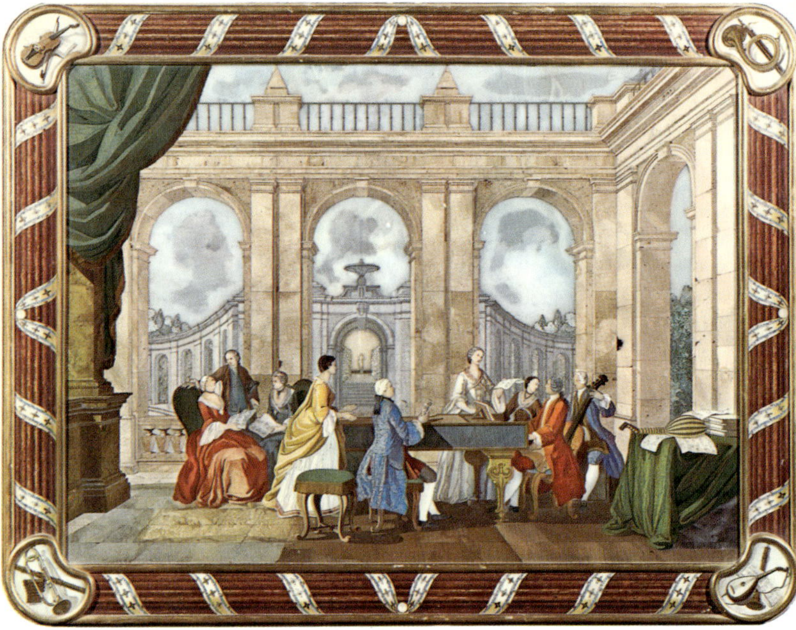

Above:
Florentine Manufactury,
The Liberal Arts: Music,
c. 1776-1780, panel inlaid
in "commesso" of oriental onyx,
Sicilian and Bohemian jasper,
lapis lazzuli and chalcedony,
gilded bronze and semiprecious
stone frame, to models
by Giuseppe Zocchi.
Museo dell'Opificio
delle Pietre Dure.

Opposite page:
Hugo Hugford, *Fluvial Landscape*,
mid-18th century, polychrome
scagliola. Museo dell'Opificio
delle Pietre Dure.

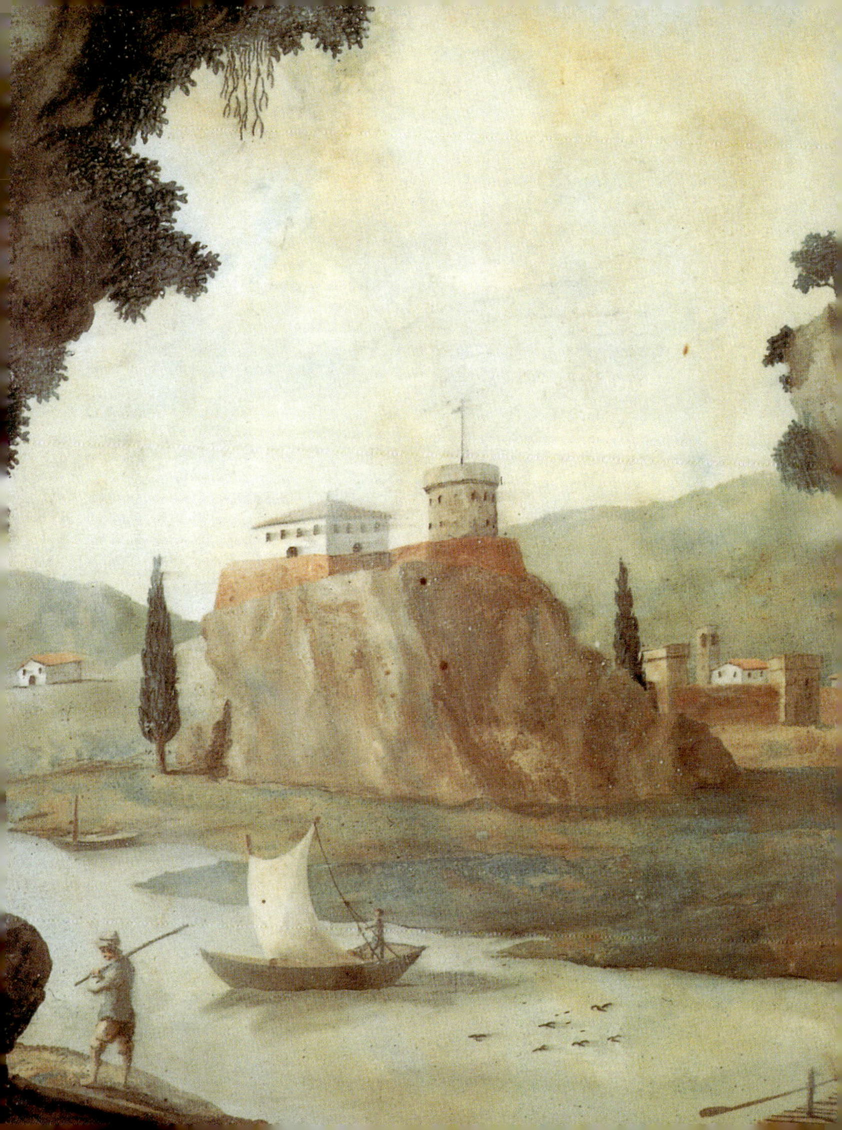

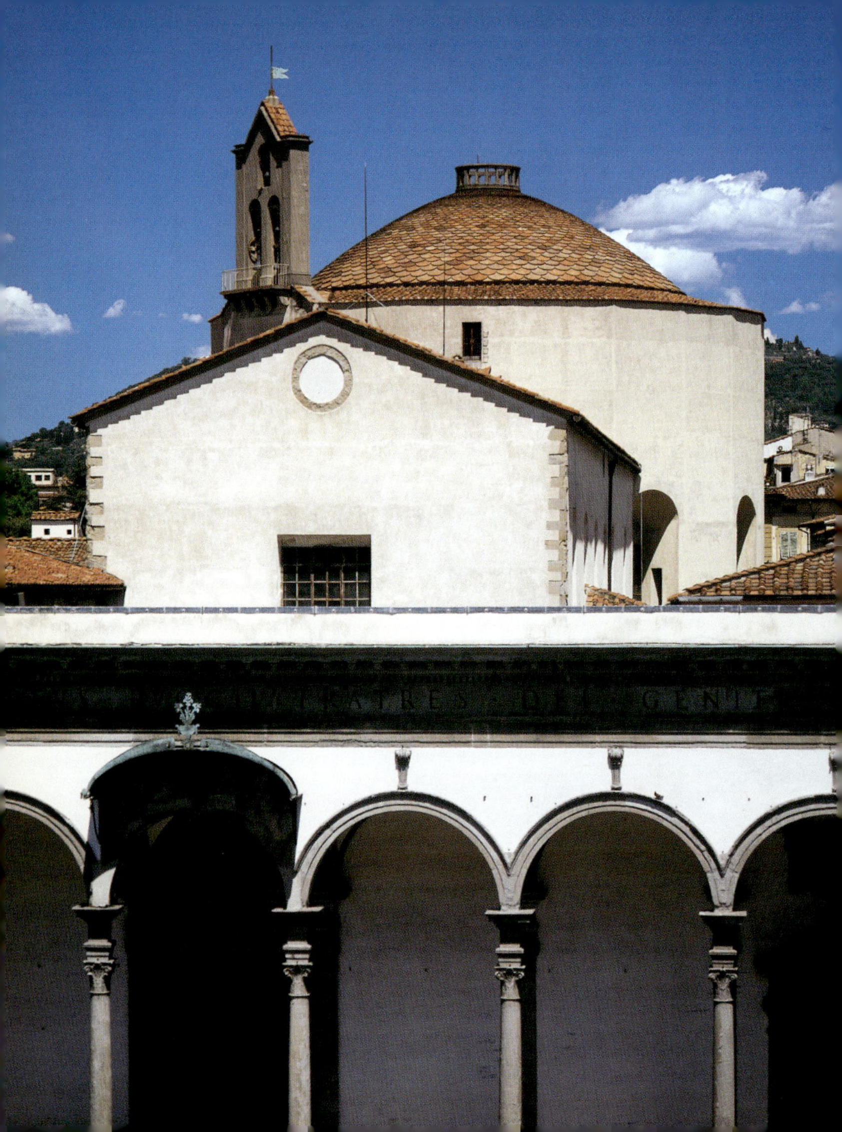

The Annunziata

The Piazza, the Church, the Spedale degli Innocenti

In every season and at any hour of the day, but especially at twilight, on winter evenings, an enchanted atmosphere pervades this piazza of subtle fascination, rich in history and works of art. Like Piazza San Marco in the 1440s, the Annunziata served as the religious "center of gravity" of the Medici family. From the Basilica of San Lorenzo the Medicean interests had in fact shifted toward the northern borders of the city. The two squares were aligned along an axis running straight north toward the family's country estates in Mugello, and were also connected through two parallel streets to Piazza del Duomo and Piazza San Giovanni. Like Cosimo the Elder at San Marco, his son Piero had at his disposal some rooms in the Convent of the Annunziata, and for him Michelozzo de-

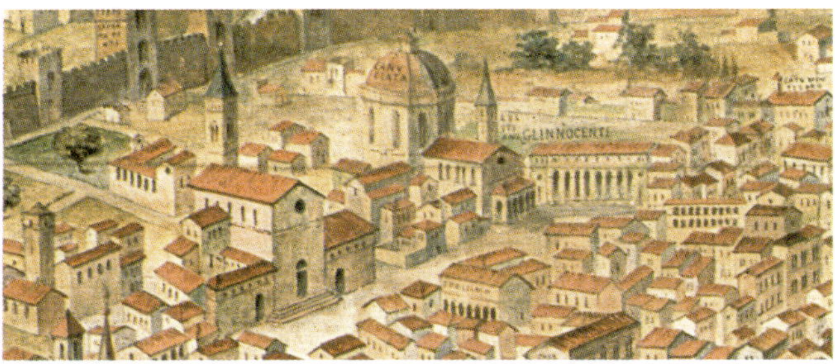

Opposite page:
Veew of the facade of Santissima Annunziata with the Rotonda by Leon Battista Alberti in the background.

Above: San Marco, the SS. Annunziata and the Spedale degli Innocenti, detail of the "*Pianta della Catena" map,* 19th century copy Museo di Firenze com'era.

signed in the Basilica a sumptuous tempietto. At the time of Grand Duke Cosimo I and his son Francesco, the area between the Annunziata, Via dei Servi and San Marco was enriched with institutions of high cultural prestige and political significance: the Orto dei Semplici (today the Botanical Gardens, one of the world's most ancient surviving ones), the Serraglio, the Stalle, and the Accademia delle Arti del Disegno in Piazza San Marco. It was expressly at the Accademia, in 1567, that the Servite Brothers granted the Chapel of San Luca in Santissima Annunziata as a burial place for artists. There was then placed in the square, in 1608, the equestrian monument to Grand Duke Ferdinando I. Accomplished between 1601 and 1608 by Giambologna using melted-down bronze from cannons coming from the booty of a battle against the Turks, the monument was completed with a base by Pietro Tacca, who also created the two zooomorphic fountains in the square, originally destined to decorate the docks at Livorno. The base of the equestrian monument, of great perspective and symbolic effect, depicts the queen bee surrounded by her swarm, accompanied by the motto MAIESTATE TANTUM, a metaphor for the Grand Duke surrounded by his subjects. Not far away, in Via dei Servi, lived some court officials, among them the Medicean secretary Ugolino Grifoni, whose palace (1557) was designed by Bartolomeo Ammannati.

Opposite page:
Pietro Tacca, *Base of the equestrian monument to Ferdinando I*,
c. 1640, bronze.
Piazza Santissima Annunziata.

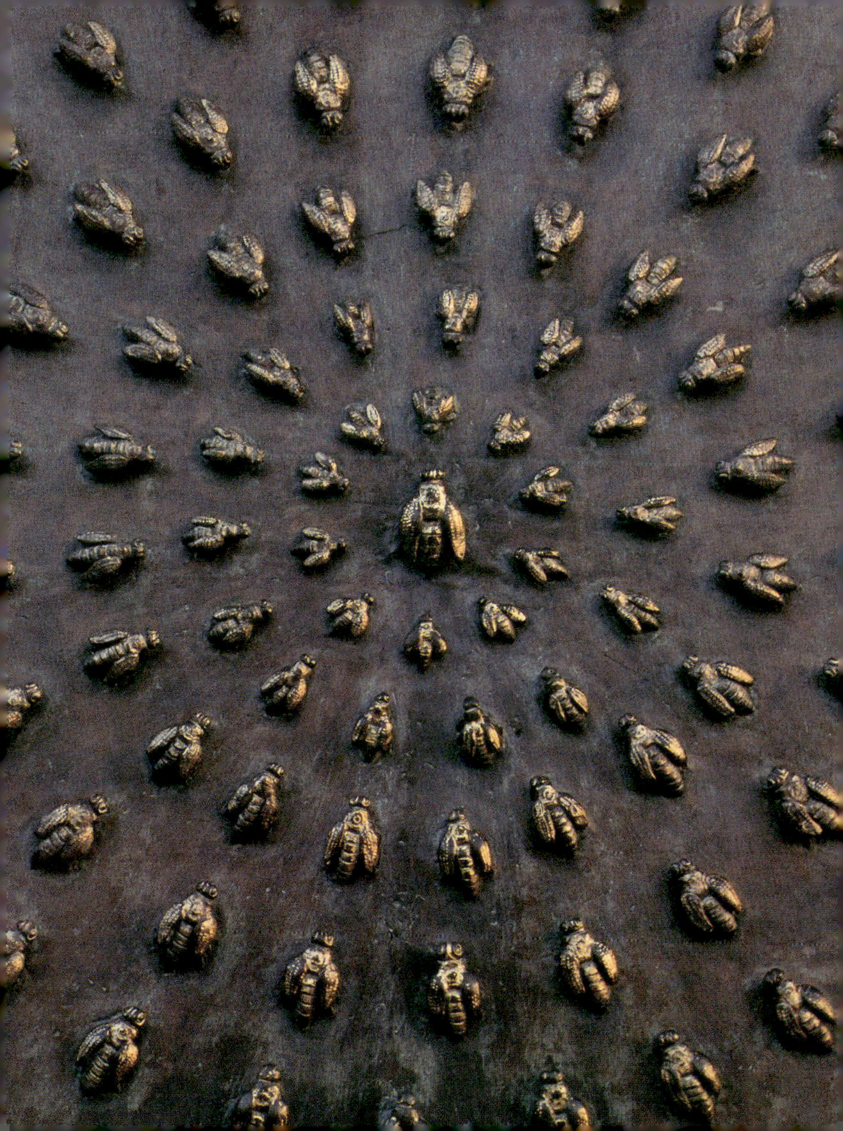

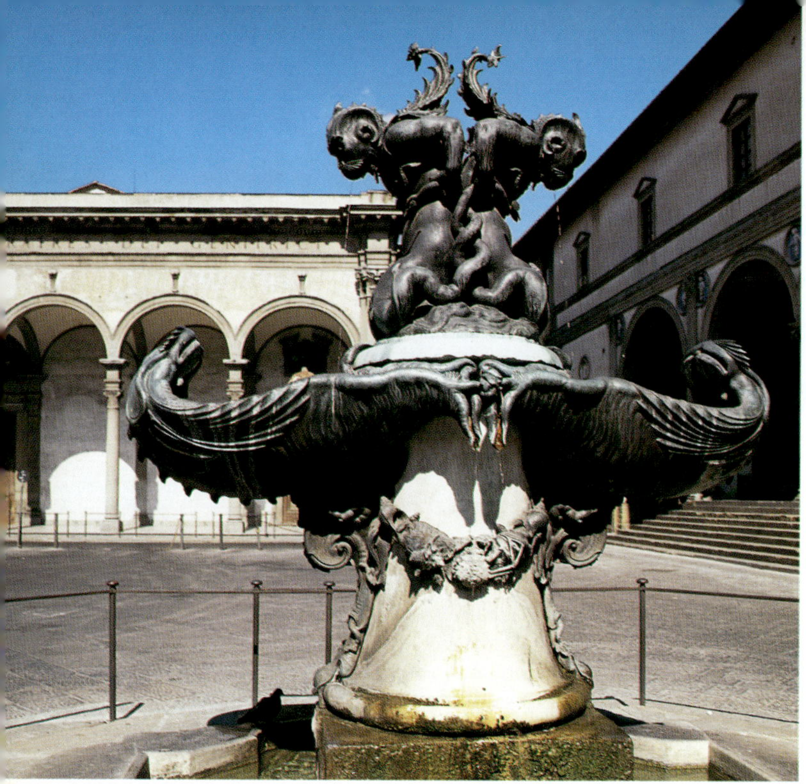

Above:
Pietro Tacca, *Fountain,*
c. 1629, bronze.
Piazza SS. Annunziata.

Opposite page:
Giambologna, *Equestrian monument to Ferdinando I*,
1608, bronze.

Following pages:
Andrea della Robbia, *Tondo of a baby in swathing bands*,
c. 1485, glazed terracotta. Façade of the Spedale degli Innocenti.

Filippo Brunelleschi,
Interior of the portico,
c. 1426. Spedale degli Innocenti.

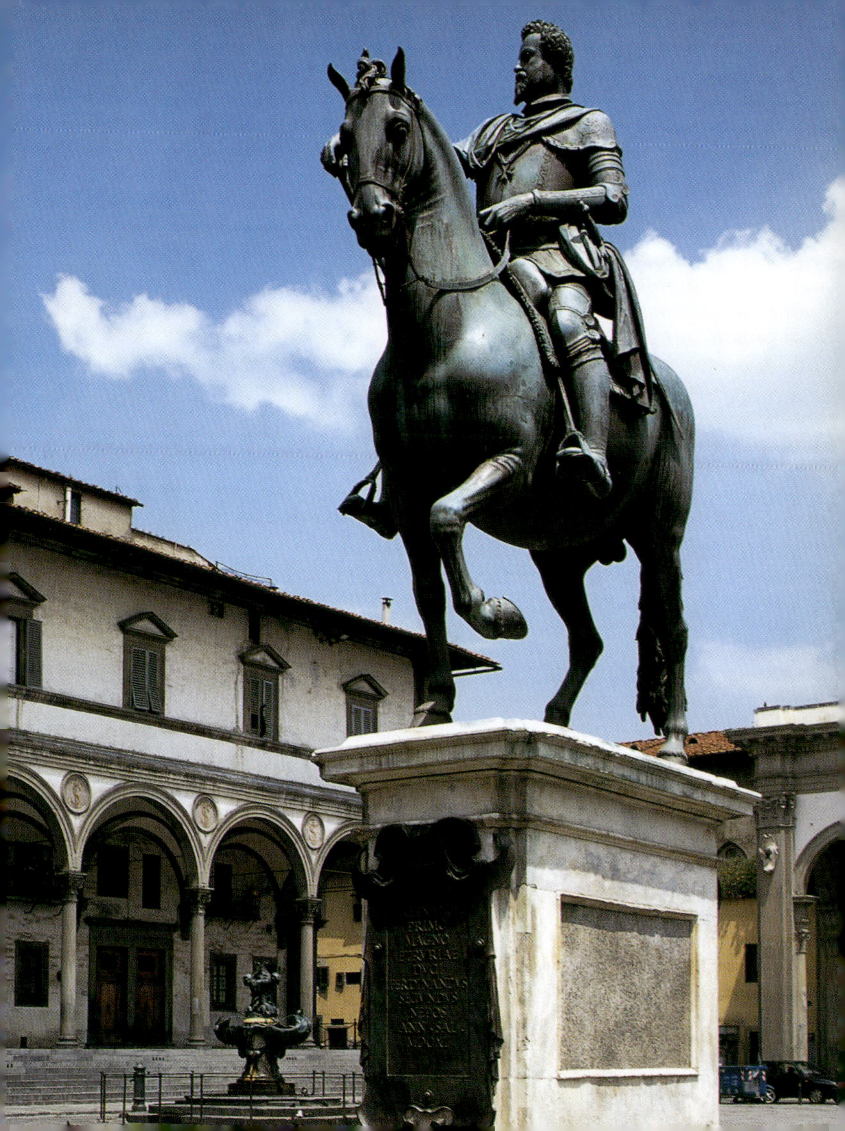

HISTORY

On the lands of Cafaggio (the present-day SS. Annunziata), outside the Balla Gate, from where packed goods ("imballate") entered, an oratory dedicated to the Madonna had stood since the 11th century. In around 1250 seven Servite monks, former Florentine merchants, took over the oratory, which became popular among the people for a miraculous fresco portraying *Our Lady of the Annunciation*. In the 14th century the territory was extended and the square was newly arranged. Starting in 1444 the Annunziata was remodeled in the form of a basilica under the guidance of Michelozzo, assisted by Pagno Portigiani and Antonio Manetti. On the eastern edge there already stood the Spedale degli Innocenti, which, under the protection of the Silk Merchants Guild, sheltered abandoned children. It had been de-

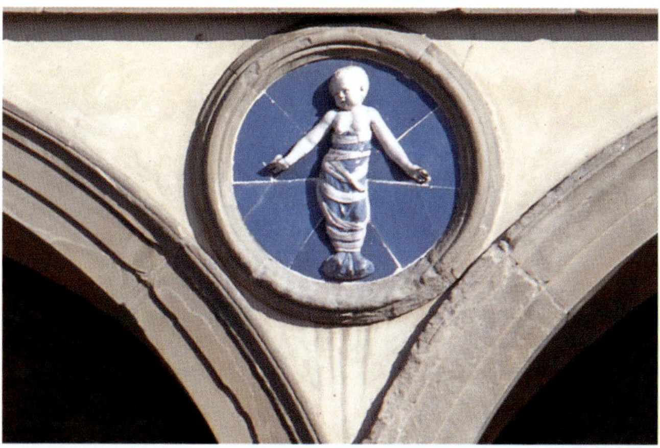

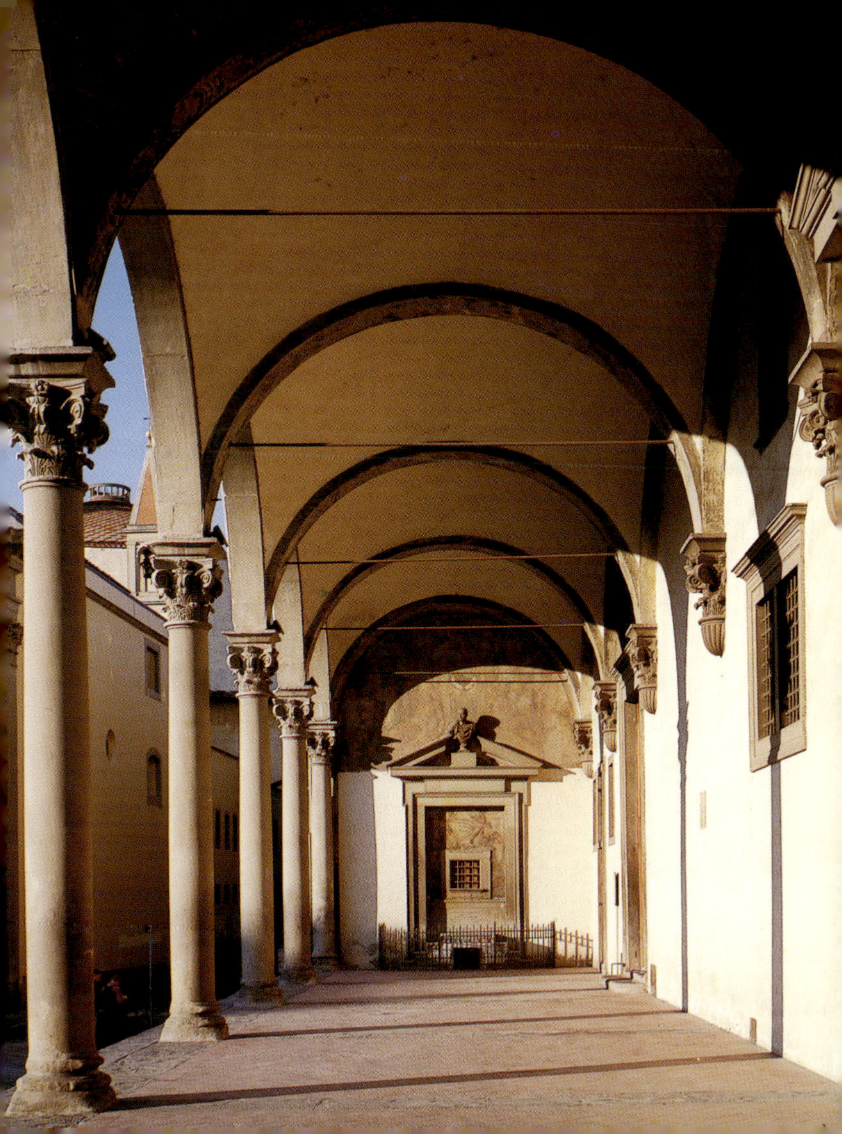

signed by Brunelleschi around 1426, and his project had then been partially modified. Around 1476 Leon Battista Alberti concluded the lengthy work of constructing the Rotonda in the Annunziata complex, financed starting from 1444 by Gianfrancesco Gonzaga and Cosimo il Vecchio, and situated in coincidence with a straight line extending from the dome of Santa Maria del Fiore. The Basilica was consecrated in 1516, the year in which Brunelleshi's portico of the Innocenti, the loggia of the Confraternita di Maria, was built on the side opposite it. Only in 1600 was the loggia on the third side of the piazza built, as completion of the church. The importance of the sanctuary in which Our Lady of the Annunciation was venerated is demonstrated by the fact that in 1416 the Florentine Republic consecrated the day of March 25 with ceremonies and festivities that have continued since then, and are still held each year, on that date, in the square. The Florentine calendar too was based on that date, which marked the end of the year. And it was at the Annunziata that Leonardo exhibited, in the early years of the 16th century, the cartoon for a *Saint Anne* commissioned of him by the Servites: an animated group of figures that aroused the fervent admiration of the Florentines, and that may have served, at least in part, as Michelangelo's inspiration for the composition of his *Doni Tondo* (Uffizi). Many are the artists who, over the centuries, have worked in this sanctuary where, among other things, the Chiostrino dei Voti is the most significant testimony to the origins of Florentine Mannerist painting.

Opposite page:
The Chiostrino dei Voti, decorated with lunettes containing frescoes dedicated to the life of the Virgin and those of the seven founders of the Order of Maria.

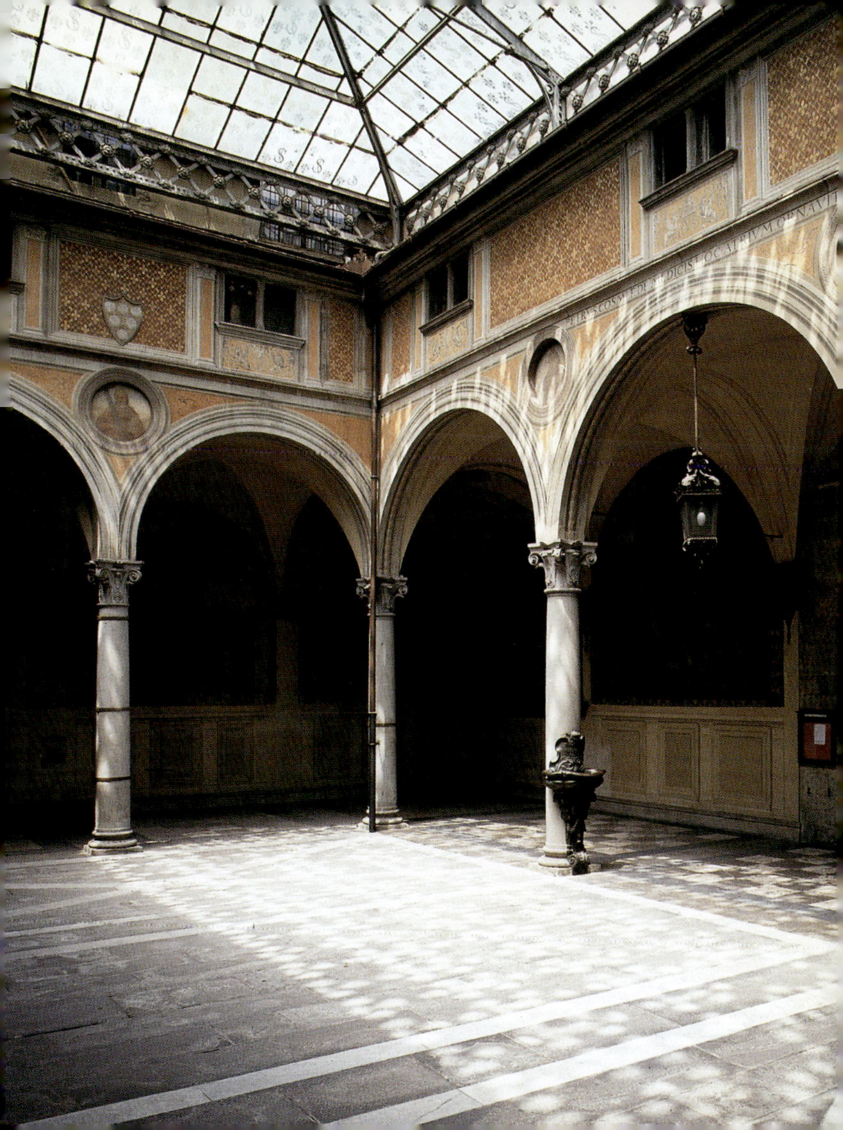

The works of art found in the monumental complex include:

- The frescoes in the Chiostrino dei Voti by Alesso Baldovinetti (c. 1460), Cosimo Rosselli (1474), Andrea del Sarto (1500, 1511-1514), Franciabigio (1513), Pontormo (1516) and Rosso Fiorentino (1517).
- The *Madonna del Sacco* (1525), a fresco by Andrea del Sarto, in the ornamental panel over the door between the Chiostro Grande (or Chiostro dei Morti, designed by Michelozzo, and the church.
- The twenty-five frescoed lunettes with *Stories of the Servite Order* in the Cloister of the Dead, painted between 1604 and 1618 by Bernardino Pocceti, Ventura Salimbeni, Donato Mascagni and Matteo Rosselli.
- The marble tempietto in the Annunciata, built between 1447 and 1461 by Pagno di Lapo Portigiani to the design of Michelozzo (who also designed the tempietto in San Miniato al Monte), commissioned by Piero de' Medici to house the miraculous fresco of the *Annunciation* (Florentine School of the 14th century). The Baroque decorations were added in the 17th century.
- The bronze Gate (1447) by Maso di Bartolomeo.
- The fresco by Andrea del Castagno depicting *St. Julian and the Redeemer* (1455), commissioned by the Gagliani family.

Opposite page:
Pontormo, *Visitation*, 1516, fresco. Santissima Annunziata, Chiostrino dei Voti.

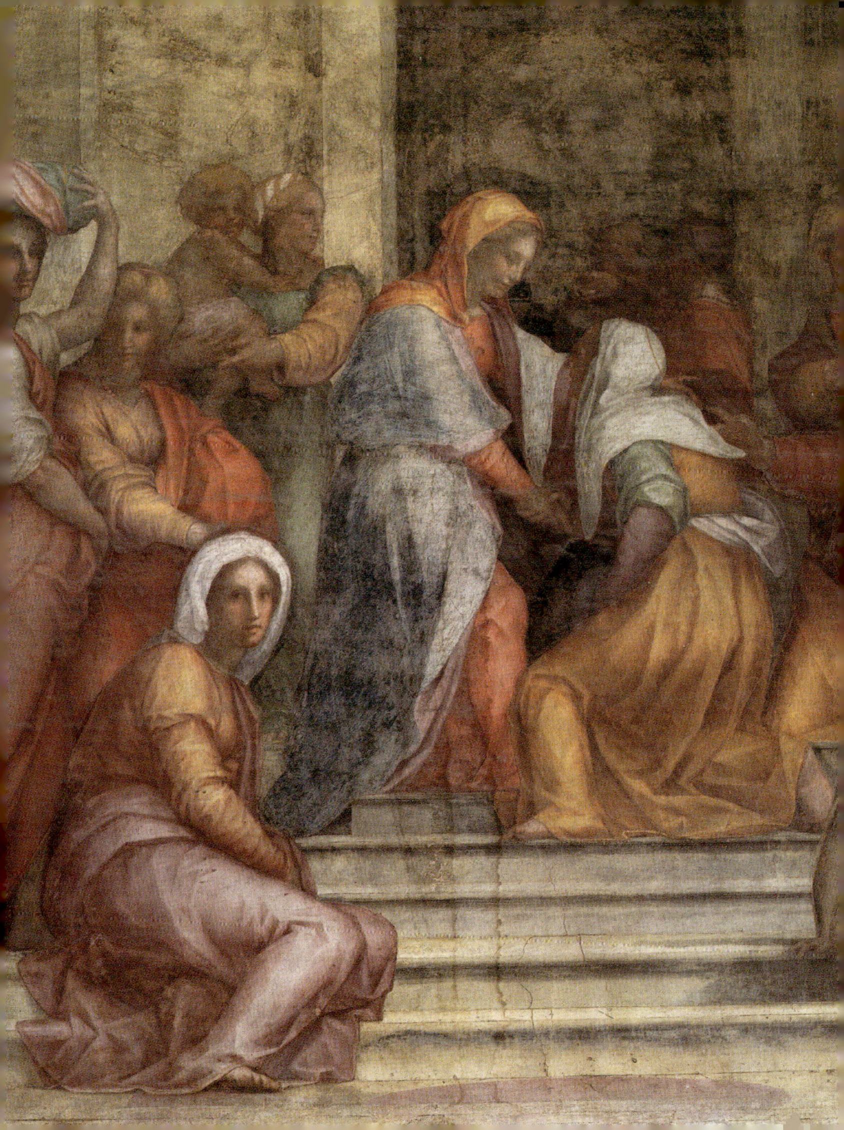

- The Feroni Chapel (1692) by Giovan Battista Foggini, one of the most interesting Baroque works designed in Florence.
- The Chapel of the Madonna del Soccorso, decorated between 1594 and 1598 by Giambologna with a *Bronze Crucifix* and some bronze bas-reliefs with *Stories of the Passion*.
- the Chapel of St. Luke, since 1563 the site of the Accademia del Disegno, whose decoration, with sculptures by Montorsoli (1533-1535), stuccoes and paintings by Alessandro Allori, Giorgio Vasari and Santi di Tito, was completed in 1572.

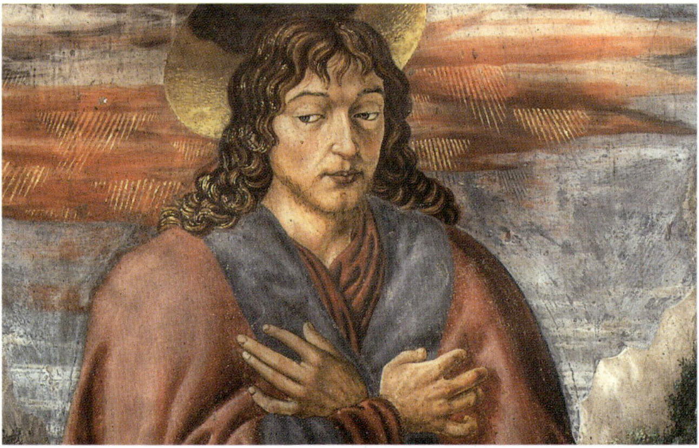

Above:
Andrea del Castagno,
Saint Julian receiving Absolution from the Redeemer, detail, c. 1455, fresco.
Santissima Annunziata.

Opposite page:
Andrea del Castagno,
Vision of St. Jerome and his Disciples,
1454, fresco. Santissima Annunziata.

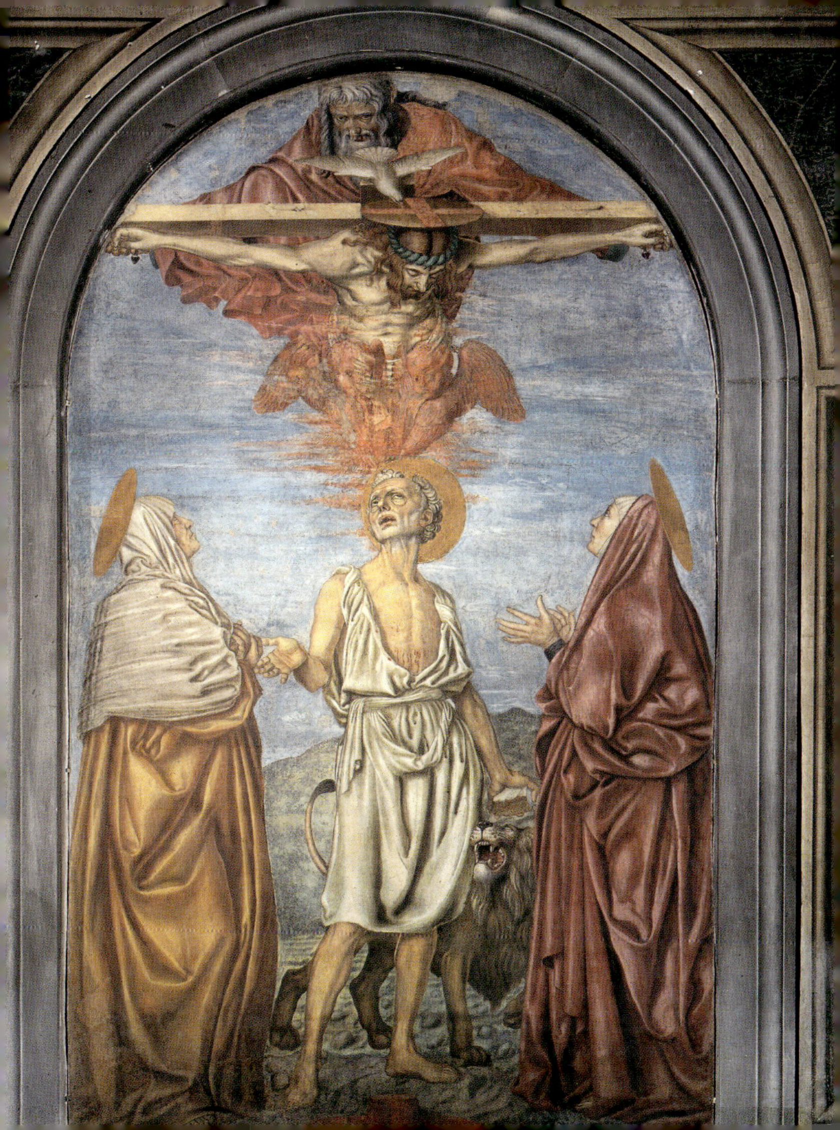

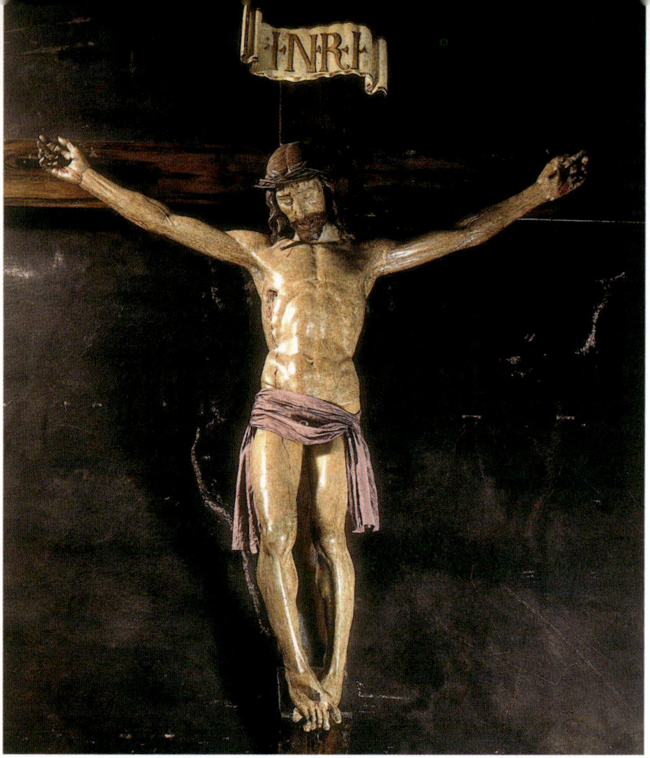

Above:
Giuliano da Sangallo, *Crucifixion*, 1481-1482, polychrome wood, the only surviving work after the destruction of the cabinets in the sacristy. Santissima Annunziata.

Opposite page:
The chapel and tempietto of the Annunciata.

Following pages:
Andrea del Sarto, *Rest during the Flight into Egypt* (*Madonna del Sacco*), 1525, fresco. Santissima Annunziata, Chiostro dei Morti.

The Chapel of San Luca, with 15th century stuccoes, scuptures and paintings.

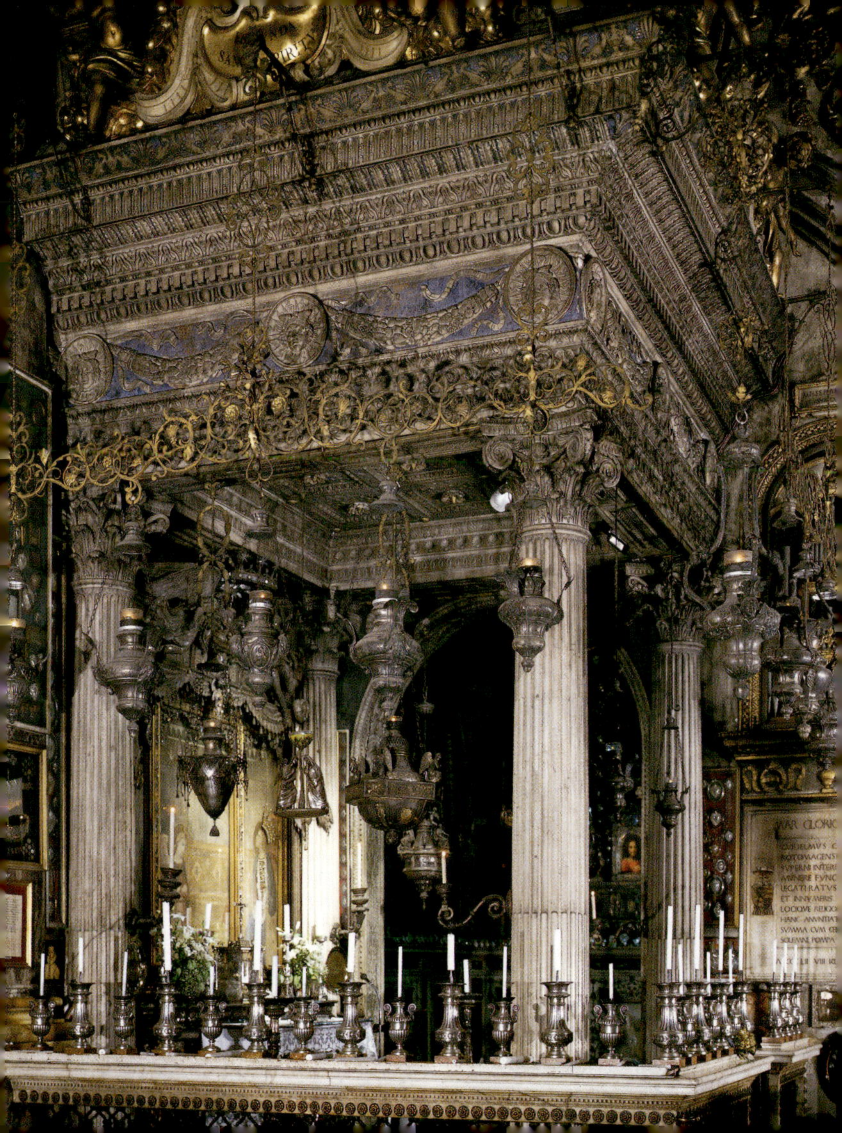

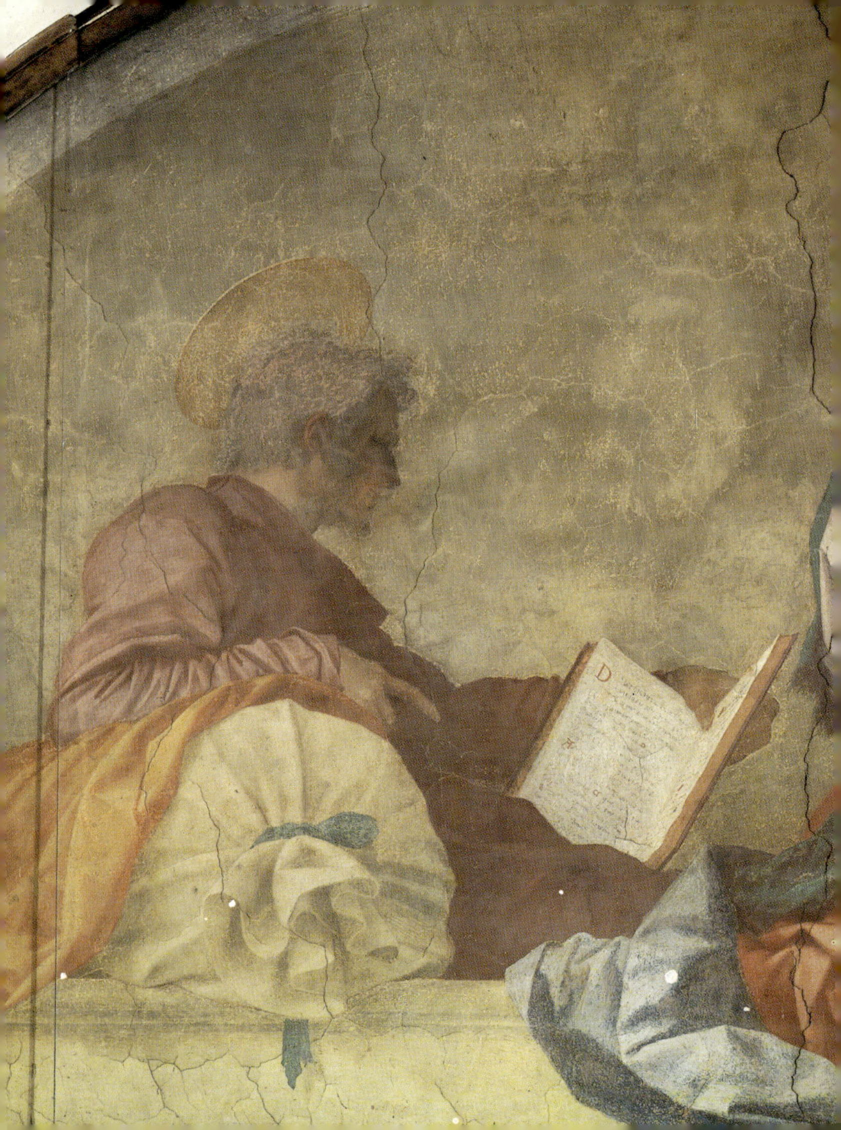

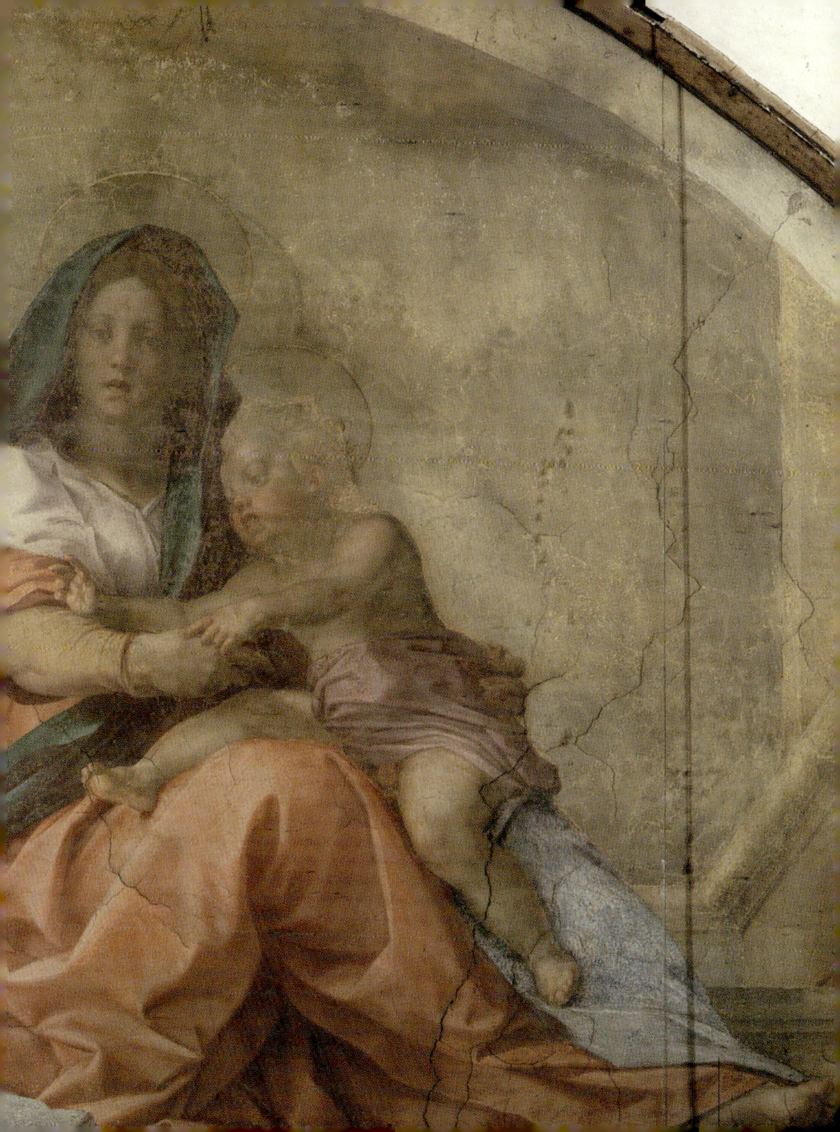

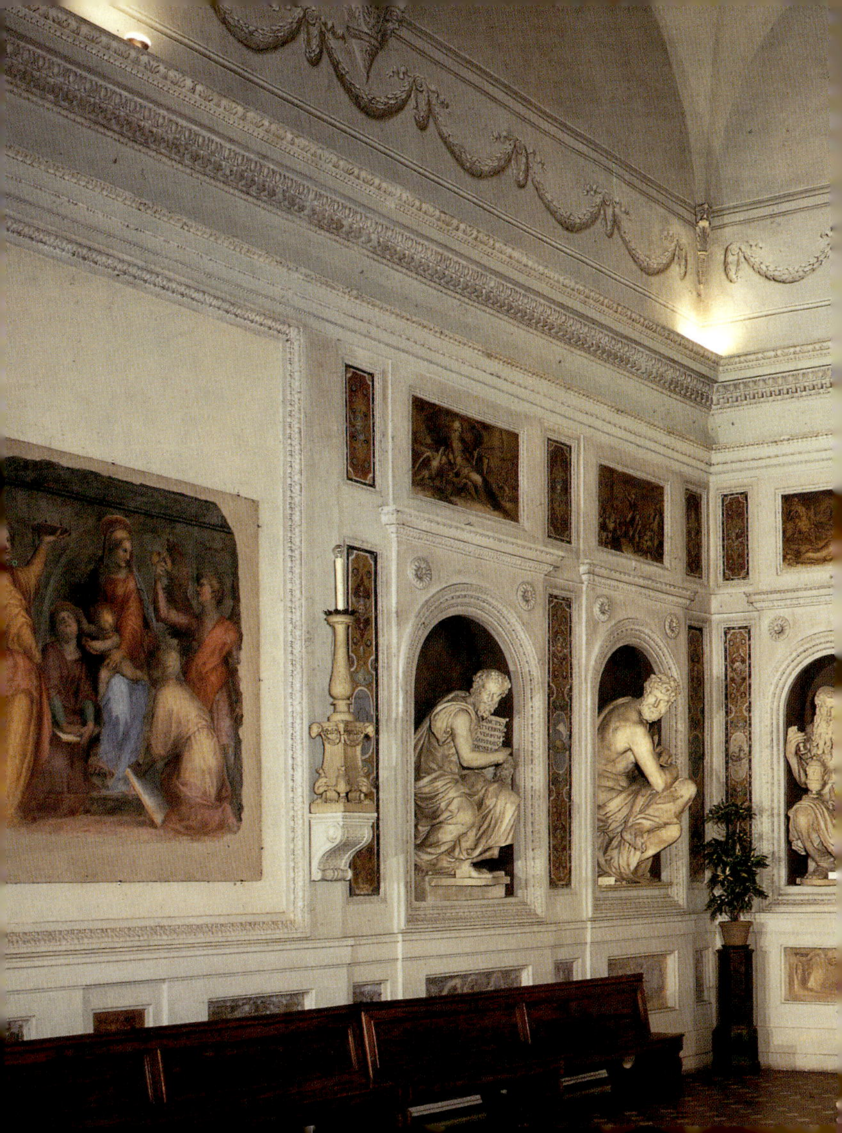

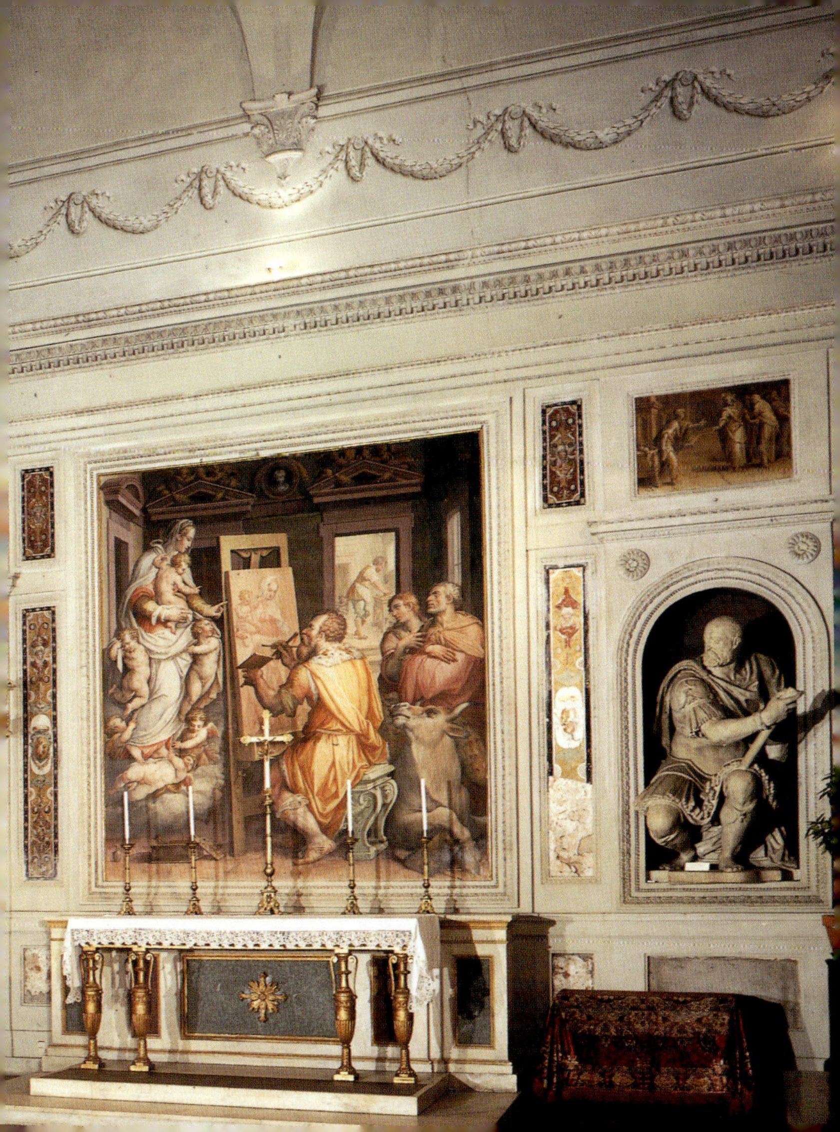

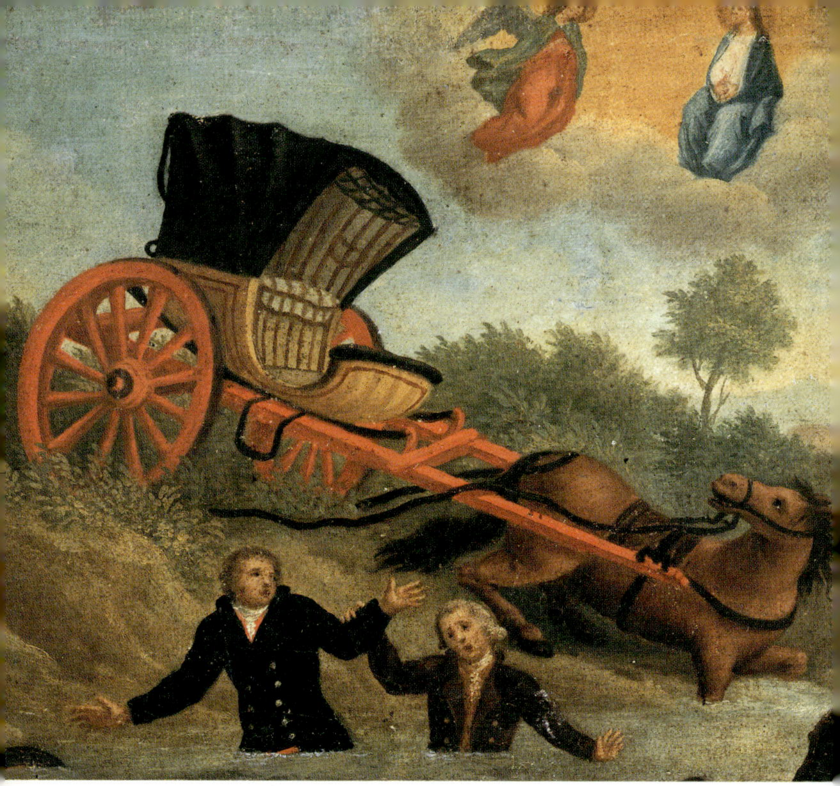

Above:
Florentine School, *Ex-voto to the Virgin in gratitude for intercession in a carriage accident,* late 18th century. Santissima Annunziata, Treasury.

Opposite page:
Florentine manufacture, *"Chinese" cape from Casa Minerbetti*, detail of embroidered fabric, 1734. Santissima Annunziata, Treasury.

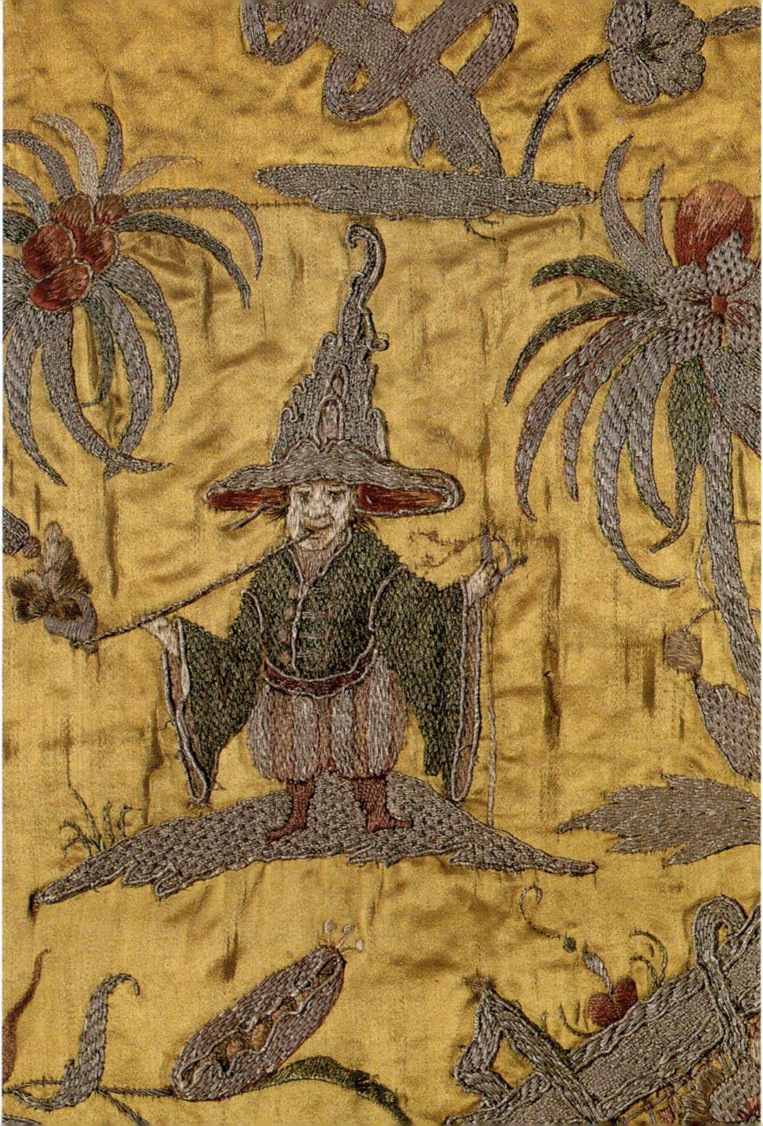

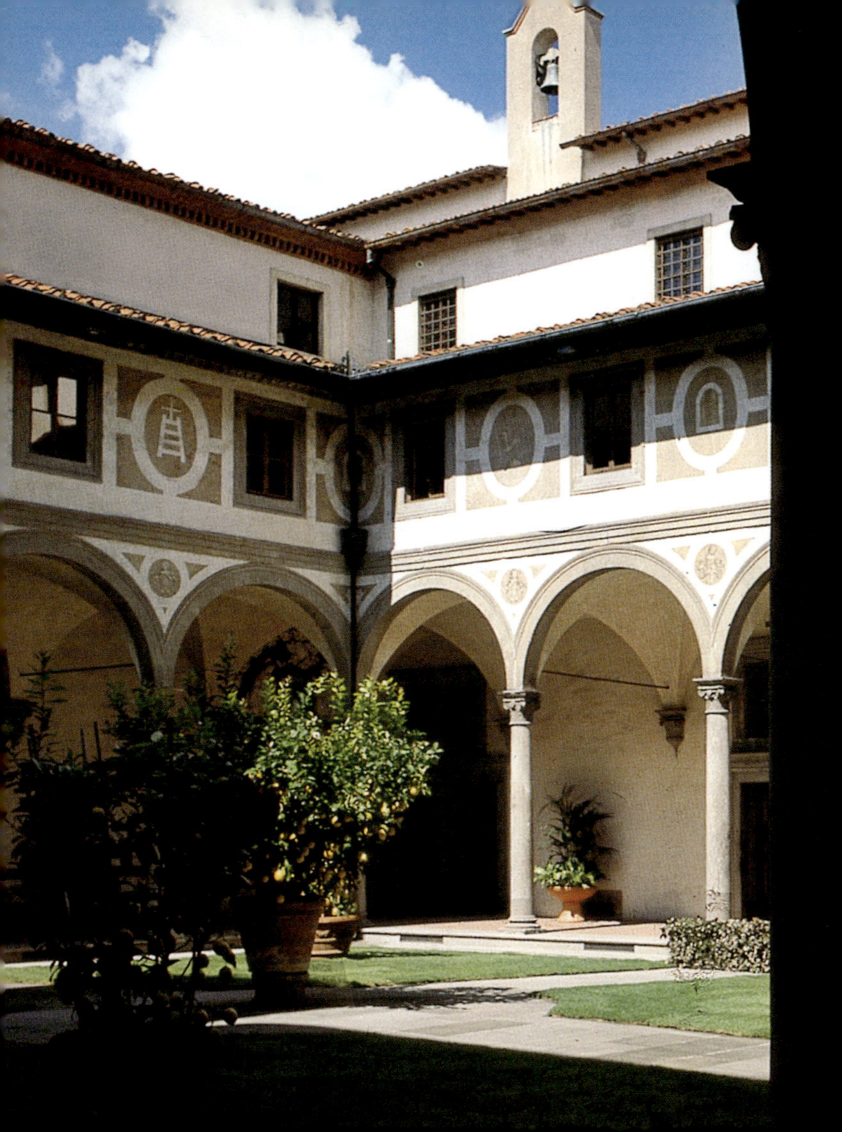

Galleria dello Spedale degli Innocenti

The pinacoteca, of notable importance although little known to the general public, is housed in the Spedale degli Innocenti, the building that, as has been seen, was designed by Filippo Brunelleschi, who supervised work on it until 1436, after which it was completed by Francesco della Luna and inaugurated in 1451. The works of art exhibited here are in part linked to the history of the Spedale, one of the city's most efficient charity organizations which, starting in the 15th century, was dedicated to taking in and raising abandoned children. Other paintings were instead brought to the museum from other religious institutions in the city following the suppression of the ecclesiastical authorities.

VISITORS' ITINERARY AND WORKS OF ART

Noteworthy among the works exhibited are:

- the *Coronation of the Virgin with Saints* (early 15th century), by the Master of the Strauss Madonna.
- the *Virgin and Child with an Angel* (c. 1466), a variation of the famous painting by Filippo Lippi in the Uffizi.

Opposite page:
The cloister of the Spedale degli Innocenti, finished around 1451 with some modifications in Brunelleschi's original project.

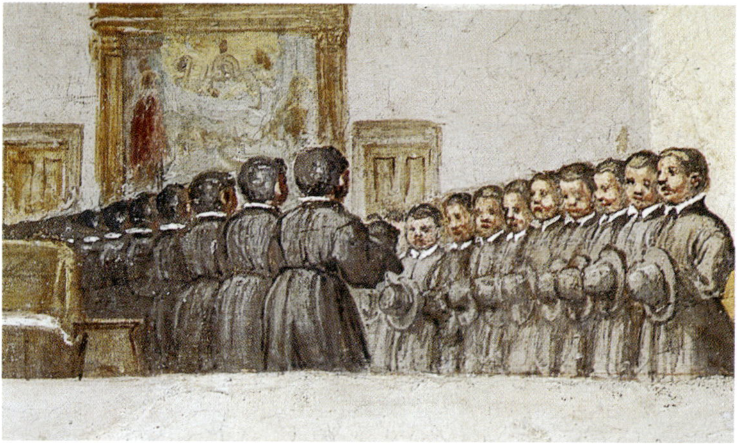

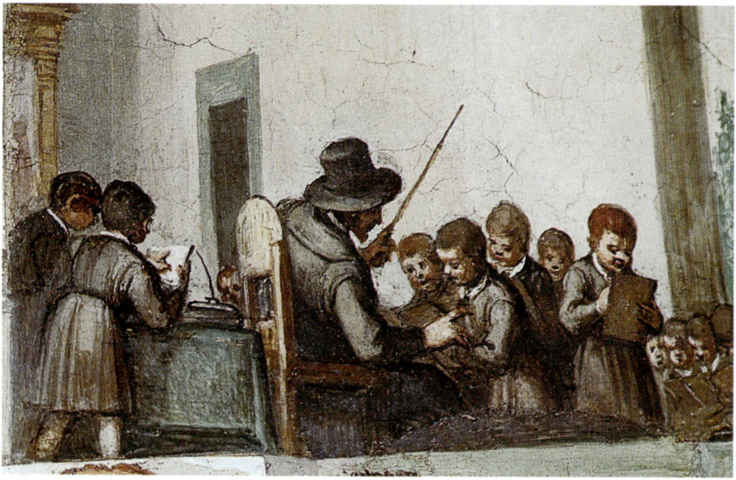

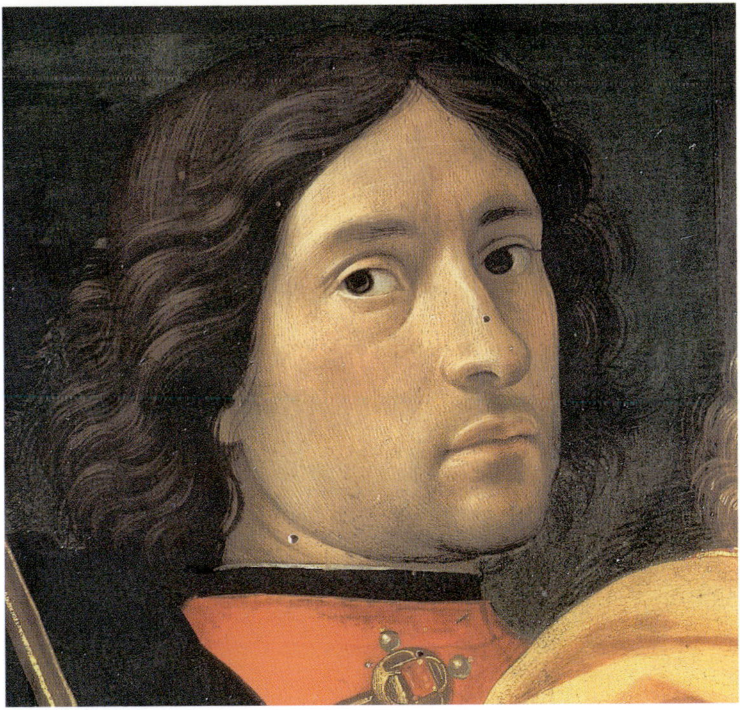

Opposite page:
Bernardino Poccetti, *Prayer in the dormitory of the Innocenti,* and *instruction of the "nocentini" (orphans)*, detail from *History of the Innocents*, 1610, fresco. Istituto degli Innocenti, former refectory.

Above:
Domenico Ghirlandaio, *Self-portrait,* detail from the *Adoration of the Magi,* illustrated on the following pages, 1488, tempera on wood. Galleria dello Spedale dell'Innocenti.

- the *Adoration of the Magi* (1488) by Domenico Ghirlandaio and Bartolomeo di Giovanni, coming from the high altar of the church of the Spedale: a work of great interest, also for the portraits of contemporaries, among them that of Ghirlandaio himself, who is gazing out at the spectator. Beside him appears the patron, Francesco di Giovanni Tesori, who donated the painting to the church of the Spedale, where it was placed above the high altar. In the procession of the Magi appear two merchants from the Silk Merchants Guild, who had participated in financing the construction of the Spedale.
- the *Virgin and Child with Saints* (1493) by Piero di Cosimo, one of the most famous paintings of the eccentric Florentine artist, commissioned of him by Piero del Pugliese, a wealthy, highly cultured figure in Florentine political life during those years, for the altar of the family chapel in the church of the Spedale. This painting too is linked to themes dear to the Spedale charity institution, since it portrays two saints considered to be "brides of Christ": Saint Catherine, guardian of young unmarried girls, and Saint Dorothy, protector of women in childbirth. The altarpiece was originally surmounted by a glazed terracotta lunette with the *Annunciation* by Andrea della Robbia, now in the courtyard.

Opposite page:
Domenico Ghirlandaio, *Adoration of the Magi*, 1488, tempera on wood. Museo dello Spedale degli Innocenti.

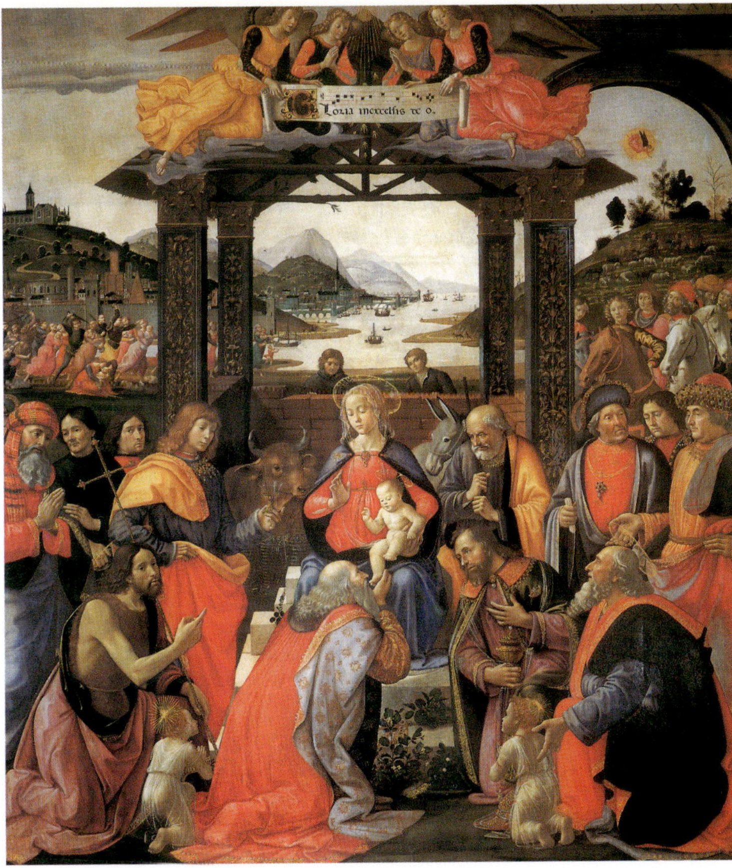

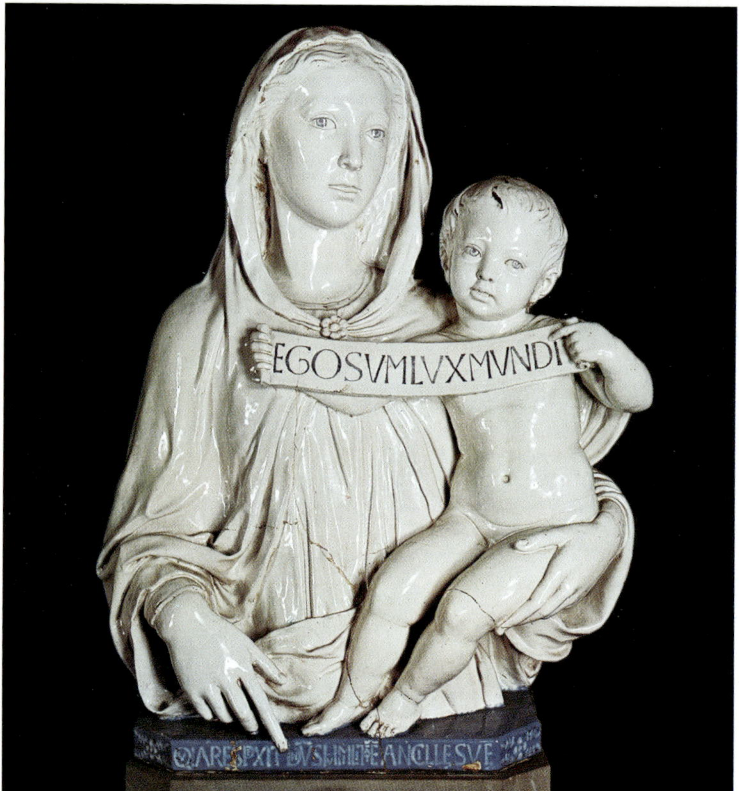

Above:
Luca della Robbia,
Madonna and Child,
c. 1450, glazed terracotta.
Museo dello Spedale degli Innocenti.

Opposite page:
Piero di Cosimo,
Madonna and Child with Saints,
1493, tempera on wood.
Museo dello Spedale degli Innocenti.

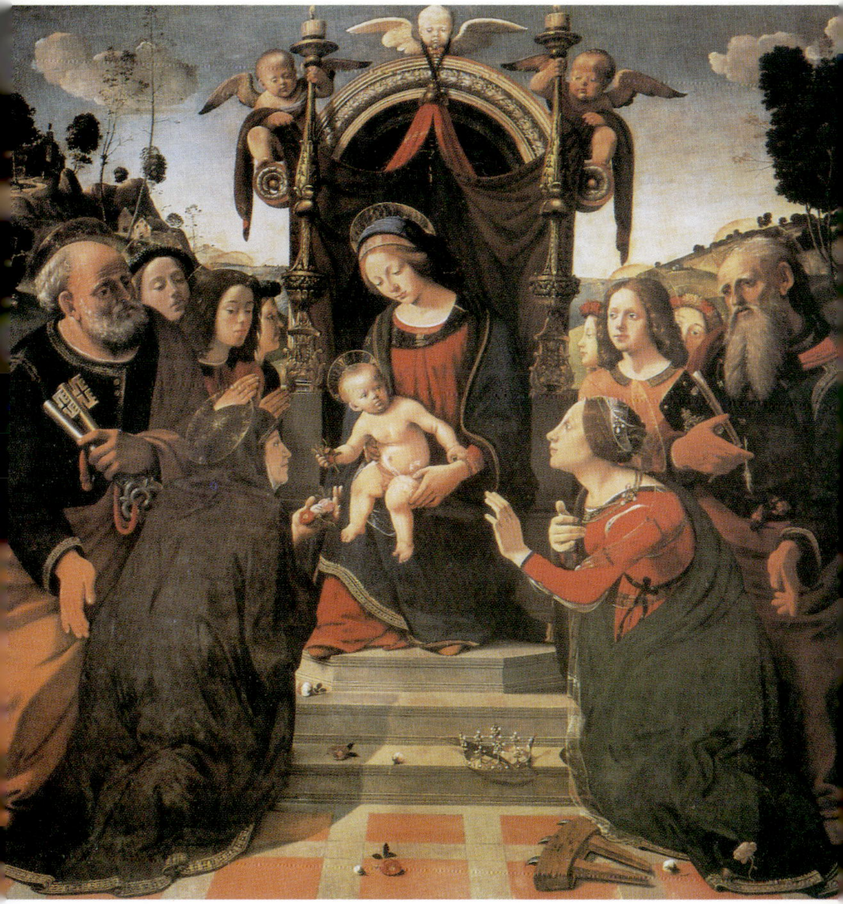

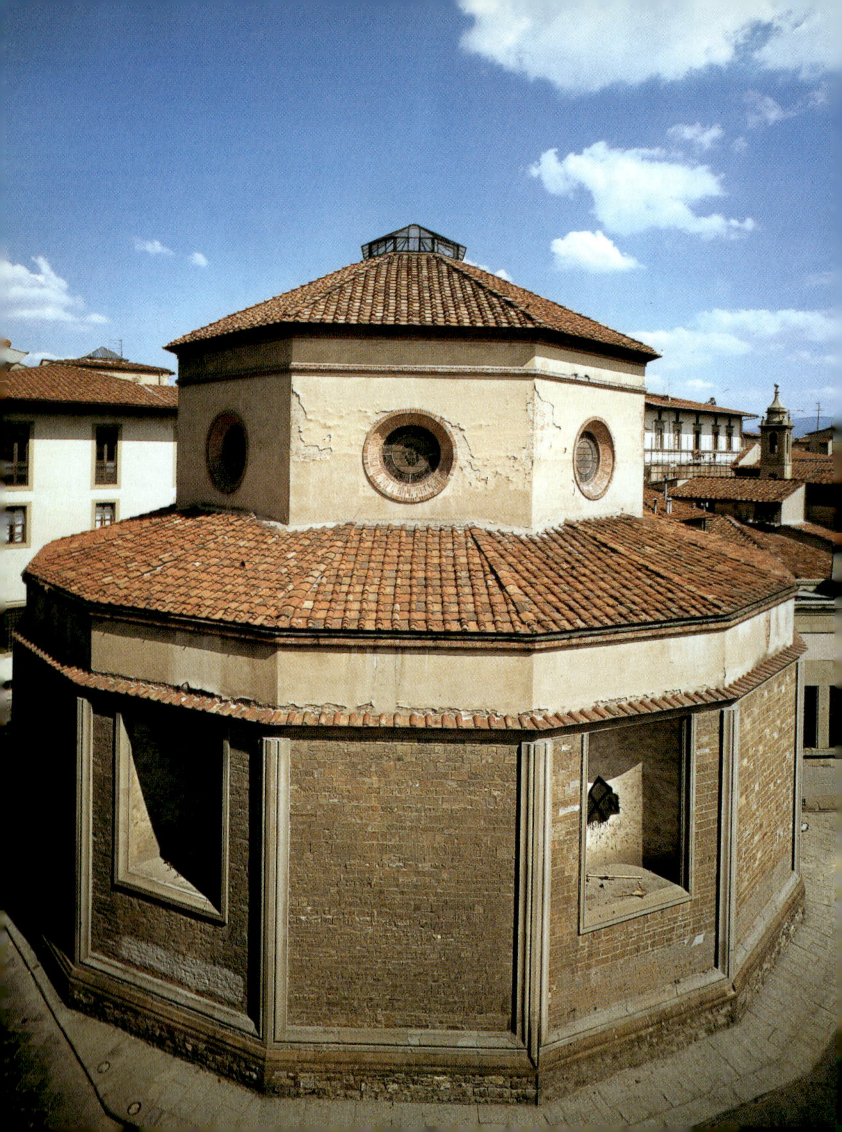

Rotonda di Santa Maria degli Angeli

In the immediate vicinity of Piazza dell'Annunziata, on the corner between today's Piazza Brunelleschi and Via degli Alfani, stands the Rotonda degli Angeli, the only example of circular plan architecture by Filippo Brunelleschi, left unfinished in 1437 due to lack of funds. Today a part of the university, the Rotonda was originally conceived as an oratory dedicated to the Virgin and the Apostles. The structure was annexed to the Camaldolensian Monastery of Santa Maria degli Angioli, the center of fervent meetings among humanists, and site, in the early 15th century, of an important school of miniaturists represented primarily by Lorenzo Monaco.

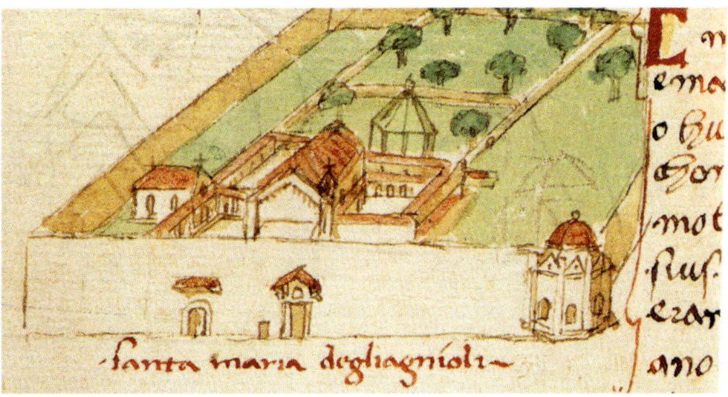

Opposite page:
Filippo Brunelleschi, *Rotonda di Santa Maria degli Angeli*, c. 1434-1437.

Above: The Monastery of Santa Maria degli Angeli with the Rotonda, from the Codice di Marco di Bartolomeo Rustici, c. 1447. Florence, Biblioteca del Seminario Maggiore.

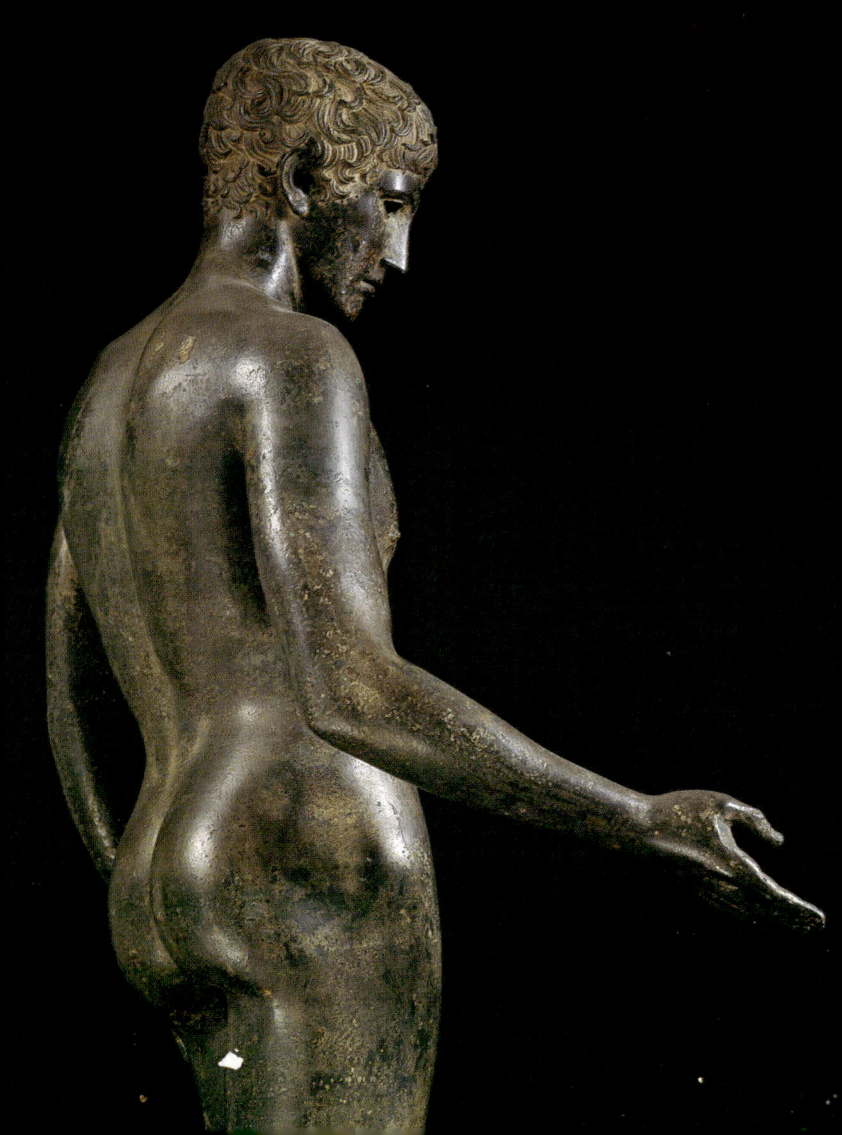

Museo Archeologico Nazionale

The Archaeological Museum, one of the most important in Italy, is situated in Palazzo della Crocetta, the building that faces on Piazza della Santissima Annunziata and was built in 1620 by Giulio Parigi for Maria Maddalena d'Austria, a sister of Grand Duke Cosimo II. It was inaugurated in 1898 as the Museo Topografico dell'Etruria, after some archaeological pieces up to then kept in the Cenacolo di Fuligno were moved here in 1881.

The original core of the exhibitions consists of the Medicean archaeological collections. The Medici were in fact, great collectors of antiquities, and had been since the time of Piero de' Medici, a passionate lover of gemstones, who spent enormous sums to purchase them. Lorenzo the Magnificent too was a great collector, and we know that in his garden on Via Larga he had formed an incomparable collection of ancient findings. Another member of the family, Cosimo I, purchased works such as the *Chimera* and the *Orator*, today exhibited in the museum but in the past kept in the Uffizi along with the *Wild Boar* (the so-called *Porcellino*, which has remained in the Gallery). Over the course of time the museum has incremented the Egyptian, Etruscan, Greek and Roman sections, and can boast

Opposite page:
Idolino di Pesaro, detail, 1st century A.D., bronze. Museo Archeologico Nazionale.

today, among other things, of being the second-ranking Italian museum, after the one in Turin, for its wealth of Egyptian findings, the fruit of numerous 19th century archaeological campaigns. Of particular importance is the collection of Attic pottery, famous among which is the *François Vase,* named after the archaeologist who discovered it at Chiusi in 1844. The work of the potter Ergotimos and the vase-painter Kleitias, who lived at the time of Pisistratus, the vase had arrived in Italy as a gift to an Etruscan nobleman. A series of mythological personages are portrayed on it in bands.

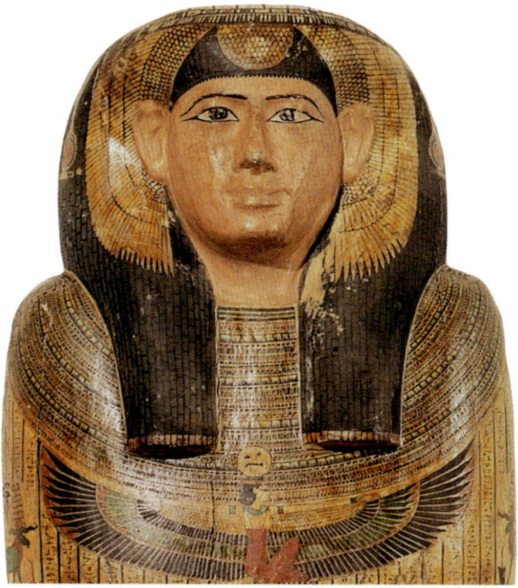

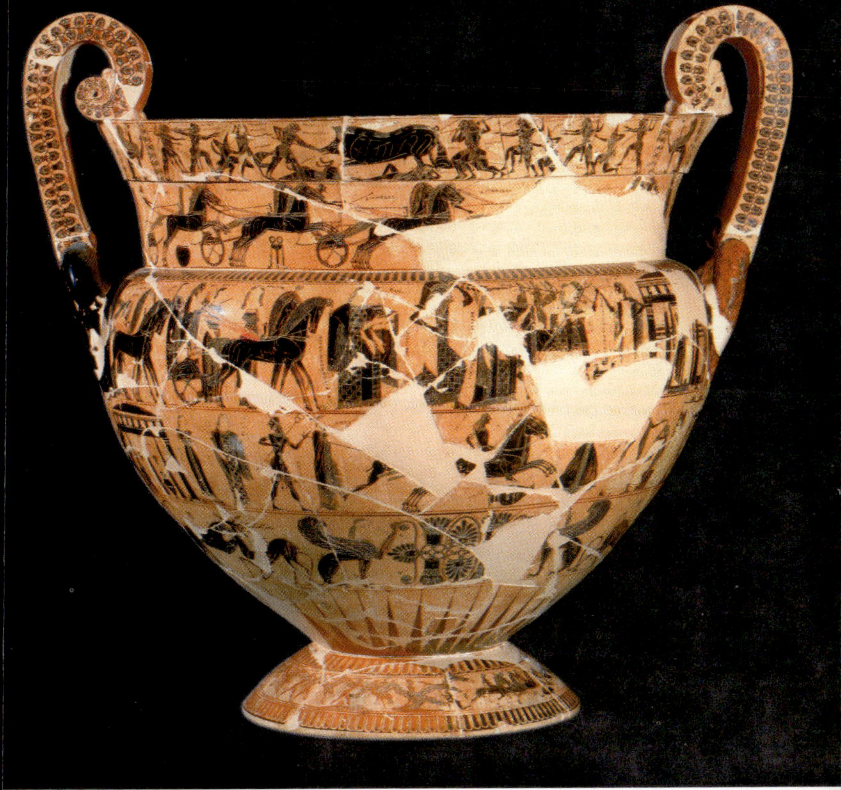

Opposite page: Egyptian art, *Sarcophagus of Cesraperet,* upper part, late epoch, xxv dynasty, stuccoed and painted wood. Museo Archeologico Nazionale.

Above:
Kleitias and Ergotimos, *François Vase*, black-figured Attic crater, 570 B.C., ceramics. Museo Archeologico Nazionale.

VISITORS' ITINERARY AND WORKS OF ART:

Among the works exhibited are:

- Etruscan tombs and a funerary monument reconstructed in the garden looking on Via della Colonna.
- The *François Vase* (570 B.C.).
- The *Apollo* and the *Apollino "Milani"*, the only two statues of Greek archaic *Kouroi* to be found in Italian public collections.
- among the Etruscan works, the *Fat Man's Sarcophagus* and that of *Larthia Seianti*, the *Mater Matuta*, and the *Chimera*, the famous bronze purchased in 1553 at Arezzo by Duke Cosimo I de'Medici. The purchase was not made at random, considering that in those years the question of the presumed origins of Florence, said to date back to a little Etruscan village, had again become a topical issue, for reasons of political and cultural prestige. With the praise of the Etruscans, heightened by the *Gello*, compiled in 1546 by the erudite Giovanbattista Giambullari, the Canon of San Lorenzo, the declared descendency of the Tuscans from this people assumed a new value: it served to establish a direct line of descent from the ancient Kings of Etruria to Duke Cosimo, a modern *Magnus Dux Aetruriae*, thus legitimizing his absolute power over the Tuscan cities.

Opposite page: Etruscan art, *Cinerary urn of the Purni, with scenes of battle between Barbarians and Greeks,* second half of the III century B.C., alabastrine marble. Museo Archeologico Nazionale.

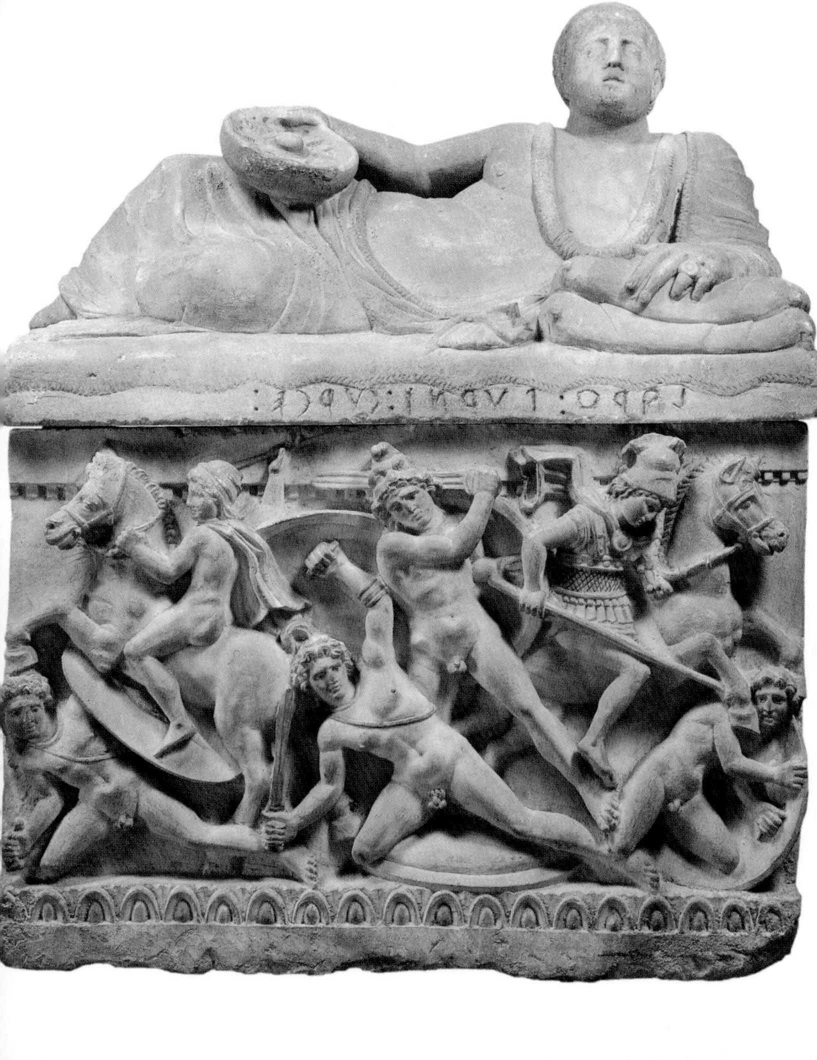

- the *Orator*, purchased in 1566 by Duke Cosimo as soon as it was found, in the vicinity of Lake Trasimeno, it seems. The only Etruscan bronze statue from the Late Hellenistic period, now identified as a portrait of the Etruscan nobleman Aulus Metellus, was recognized in the grand-ducal period as a sort of "Scipione Minor" rather than an Etruscan aristocrat, as was actually the case. A few years after the "political use" of the *Chimera*, the times had changed and interest in classical antiquity had forcefully emerged again.
- The *Idolino*, a refined bronze from the Augustan age orginally used as lamp-holder. Found in 1530 at Pesaro, it entered the Medicean collections as a gift from Francesco II della Rovere to his grand-daughter Vittoria on the occasion of her wedding to Grand Duke Ferdinando II dei Medici.

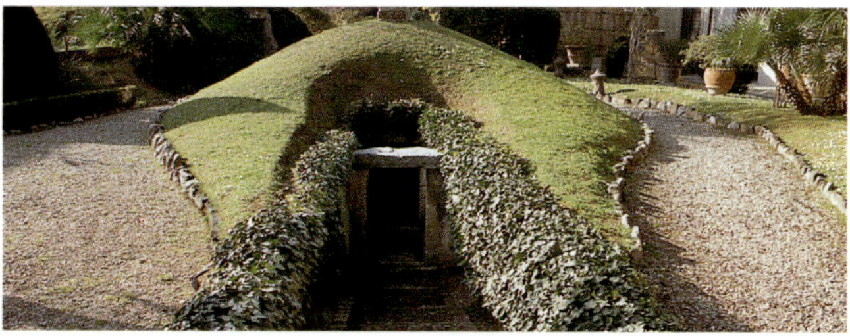

Above:
Tholos from Casale Marittimo, Garden of the Museo Archeologico Nazionale.

Opposite page:
Etruscan art, *The Orator,* beginning of I century B.C or first half of II century B.C.

Following pages:
Chimera, late V-early IV century (modern restoration), bronze. Museo Archeologico Nazionale.

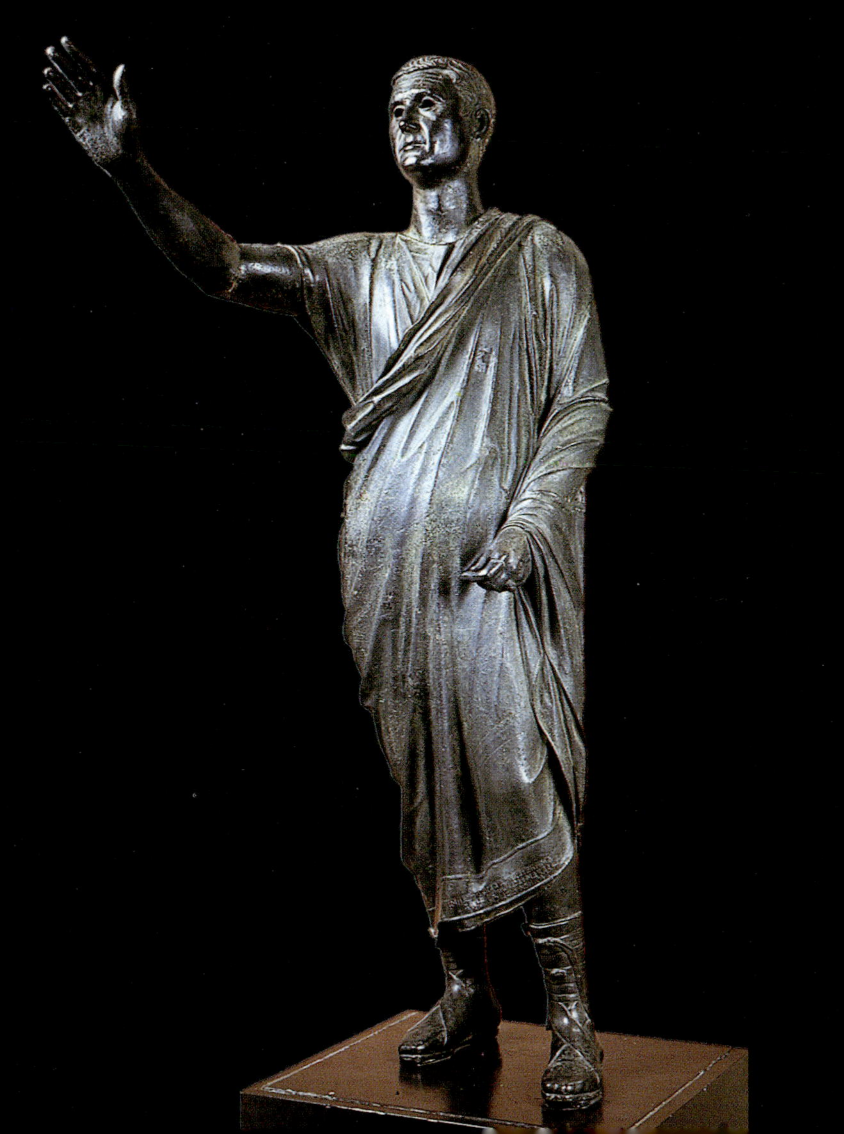

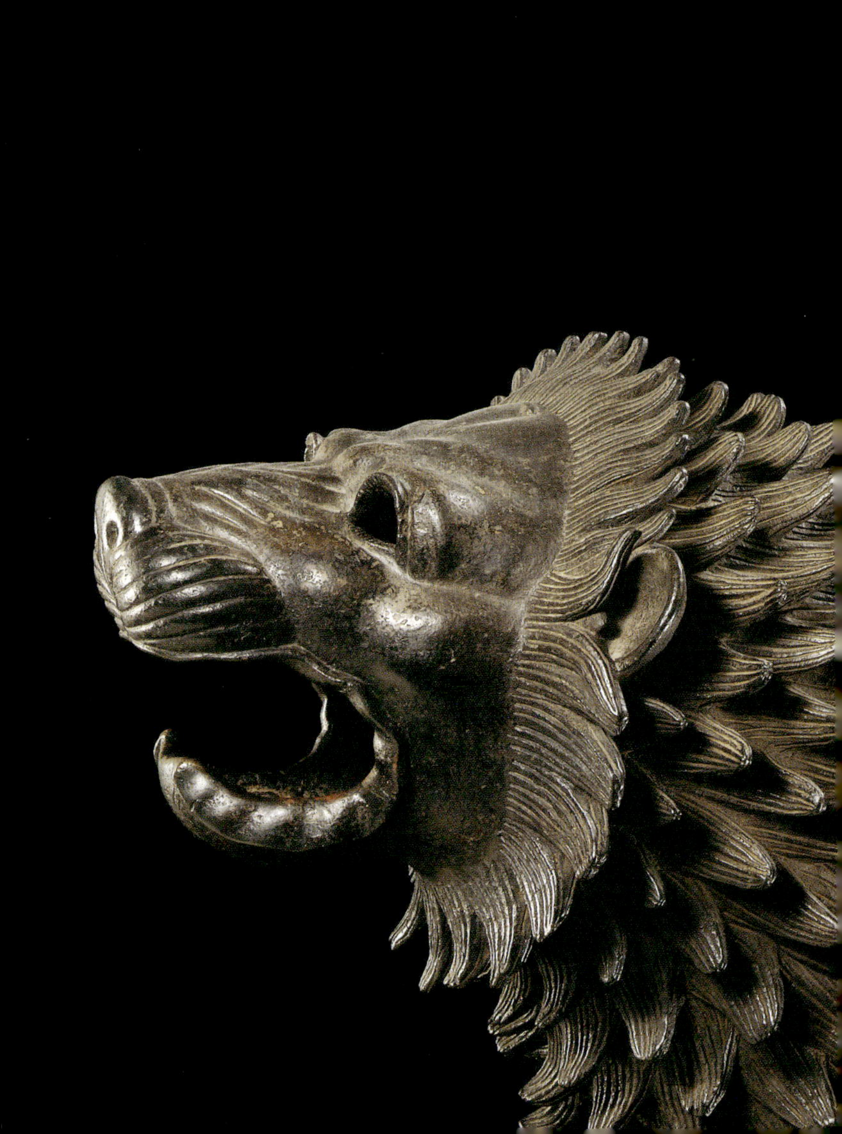

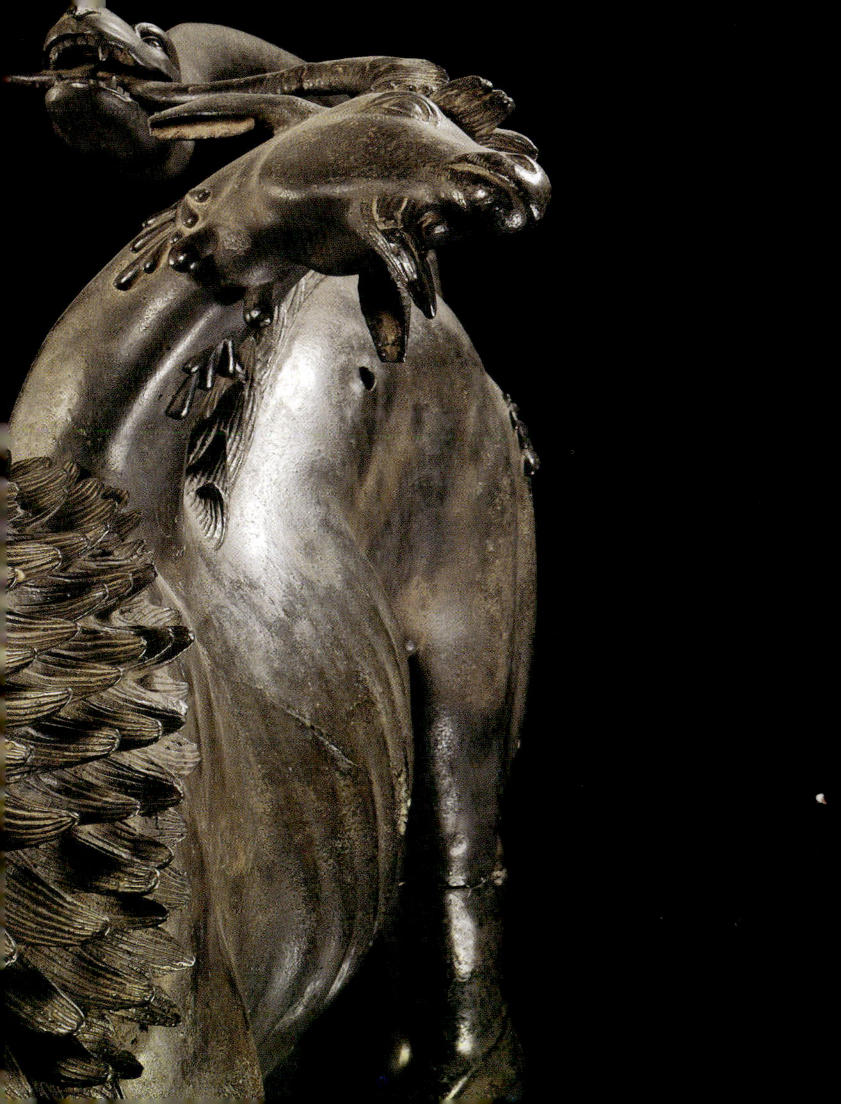

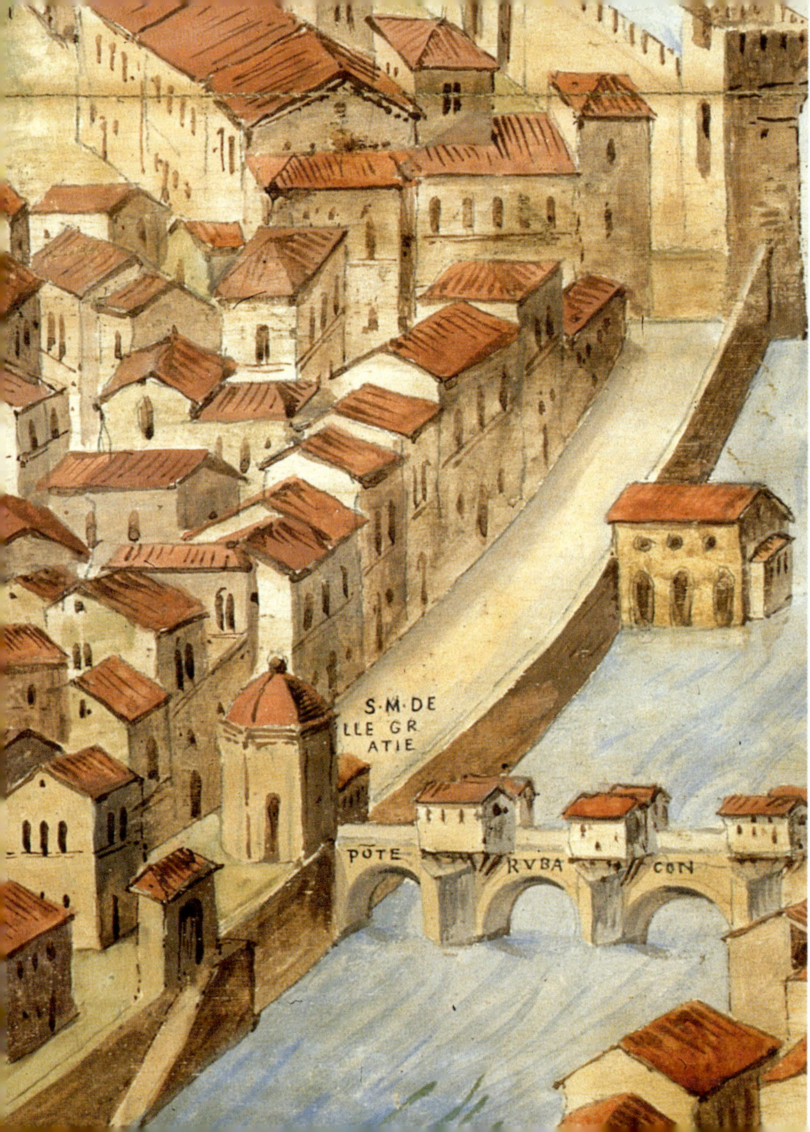
S·M·DE
LLE GR
ATIE
POTE
RVBA
CON

MUSEO DI FIRENZE COM'ERA

Founded in 1908 by the art historian Corrado Ricci and first situated in Casa Buonarroti in Via Ghibellina, the historical-topographical museum of Florence was transferred in 1955, after having been moved several times, to the former Convent of the Oblate in Via Sant'Egidio, where it remains today, and has been rearranged on the ground floor, in the vicinity of the Library. The museum offers abundant documentation consisting of paintings and engravings that depict, from medieval times to the 19th century, more or less well-known aspects of the city of Florence, some of which have by now disappeared or been totally transformed.

Among the works exhibited are:

- a watercolor reproduction of the oldest known semi-perspective view of Florence (called *Pianta della Catena* or map of the chain) for the drawing around its border), whose 15th century original is now in Berlin.
- the 16th century lunettes by the Flemish artist Giusto Utens, with birds-eye views of the Medicean villas.
- the 18th century vedutas of Florence by Giuseppe Zocchi.
- tempera paintings by Giuseppe Maria Terreni representing festivities at the Cascine Park and etchings by Signorini.

Opposite page:
Francesco and Antonello Petrini, *View of Florence from Monte Oliveto*, detail, 1887, color copy of woodcut attribuited to Francesco di Jacopo Rosselli, *Fiorenza. View known as "Pianta della Catena"* (1471-1482, at the Kupferstichkabinett of Berlin). Museo di Firenze com'era.

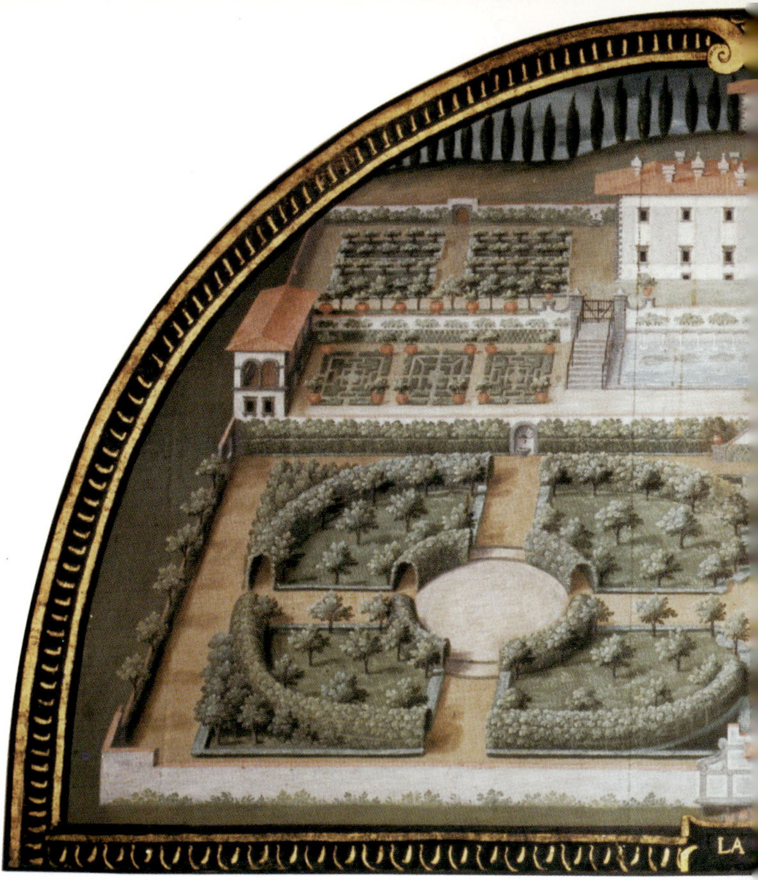
LA

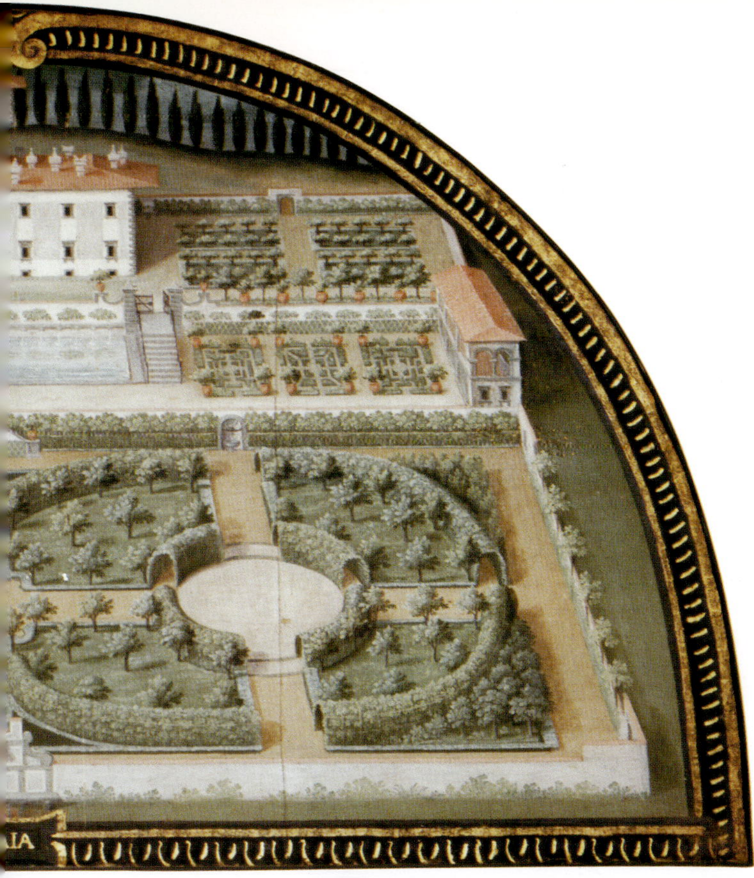

Giusto Utens, *La "Pretaia"*, lunette in tempera depicting the Medicean villa of Petraia outside of Florence, 1559. Museo di Firenze com'era.

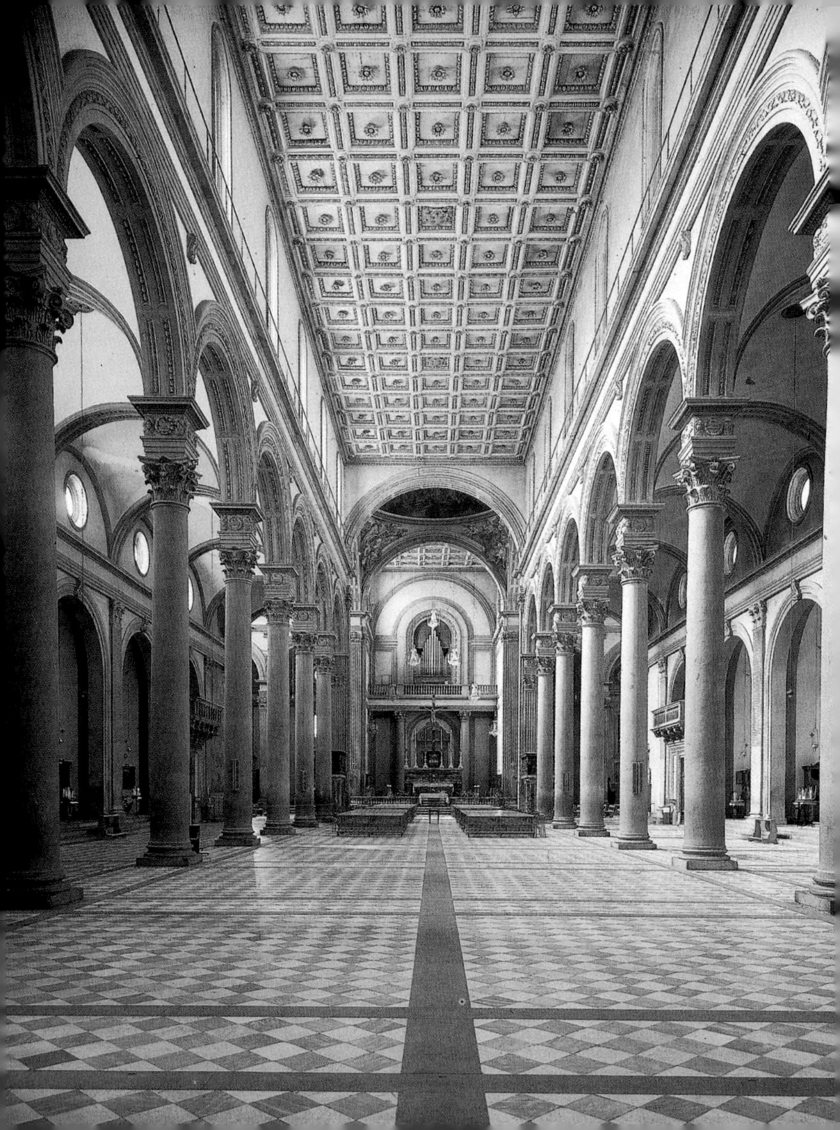

San Lorenzo

The Piazza, the Basilica, the Library, the Medici Chapels

The Basilica of San Lorenzo, set in a lively square filled with the stalls of a market frequented by tourists but also beloved by Florentines, was, starting from the late 15th century, the Medici's favourite church. The ecclesiastical building in Renaissance style, to which is annexed a prestigious library, the Biblioteca Medicea Laurenziana, stands on the site occupied by one of the oldest churches in Florence, consecrated in 393 by Saint Ambrose and remodelled several times over the centuries before the final project of Filippo Brunelleschi, who began working on it in 1421, suspended work for several years and resumed it in 1442.

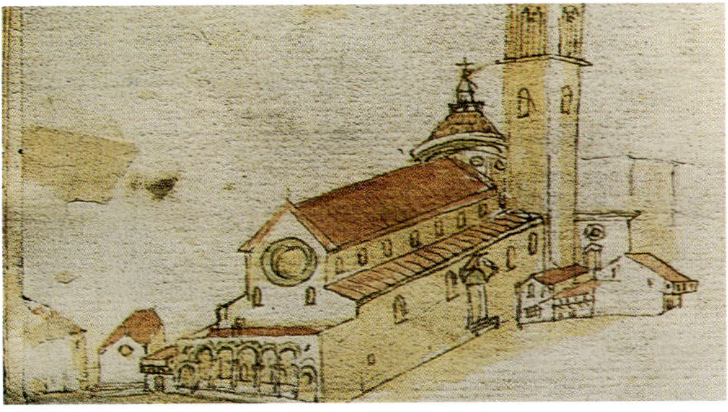

Opposite page:
Interior of the Basilica of San Lorenzo looking toward the transept.

Above: The old Romanesque façade of San Lorenzo, from the *Codice* by Marco di Bartolomeo Rustici, c. 1447. Biblioteca del Seminario Maggiore.

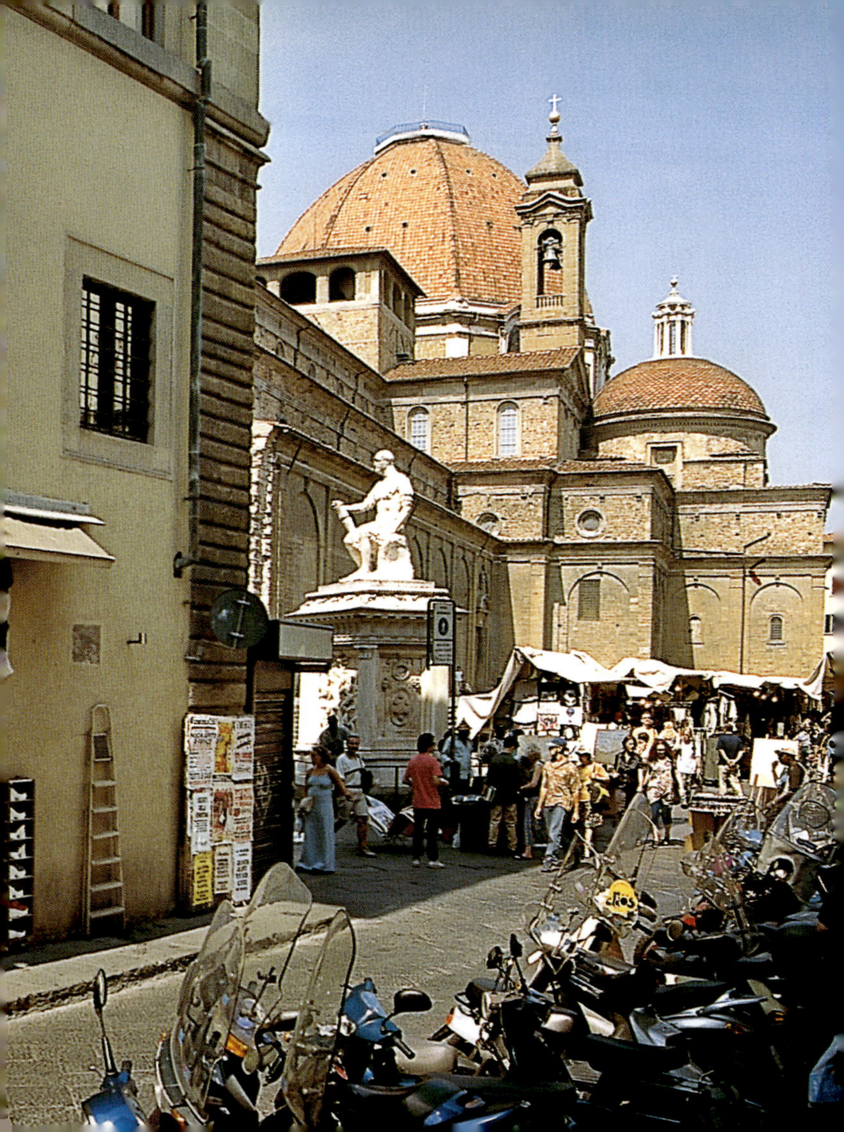

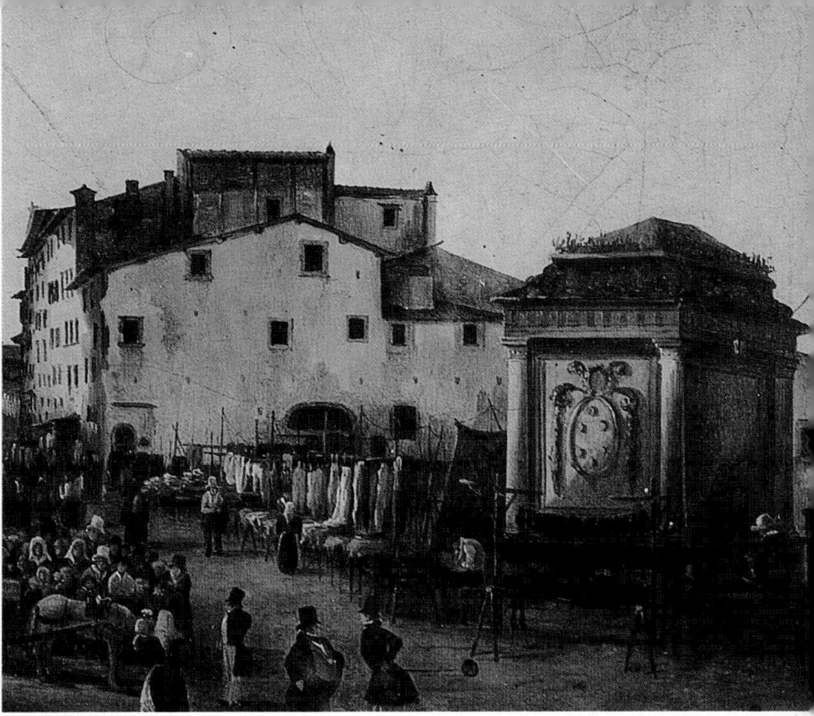

Opposite page:
The lively market around the north side of San Lorenzo. Here stands the monument to Giovanni dalle Bande Nere, the father of Cosimo I (1540-1554), one of the most intense and least "known" works of Baccio Bandinelli, originally conceived for the condottiero's tomb in the Neroni Chapel in San Lorenzo. The marble statue was moved into the square only in 1850, and was placed on a beautiful classic-style base, taken from the chapel and put here in 1620.

Above:
Piazza San Lorenzo in a canvas by Giovanni Signorini (1820). On the marble base with the Medici coat of arms, almost in ruins at the time, the statue of Giovanni dalle Bande Nere had not yet been placed.

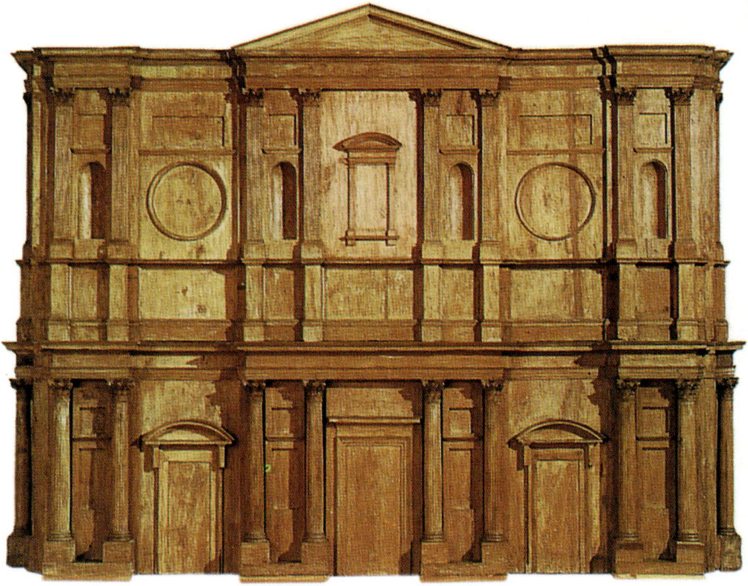

Above:
Michelangelo Buonarroti, *Wooden model of the project (never realized) for the façade of the Basilica of San Lorenzo*, c. 1519.
Museo della Casa Buonarroti.
In Michelangelo's project, the façade was to be decorated with twelve giant marble statues, six bronze statues and seven great relief carvings.

Opposite page :
The cloister of the Basilica of San Lorenzo.

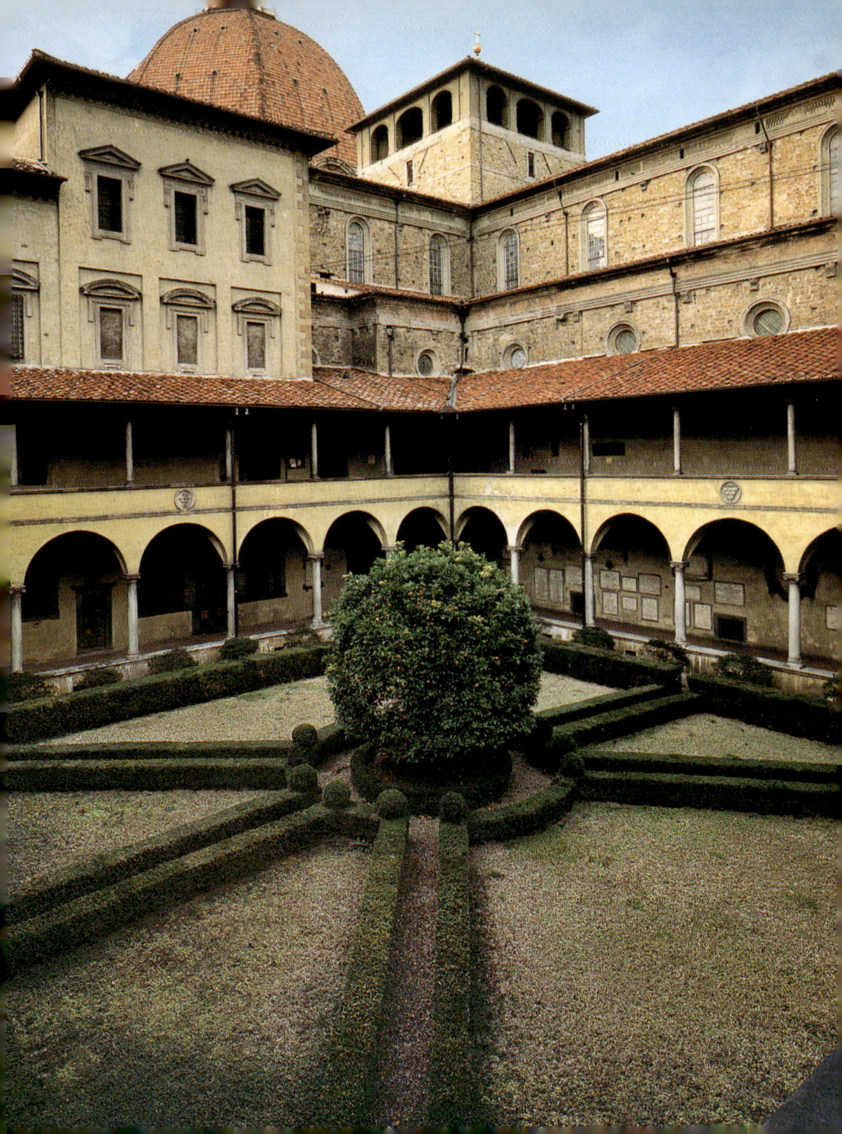

HISTORY

Commissioned by Giovanni di Bicci de' Medici, father of Cosimo the Elder, Brunelleschi had begun the Old Sacristy in 1422, to then proceed with a chapel in the transept and later with the whole church building. Work continued after the death of the architect (1446) up to 1461; the facade has remained unfinished, in spite of monumental projects for it such as that of Michelangelo. Around 1520, work began on the Biblioteca Medicea Laurenziana, located to the left of the main body of the building, and on the New Sacristy which, along with the 17th century Chapel of the Princes, entered from Piazza Madonna degli Aldobrandini at the back of the church, now make up the museum complex of the Medici Chapels. The interior of the church is built in the shape of a Latin cross, with chapels along the sides and a dome over the transept. Although in general appearance the church may seem reminiscent of Gothic ones such as Santa Croce and Santa Maria Novella, the space of the building is in reality innovatively organized according to the multiples of a module corresponding to the height of one of its square bays. Although the church was designed with perspectives based on principles of maximum rationality and classicism, its original project by Brunelleschi has been modified. It is enriched by numerous works of art, most of them found in the family chapels

Opposite page:
View of the right nave of San Lorenzo, showing some of the chapels. Brunelleschi had planned the arches of the naves and of the side chapels to have a common vanishing point, establishing ratios of proportional height that accentuate the sense of depth and plasticity of the whole.

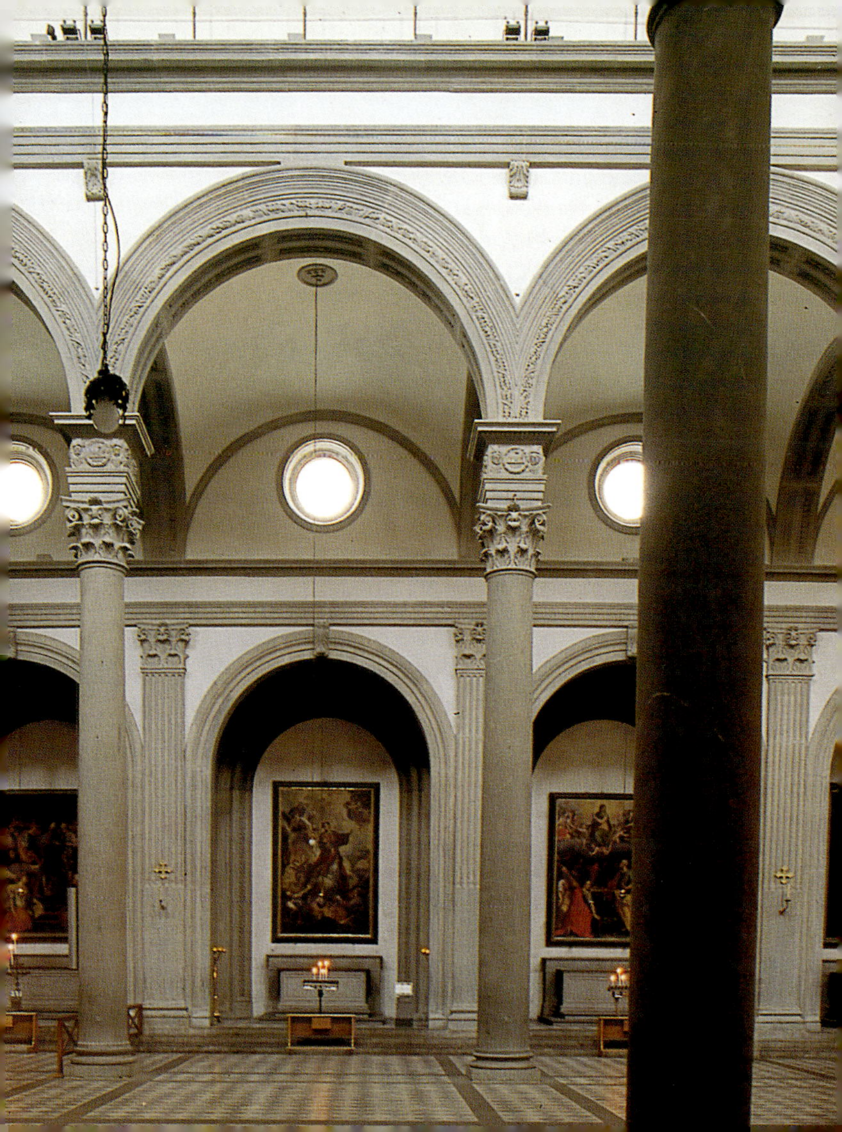

of the nobility. At the opposite ends of the transept are the Old Sacristy designed by Brunelleschi (on the left) and the new one by Michelangelo (on the right). The Old Sacristy is a supremely harmonious cubical room, covered by an umbrella-shaped cupola decorated with stucco tondoes. The dome of the "scarsella" is adorned with a representation of heavenly bodies, perhaps painted by Pesello, highly esteemed at the time, influenced by the astronomer Paolo dal Pozzo Toscanelli, a friend of Cosimo the Elder. It should also be recalled that, for the choir of San Lorenzo, Pontormo painted a grandiose cycle of frescoes (*Genesis* and the *Last Judgement*), inspired by Michelangelo's Sistine Chapel, later destroyed in a fire, of which the preparatory drawings remain. Bronzino completed the cycle in 1569 with the *Martyrdom of St. Lawrence*, still to be seen.

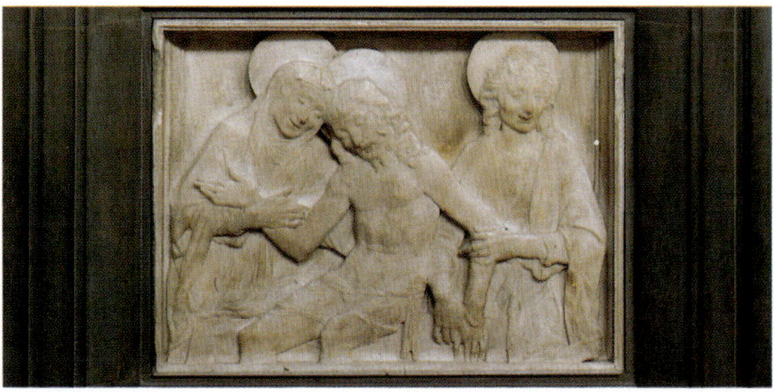

Above and opposite page:
Desiderio da Settignano, *Tabernacle of the Corpus Domini,* detail (above) of the lower part with the *Pietà,* and of the lunette and the door flanked by angels holding candelabra (this page), 1453-1455, marble.
San Lorenzo, nave (formerly in the Chapel of the Sacrament).

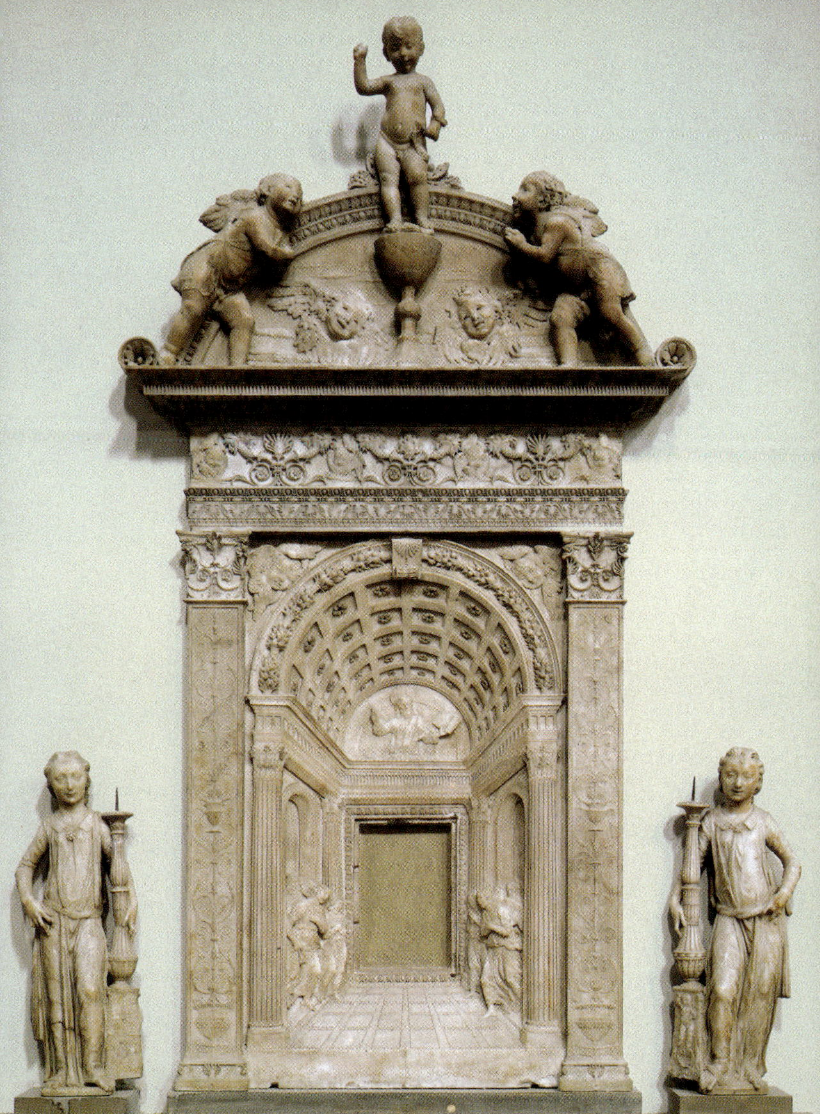

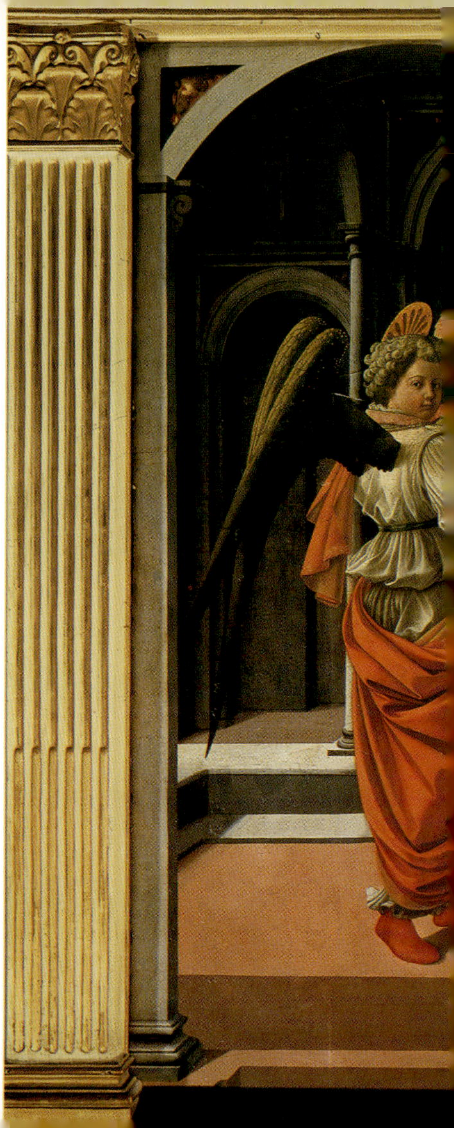

Filippo Lippi, *Annunciation,* commissioned by Niccolò Martelli between 1437 and 1441, tempera on wood. Basilica of San Lorenzo.

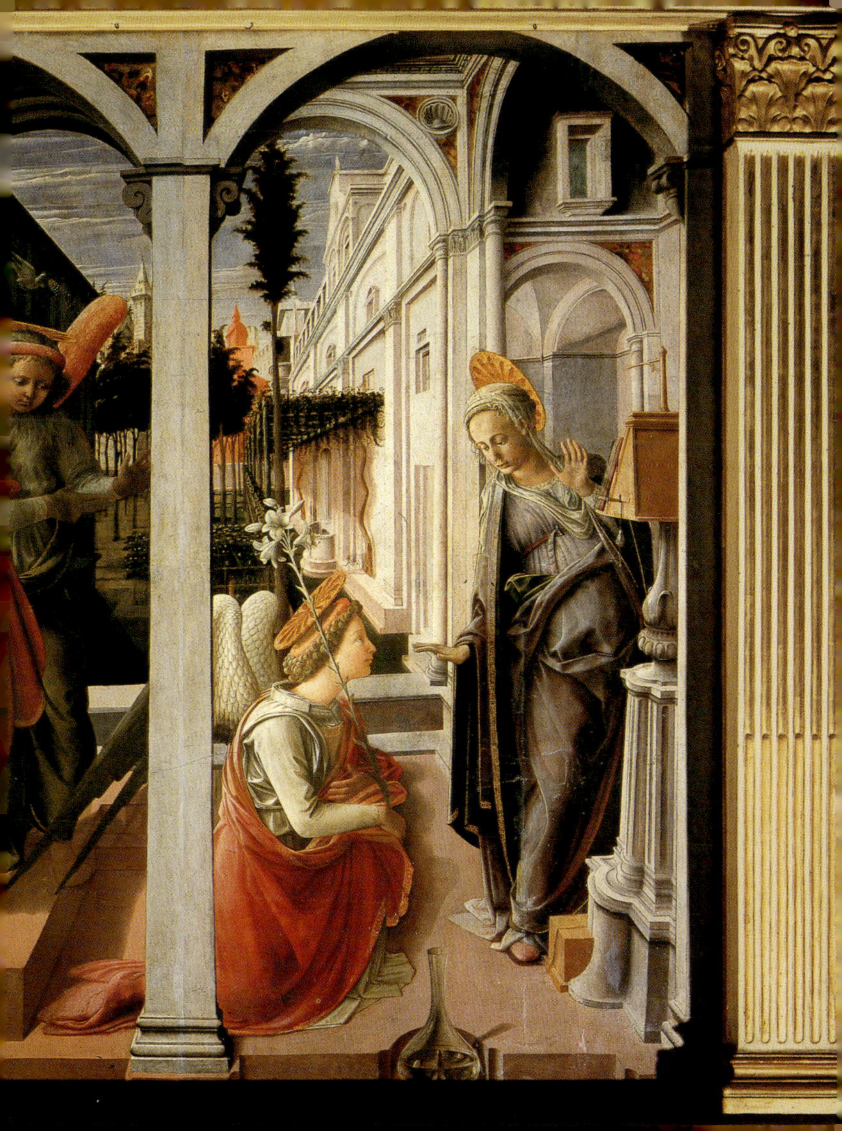

Noteworthy are:

- the *Annunciation and two Angels* (*Martelli Altarpiece*, 1437-1441), by Filippo Lippi, with a view of the city in the background, and in the foreground an ethereal cruet of transparent glass.
- the marble tabernacle (1453-1455) by Desiderio da Settignano, inspired by the most refined classicism.
- the two bronze pulpits (c. 1465) accomplished by Donatello, now in his old age, assisted by Bellano and Bertoldo.
- the *Marriage of the Virgin* (1523), one of the most famous altarpieces by Rosso Fiorentino, a composition of exceptional scenography.
- the fresco depicting the *Martyrdom of St. Lawrence* (1565-1569) by Bronzino, which bears witness to the artist's anatomical studies from nature as well as to the influence of Michelangelo's *ignudi* in the Sistine Chapel.
- the altar made of semiprecioius stones in the Cappella Maggiore (1787).
- in the Old Sacristy, the *Tombs of Piero and Giovanni de' Medici* (1472) by Verrocchio, with the legs and the bronze gate distinguished by splendid naturalist details.

Opposite page:
Andrea del Verrocchio, *Tomb of Piero and Giovanni de' Medici*, 1472, marble, porphyry and bronze. San Lorenzo, Old Sacristy.

Following pages:
Pesello, *Signs of the zodiac and map of the heavens*, 1442, fresco. Old Sacristy, cupola.

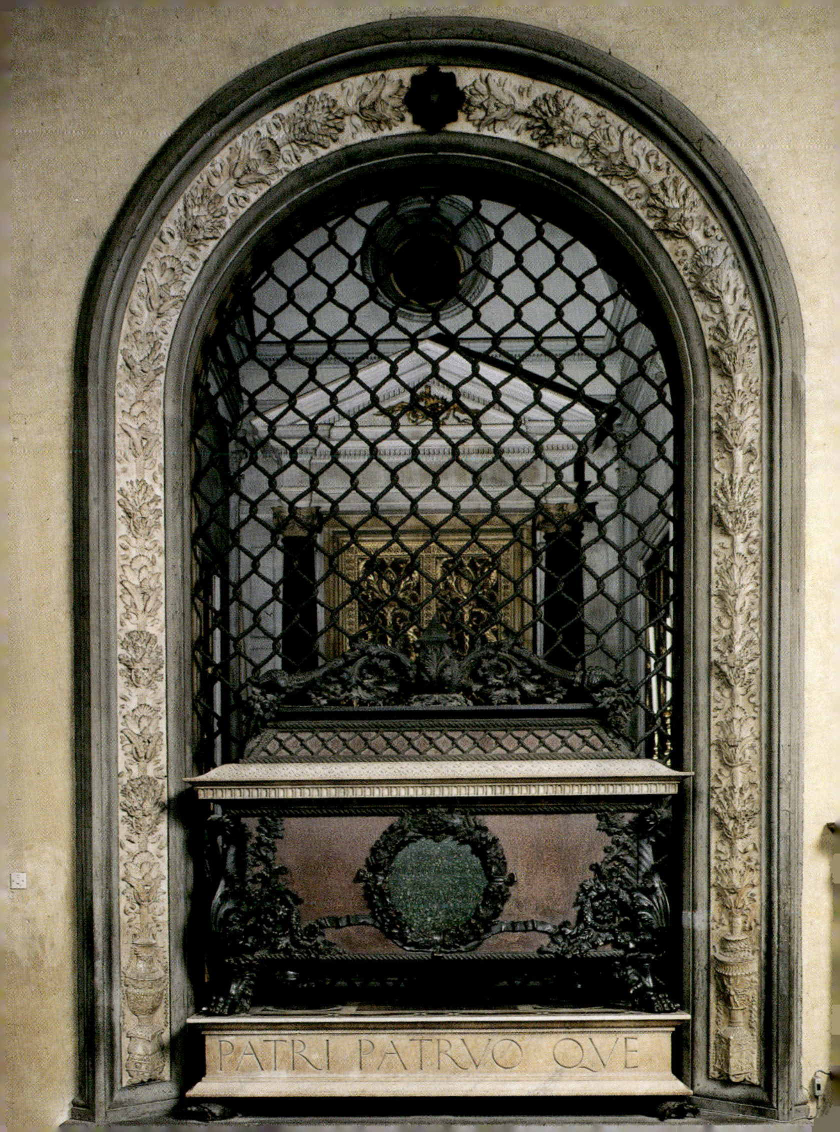
PATRI PATRVO QVE

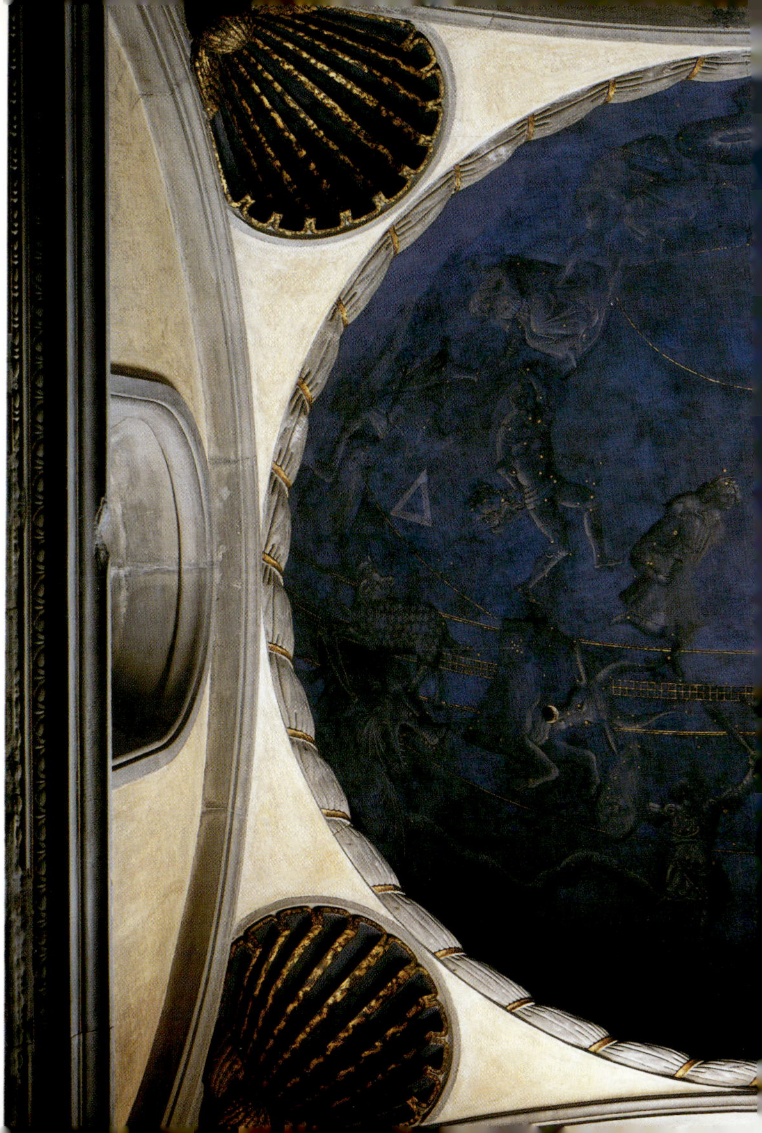

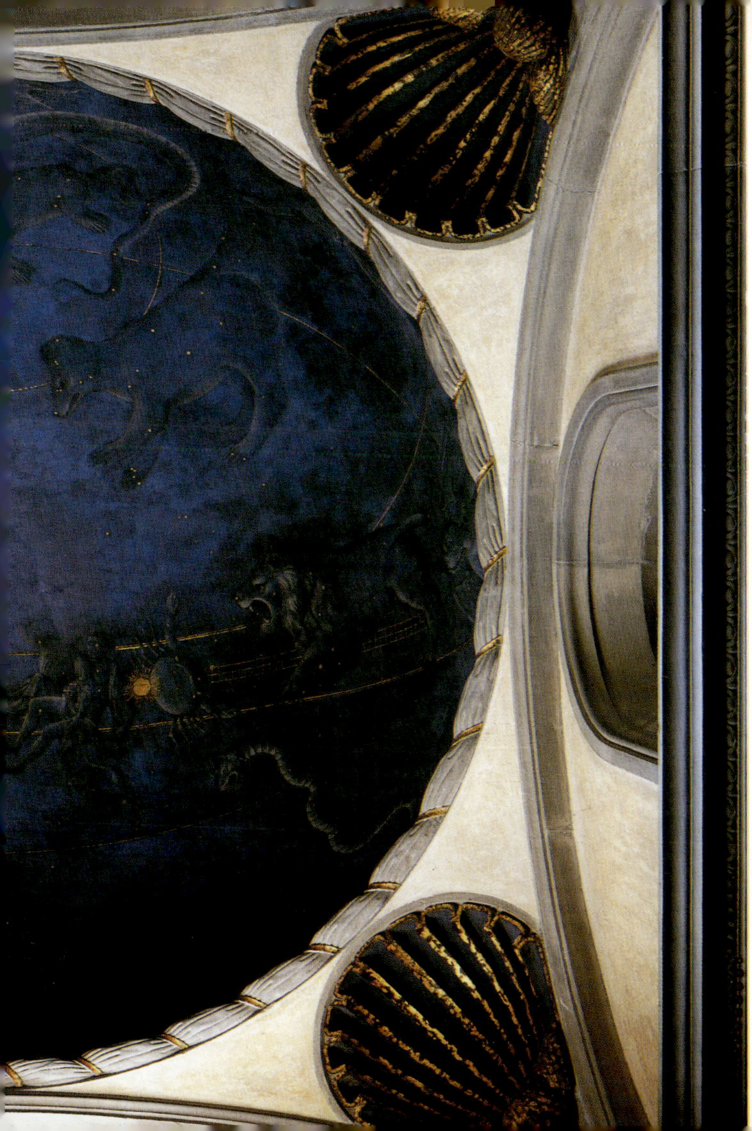

Below:
Donatello, *St. Lawrence reviving Drusiana*, c. 1428-1429, polychrome stucco.
San Lorenzo, Old Sacristy.

Opposite page:
View of the Old Sacristy of San Lorenzo. Designed by Filippo Brunelleschi between 1422 and 1428, it was decorated in stucco by Donatello with *Stories of St. John* in tondoes (1428-1432), and with the *Patron Saints of the Medici, Cosmus and Damian, Lawrence and Stephen*, in the two great curved spaces above the bronze doors, they too in stucco against a polychrome background accomplished through the technique "del buon fresco". These latter decorations, begun by Donatello around 1442-1443 and left unfinished when he departed for Padua, were completed in all probability by another artist (perhaps Michelozzo or Luca della Robbia).

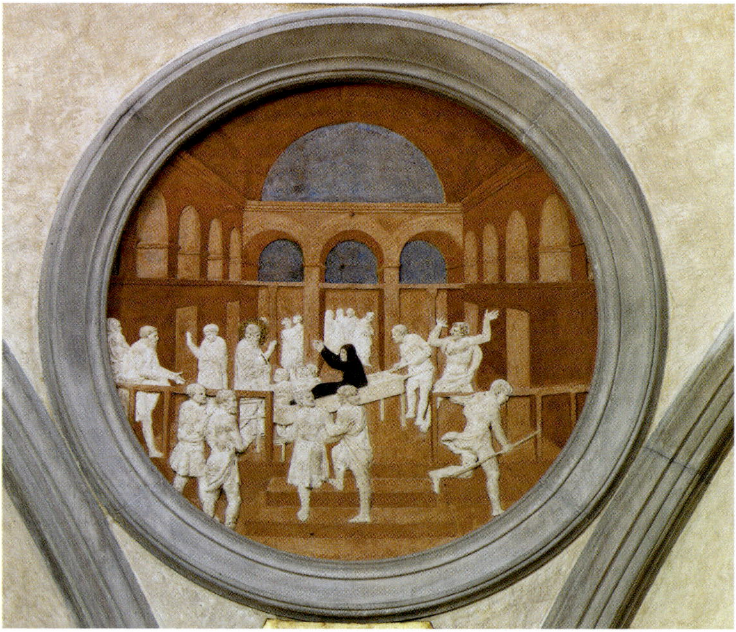

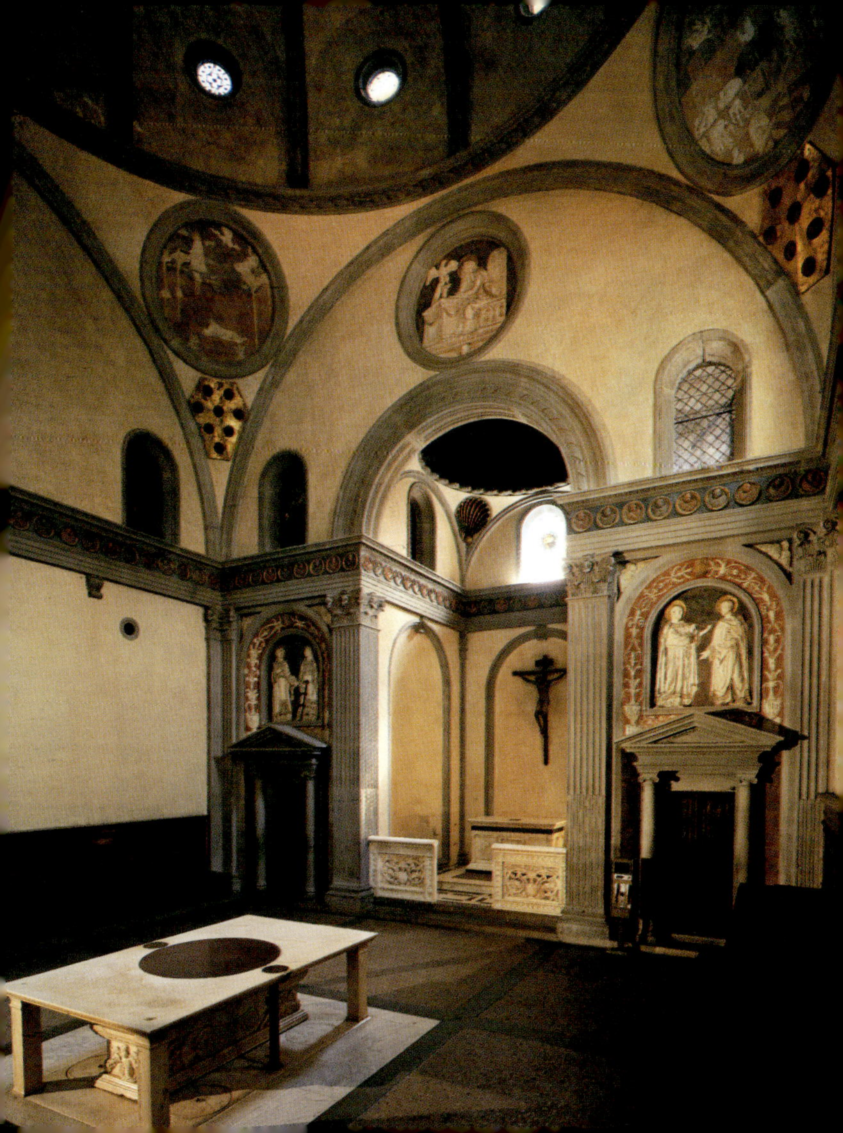

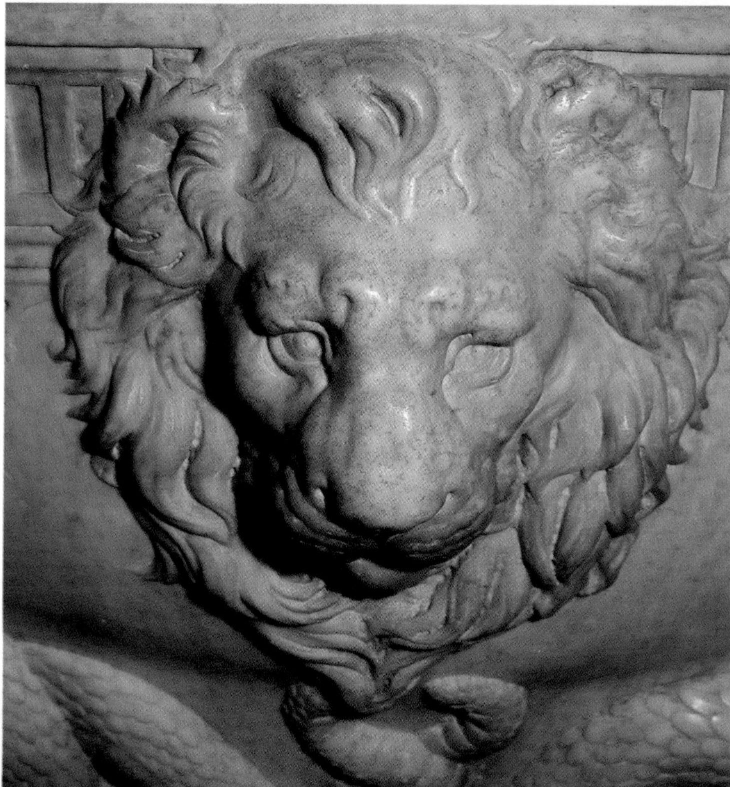

Above and opposite page:
Lavabo with Medici crests, animal protomes and plant elements, 15th century. San Lorenzo, niche to the left of the Old Sacristy.

Following pages:
Donatello, Bellano and Bertoldo, *Pulpit on the right,* detail, c. 1465, bronze.
San Lorenzo, nave.

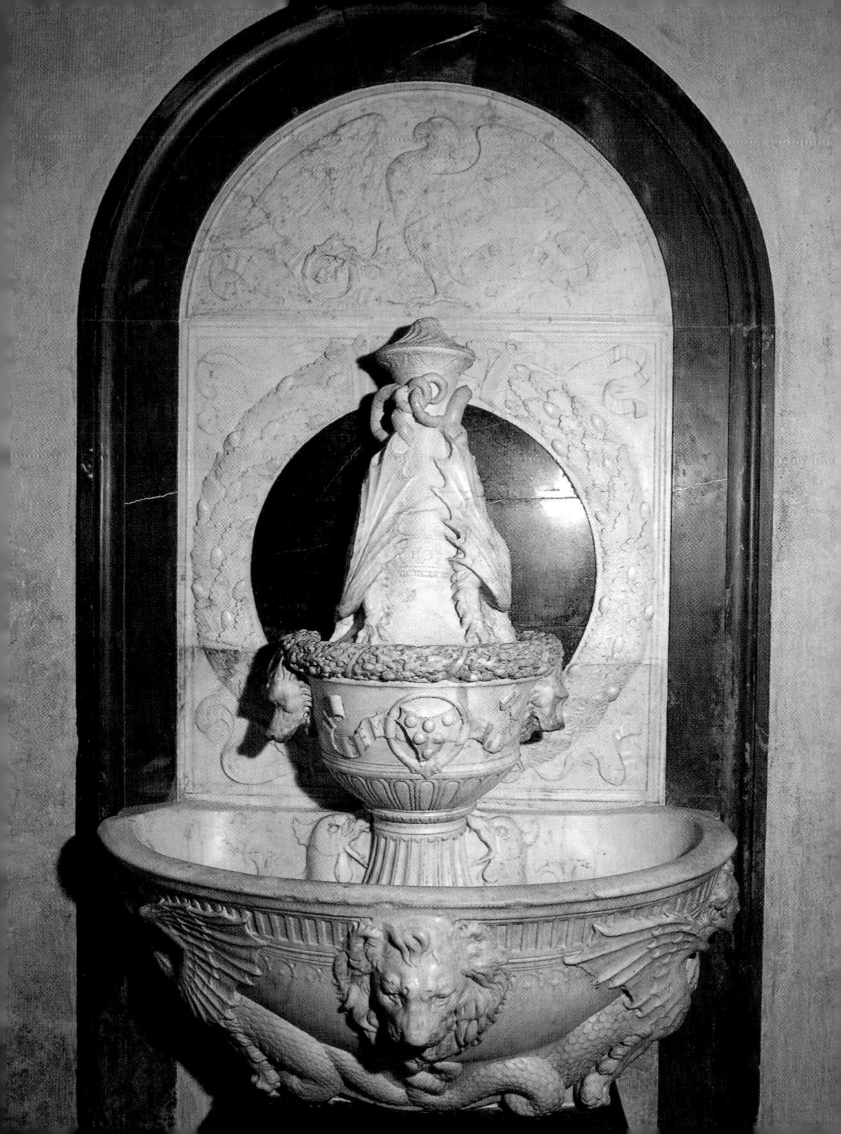

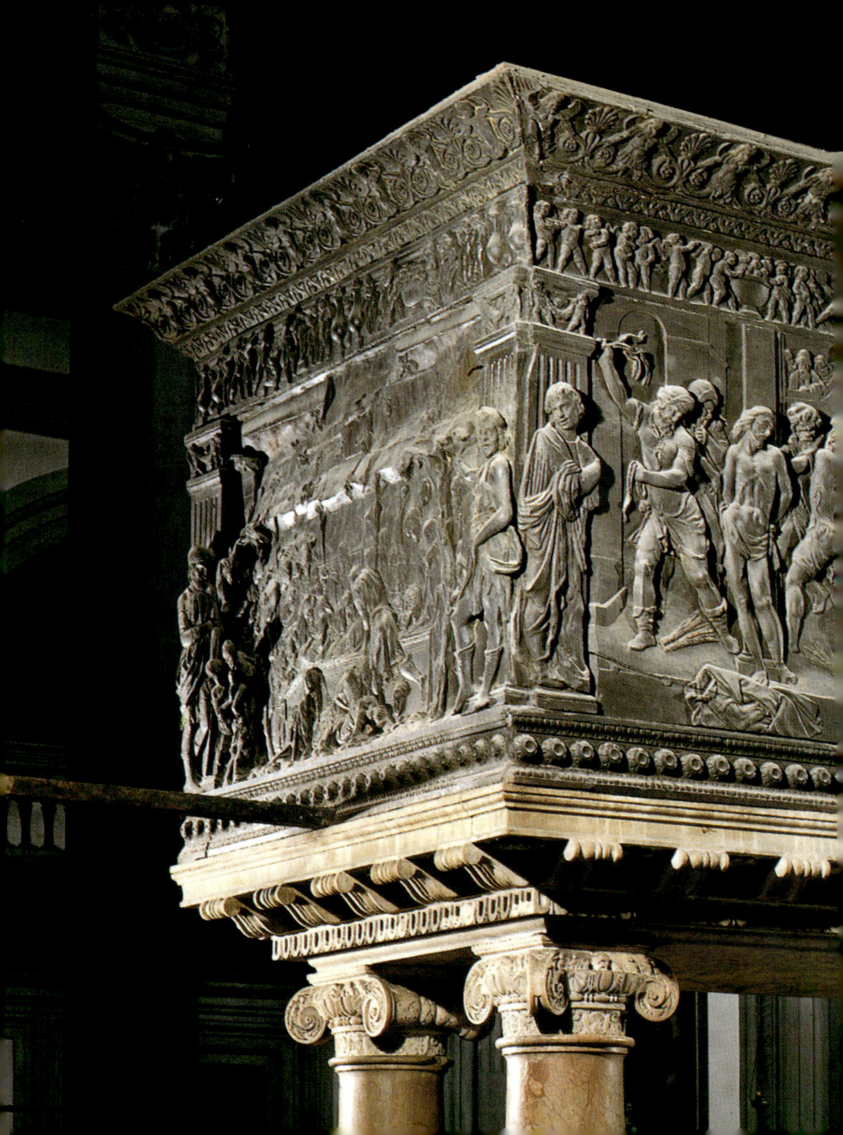

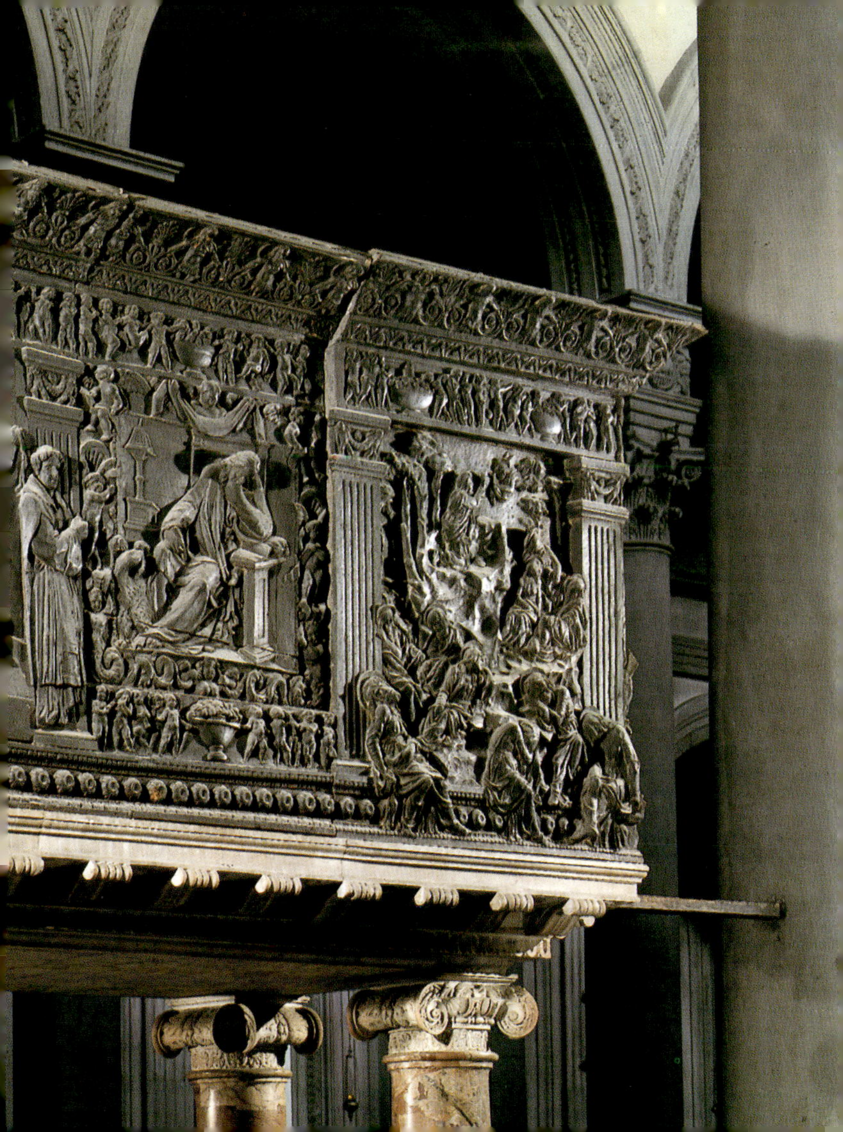

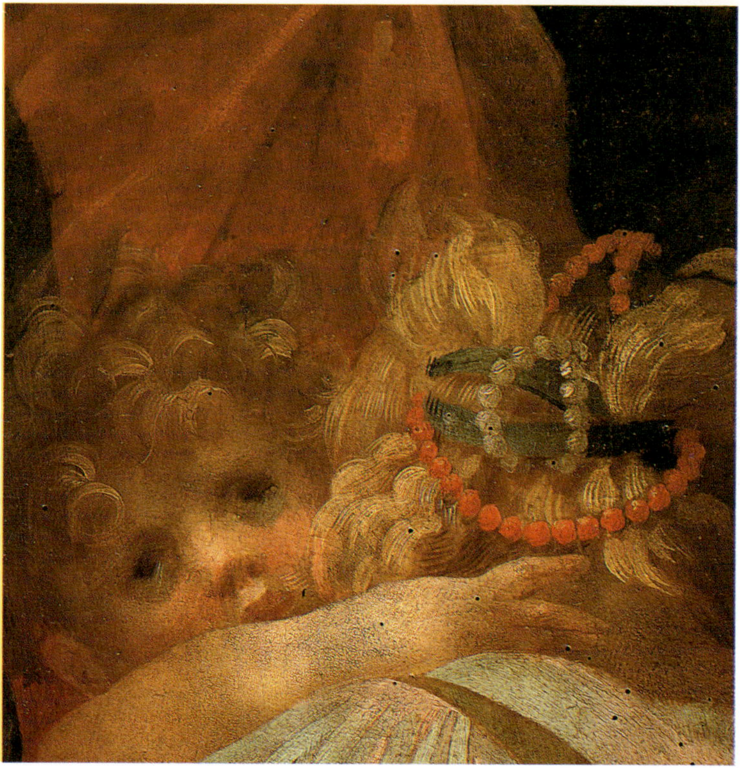

Above and opposite page:
Rosso Fiorentino, *Marriage of the Virgin*, whole and detail, 1523, oil on canvas. San Lorenzo.

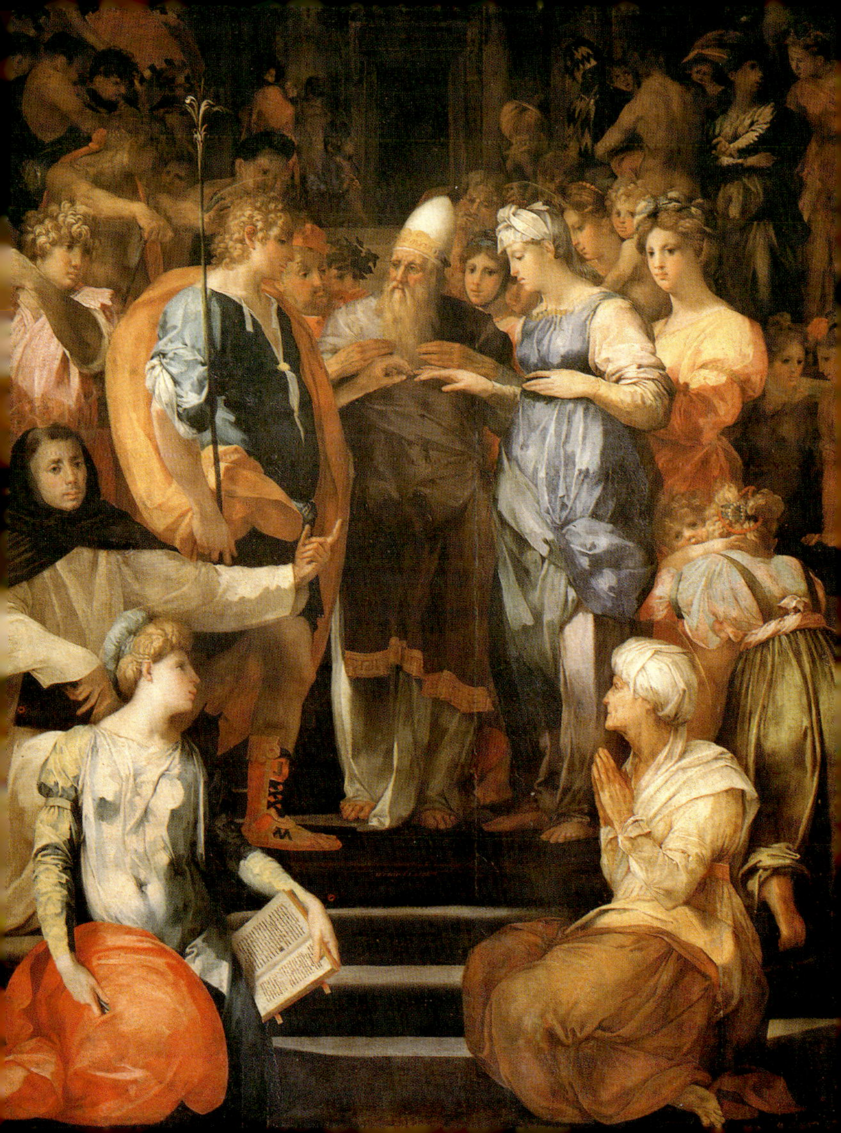

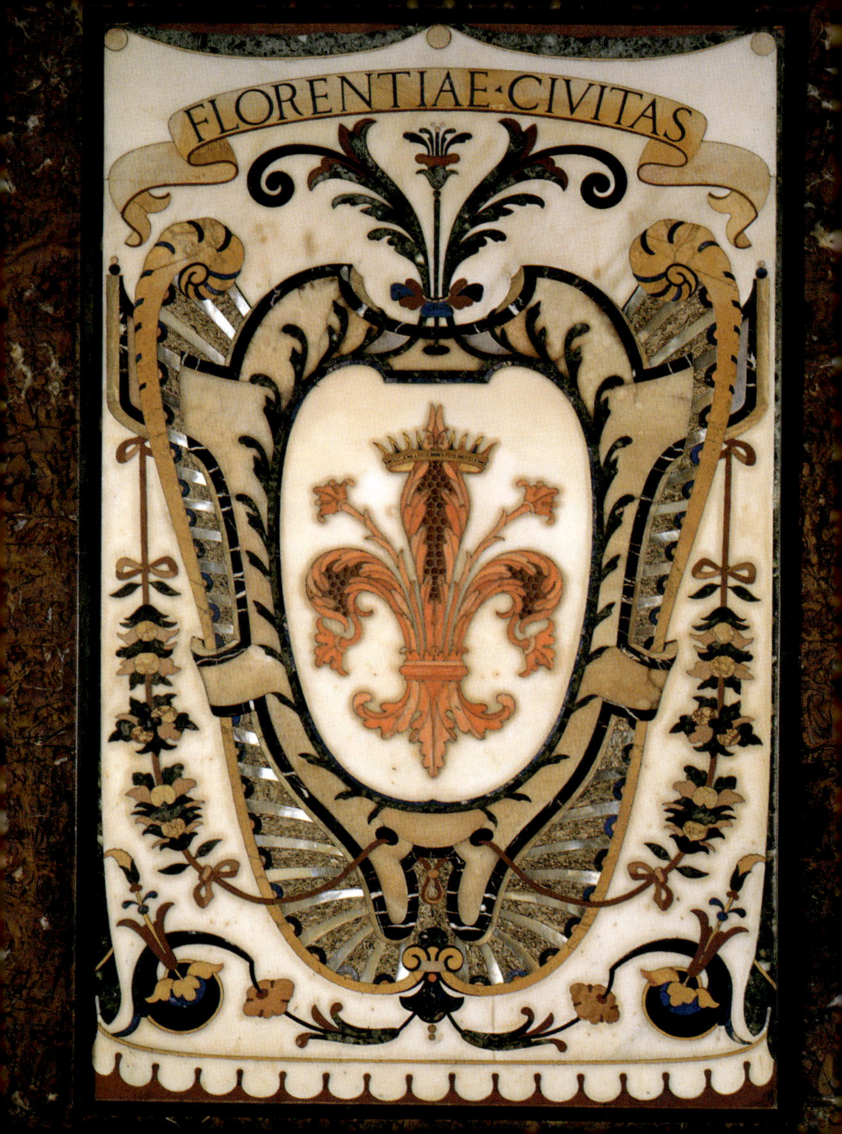
FLORENTIAE·CIVITAS

Museo delle Cappelle Medicee

The Museum of the Medici Chapels (entered from Piazza Madonna degli Aldobrandini, at the back of the Basilica di San Lorenzo) consists of the splendidly opulent Chapel of the Princes, the most ambitious project carried out by the Opificio delle Pietre Dure over the course of a very long period, starting in the 17th century, and the crypt designed by Buontalenti (1508), in which some members of the Medici and Lorraine families are buried, as well as the world-famous New Sacristy of Michelangelo, with its masterpieces of sculpture.
The idea of building the Chapel of the Princes, which contains six monumental sarcophaguses of the Medici Grand Dukes (from Ferdinando I to Cosimo III), had already, it seems, been thought of by Cosimo I de' Medici, but it is certain that work on it began at the time of Ferdinando I, who in 1602 announced a competition for its architectural design. The Chapel of the Princes, an imposing and extremely expensive work, all decorated in semiprecious stone, was finished only in the 19th century, although most of the decoration dates from the 17th and 18th centuries. The octagonal plan, desgined by the architect Matteo Nigetti from 1605 to 1640, follows the original project of Don Giovanni de'Medici, the illegitimate son of Cosimo, re-elabo-

Opposite page:
Crest of Florence,
late 17th-early 18th century,
inlaid marble.
Chapel of the Princes, moulding.

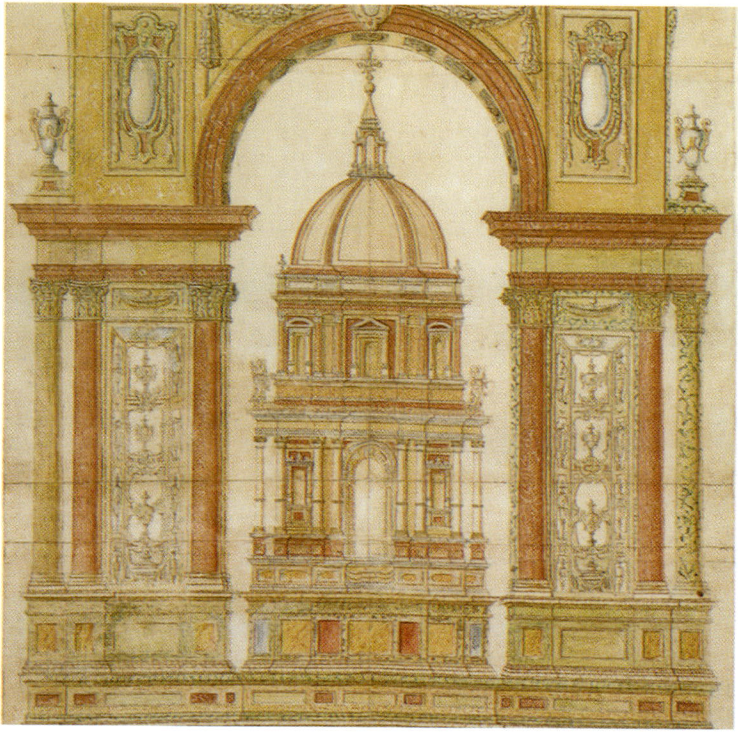

Above:
Don Lorenzo de' Medici and Matteo Nigretti with suggestions from Cristina di Lorena, *Reliquary/shelves in rock crystal,* water-color drawing, detail of the *Project for the altar in the Chapel of the Princes,* 1602-1604.
State Archives, Lorraine Imperial Royal Court, no. 5444,2.

Opposite page:
A view of the Chapel of the Princes.

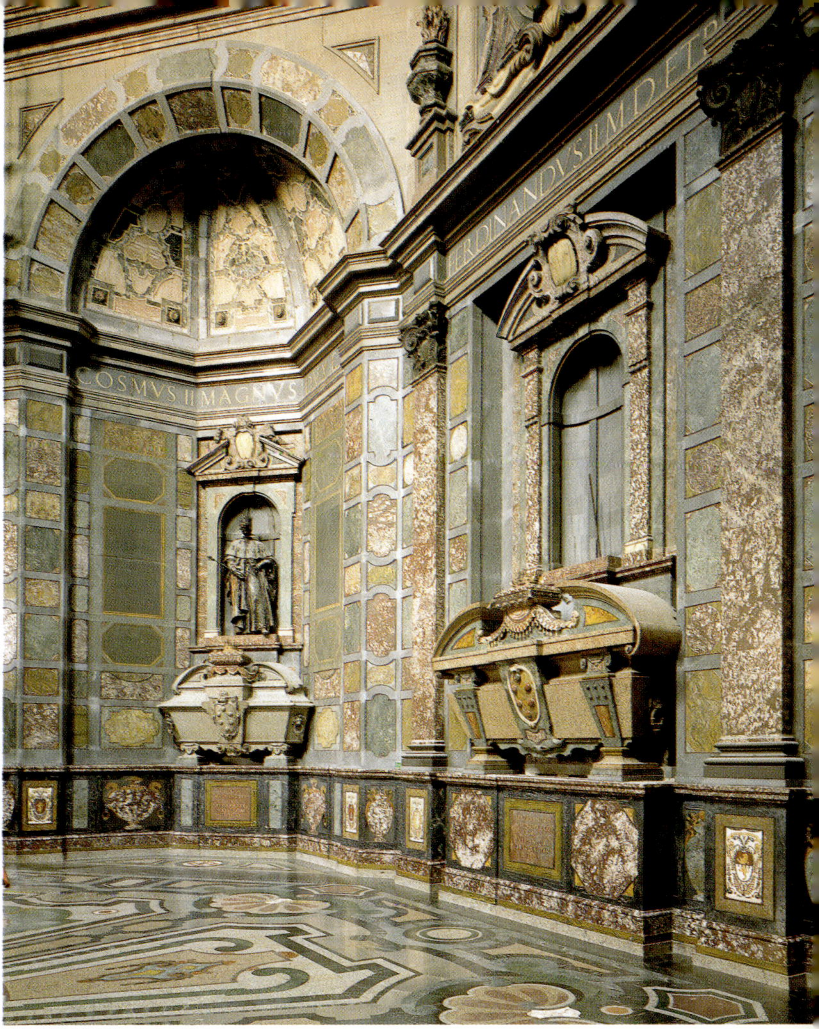

rated by Buontalenti. Two of the six sarcophaguses are decorated with large statues in gilded bronze, the work of Pietro and Ferdinando Tacca. Along the moulding are sixteen magnificent crests of the cities belonging to the Grand Duchy of Tuscany. Behind the altar, made of marble and semiprecious stones, are two sacristies, today called the Chapel of the Relics and the Chapel of the Treasury, which contain various liturgical objects from the Basilica of San Lorenzo, among them a beautiful gilded silver Pastoral, which was donated to the Basilica in 1520 by Pope Leo X.

The New Sacristy, so called to distinguish it from the 15th century one designed by Brunelleschi in a position symmetrical to the one designed later by Michelangelo, was built at the desire of Cardinal Giulio de' Medici and Pope Leo X (who was also a member of the Medici family) to house the last Medici tombs in the Basilica of San Lorenzo, where Giovanni and Piero de'Medici had been buried earlier in the Old Sacristy.

"I work as hard as I can", wrote the tormented Michelangelo to Pope Clement VII de' Medici in 1526, referring to the grandiose sculptures that he was laboriously completing for the Sacristy. After a pause during the siege of 1530, at the time when the great artist was engaged in supervising the fortifications of the city of Florence, and when he left the city definitively in 1534, the Sacristy was only partially completed.

Opposite page:
Crest of the city of Pisa, late 16th-early 17th century, inlaid marble. Chapel of the Princes, molding.

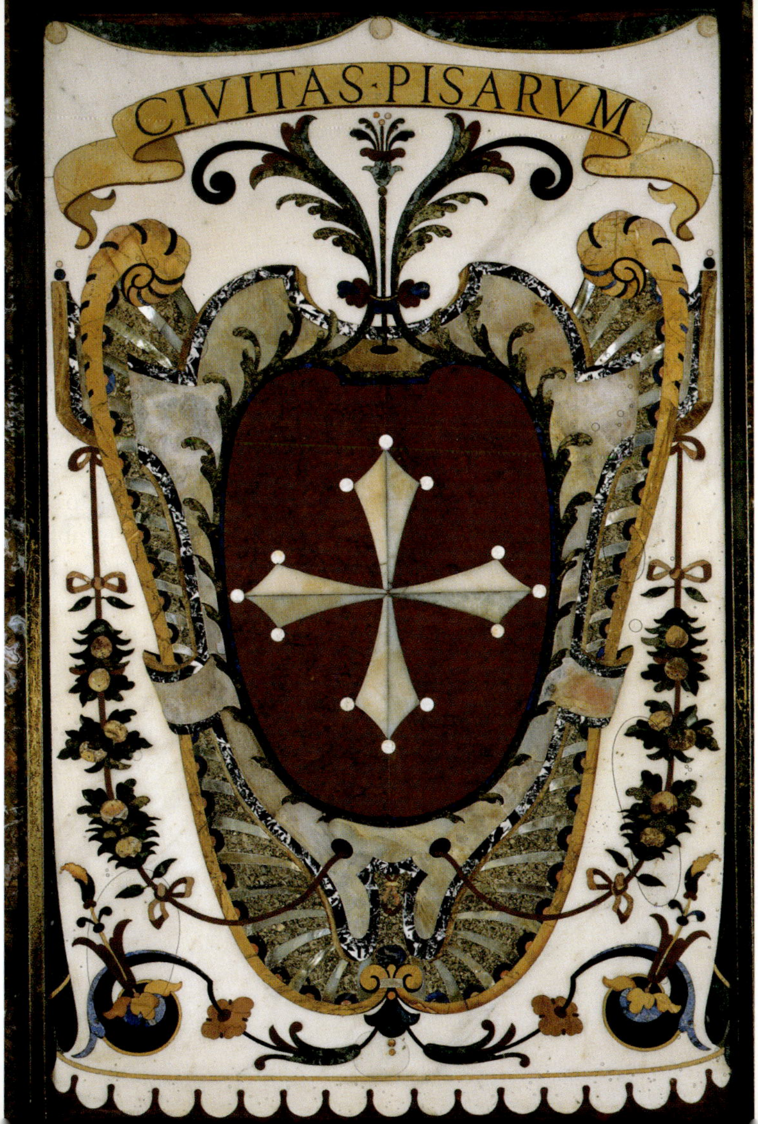
CIVITAS·PISARVM

There remain the tormented, enigmatic figures of *Dawn* and *Dusk*, of *Day* and *Night* (whose symbolic meanings are still the subject of debate). Regarding the *Night*, Michelangelo himself, who was also a sensitive poet, wrote intense verses, reflecting his grief at the undertain situation of his city:

Dear to me is sleep, and even more
to be of stone, / while shame and evil last; /
not to see, not to hear is my great fortune; /
but do not wake me, speak softly.

In addition to the sculptures mentioned above, in the chapel with its square layout and domed ceiling, we may admire the colossal statues of *Lorenzo de' Medici Duke of Urbino* (1525) and *Giuliano Duke of Nemours* (1526-1531). That of Lorenzo, grandson of Lorenzo the Magnificent, stands over the sarcophagus with the statues of *Dawn* and *Dusk*; the other, of Giuliano, the third-born child of the Magnificent, is over the sacophagus bearing the statues of *Night* and *Day*.
On the right wall is another masterpiece by Michelangelo, the *Virgin and Child*, planned to occupy a niche that was never built, and flanked by statues of *Saints* completed by the artist's pupils.

Opposite page:
A view of the New Sacristy, built in several stages (between 1521 and 1534) by Michelangelo, and completed by Giorgio Vasari and Bartolomeo Anmmannati. It is a very high-ceilinged room, with a striking perspective effect. The sculptures on the walls are spaced by double pilasters.

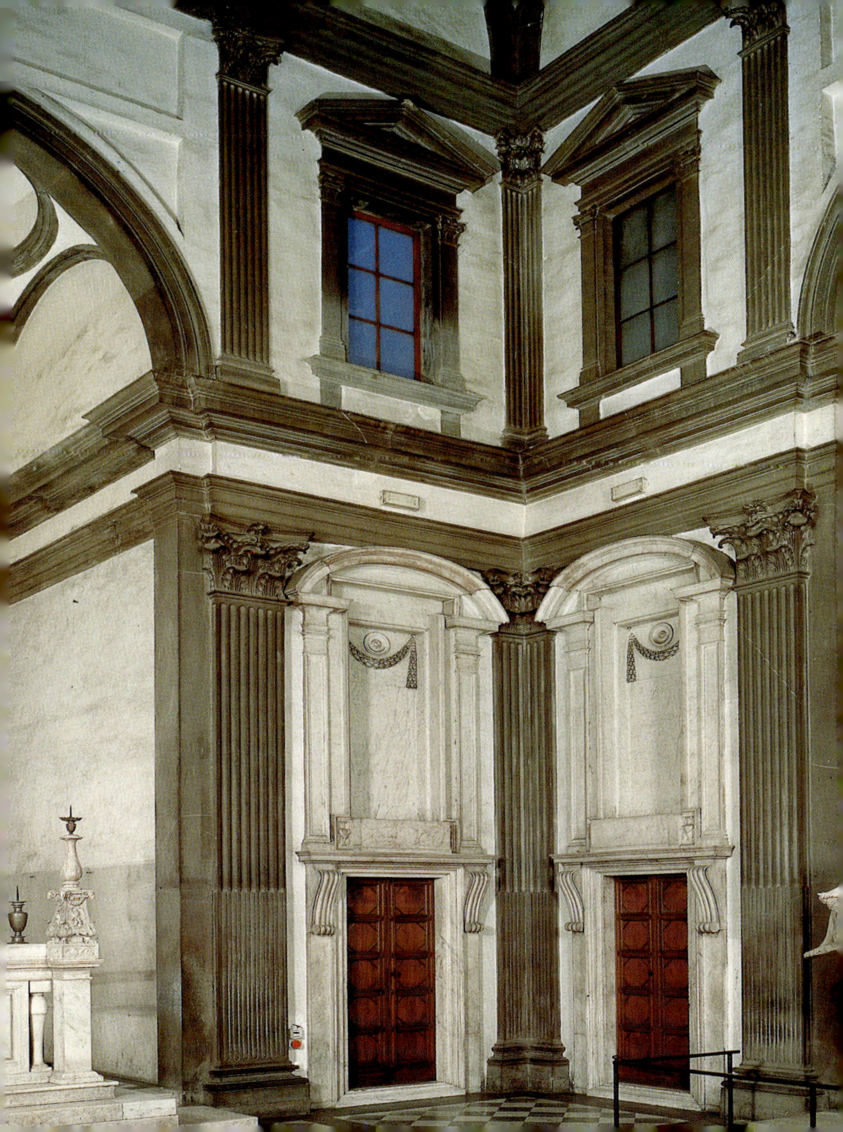

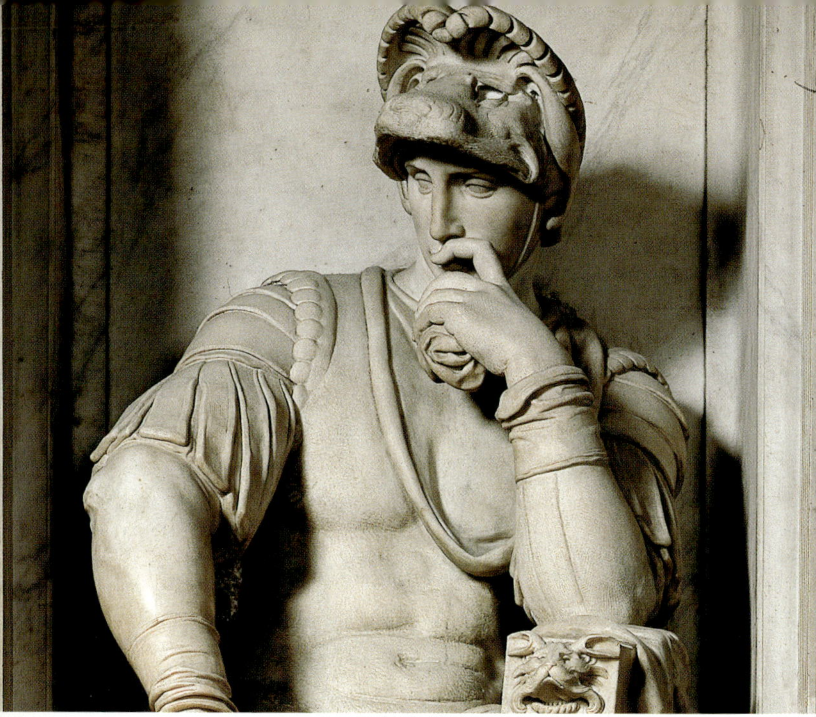

Above:
Michelangelo, *Lorenzo Duke of Urbino*, detail, 1525-1527, marble. Medici Chapels, New Sacristy.

Opposite page:
Michelangelo, *Tomb of Lorenzo Duke of Urbino*, with the statues of *Dawn* and *Dusk* on the sarcophagus. Medici Chapels, New Sacristy.

Following pages:
Michelangelo, *Tomb of Giuliano Duke of Nemours*, with the statues of *Night* and *Day* on the sarcophagus, whole and detail, 1526-1534, marble. Medici Chapels, New Sacristy.

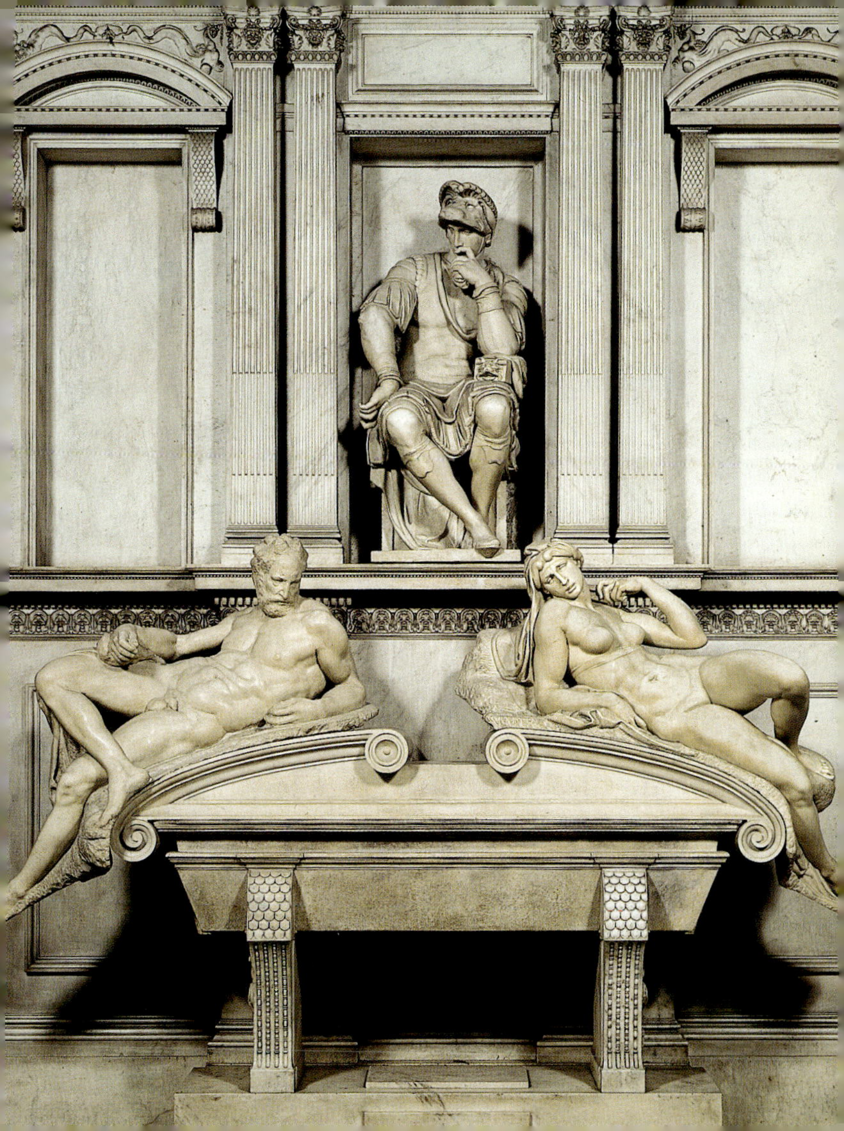

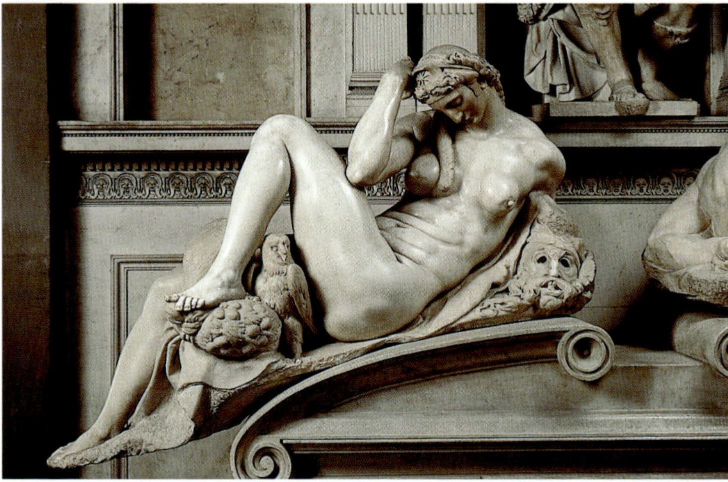

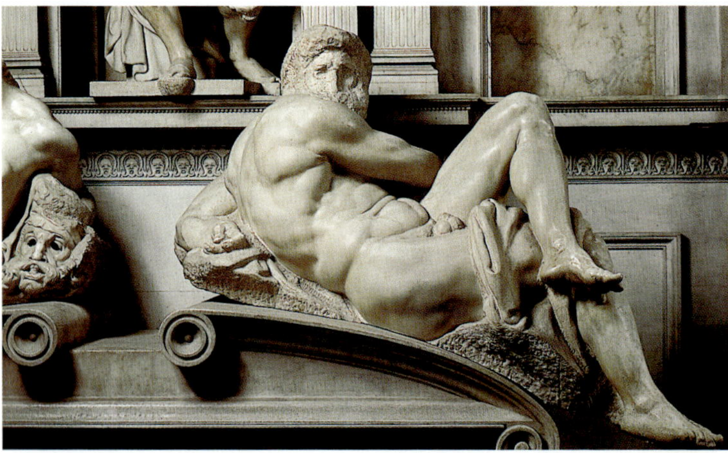

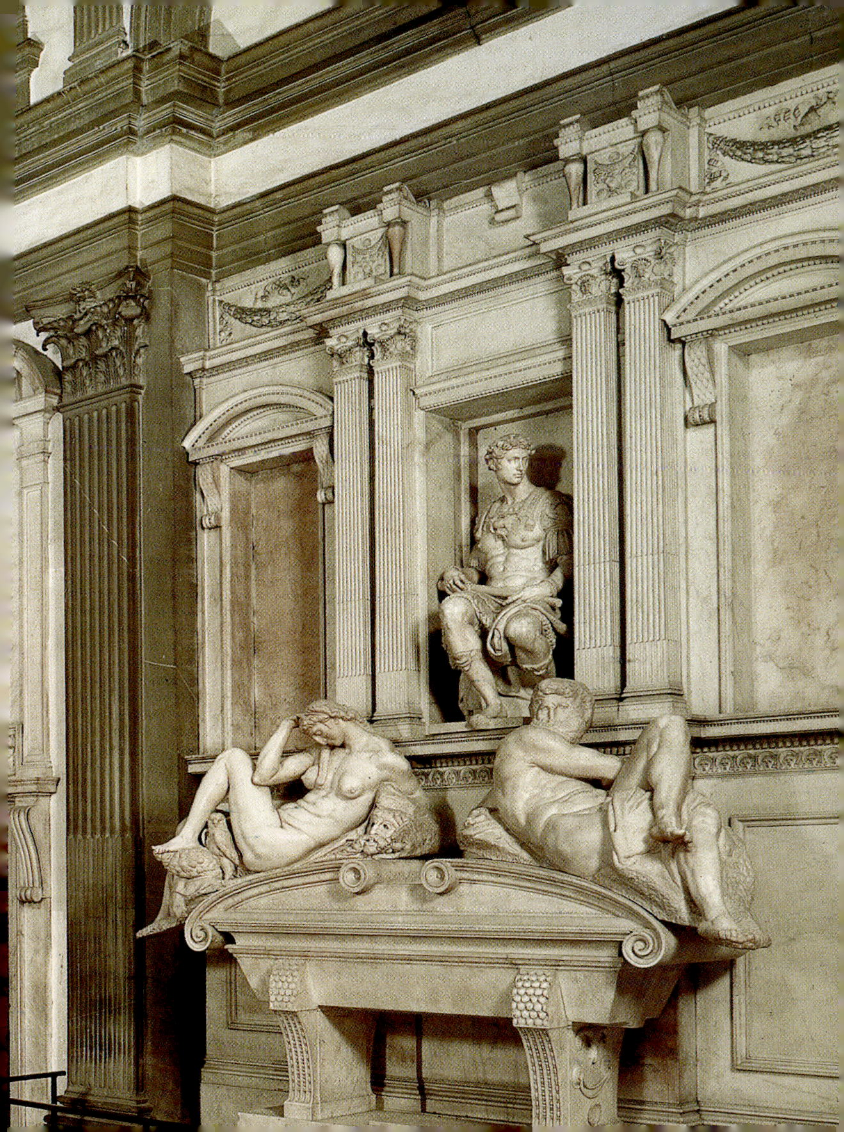

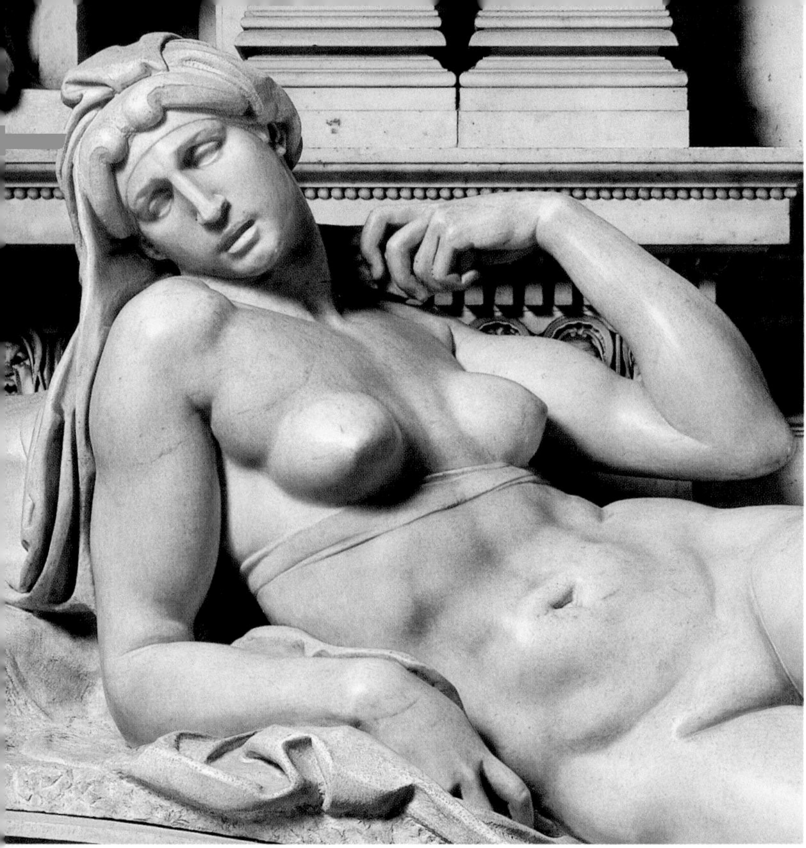

Above:
Michelangelo, *Dawn*,
detail, 1524-1527,
marble. Medici Chapels,
New Sacristy.

Opposite page:
Michelangelo,
Virgin and Child,
detail, 1521-1534, marble.
Medici Chapels, New Sacristy.

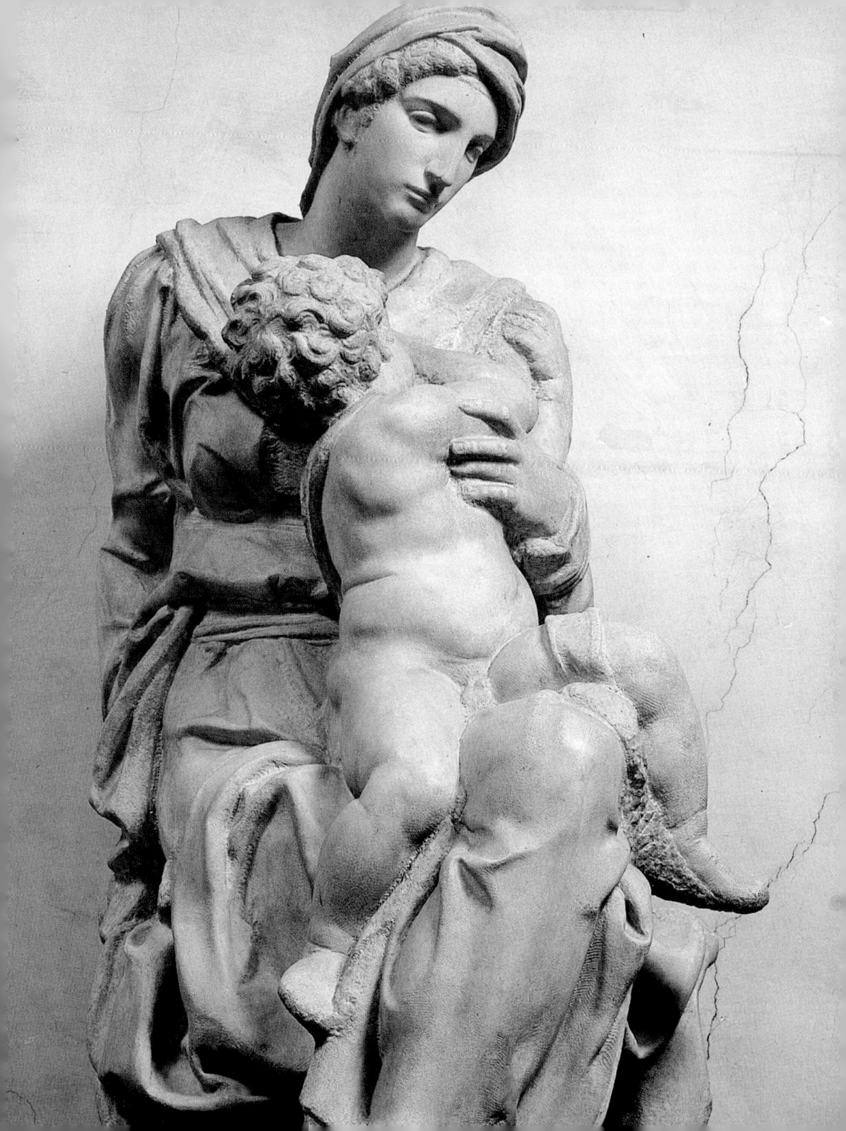

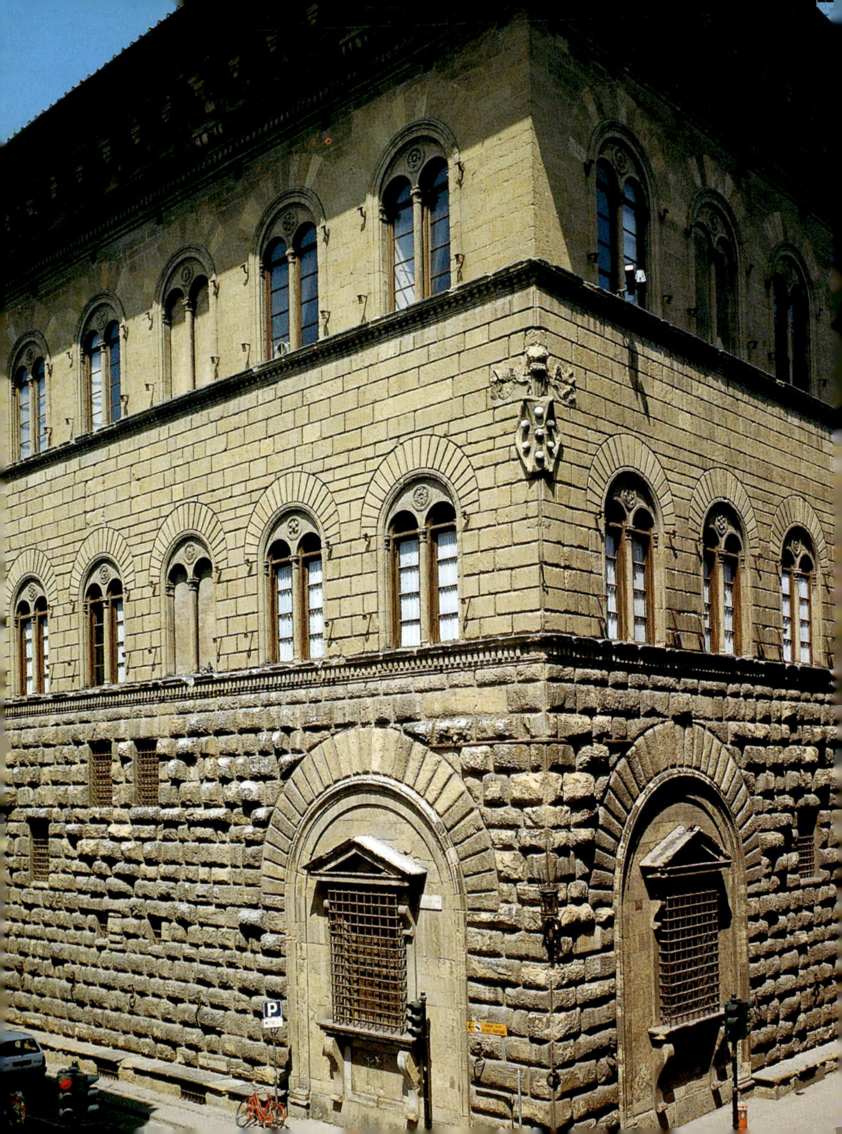
P

PALAZZO MEDICI RICCARDI

The Palace, the Chapel of the Magi and the Biblioteca Riccardiana

Appearing relatively modest as compared to the palaces then being built by other wealthy Florentines such as Palla Strozzi and Luca Pitti, the palace erected for Cosimo the Elder as his new residence in Via Larga (today's Via Cavour) was also designed to serve as headquarters for the highly efficient Medici "holding company". On the ground floor of the sober edifice, praised at the time by the erudite Filarete for its rationality, the financial business of the Medici Bank was in fact conducted throughout the 15th century. Cosimo, a businessman as well as shrewd politician, capable of adroit diplomatic operations (such as that of financing the transferral of the Council from Ferrara to Florence in 1439 to strengthen his ties to the pope), had been very careful, upon his triumphant return in 1434 after a year of exile, not to display his power ostentatiously. The palace commissioned of his favorite architect Michelozzo is thus much less grandiose than the one originally designed by Brunelleschi, which was to have faced on Piazza San Lorenzo. Although Brunelleschi's design was part of an intelligent urban planning initiative, having the palace face the Medicean basilica par excel-

Opposite page: Palazzo Medici Riccardi, on the corner between Via Gori and today's Via Cavour. Designed by Michelozzo for Cosimo the Elder (1444-1464), the building has undergone various changes and additions. On the ground floor can be seen the "kneeling windows", resting on consoles designed by Michelangelo.

lence, so beloved by Cosimo's father, would have been too brazen a reminder to the Florentines of the enormous political influence exerted in the city by the Medici family. Accordingly, on the ground floor of the building designed by Michelozzo, almost as in the traditional severe, square Town Hall, the ethical values of "decorum" and morality had to be displayed above all else, as in a medieval cloister. Here were placed Donatello's bronze *David* (now in the Bargello) which, along with the *Judith* by the same artist that stood in the second courtyard, would remind the Florentines of the republican ideals they held dear, and reassure them that there was no danger that a Medicean government would fail to respect such principles. The decorations were instead more splendid on the upper floors, where access was restricted to family members and illustrious guests (one of the first to visit the just-finished palace was, in 1459, Giangaleazzo Sforza). In the frescoes adorning the private chapel commissioned of Benozzo Gozzoli da Piero, son of Cosimo, the Medici thus decided to openly display the family's virtues and salient characteristics by having the eldest son Lorenzo portrayed as one of the Magi, an earthly king kneeling before the King of Heaven. The "studiolo" of Piero, decorated with glazed terracottas by Luca della Robbia and filled with precious objects, has instead been lost. In the palace, moreover, the first Medici gathered extraordinary works of art, as shown by the 15th century invento-

Opposite page:
The first courtyard of
Palazzo Medici Riccardi.

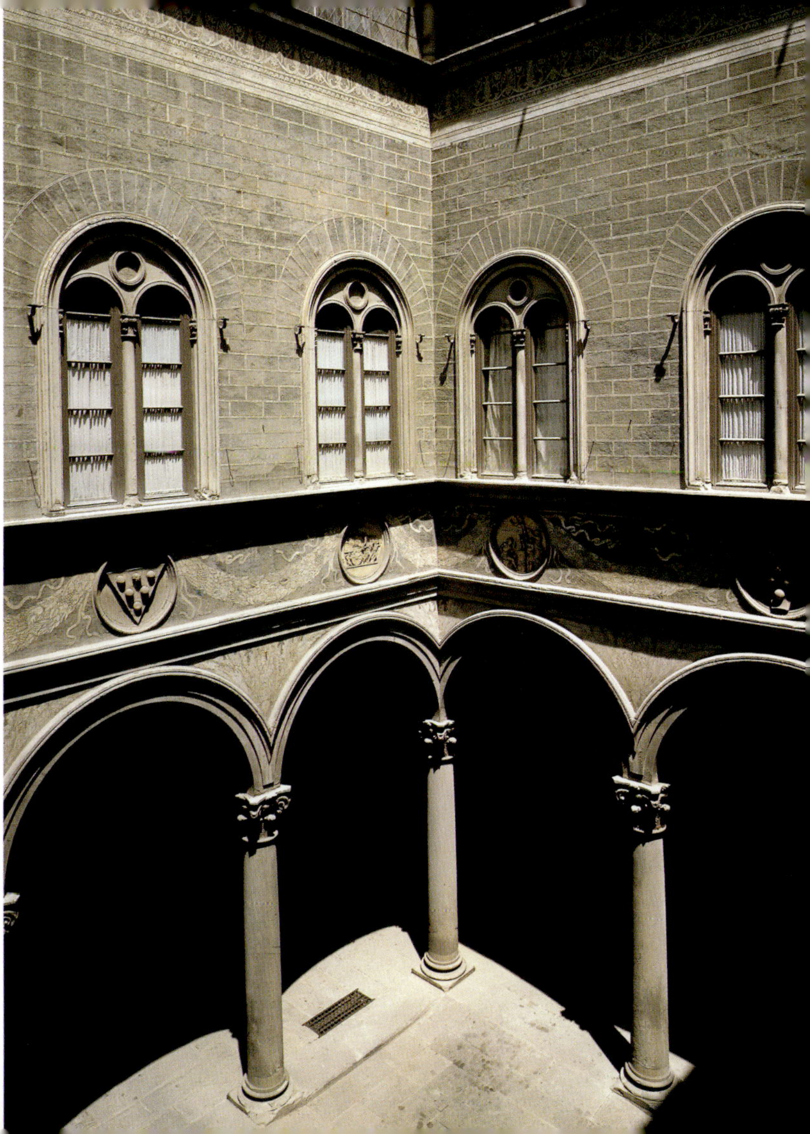

ries, which document the presence of paintings by Jan van Eyck and sculptures by Pollaiolo. Over the centuries, the building underwent several changes, one of the most important being the walling off in 1517 of the loggia on the ground floor that faced on the so-called Canto dei Medici. When the palace passed into the hands of the Riccardi family in 1659, it was enlarged with a new wing on Via Ginori, bounded on the long side by today's Via Cavour. Dating from 1682 are the frescoes representing the *Apotheosis of the Medici* painted by Luca Giordano in the gallery decorated with Baroque stuccoes. In the same building is the Biblioteca Riccardiana, founded by Riccardo Romolo Riccardi and opened to the public in 1715, which contains 60,000 volumes, ancient manuscripts and incunabola.

VISITORS' ITINERARY AND WORKS OF ART

Noteworthy are:

- on the outside of Palazzo Medici, distinguished by round-arch windows alternating with two-light mullioned ones and Medici coats of arms, the rusticated stone revetment, whose relief is less prominent on the first floor and disappears entirely on the second.
- inside, the two courtyards (the first decorated with epigraphs, Medicean coats of arms and graffiti, the second containing a garden, the site of memorable theatrical performances in the 16th century).

Opposite page:
The garden in the second courtyard of Palazzo Medici.

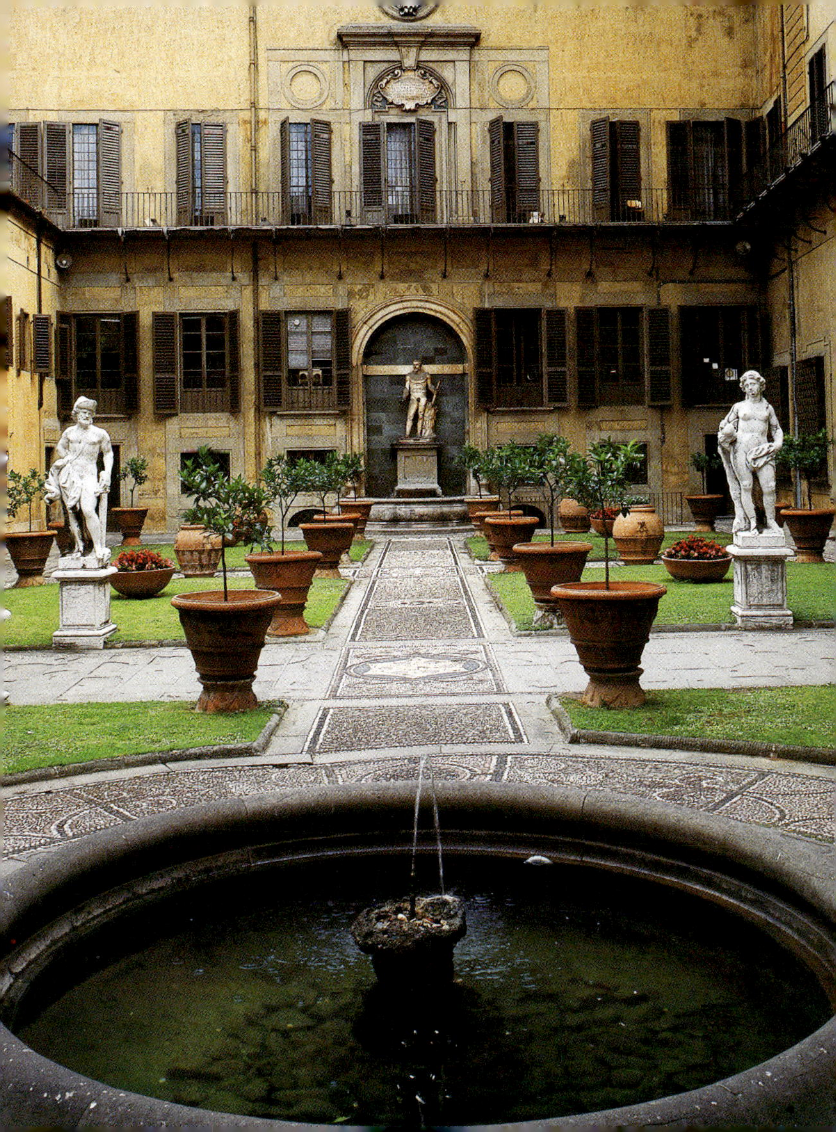

- on the upper floor, the Chapel of the Magi (1459) frescoed by Benozzo Gozzoli with the *Cavalcade of the Magi*, set in a luxuriant landscape, with castles and wild animals. The procession evokes the solemn cavalcade of the Greeks held twenty years earlier in Florence for the arrival of Pope Pius II on the occasion of the Council; among the personages in the Medicean entourage of the mid-15th century appears the Byzantine Emperor John VII Paleologus, who had participated in the Council held in 1439, in the guise of one of the Three Kings. Note also in this chapel the marble floor by Michelozzo, the inlaid wooden choirstalls by Giuliano da Sangallo, and the altarpiece with the *Adoration of the Child and the Infant St. John* by Pseudo Pierfrancesco Fiorentino (c. 1459).
- the *Madonna and Child* (c. 1450) by Filippo Lippi, an artist who at times resided as a guest in the palace of his patron and great admirer, Cosimo il Vecchio.
- in the gallery (c. 1670-1688), the frescoes by Luca Giordano (1683) and the stuccoes (1687) by Giovan Battista and Marco Andrea Ciceri.

Opposite page:
A view of the Chapel of the Magi in Palazzo Medici, frescoed by Benozzo Gozzoli (1459) and embellished by a refined marble floor designed by Michelozzo. The inlaid choirstalls (1469) were carved by Giuliano da Sangallo.

Following page:
Some details from the *Cavalcade of the Magi* by Benozzo Gozzoli. Among the personages identified are the young Lorenzo dressed as one of the Magi, his brother Giuliano with a leopard on his horse, his grandfather Cosimo, still grasping the reins in his hands, and his father Piero, with his hand on his horse's mane.

- in the Biblioteca Riccardiana (access from Via Ginori), the frescoes by Luca Giordano on the ceiling, with stuccoes by Giovan Battista Ciceri and Anton Francesco Andreozzi (before 1689). The library, open to scholars, contains priceless 15th century manuscripts.

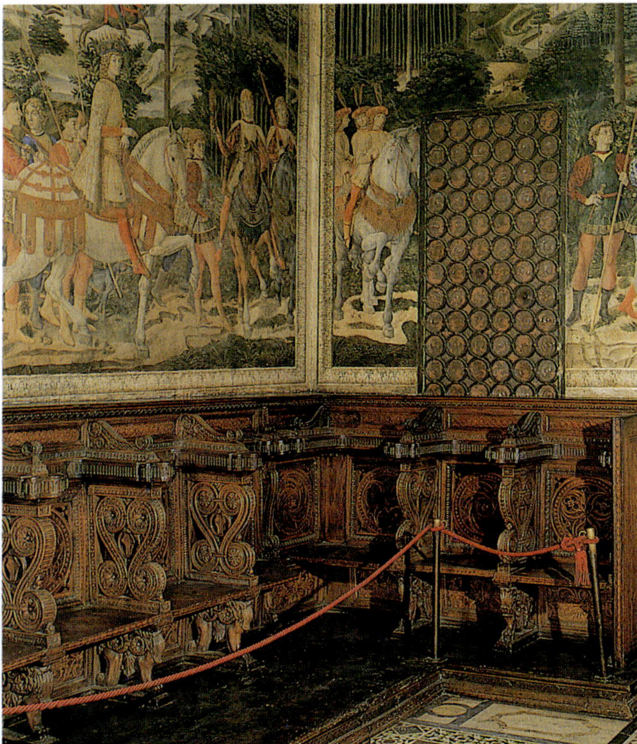

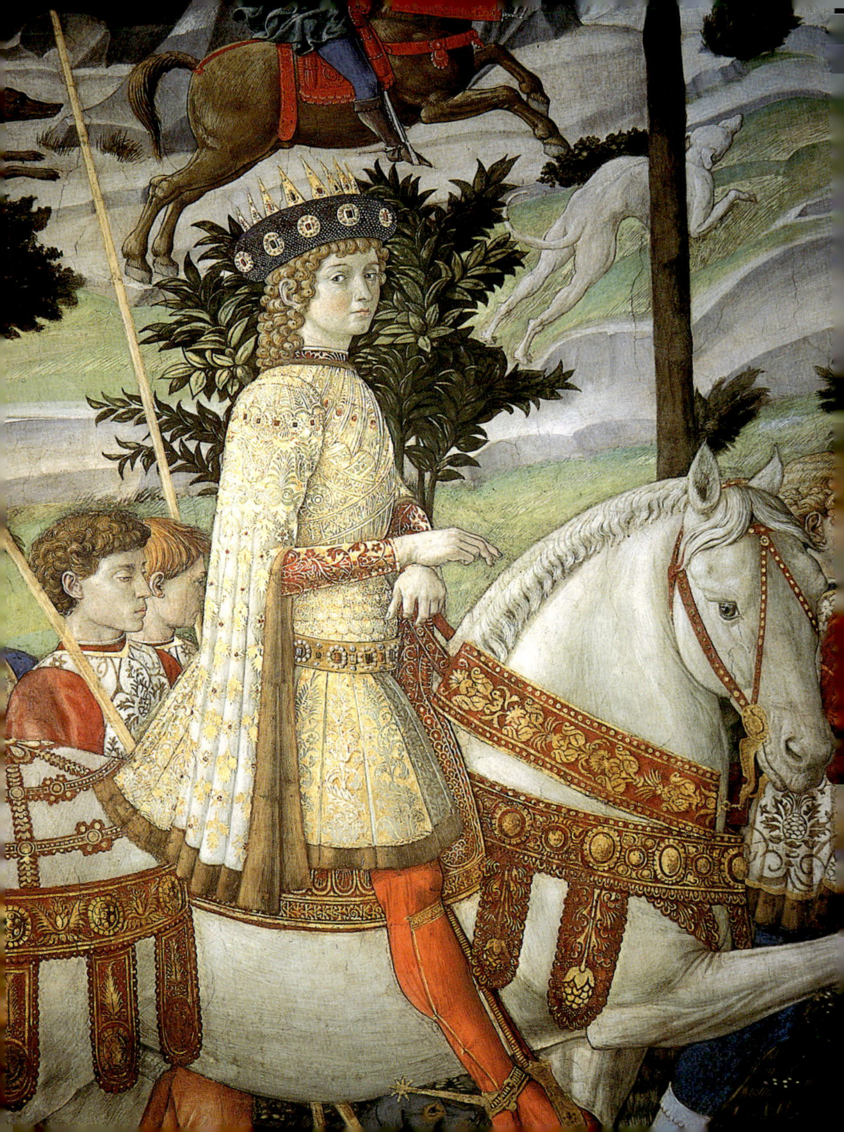

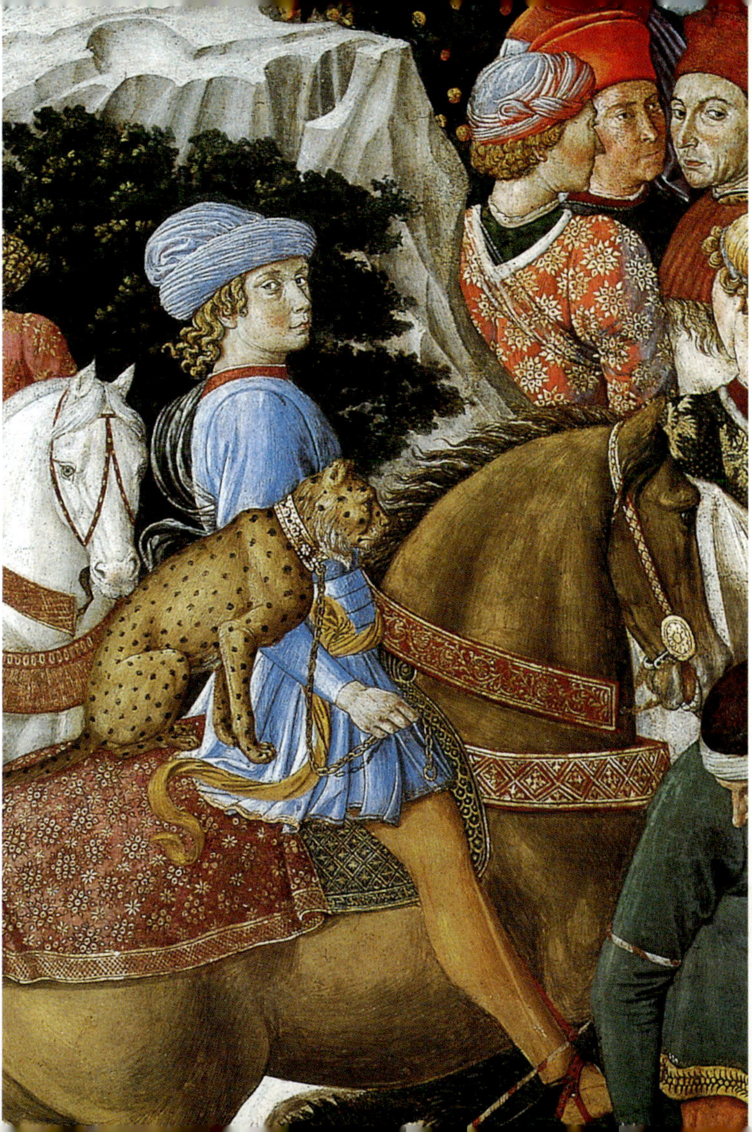

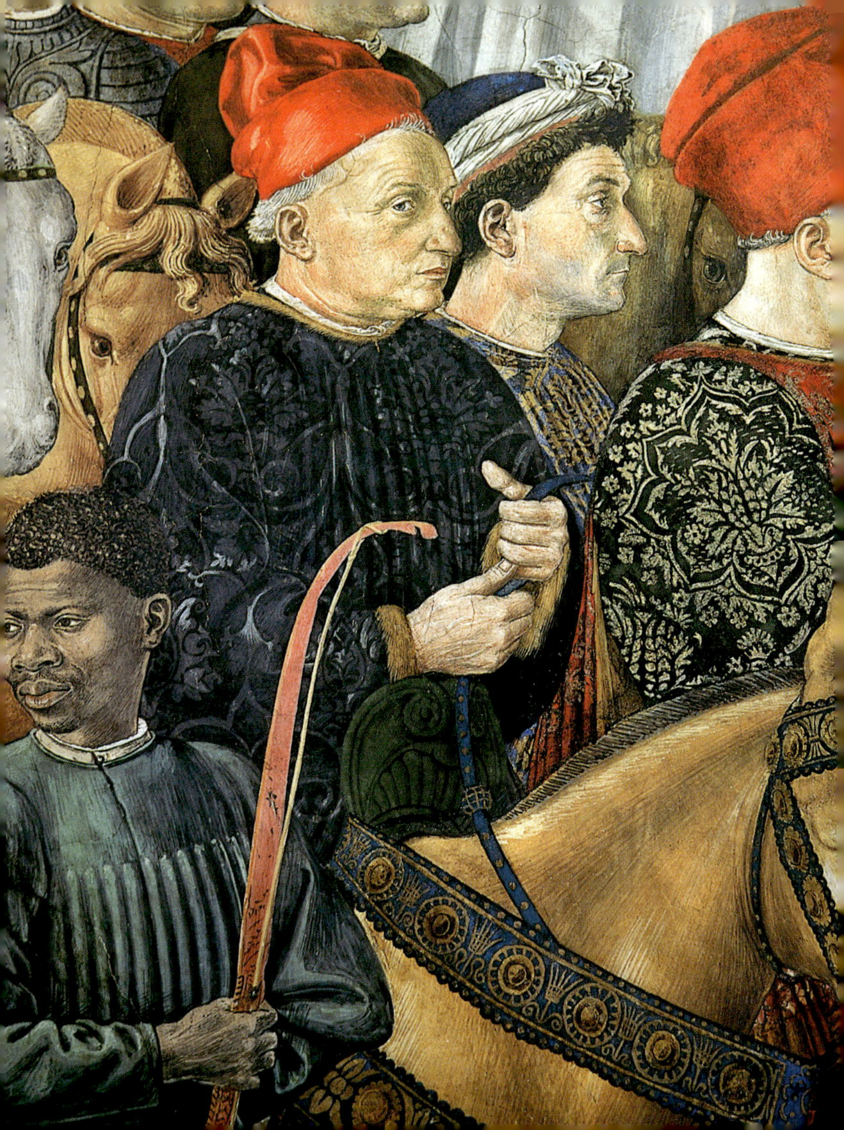

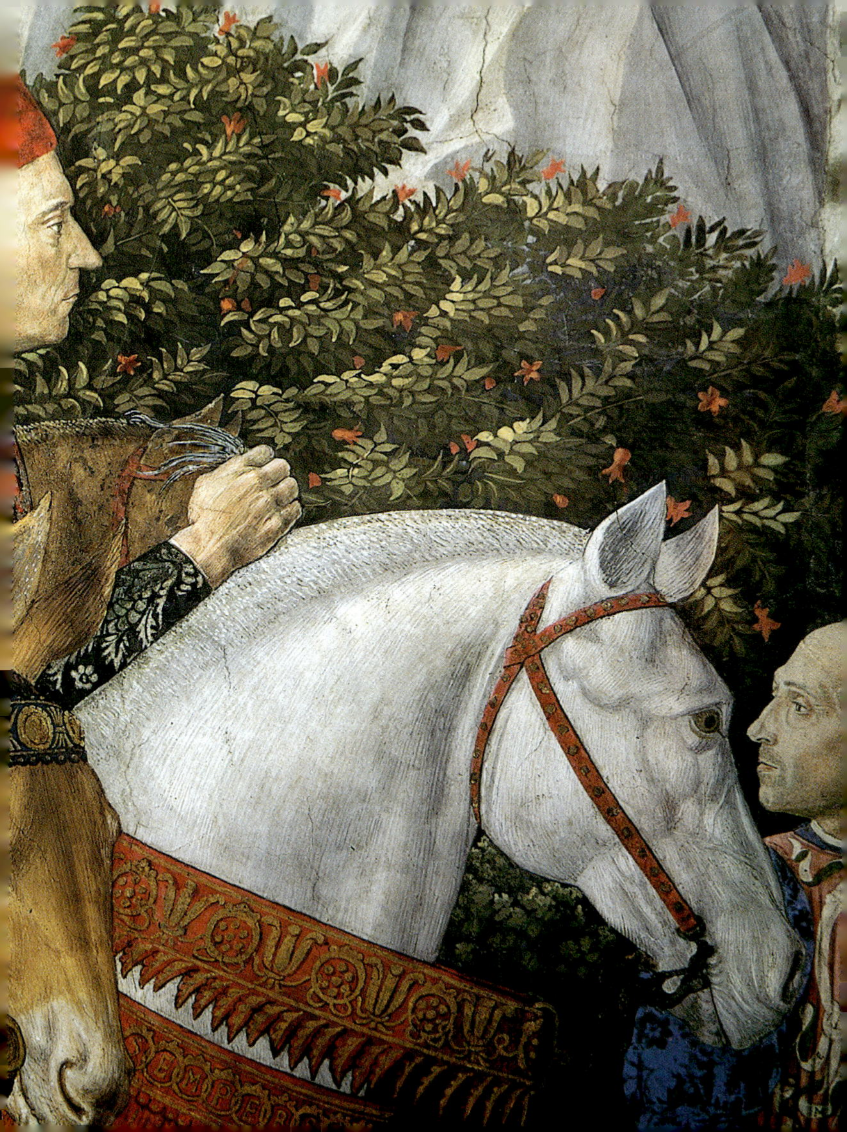

Opposite page and below:
Pseudo Pierfrancesco Fiorentino, *Adoration of the Child and the Infant St. John*, whole and detail, c. 1460, tempera on wood (coeval copy of the altarpiece painted by Filippo Lippi for the chapel in Palazzo Medici, now in the Berlin Museums). Palazzo Medici Riccardi, altarpiece of the Chapel of the Magi.

Following pages:
Benozzo Gozzoli, *Angels gathering flowers in the garden*, detail of the fresco on the walls of the tribune in the Chapel of the Magi, representing *Angels in glory and in adoration* at the sides of the *Adoration of the Child* by Pseudo Pierfrancesco Fiorentino, 1459.

Giovan Battista and Marco Andrea Ciceri, *Stucco decoration,* 1687. Palazzo Medici Riccardi, Luca Giordano Gallery.

View of the library ceiling, with frescoes by Luca Giordano and stuccoes by Giovan Battista Ciceri and Anton Francesco Andreozzi (before 1689). Biblioteca Riccardiana.

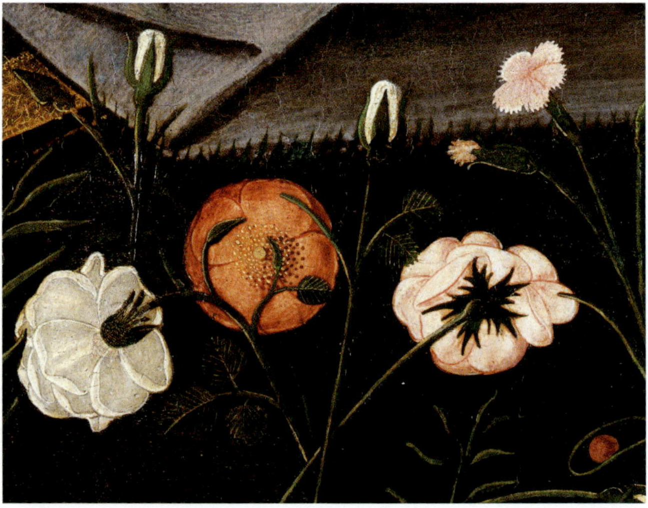

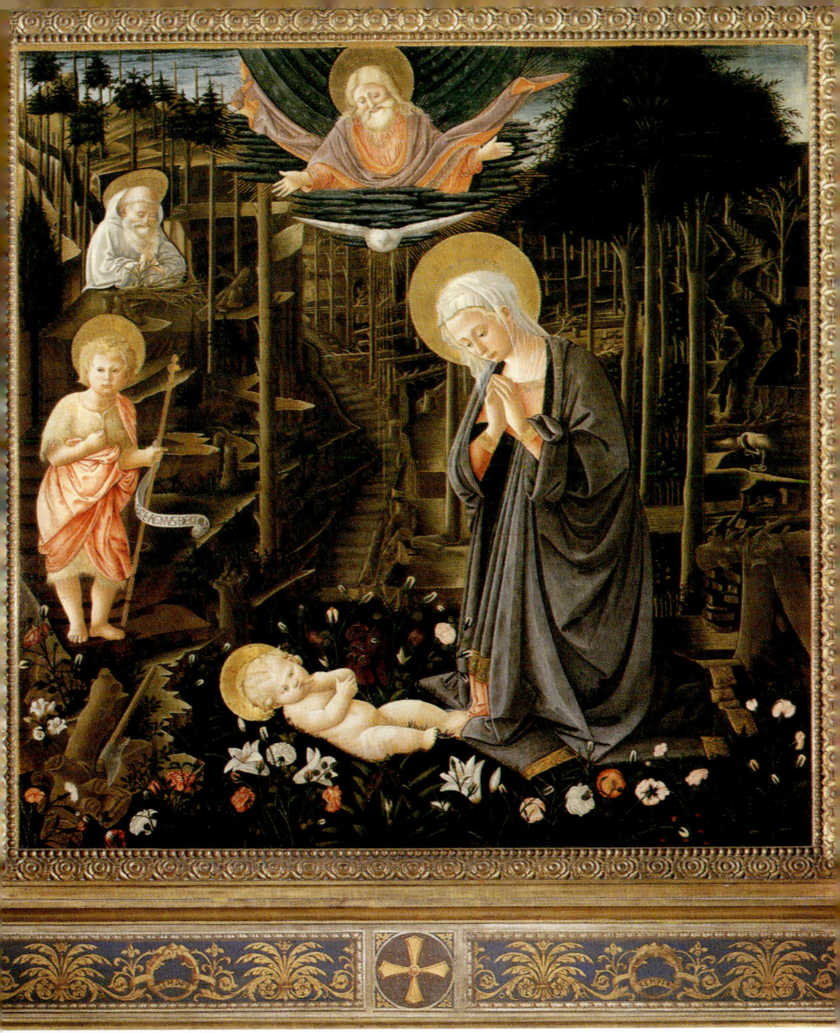

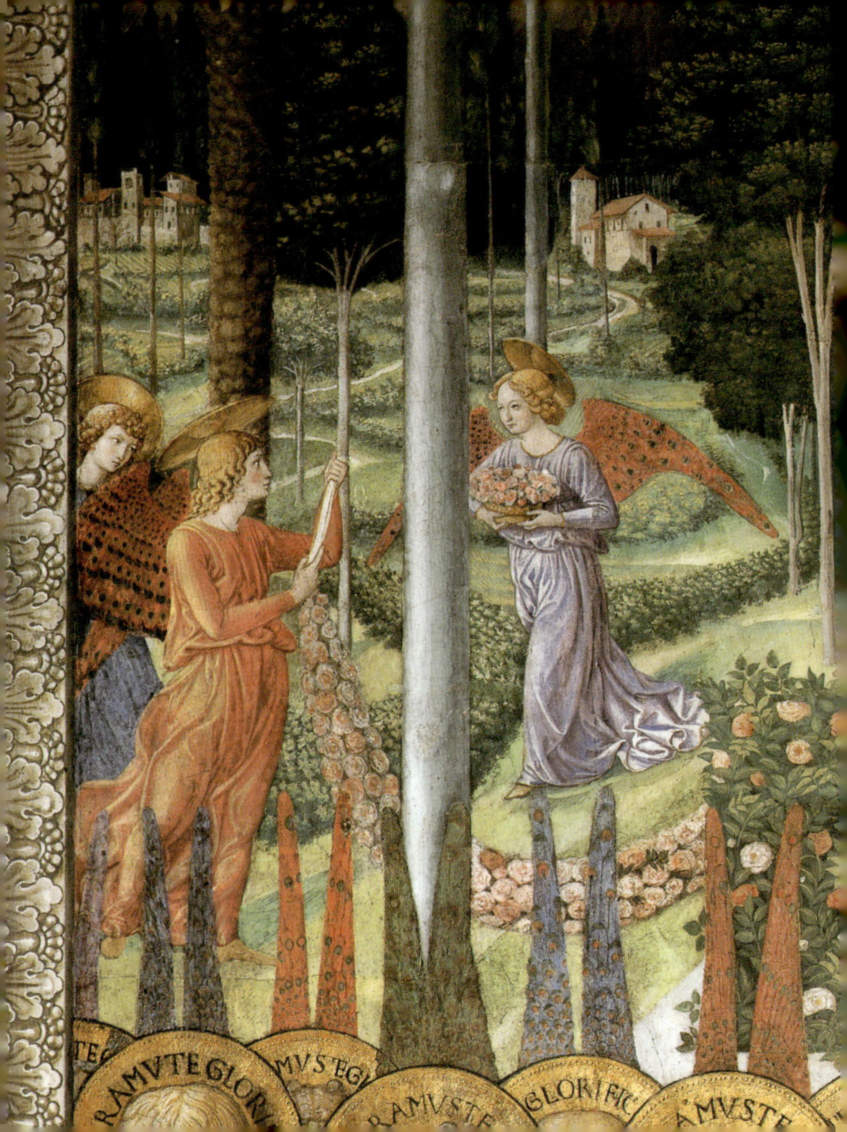
RAMVTEGLORI
MVS EGI
RAMVSTE
GLORIFIC
AMVSTE

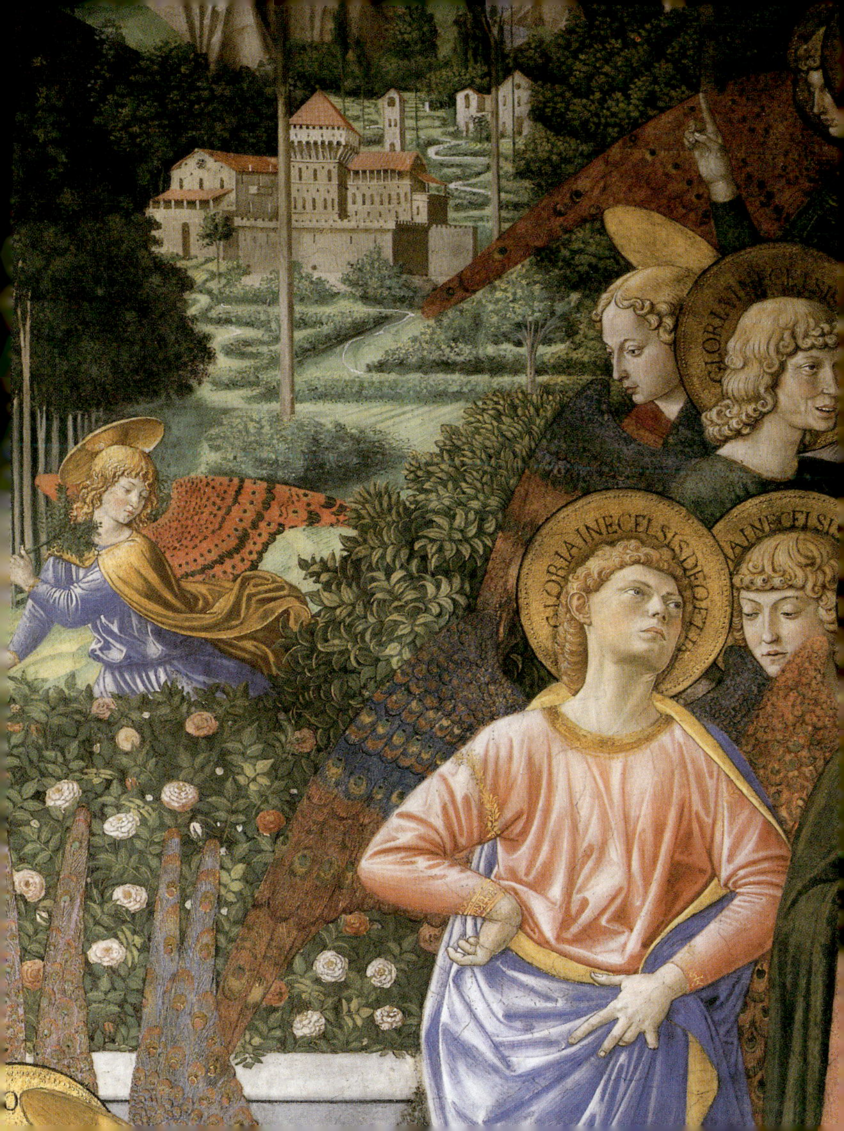
GLORIA INECELSIS DEO ET

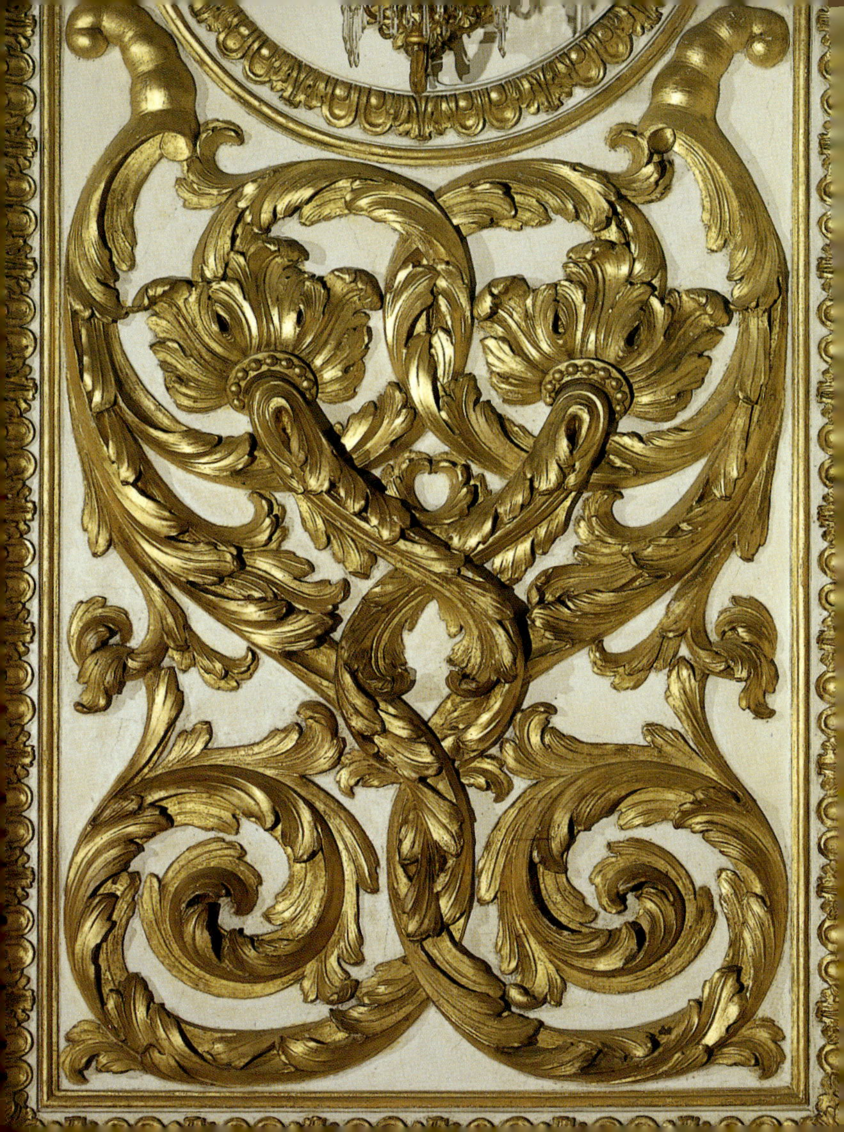

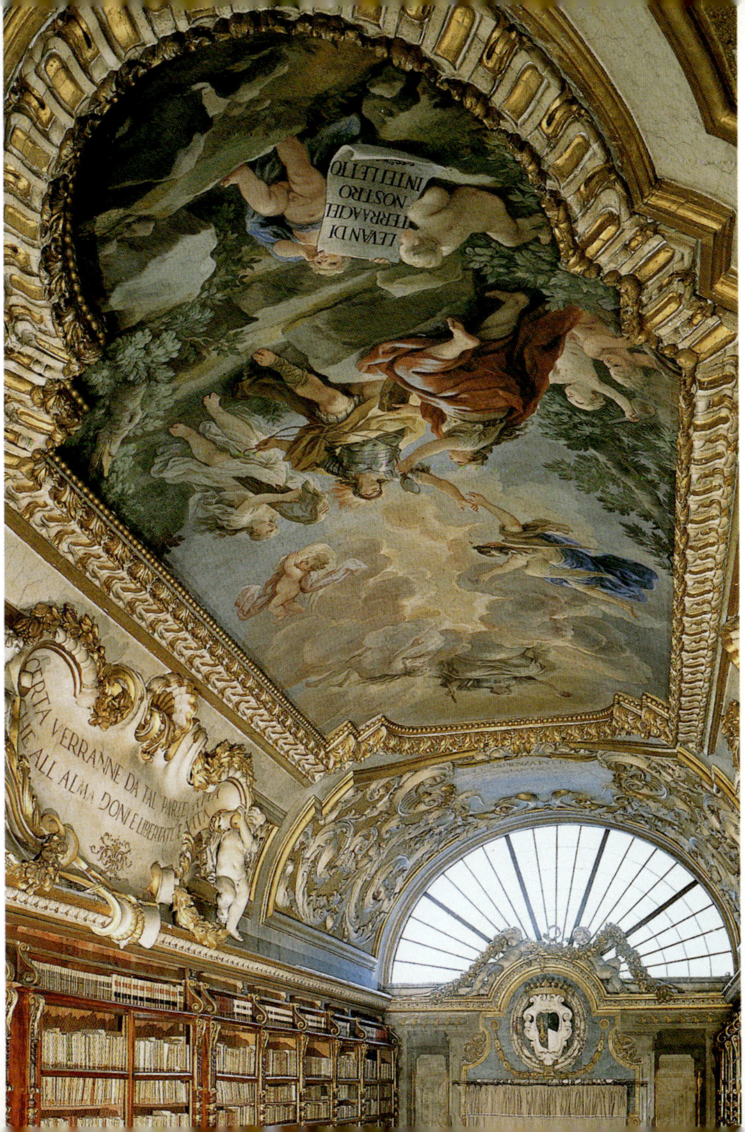

LEVAN DI TERRA CHE NOSTRO INTELLETTO
CERTA VERRANNE DA TAL PARTE AITA
CHE ALL ALMA DONI E LIBERTATE E VITA

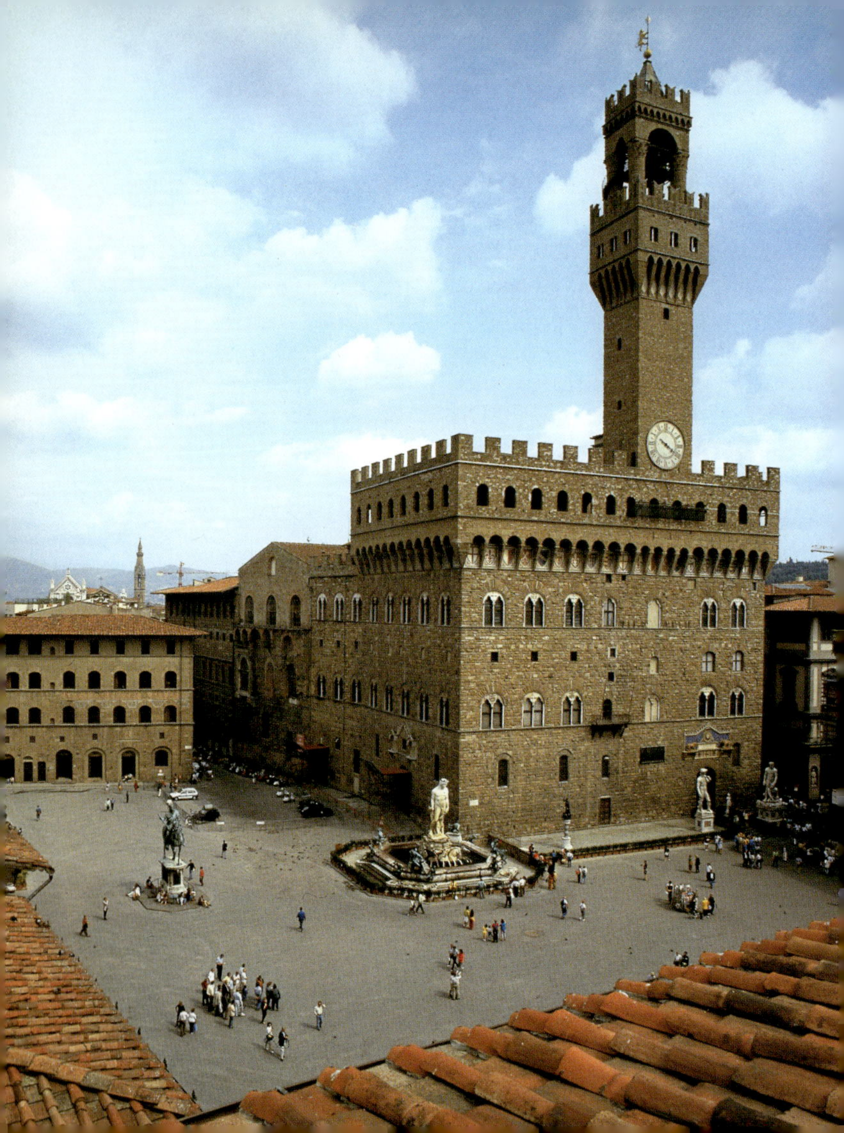

Piazza della Signoria

The Piazza, the Statues, the Loggia, the Palaces

For centuries the heart of Florence's civil and political life, today a meeting place and pedestrian zone closed to traffic, Piazza della Signoria has a long and fascinating history; under its present-day paving archaeologists have found the remains of the ancient Roman *Florentia*, which also had its ideal center in today's Piazza della Repubblica (where the Forum once stood, and where the Old Market was later to exist). Connected to the religious center of the city, that is, to the Duomo and the Baptistery, through Via Calzaiuoli (from the name of the shops that sold woollen stockings), the square grew up in the late 13th century around Palagio dei Priori (later called Palazzo Vecchio). At first included in the Sestiere of San Pier Scheraggio (from the name of the church partially demolished in the 16th century to make room for the Uffizi), the area was encapsulated in the Santa Croce quarter around 1343. The square is distinguished by the asymmetric position of the great palace which, according to the chronical writers, was built on the western edge to avoid the cursed land on which the houses of the Ghibellines had been torn down by the Guelphs. In addition to Palazzo Vecchio, the

Opposite page:
Piazza della Signoria seen from the rooftops: on the left, in the background, the façade of Palazzo di Mercatanzia, on the corner of Via dei Gondi, whose downward slope indicates the presence of the tiered seats in the Roman theater. Standing before the corner of Palazzo Vecchio, the fountain of Neptune, known as the "Biancone".

Loggia dei Priori (later called Loggia dei Lanzi), the Tribunale di Mercatanzia, the square was adorned in the 15th and 16th centuries with symbols of republican virtue (Donatello's *Marzocco*, Michelangelo's *David*) and in grand-ducal times with the statues alluding to Medicean power. And it was here, in the early 15th century, that Brunelleschi chose to carry out one of his two famous experiments in perspective (the other of which involved the Duomo and the Baptistery).

HISTORY

The Piazza Signoria area has been inhabited since the remote past, and excavations carried out in the 20th century bear witness to the continuous presence of mankind since proto-historic times. At various depths, the remains of constructions from different epochs (thermal baths, wells, tombs, towers) have been found. Near the southeast corner of the most ancient circle of walls was the Roman theater, which exploited the natural slope of today's Via dei Gondi. As previously mentioned, the square took shape around Palazzo dei Priori on the place where the ancient towers of the Uberti had stood. The Loggia dei Priori (also known as Loggia dell'Orcagna), positioned transverse to the palace, on the south side of the square, was begun in the last quarter of the 14th century by Benci di Cione and Simone di

Opposite page:
Giambologna, *Equestrian monument to Cosimo I*, detail of the bronze horse, c. 1598. Piazza Signoria.

Following pages:
Piazza Signoria, with the paving made of terracotta tiles bordered in blue, detail of the *Festa degli omaggi*, early 16th century. Uffizi.

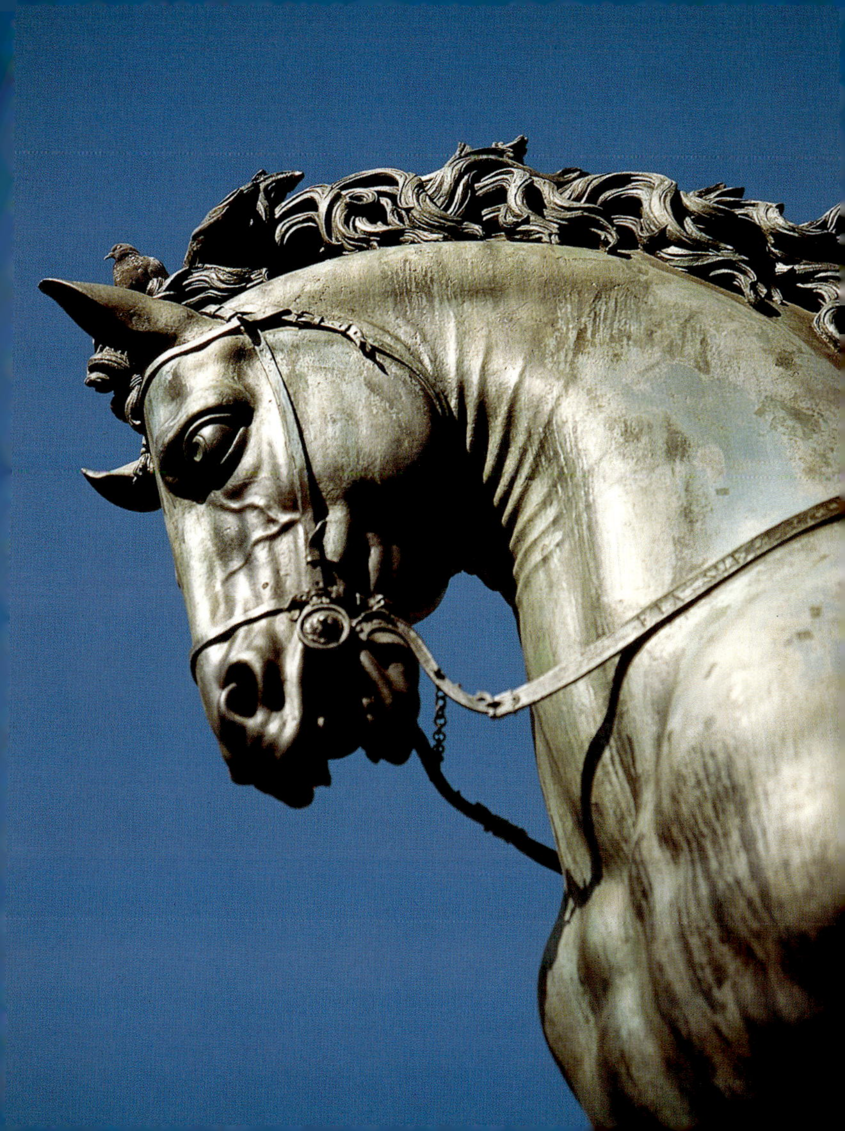

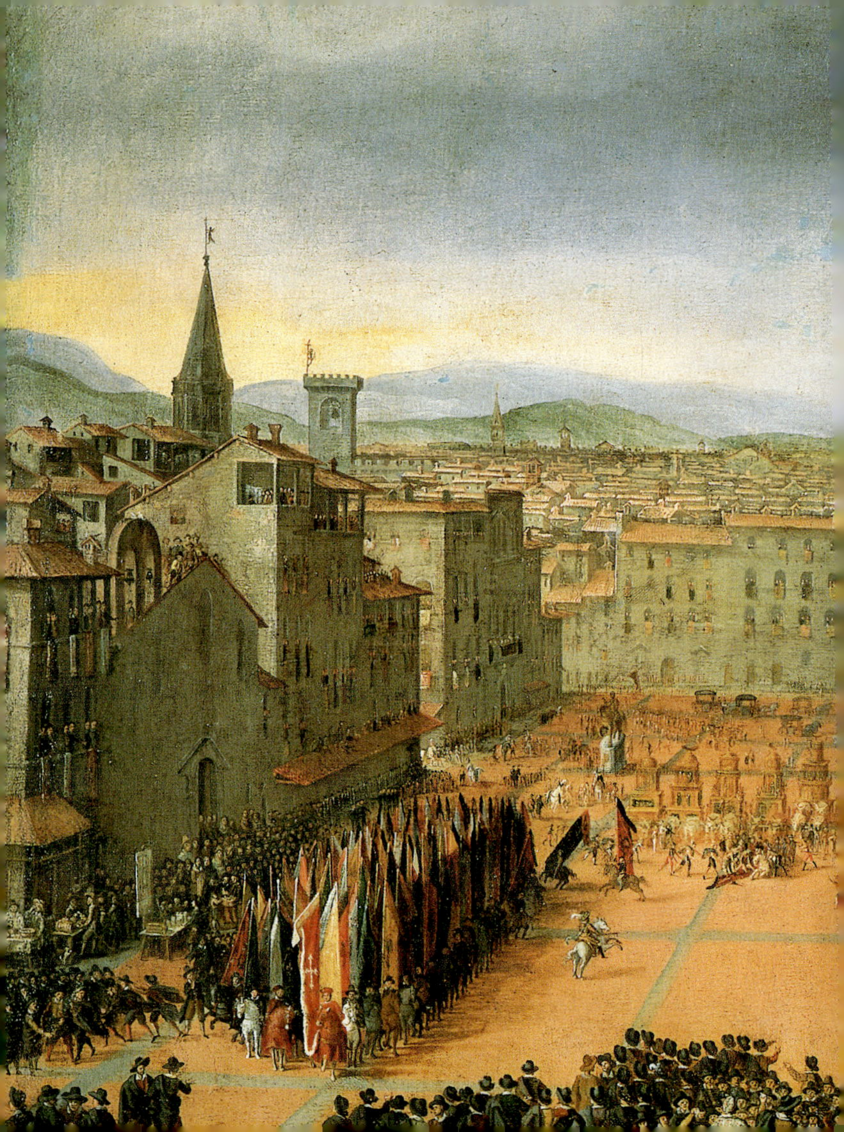

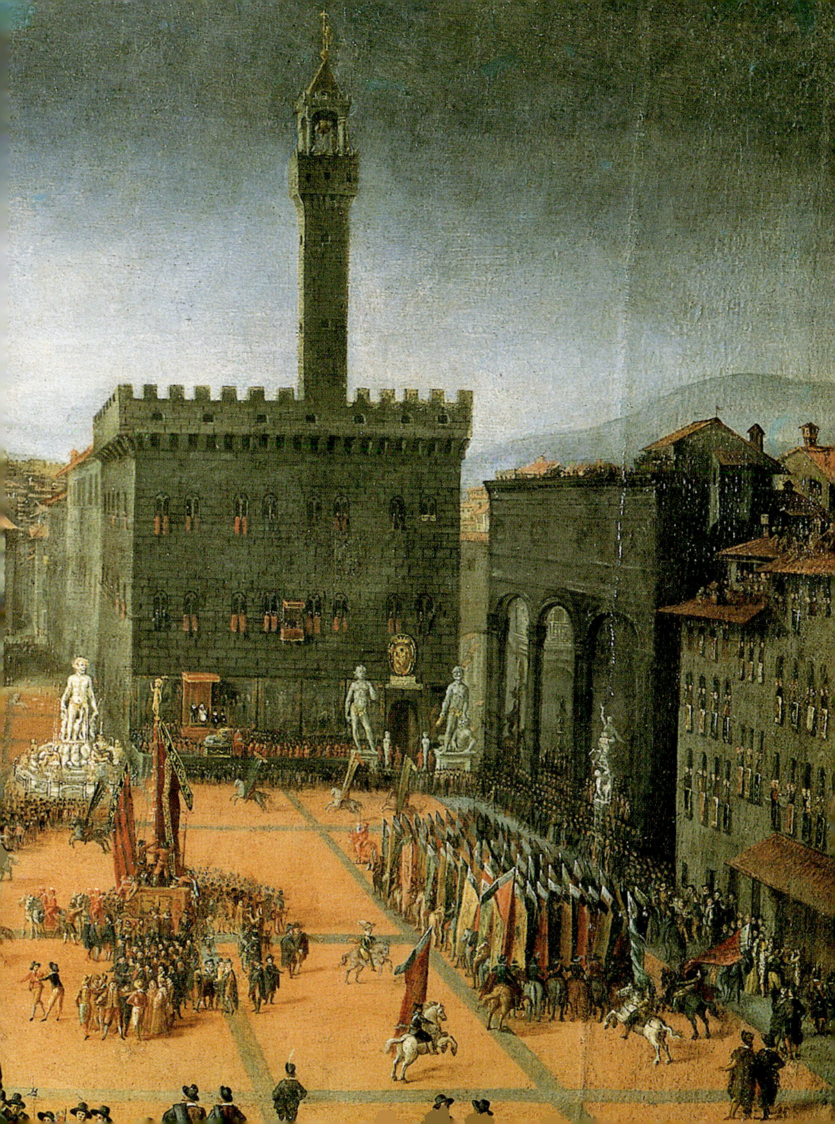

Francesco Talenti, probably to the design of Orcagna. It was here that the public ceremonies of the Signoria were held, and here that in the 16th century Cosimo I stationed a guard of Lanzichenecchi, the derivation of the name Loggia dei Lanzi. Around 1585 the loggia was connected to the Uffizi by a hanging garden. Also dating from the 14th century is the original structure of the Palazzo di Mercatanzia, on the east side of the square, on whose facade can be seen, although worn, the stone coats-of-arms of all of the Guilds. On the north side stood the church, later demolished, of San Romolo, and on the same side was later built Palazzo Uguccioni, sometimes attributed to Raphael.
The history of the piazza is also linked to famous sculptural groups. In addition to the statues by Donatello and Michelangelo that stood in front of Palazzo Vecchio (the *David* was later moved to the Galleria dell'Accademia), we may recall primarily the marble group of *Hercules and Cacus* (1525-1534) by Baccio Bandinelli, which had first been commissioned by Pier Soderini to serve as companion piece to Michelangelo's *David* and was then sculpted at a later time, to be met with some derision and biting criticism. By the end of the 16th century this area had become a Medicean emblem par excellence: on the edge of the square, near where Via delle Farine enters it, stands the *Equestrian Monument to Cosimo I* by Giambologna (c. 1598),

Opposite page:
Giambologna,
Equestrian Monument to Cosimo I,
c. 1598, bronze.
Piazza della Signoria.

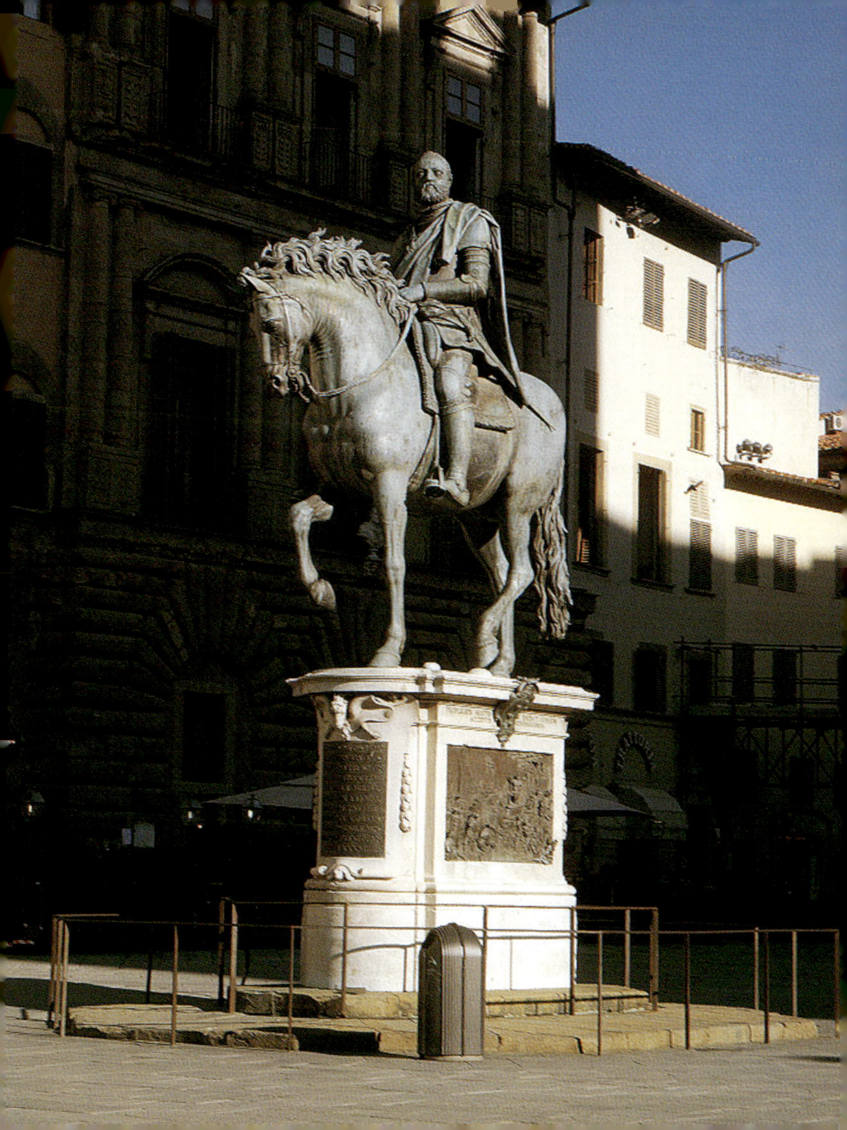

inspired by the model of *Marcus Aurelius* (the base, illustrating episodes from Cosimo's political career, was finished by his assistants). The *Fountain of Neptune* (the *Biancone,* c. 1565, dearly beloved by the Florentines but also frequently damaged by vandalism), suggests with its multiform marine figures the naval interests of Cosimo I, who had incremented the Port of Livorno. Under the Loggia dei Lanzi, the famous *Perseus* (1545-1554) by Benvenuto Cellini was commissioned by Cosimo I in 1545. The process of casting the bronze statue (over three meters high) was so difficult that the artist is said to have sacrificed the family tableware, throwing it into the molten metal to make it flow more freely.
The dynamic *Rape of a Sabine Woman* (1583) by Giambologna is the first marble group with several figures in European sculture designed to be seen from any viewing point.
Over the centuries, Piazza della Signoria has been the theater of historic events of exceptional importance, as exemplified by two episodes: on 26 July 1343, Saint Anne's Day, the revolt against the Duke of Athens Gualtieri di Brienne and his expulsion from Palazzo Vecchio (an event still today recalled with a ceremony held in Orsanmichele every July 26), and the agony of Girolamo Savonarola, who was burned at the stake here in 1498, after the downfall of his short-lived republic.

Opposite page:
Bartolomeo Ammannati,
Fountain of Neptune,
c. 1565,
marble and bronze.
Piazza della Signoria.

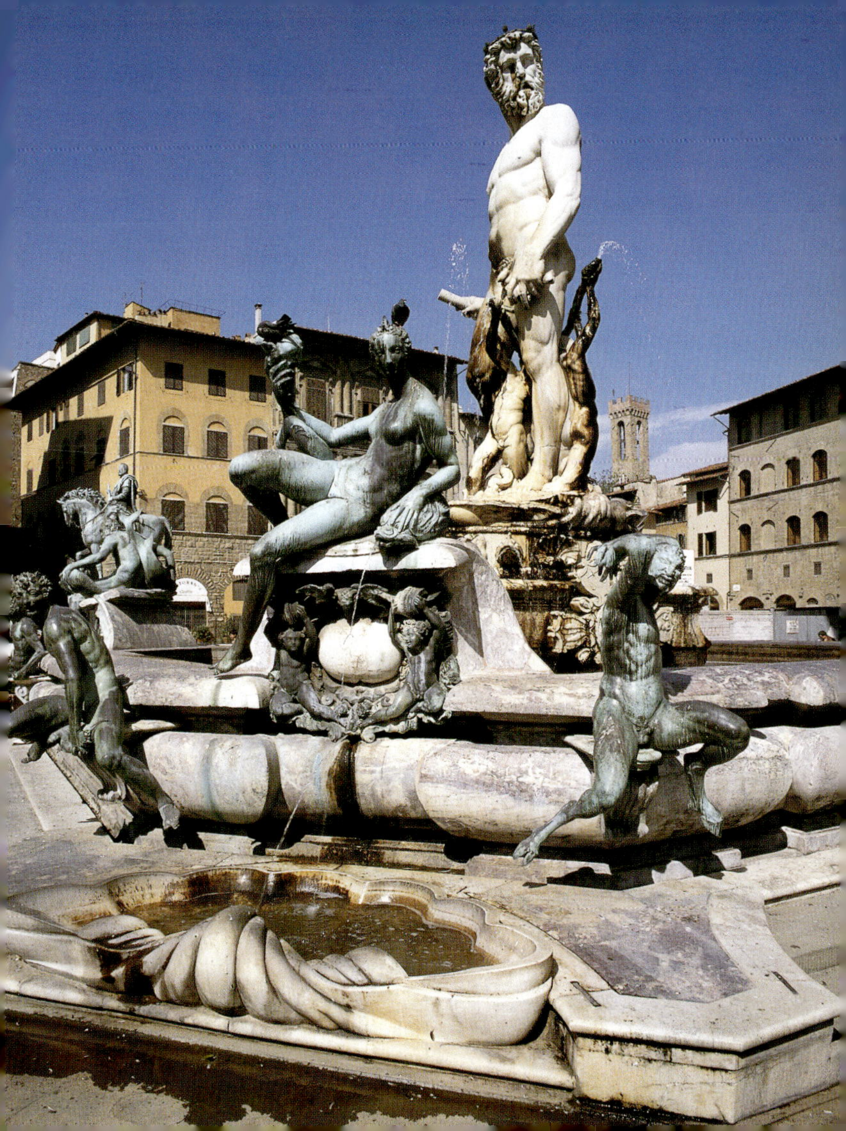

Below:
Carpenters' shops in Piazza Signoria, detail from the *Approval of the Rule of St. Francis*, 1483, from Ghirlandaio's cycle of frescoes in the Sassetti Chapel in Santa Trinita.

Opposite page:
Baccio Bandinelli, *Hercules and Cacus*, 1525-1534, marble. Piazza Signoria.

Following pages:
Bernardino Gaffurri and Jacques Bylivelt, *Veduta di piazza Signoria*, c. 1599, gold and semiprecious stones. Florence, Palazzo Pitti, Museo degli Argenti.

The precious oval inlaid in semiprecious stones shows Piazza Signoria viewed from the side, with the colossal bronze and marble statues symbols of Medici prestige appearing aligned (the *Equestrian Monument to Cosimo I* by Giambologna, the *Fountain of Neptune* by Bartolomeo Ammannati, the *Marzocco* by Donatello, the *David* by Michelangelo, the *Hercules and Cacus* by Baccio Bandinelli) in continuity with the perspective view of Palazzo Vecchio and the Uffizi further off. In the background appears the Loggia dei Lanzi, with the *Perseus* by Benvenuto Cellini and the *Rape of a Sabine Woman* by Giambologna.

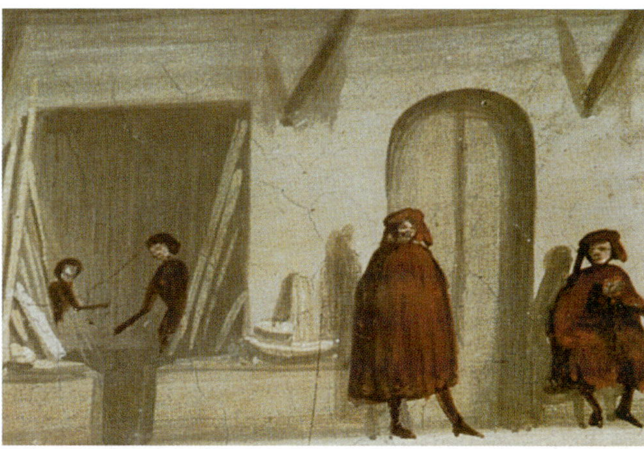

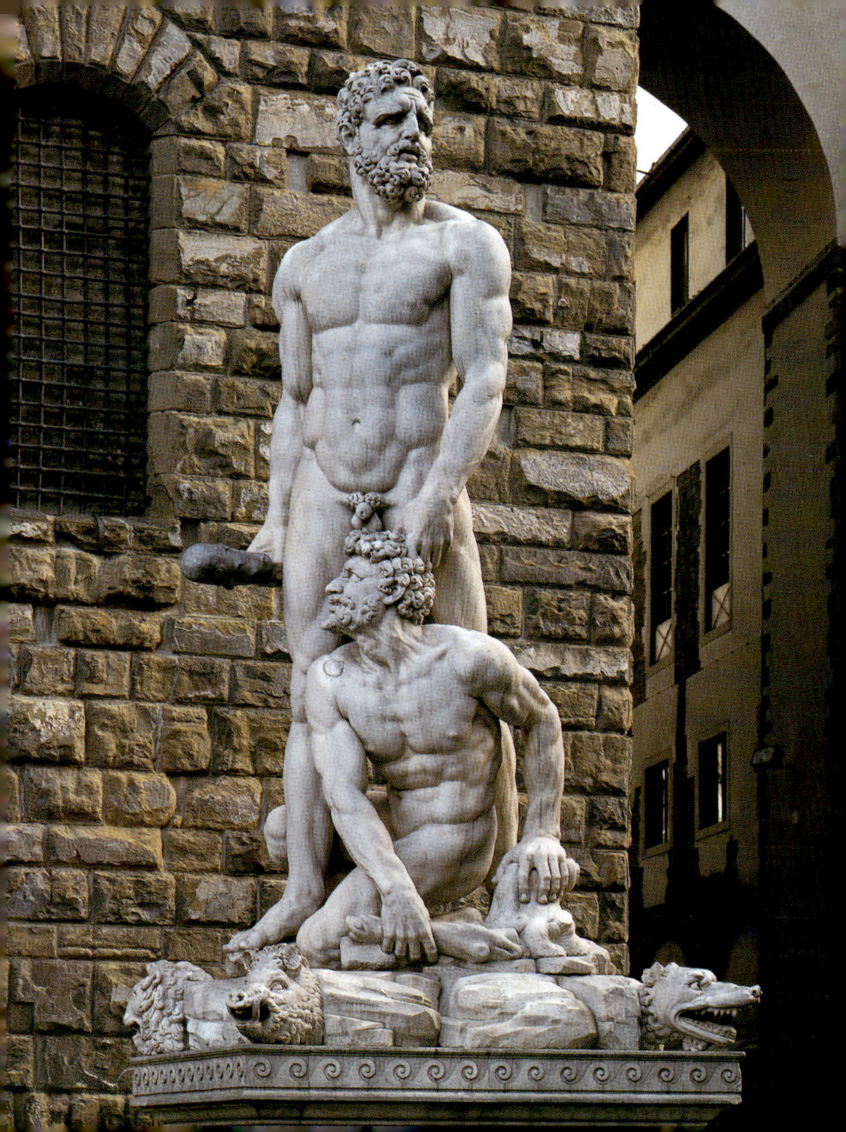

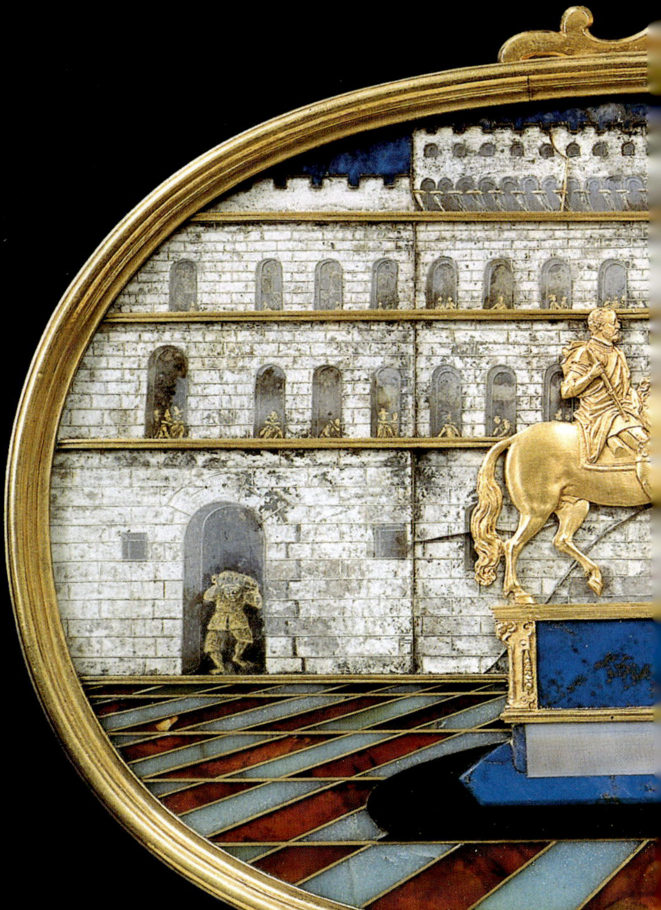

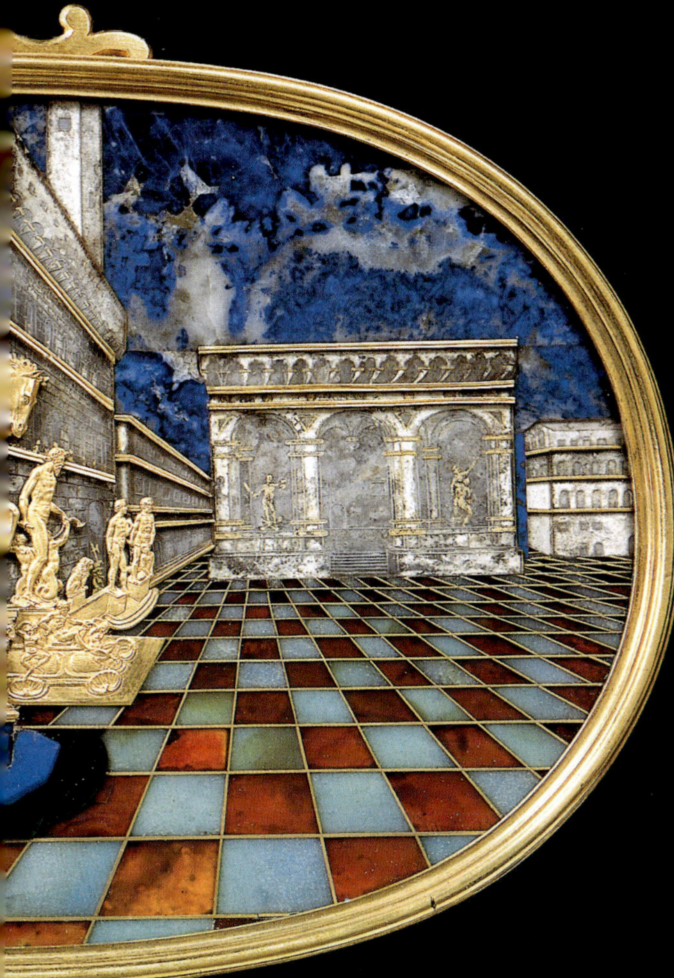

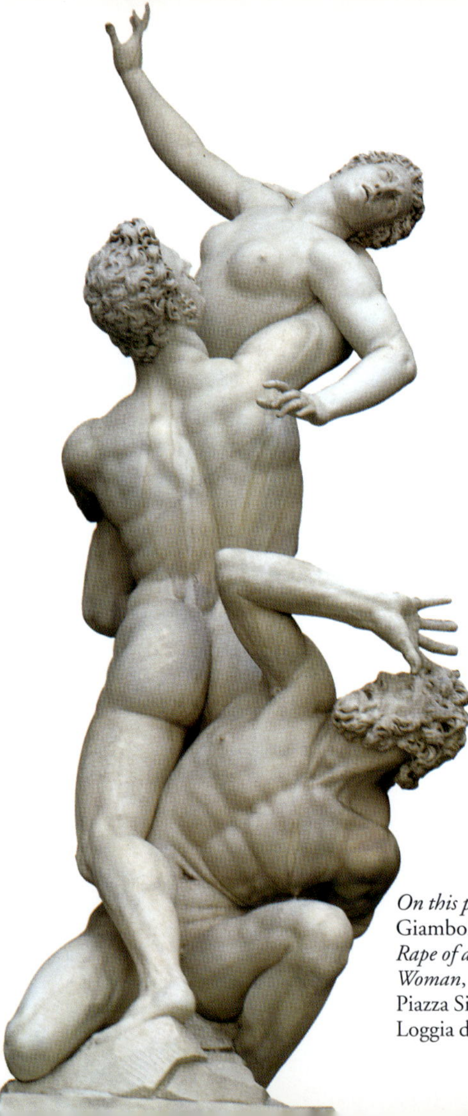

On this page:
Giambologna,
Rape of a Sabine Woman, 1583, marble.
Piazza Signoria,
Loggia dei Lanzi.

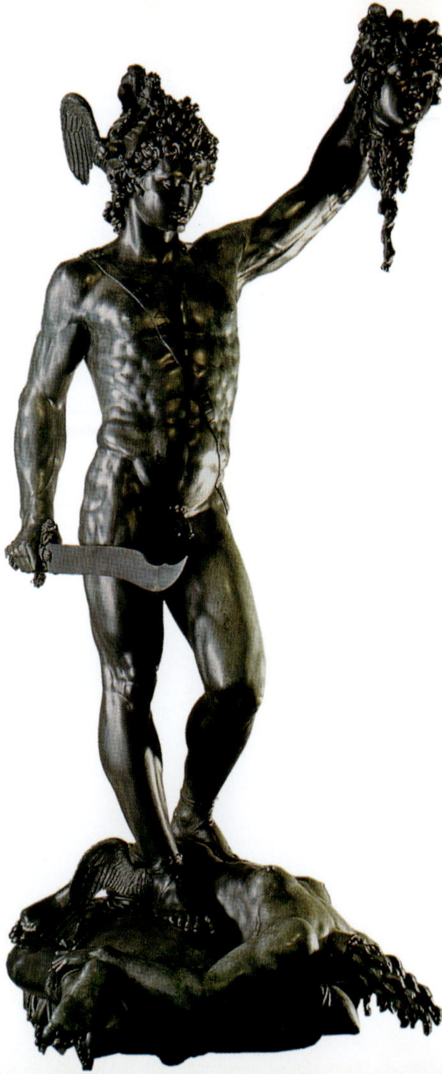

On this page:
Benvenuto Cellini,
Perseus, 1545-1554,
bronze.
Piazza Signoria,
Loggia dei Lanzi.

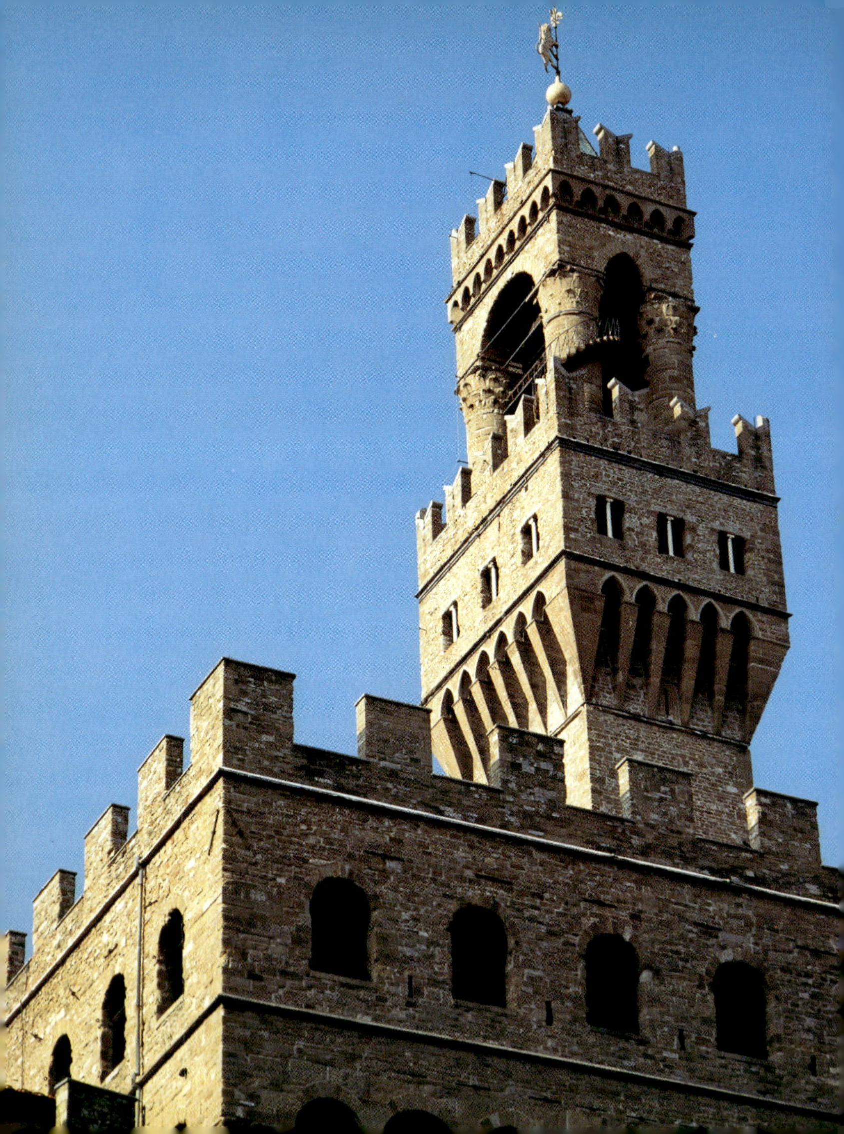

Palazzo Vecchio

Palazzo dei Priori (or "del Popolo", later called Palazzo Vecchio, the Old Palace, to distinguish it from the new grand-ducal residence, Palazzo Pitti) is the most important monument in Piazza della Signoria. Its origins are linked to the time of peace that prevailed after 1250 subsequent to the bitter struggles between Guelphs and Ghibellines, from which the Guelphs had emerged victorious. After years of conflict, the city had at last reached a state of relative calm and flourishing activity, and in 1282 the "Arti", or Guilds, had prevailed upon the Ordinamenti di Giustizia to accept their own representatives, the Priors, who took their places alongside the Podestà and the Capitano di Parte Guelfa. In 1285 it was thus decided to build Palazzo dei Priori, "for the Comune and the people of Florence", that is, to house the Gonfalonier of Justice and the Priors ("the Signoria") who, in a two-months' term of office, governed public affairs with the obligation to live in seclusion. The building project, begun in 1299 by Arnolfo di Cambio, was completed within a few year's time: a palace-fortress, built of *pietra forte*, with a jutting crenallated gallery, gutters from which boiling oil could be poured as in a castle, and a tower 97 meters high, like the structure of the palace, which rested on the foundations of the Foraboschi fam-

Opposite page:
A view of Palazzo Vecchio, with its top floor crenellated like a castle, and its tower.

ily's ancient towers. In 1323 the "aringhiera" (orator's platform) was built (removed in the 19th century): three tiers of steps running along the facade and to the north, as a place for the Signoria to gather during ceremonies, clearly visible in frescoes from the time. During the brief reign of the Duke of Athens Gualtieri di Brienne (1342), the palace was probably enlarged along Via della Ninna and on the north side. Large-scale modifications, especially in the inner courtyard, were to be made later by Michelozzo, starting in 1453, and then by Vasari. In the early years of the 16th century the Gonfalonier Pier Soderini and his family came to live in halls already completed by Benedetto and Giuliano da Maiano, the Audience Chamber, the Hall of Lilies, and on the floor below the Hall of the Two Hundred. Dating from those years is the competition for the frescoes in the High Council Hall. Leonardo da Vinci participated with cartoons for the *Battle of Anghiari*, Michelangelo with those for the *Battle of Cascina*. In 1543 the palace became the residence of Cosimo I (who with his wife Eleonora di Toledo left the palace in Via Larga), and was subjected to a vast program of remodeling and decoration of the interiors conducted by Battista del Tasso and later by Giorgio Vasari. These initiatives included the decoration of the monumental Hall of the Five Hundred, destined to the councillors elected by the people (designed by Cronaca, 1496) and of the more secluded chapel of Eleonora di Toledo, frescoed by Bronzino, in the so-called Quartiere di Eleonora. In a little

Opposite page:
The "aringhiera" before the façade of Palazzo Vecchio, detail from Ghirlandaio frescoes representing *The Approval of the Rule of St. Frances by Pope Honorius III*, c. 1483. Santa Trinita, Sassetti Chapel.

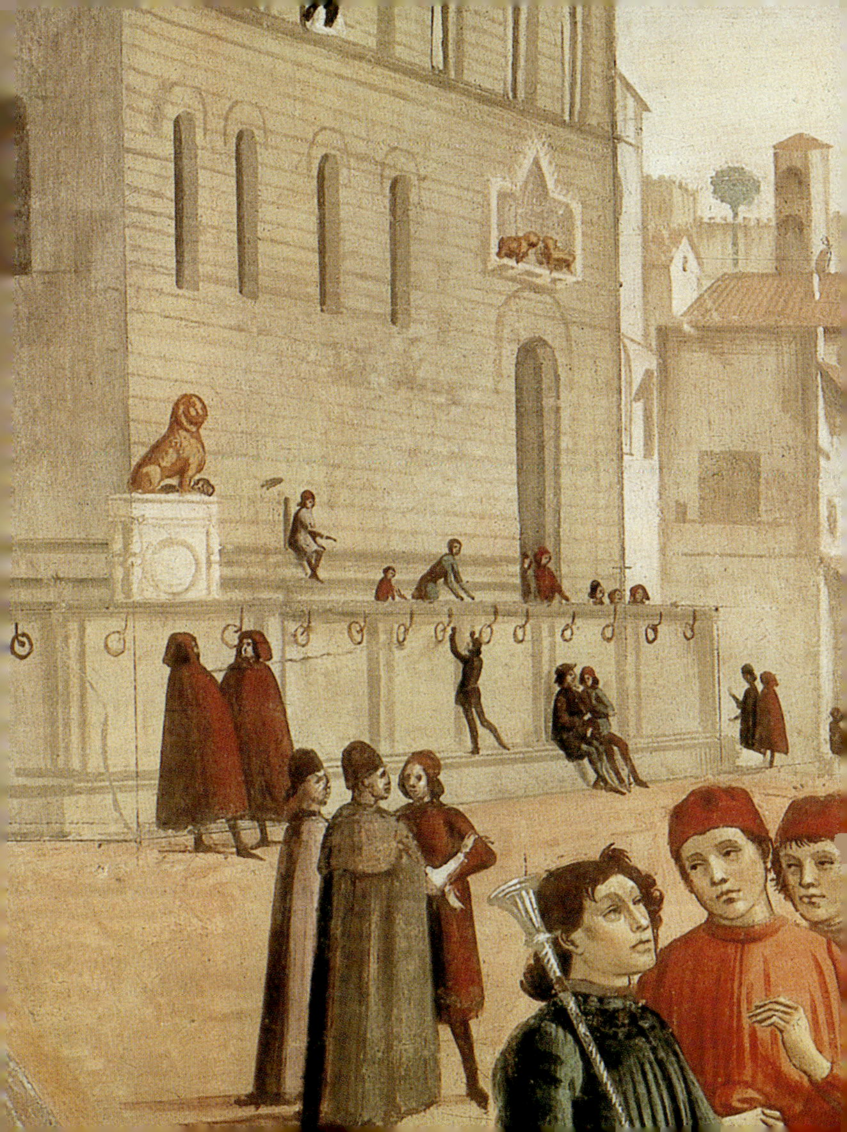

room adjacent to the Hall of the Five Hundred, Francesco I, having succeeded his father even before the death of the latter, had the Studiolo decorated in 1570. Receiving no light from outside, adorned with little sculptures and lined with Mannerist panels alluding to Francesco's multifarious scientific and alchemistic interests, the Studiolo was a compendium of everything in nature that appeared strange, monstrous and uncommon. Rare metals, substances used in alchemy, quartzes, crystals, pearls are all depicted on its walls and ceiling, according to a complex allusive program dictated by the erudite Don Vincenzo Borghini. After 1555 the palace was called "Vecchio" (old) to distinguish it from the "new" one in Oltrarno, which had previously belonged to Luca Pitti and was purchased in 1549 by Eleonora di Toledo as the new residence for the grand-ducal family. Palazzo Vecchio is still today the seat of the municipal administration, with various offices, and is as a whole considered a museum complex, the following parts of which are open to visitors: Michelozzo's courtyard, the Sala d'Arme on the ground floor (where exhibitions are held), and various sections of the upper floors, among them the Hall of Lilies, the Audience Chamber, the Hall of the Five Hundred with the Studiolo di Francesco I, the apartment of Eleonora and that of the Elements.

Opposite page:
Florentine Master, *The Expulsion of the Duke of Athens (St. Anne offers armed gonfaloniers to recapture Palazzo Vecchio)*, c. 1343, fresco detached from the Stinche prison. Palazzo Vecchio. Against the background of the palace in which he had taken residence, the duke is shown here fleeing from the throne, holding an animal with the head of a man, a sign of trickery; on the ground lie the broken attributes of Justice; in the sky is an avenging angel, surrounded by the signs of the Zodiac.

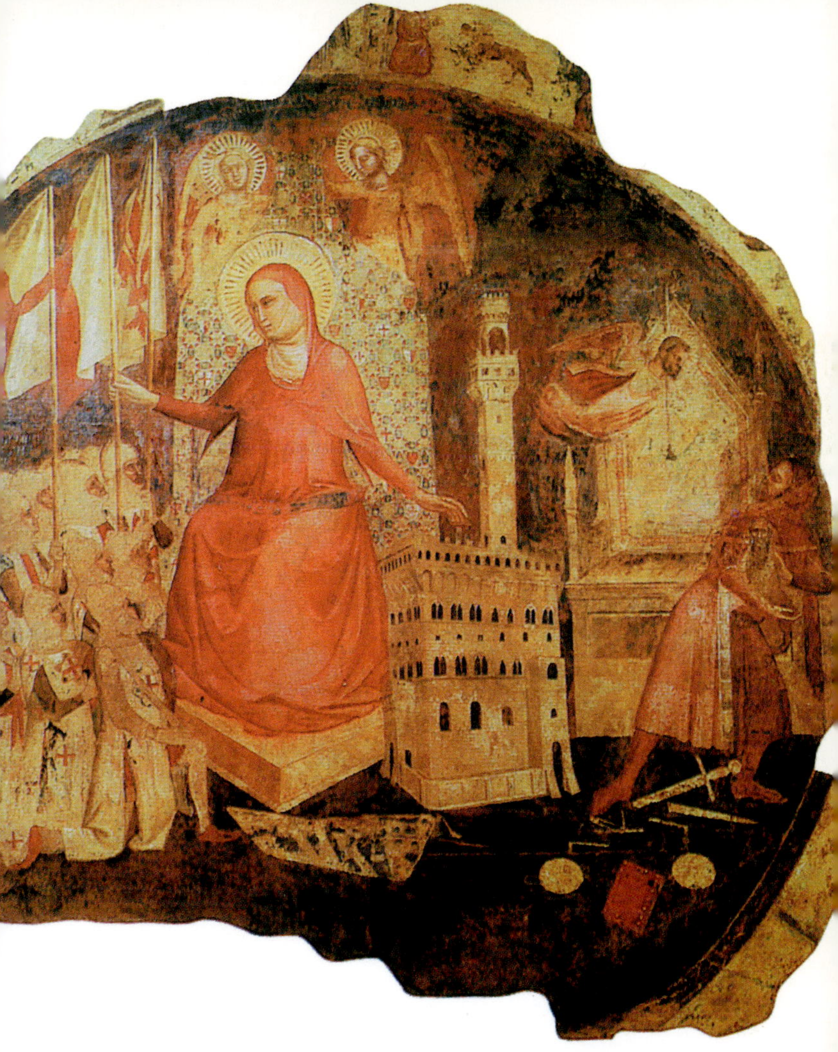

- In the Hall of the Five Hundred, the *Genius of Victory* (1532-1534), marble statue by Michelangelo, and on the walls panels with frescoes of Florentine battles (1563-1565) by Giorgio Vasari and assistants.
- the Studiolo of Francesco I, with *Pearl Fishing* by Alessandro Allori, the *Alchemist's Laboratory* by Giovanni Stradano, and other paintings by Mannerist artists such as Mirabello Cavalori, Naldini, Poppi, Maso da San Friano, Santi di Tito and Vasari.
- the Geographic Maps Room, with 53 plates depicting the known countries, begun by Egnazio Danti for Cosimo I, and finished by the monk Stefano Bonsignori for Francesco I, who for unknown reasons had excluded Danti.
- the Hall of the Two Hundred, rebuilt by Benedetto and Giuliano da Maiano (c. 1472).
- the marble portal by Benedetto da Maiano (c. 1476-1481), which opens from the Hall of Lilies into the Audience Chamber, and the marquetry of the inlaid door.

In the Apartment of Eleonora, the chapel of Eleonora, with frescoes by Agnolo Bronzino, and the chamber of Gualdrada, with frescoes depicting Florentine streets and squares.

Opposite page:
The Hall of the Five Hundred in Palazzo Vecchio.
The ceiling of the hall (1563-1597) was raised by Giorgio Vasari, who also accomplished the decorative program, aided by various assistants, on the walls and on the ceiling divided into compartments framed in wood.

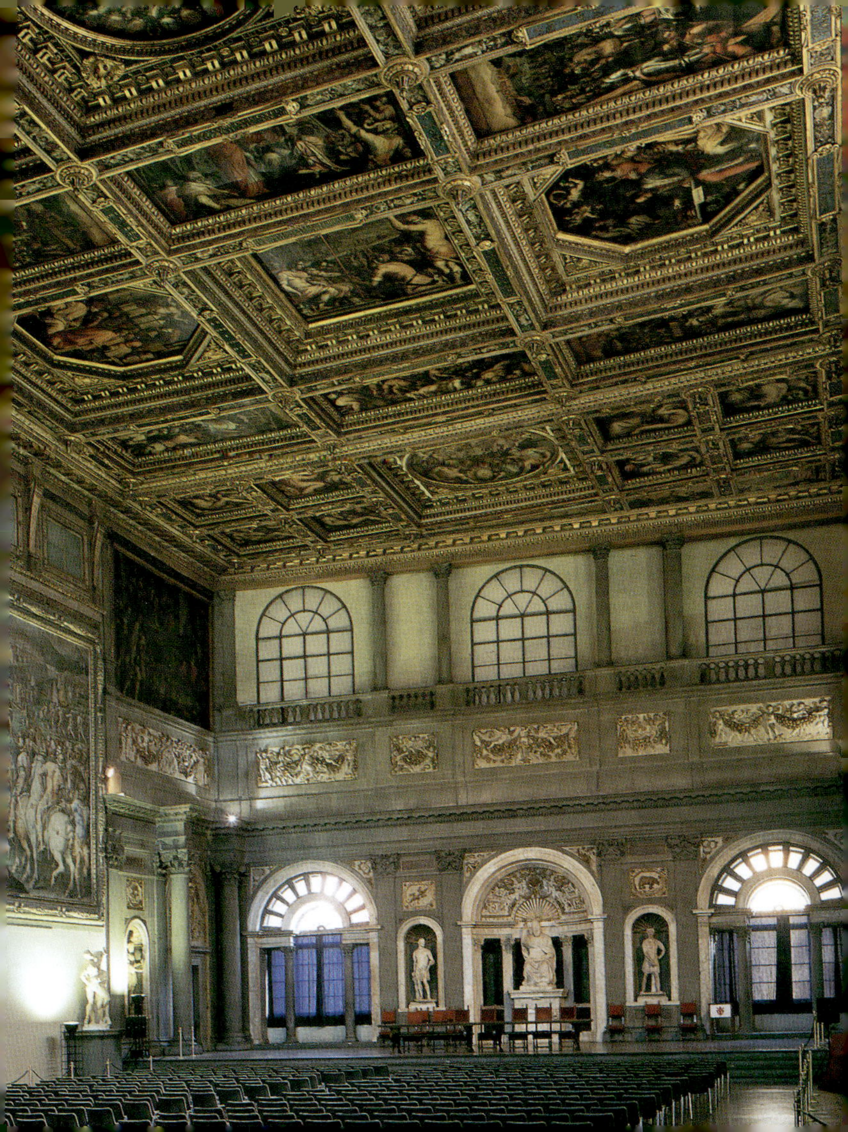

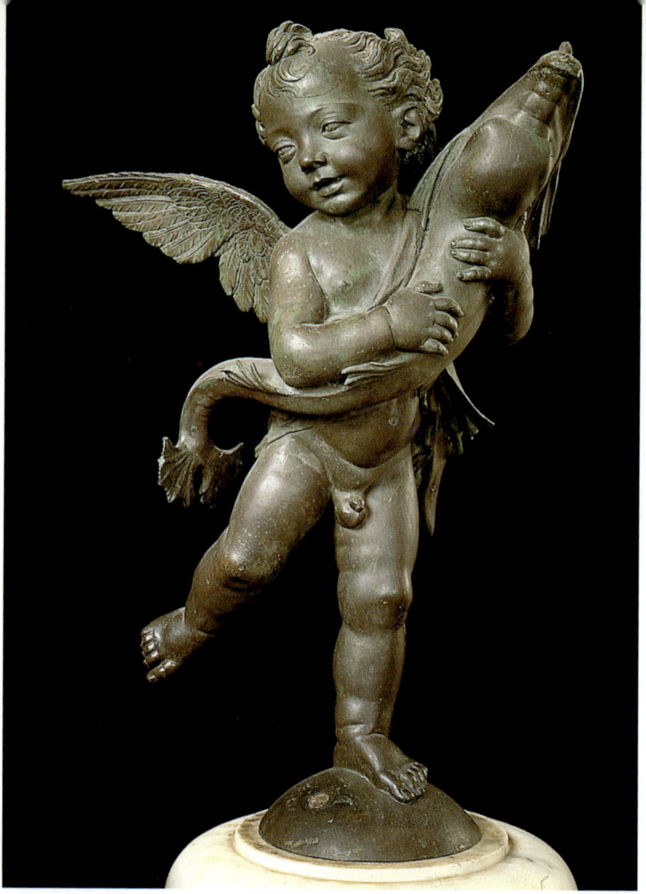

Above:
Verrocchio, *Putto with a Dolphin*, c. 1476 Palazzo Vecchio, Juno's Terrace.

Opposite page:
Michelangelo, *Genius of Victory*, 1534, marble. Palazzo Vecchio, Hall of the Five Hundred.

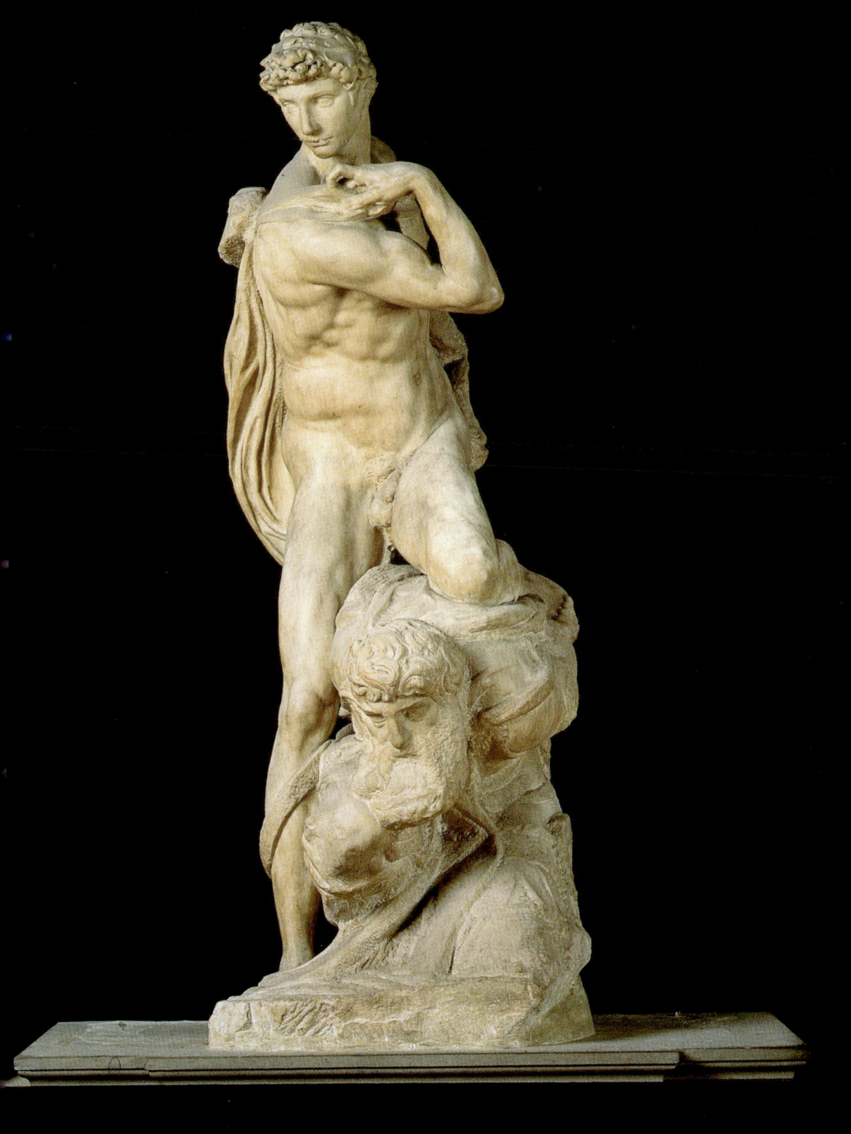

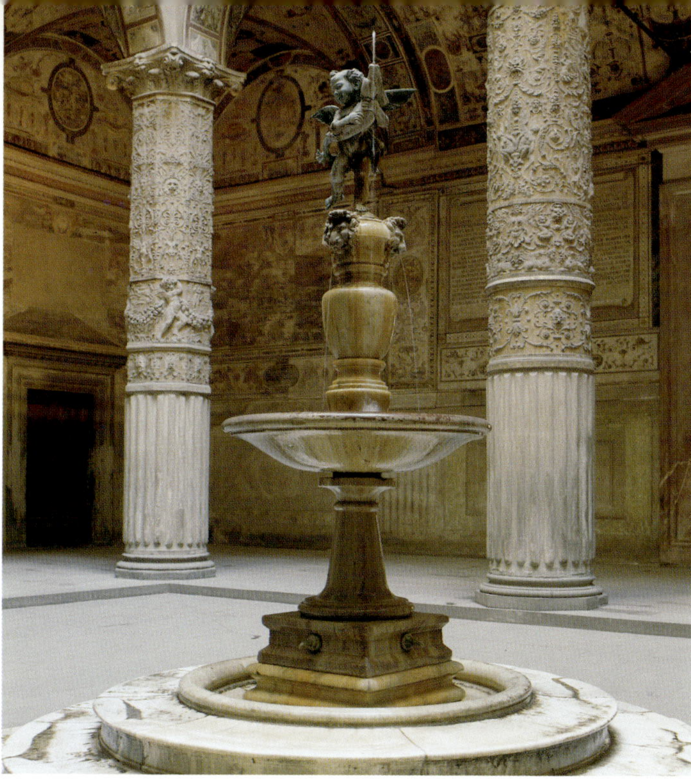

Above:
Michelozzo's courtyard
with the fountain, on the ground
floor of Palazzo Vecchio.

Opposite page:
Giuliano da Maiano and
Francesco di Giovanni, known
as Francione, *Dante and Petrarch,*
detail of the inlaid door,
1476-1480.

Following pages:
Giuliano da Maiano, Francione and
Francesco di Domenico, known
as Monciatto, *Ceiling and frieze
in the Hall of Lilies,*
1475-1478. Palazzo Vecchio.

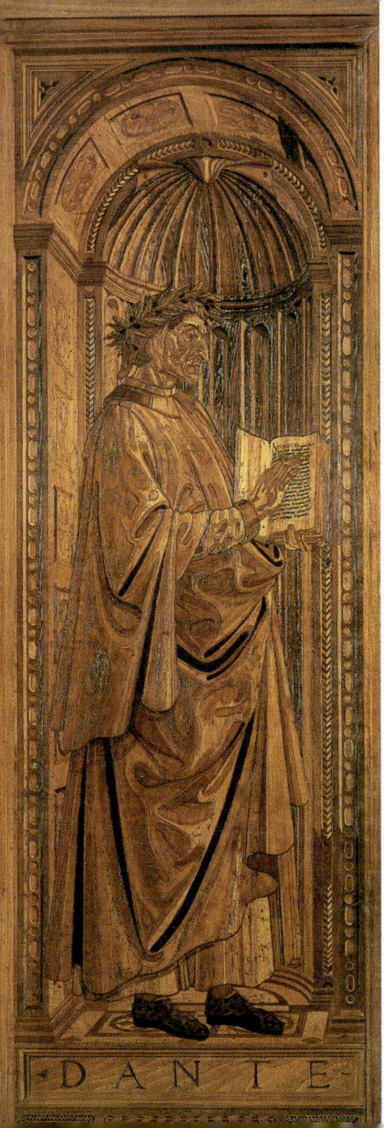
DANTE

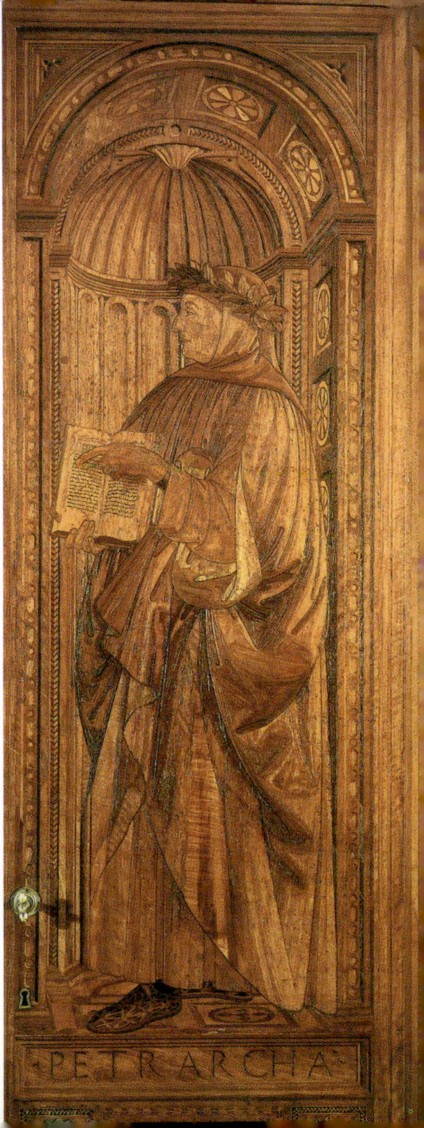
PETRARCHA

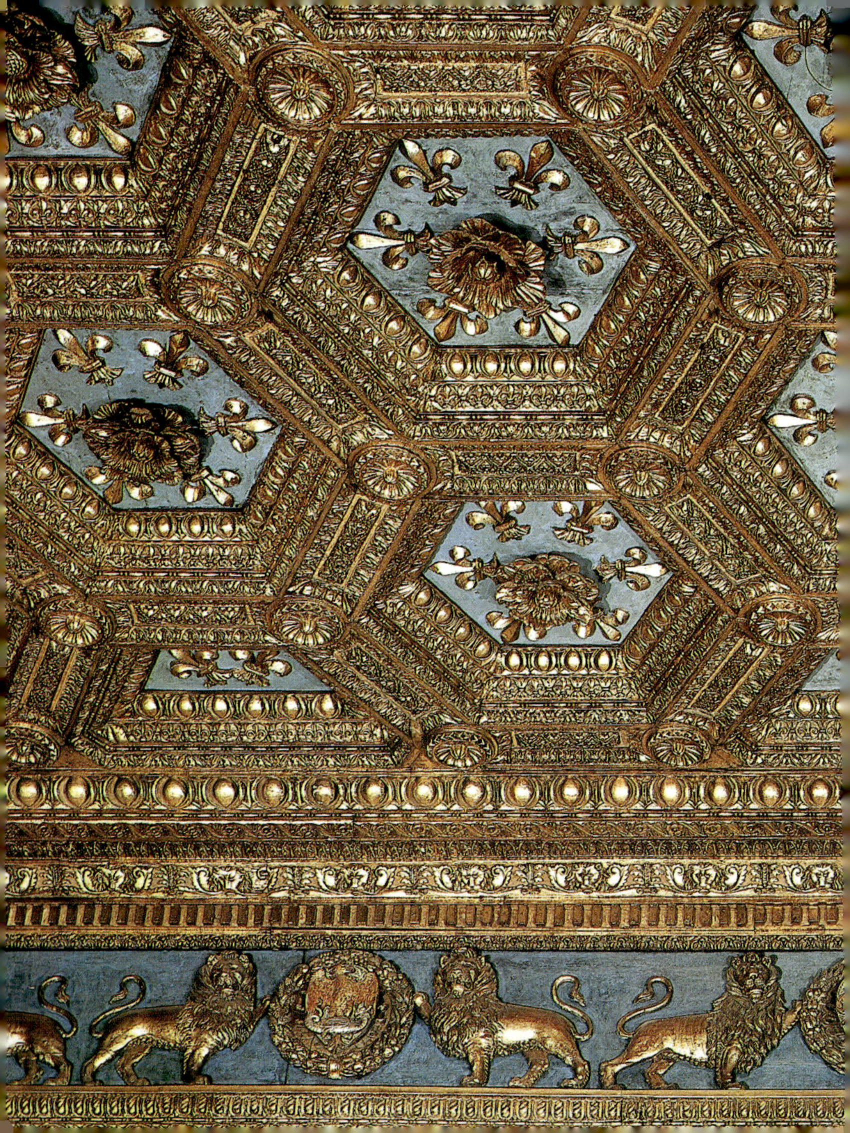

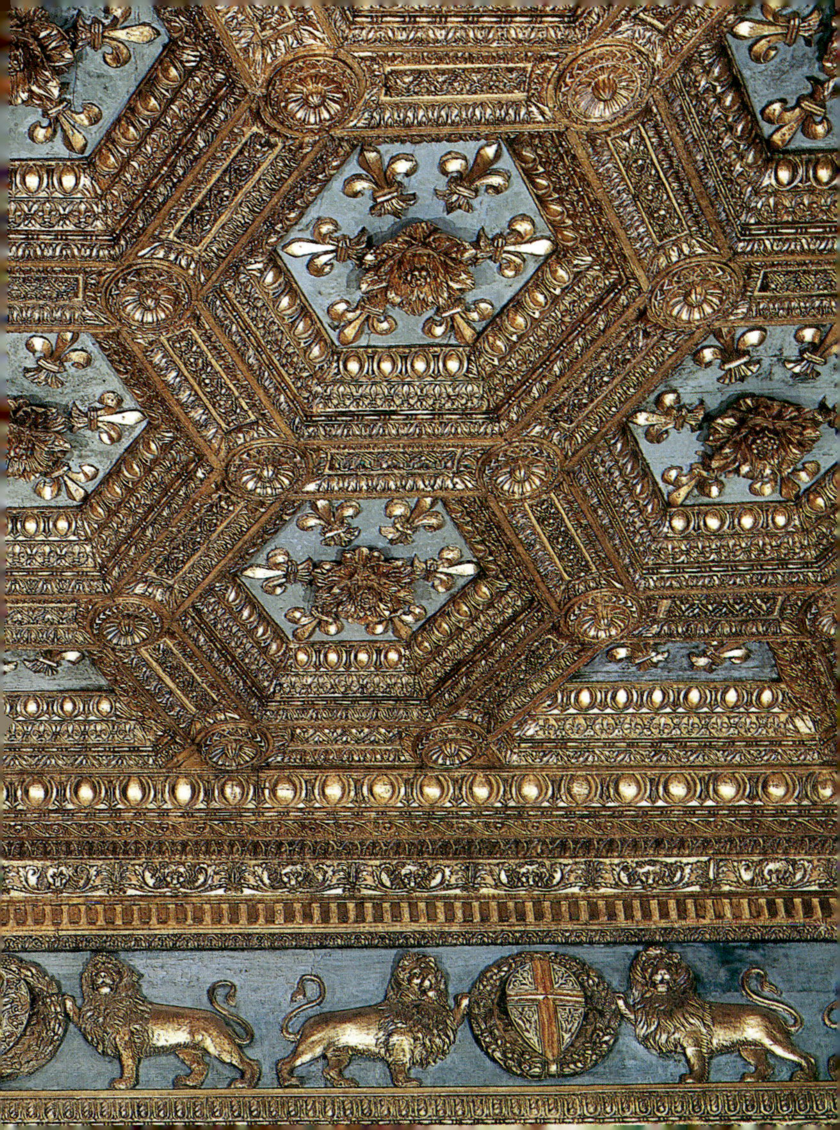

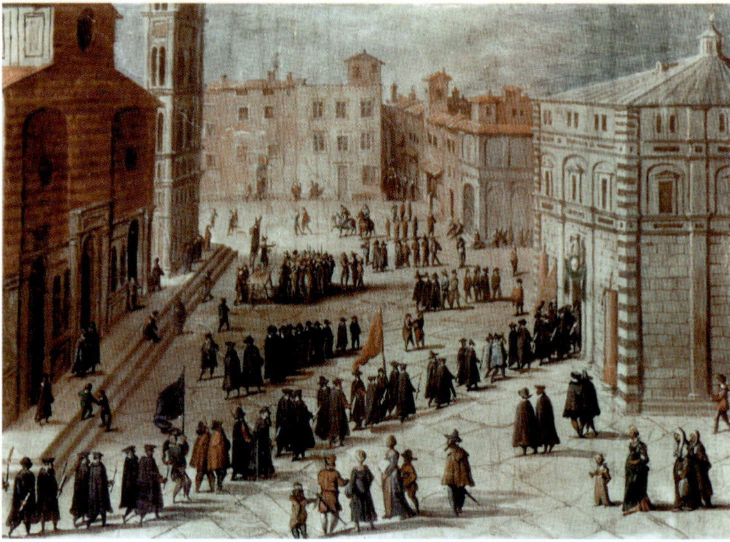

Above:
Giovanni Stradano,
The procession of Corpus Domini in Piazza San Giovanni,
c. 1562, fresco. Palazzo Vecchio,
Hall of Gualdrada.

Opposite page:
Alessandro Fei, *The Goldsmith's Shop*, 1570, painted panel.
Palazzo Vecchio,
Studiolo of Francesco I.

Following pages:
Maso da San Friano,
The Diamond Mine,
1579, painted panel.
Palazzo Vecchio,
Studiolo di Francesco I.

Giorgio Vasari, *Coral Fishing*,
detail from *Perseus and Andromeda*,
1570, painted panel.
Palazzo Vecchio,
Studiolo of Francesco I.

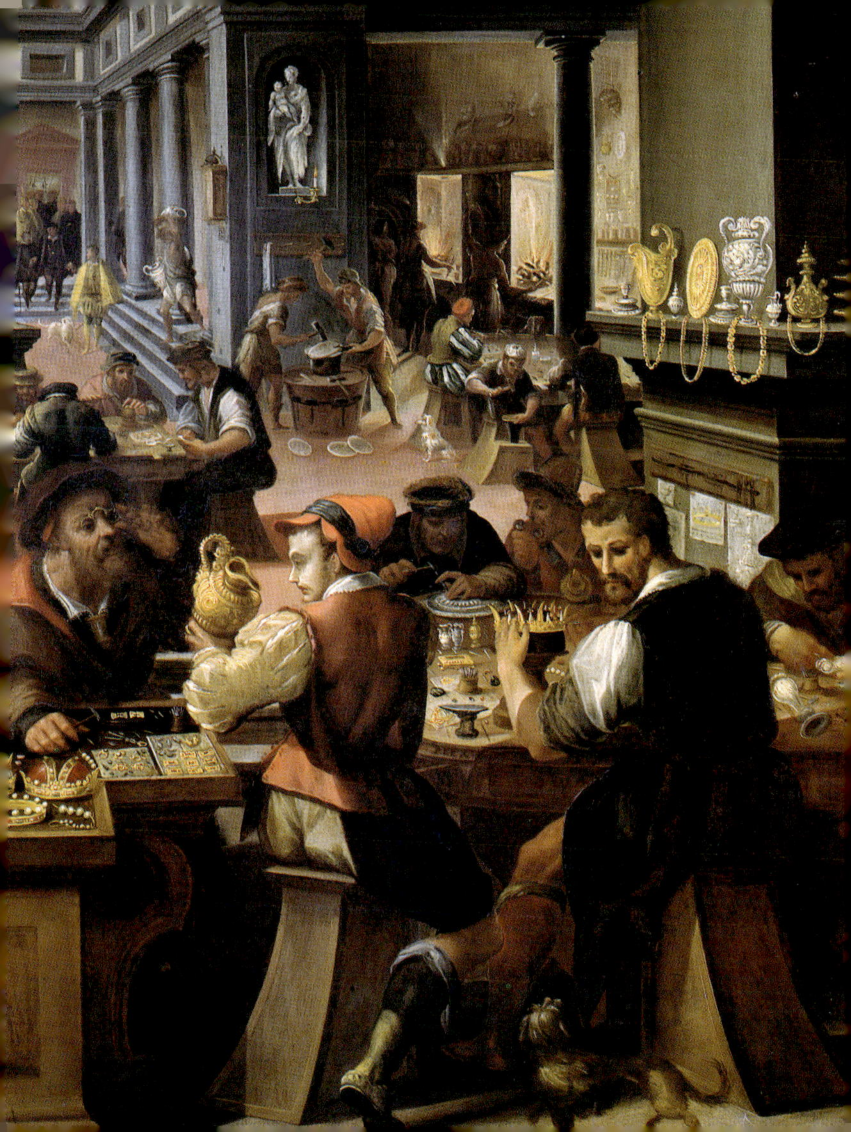

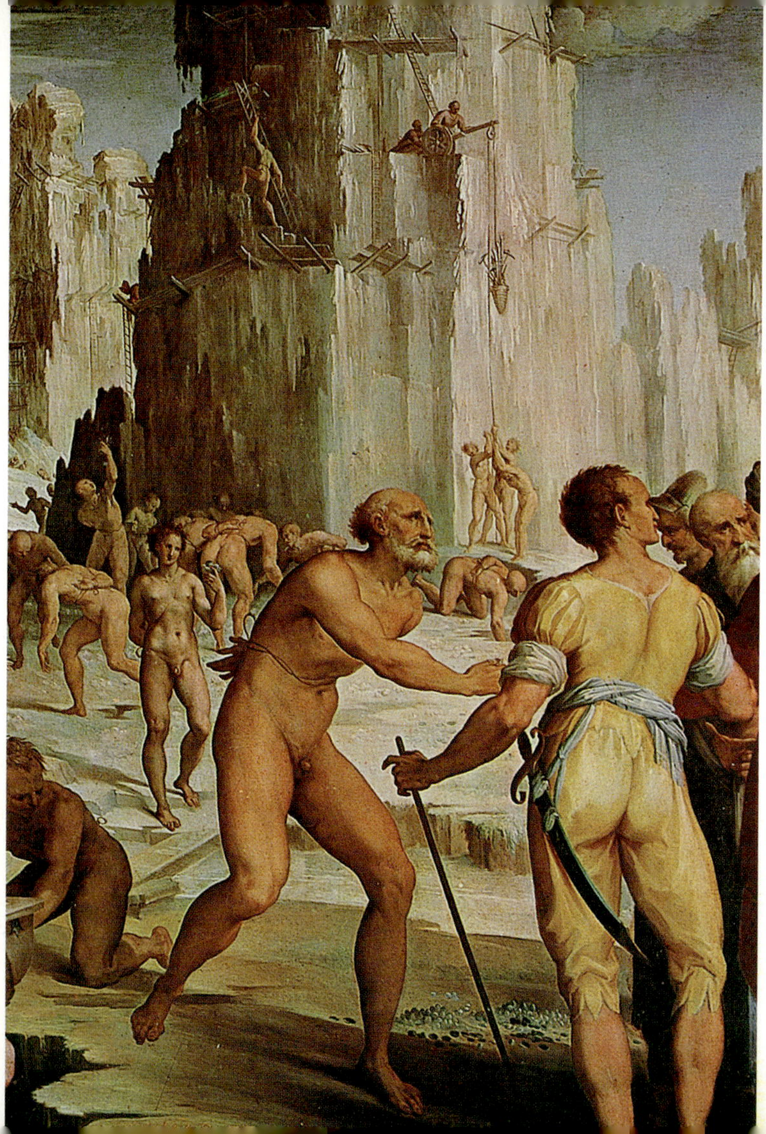

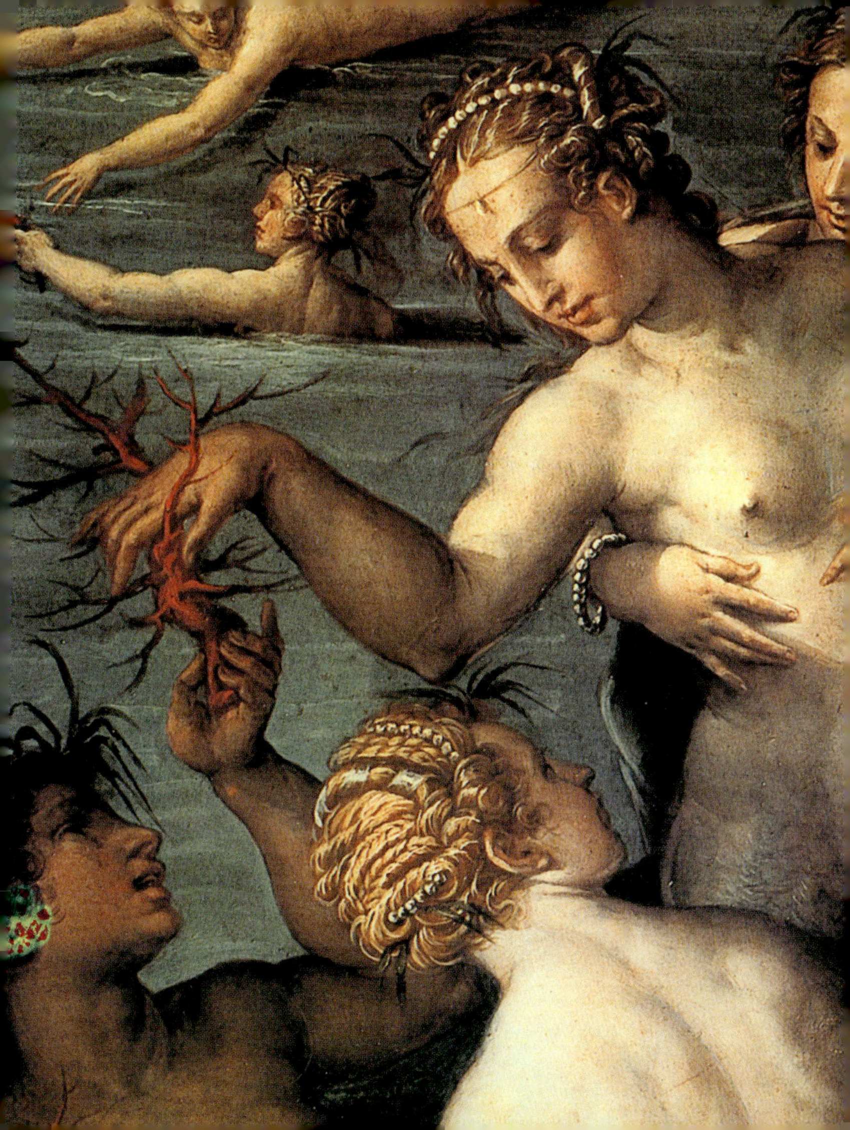

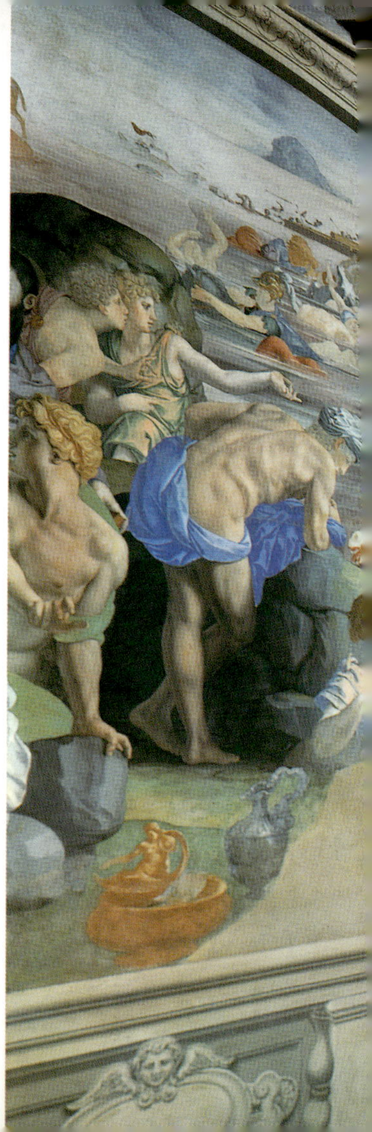

The Chapel of Eleonora
in Palazzo Vecchio, decorated
with frescoes and an altarpiece
by Agnolo Bronzino.

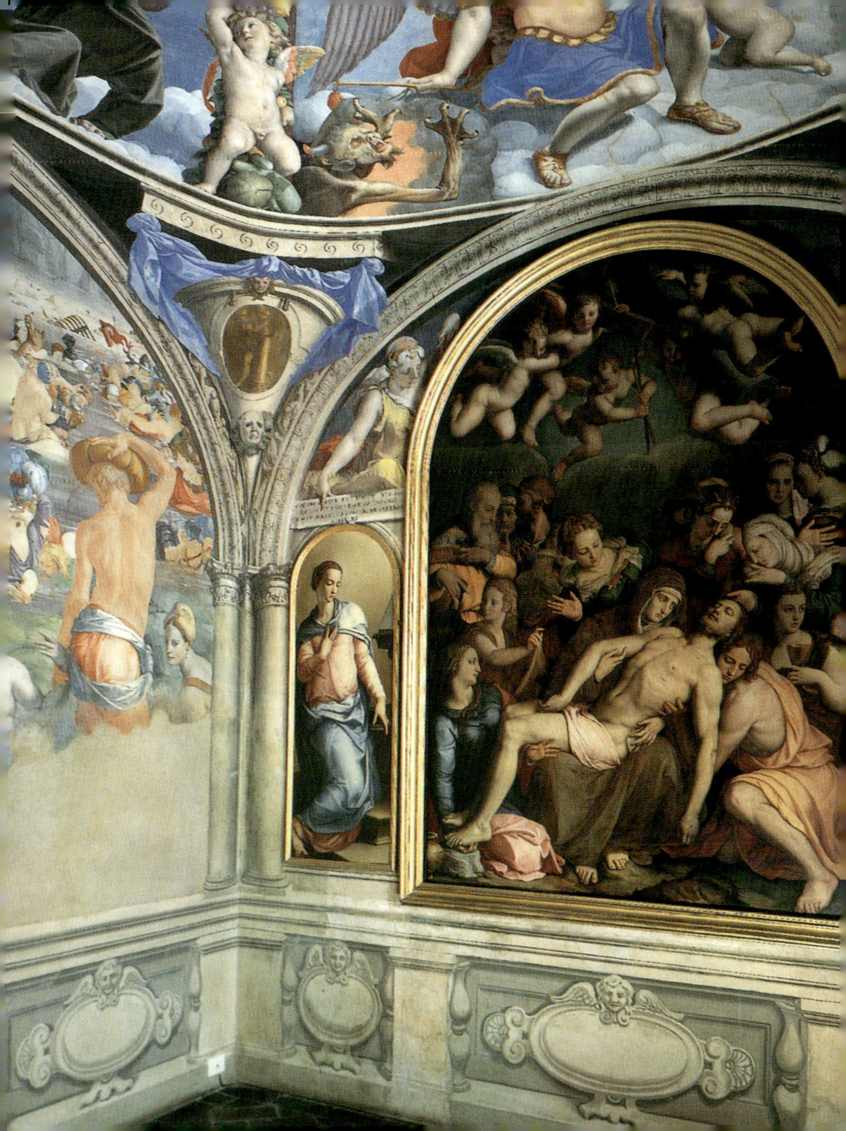

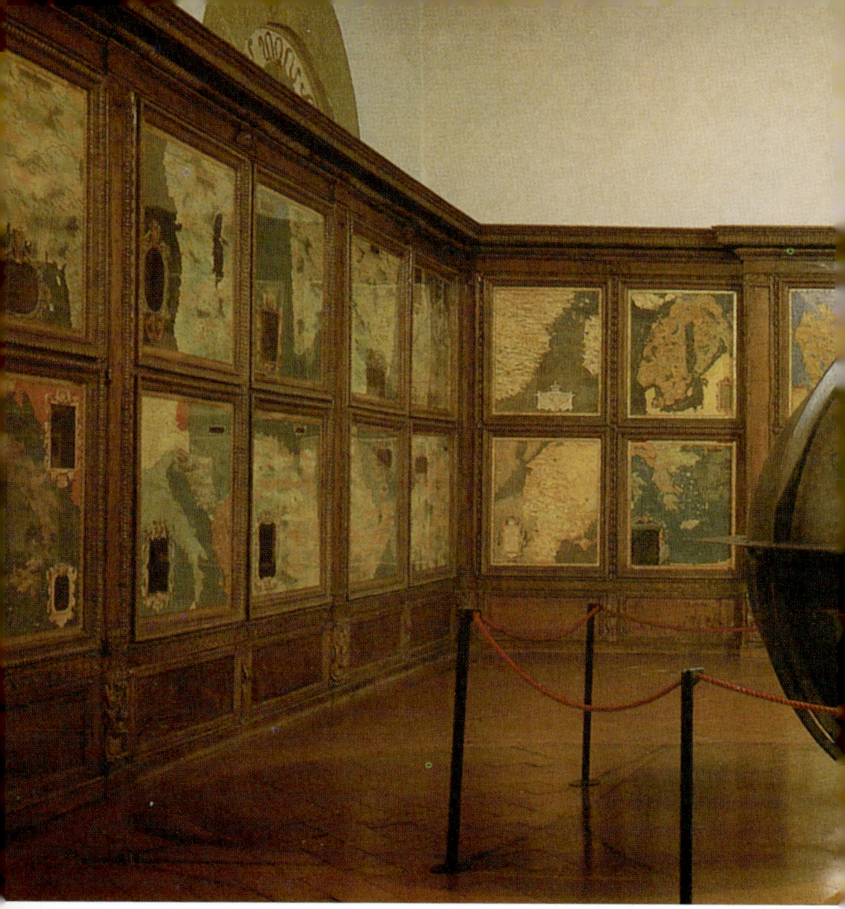

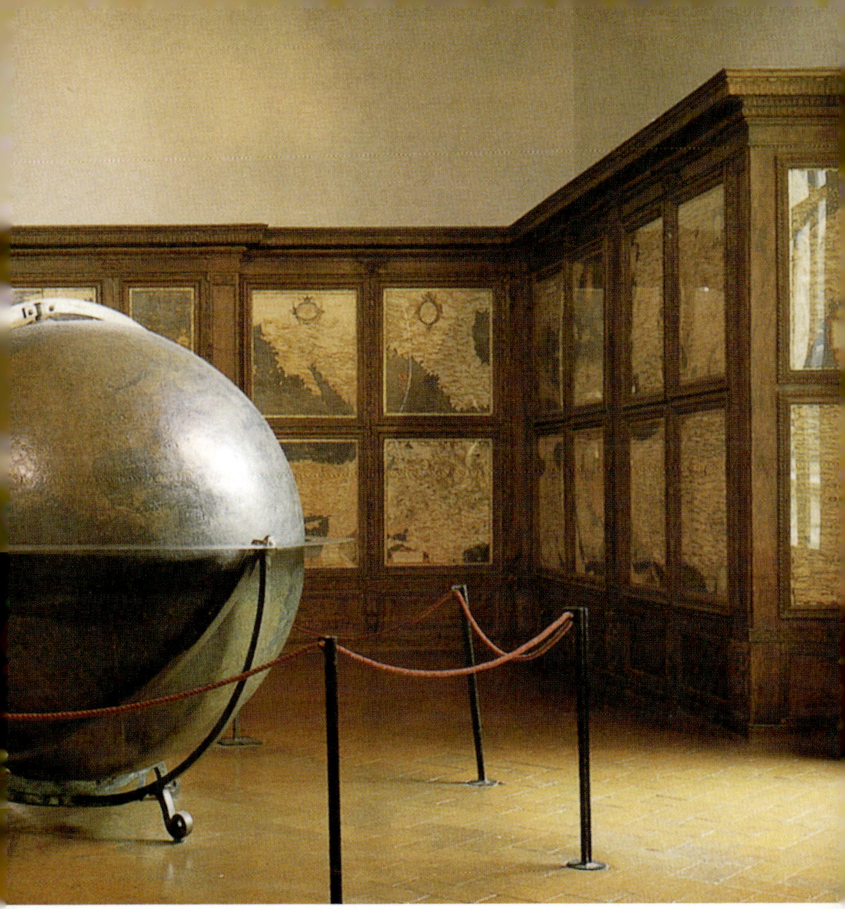

The Geographic Maps Room in Palazzo Vecchio, decorated in the 16th century with maps by Egnazio Danti and Stefano Buonsignori.

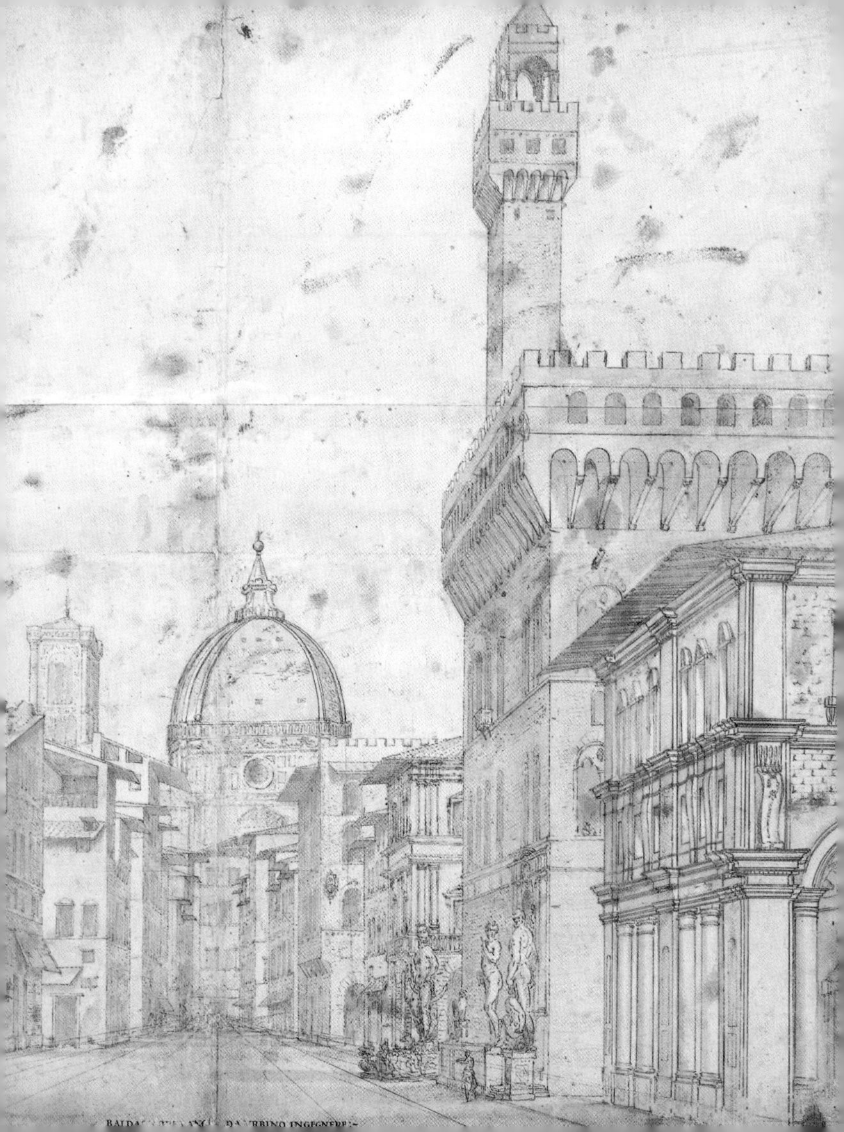
BALDA
INGEGNERE

Galleria degli Uffizi

The fascination of what is considered one of the world's most important museums, with millions of visitors each year, may also lie in its severe, imposing aspect, in its unique panoramic views over the river, in its broad corridors which – even when thronged by visitors – convey a true sense of "art gallery". The Galleria degli Uffizi is, not by chance, the oldest museum in modern Europe. Its origins date back to 1581, the year when Francesco I de' Medici set up a gallery "with pictures, statues and other precious things" on the top floor of the East Wing of the Uffizi (which served at the time, as will be seen, as the seat of the Magistrature). In 1591 Francesco Bocchi described the gallery as "so magnificent, so regal [...] filled with statues, with noble paintings and extremely precious objects [...] where the eye sweeping over so many magnificent things, so different, so rare, so sublime, is overcome by such delight that the soul almost faints." The ceilings were frescoed with the grotesque motifs that were later to adorn, with themes alluding to the objects displayed, the adjacent rooms containing armor, scientific instruments and geographic charts.

The Grand Duke recommended to his ministers that they "use courtesy" with those who wished to see the gallery.

Opposite page:
Idealized view of the East Wing of the Uffizi, still without the second floor, detail from the *Sketch for stage settings of the "Widow" by G. Battista Caccini,* performed in 1569, pen, sepia and watercolor. G.D.S.U., 404P.

Remarking on this "public" service, Bocchi commented that the works of art could be seen better here "than if they were placed in public squares; because outside, they would be stained by water and wind, but here they are conserved in cleanliness."

HISTORY

The imposing building complex of the Uffizi had not been created to serve as a museum. The building ordered by Cosimo I in 1560 was designed to house the Magistrature, or administrative and judiciary offices (*uffici*, the derivation of the name Uffizi). To design and supervise this great project, Cosimo called upon his favorite artist, Giorgio Vasari from Arezzo. For years Vasari had been working, with vast expenditure of means, on the restructuring and decoration of Palazzo Vecchio, at the time a Medici residence. While Palazzo Vecchio was to assume the aspect of a royal palace, the Uffizi appeared from the very start as a structure useful to the public. The building has a U-shaped layout, consisting of two long wings, to the east and the west, joined on the southern side by a body overlooking the river with an airy loggia on the first floor and a portico on the ground floor opening onto the square. The East Wing is linked by an over-

Opposite page:
The Tribune of the Uffizi
as it appears today.

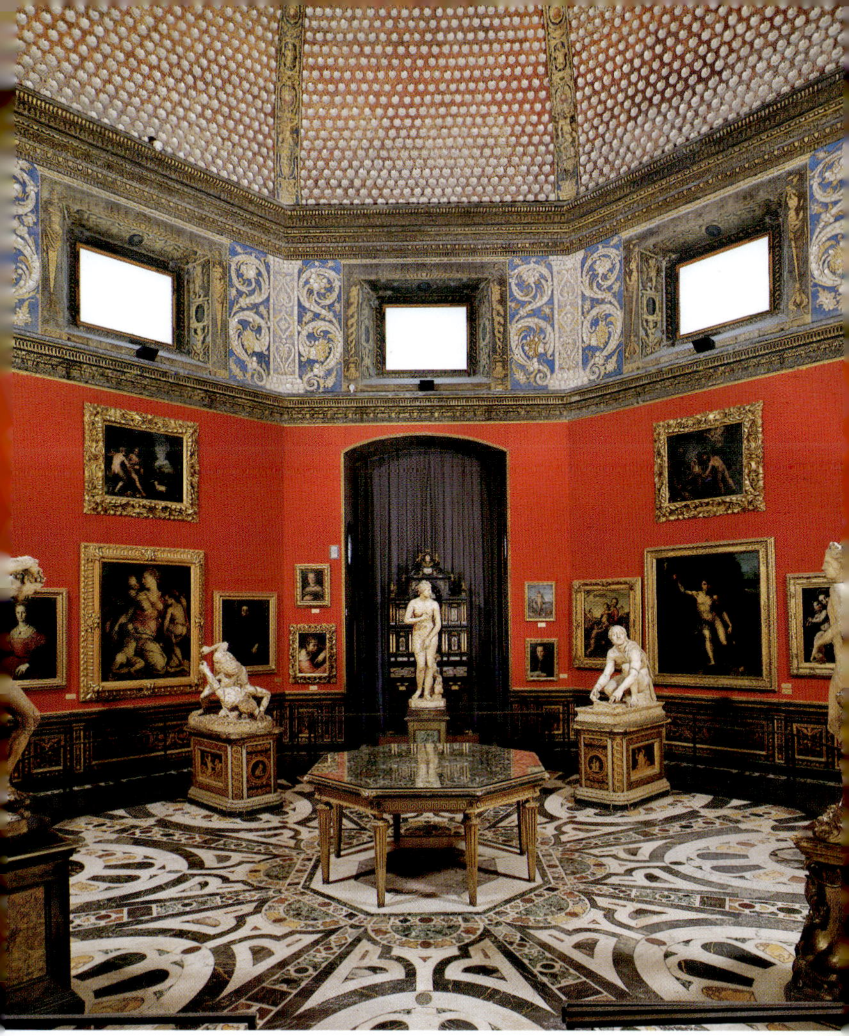

head passage to Palazzo Vecchio. The West Wing is connected to the Loggia dei Lanzi by a bridge suspended over Via Lambertesca. A grandiose, imposing edifice, built to the serial design common to most Magistratures, the Uffizi was constructed of the typical Florentine material, *pietra serena*, a gray stone against which the white plaster of the walls stands out. To make space for the building, many constructions in the area were demolished, and on the ground floor, facing Palazzo Vecchio, the remains of the Romanesque church of San Pier Scheraggio, already partially demolished in 1410 to widen Via della Ninna, were encapsulated into the new building. Into the Uffizi were then moved various manufacturies, such as that of tapestry, directed by expert Flemish masters purposely called to Florence. Both Cosimo I and Vasari died in 1574, and the Uffizi was finished by Buontalenti, who in 1586 also built the Medicean Theater, a place where memorable performances were held. Vasari remains however the architect of an arduous undertaking. For the wedding of Francesco I and Joan of Austria he built, from March to September 1565, a spectacular Corridor that joins the Uffizi to the Pitti Palace. The Vasari Corridor starts from the West Wing, runs across the Arno above the shops on the left side of the Old Bridge, emerges at the church of Santa Felicita, then called Palatine Chapel, and ends in the Boboli

Opposite page:
The section of the Vasari Corridor that runs from Lungarno degli Archibusieri to Ponte Vecchio.

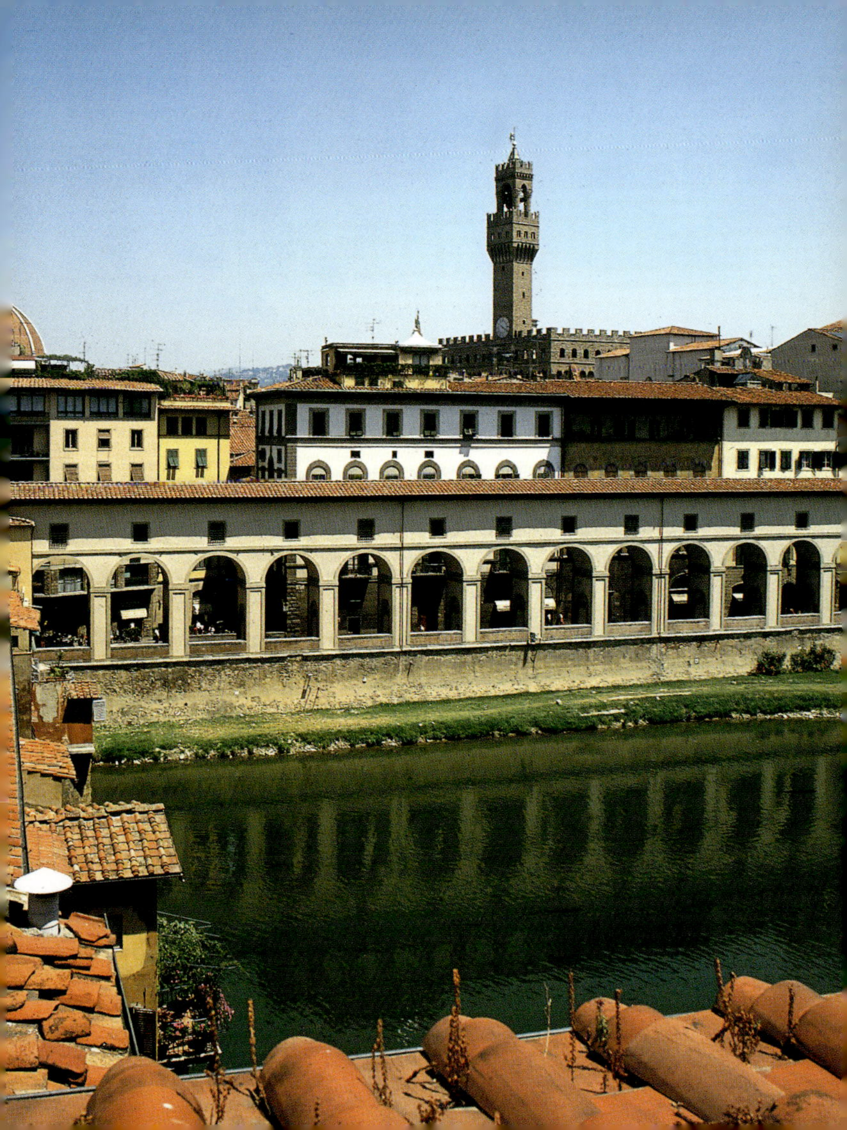

Gardens. An urban project of highest symbolic significance in the city of the Grand Duke, the Corridor, almost a kilometer long, was reserved exclusively to the Medici family and the court dignitaries, who traversed it in a two-seat cart "pulling themselves by hand with the greatest of ease" (Cinelli 1677).
This is, in brief, the origin of a museum that was to become much vaster, its collections incessantly enriched up to the last heir of the Medici dynasty: Anna Maria Luisa (also called Ludovica) de' Medici, who before dying in 1743 declared the gallery to be "public and inalienable property", thus instilling new vitality in the Uffizi at the time of the Lorraine Grand Duchy. The Galleria degli Uffizi is not only the oldest museum, but also the one whose history is closely interwoven, more than anywhere else in Europe, with that of its city and its sovereigns. The terrorist attack in 1993 has not halted the difficult process of modernizing the museum, and in the last few years its exhibition space has been doubled by extending the visitors' itinerary to the rooms on the floors below the historic gallery.

Opposite page:
View of the first Corridor
(East Corridor) of the Uffizi
looking south.

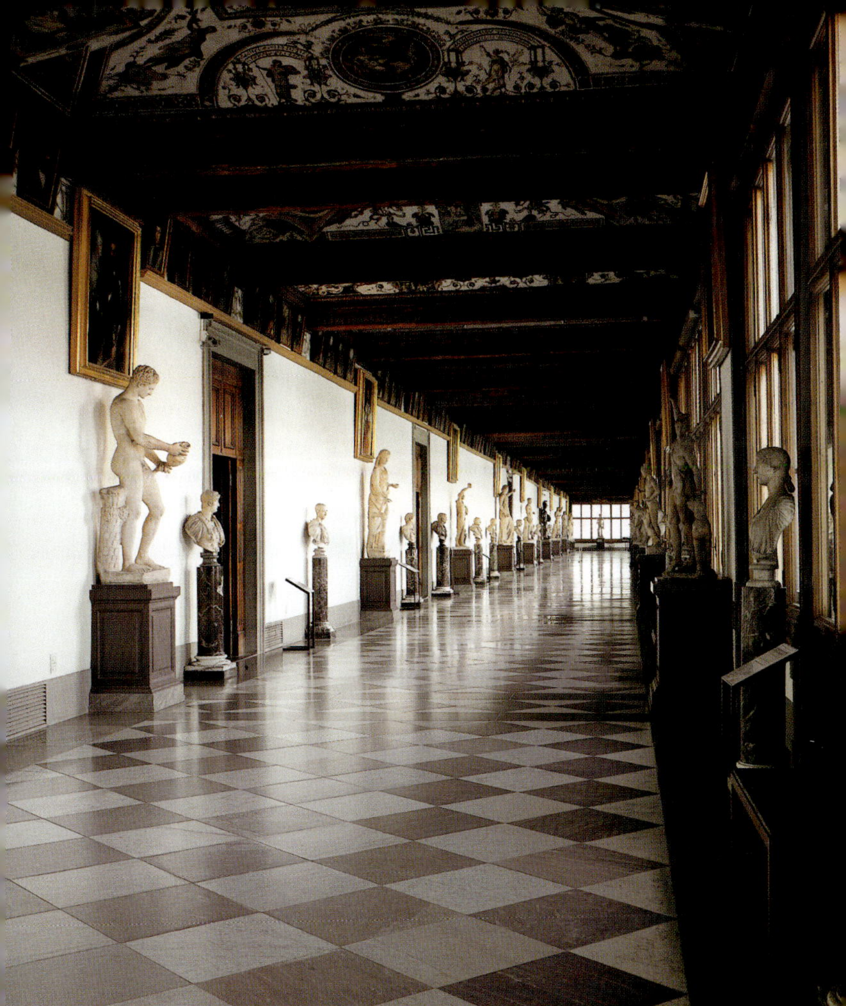

THE TRIBUNE

The Tribune, the "heart" of the original museum, was completed by Bernardo Buontalenti in 1584 for Francesco I. It is an octagonal room, unique and welcoming, with a cupola encrusted with mother-of-pearl shells gleaming against a background of scarlet lacquer like an immense jewel. In this room were exhibited, as "emblems of the Grand Duke's wealth and power" (Heikamp 1997), the most amazing objects in the already fabulous Medici collections. In 1591 Francesco Bocchi described in wonder this "jewel-casket of rare and precious things": light falling softly from windows of Oriental crystal on the bronzes, the gemstones and "the most rare instruments" arranged "in certain ebony cabinets" running around the walls lined in red velvet, on which hung an outstanding group of 16th century paintings, including seven by Raphael and nine by Andrea del Sarto. Above is the lantern with the wind rose that symbolizes the air; the shells, water; the red walls, fire; and the marble and semiprecious stones of the floor, earth. This is the cosmos, with its elements, which surrounds and glorifies the Prince. At the center, an octagonal jewel case (lost) echoed the shape of the room.

Opposite page:
The Wind Rose in the lantern over the Tribune.

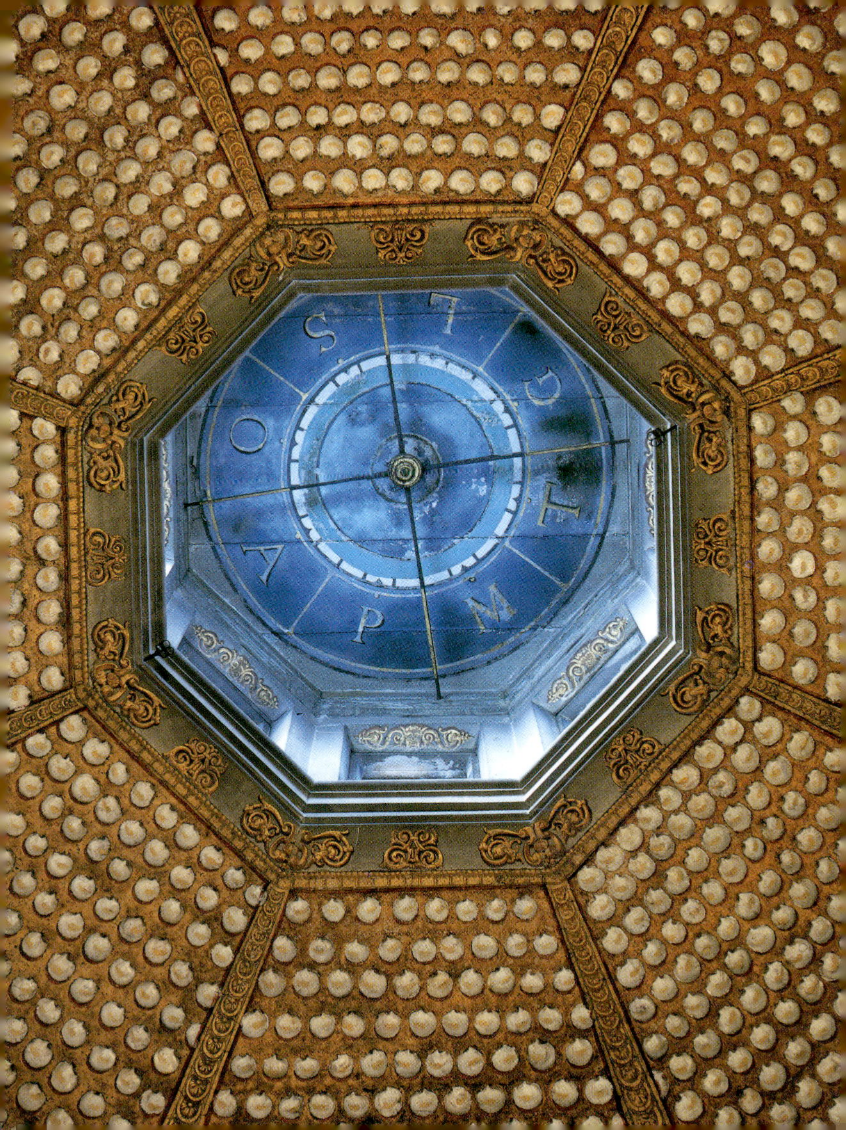

CABINET OF PRINTS AND DRAWINGS

From its very origins, Florentine art has boasted a special vocation for drawing, and not by chance, since the time of Lorenzo the Magnifient, the Medici collected drawings. In the 15th century Cennino Cennini, painter and author of a treastise on techniques, hailed drawing as "the foundation of art" and in the 16th century the great draftsman Pontormo, in comparing the various artistic disciplines, called it the noblest of them all. Among the first to recognize drawing as a work of art in itself was Giorgio Vasari, fervent collector, skilled draftsman and an expert on technique. The Uffizi's extraordinary collection of drawings, today the most conspicuous in Italy and one of the largest in the world, may be said to have started at the time of Cardinal Leopoldo (1617-1675). The collection, originally kept in Palazzo Pitti and for years now at the Uffizi, in the Cabinet of Prints and Drawings (Gabinetto Disegni e Stampe - G.D.S.U.), boasts drawings of fundamental importance from the 14th-15th centuries to the present day, with important works by such great masters as Leonardo, Michelangelo, Raphael, Andrea del Sarto and Pontormo.

Opposite page:
Leonardo da Vinci,
Study of a girl's head,
1475-1480. Uffizi, G.D.S.U.

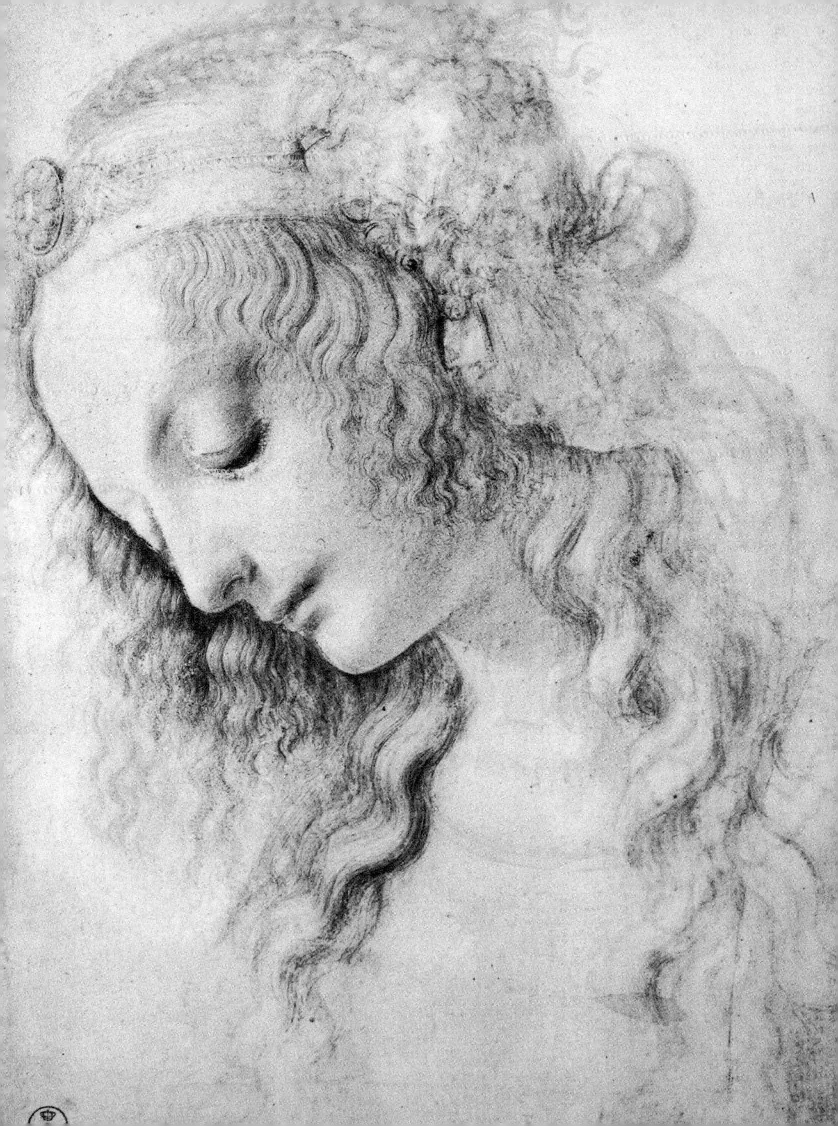

THE GROTESQUE DECORATIONS

The grotesque, a fantastic decoration inspired by the friezes in Imperial Roman residences, takes its name from the so-called "grottoes" in Nero's *Domus Aurea* in Rome, rediscovered around 1480. The fashion for these imaginative decorations reached its peak about a century later, and in keeping with late-Mannerist taste, the ceilings of the Uffizi were frescoed, between 1579 and 1581, with a series of grotesque motifs of remarkable iconographic variety. The decorations continue in the four rooms named after the Medici Armory and the Geographic Charts, as well as in the Mathematics Room, where they can still be admired today.

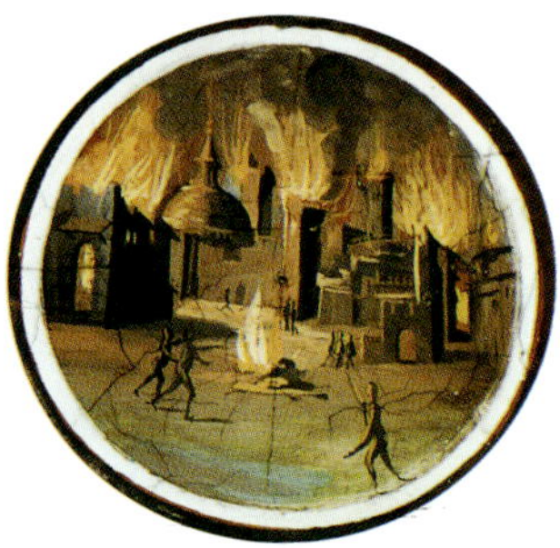

Above:
Grotesque with city in flames,
c. 1580, fresco.
Uffizi,
First Corridor, bay 33.

Opposite page:
Grotesque with pergola and coats of arms of the Medici, the House of Austria and Bianca Cappello,
c. 1581, fresco touched up in tempera. Uffizi, First Corridor.

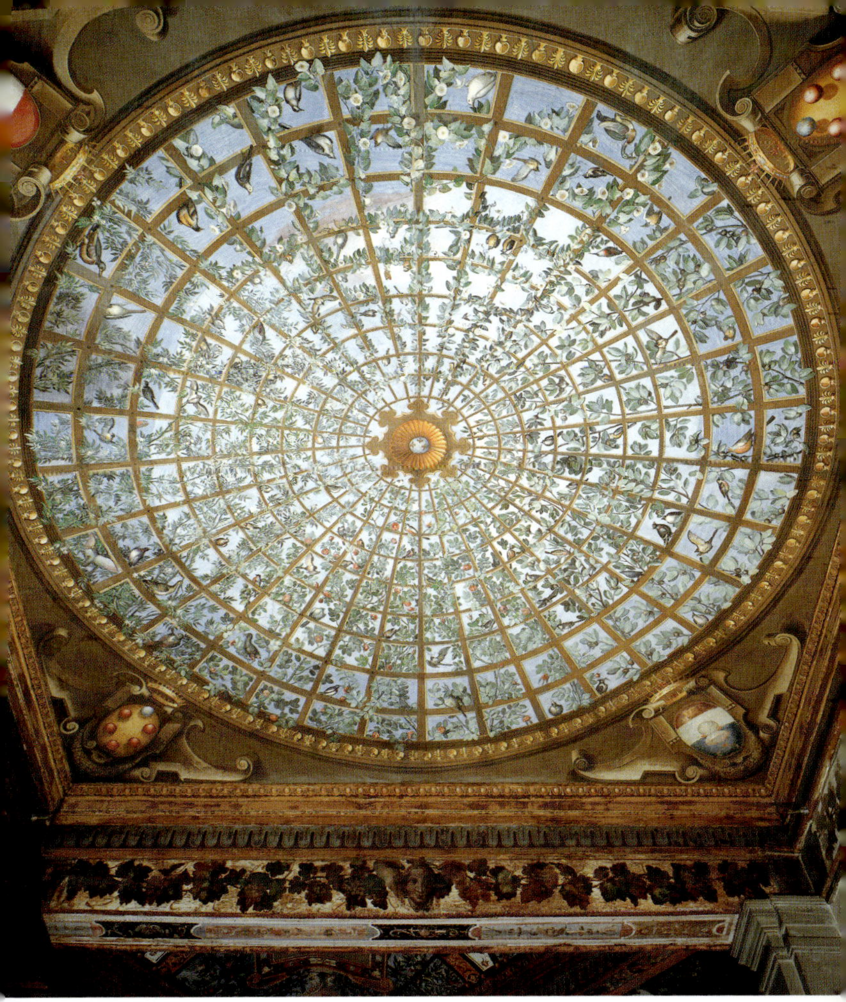

THE ANCIENT SCULPTURES

The Uffizi's archaeological collection is one of the world's oldest, originating from the early Medici's passion for collecting antiquities. Since the 15th century, in fact, the Medici had collected cameos, bas-reliefs and sculptures, in keeping with the renewed humanistic interest in every aspect of antiquity. Unfortunately for posterity, neither the collections of the founding father Cosimo the Elder nor those of Lorenzo the Magnificent, who allowed his most important pieces to be studied by artists in the Garden of San Marco, have survived. With Cosimo I a new, fundamental trend emerged; the pieces he purchased bore political significance, as with the Etruscan bronzes of the *Chimera* and the *Orator*, which served to establish a direct relationship with the ancient kings of Etruria, and the busts of Roman emperors still present today in the three corridors of the Uffizi. Dozens of sculptures were then purchased by his son Francesco I, and others by Cardinal Ferdinando for Villa Medici in Rome, which were later to enter the collections in the Uffizi. Sculptures such as the *Venus*, the *Knife-grinder*, and the *Wrestlers* were exhibited in the Tribune, while later, for the Niobe group, a special room was

Opposite page:
The *Medici Venus*, copy from a Greek original of the II century B.C., Greek marble, coming from Villa Medici.

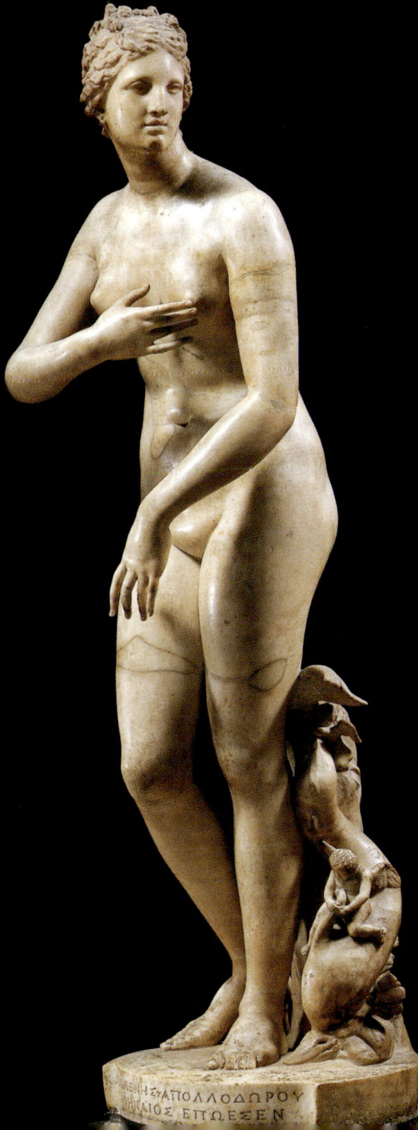
ΑΠΟΛΛΟΔΩΡΟΥ
ΕΠΩΕΣΕΝ

created in the Third Corridor. In the recent restoration of the three corridors in the Gallery, the exhibition scheme documented in 1748, in which statues alternate with portrait busts, has been reproduced as closely as possible.

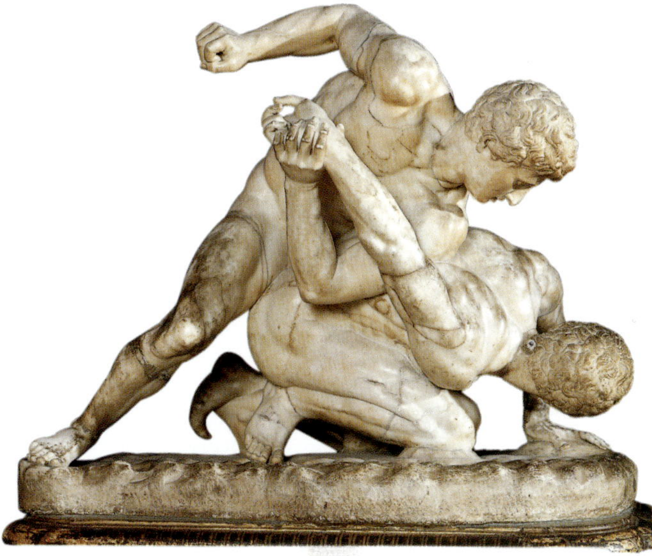

Above:
The *Wrestlers*, copy from the second half of the III century B.C. of a Hellenistic bronze original, Greek marble, coming from Villa Medici in Rome, in the Tribune since 1677.

Opposite page:
Head of the so-called "Dying Alexander",
Hellenistic Art, Parian marble.

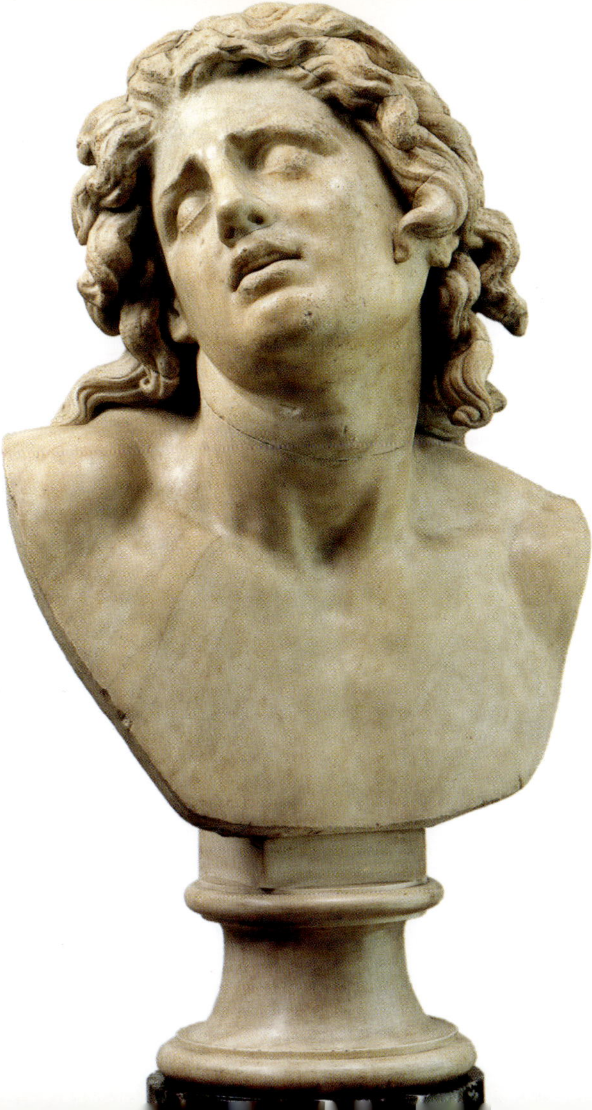

THE COLLECTION OF SELF-PORTRAITS

While Giorgio Vasari, in the second edition of his monumental work on the lives of the artists (1568), had already thought of supplementing each biography with a picture, real or presumed, of the artist, it was only in 1664 that a particular collectors' interest in the self-portrait genre arose in Florence. In that year, in fact, Leopoldo de' Medici began to form an extraordinary systematic collection, purchasing self-portraits all over Europe through his agents or having them specially painted by the greatest masters of the time. Having grown enormously over time, the collection of self-portraits in the Uffizi, at present still partly exhibited in the Vasari Corridor, is the world's largest and most important, extending down to our own day, with many contemporary artists represented as well.

Opposite page:
Elisabeth Vigée-Lebrun, *Self-portrait with painting of Queen Marie Antoniette*, 1790, oil on canvas. Galleria degli Uffizi. This self-portrait was painted in Rome by the French artist for Grand Duke Pietro Leopoldo.

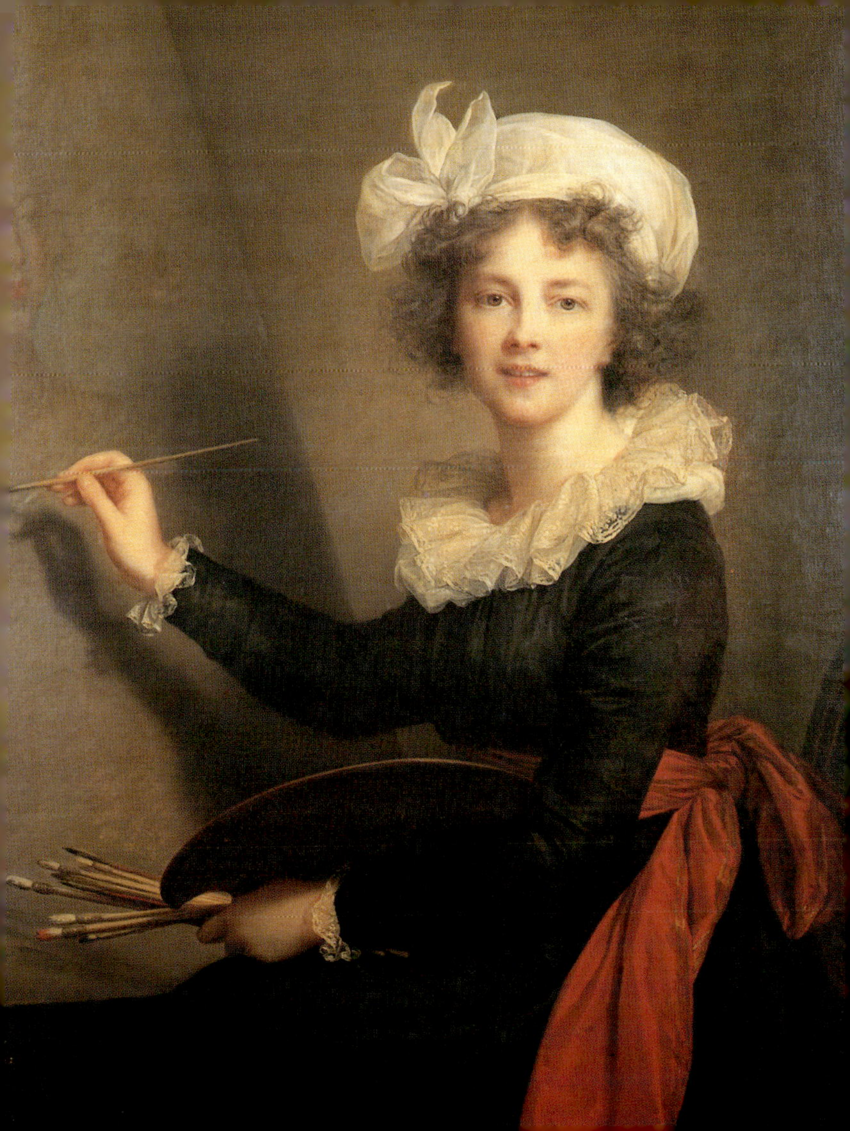

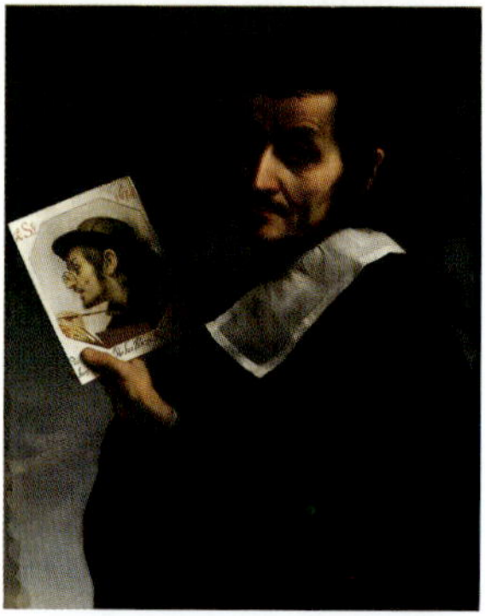
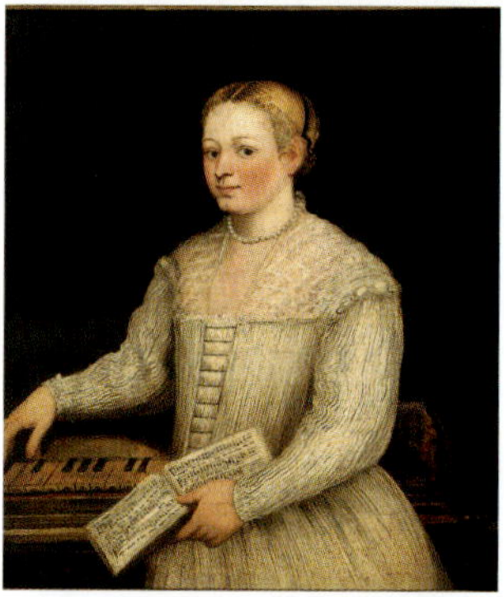
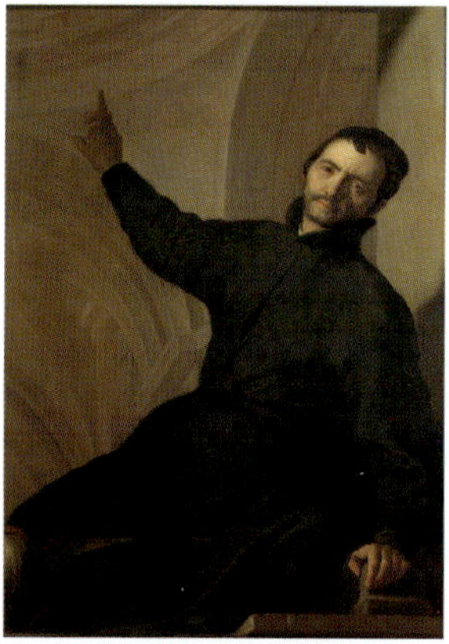
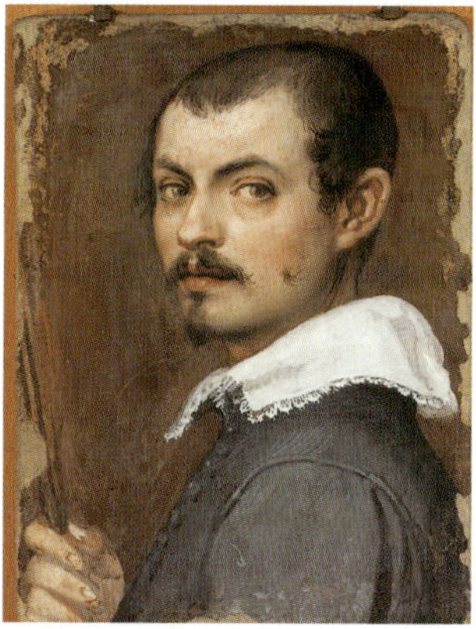

Above: Self-portraits of: Carlo Dolci, 1674; Marietta Robusti la Tintoretta, c. 1580; Andrea Pozzo, c. 1688; Giovanni da San Giovanni, 1616.

Opposite page: *Sir Joshua Reynolds, Self-portrait dressed as a Doctor of Oxford*, 1775. Uffizi.

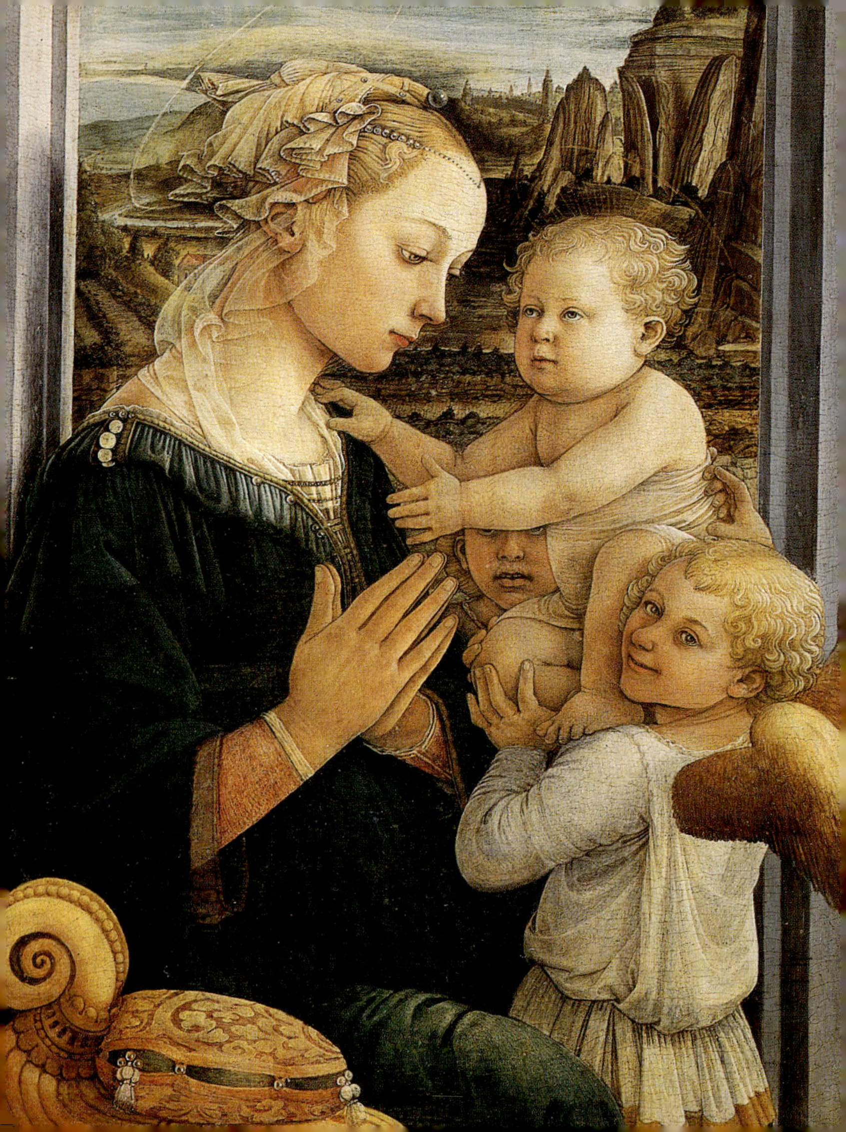

MASTERPIECES IN THE GALLERY

Most of the vast collection of paintings in the Uffizi is to be found on the second floor of the museum, but the exhibition area is now being extended to the first floor, where many works formerly relegated to storage will be suitably arranged according to schools and geographic areas, bearing testimony not only to the Tuscan schools but also to those of other regions in Italy and other countries. The collections include important groups of Flemish, German, French and Spanish paintings from various periods, some of which arrived here very early, purchased by the Medici and Lorraine families, great connoisseurs and collectors of wide-ranging taste, and some coming from other acquisitions. A number of Tuscan paintings were moved here in the 19th century from monasteries and churches suppressed in accordance with Napoleonic law; these works had been commissioned, over the centuries, by religious associations or wealthy Florentines. The main historic groups are described below, regardless of their location in the gallery and in the Contini Bonacossi collection, which has been annexed to the Uffizi for several years now and is included in the museum itinerary.

Opposite page:
Filippo Lippi,
Madonna and Child with Two Angels,
c. 1465, tempera on wood.
Uffizi.

This is one of the most admired and copied paintings in the Uffizi, where it arrived in 1796 from the Medicean villa of Poggio Imperiale.

13TH AND 14TH CENTURY PAINTING

The artists represented are for the most part Tuscan, documenting the origins and development of Florentine, Sienese, Pisan and Aretine painting, with important crucifixes and gold-leaf paintings by 13th century masters (among them Meliore, Bonaventura Berlinghieri, and several who have remained anonymous) up to the highest achievements of Florentines such as Cimabue, Giotto and his pupils (among them Taddeo Gaddi, Giovanni da Milano, Bernardo Daddi, and Giottino). The 12th-14th century Sienese school is also well represented, with splendid masterpieces by Duccio da Boninsegna, Simone Martini, Ambrogio and Pietro Lorenzetti, and Ugolino di Nerio; some of these artists, such as Duccio and the two Lorenzettis, also worked for Florentine churches.

VISITORS' ITINERARY AND WORKS OF ART

Noteworthy in the collections are:

- the three *Maestà* by Cimabue, Duccio and Giotto, coming from Santa Trinita, Santa Maria Novella and Ognissanti.
- the *Presentation in the Temple* (1342) by Ambrogio Lorenzetti, formerly above the Patron Saint's altar in the Duomo of Siena.

Opposite page:
Cimabue,
Santa Trinita Maestà,
c.1280-1290,
tempera on wood. Uffizi.

Following pages:
Duccio di Boninsegna, *Maestà*, c. 1285, tempera on wood. Uffizi.
Giotto, *Maestà*, c. 1310, tempera on wood. Uffizi.

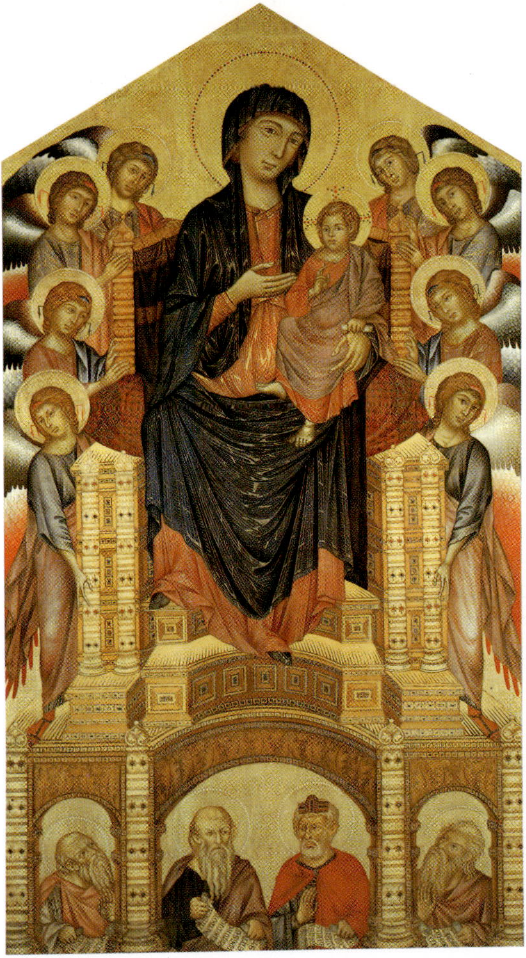

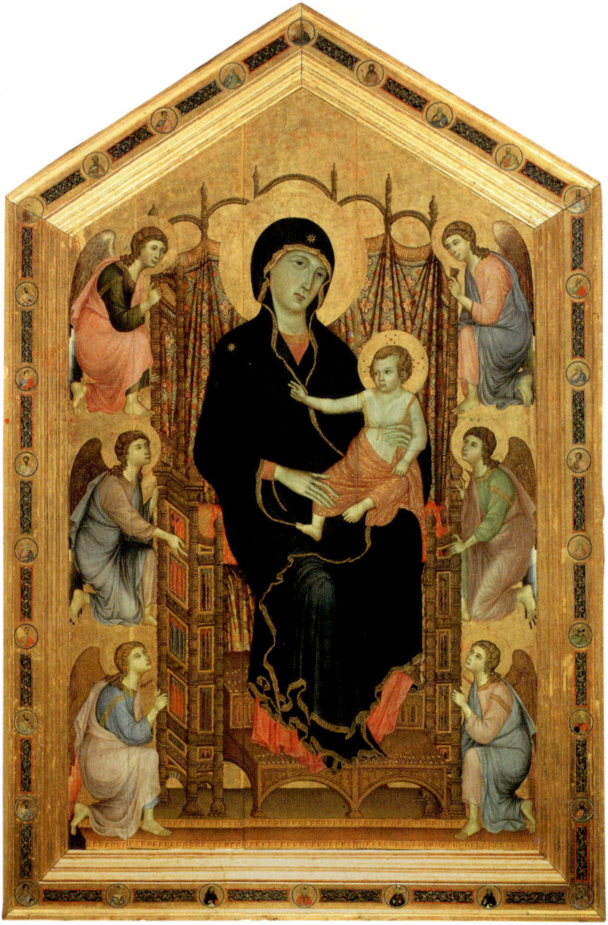

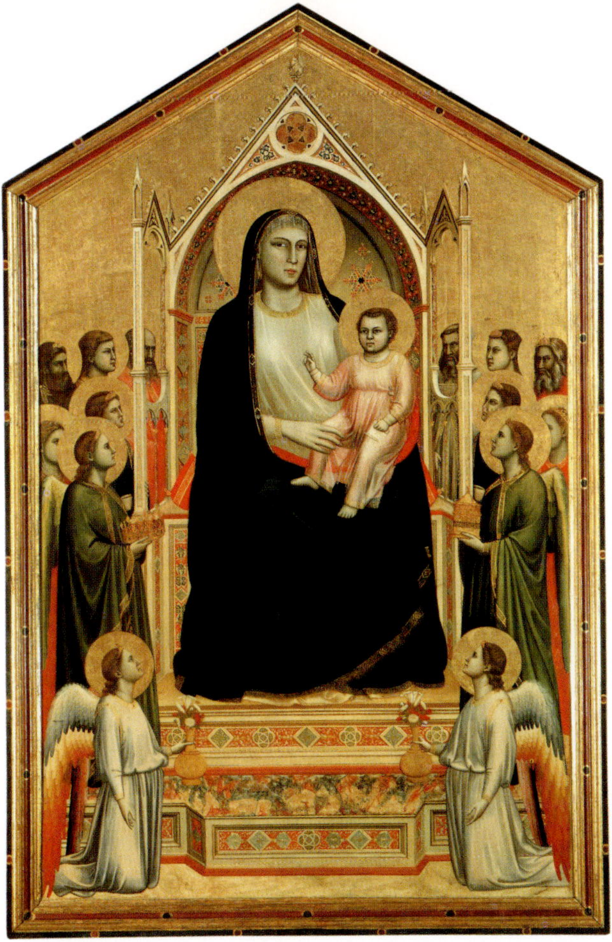

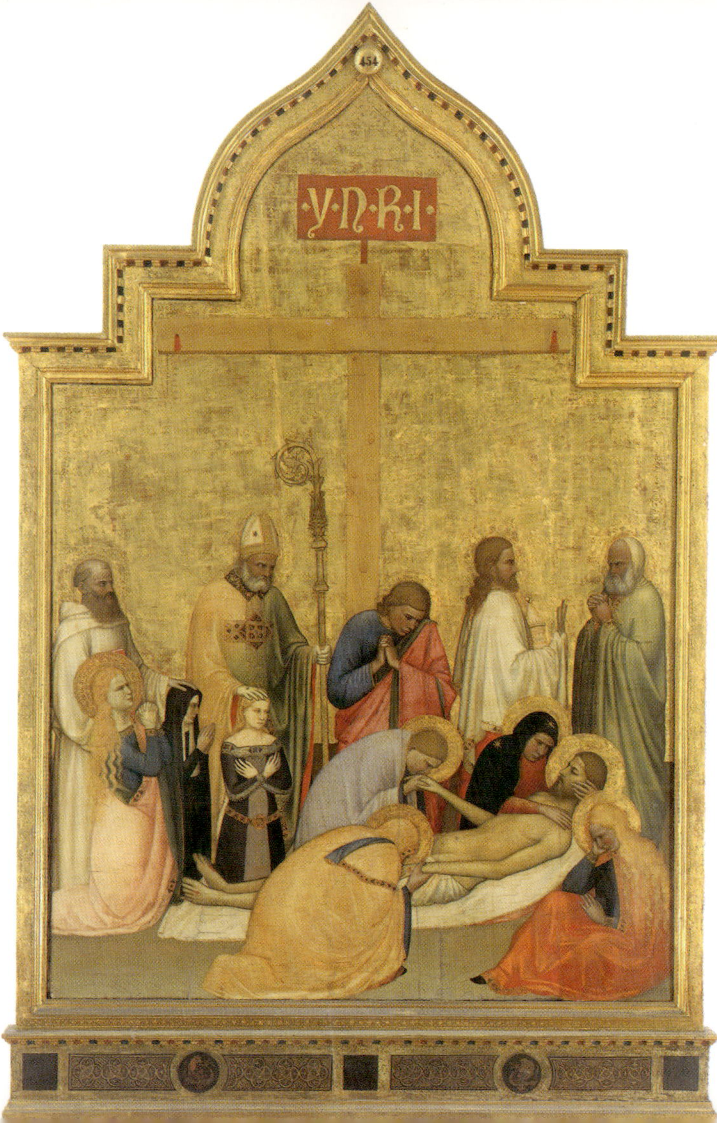
454
·Y·N·R·I·

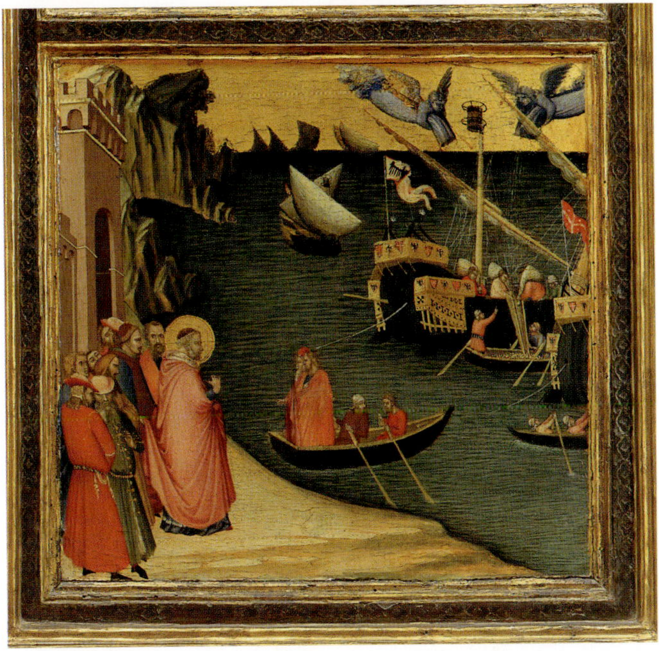

Opposite page:
Giottino, *Pietà*, c. 1360-1365 tempera on wood (from the rood-screen of the Florentine church of San Remigio). Uffizi.
Giottino was one of the greatest Florentine artists of the second half of the 14th century, remarkably inventive in composition, capable of expressing a broad range of emotions.

Above:
Ambrogio Lorenzetti, *Miracle of the Grain*, detail from the *Four Episodes in the Life of St. Nicholas*, c. 1327-1332, tempera on wood, (part of a dismembered altar-frontal, from the Florentine church of San Procolo). Uffizi. The invention of the marine landscape is accomplished through a "herring-bone" perspective.

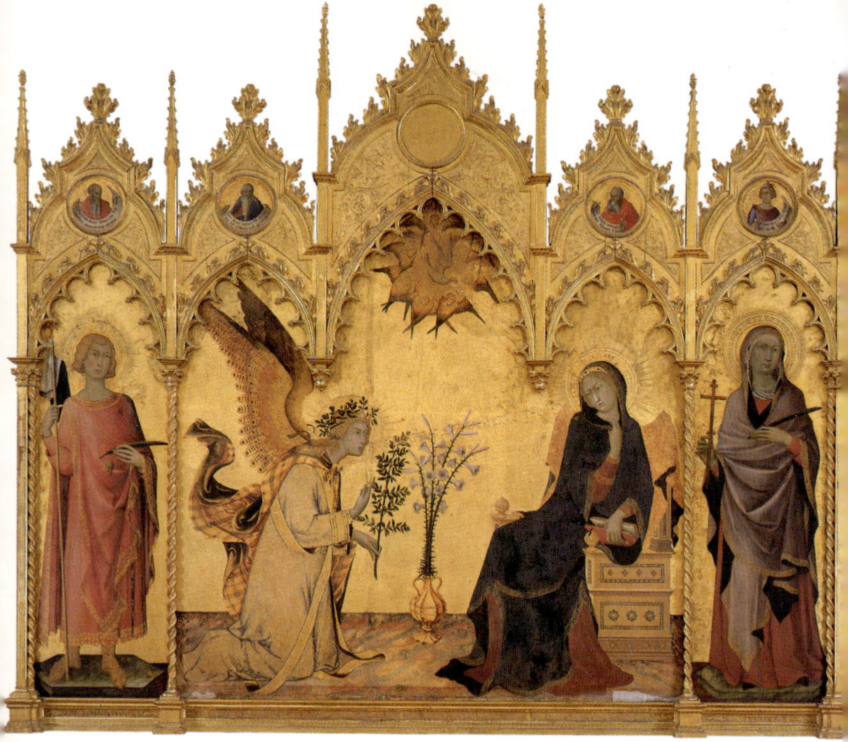

Above:
Simone Martini and Lippo Memmi, *Annunciation*, signed and dated 1333, tempera on wood (from the altar of Sant'Ansano in the Duomo of Siena, purchased through the offices of the Grand Duke of Tuscany, in the Uffizi since 1799).

Opposite page:
Ambrogio Lorenzetti, *Presentation in the Temple*, signed and dated 1342, tempera on wood (from the altar of St. Crescenzius in the Duomo of Siena, in the Uffizi since1913). Uffizi.

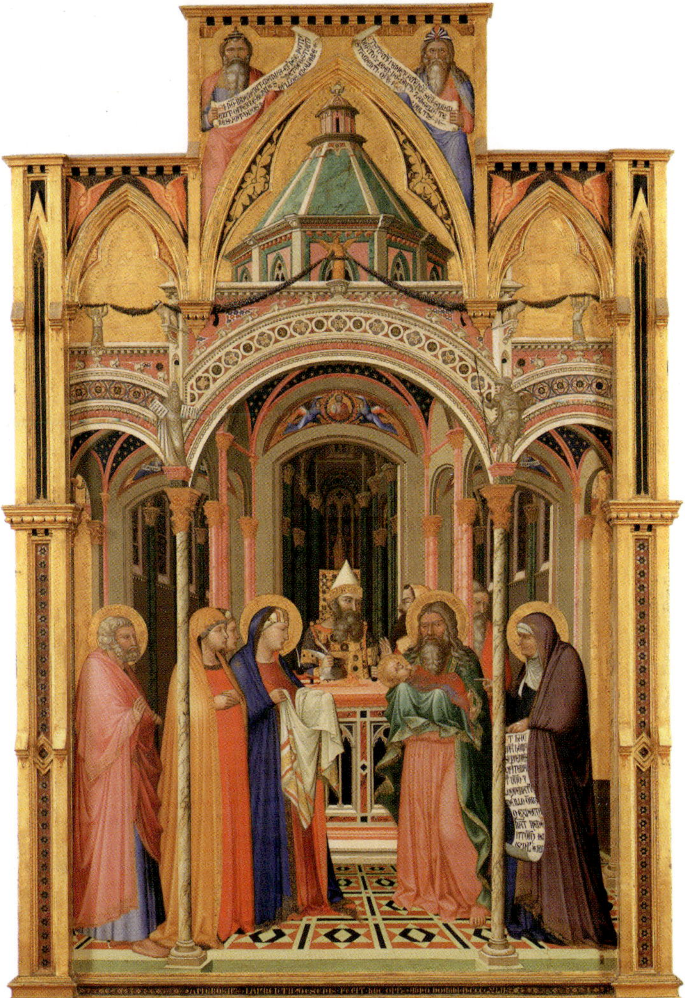

- the *Annunciation* (1333) by Simone Martini and Lippo Memmi, also originally in the Duomo of Siena.

15TH CENTURY ITALIAN PAINTING

The 15th century Italian paintings constitute one of the most important selections in the world, and one of the most significant in the Uffizi, especially as concerns Florentine art. The collection includes, among other things, the largest group existing in a single museum of works by Botticelli and Filippo Lippi. There are also masterpieces from the schools of Northern and Central Italy, representing the developments in figurative style from International Gothic to High Renaissance. A very brief summary of the most important works is given here, without claiming to present a thorough description of all, for which reference should be made to our catalogue of the works exhibited in the Gallery (*The Uffizi Gallery. Art. History, Collections*, Florence 2004).

VISITORS' ITINERARY AND WORKS OF ART

Noteworthy in the collections are:

- the *Thebaide* (1418), now attribuited to Fra Angelico.
- the *Coronation of the Virgin* (1414) by Lorenzo Monaco.

Opposite page:
Lorenzo Monaco,
Coronation of the Virgin,
1414, tempera on wood, Uffizi.

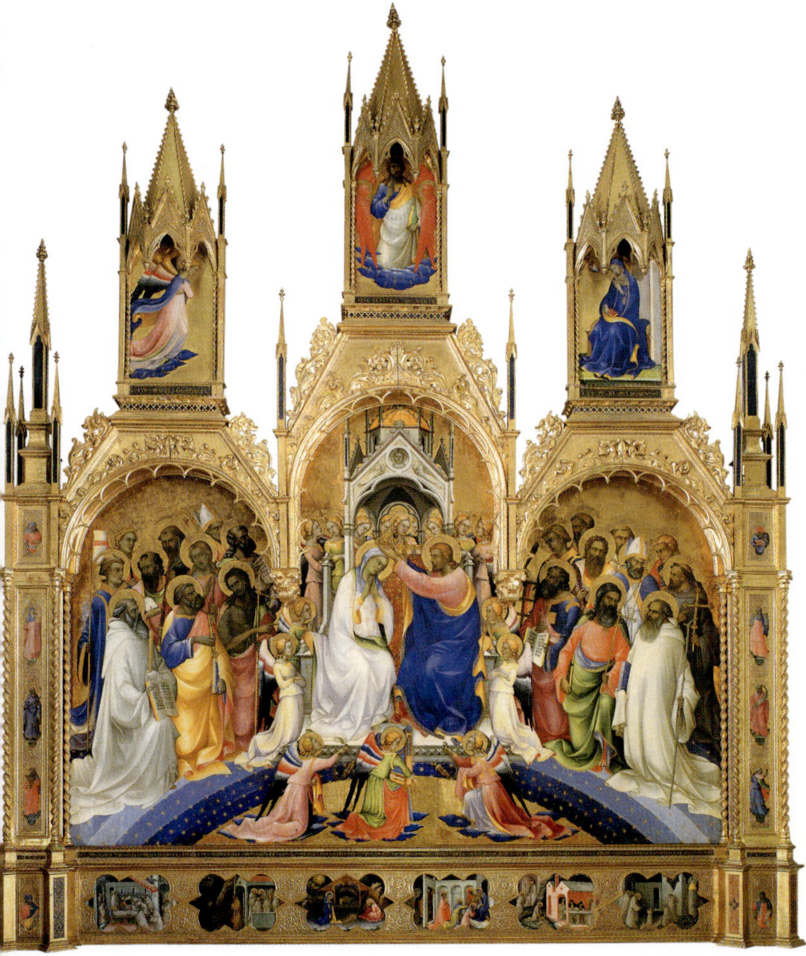

- the *Adoration of the Magi* (1423), painted by Gentile da Fabriano for the chapel of Palla Strozzi in Santa Trinita.
- the *Saint Anne Metterza* (c. 1424) by Masaccio and Masolino.
- the *Battle of San Romano* (c. 1438) by Paolo Uccello, once believed to have been painted, along with two other panels now in London and Paris, for Palazzo Medici, but instead commissioned by a member of the Salimbeni family.
- the *Santa Lucia dei Magnoli Altarpiece* (c. 1440) by Domenico Veneziano, an artist attentive to the effects of light, who also worked in Florence with Piero della Francesca.
- the cycle of *Illustrious Men* (c. 1448) by Andrea del Castagno, frescoes detached from Villa Carducci di Legnaia.
- numerous works by Filippo Lippi, including: the *Novitiate Altarpiece* (c. 1445); the *Coronation of the Virgin* (1439-1447) from the church of Sant'Ambrogio; the famous gentle, sweet *Madonna and Child with Two Saints* (c. 1465).
- the *Uffizi Triptych* (c. 1470), the *Portrait of Carlo de' Medici* (1466), and the *Madonna of the Caves* (1488-1490), by Andrea Mantegna, who, it seems, worked for the Medici.
- the *Diptych of the Duchess and Duke of Urbino* (c. 1472) by Piero della Francesca, which arrived in Florence in 1631 with the inheritance of Vittoria della Rovere.

Opposite page:
Gentile da Fabriano,
Adoration of the Magi,
1423, tempera on wood, Uffizi.

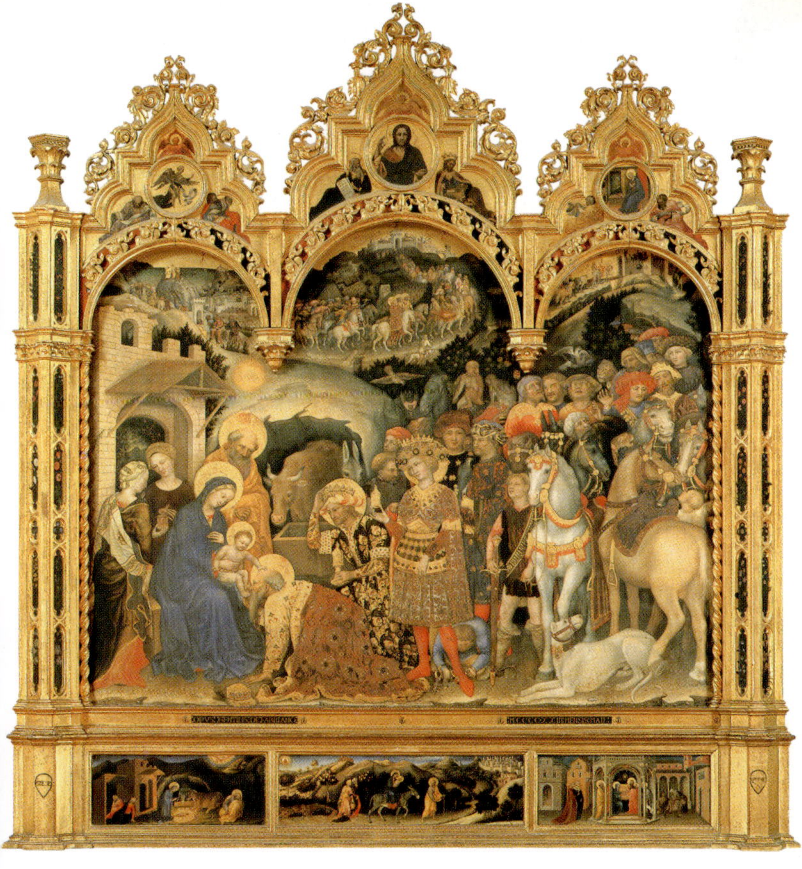

- the *Labors of Hercules* by Antonio del Pollaiolo and the *Cardinal of Portugal Altarpiece* (1466-1468), painted in collaboration with his brother Piero for the chapel in San Miniato al Monte.
- among the works of Sandro Botticelli, the *Fortitude* (1470), painted for the series of six *Virtues* for the Tribunale di Mercatanzia (the other panels are by Piero del Pollaiolo); the *Portrait of a Youth with a Medal* (c. 1475); the *Adoration of the Magi* (1475), commissioned by the broker Guasparre del Lama for his chapel in Santa Maria Novella; the *Primavera* and the *Birth of Venus*, his two most famous paintings, still subject to debate as regards their dating, their symbolic meaning, linked in any case to the neo-Platonic culture predominating at the time of Lorenzo the Magnificent, and their destination and provenance (the former has been documented in the home of Lorenzo and Giovanni di Pierfrancesco de' Medici, cousins of the Magnificent, where another masterpiece by Botticelli, *Pallas and the Centaur*, c. 1482, also hung; the latter was seen by Vasari in the suburban Villa of Castello); the tondo with the *Madonna of the Pomegranate*, painted in 1487 for the Audience Chamber of the Massai di Camera in Palazzo Vecchio; among his late works, the monumental *Coronation of the Virgin* (c. 1490) for the Goldsmiths Chapel in the church of San Marco and the *Calumny* (1495), inspired by a painting of Apelles.

Opposite page:
Masaccio and Masolino,
Saint Anne Metterza, c. 1424,
tempera on wood. Uffizi.

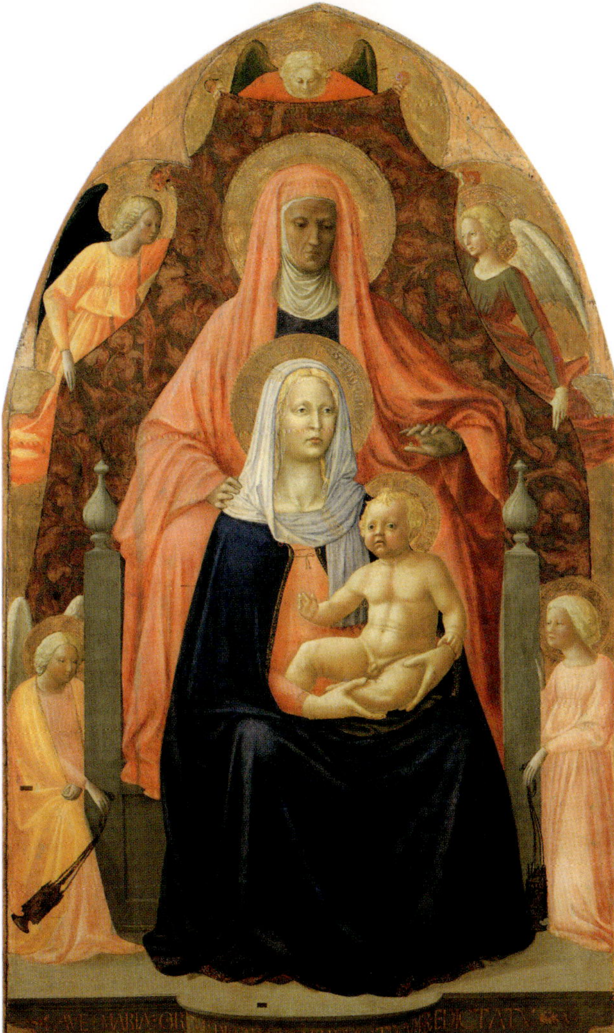

- the *Baptism of Christ* (1470-1475), painted by Verrocchio with the collaboration of Leonardo, whose youthful, luminous *Annunciation* (c. 1472) and unfinished *Adoration of the Magi*, commissioned in 1480 by the monks of San Donato a Scopeto and then replaced by one by Filippino, are also exhibited.
- the *San Giusto degli Ingesuati Altarpiece* (c. 1486) by Domenico Ghirlandaio, of which Vasari praised the invention of the angel's gilded breastplate, an effect created by the artist with color alone.
- the *Madonna and Child with Saints* (1486), a great altarpiece by Filippino Lippi, who also painted the *Adoration of the Magi* (1496), as replacement for the one by Leonardo, containing many portraits of contemporaries, in particular members of the cadet branch of the Medici family who renounced power in fidelity to Savonarola's republic.
- A number of altarpieces painted by Perugino for Florentine churches, and his intense *Portrait of Francesco delle Opere* (1494).

Opposite page:
Andrea del Castagno, *Niccolò Acciaiuoli*, detail from the cycle of *Illustrious Men* from Villa Carducci at Legnaia, c. 1449-1450, detached fresco. Uffizi.

Following pages:
Paolo Uccello, *Battle of San Romano*, c. 1438, tempera on wood. Uffizi.

Piero della Francesca, *Diptych of the Duchess and Duke of Urbino*, with the portraits of Battista Sforza and Federigo II da Montefeltro on the front, and on the back the couple riding in triumphal chariots, c. 1472, tempera on wood. Uffizi.

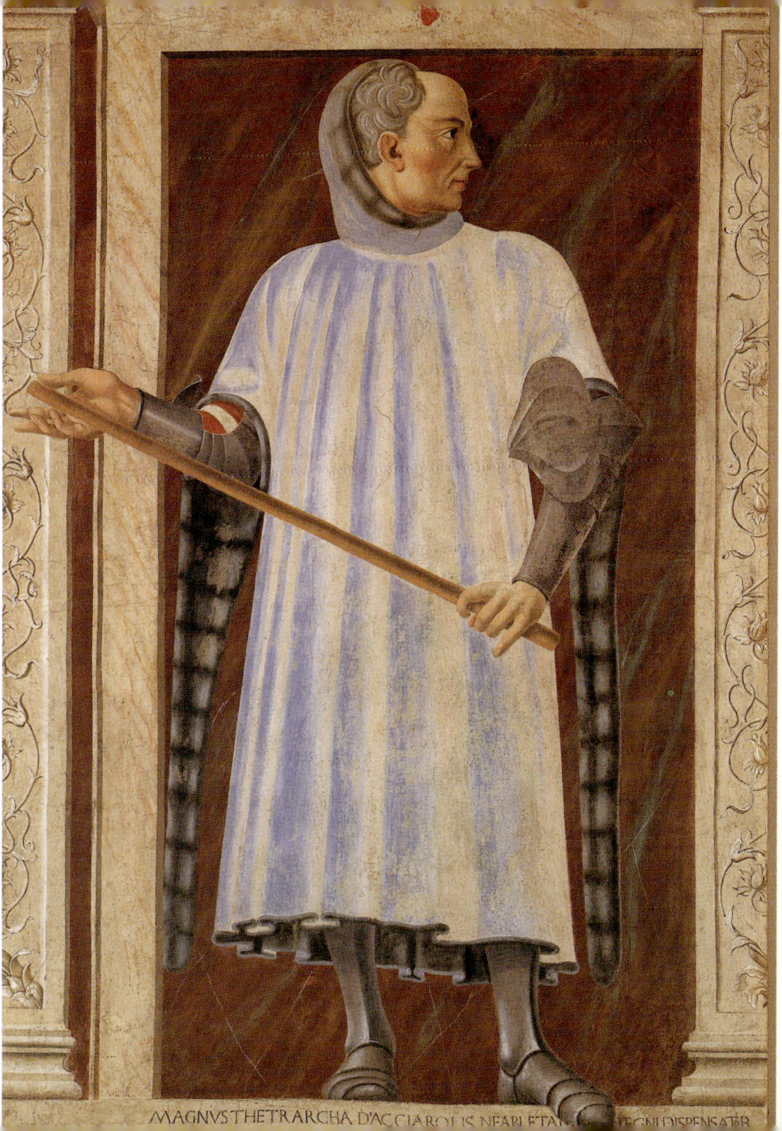
MAGNVS THETRARCHA D'ACCIAROLIS

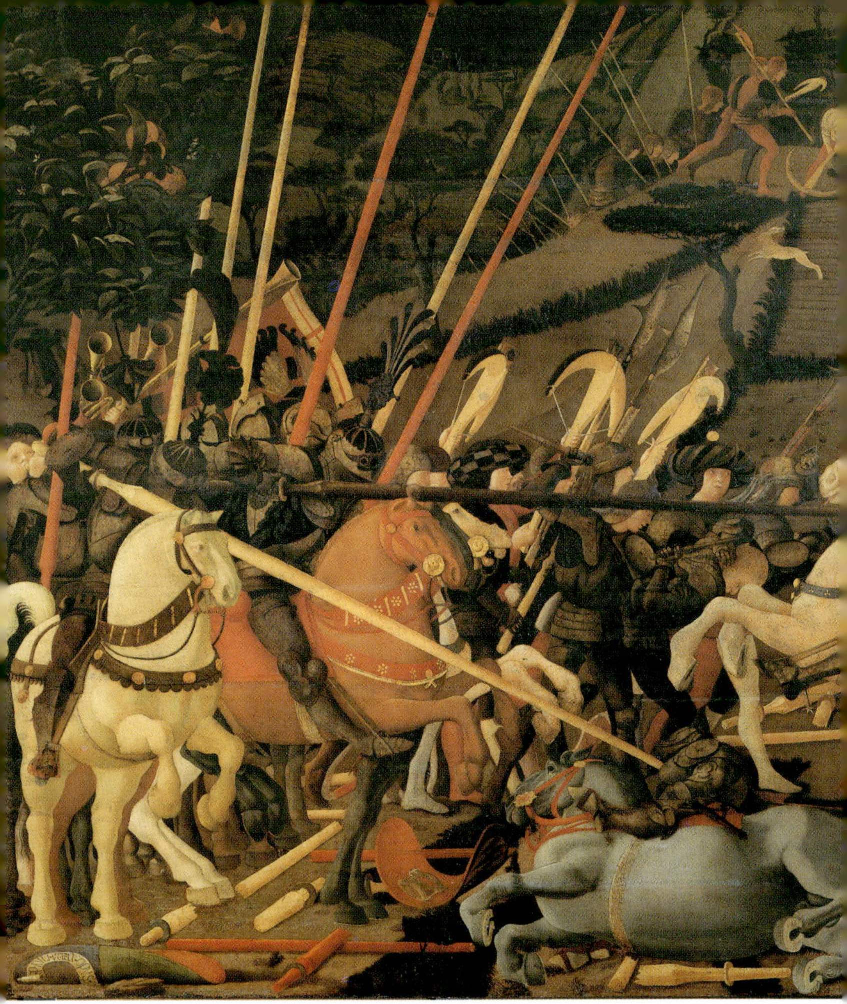

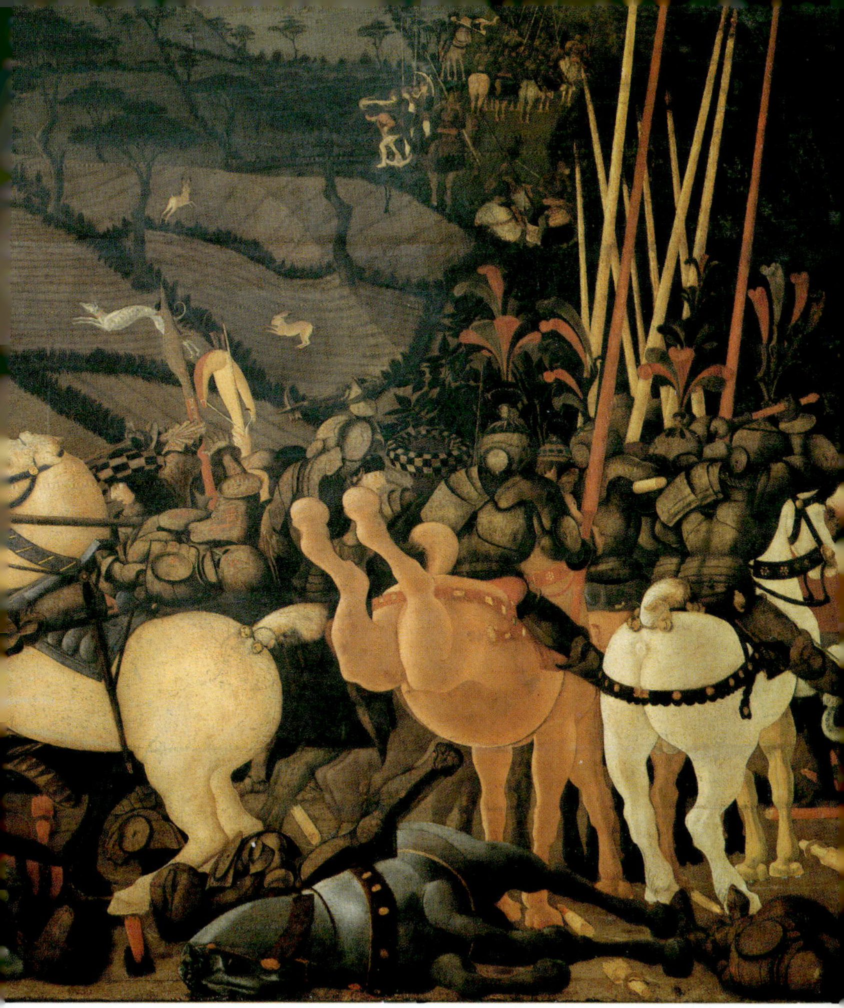

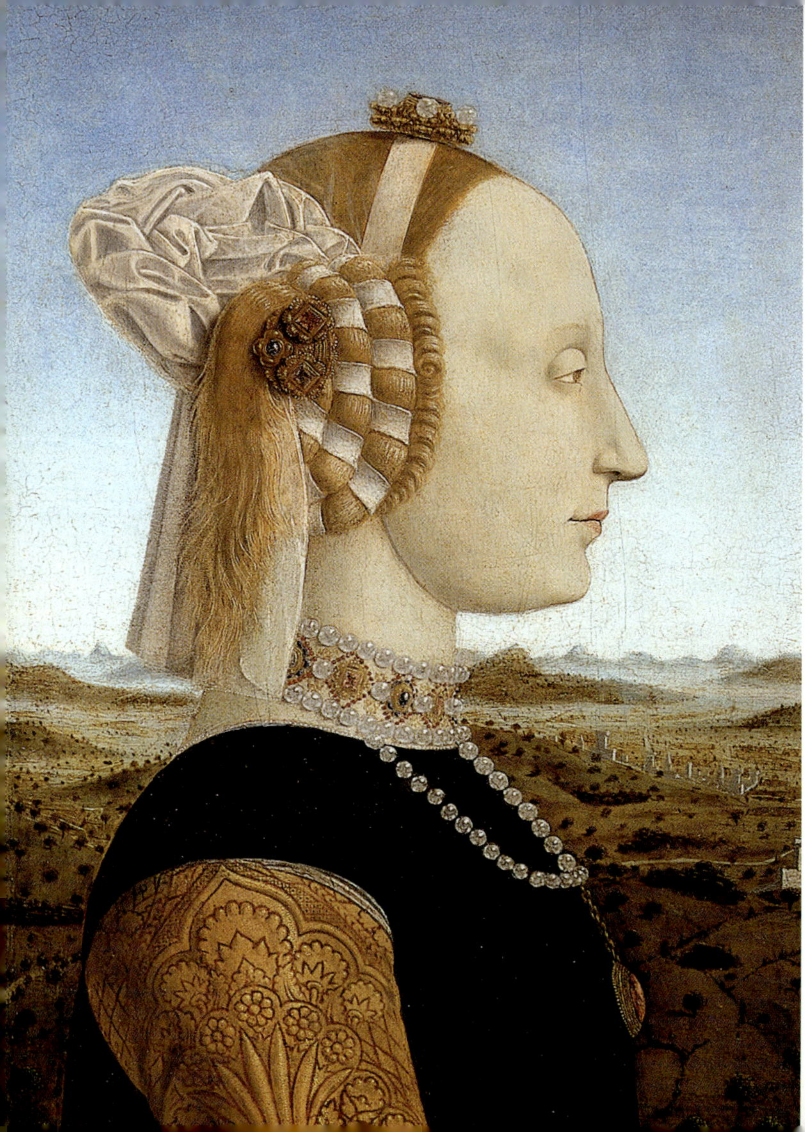

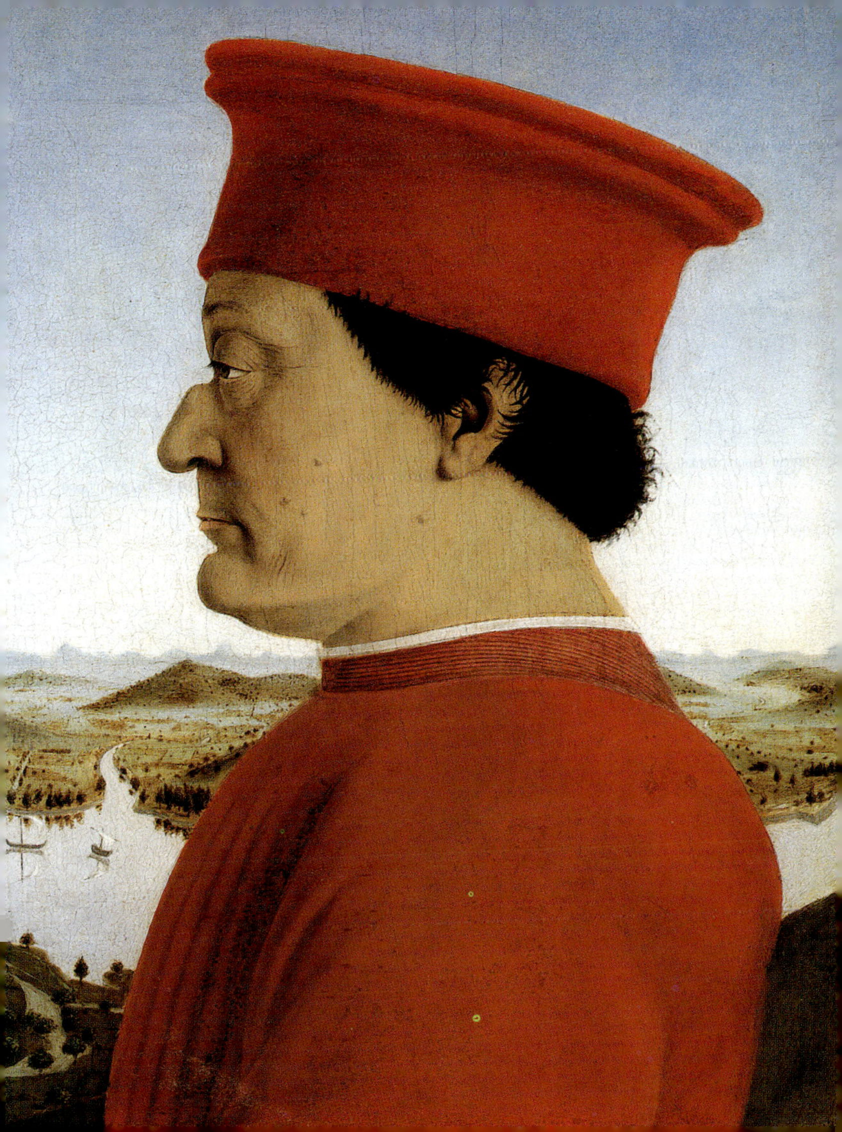

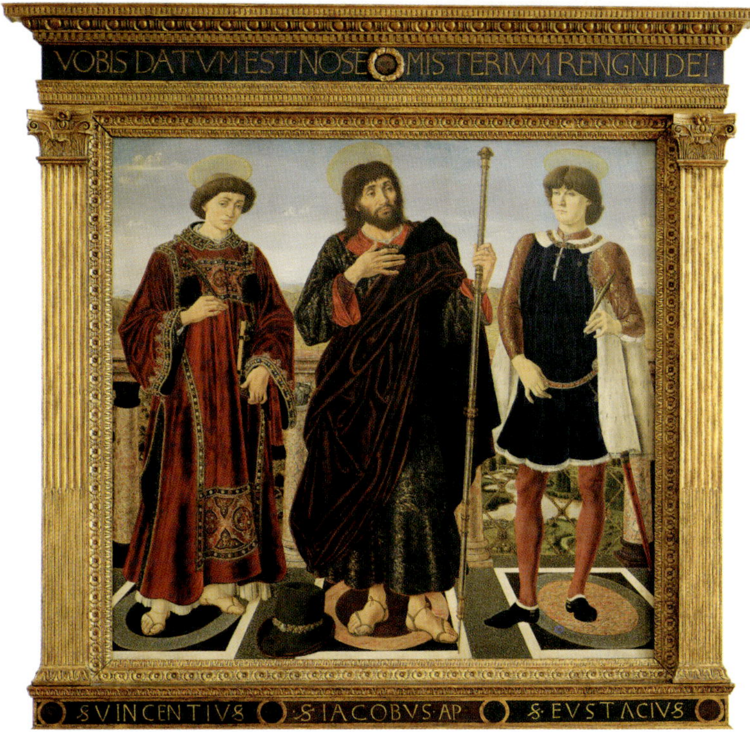

Above:
Antonio and Piero del Pollaiuolo,
The Cardinal of Portugal Altarpiece,
c. 1466-1468 , tempera on wood.
Uffizi, from the Cardinal
of Portugal's Chapel in
San Miniato al Monte.

Opposite page:
Sandro Botticelli,
Portrait of a Young Man with a Medal,
c. 1475 , tempera on wood
and gilded stucco.
Uffizi.

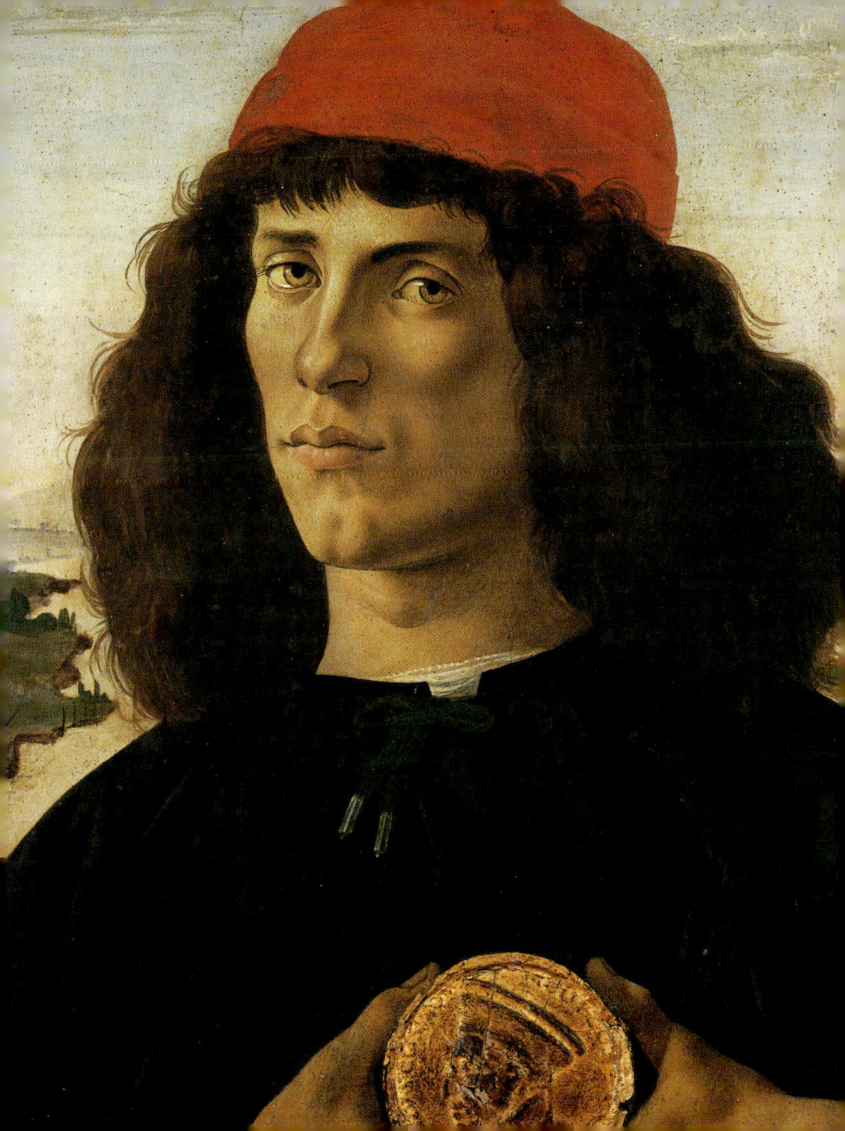

Opposite page:
Andrea del Verrocchio, Leonardo da Vinci and collaborators, *Baptism of Christ*, 1470-1475, tempera and oil on wood. Uffizi. The work was painted for the monastery of San Salvi in Verrocchio's shop, where the young Leonardo was working at the time; his hand may be recognized in the angel seen in profile and in the landscape in the background, retouched in oil. It has been hypothesized that the angel on the right was painted by Botticelli.

Following pages:
Sandro Botticelli, *Primavera*, 1481-1482, grease tempera on wood. Uffizi.
Sandro Botticelli,
The Birth of Venus, c. 1484, tempera on linen. Uffizi.
The symbolic meaning of Botticelli's two most famous paintings is still debated. The *Primavera* is thought to be either a complex nuptial allegory inspired by classical texts and by the verses of Poliziano for the *Giostra* of Giuliano de' Medici (1475), or a metaphor of the Liberal Arts.
It has been hypothesized that the *Birth of Venus* alludes to the fusion of Spirit and Matter, to the harmonious connubium of Idea and Nature, according to Laurentian neo-Platonic theories.

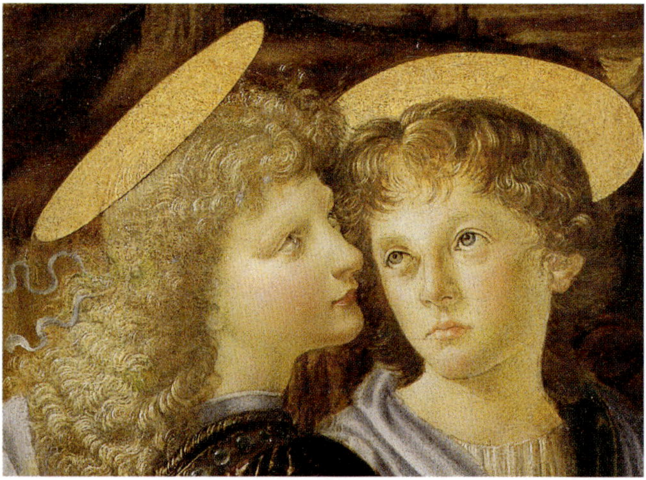

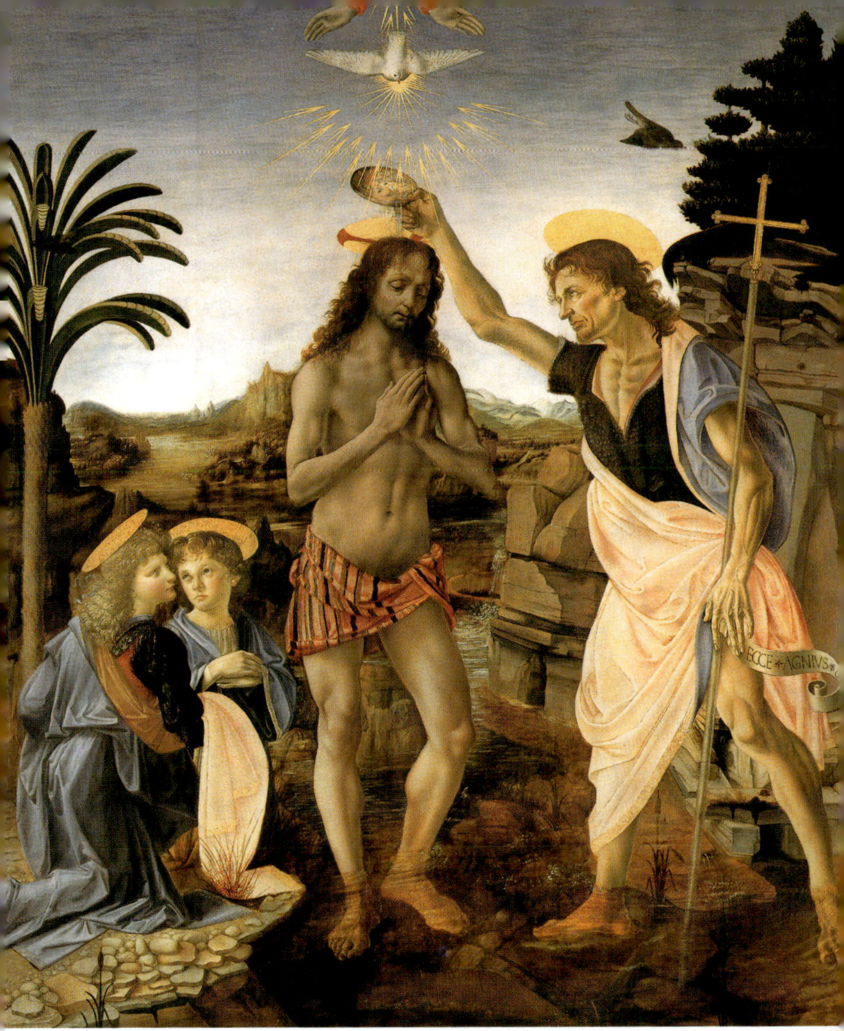
ECCE AGNIVS

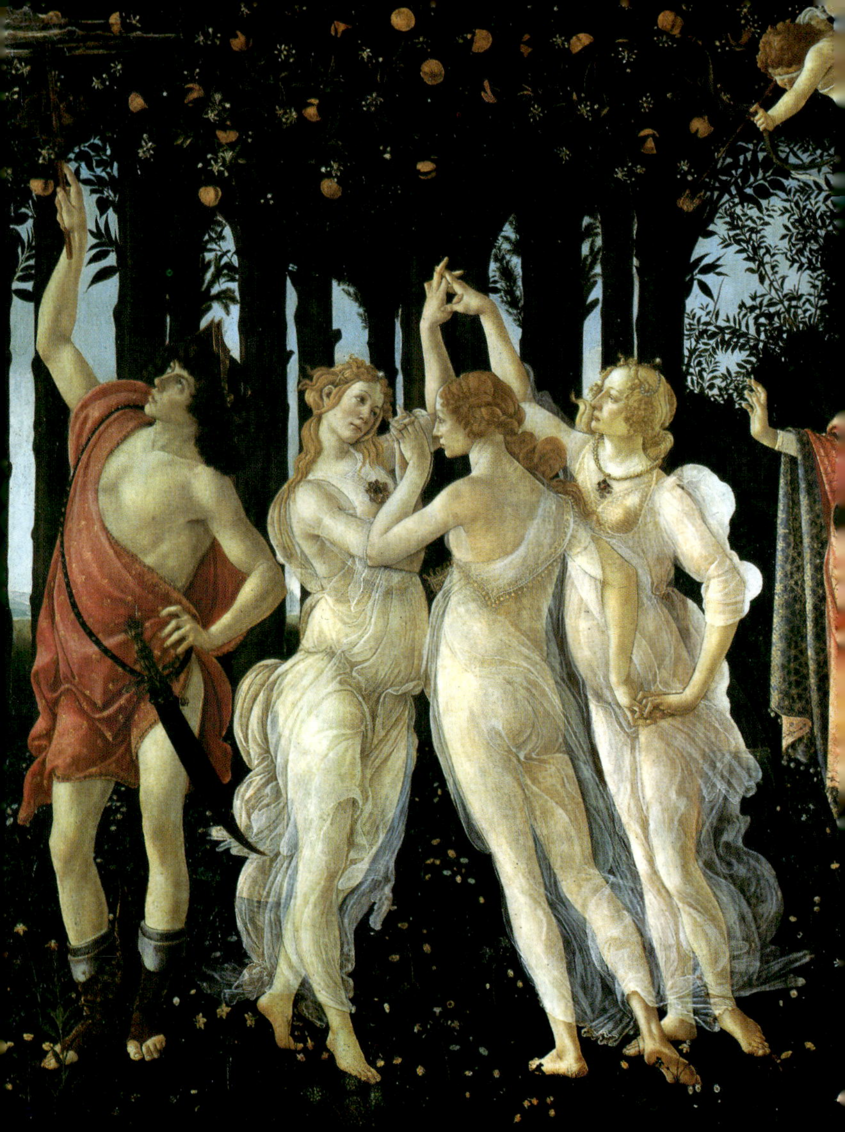

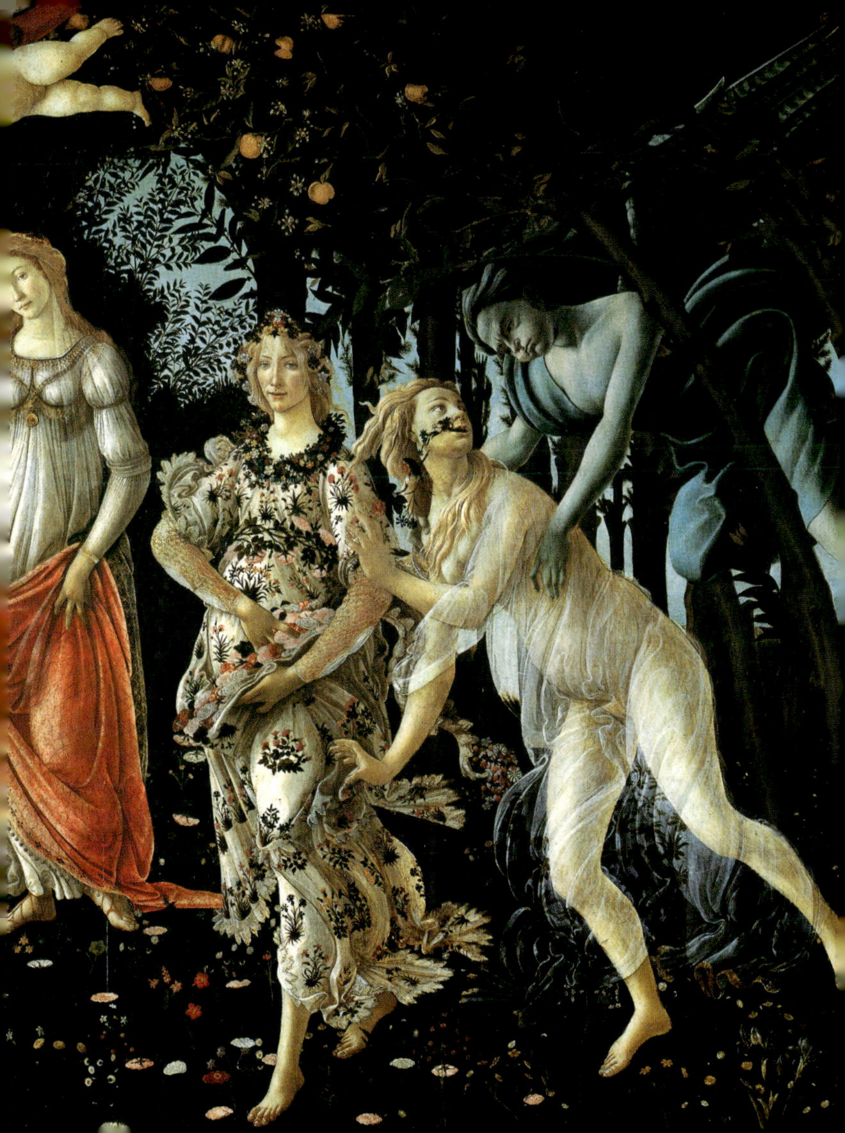

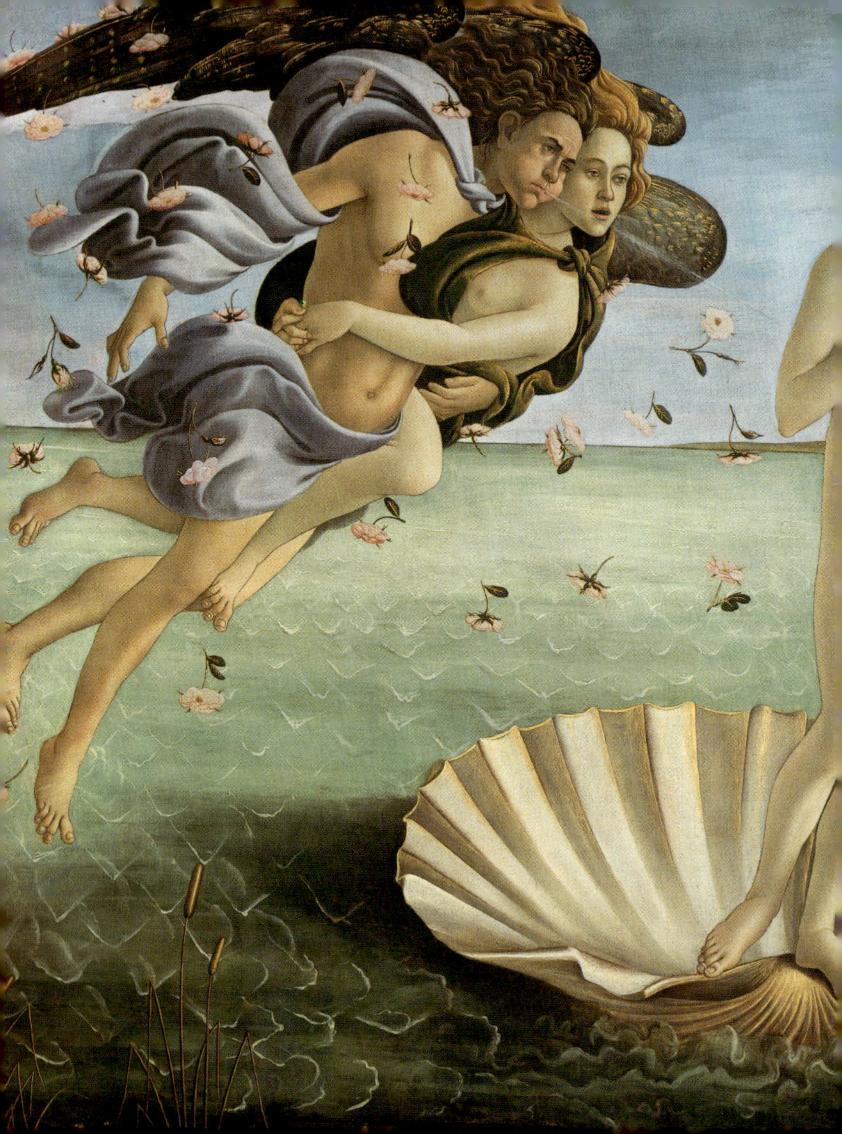

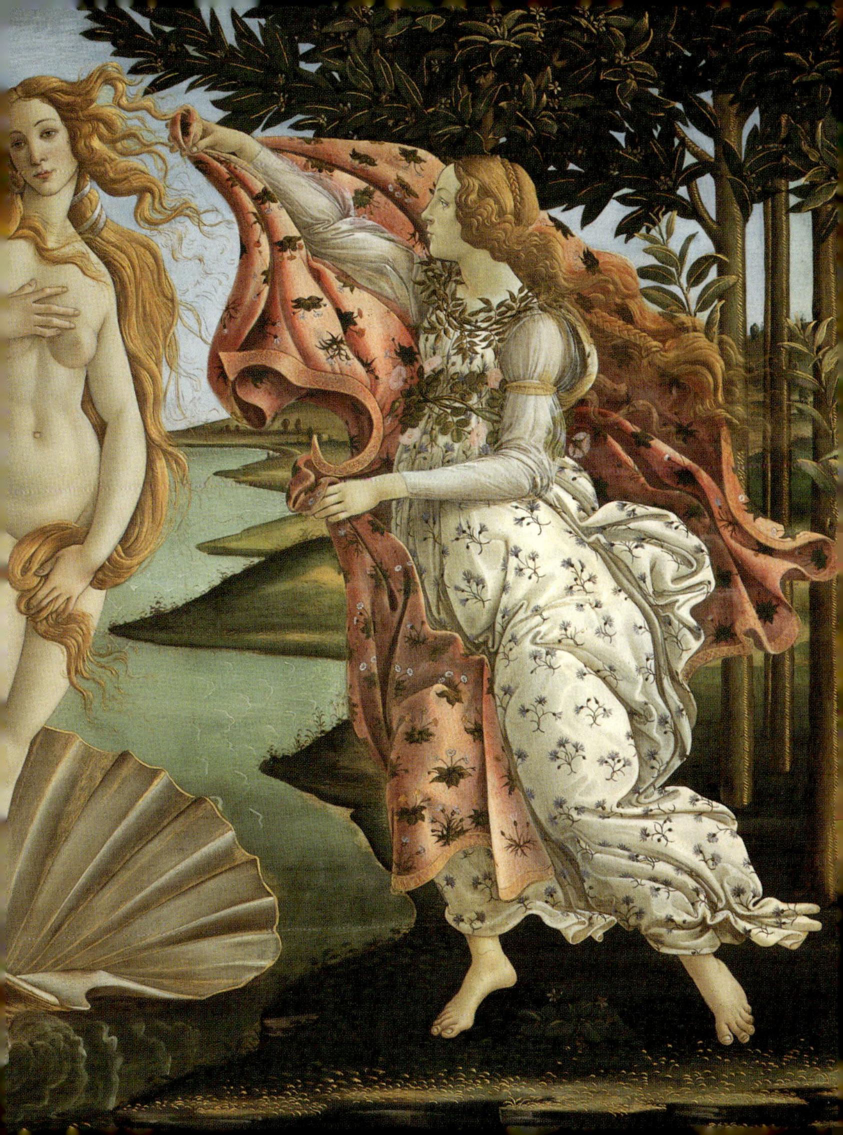

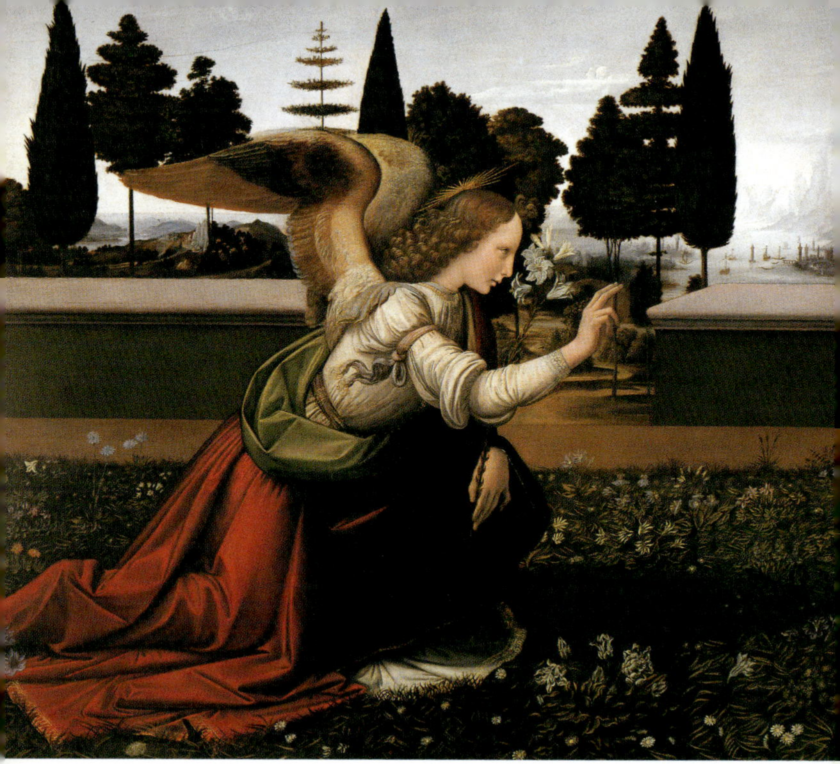

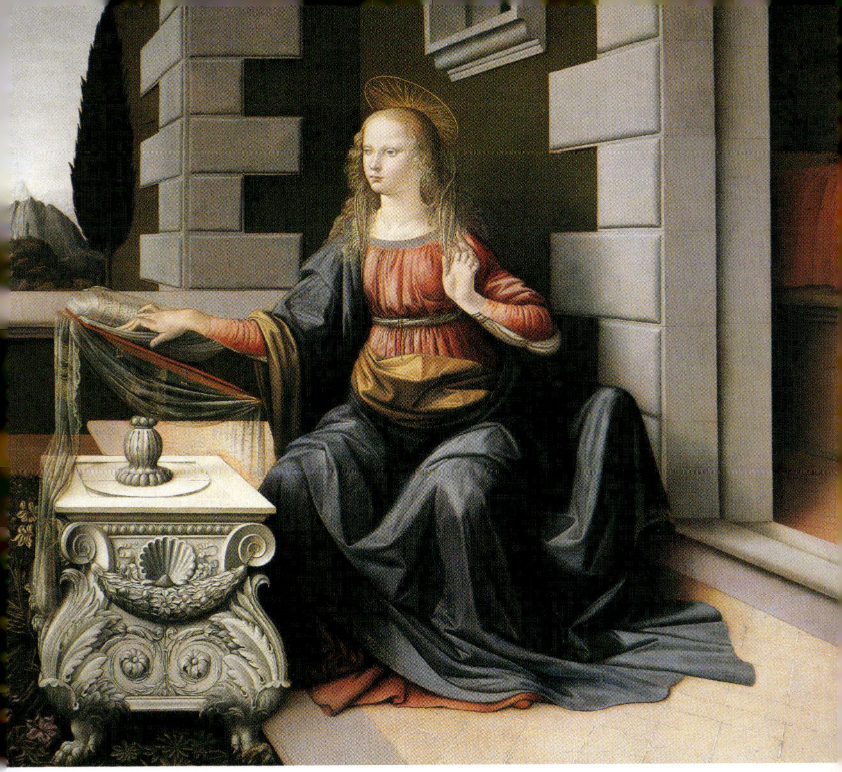

Above:
Leonardo da Vinci, *Annunciation*,
c. 1472, tempera mixed with oil on wood. Uffizi.

Following pages:
Filippino Lippi, *Madonna and Child with Saints*,
1486, tempera on wood. Uffizi.
Pietro Perugino, *Portrait of Francesco delle Opere,*
1494, oil on wood. Uffizi.

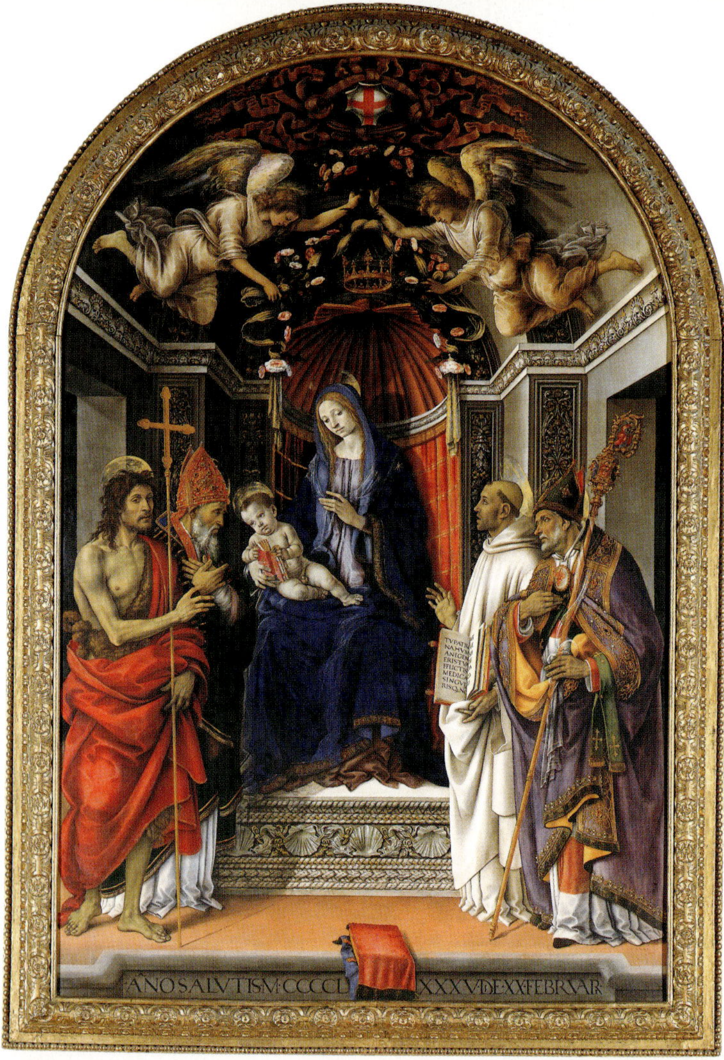
ANOSALVTISM·CCCCL
XXXV·DIE·XX·FEBRVAR

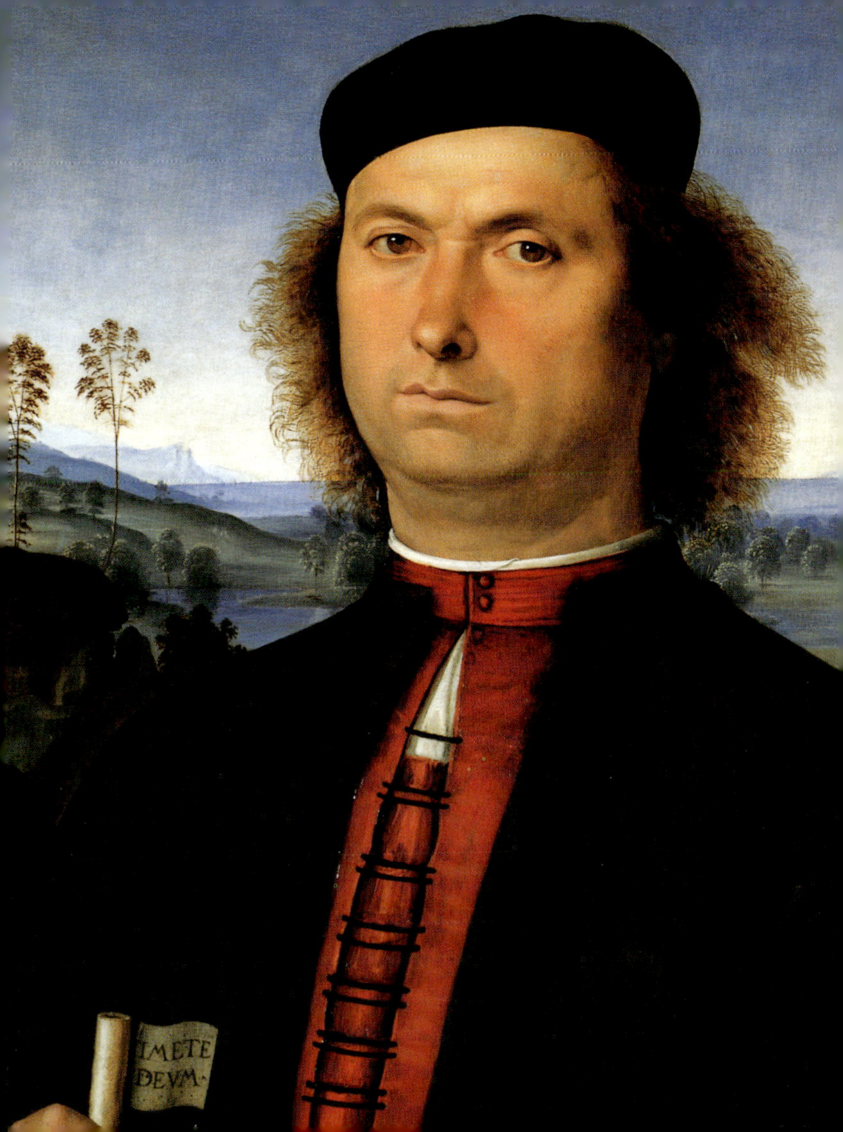
IMETE
DEVM·

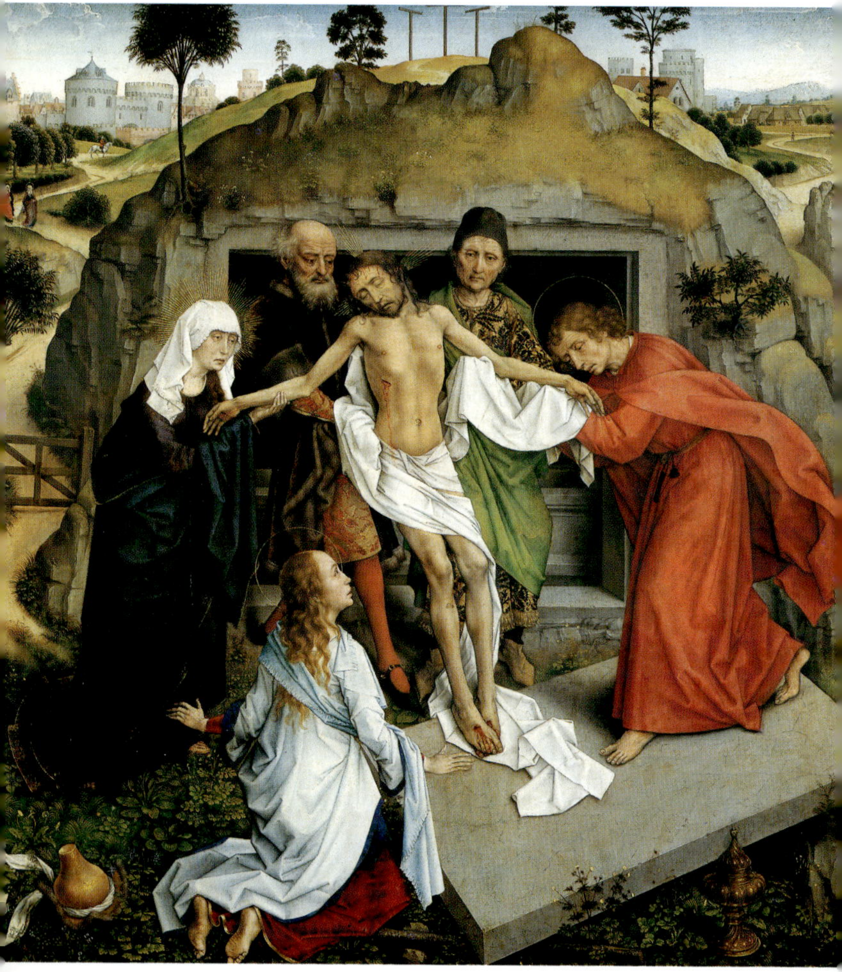

FOREIGN PAINTING IN THE RENAISSANCE

The group of Flemish, Dutch and German 15th and 16th century paintings, many of them documented in Florence at a very early time, is represented primarily by two works by Rogier van der Weyden and Hugo van der Goes, both of them linked, for different reasons, to the history of Florence. The splendid *Deposition in the Sepulchre* (c. 1460) by Rogier van der Weyden was documented in the Medicean villa of Careggi at least from 1482. It has been suggested that it was commissioned by Cosimo the Elder, whose features have been recognized in the figure of Nicodemus, sumptuously arrayed. For this composition Rogier drew inspiration from the predella (now in Munich) of the *St. Mark Altarpiece,* painted by Fra Angelico for the Medici in 1440. It is thus probable that the Flemish artist had been to Florence, perhaps during a voyage to Italy for the Jubilee of 1450. The fertile exchange between Flemish and Florentine art, which was to continue throughout the century, is confirmed by the great *Triptych* of Hugo van der Goes, painted in Bruges around 1478 for Tommaso Portinari, who was director of the Medici bank in that city. The great painting, its side panels painted with

Opposite page:
Rogier van der Weyden, *Deposition in the Sepulchre,* c. 1460, oil on oakwood. Uffizi, from the Medicean villa of Careggi.

monochrome figures on the back too according to Flemish tradition, made its solemn entry into Florence in 1483, to be placed over the high altar of Sant'Eligio, the favorite church of the Portinari family. The Portinari also commissioned portraits of another Flemish painter, Hans Memling, who is well represented in the Gallery with paintings on religious themes. At the end of the century, German artists too began to approach Italian art, were attracted and influenced by it. First among them was Albrecht Dürer (represented in the Uffizi by masterpieces from both his youth and his maturity), who had studied the paintings of Mantegna, Giovanni Bellini and Leonardo in Venice and whose engravings attracted the interest, in Florence, of early Mannerist artists such as Pontormo. Of Holbein, instead, an original, superbly skilled portrait painter from Augsburg who died of plague in London in 1543, we have the intense *Portrait of Richard Southwell*, acquired in 1620 by Cosimo II de' Medici, as well as the artist's *Self-portrait* (1542), a pastel on paper purchased in London in 1681 on behalf of Cosimo III de' Medici. And a beautiful Italianized portrait by the German artist Georg Pencz, considered the most talented among the *petites maitres* influenced by Dürer, also hangs in the Uffizi.

Opposite page:
Hans Memling,
Madonna enthroned with Child and Musical Angels,
c. 1490, oil on wood. Uffizi.
Already by the end of the century this painting must have been in Florence, since the landscape in the background, typically Nordic, was faithfully copied by Fra Bartolomeo in a painting now in New York.

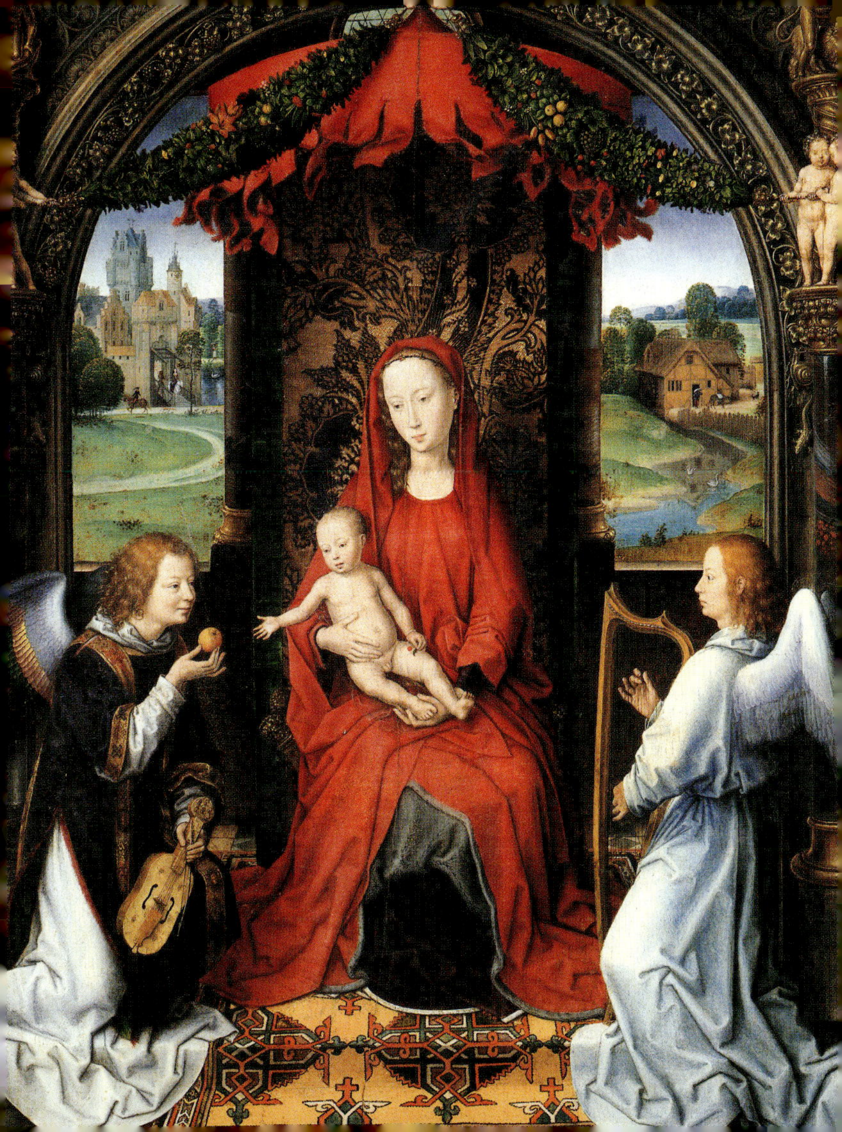

These pages:
Hugo van der Goes,
Portinari Triptych, detail from the central panel, c. 1478. oil on wood. Uffizi.
For Florentine artists such as Ghirlandaio and Filippino Lippi, the most striking element in Flemish painting was its meticulous care for detail.

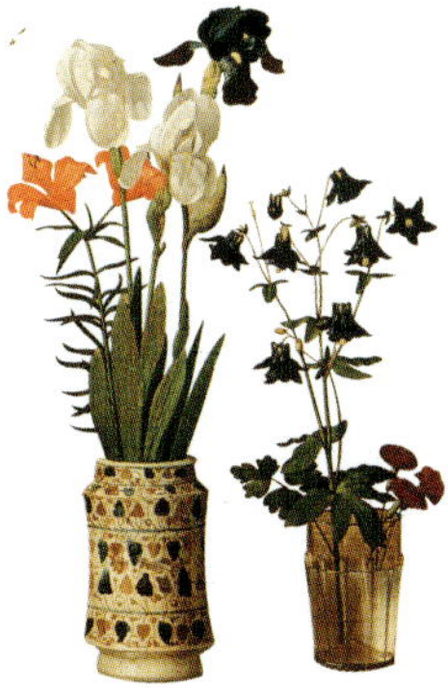

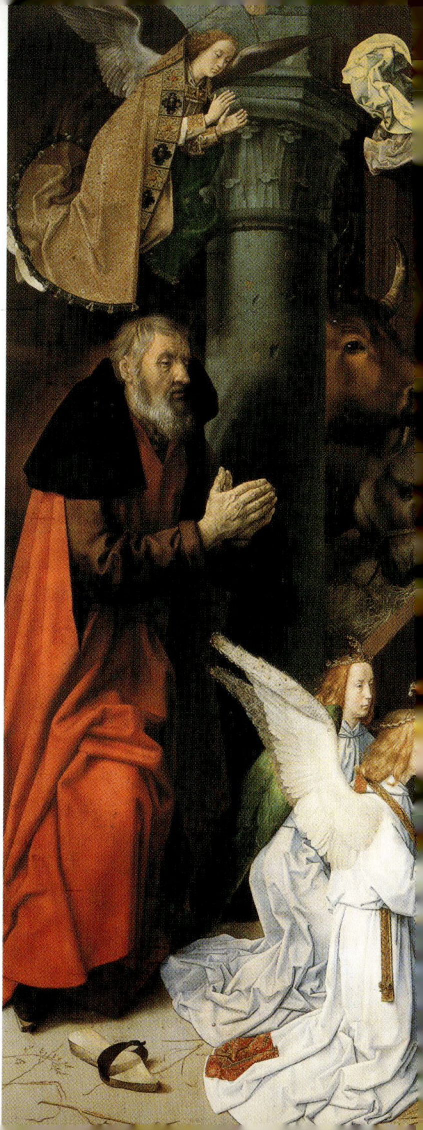

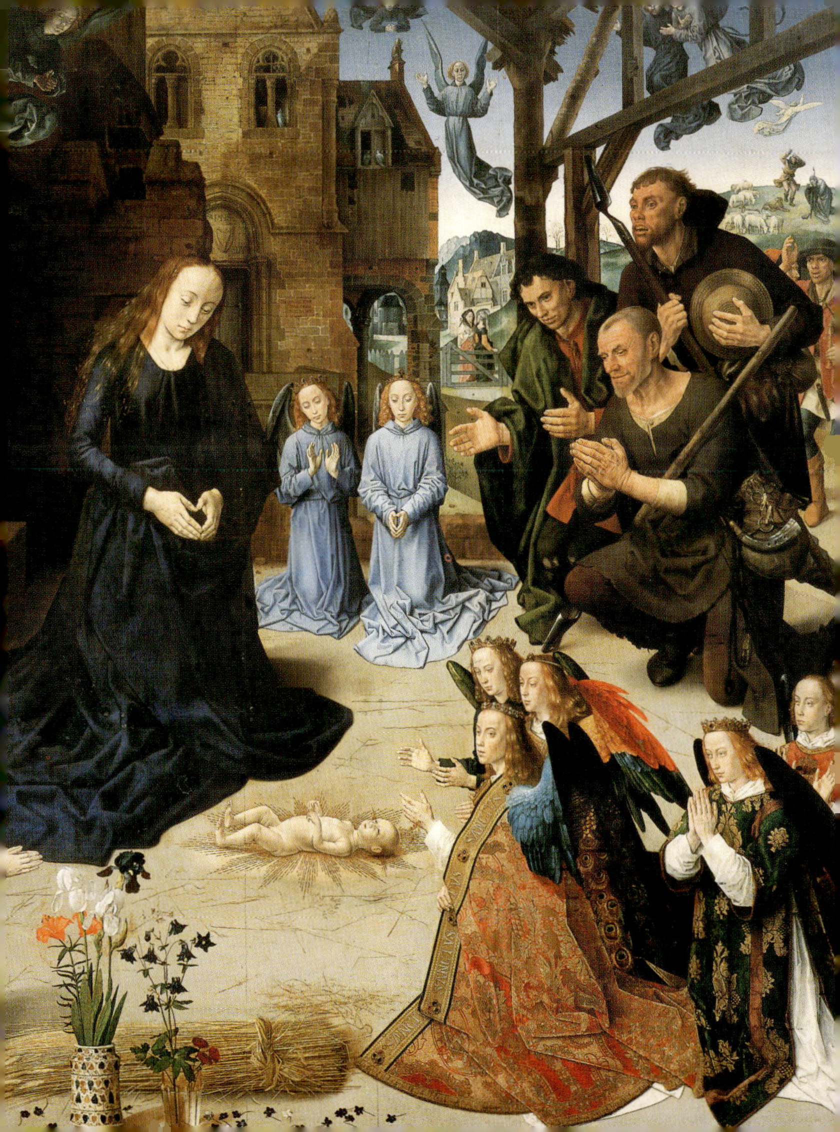

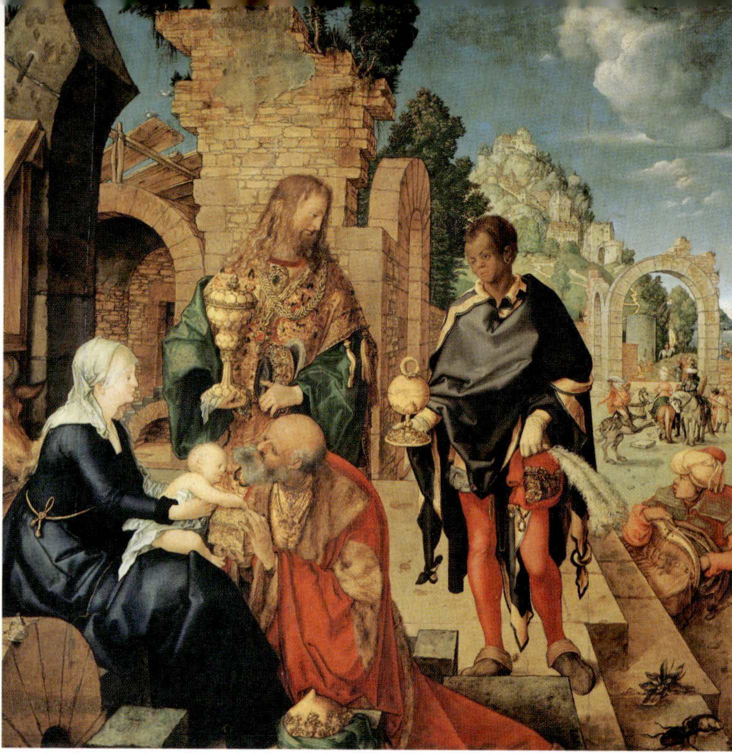

Above:
Albrecht Dürer, *Adoration of the Magi*, 1504, oil on wood. Uffizi.

Opposite page:
Hans Holbein, *Portrait of Richard Southwell, testamentary executor of Henry VIII of England*, 1536, oil on wood.
Uffizi, requested of the Duke of Arundel as a gift by Cosimo II de'Medici in 1620.

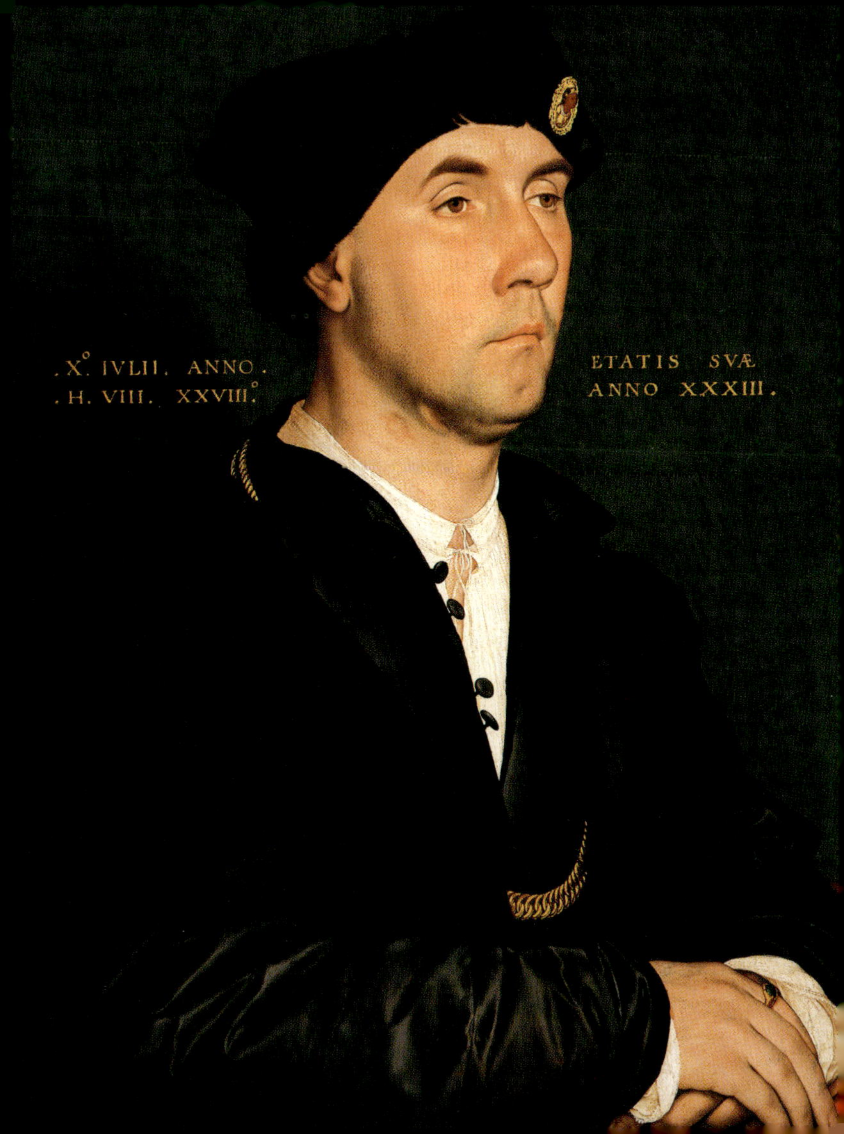
.X°. IVLII. ANNO.
.H. VIII. XXVIII°.
ETATIS SVÆ
ANNO XXXIII.

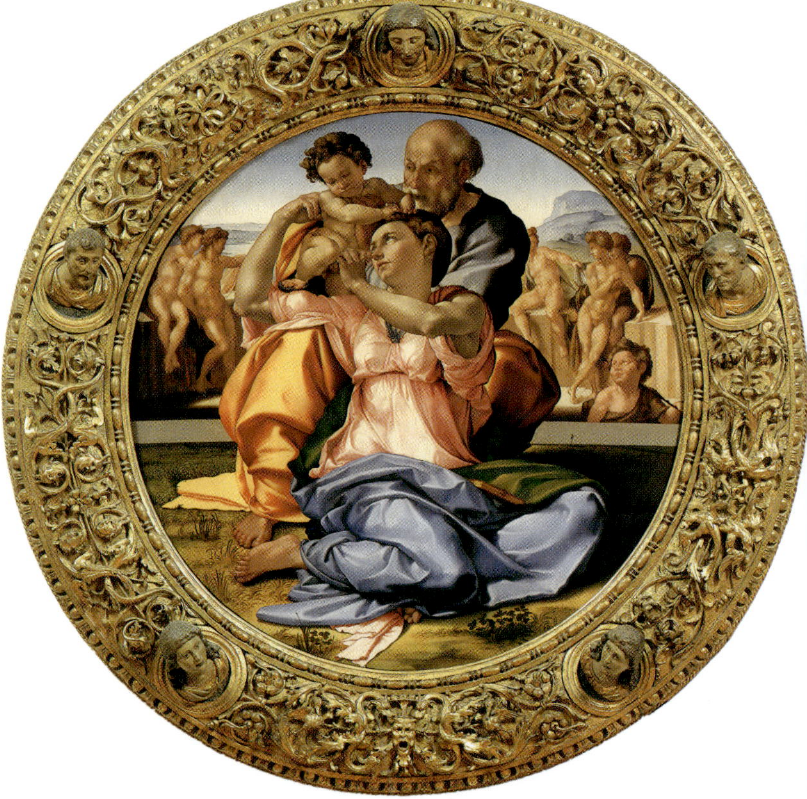

The collection of 16th century paintings, representating practically all of the Italian schools, is so vast as to make it impossible here even to summarize a full list, for which reference may be made once again to our *Uffizi. Art, History, Collections*. Among the main groups, the first is that of the great 16th century Florentine masters, foremost among them Michelangelo. His *Doni Tondo* (1506-1508) is rightly considered the most emblematic painting of the century. Painted after the disinterrment in 1506 of the Hellenistic group the *Laocoön,* from which derives the pose of the nude sitting behind St. Joseph, the tondo, thought to be linked to a birth or a wedding, portrays an unusual *Holy Family* portrayed in gelid colors, with a revolutionary serpentine composition. It was commissioned by the Florentine merchant Agnolo Doni, perhaps on the occasion of the birth of his daughter Maria in 1507. The frame, with its richly carved all-round medallions, is original; on it, the presence of Christ, angels and prophets seems to refer to the still unknown symbolic meaning of the composition, animated in the background by sculptural nudes with an abstract landscape fading into the distance. Some paintings by Raphael,

Opposite page:
Michelangelo, *Doni Tondo (Holy Family with the Infant St. John the Baptist,* c. 1506-1508, tempera on wood, coeval frame in carved and gilded wood. Uffizi.

who sojourned in Florence as a young man, working for important clients such as the Nasi and Doni families, belong to the early years of the century. The intense *Portrait of Leo X with two Cardinals* (1518), commissioned by the Medici pope after the artist had moved to Rome, is also his work. A precious testimony of important clients are the panels painted by Perin Del Vaga and Francesco Granacci, friend and collaborator of Michelangelo, to decorate the bridal chamber of Pierfrancesco Borgherini in Borgo Santi Apostoli, of which marvelous descriptions remain. Other artists who worked on it were Andrea del Sarto and his pupil Pontormo, who together with Rosso Fiorentino represent the most transgressive, by now Mannerist, wing of early

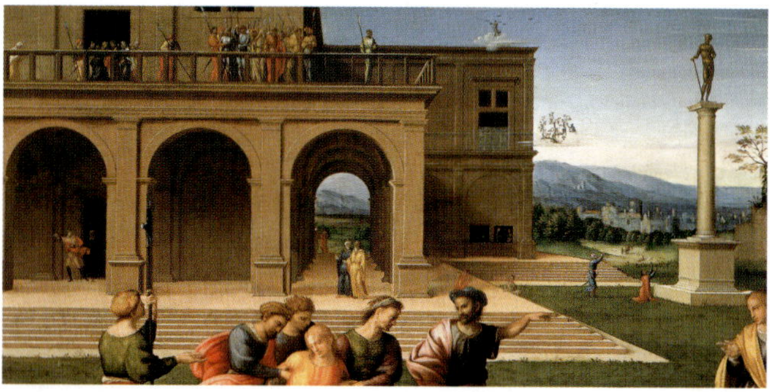

Above: Francesco Granacci, *Joseph led away to Prison*, detail, c. 1515, tempera on wood. Uffizi, from the bridal chamber of Pierfrancesco Borgherini.

Opposite page: Raphael, *Leo X with Two Cardinals* 1518, oil on wood. Uffizi.

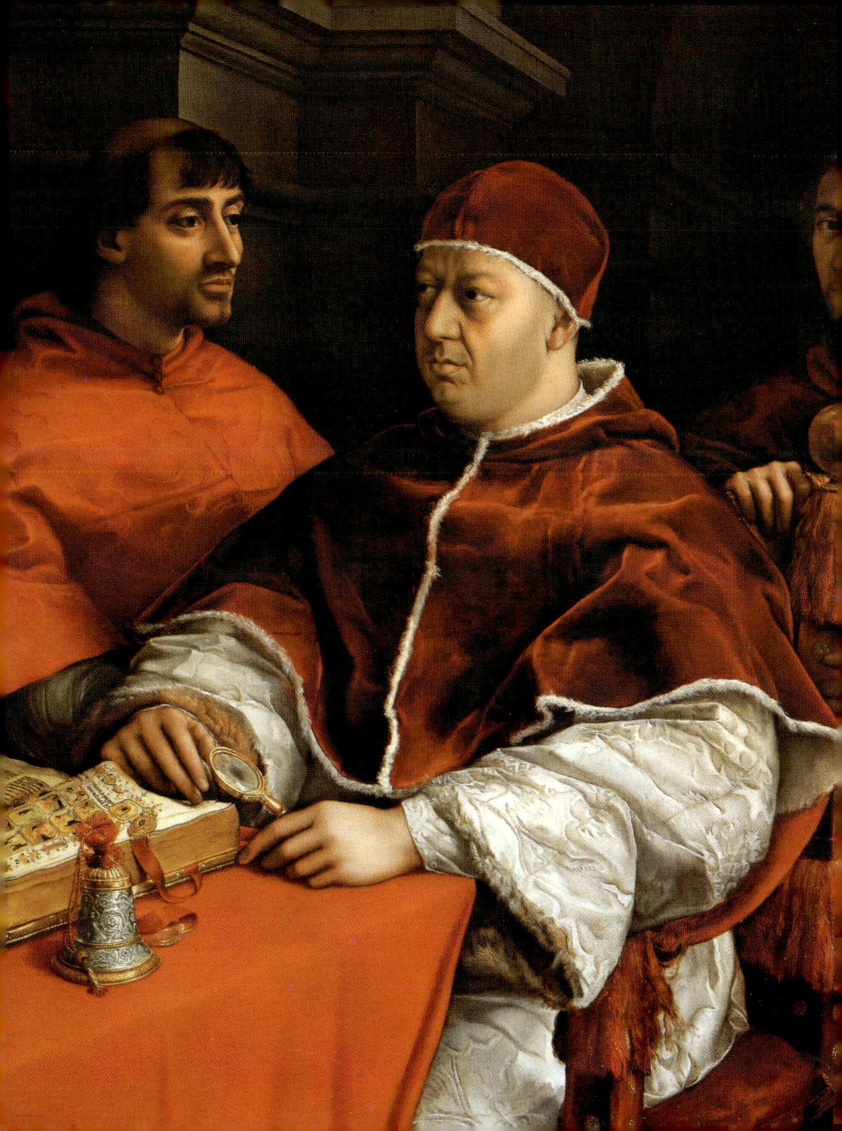

16th century Florentine art. A bizarre, highly eccentric artist was Piero di Cosimo, who worked for religious clients (*The Incarnation of Christ* for the Tedaldi Chapel in the Annunziata) and secular ones such as Filippo Strozzi. Agnolo Bronzino, a friend of Pontormo and author of magnificent Petrarchian verses, a refined, intellectual artist, was a prolific portrait painter of courtiers and high-ranking personages. His many works in the Uffizi include the *Holy Family* (c. 1541) for the Panciatichi, to whom he also dedicated two famous portraits now in the Tribune. Paintings from other schools include the unusual *Sacred Allegory* (1490 or 1504), one of the most fascinating enigmas in the art of the western world, by the Venetian Giovanni Bellini, and the strikingly inventive *Chastity of Susannah* (1517) by the isolated itinerant painter Lorenzo Lotto. Among the Emilians, Correggio and Parmigianino are well represented; by the latter, the *St. Zaccariah Madonna* (c. 1533) was in the Tribune in 1605. But it is perhaps the Venetian school to predominate, with superb masterpieces by Titian (*Flora*, the *Portraits of Francesco and Eleonora della Rovere*, and above all the perturbing *Venus of Urbino*, one of the most sensual paintings of all times), Sebastiano del Piombo, Veronese and Tintoretto. An entire section is dedicated to

Opposite page:
Pontormo, *Portrait of Cosimo the Elder*, c. 1519-1520, oil on wood. Uffizi. This portrait of the founder of the Medici family, who died in 1464, was painted for Goro Gheri, responsible from 1519 for the extraordinary administration of Florence after the death of Lorenzo Duke of Urbino.

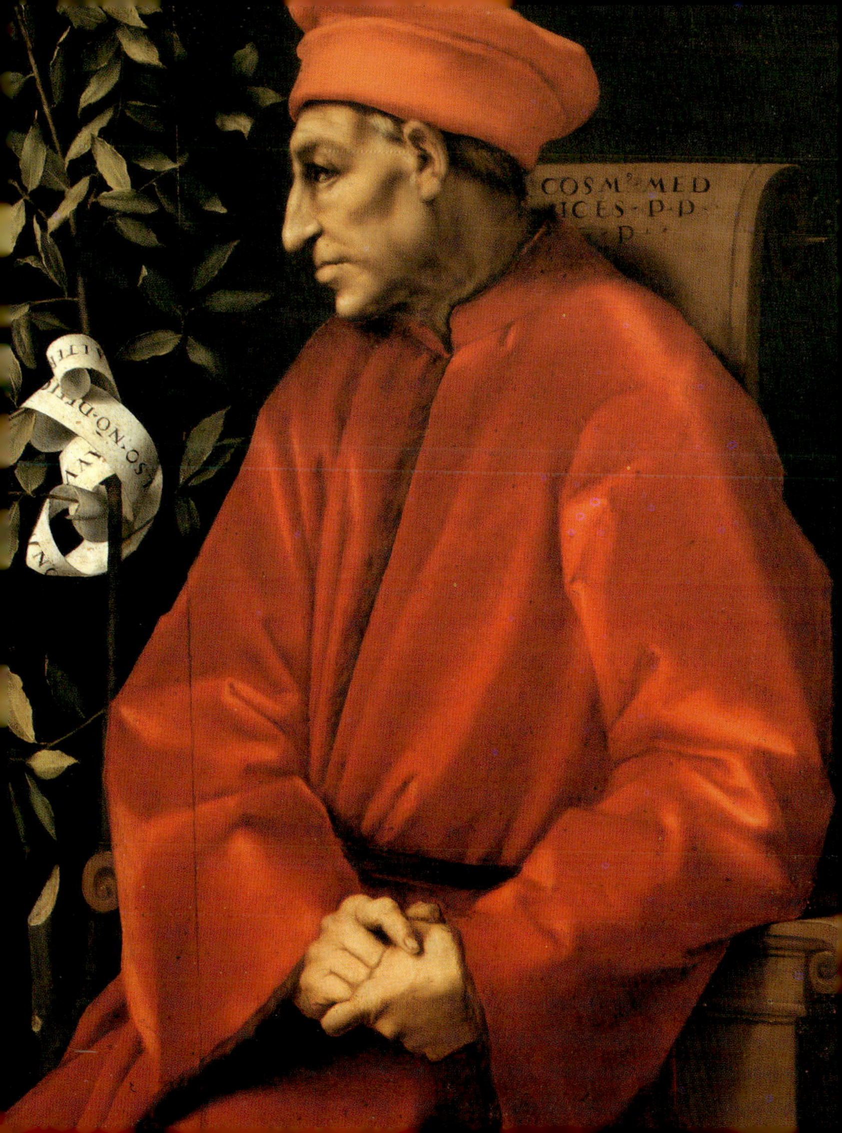

Mannerist painting in the European courts, represented both by Italian artists such as Vasari and Jacopo Zucchi, and French ones such as François Clouet. Outstanding among the Reformation artists is Federico Barocci, who painted the monumental *Madonna of the People* (1579).

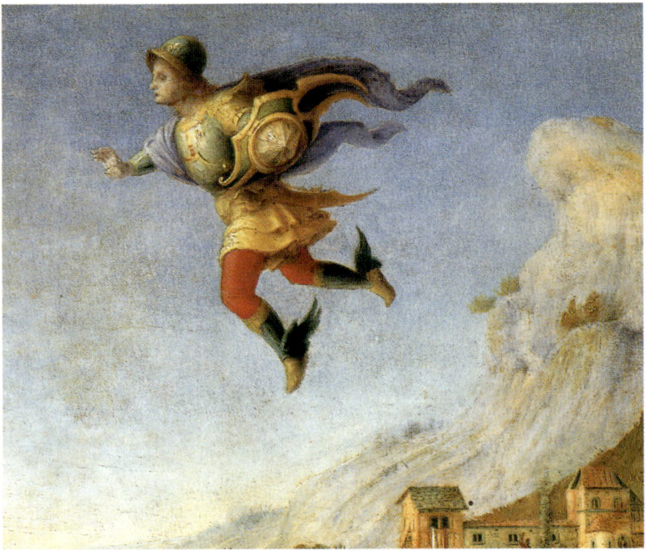

Above:
Piero di Cosimo, *Liberation of Andromeda*, detail, 1510 or 1513, oil on wood. Uffizi.

Opposite page:
Andrea del Sarto, *Woman with the "Petrarchino"*, c. 1528, oil on wood. Uffizi, in the Tribune since 1589.

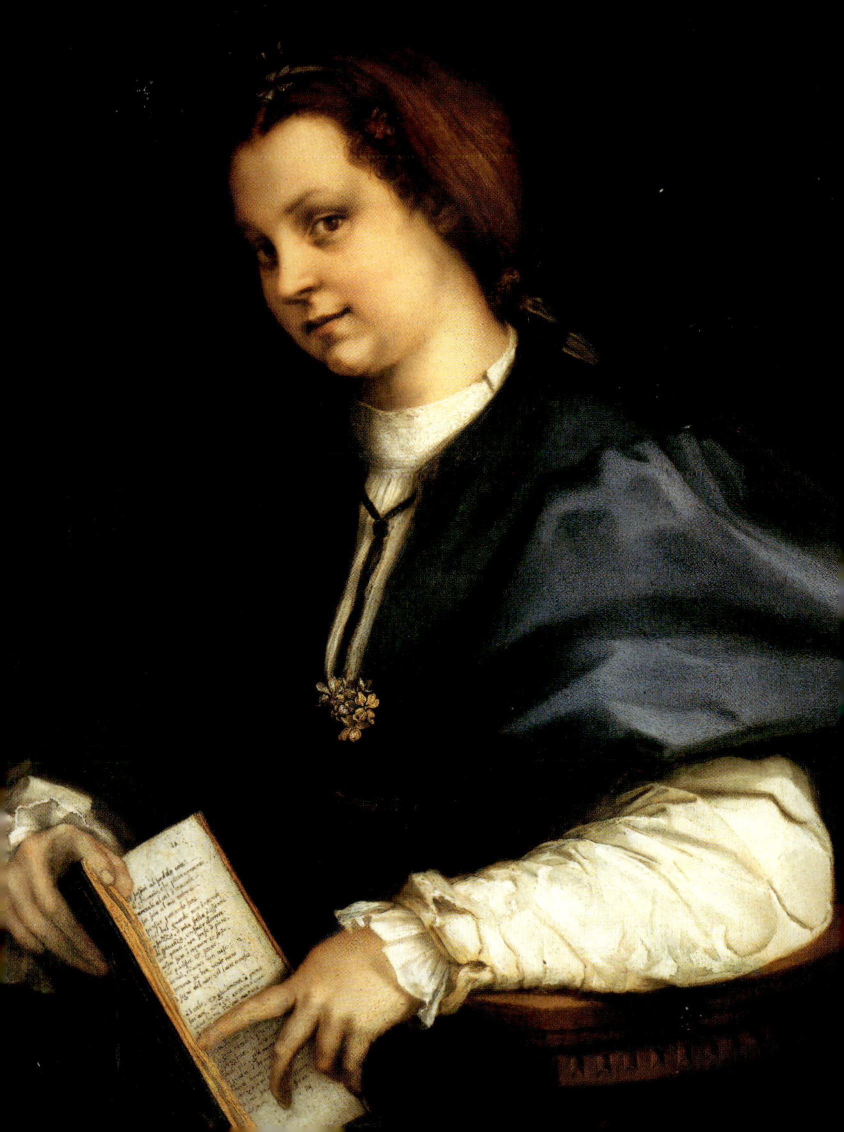

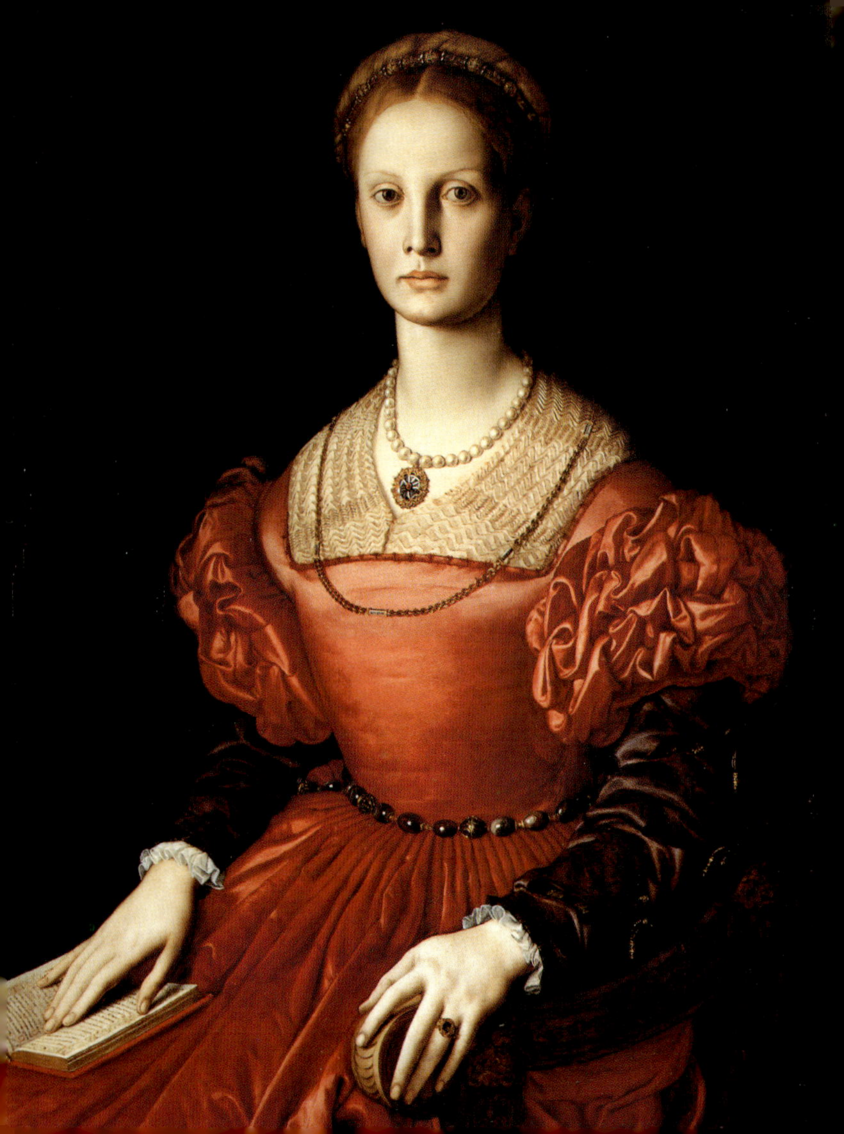

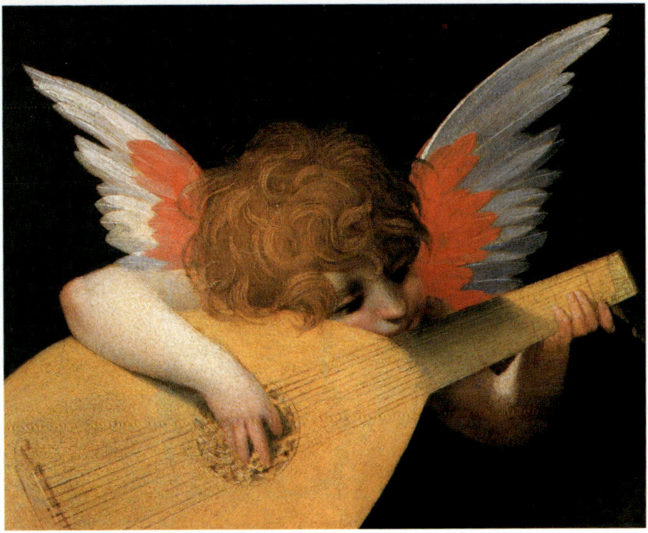

Opposite page:
Agnolo Bronzino, *Portrait of Lucrezia Panciatichi*, c. 1541, oil on wood. Uffizi.
In 1528 Lucrezia di Gismondo Pucci married Bartolomeo Panciatichi, ambassador of Cosimo I to France. Bronzino painted their two portraits in Florence, at a time when Bartolomeo held important positions. Lying against the sumptuous dress of the woman with the melancholy gaze, the gold and enamel placques of her necklace bear the words *amour dur sans fin*, which can be read in circular order without any loss of meaning.

Above:
Rosso Fiorentino, *Musical Angel*, 1521, oil on wood. Uffizi, in the Tribune since 1521.
Over the centuries, this has been one of the works most admired by visitors to the Tribune, where it has hung since 1605. Once believed to be a complete painting, it is instead the fragment of a composition in which the little angel with the lute was seated on tiered steps.

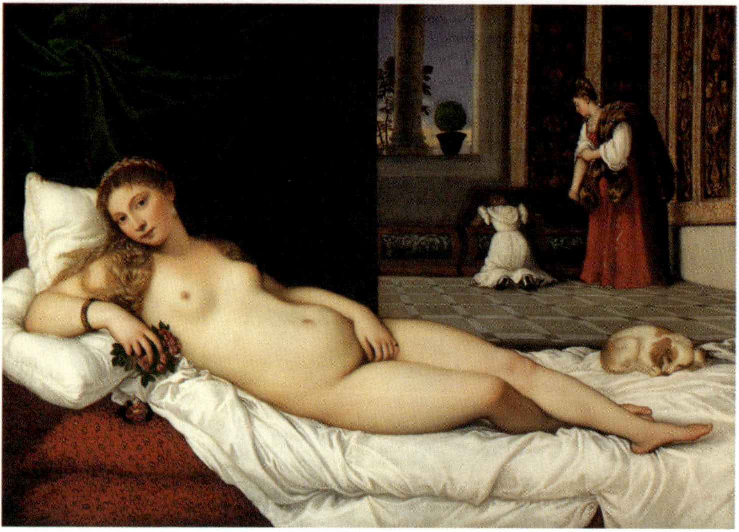

Above and opposite page:
Titian, *Venus of Urbino*,
whole and detail,
1538, oil on canvas.
Uffizi.

Arriving in Florence from Urbino in 1631 as part of the heredity of Giulia della Rovere, the canvas was painted for Guidubaldo II della Rovere, later Duke of Urbino.

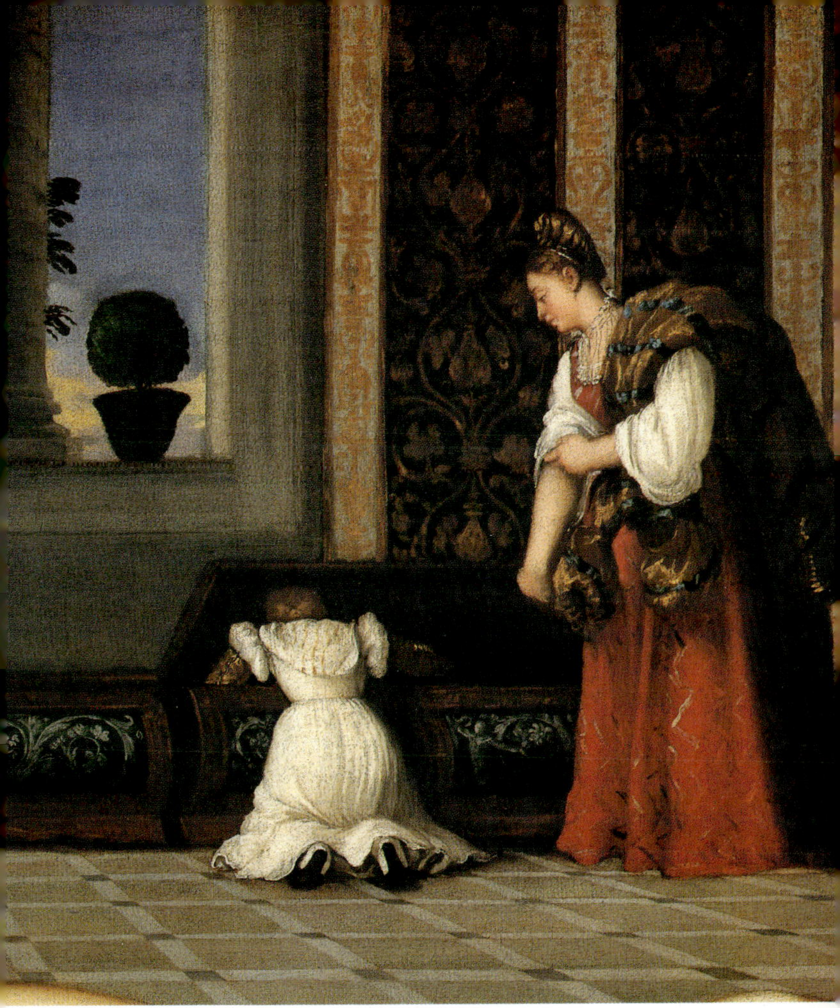

17TH AND 18TH CENTURY PAINTING

The conspicuous nucleus of 17th and 18th century paintings in the Uffizi is highly significant to the history of Medici and Lorraine collecting. The collection includes portraits, still lifes, genre and religious scenes, some of them still in the Vasari Corridor, from where they will be moved to the *pian nobile* of the museum, now undergoing remodeling. Exhibited on the second floor are masterpieces by Caravaggio, Artemisia Gentileschi, Carracci, Guido Reni, Rubens, Rembrandt, Velázquez and 18th century European masters.
Caravaggio, one of the greatest artists of all time, is represented by some of his greatest works, among them *The Adolescent Bacchus* (c. 1598), which may have been donated to Ferdinando I de' Medici by Cardinal Francesco Maria Del Monte, his protector in Rome, known for certain to have sent the Grand Duke the frightful *Head of Medusa* (1595-1598) painted on a tondo covered with canvas. Among the paintings by Rubens are the *Triumph* and the *Battle*, two enormous canvases from the series, uncompleted, dedicated to the victories of Henry IV, commissioned by his widow Maria de' Medici; by Rembrandt, the *Self-portrait as a Young Man* painted in Amsterdam around 1634; and by Goya, the delicate *Countess of Chinchón.*

Opposite page:
Caravaggio,
The Adolescent Bacchus,
c.1598, oil on canvas.
Uffizi.

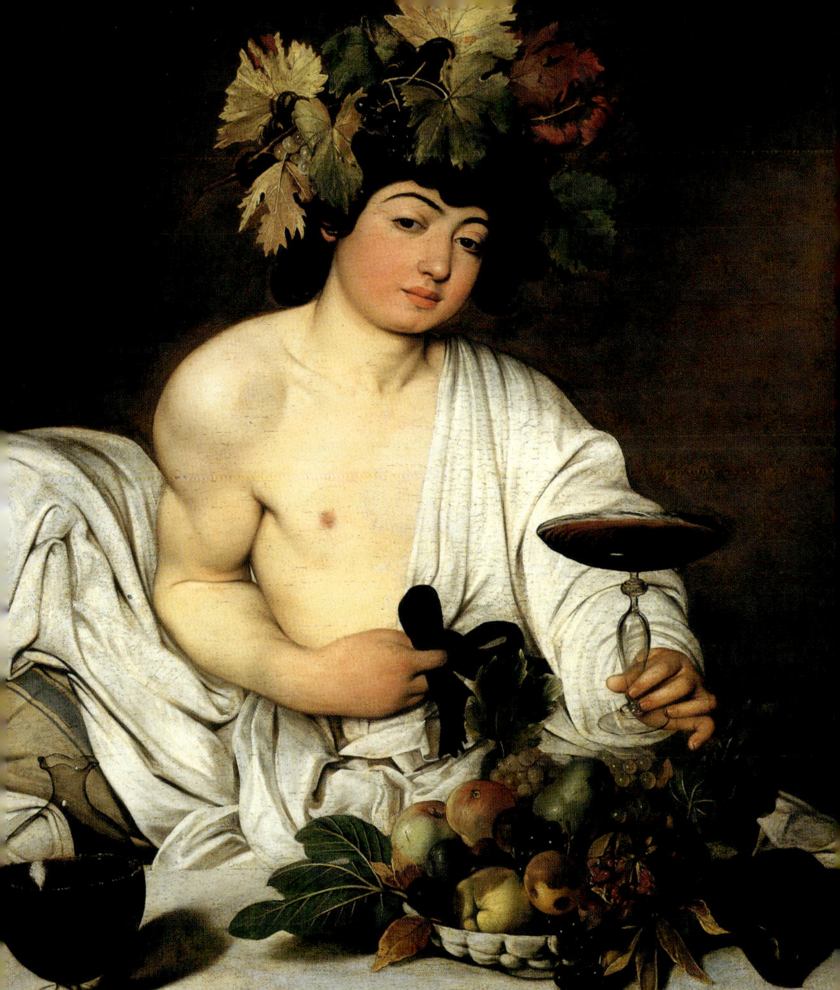

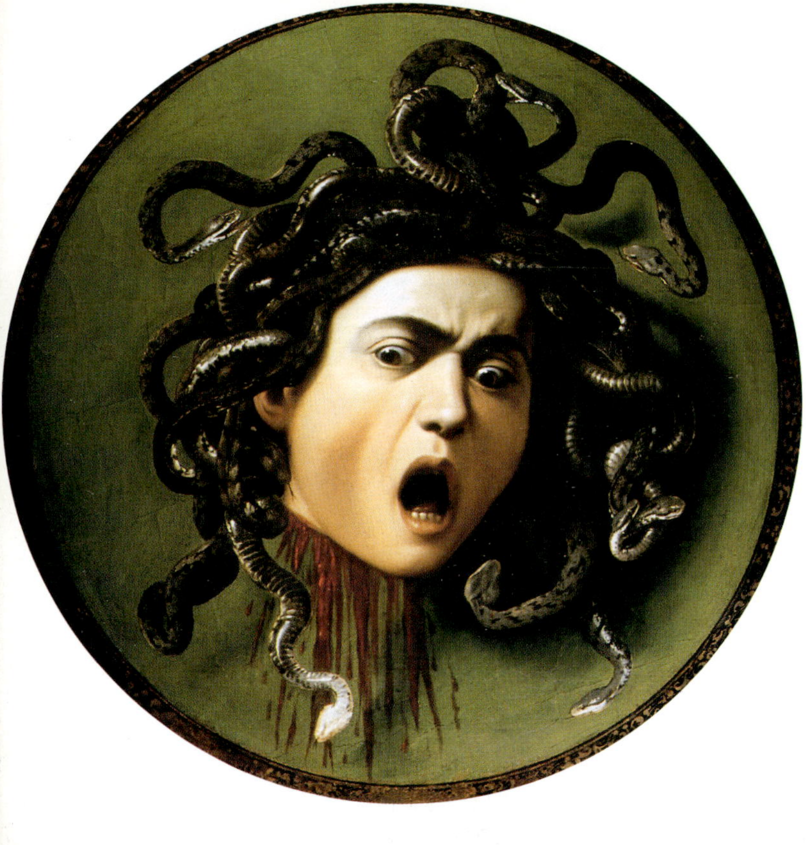

Following pages:
Caravaggio, *Head of Medusa*, 1595-1598, oil on wood covered with linen. Uffizi.

Opposite page:
Artemisia Gentileschi, *Judith and Holophernes*, c.1620, oil on canvas. Uffizi.

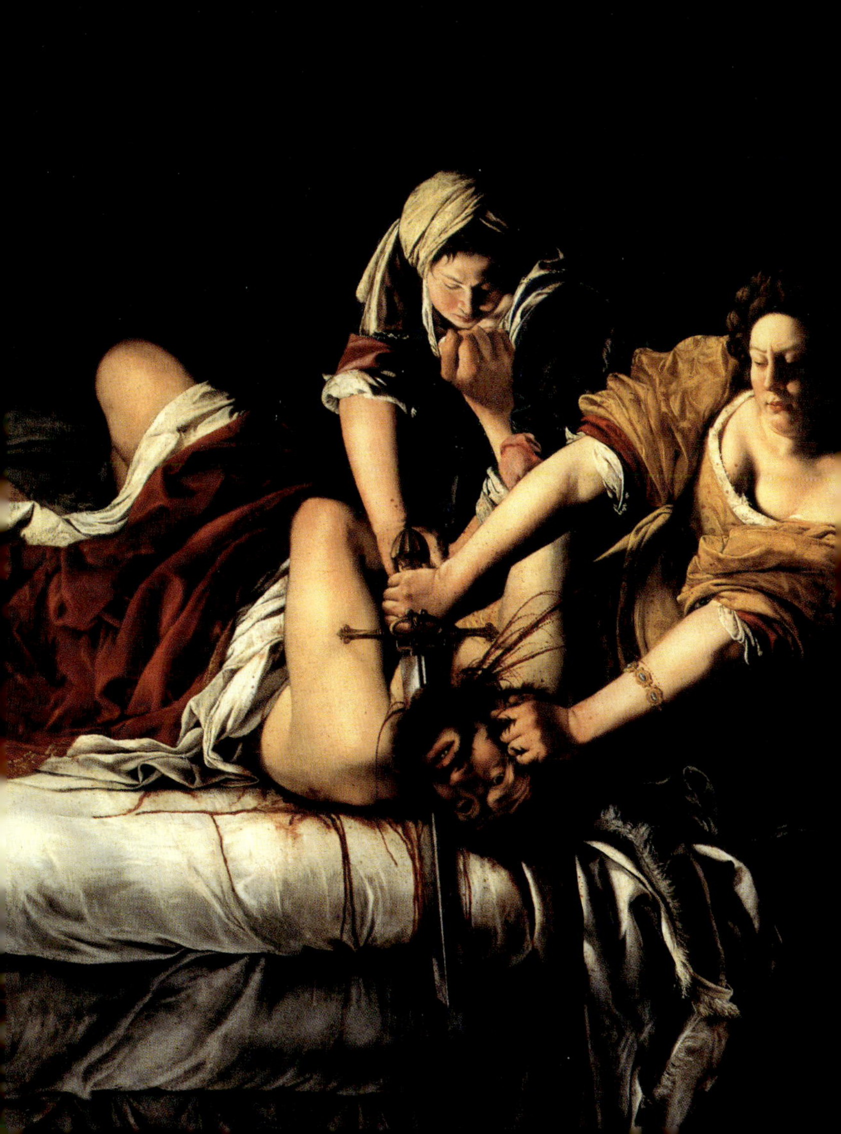

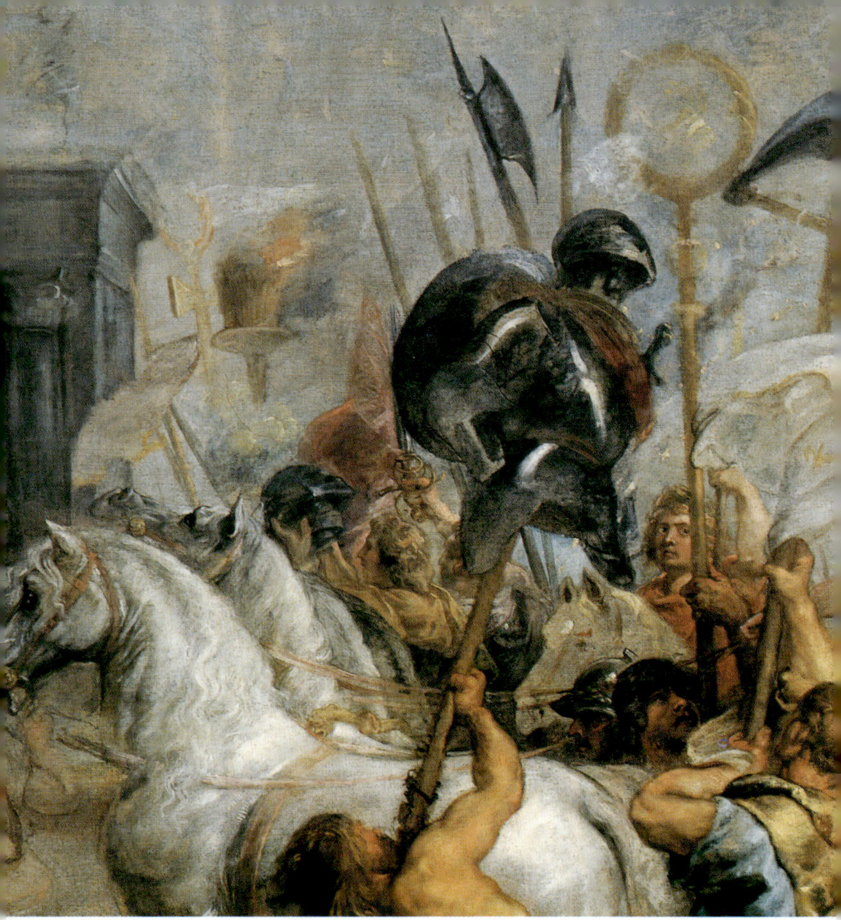

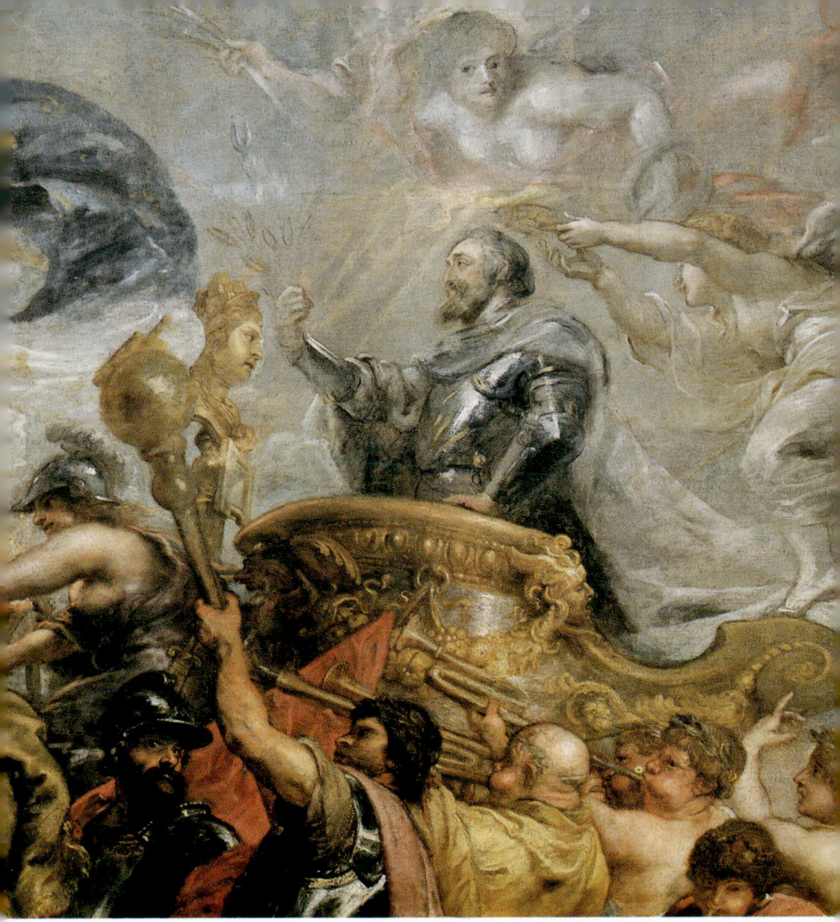

Above:
Pieter Paul Rubens, *Triumph*,
detail, 1627-1630, oil on canvas. Uffizi.

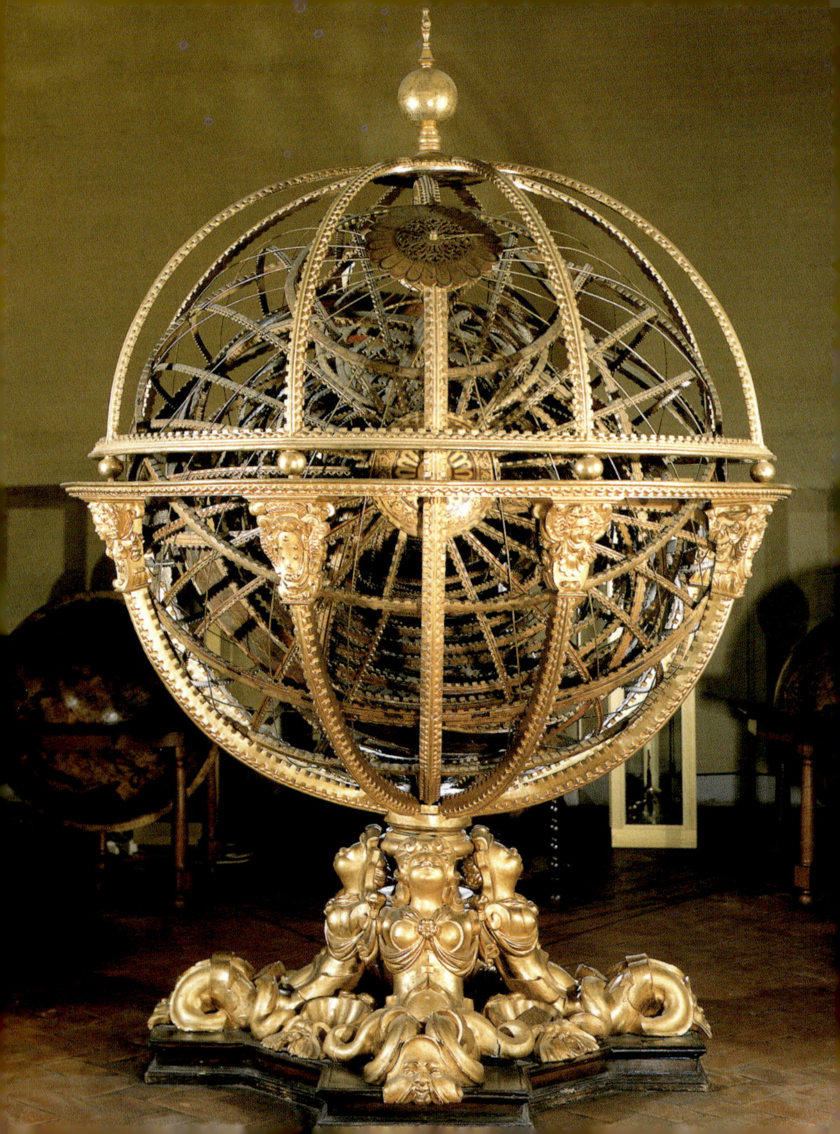

Museo di Storia della Scienza

In Palazzo Castellani, located in Piazza dei Giudici, with a splendid loggia overlooking the Arno, the Museo di Storia della Scienza, organized according to modern canons, contains what remains of the Medici-Lorraine collection of scientific instruments: objects that often possess exceptionally high historical/artistic value and that bear witness to the vast interests and the research promoted in Florence by the Medici and Lorraines in many fields of science, starting from the 15th century. The Institute annexed to the museum is engaged in conducting historical research on the collections and acquiring and disseminating knowledge on them through studies, archival research and the organization of important exhibitions. Annexed to the museum is a library containing precious ancient sources and and a number of laboratories.

VISITORS' ITINERARY AND WORKS OF ART:

Noteworthy are:

- the great armillary sphere by Antonio Santucci, over three meters high, decorated with the coats of arms of the Medicean Grand Duchy.
- the collection of sun dials, both nocturnal and diurnal and the original instruments of Galileo.

Opposite and following pages: Antonio Santucci, *Armillary sphere,* whole (this page) and detail (following page) with the Medici coats of arms and the hole into which a crank was inserted to move the sphere, 1588-1593. Istituto e Museo di Storia della Scienza.

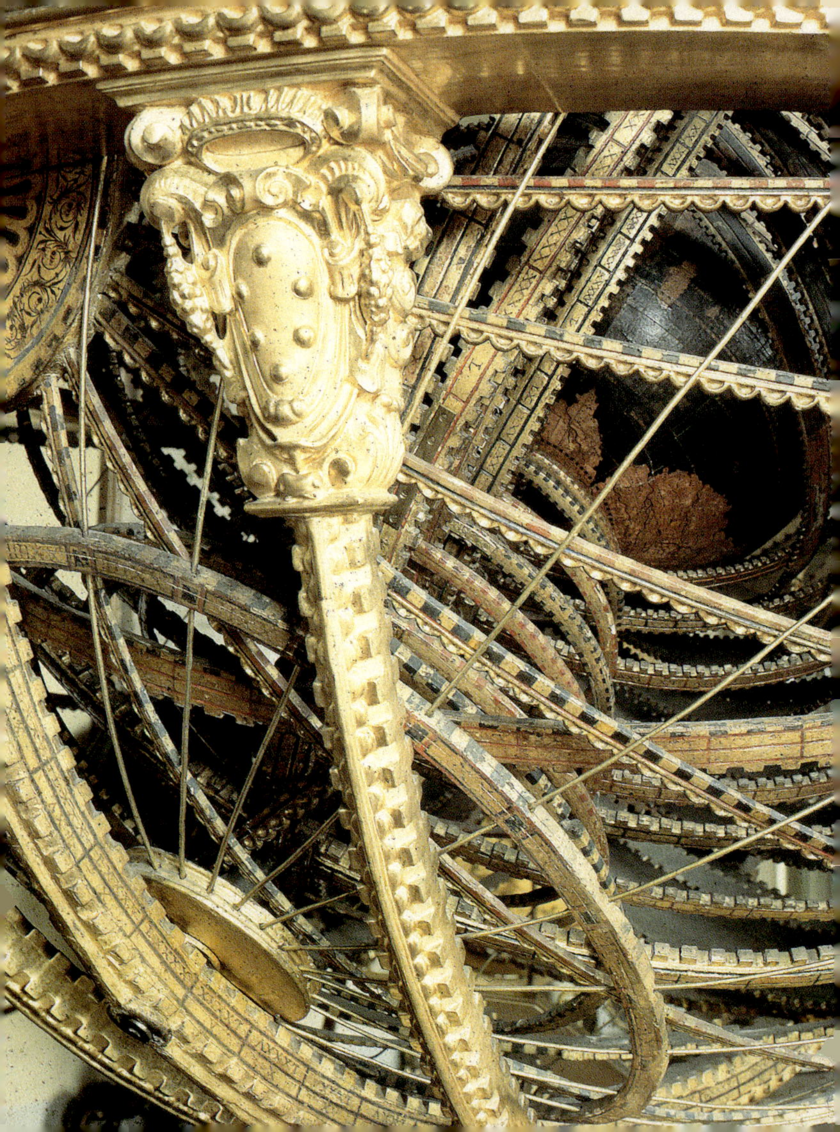

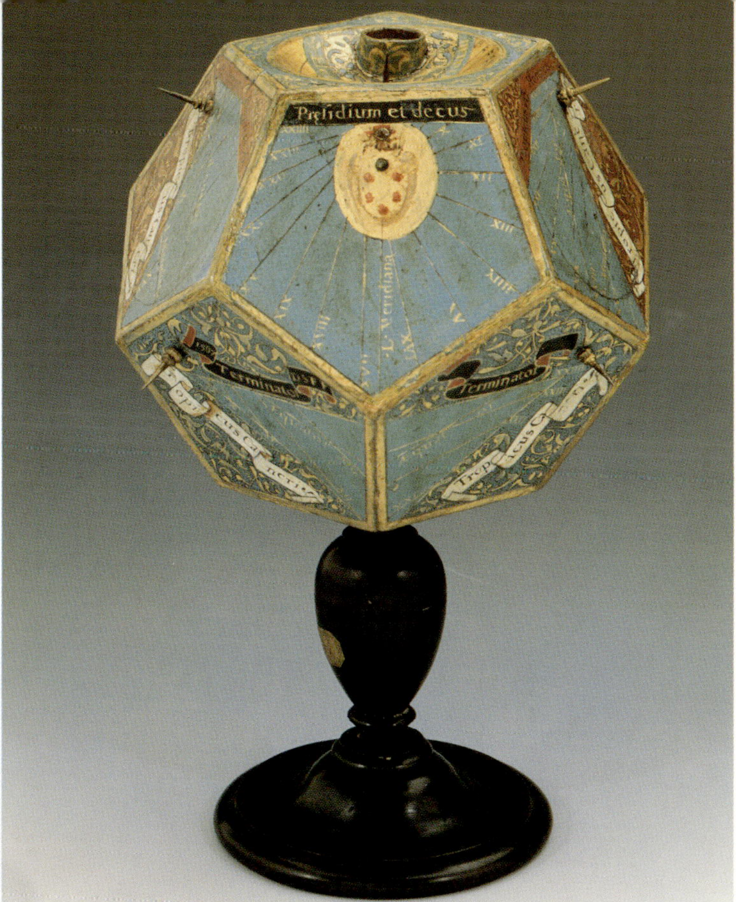

Above: Stefano Buonsignori, *Polyhedric sun dial*, 1587.

Istituto e Museo di Storia della Scienza.

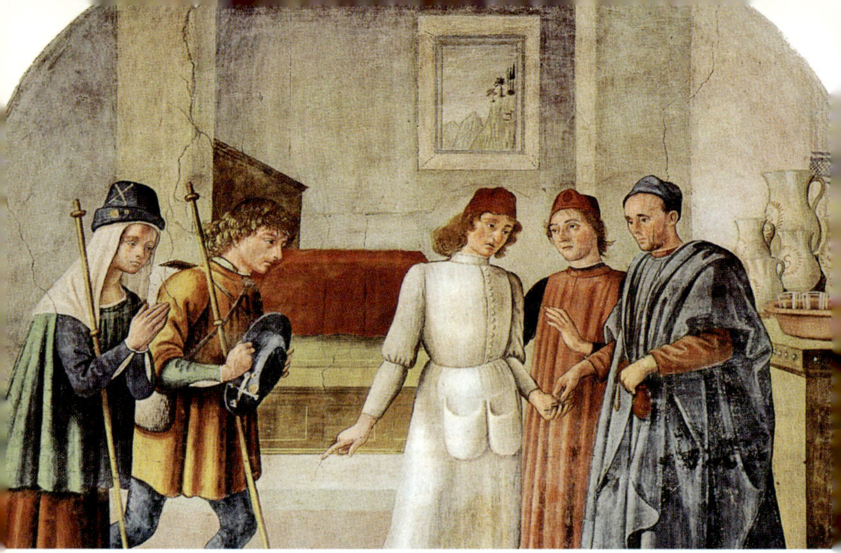

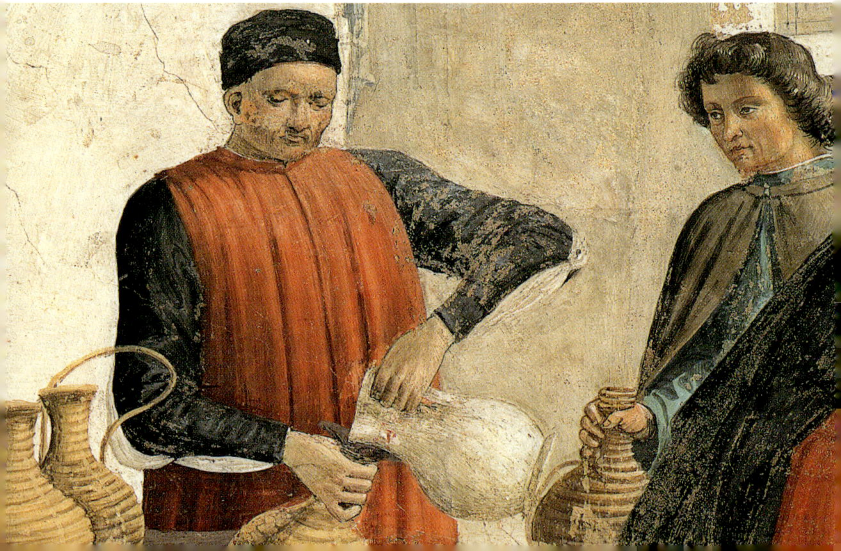

ORATORIO DEI BUONOMINI

The Oratorio dei Buonomini , charming and secluded, is located in the heart of medieval Florence, in the little Piazza di San Martino, the parish of the Alighieri and Donati families, between Via Dante and Via dei Cimatori, where the medieval Castagna Tower, the first residence of the magistrature of the Priori delle Arti (1282), once stood. Only a few steps away we find what is erroneously called "Dante's house", but is in reality a 19th century reinvention of the medieval legend surrounding the great poet. The little church of San Martino al Vescovo, site of the Oratorio dei Buonomini, was founded by Saint Antonino Pierozzi, Bishop of Florence, in 1432, the year in which the ancient church of San Martino, thought to be the place where Dante married Gemma Donati, was abandoned. Starting in 1478 the Oratorio was the headquarters of the Compagnia dei Buonomini, an organization which assisted families that had fallen in the world and were thus "vergognose", or shameful. On the outside wall is a slit for anonymous offerings. The oratory still has frescoes representing *Stories of Saint Martin*, patron saint of the needy, and *Works of Charity*, attributed to the school of Ghirlandaio.

Opposite page:
School of Ghirlandaio, *Works of Charity*, details from the cycle of frescoes, last quarter of the 15th century. Oratorio dei Buonomini.

The Compagnia dei Buonomini was founded by St. Antonino; the frescoes on charity contain interesting scenes of domestic life in the 15th century.

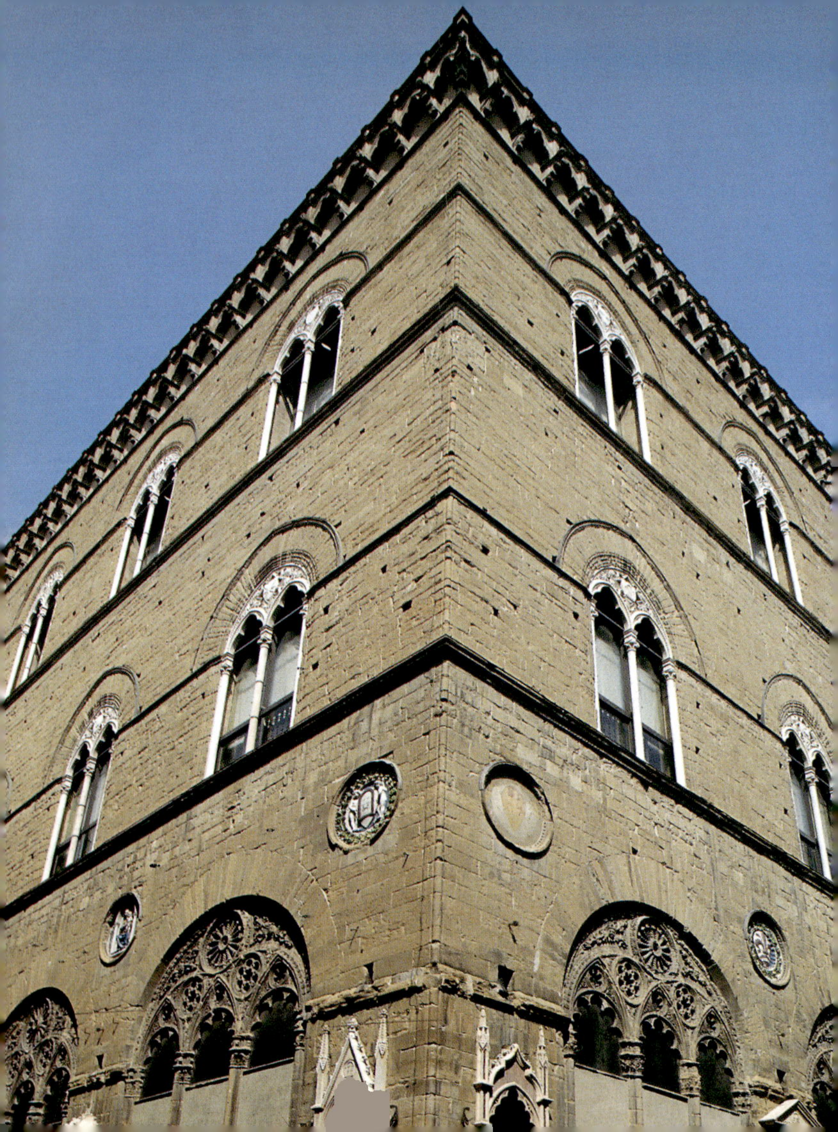

Orsanmichele

During the course of the Middle Ages the "Arti", or Guilds, became the cornerstone of economic structures and social relationships in Florence. Orsanmichele, a building unique of its kind, an unusual "stone cube" considered the pantheon of the "Arti", is the symbolic monument of this phenomenon. Originally an oratory surrounded by orchards and cultivated lands, then a loggia where grain was stored and sold, it ultimately came to be the church consecrated by the Guilds to their patron saints, represented outside of the building by monumental sculptures in niches created by the most famous artists of the early Renaissance period.

HISTORY

The origins of the church of Orsanmichele are to be found in the ancient orchard called Orto di San Michele (the derivation of the name), in the vicinity of which an oratory stood in the late Middle Ages. Around 1290, it seems, Arnolfo built there a loggia to be used as a grain market (the prices were controlled by the Comune), which was destroyed by fire in 1304. A larger loggia designed as a grain storage and market place, perhaps the biggest in the Medieval western world, over forty meters high and with

Opposite page:
View from the outside of the upper floors of Orsanmichele.

a square layout, was begun in 1337 and completed in 1404. The work, sponsored by the Silk Merchants Guild, was begun following projects by Francesco Talenti, Neri di Fioravante and Benci di Cione (the latter also designed the Loggia dei Priori, later called Loggia dei Lanzi, in Piazza Signoria). In 1380 Simone di Francesco Talenti finished the building, closing the great loggia on the street (where the market had been, while the upper floors had been used as storehouse) with delicate, refined mullioned windows and stained glass windows. This was the origin of the religious building, which was also the seat of the charitable brotherhood of Orsanmichele. The grain market was moved elsewhere, and inside the church was placed the monumental tabernacle all made of delicate marble tracery created by Orcagna (1352-1359), commissioned by the Brotherhood of Orsanmichele to frame the panel portraying the *Madonna delle Grazie*. The altarpiece, painted by Bernardo Daddi in 1344 as replacement for a previous one deemed miraculous and perhaps destroyed by fire in 1304, was the object of great devotion, and the tabernacle, which cost an exorbitant amount, was partially financed by alms donated in thanks for salvation from the devastating plague of 1348. Over the course of the 15th century the loggia was decorated on the outside with the tabernacles of the Guilds. It is not surprising that the powerful Guilds had chosen just this monument. Orsanmichele, in fact, was located at a

Opposite page:
Bernardo Daddi, *Madonna delle Grazie*, 1344, tempera on wood. Orsanmichele, Tabernacle of Orcagna.

Following pages:
The interior of Orsanmichele with pillars decorated all over, the altar dedicated to St. Anne (left) and the Tabernacle of Orcagna.

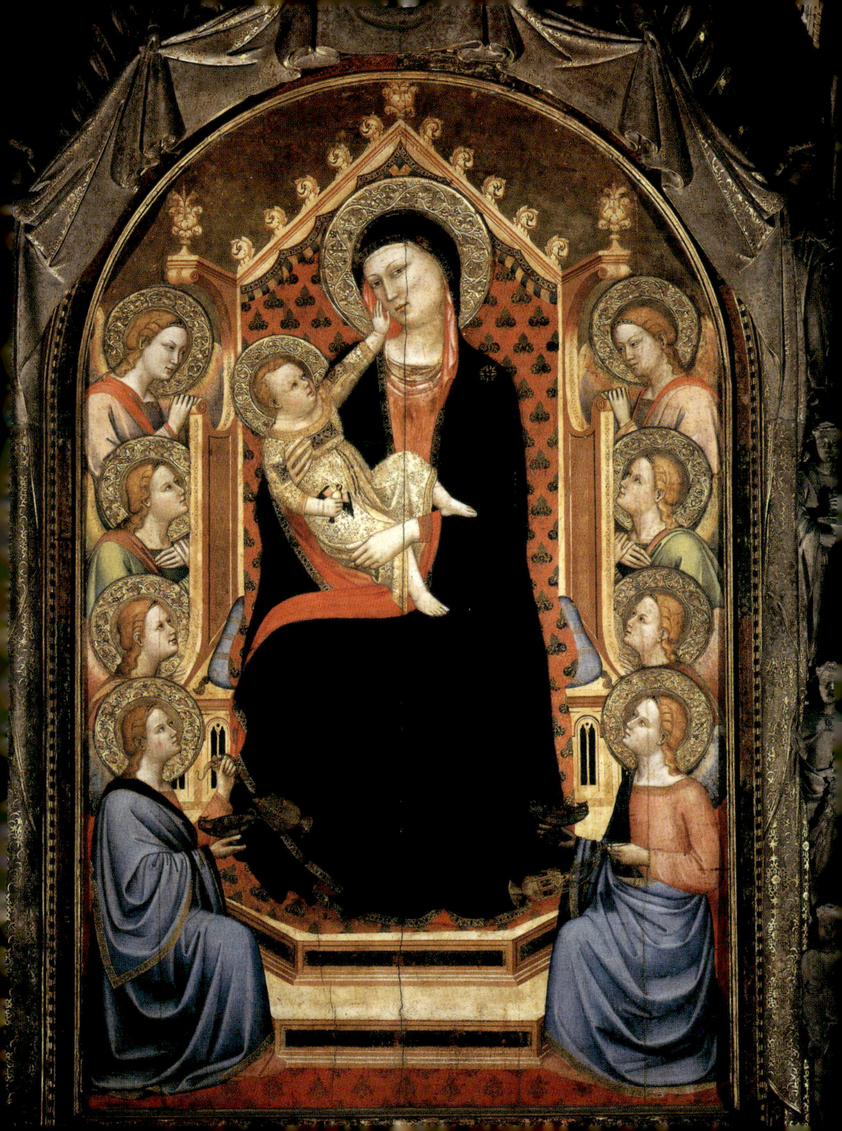

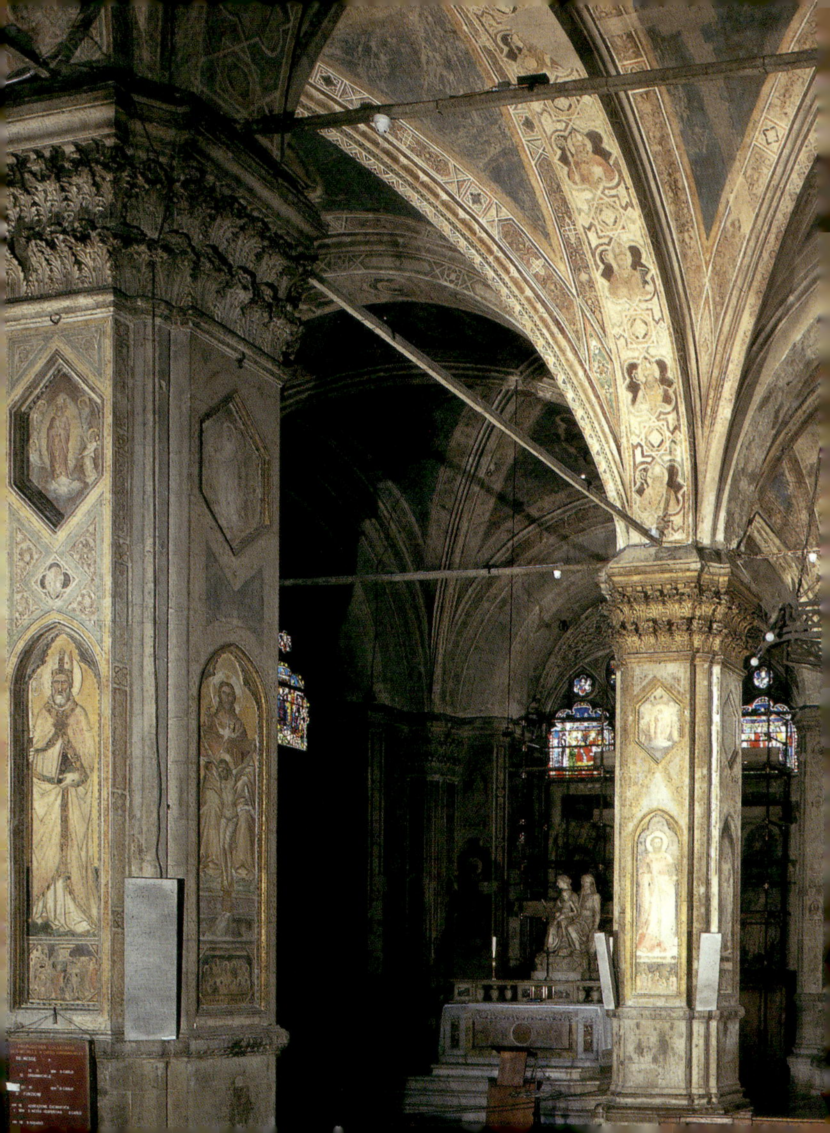

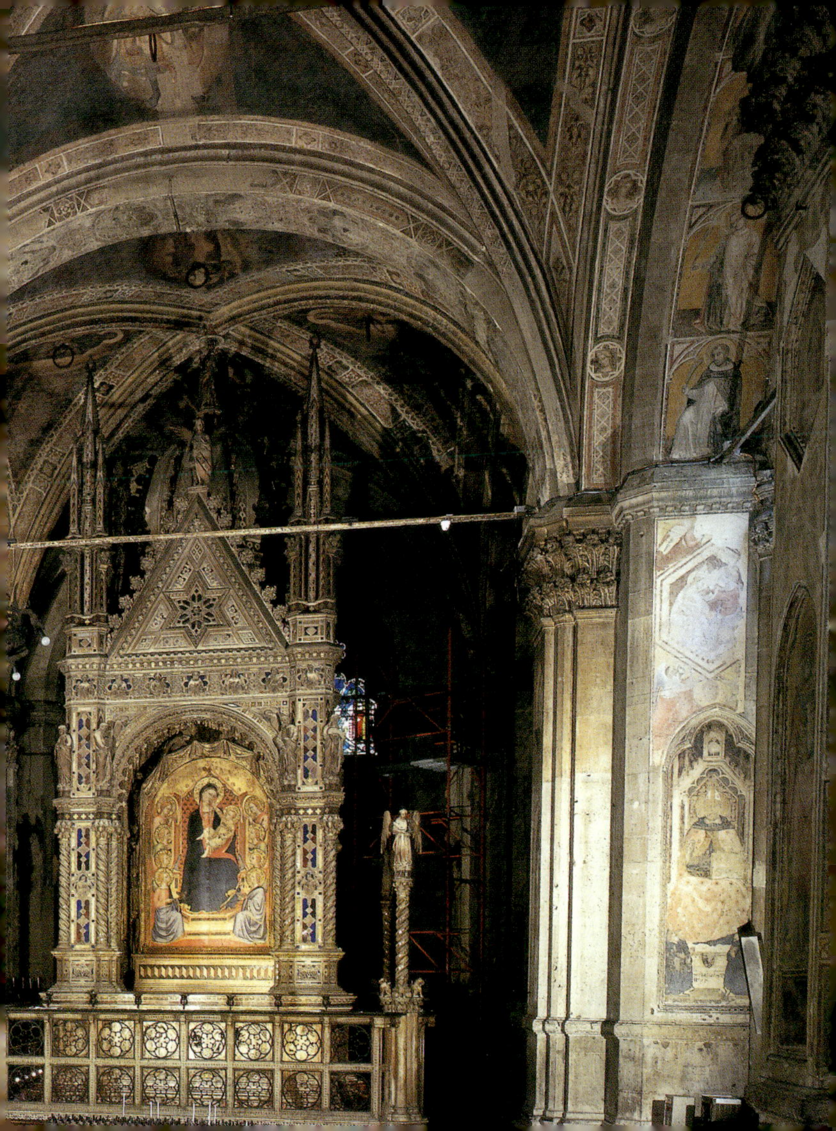

strategic point in the city, directly connected by a network of streets to the main economic, religious and power centers. Already in 1298, during a time of particularly active urban initiatives, an avant-garde plan had been formulated: the opening of a remarkably beautiful street (*Via Pulcherrima*) that was to link Orsanmichele to the Bargello, then called Palazzo del Podestà, a plan opposed by the monks of the Badia, who owned property in that area. Finally, between 1322 and 1325, Via Larga (today's Via Cavour) was opened, to allow the transit of wagons transporting grain from the territory of Mugello, north of the city, straight to the grain market loggia of Orsanmichele. Moreover, Orsanmichele was situated halfway between the two poles of political and religious life, Piazza dei Priori (later Piazza della Signoria) and the Duomo and Baptistery complex. The building also came to constitute the ideal barycenter of the triangle marked by the city's three most important spiritual centers: Santo Spirito, Santa Croce and Santa Maria Novella. And in addition, it was a only a few meters from the Palagio dell'Arte della Lana, the Wool Merchants Guild that exerted the strongest influence on Florentine economic life, which the chronical writer Giovanni Villani had significantly placed at the ideal center of the city. In 1389, for the "decorum" of Florence, it was also decided to widen the section of street that connected the Duomo and Orsanmichele to Palazzo dei Priori, and it was es-

Opposite page:
Luca della Robbia,
Coat of Arms of the Masters of Stone and Wood Work,
c. 1445, glazed terracotta.
Orsanmichele, exterior.

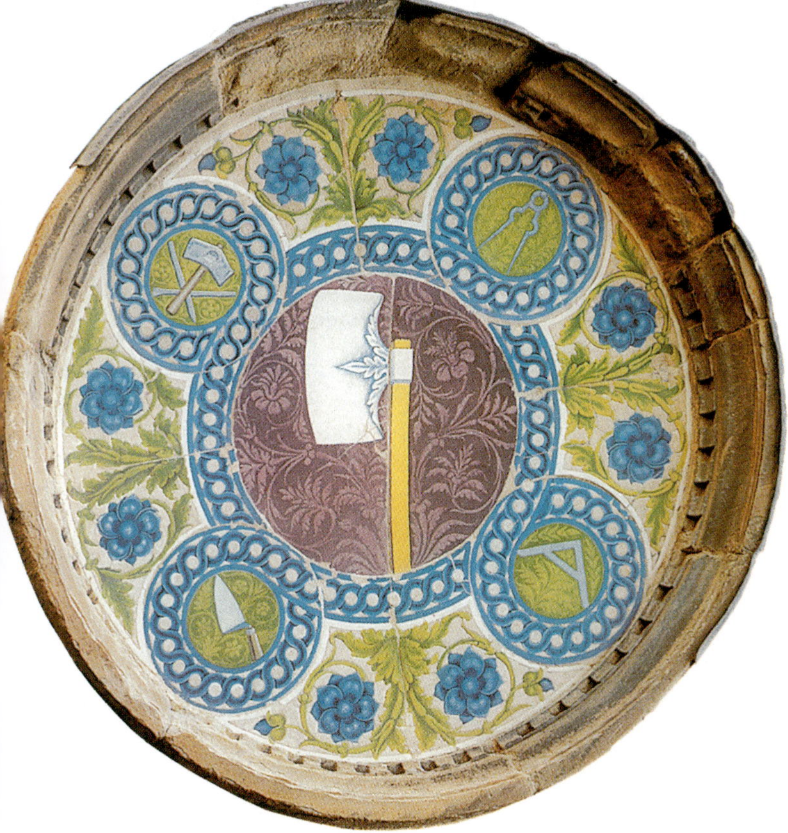

tablished that the facades of the houses in this street (Via dei Calzaiuoli) should all be faced in *pietra forte*, but this project was carried out only partially.
The upper floors of Orsanmichele, rebuilt by Buontalenti in the 16th century, are today the site of a museum that houses the original scuptures of the patron saints removed from the outside of the building for reasons of conservation and replaced by copies. In the 14th and 15th centuries many artists worked here, and not only the master sculptors commissioned by the Guilds to decorate their niches (among them Donatello, Nanni di Banco, Ghiberti, Michelozzo and Verrocchio). Inside the church, for instance, on a pillar of the Money-changers Guild, Orcagna had painted in 1367 the *Triptych of St. Matthew,* patron saint of money-changers (finished by his brother Jacopo di Cione, now in the Uffizi). It should also be recalled that the church was dedicated to St. Anne, who in 1343 had become the symbol of the expulsion of the Duke of Athens from Florence, an event which took place on July 26th of that year, her Saint's Day. Every year on that day, which had become a liturgical and religious festival, the banners of the Guilds were hung outside the walls of Orsanmichele, where there was and still is today a votive altar dedicated to St. Anne.

Opposite page:
Andrea Orcagna and Jacopo di Cione, *Triptych of St. Matthew*, 1367-1368, tempera on wood. Florence, Galleria degli Uffizi, formerly on the pillar of the Money-changers Guild in Orsanmichele.

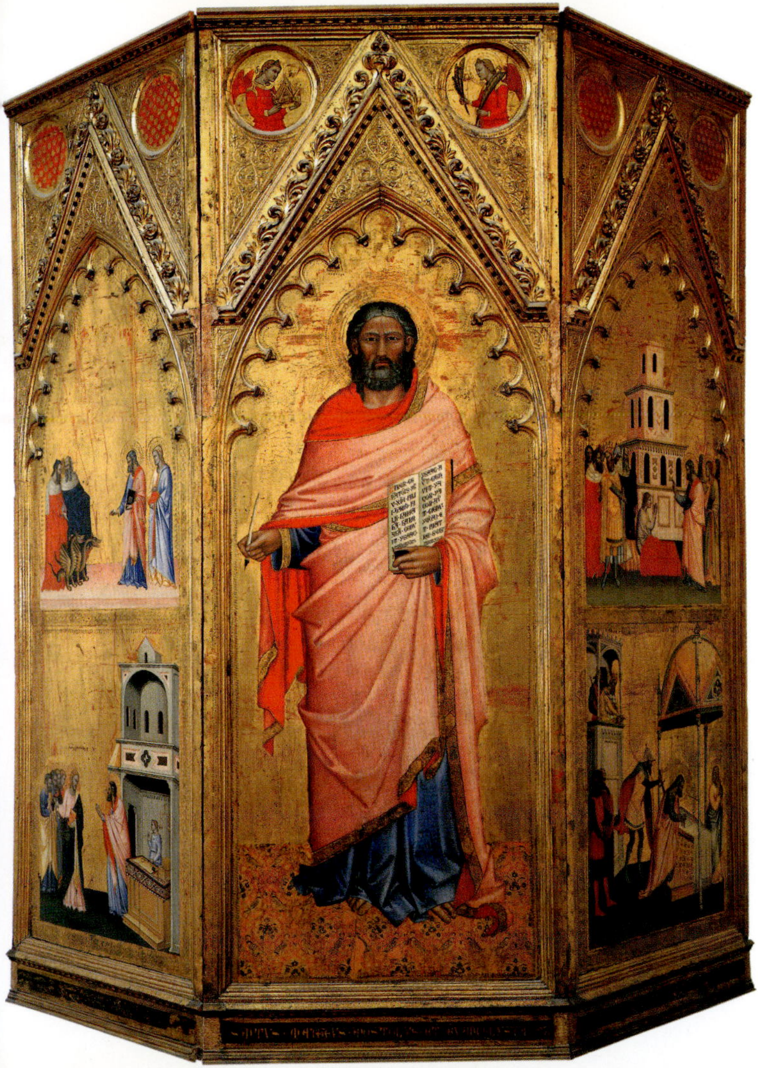

Noteworthy are:

• ON THE OUTSIDE:

- the tabernacle of the Money-changers Guild (early 15th century) by Lorenzo Ghiberti and Michelozzo.
- the tabernacle of the Blacksmiths Guild, with *St. Eligius* (1415) by Nanni di Banco, and that of the Masters of Stone and Wood Working with the statues of the *Four Saints Crowned* (c. 1415), also by Nanni di Banco.
- the tabernacle of the Armor-makers and Sword-makers Guild with *St. George* (1420) by Donatello (original at the Bargello Museum): a crucially important work for the artists active in those years, which shows perfect comprehension of Brunelleschi's research in the bas-relief of *St. George and the Princess*, a perspective scene later to be emulated by Masaccio in the *Tribute* in the Brancacci Chapel.
- the tabernacle of the Merchants Guild by Donatello and Michelozzo (1425), with the *Incredulity of St. Thomas* (1486) by Verrocchio.

Opposite page:
Mariotto di Nardo (attr.), *Saint Anne with a model of the city of Florence,* detail from the *Age of Grace*, 1398, fresco.
Orsanmichele, third bay in the north nave.

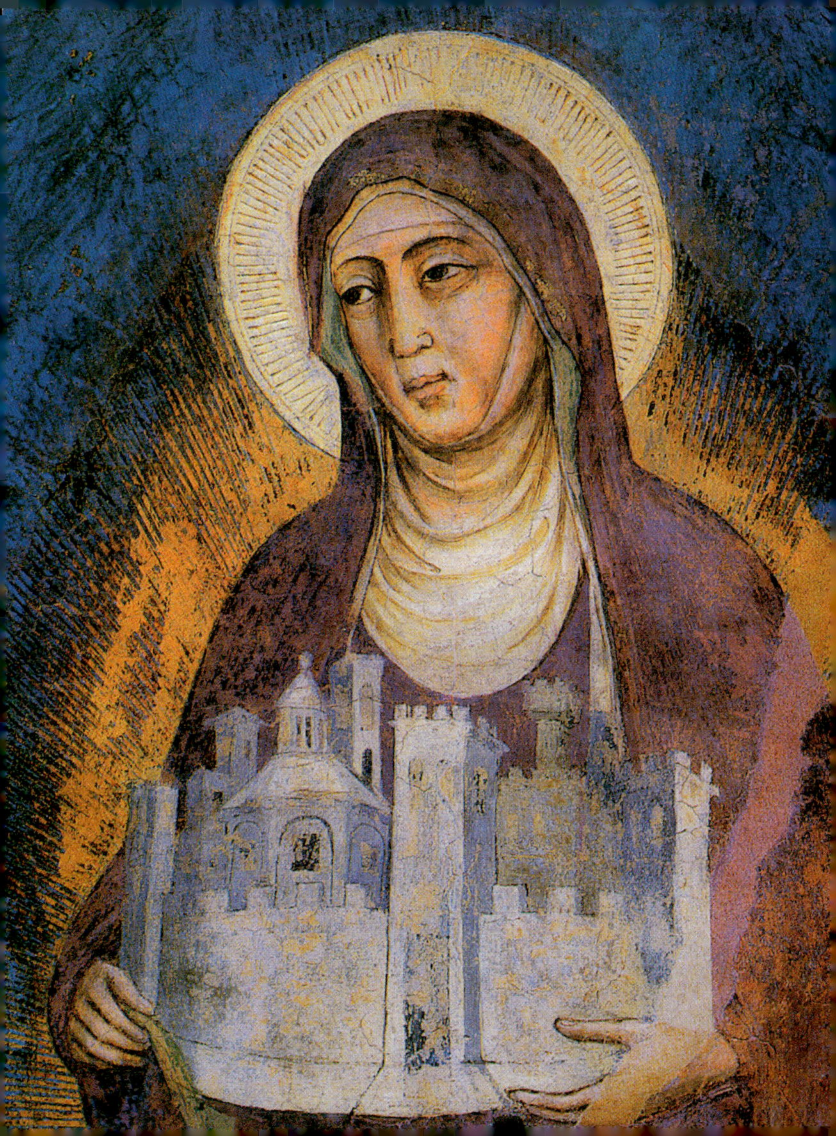

• ON THE INSIDE:

- the marble tabernacle of Orcagna, which evokes in monumental dimensions a precious object of the goldsmith's art, with arcades embroidered like lacework, bas-reliefs and all-round sculptures. The little cupola, surrounded by Gothic-style spires, probably derives from Arnolfo's project for a dome, never realized, over the Cathedral.

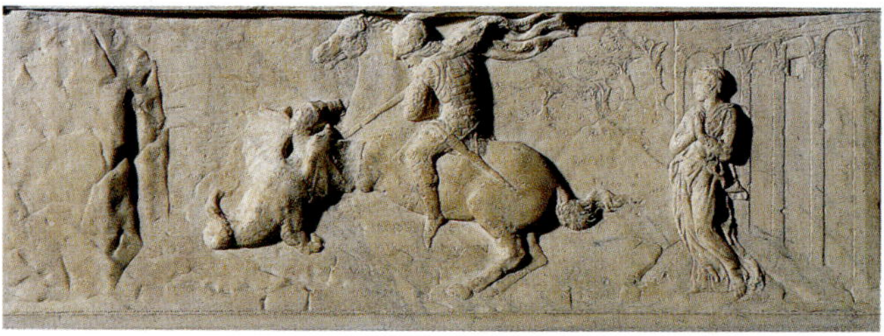

Opposite page e above: Tabernacle of the Armor-makers and Sword-makers Guild, with the statue of *St. George* by Donatello (copy, original in the Bargello), and bas-relief on the predella depicting *St. George freeing the Princess from the Dragon*, c. 1417. Orsanmichele, north side.

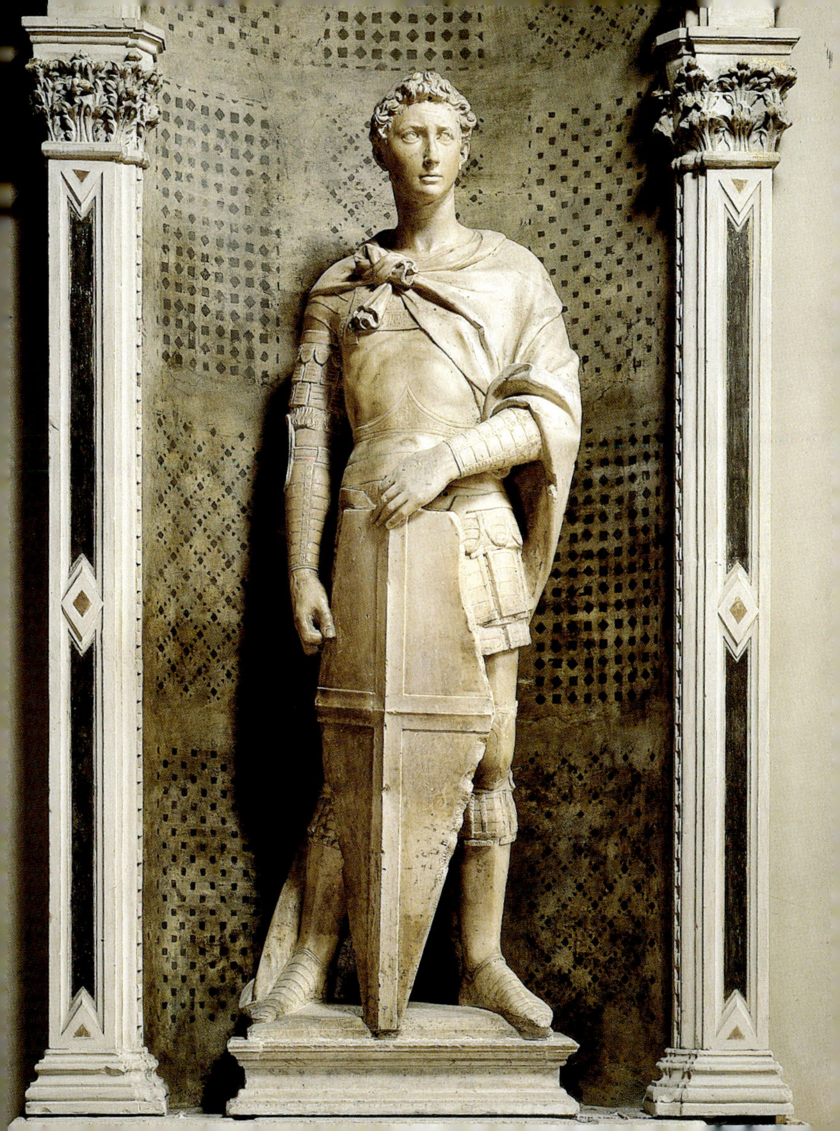

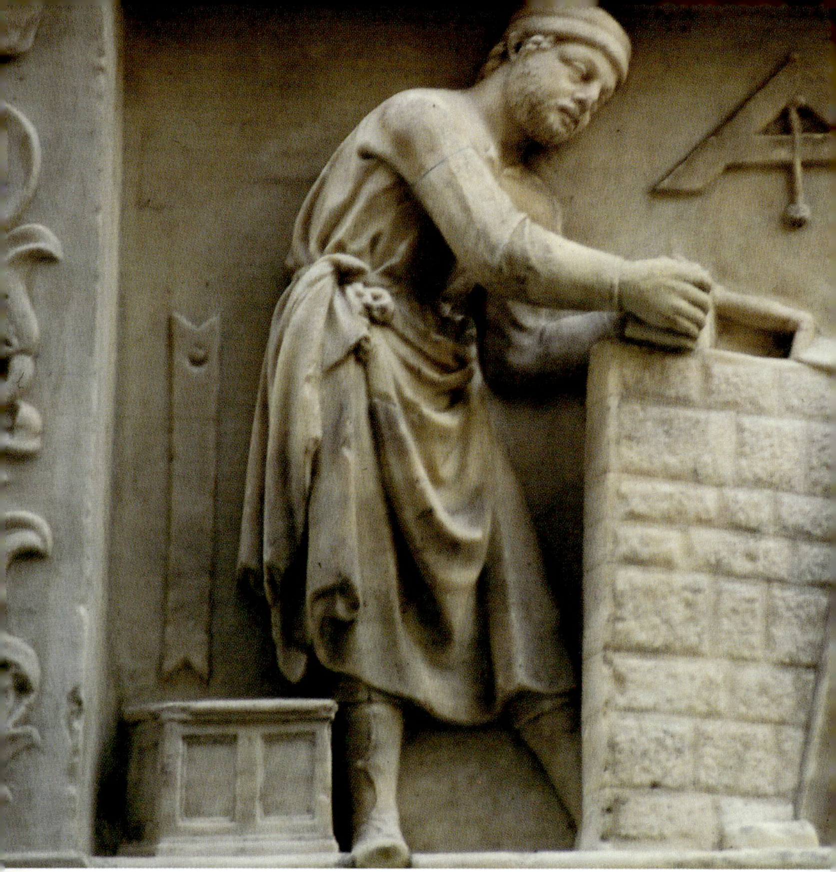

Above:
Nanni di Banco, *Craftsmen at work,* detail from the base of the Masters of Stone and Wood Work Tabernacle and with the bronze group of the *Four Saints Crowned* in the niche illustrated on the following page, c. 1415, marble. Orsanmichele Museum.

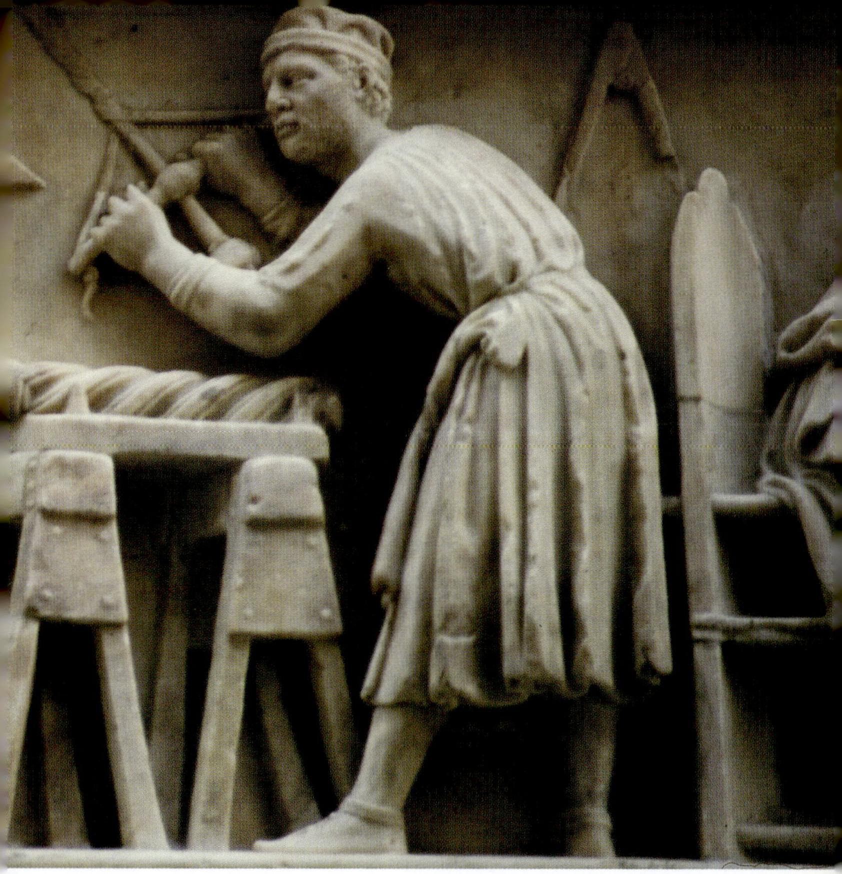

Following page: Andrea del Verrocchio, *Incredulity of St. Thomas*, 1486, bronze, in the niche of the Tabernacle of the Tribunale di Mercanzia. Orsanmichele Museum.

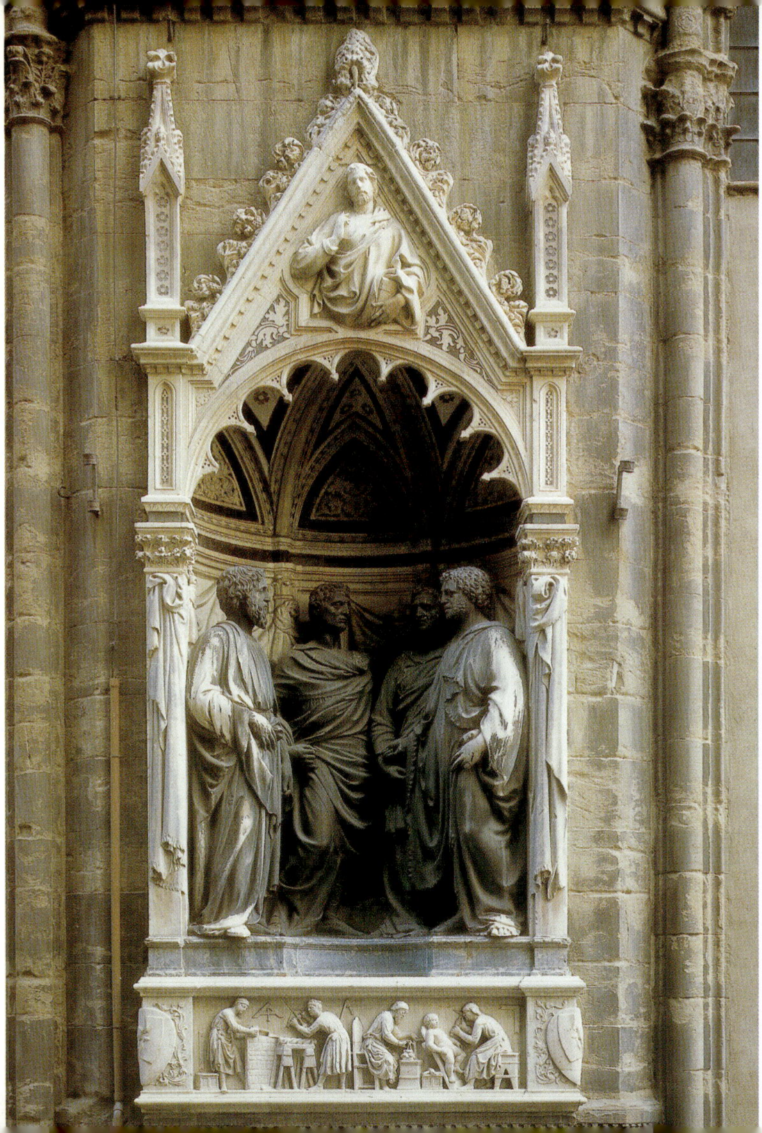

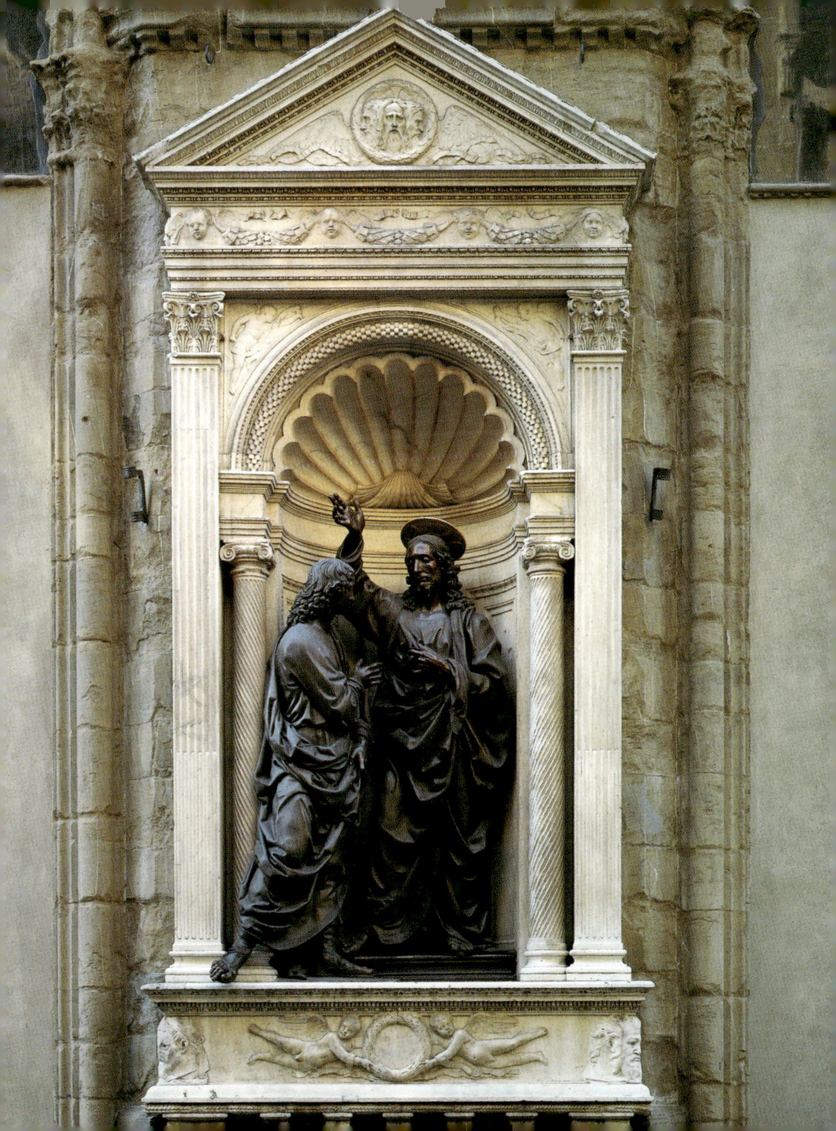

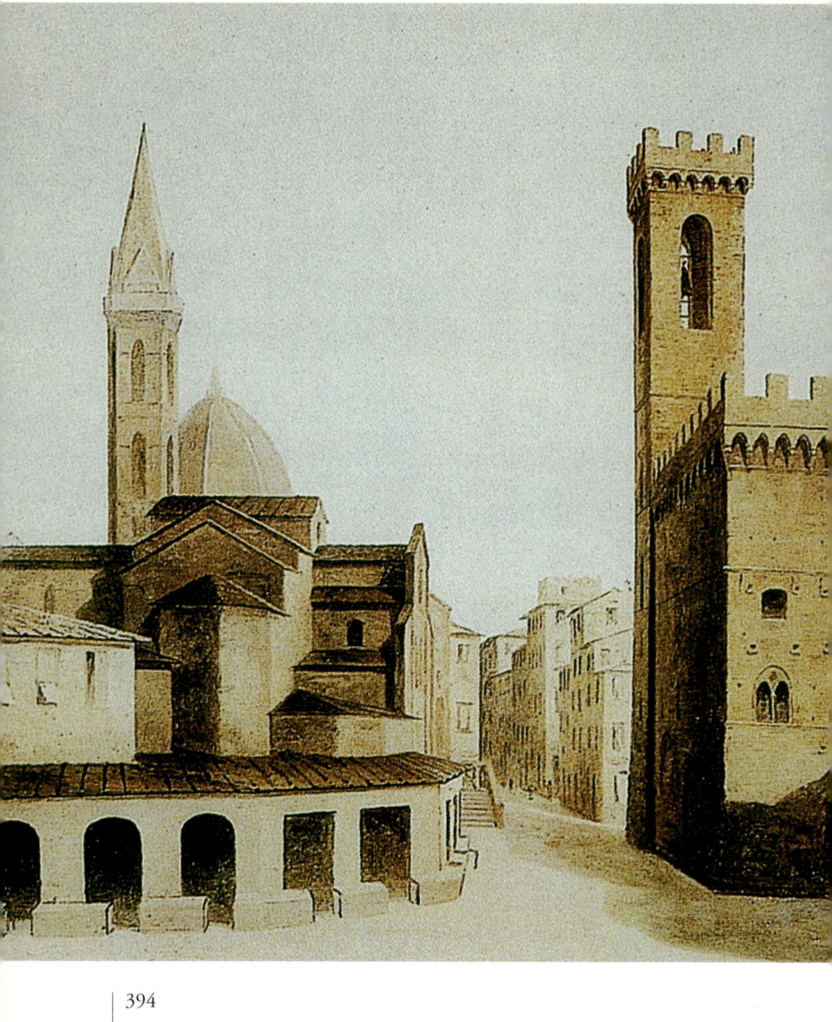

Badia Fiorentina

Behind Piazza Signoria, on Via del Proconsolo in front of the Bargello, on the straight line running from the apse of the Duomo to Piazza San Firenze, the Badia Fiorentina is the oldest monastic structure in the city. Dedicated to Our Lady of the Assumption and to St. Stephen, the Benedictine complex stood right against the eastern side of the Carolingian walls, which from Porta San Piero (at the crossroads of today's Corso and Via del Proconsolo) to the Porta Aurea (where Via de' Gondi enters Piazza San Firenze) bounded the extension of the monastery's territory. For many years, as recalls Cacciaguida in the *Paradise*, the bell tower of the Badia, which appears in the oldest drawings of the city, marked the rhythm of the working hours and daily life of the Florentines: "Fiorenza within the ancient circle/ where she still tolls the third and ninth [hours]" (xv, 97-98). It was thus a religious complex of great historic significance, the most important one founded in late medieval Florence. The monastery originated in 978 through the donation of Marchesa Willa, widow of the Margrave Uberto and mother of Ugo, Marchese of Tuscia, who died on 21 December 1001 after having further enriched the monastery. Buried in the chuch (his funerary monument, one of the most expressive works of Mino da Fiesole, ren-

Opposite page:
The Badia Fiorentina, with the bell tower and the three apses turned toward Piazza San Firenze, with the stationery shops in the square huddled against it, as it appears in a painting by Fabio Borbottoni (c. 1890) now in the collection of the Cassa di Risparmio di Firenze.

ovated around 1481), Ugo traditionally remains the true patron of the Badia, who is still solemnly commemorated every year on December 21st.

The original church was oriented by ninety degrees in respect to the present-day façade opposite the Bargello. With a square plan, it had apses to the east toward the wall, demolished in 1172 to allow a more ample circle. The church was enlarged in 1285, probably under the supervision of the greatest architect of the time, Arnolfo di Cambio, who worked on most of the major construction sites in the city. In 1307 the hexagonal bell tower was partially lowered by order of the Comune to punish the monks who had failed to pay a tax, but in 1330 the last two orders of two-light mullioned windows and spires were rebuilt. Proof of its importance is the fact that the church was at the time rich in works of art: the chapels in the apse decorated with frescoes, polychrome majolica floors, and gold-leaf paintings such as the cuspidate polyptych by Giotto (c. 1300) over the high altar, now in the Uffizi. After a period of relative decline the Badia rose to importance again under Abbot Gomezio, an erudite Portuguese humanist (1419-1439). Dating from this time is the delightful Cloister of the Orange Trees, designed by Antonio di Domenico with the collaboration of Bernardo Rossellino, one of the earliest in the Florentine Renaissance. On the frescoes in the cloister representing *Stories of St. Benedict*, attributed to an

Opposite page:
Filippino Lippi, *Apparition of the Virgin to St. Bernard*, detail, c. 1480, panel painting. Badia Fiorentina, formerly in the monastery of the Campora.

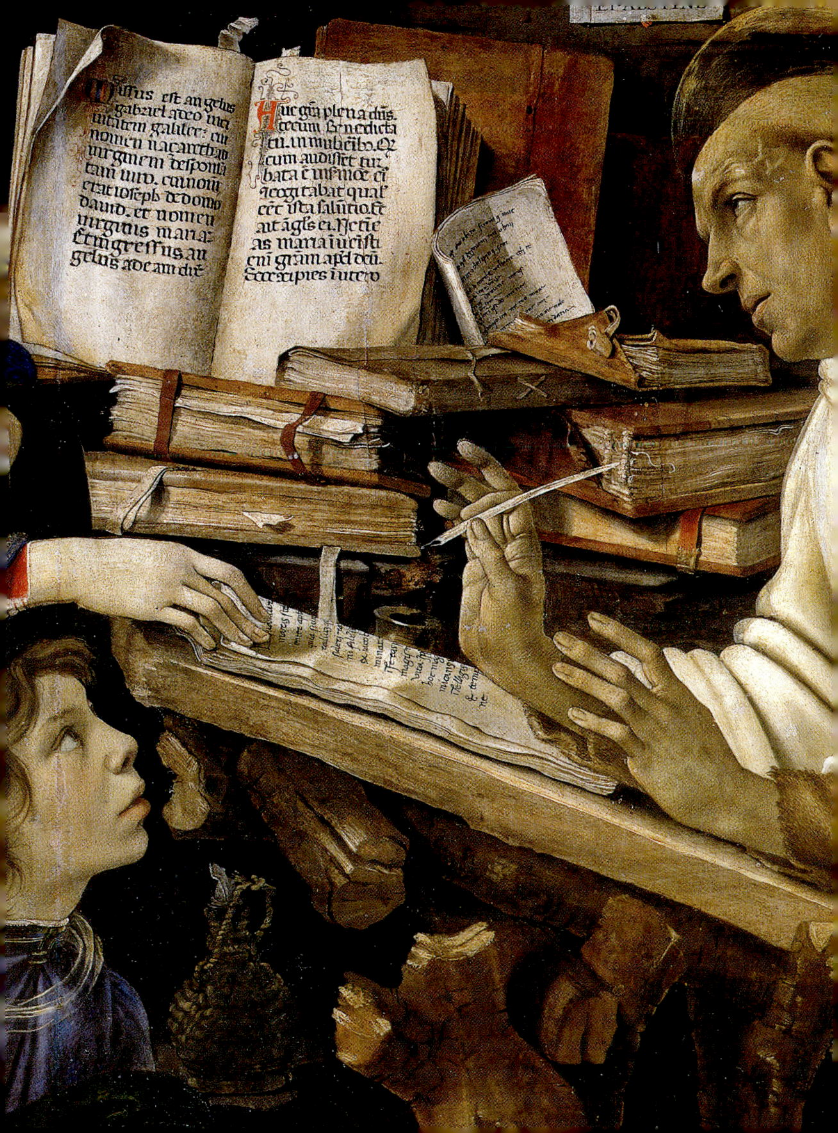

unknown painter called the Master of the Cloister of the Orange Trees, the Portuguese artist Giovanni di Consalvo, who may have come to Florence in the entourage of the Abbot his countryman, collaborated in all probability. In the early years of the 16th century other refined furnishings were placed in the church, among them the wooden choirstalls, exquisitely carved in the workshop of the Del Tasso family, only some of which have survived. In 1529 there was placed in the Badia, where it still remains today, the famous altarpiece by Filippino Lippi representing the *Apparition of the Virgin to St. Bernard*, commissioned for the monastery of the Campora outside of Porta Romana by Piero del Pugliese, a leading figure in Florentine cultural and political life, here shown at the foot of the "Sacra Rappresentazione": a work rich in symbolic references and strongly influenced by Flemish art. In the following centuries the church underwent important changes, starting with major modifications in its layout, transformed into a Greek cross by Matteo Segaloni, and the erection of a Baroque chapel dedicated to St. Bernard.

Opposite page:
Marco and Francesco di Domenico del Tasso, *Choirstalls*, detail, 1501-1502, inlaid wood. Badia Fiorentina.

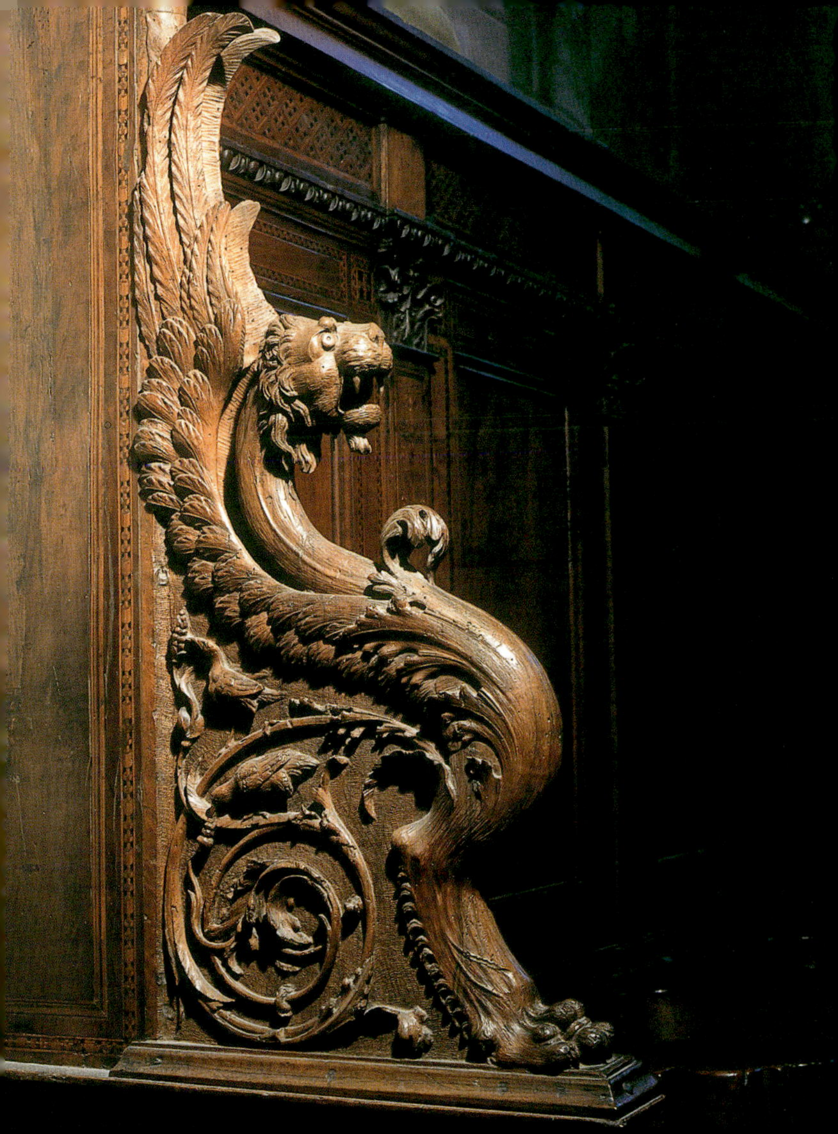

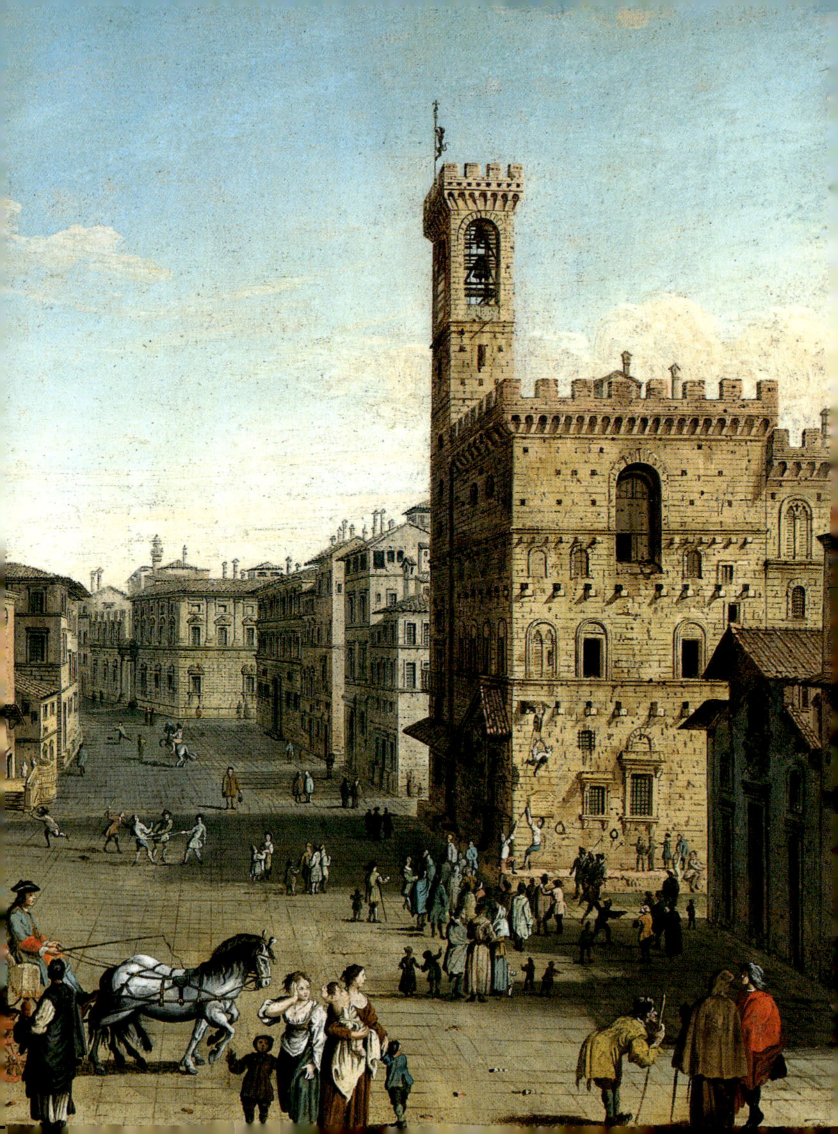

Palazzo e Museo del Bargello

One of the most interesting of the Florentine museums, established in 1859 to house sculptures and works of the minor arts, the Museo Nazionale del Bargello, whose original collections have been greatly extended over the years, is located in the oldest, most important civic building of medieval Florence: the Palazzo del Podestà, on the corner between Via del Proconsolo (the magistrate who presided over the Consuls of the Guilds) and today's Piazza San Firenze. The courtyard richly adorned with coats of arms of the Guilds, the Quarters, the Podestà and the Judges of the Rota, the balcony on which stand the stupendous bronze figures of animals and birds by Giambologna, and the austere halls of the museum are all enveloped in a unique atmosphere.

HISTORY

The building was erected around the middle of the 13th century as a meeting place for the Councils of the People and as headquarters for the magistrate who protected the interests of the people against the Ghibelline nobility. When the Guelph faction returned to power in 1261 it became the seat of the Podestà

Opposite page:
The Palazzo del Bargello, on the corner between Via del Proconsolo, Via della Vigna Vecchia and Piazza San Firenze, in a detail from a painting by Giuseppe Zocchi, *Piazza San Firenze*, fifth decade of the 18th century. Ente Cassa di Risparmio di Firenze.

(the magistrate brought in from elsewhere to ensure balance between the various factions). Older by several decades than Palazzo Vecchio, the Bargello (which takes its name from the Captain of Justice who resided there starting from 1547) is the first important example of Florentine civic architecture, built in sturdy *pietra forte*, perhaps to the project of the Dominican architects of Santa Maria Novella, Fra Sisto and Fra Ristoro. The high tower at the corner, crennellated like the whole perimeter of walls, still has the bell called "La Montanina", which tolled in case of danger to call out the Florentines. The building was enlarged in 1261 toward Via dell'Acqua, then on the Via della Vigna side. Between 1280 and 1285 the inner courtyard was built, while the spectacular balcony on the first floor with its monumental staircase dates from 1345-1367, the years in which Neri di Fioravante created the great cross-vaulted hall with mullioned windows on the second floor. Almost from the start, the palace was a place to be feared by the Florentines. As public admonishment, traitors and political victims were, in fact, painted as hanged men on one of its outer walls. Andrea del Castagno, one of the artists obliged to produce this "pittura infamante", unable to refuse the task of portraying one of the exiles after the Battle of Anghiari in 1440, became known as "Andreino of the hanged men." In 1530 Andrea Del Sarto, to keep from being labeled with such a nickname, erected a paling to hide behind while he painted by night the notorious figures

Opposite page:
The courtyard of the Bargello, with the monumental staircase leading to the balcony.

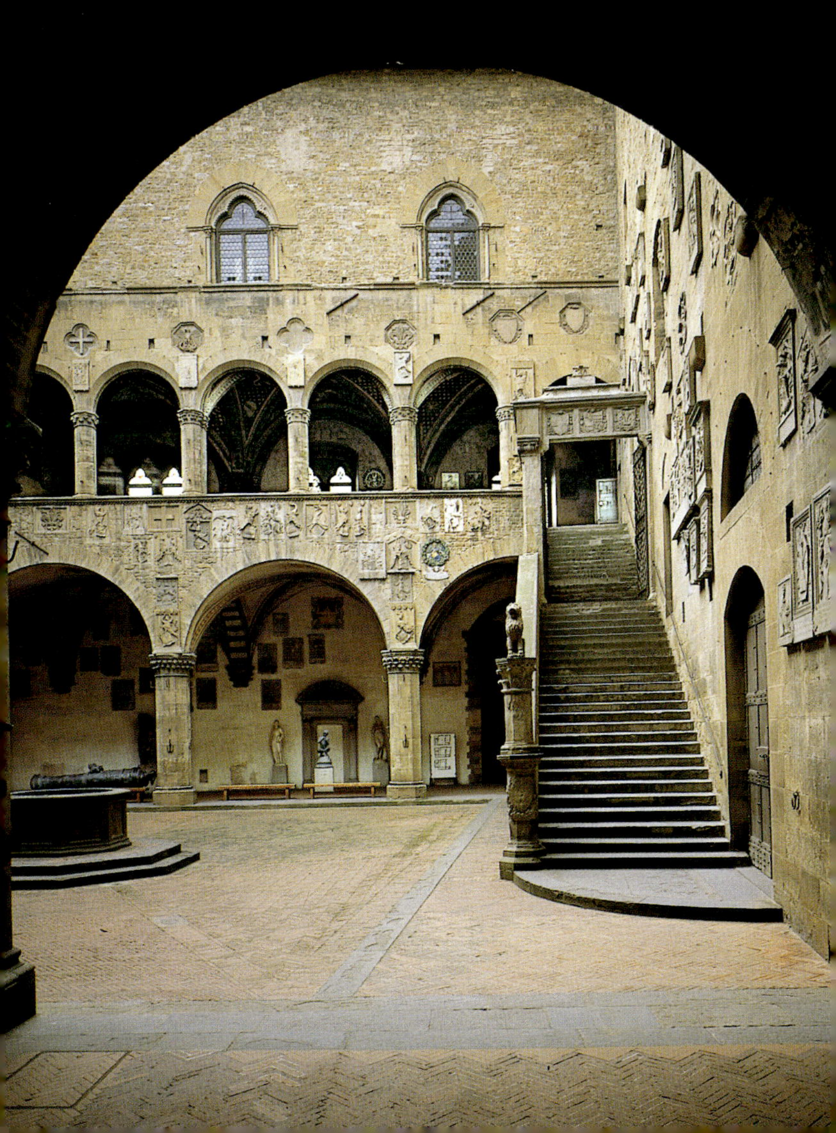

of the mercenaries who had run away with the soldiers' wages during a siege by Imperial troops. At the time when the palace was the seat of Justice many Florentines were hanged there, and many others were imprisoned and tortured.

MUSEO NAZIONALE DEL BARGELLO

Incremented in concurrence with the celebrations for Dante held in 1865, and later through important donations such as those made by Louis Carrand in 1888 and Giulio Franchetti in 1907, the museum displays a conspicuous collection of works, so vast that only its most important groups can be listed here.

Among these are:

- the remarkably rich collections of Medicean porcelain, seals, medals, bronze statuettes, weapons, ivory carvings, chests, furnishings, gold and silver work, and Islamic objects.
- by Donatello: from Orsanmichele, the marble statue of *St. George* with its predella (c. 1417, illustrated on the pages dedicated to Orsanmichele); the *Atys* (c. 1440); the marble *David* (1409) and the bronze *David* (c. 1440-1450).
- the bronze panels by Lorenzo Ghiberti and Brunelleschi for the competition for the second door of the Baptistery (1402).
- numerous reliefs and sculptures by Desiderio da Settignano, Rossellino, Mino da Fiesole, Sansovino, and Bertoldo.

Opposite page:
Donatello, *David*, c. 1440-1450, bronze.
Museo Nazionale del Bargello.

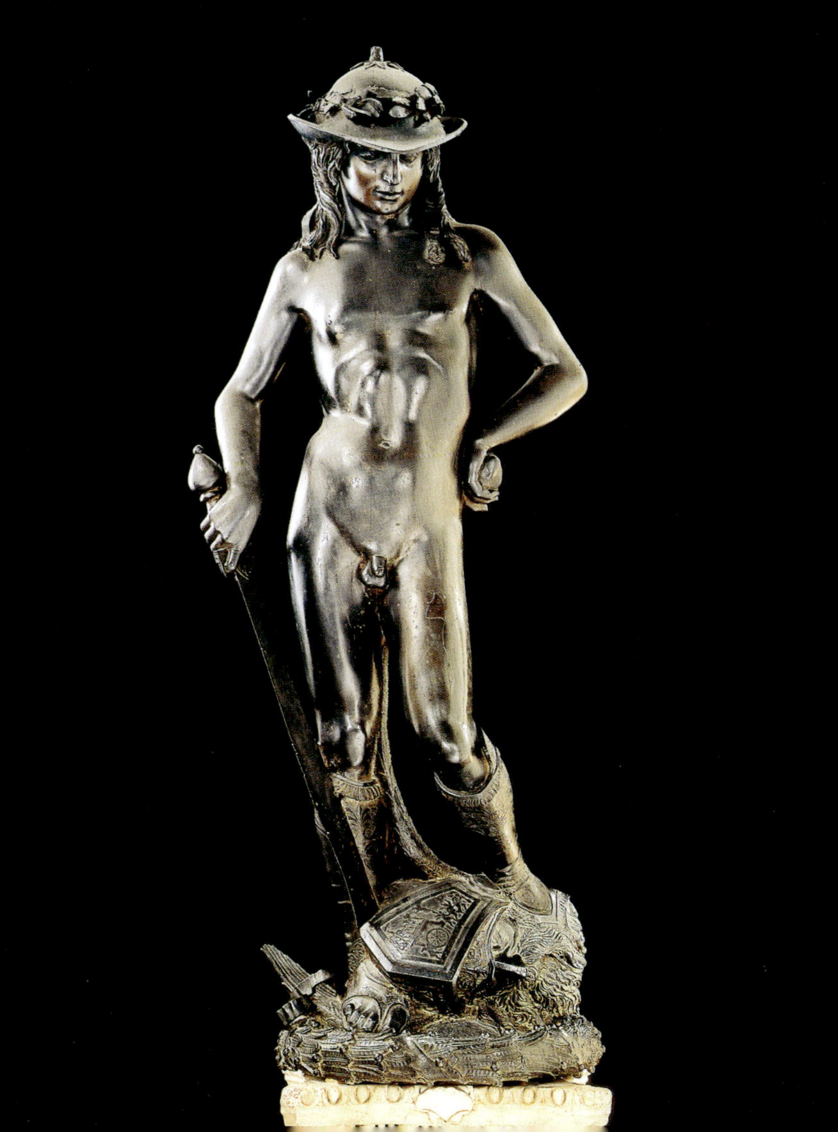

- by Andrea Verrocchio: the bronze *David* (1465), and the delicate marble bust of the *Lady with a Flower* (1475-1480).
- by Pollaiuolo, the bronze statuette of *Hercules and Antheus* (c. 1478).
- by Michelangelo: the *Bacchus* (1496-1497), the *Brutus* (c. 1540), the *Madonna and Child with the Infant St. John* (1504-1505), and the *David-Apollo* (1530-1532).
- by Giambologna: the bronze animals (1567), from the grotto of the Medicean villa of Castello and the *Mercury* (c. 1580).

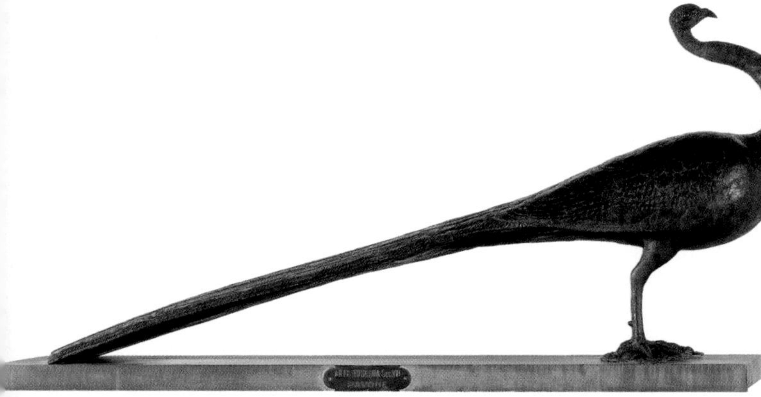

Above:
Giambologna, *Peacock*,
1567, bronze.
Museo Nazionale del Bargello.

Opposite page:
Andrea del Verrocchio, *David*,
c. 1465, partially gilded bronze.
Museo Nazionale del Bargello.

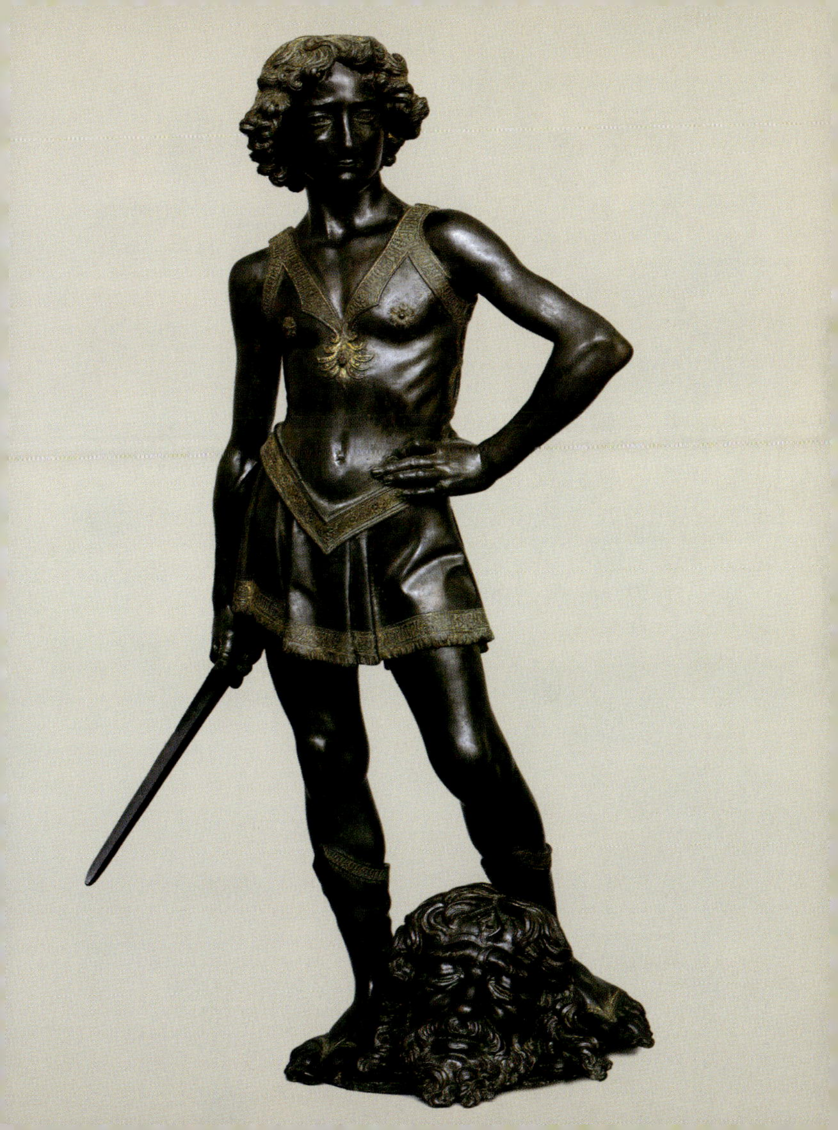

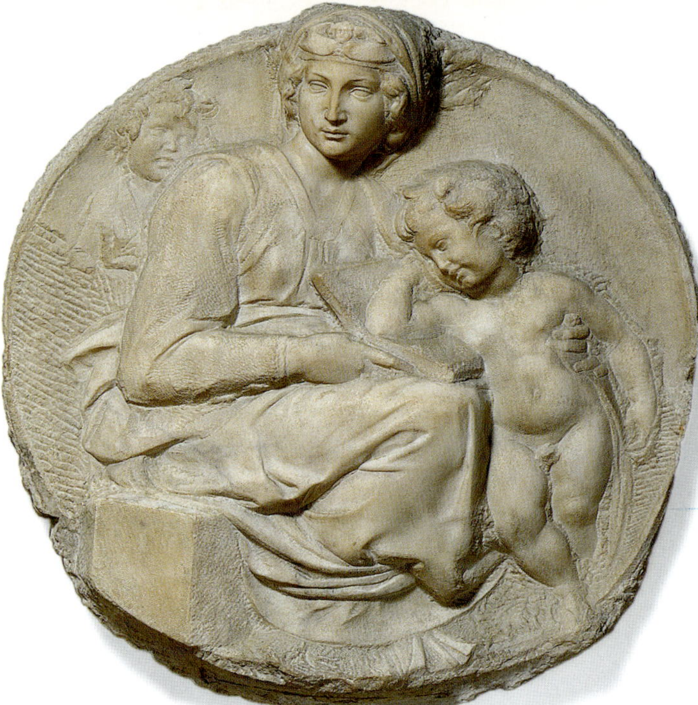

Above:
Michelangelo, *Madonna and Child with the Infant St. John,* 1504-1505, marble.
Museo Nazionale del Bargello.

Opposite page: Michelangelo, *Bacchus*, 1496-1497, marble.
Museo Nazionale del Bargello.

Following pages:
Andrea Verrocchio, *Lady with a Bouquet*, c. 1480, Museo Nazionale del Bargello.

Benvenuto Cellini, *Cosimo I*, c. 1547, bronze.
Museo Nazionale del Bargello.

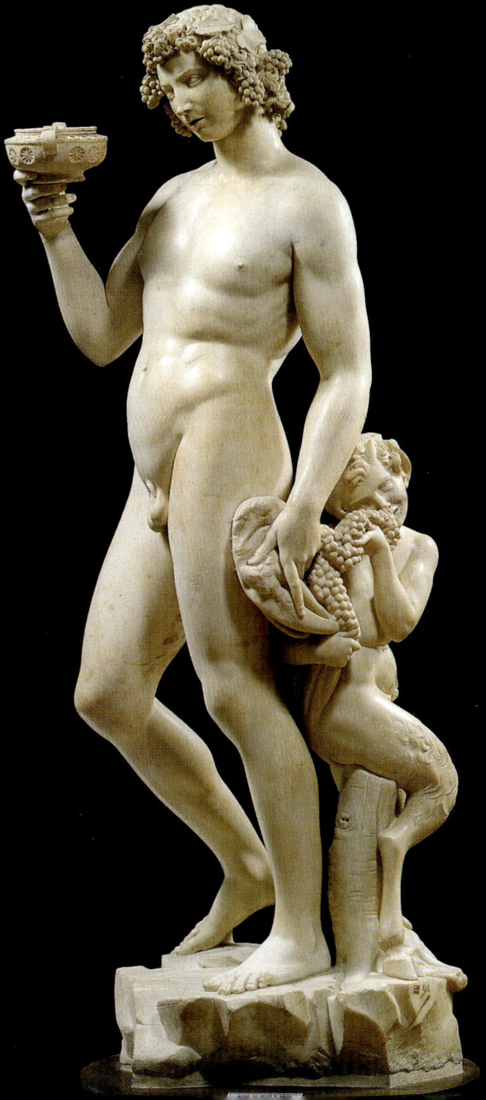

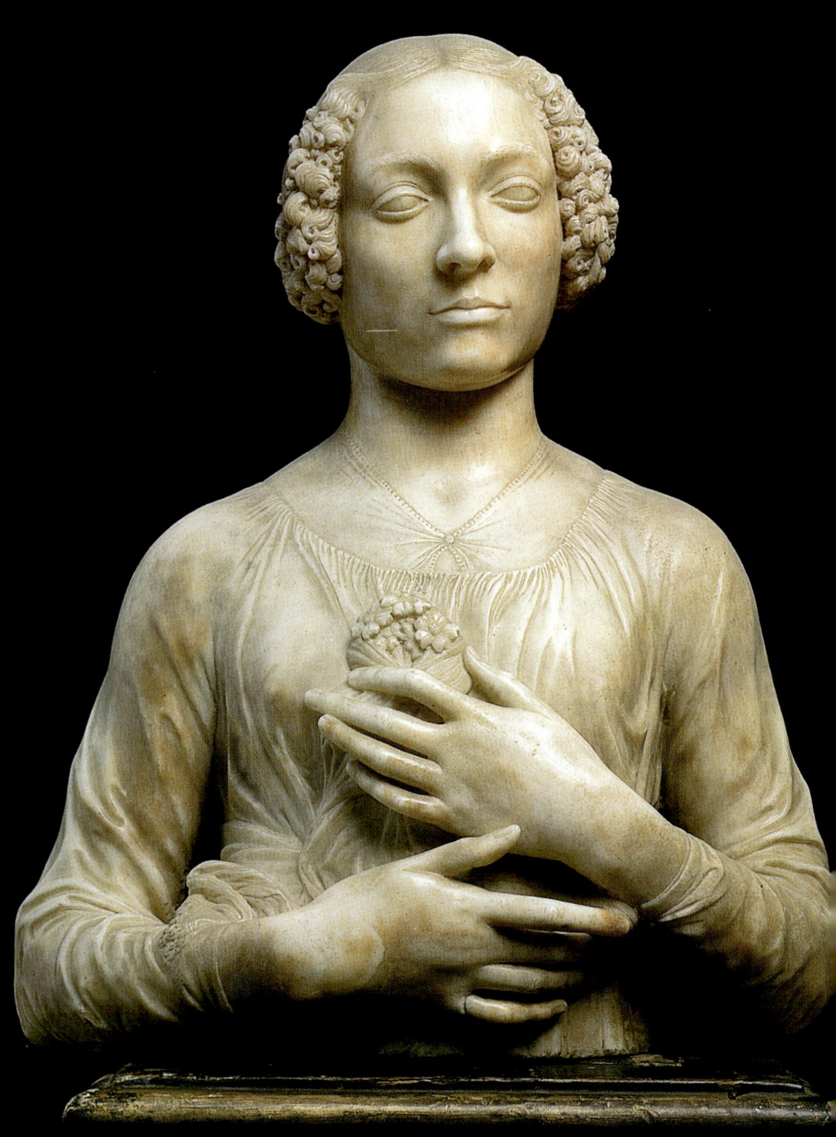

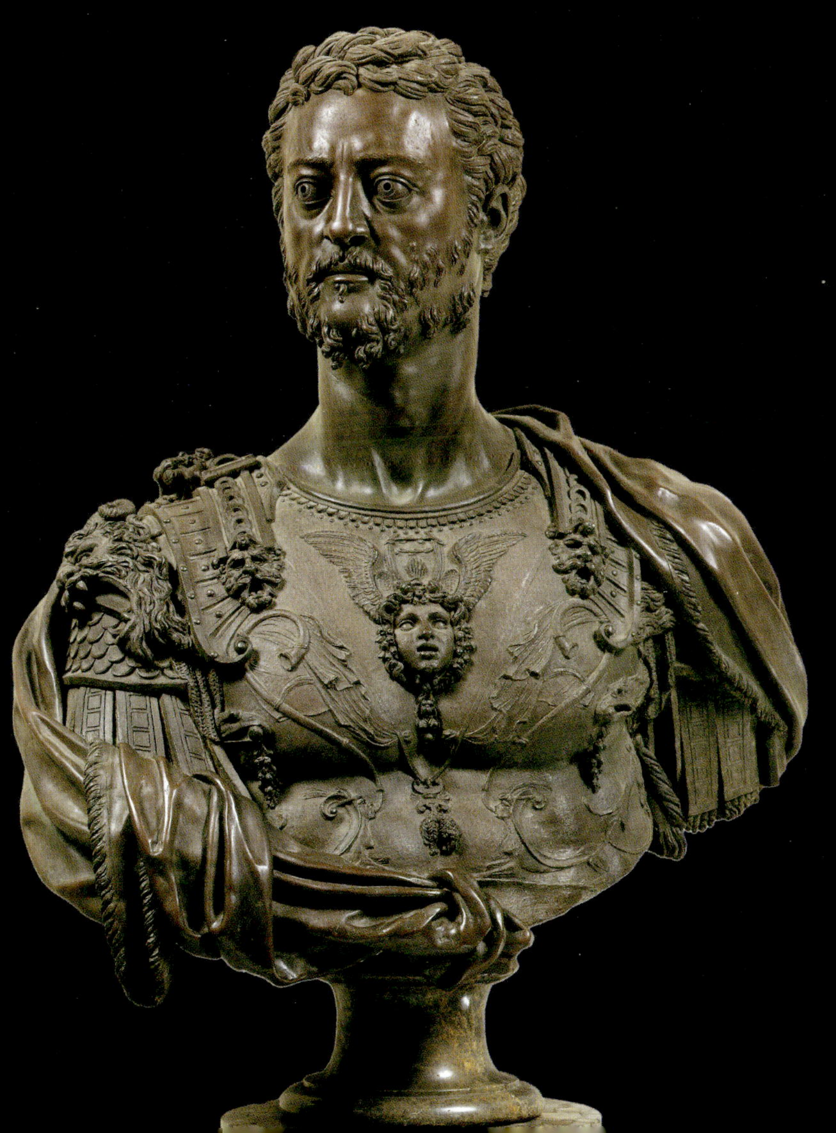

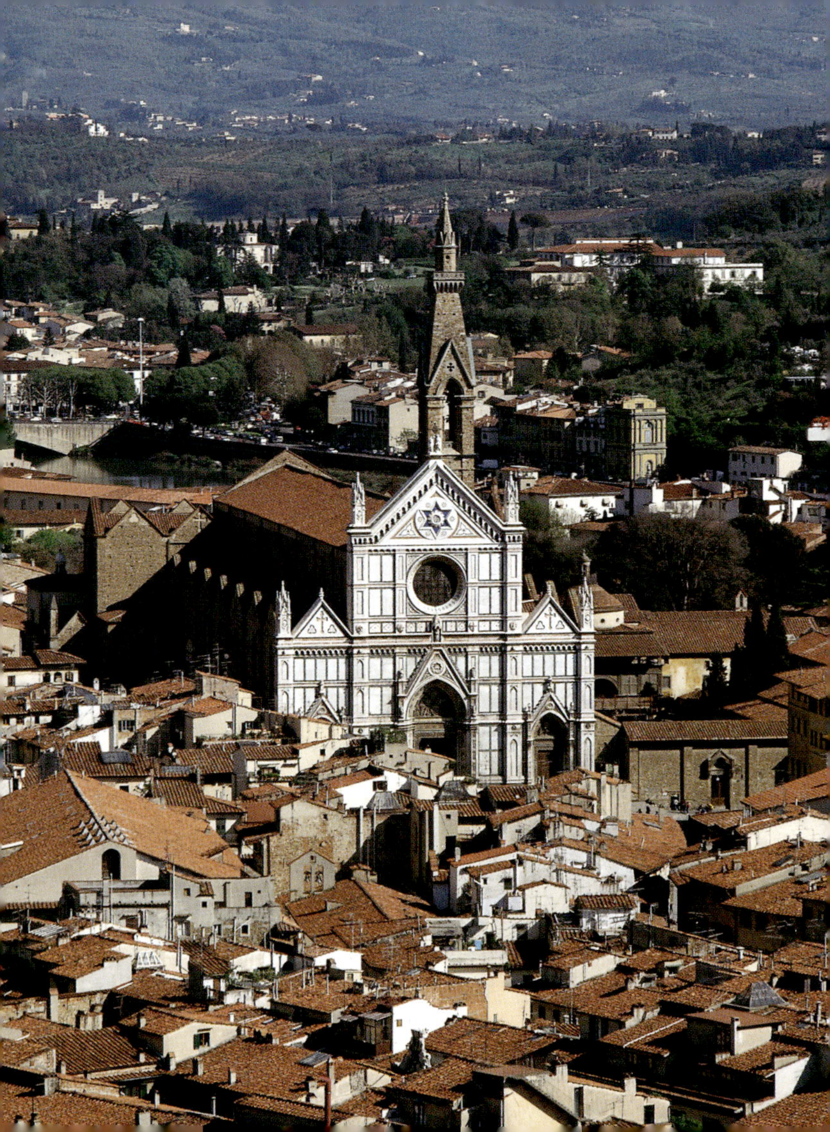

PIAZZA SANTA CROCE

The Piazza, the Church, the Chapels, the Museum

In the collective memory of the Florentines, Piazza Santa Croce remains the theater of historic events linked to their ancestral fortitude: such as that football game, played by them at one of the most dramatic moments in the city's history, on 17 February 1530, "in scorn and ridicule" of the Imperial troops beseiging them, as reported by the 16th century historian Benedetto Varchi. Although worn out by the siege, the Florentines stationed heralds with trumpets and other instruments "on the roof ridge of Santa Croce", so as not to be merely heard but also seen by the enemy ranked just outside of the walls. More recently, in the last century, on Christmas night of 1966, the charismatic presence of Pope Paul VI, who spoke after nightfall from the parvis of Santa Croce, instilled courage and hope in the residents of the Florentine district most heavily damaged by the flood that, on November 6th, had swept through the city. Among so many other things, thousands of books in the nearby National Library had been destroyed and the famous *Crucifix* by Cimabue has been damaged, almost irreparably it seemed. Those who lived through those days, and the long period of recovery, still recall the persistent smell of mud and heating oil, but

On the eastern edge of the city, the Santa Croce quarter is dominated by the grandiose basilica, founded by Franciscan monks in the 13th century.

also the smiling faces of the young people who came from all over the world to clean the mildew from books and precious manuscripts, and the monks of Santa Croce frantically searching through the mud for even a single tiny fragment of that Crucifix which, thanks to the work of expert restorers in the laboratories of Fortezza da Basso, has now returned to the Santa Croce Museum, not intact but in part still legible.

The Santa Croce district is located, in fact, in the lowest part of the city, easily subject to flooding from the Arno. When the Franciscans first settled here, in the early 13th century, it was no more than a swampy plain, still outside the city walls, protected only by an embankment along the Arno. It was here that the poorest citizens lived, although later luxurious palaces were built and it was inhabited (and still is today) by many illustrious personages. The Santa Croce Quarter was established in 1343, incorporating the previously-existing Sestiere di San Pier Scheraggio and a part of the Sestiere di San Pier Maggiore. It had as its emblem a cross of gold on a blue field and its standards were the Chariot, the Black Lion, the Ox and the Wheel. The predominant activities of this area depended on the nearness of the river. The dyers' industry, in particular, provided work for many people. It was here that, in the "tiratoi", or drying shops, on the

Opposite page:
Andrea Orcagna,
Earthquake,
c. 1345, fragmentary fresco.
Museo dell'Opera
di Santa Croce (entered from the church).

Following pages: Cimabue, *Crucifix*, c. 1287, panel painting. Museo dell'Opera di Santa Croce.

Donatello, *Annunciation*, c. 1433, pietra serena with gilded highlighting. Santa Croce.

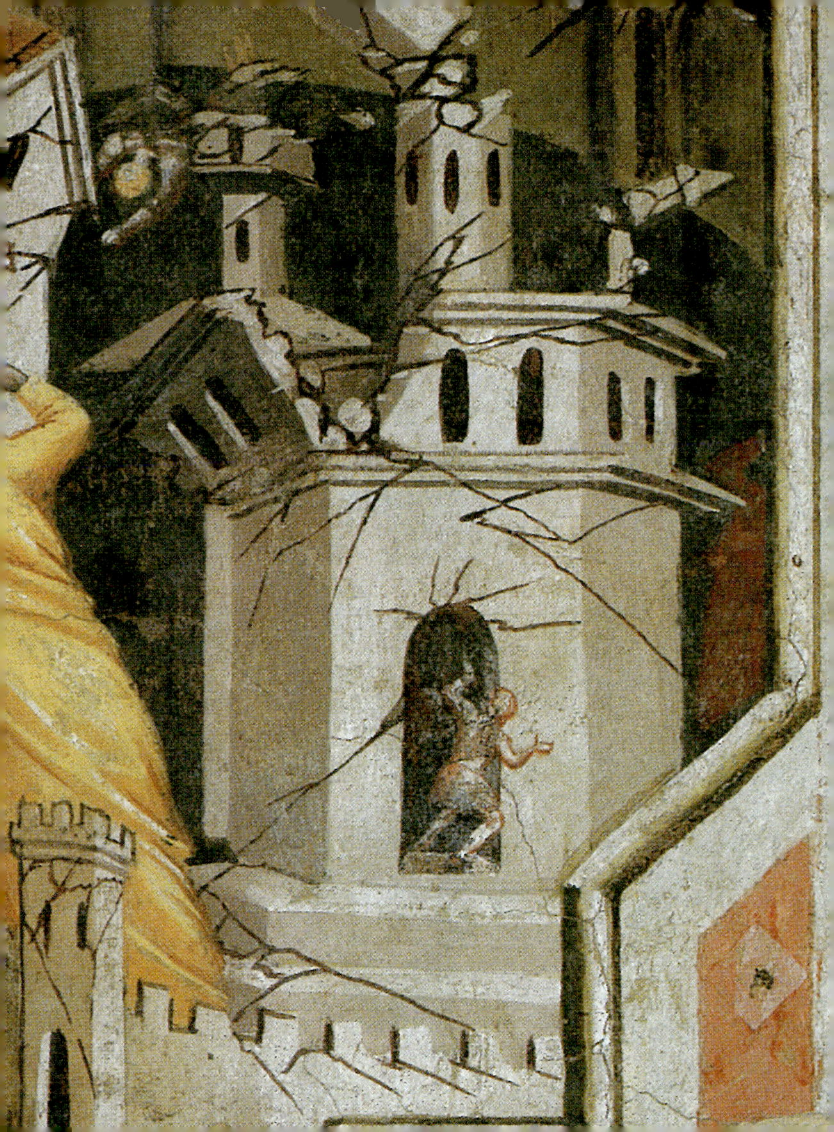

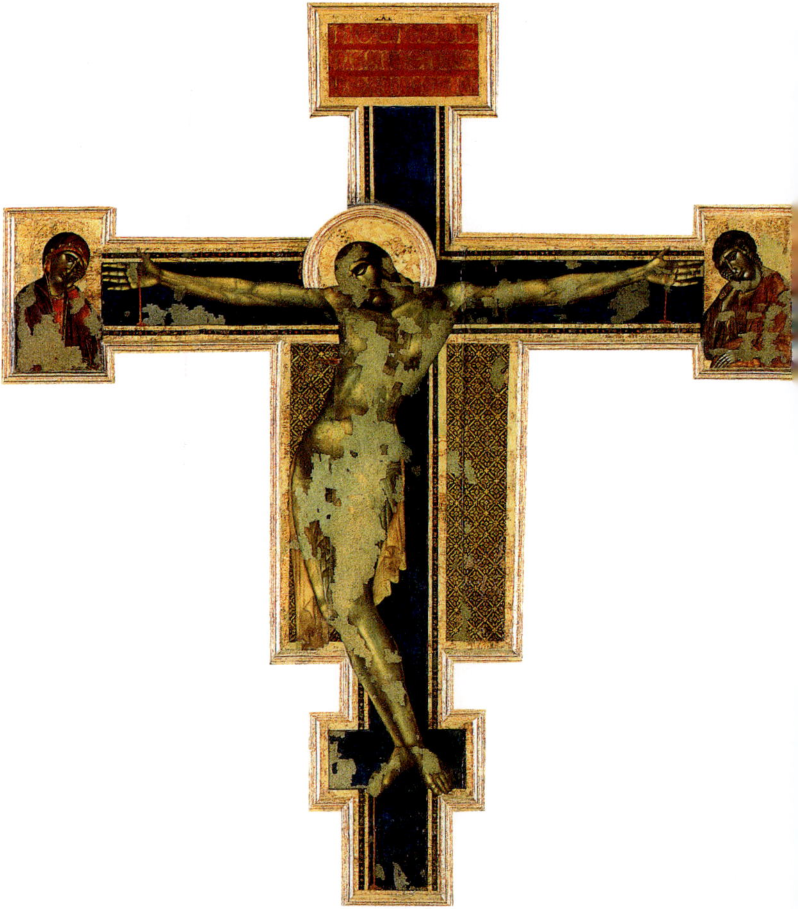

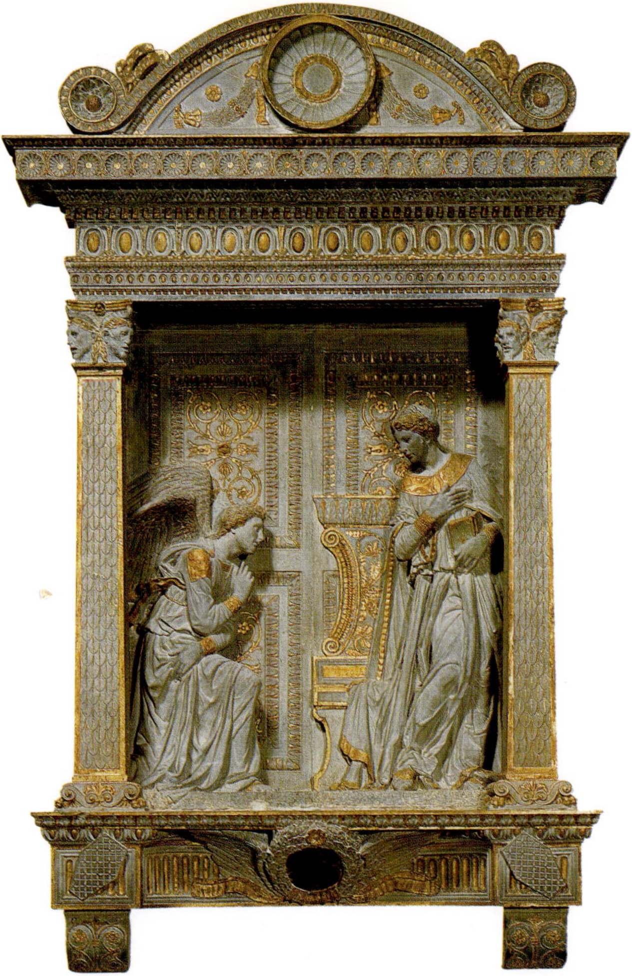

Arno, woollen cloth was dyed (from which derives the name of the street linking today's Piazza Cavallaggeri, the site of the National Library, with Via de' Benci, named after the Benci family). The district was inhabited by workmen who had moved to town from the country but also by powerful families such as the Alberti (their tower, on the corner between Via de' Benci and Borgo Santa Croce, still has its ancient "loggetta" on the ground floor). Wealthy bankers came to live here too – the Rinuccini, Baroncelli and Peruzzi – who earned high profits from their profession and immortalized their names in the chapels of the Basilica, frescoed by the greatest painters of the time, from Giotto to Taddeo and Agnolo Gaddi, from Nanni di Banco to Giovanni da Milano. The Peruzzi, who lost their fortune between 1340 and 1346 in a sensational bankruptcy, lived in the area once occupied by the Roman amphitheater. Looking at a map of Florence, we can trace the perimeter of the ancient building, whose shape survives today in the curving lines of Via Torta (i.e., curved), Via Bentaccordi and Piazza Peruzzi. Adjacent to these streets, in the Stinche block (Via Isola delle Stinche) stood the prison, erected between 1299 and 1301 on lands expropriated from the Uberti, around the present-day Via Verdi.

Opposite page:
Giotto, *Funeral of St. Francis*, detail from the *Stories of St. Francis*, after 1317, fresco.
Santa Croce, Bardi Chapel.

Following pages:
The façade of Santa Croce, designed in neo-Gothic style by Nicolò Matas between 1854 and 1863. The Bell Tower also dates from the 19th century.

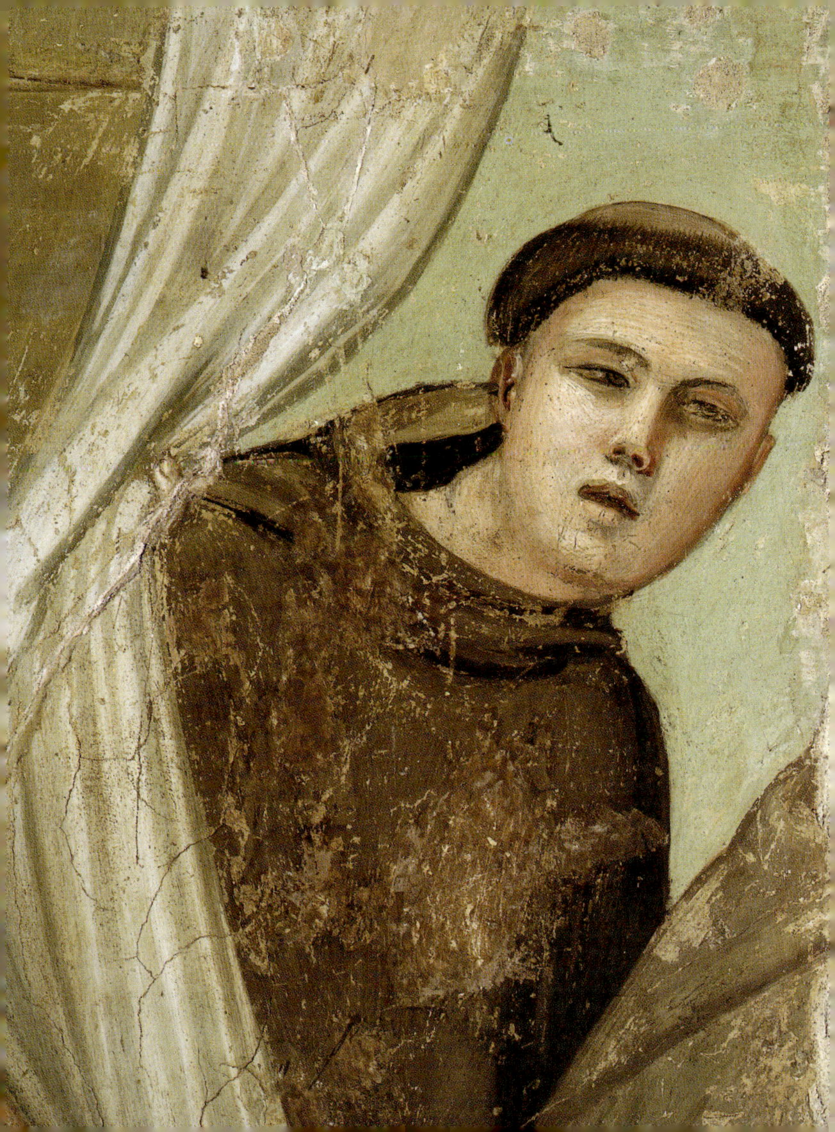

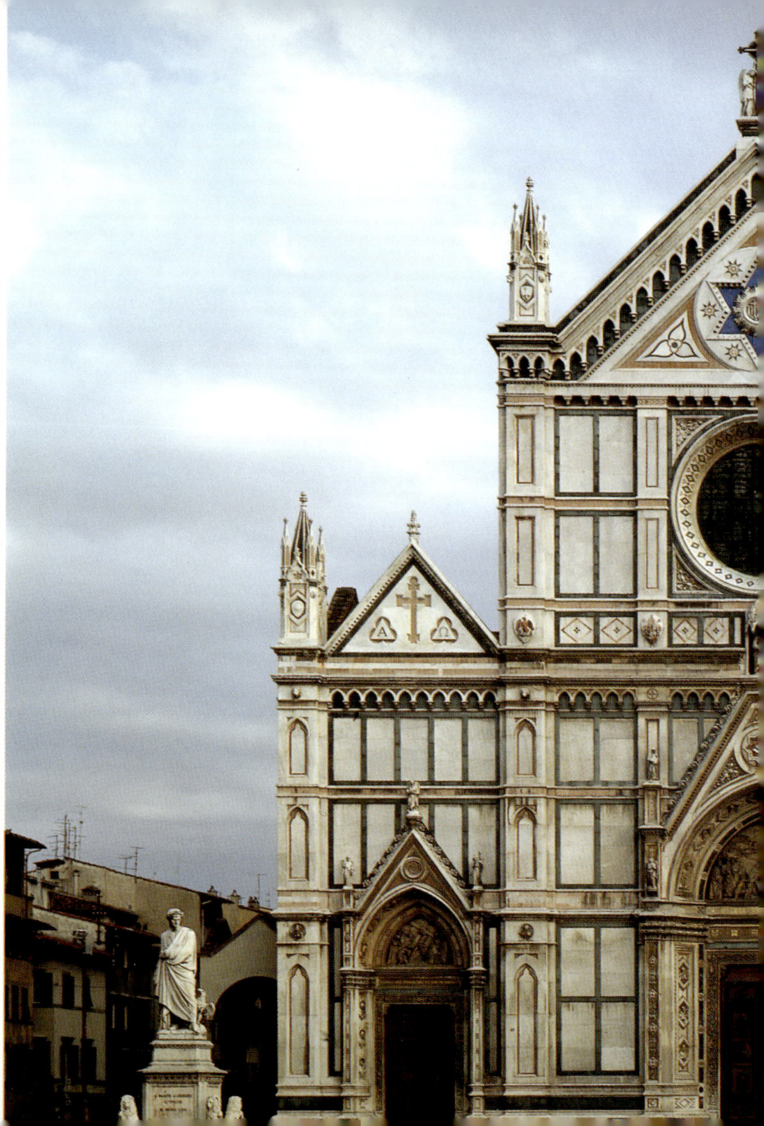

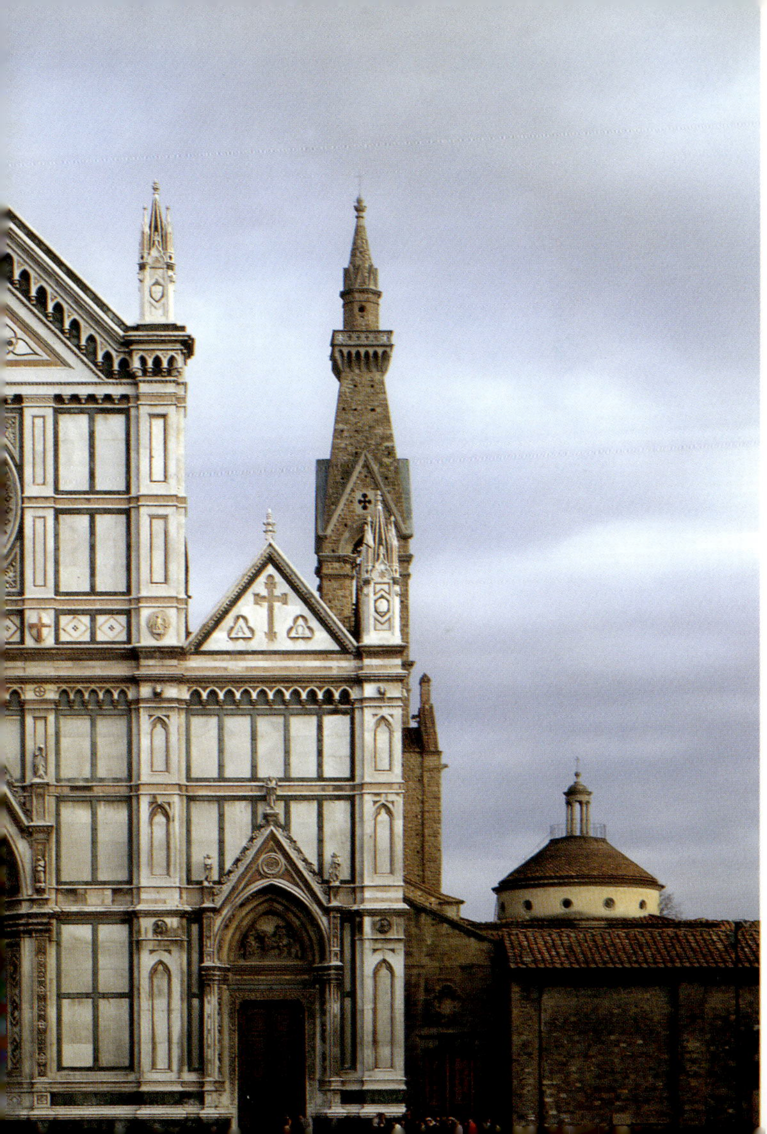

HISTORY

On the eastern edges of the city, and at the opposite pole from the Dominican church and monastery of Santa Maria Novella, the church of Santa Croce was begun around 1294 on the site of a primitive oratory built by a small group of followers of "God's minstrel", who came to live here in 1209, a few years before St. Francis passed through Florence. The project for the new church was drawn up by the greatest architect of the times, Arnolfo di Cambio. The earlier building continued to co-exist for some time with the new one, begun, it seems, starting from the grandiose apse section. In the last quarter of the 14th century the main structures of the Basilica, financed by public funds and by the wealthiest families in the area, were finished: a great T-shaped plan, with three naves divided by octagonal pilasters supporting pointed arches; a gallery that runs along the middle nave, below the double row of ogival windows; the ceiling with its exposed wooden trusses, brightly painted. The work of finishing and decorating the church, whose proportions are almost the same as those of the Basilica of St. Peter's in Rome, continued for years. In the apse section, no less than ten chapels provide a magnificent extension of the frescoed surface, constituting the manifesto of Florentine Medieval figurative art. During the course of the 16th century the monastery was also enlarged

Opposite page:
View of the interior of Santa Croce looking toward the transept.

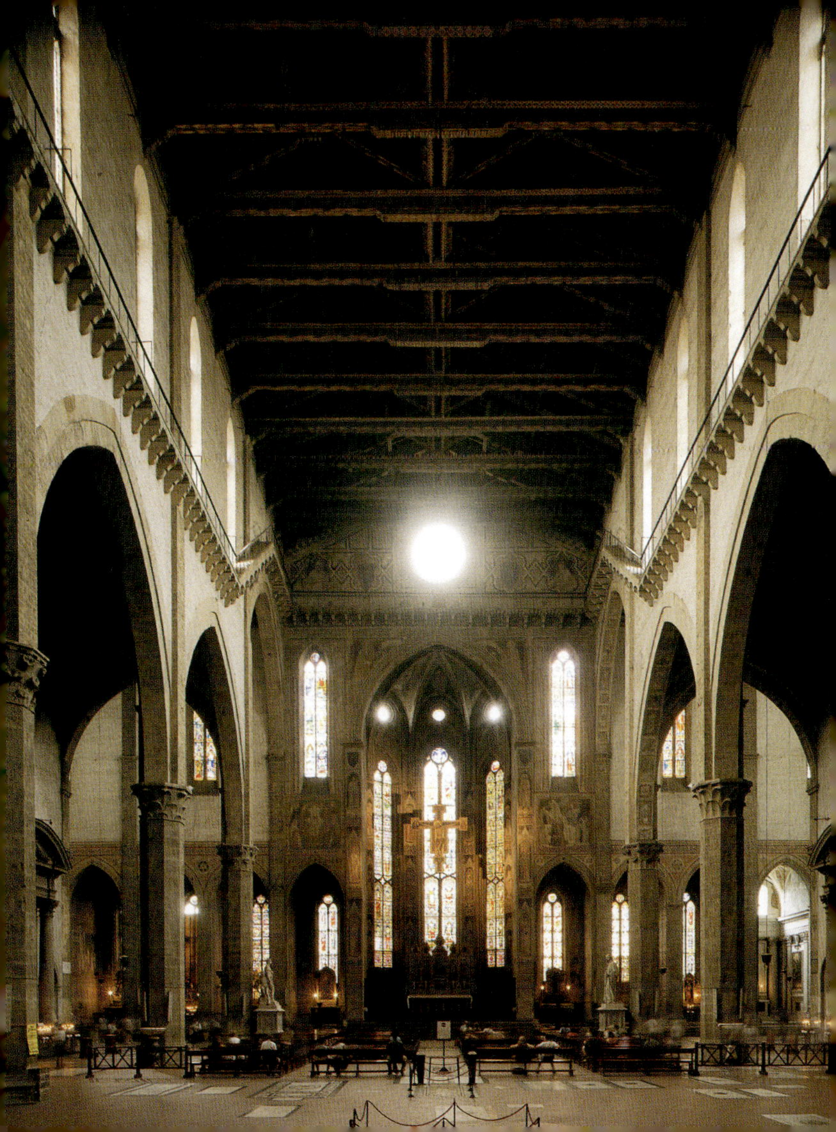

and decorated, while in 1423, after a fire, the dormitory and library were rebuilt. Then came the Pazzi Chapel, commissioned in 1429 by Andrea dei Pazzi (exterior modified in the 19th century), and the large cloister, designed, like the chapel, by Filippo Brunelleschi (c. 1453) and finished after his death, perhaps by Bernardo Rossellino. In 1445 Michelozzo had instead built for his patron, Cosimo the Elder, the Novitiate Chapel. As in other Florentine churches, in the sixth decade of the 16th century the "modernizing" initiatives of Giorgio Vasari, in keeping with changing taste and the dictates of the Counter Reformation, led to the demolishing of the choir in front of the transept. Vasari raised part of the floor, whitewashed many of the frescoes adorning the walls of the Gothic church and placed against them simple altars in *pietra serena*, changing the original appearance of the building. As in the Cathedral of Santa Maria del Fiore, the façade of Santa Croce is not original, despite its appearance. It was in fact built in Neo-Gothic style, between 1857 and 1863, by Nicolò Matas, and decorated with antique-style sculptures.
The church is also famous for containing the tombs of illustrious men, and for this reason it is known as the Pantheon "*delle itale glorie*" (of Italy's glories) (from the poems of Ugo Foscolo in *Sepolcri*, 1806).

Opposite page:
View of the nave of Santa Croce, from the transept crossing.

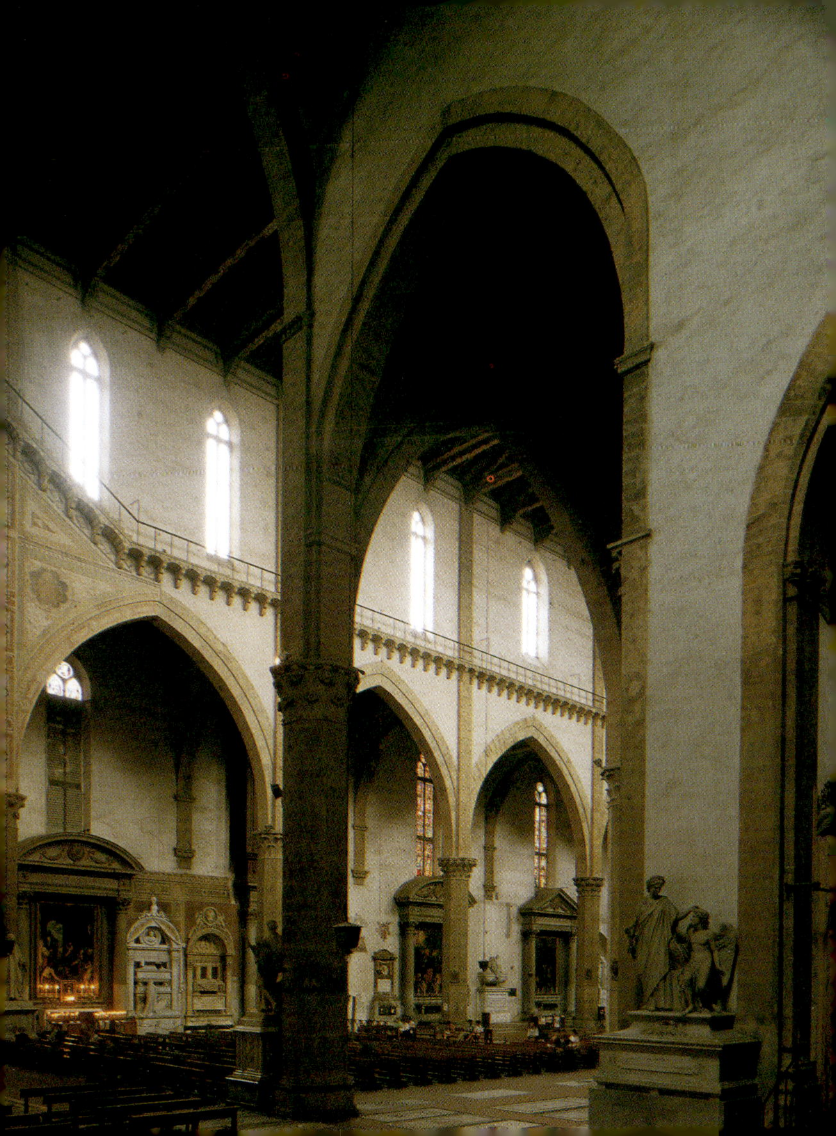

Annexed to the church, in the ancient refectory and other adacent rooms, among them the former Cerchi Chapel, the Museo dell'Opera di Santa Croce, inaugurated in 1900, exhibits works some of which have been restored after having been damaged by the flood.

VISITORS' ITINERARY AND WORKS OF ART

- INSIDE THE CHURCH:
  - the Bardi and Peruzzi Chapels (to the right of the transept), decorated between 1320 and 1328 for the most powerful families of Florentine bankers. The frescoes, restored several times over the centuries, representing *Stories of St. Francis* and *Stories of St. John the Evangelist and St. John the Baptist*, mark the peak of Giotto's artistic maturity as regards conception of space, complexity and profundity of the architectural backgrounds, and the powerful plasticity of the forms. Restoration has revealed that in the Bardi Chapel he worked on fresh plaster, while in the Peruzzi Chapel he painted his scenes on a dry wall, allowing him to work on larger surfaces at a time.

Opposite page: Giotto, *The trial by fire before the Sultan*, detail from the *Stories of St. Francis*, after 1317, fresco. Santa Croce, Bardi Chapel.

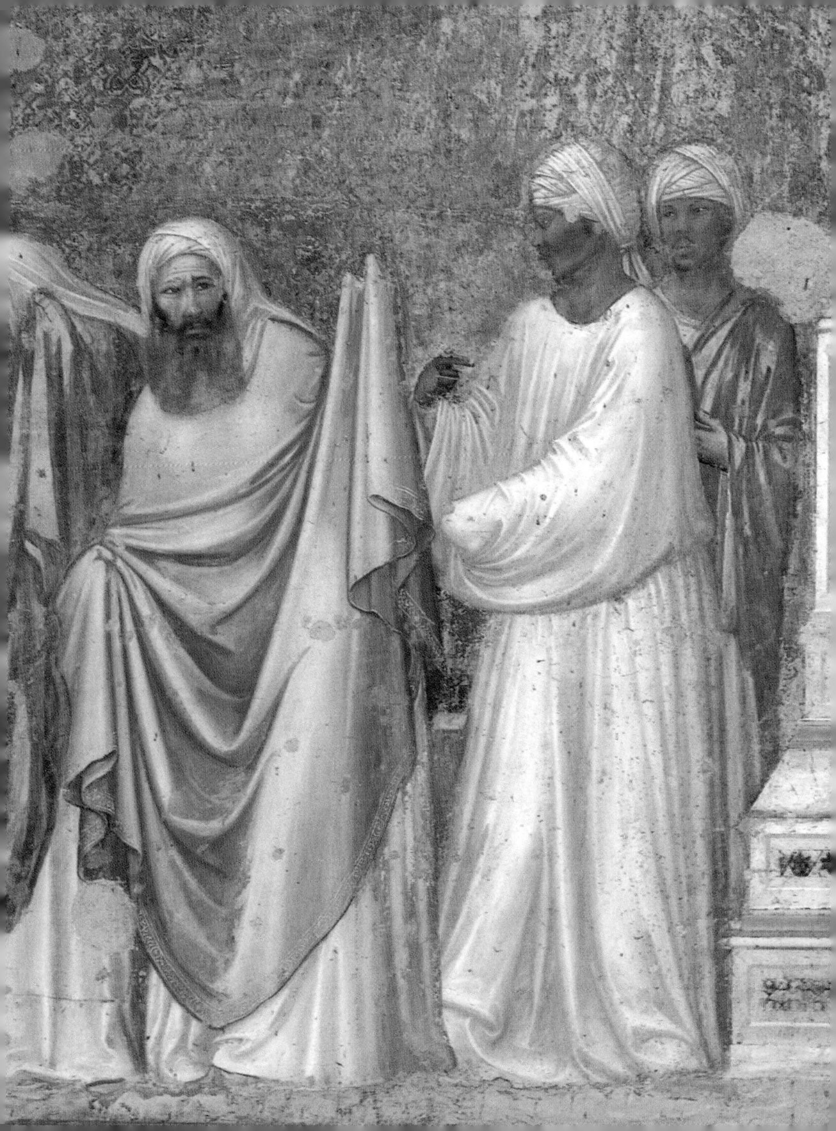

- in the Baroncelli Chapel, the Polyptych (c. 1328) by Giotto and assistants, and the frescoes illustrating *Stories of the Virgin* (third decade of the 14th century) by Taddeo Gaddi.
- In the Magna (or Alberti) Chapel, the cycle with the *Legend of the Holy Cross* (c. 1385) by Agnolo Gaddi.
- in the Bardi di Vernio Chapel (at left of the transept), the *Stories of St. Silvester* (c. 1340) by Maso di Banco.
- the numerous stained glass windows, some designed in the 14th century by Taddeo Gaddi and Maestro di Figline.
- on the wall of the right nave, the *Annunciation* (c. 1433), by Donatello, a supremely refined high-relief in *pietra serena* with gold highlighting.
- on the third pillar in the central nave, the octagonal marble Pulpit (c. 1475) by Benedetto da Maiano.
- the two marble humanist tombs par excellence, almost opposite each other: on the right nave, the *Tomb of Leonardo Bruni* (c. 1444-1450) by Bernardo Rossellino, on the left one, the *Monument to Carlo Marsuppini* (1455) by Desiderio da Settignano.
- in the left wing of the transept, the wooden *Crucifix* (1412) by Donatello.

Opposite page:
Taddeo Gaddi,
False niche with domestic objects,
third decade of the 14th century,
fresco. Santa Croce,
Baroncelli Chapel.

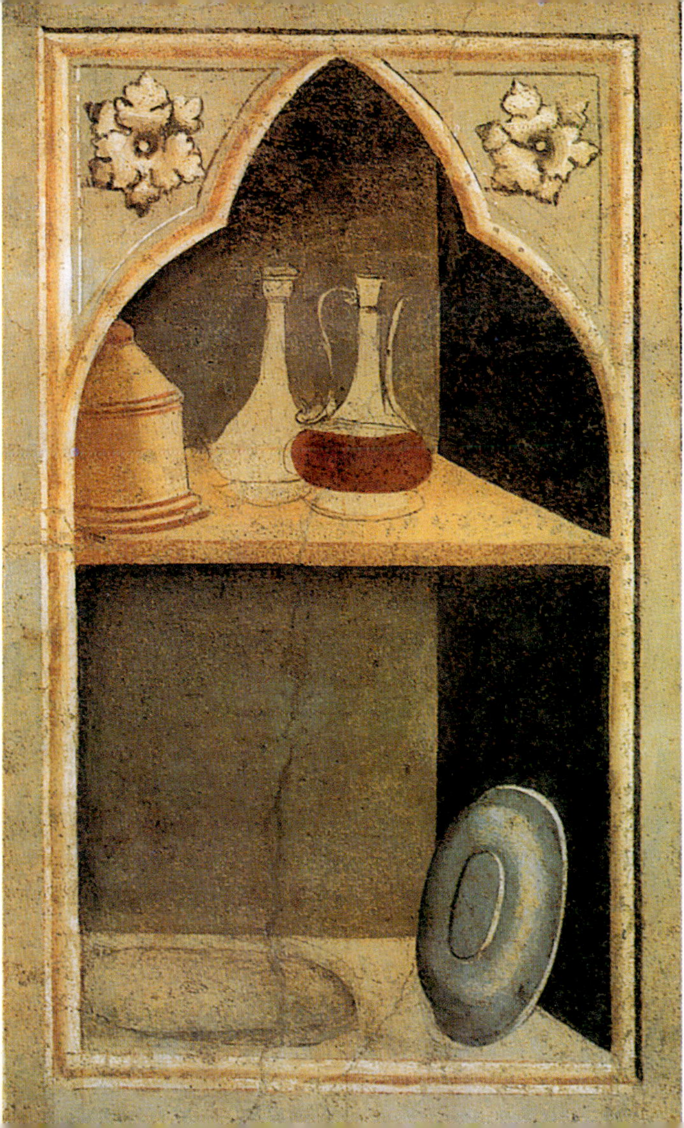

- among the tombs and monuments to illustrious men, those of Michelangelo (1574, by Giorgio Vasari); Vittorio Alfieri (1806-1810, by Antonio Canova); Michele Skotniki (1808, by Stefano Ricci); and Princess Zamoysky (1844, by Lorenzo Bartolini).

• THE PAZZI CHAPEL

- the luminous chapel, reached through the Museum, to the right of the church, was commissioned of Brunelleschi in 1429 by the banker Andrea di Gugliemo Pazzi, and finished after years of work. The layout is similar to that of the Old Sacristy in San Lorenzo, but with a rectangular plan rather than a square one. On the cupola, in the oculi of the pendentives, appear the crests of the Pazzi family and glazed terracotta tondoes portraying the Evangelists, perhaps designed by Brunelleschi himself.

• IN THE MUSEUM

- the *Crucifix* (c. 1287) by Cimabue.
- The *Tree of the Cross* (sixth-seventh decade of the 14th century) by Taddeo Gaddi, a grandiose fresco in the Refectory.
- the *St. Ludovic of Toulouse* (1423) by Donatello.
- the fragments of a *Triumph of Death* (c. 1350) by Orcagna.

Opposite page and following pages:
Desiderio da Settignano,
Monument to Carlo Marsuppini,
details, 1454, marble.
Santa Croce.

Following pages:
Bernardo Rossellino,
Tomb of Leonardo Bruni,
detail, 1444, marble.
Santa Croce.

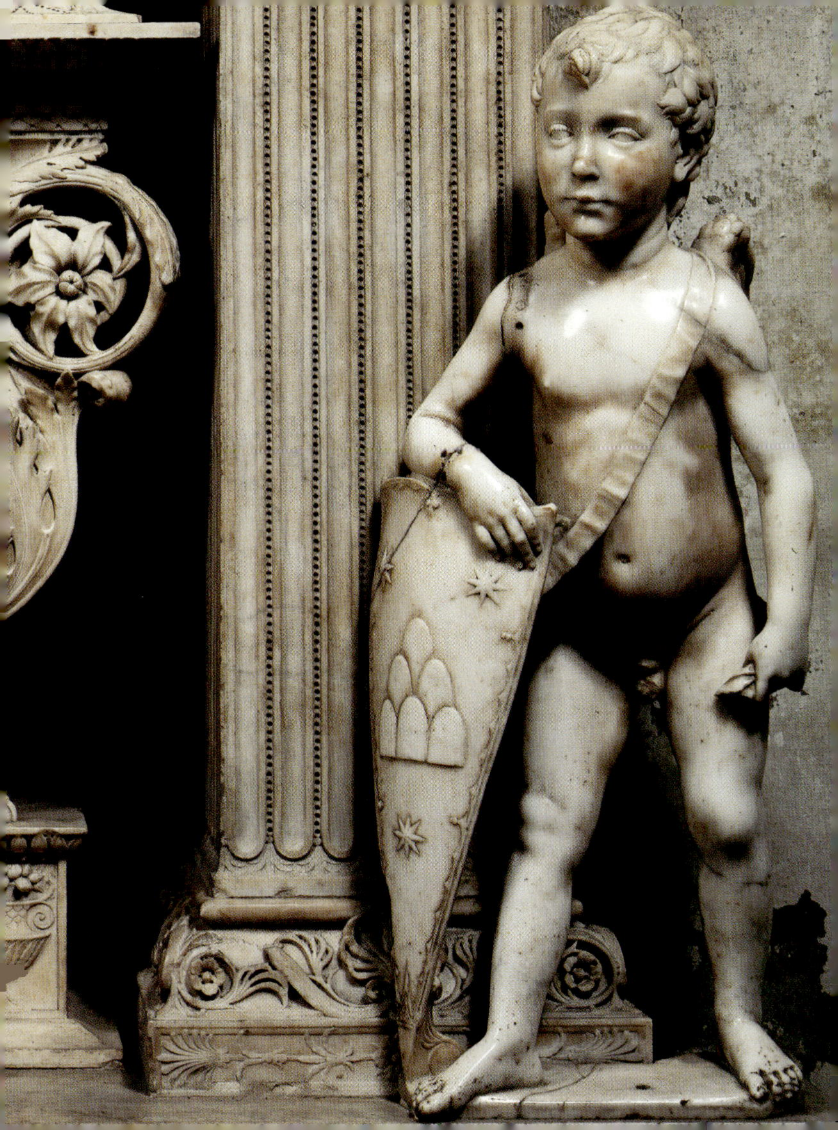

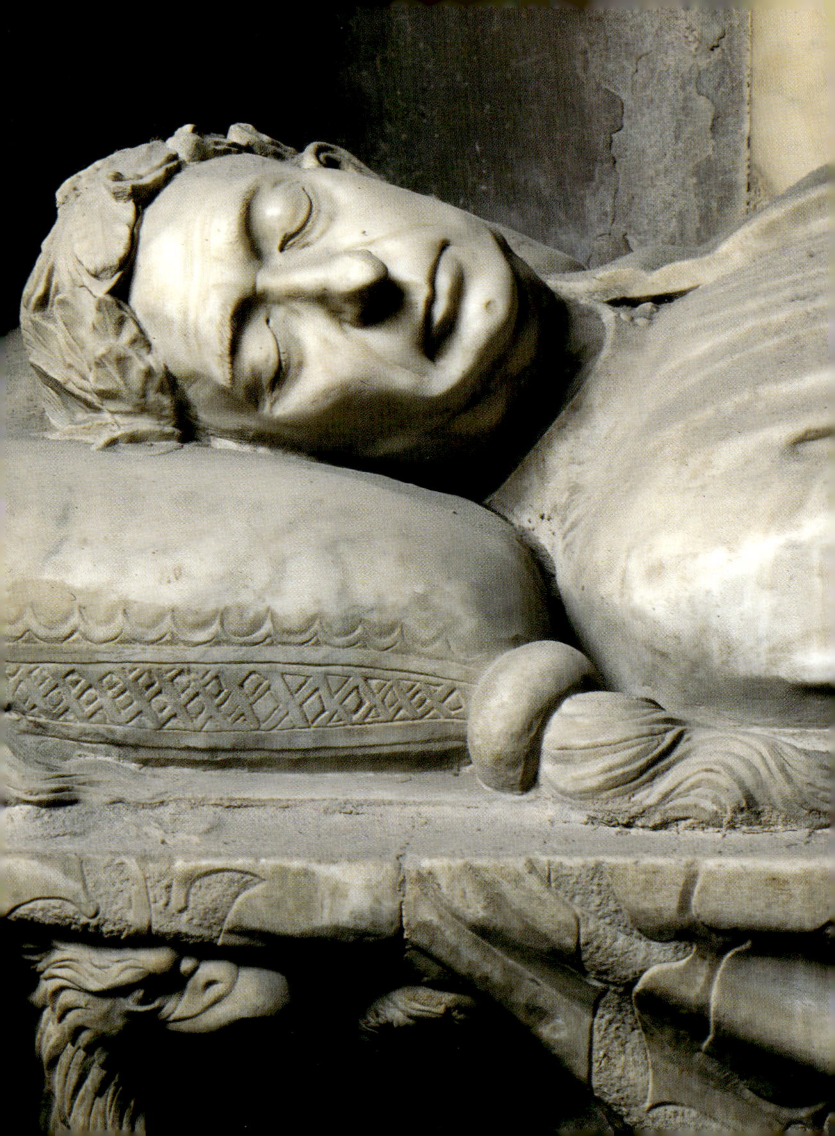

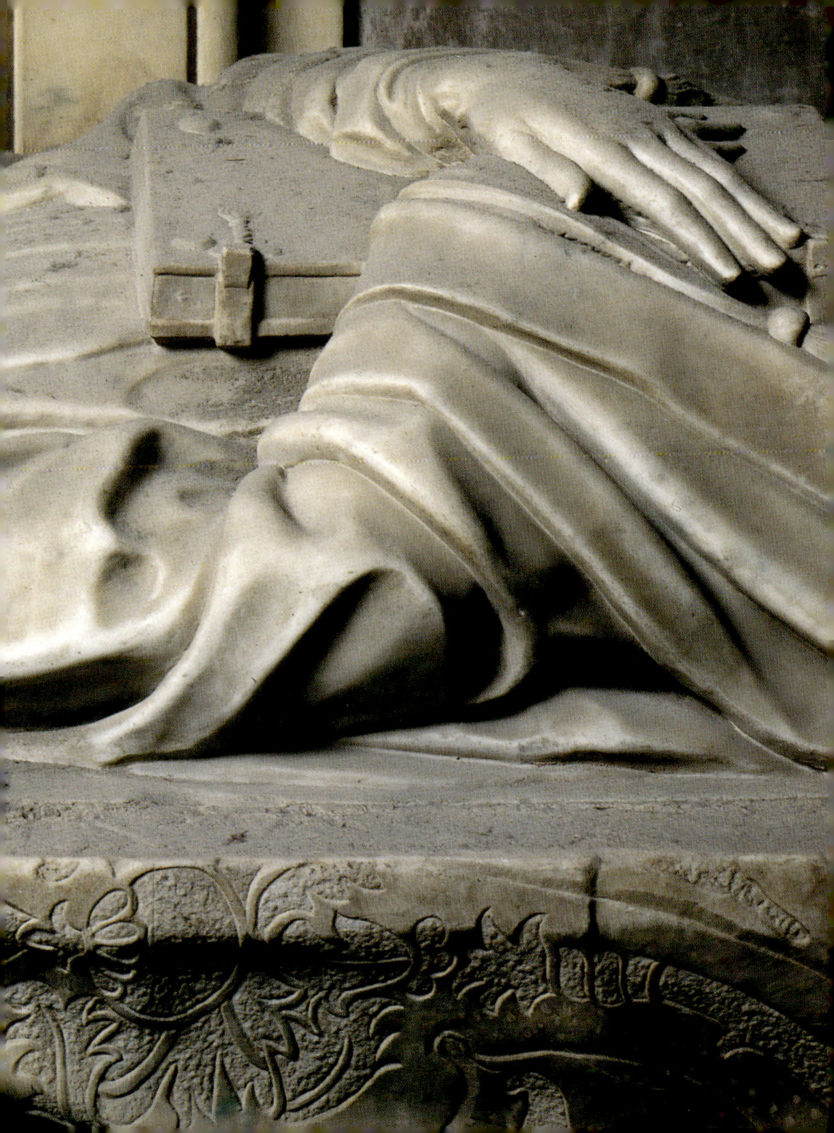

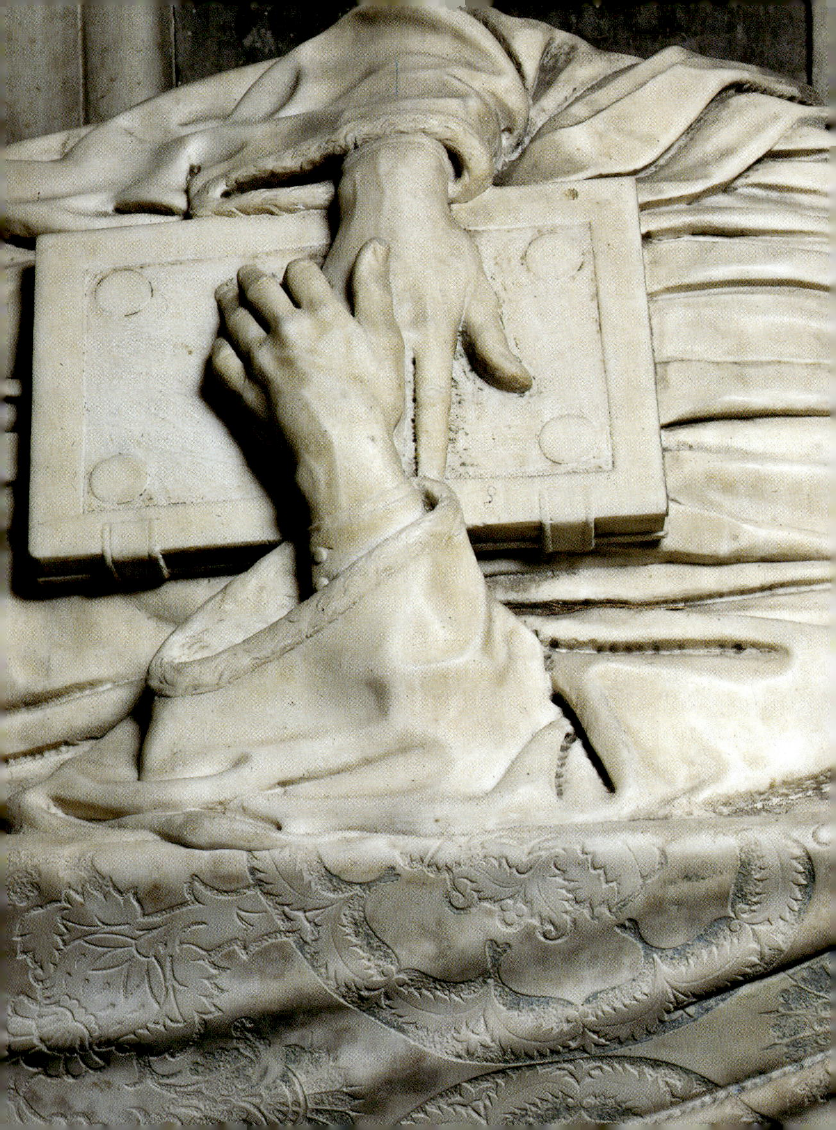

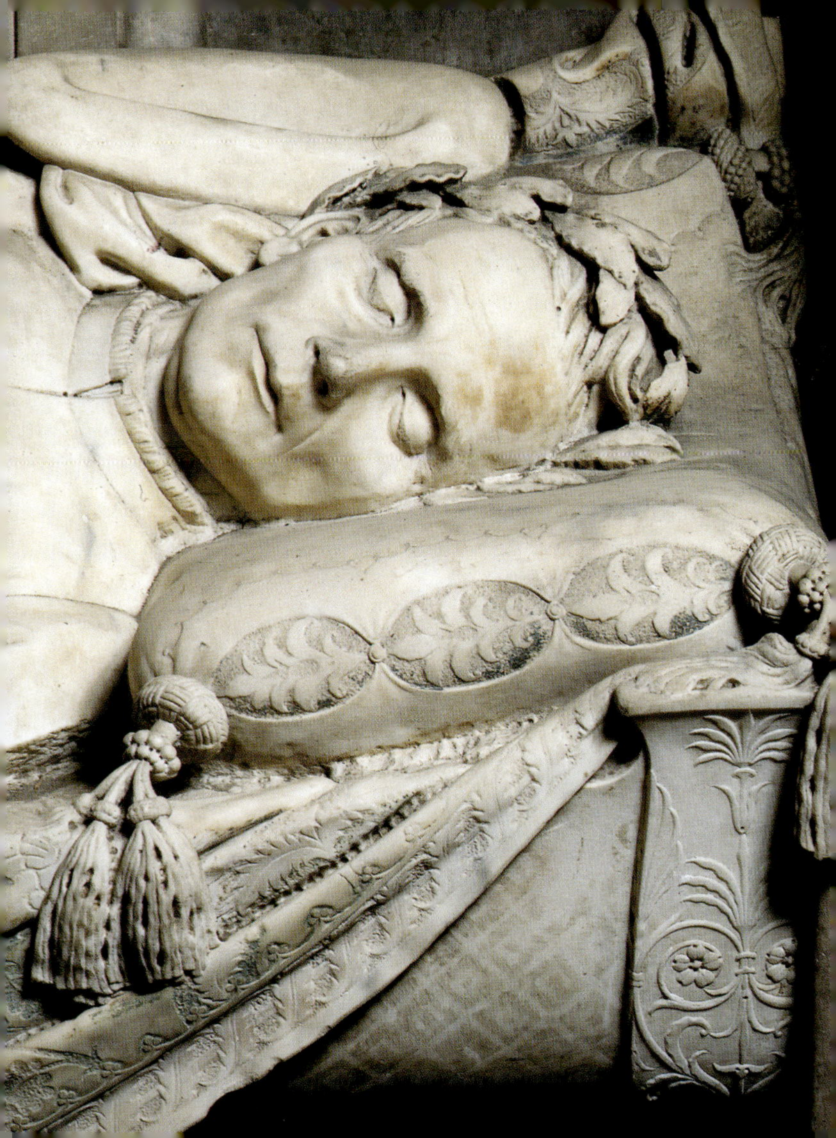

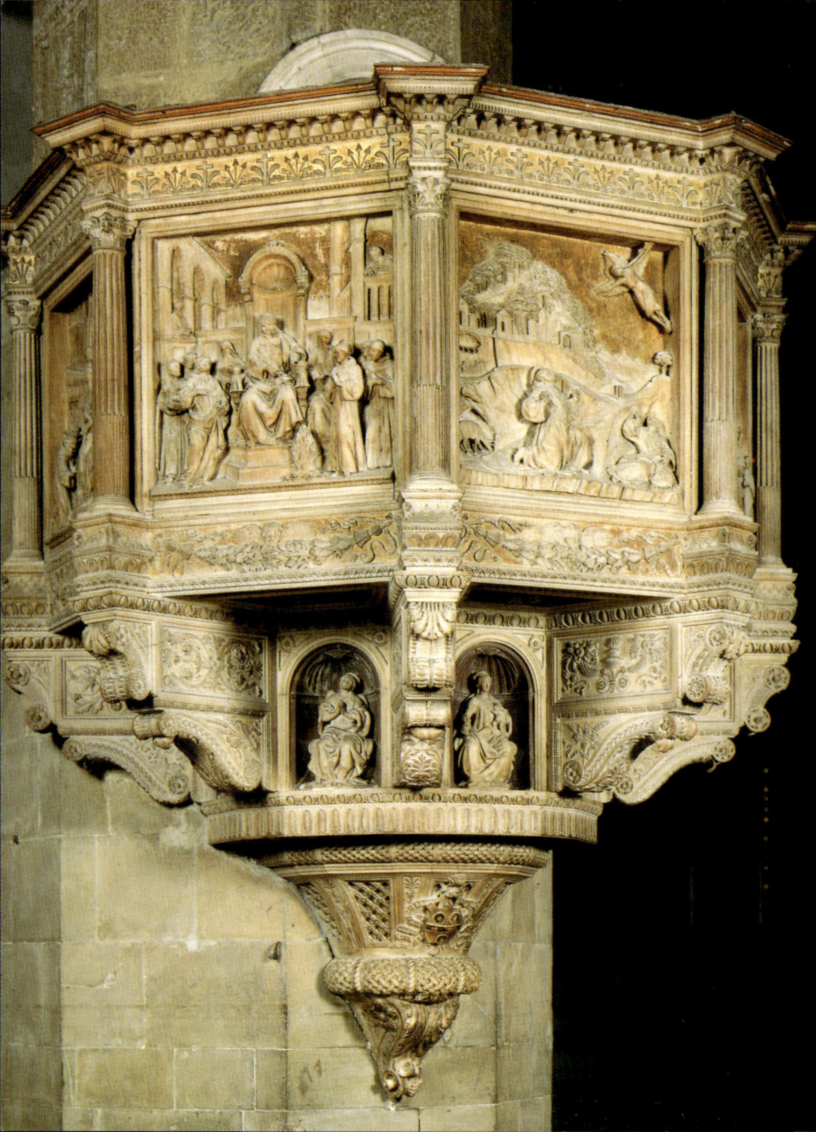

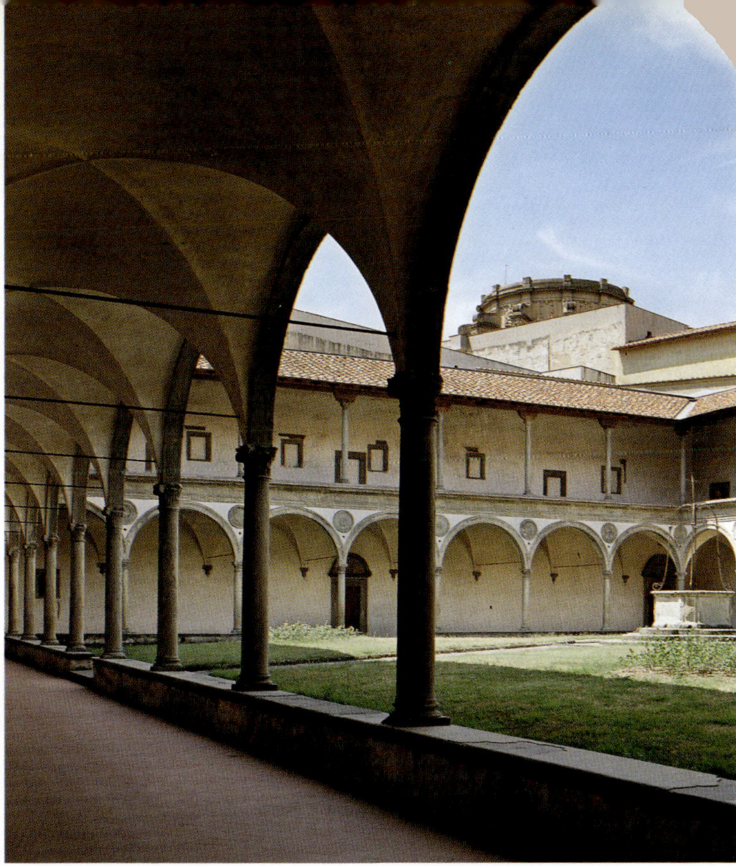

Opposite page:
Benedetto da Maiano, *Octagonal pulpit*, with *Stories of St. Francis* in the five panels, 1454, marble. Santa Croce.

Above:
View of the second cloister, designed by Filippo Brunelleschi in 1429 and finished in 1453.

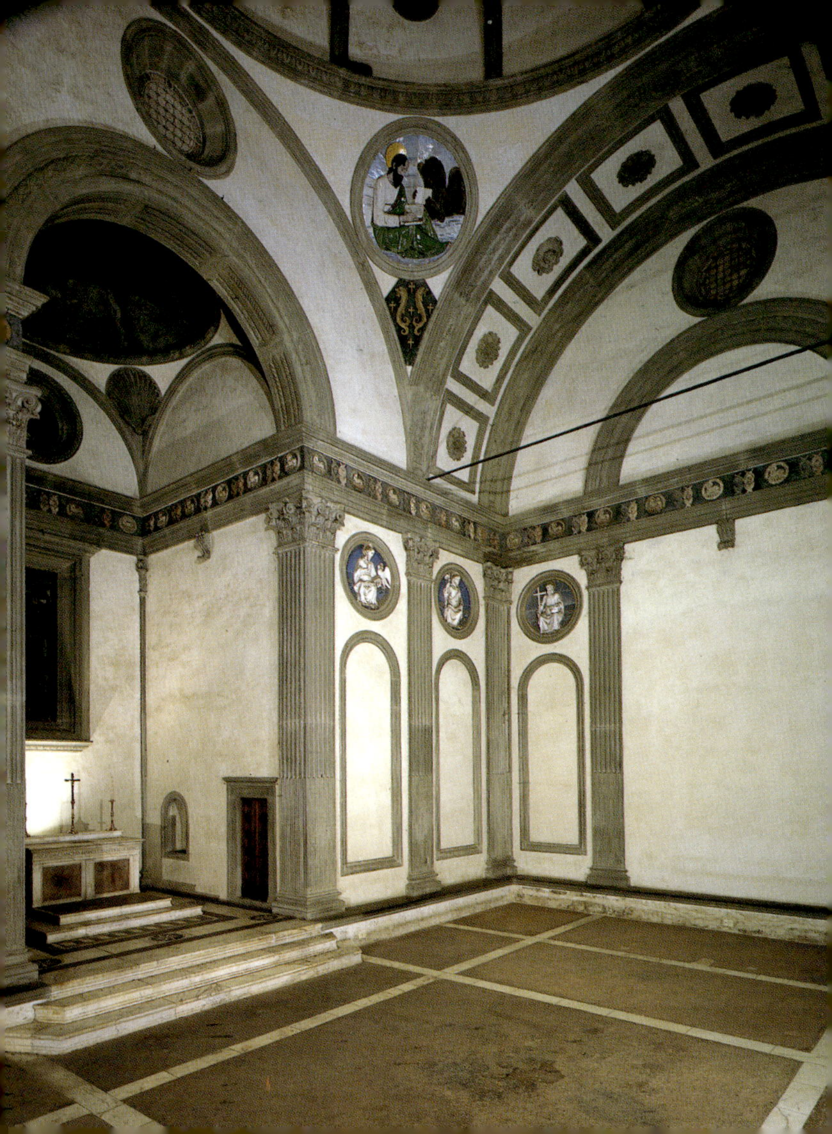

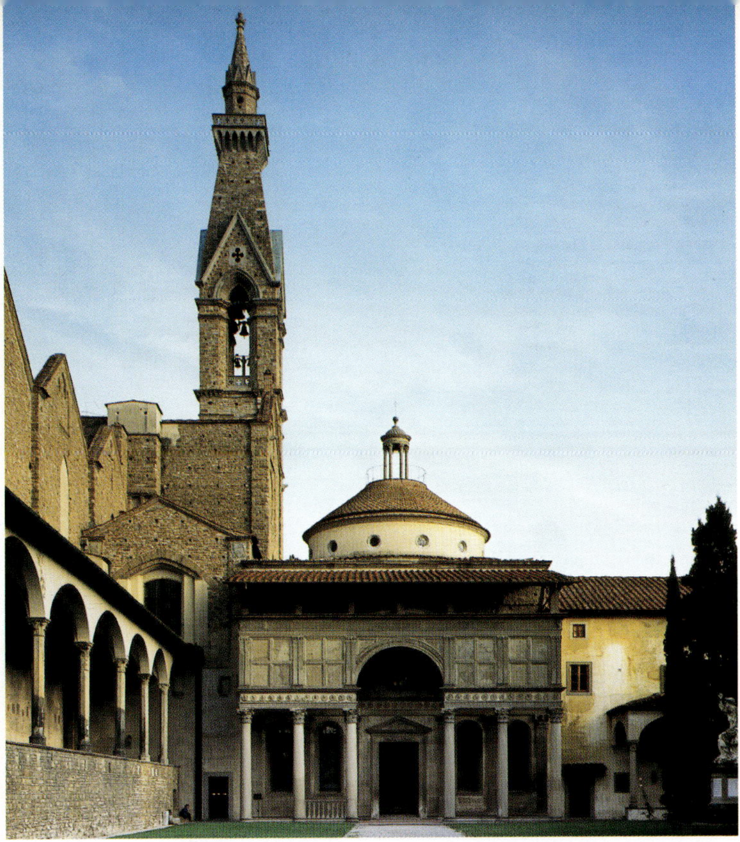

Opposite page and above:
View of the Pazzi Chapel, designed by Brunelleschi in 1429 and finished after his death.
Following pages:
Donatello, *St. Ludvic of Toulouse*, 1423, gilded bronze. Museo di Santa Croce (from Orsanmichele).

Stefano Ricci, *Tomb of Michele Skotniki*, with the allegory of Music, 1808, marble. Santa Croce.

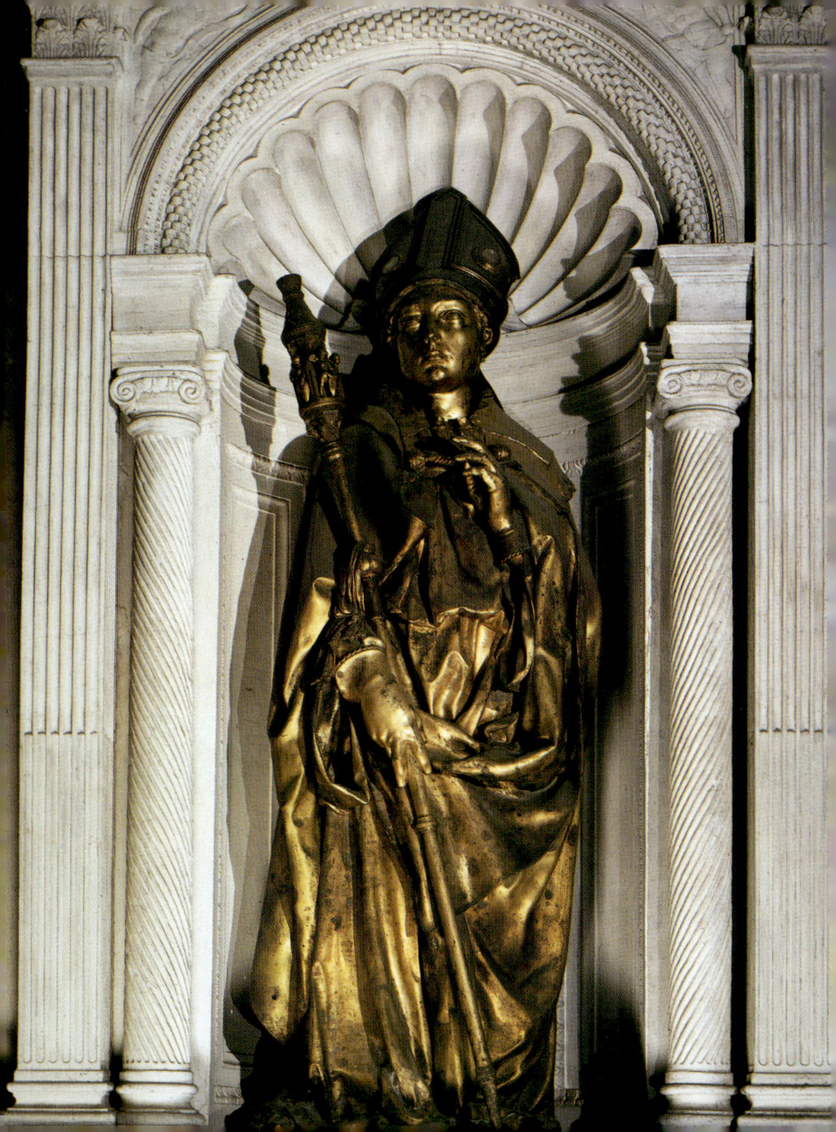

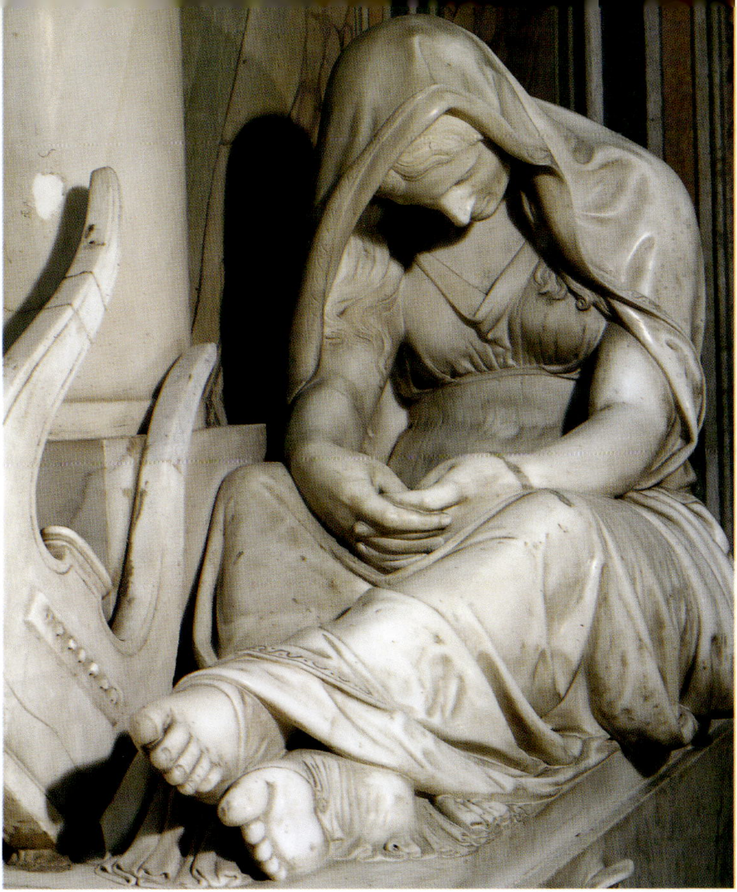

Following pages:
Taddeo Gaddi, *Tree of the Cross* and *The Last Supper*, sixth-seventh decade of the 14th century, fresco in the Refectory. Museo di Santa Croce.

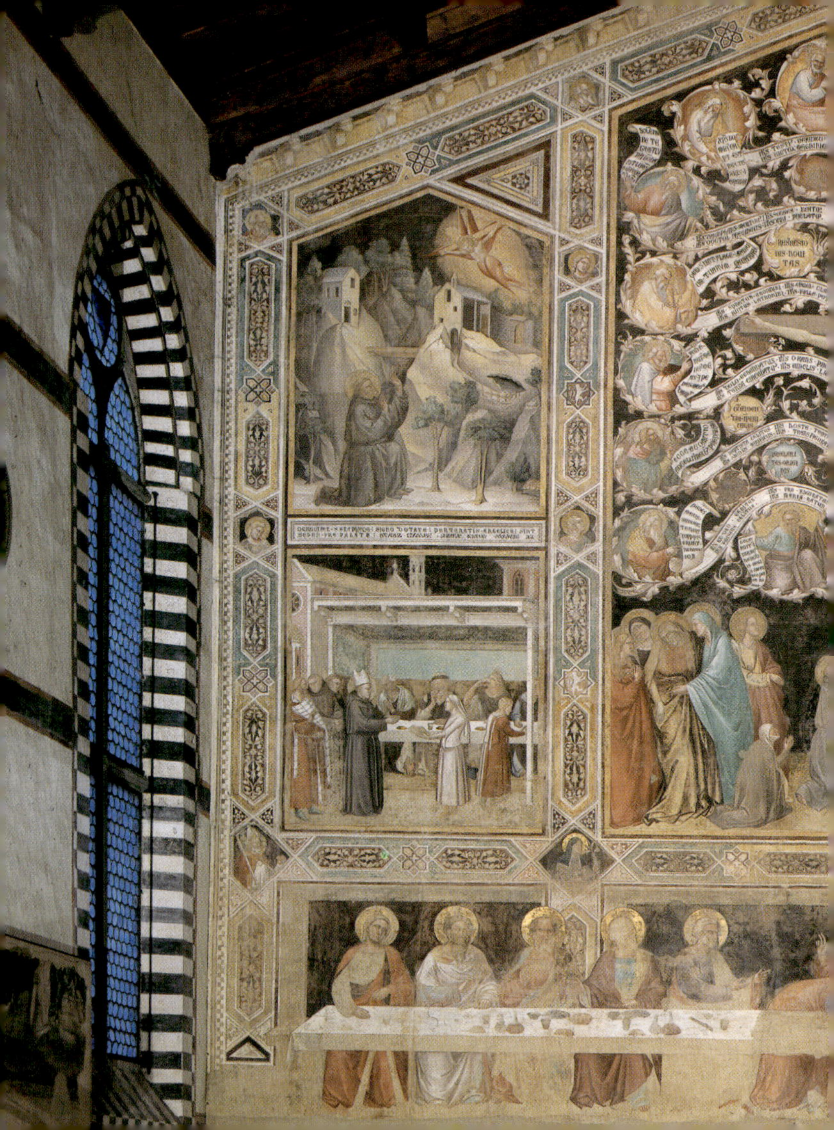

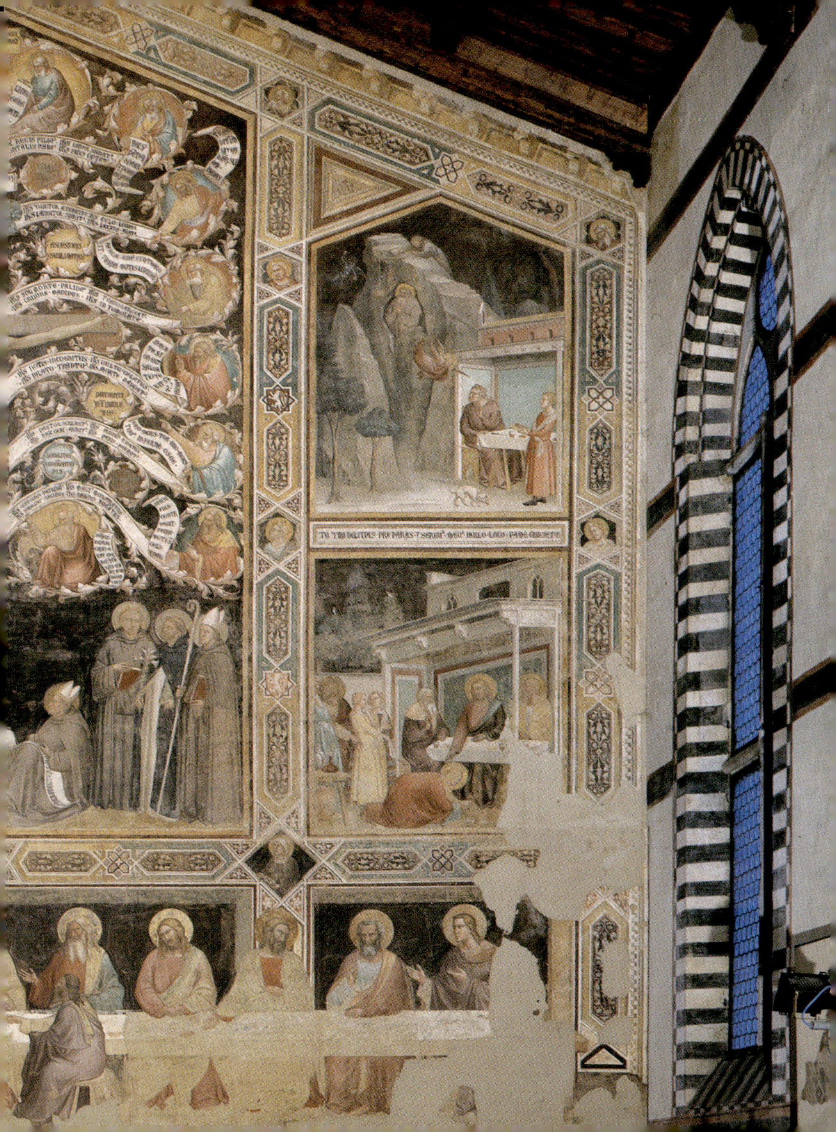

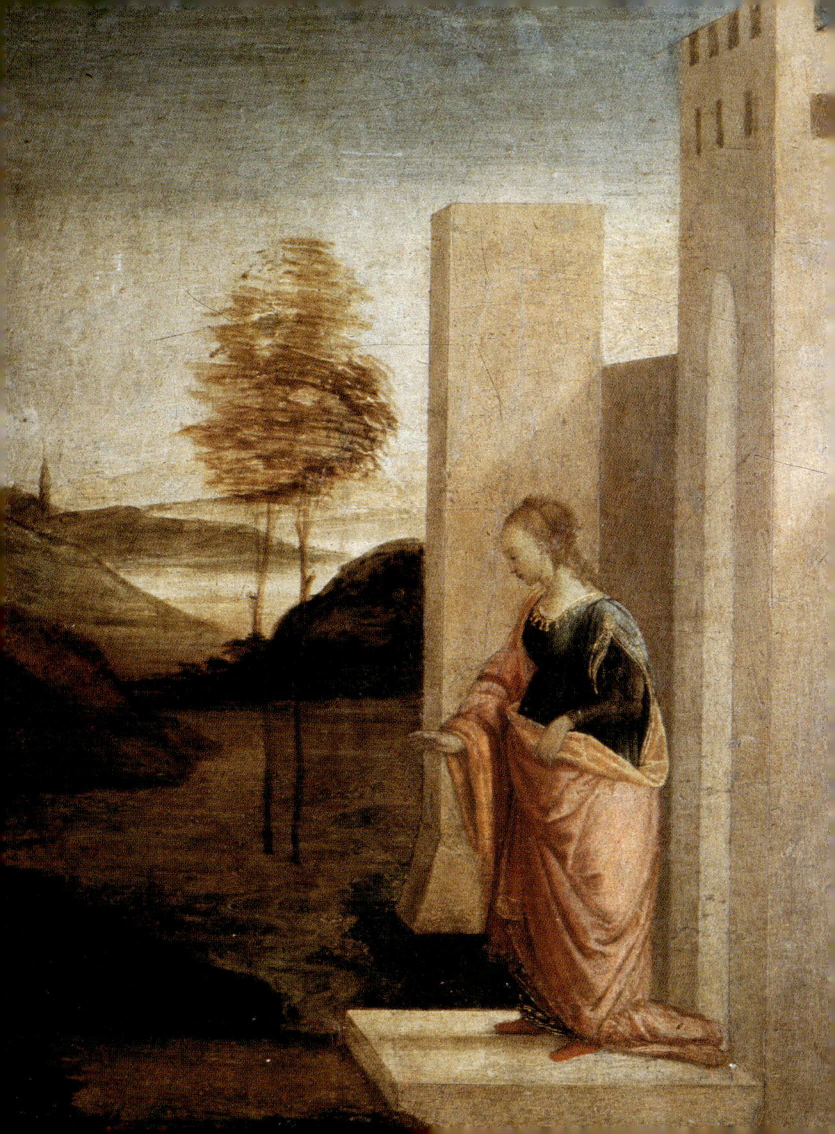

Museo Horne

In the Santa Croce quarter, in a beautiful Renaissance palace, the Horne Museum, with its Foundation of the same name, is situated on the corner between Via de' Benci and Corso dei Tintori. The late 15th century design of the palace (at the time owned by the Corsi family, but in the 14th century by the Alberti, who also owned, not far from here, a famous tower), has been variously attributed to Giuliano da Sangallo, to Cronaca or to Baccio d'Agnolo.

Starting in 1911 the palace was inhabited by a British intellectual of eclectic interests, Sir Herbert Percy Horne (who died in 1916), an architect and the author of a monumental study on Botticelli. Horne had the palace renovated with the intention of recreating a typical lordly residence of the Renaissance. He furnished it with a great quantity of Florentine antiques, and with works of art of the very highest level, outstanding among which are the *Saint Stephen* (c. 1320) by Giotto, a triptych by Pietro Lorenzetti, a predella representing *Stories of St. Julian* (c. 1420) by Masaccio, a polychrome stucco portraying the *Virgin of the Candelabrum* (c. 1470) by Antonio Rossellino, and a beautiful tondo by Beccafumi.

Opposite page:
Filippino Lippi, *Queen Vasthi leaving the Royal Palace*, 1480, oil on panel.
Museo Horne.

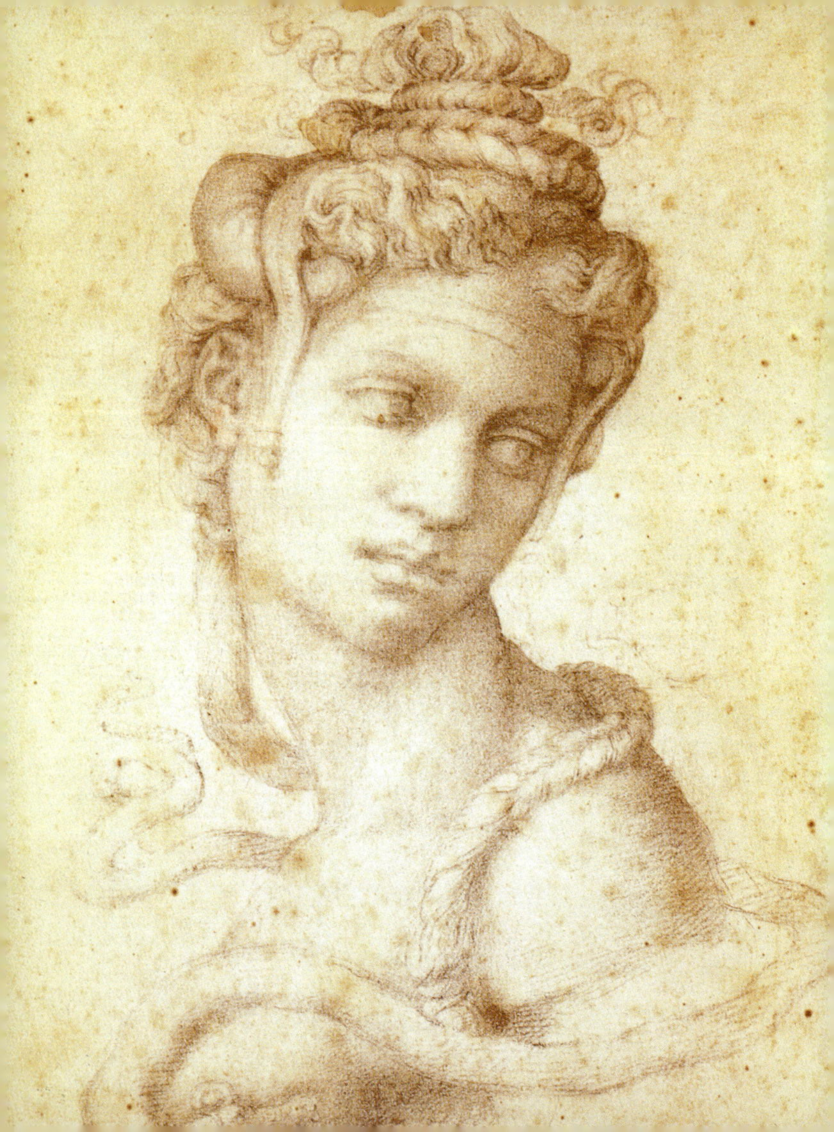

MUSEO DI CASA BUONARROTI

A typical example of museum/house linked to the life and career of an artist, in this case one of the very greatest in history, Casa Buonarroti is situated in Via Ghibellina, on the site where Michelangelo himself bought land for the family residence in 1508. The palace was then built, between 1546 and 1553, by Leonardo's nephew, while around 1620 his grand-nephew Michelangelo the Younger (1568-1657) had the interior, which contained a picture gallery with paintings by the finest artists of the Florentine Baroque period as well as an exquisite studiolo, frescoed by Baccio del Bianco. Casa Buonarroti was donated to the City of Florence in 1858, and opened to the public a year later, bearing witness to Michelangelo's career, as illustrated by some of his works of arts (including two youthful bas-reliefs representing the *Battle of the Centaurs* and the *Madonna of the Stairs)*, as well as to the antiquarian interests of his descendents. The Casa Buonarroti Foundation, which possesses a specialized library and one of the most important collections of Michelangelo's drawings and studies, periodically organizes important thematic exhibitions on the great master and the art of his times.

Opposite page:
Michelangelo, *Cleopatra*,
1533, drawing.
Museo di Casa Buonarroti.

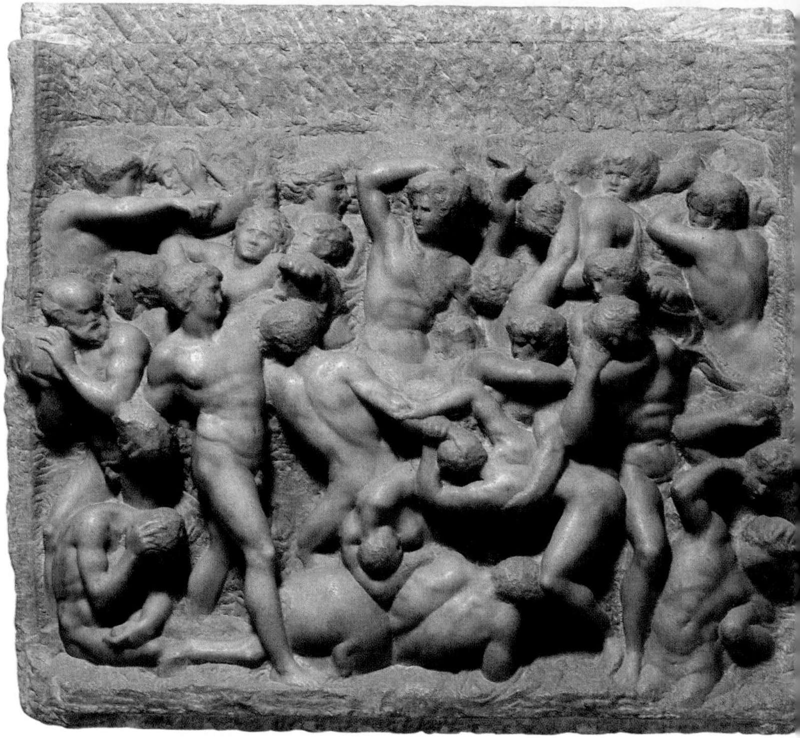

Above:
Michelangelo,
Battle of the Centaurs,
1490-1492, marble.
Museo di Casa Buonarrotti.

Opposite page:
Michelangelo, *Madonna of the Stairs*,
c. 1490-1492, marble.
Museo di Casa Buonarroti.

MyChef Rist. Comm. Srl - PizzaChef
Aeroporto "A.Vespucci"-Firenze (Cs3)
P. Iva 04628730964
info@mychef.it

	EURO
BIRRA SPINA GRANDE	3,10
BIRRA SPINA GRANDE	3,10

T.75401 C.3 0.31

TOTALE EURO 6,20

PAGAMENTO CONTANTI 6,20

RESTO 0,00

26/10/07 16-44 752 31 3 SC.N. 140
RR 52300178

errebi
KOEHLER
KT55 F18

ISPT/DCA/SLA/3/3/14/TRF/99 DEL 23.06.99 N° 0008277 SCAD.12/10

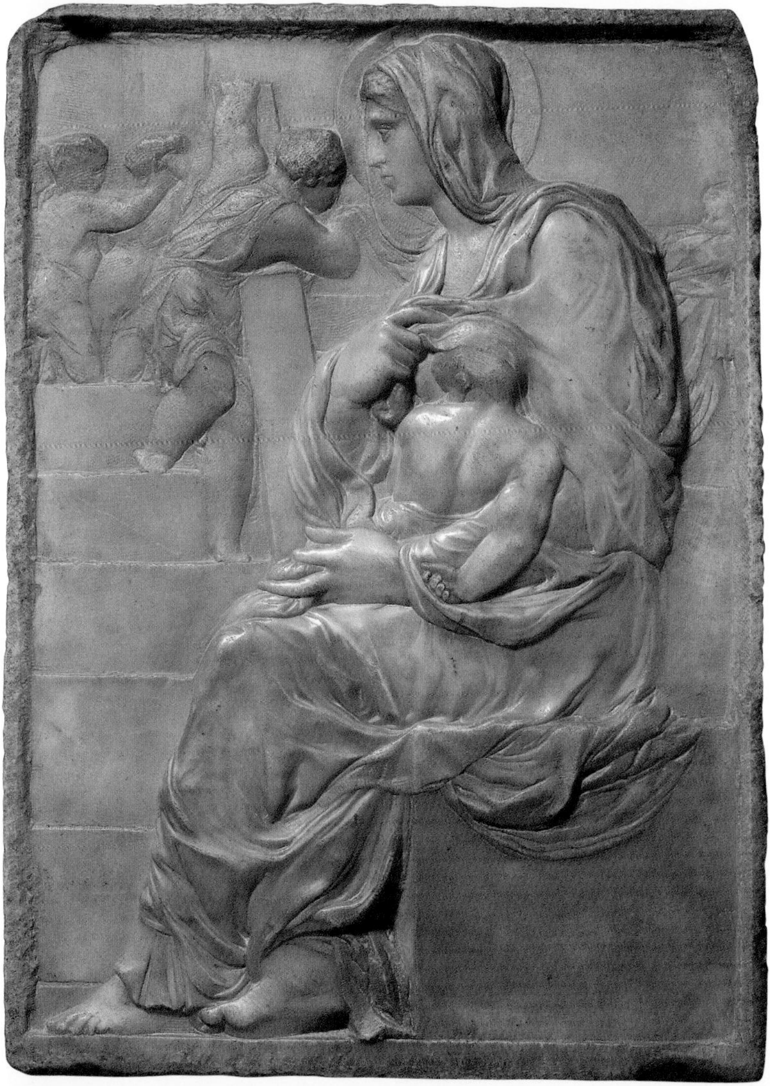

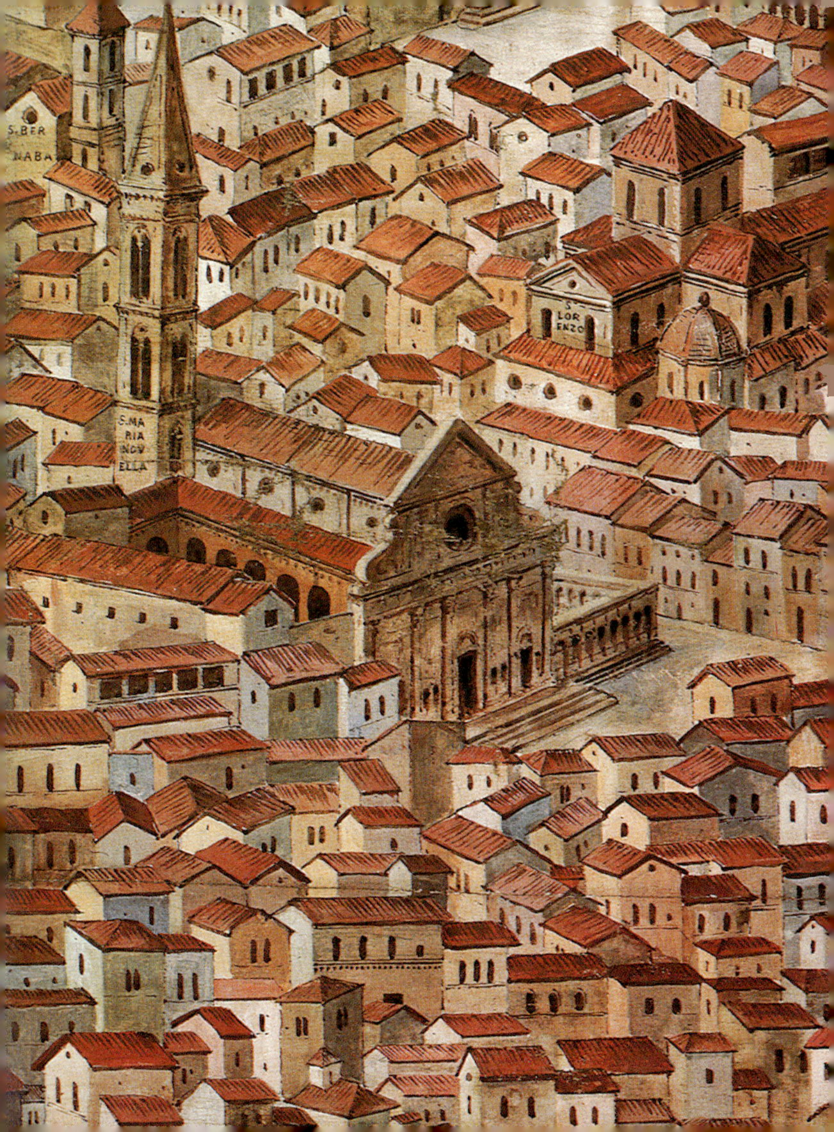
S.BER NABA
S.MA RIA NOV ELLA
S. LOR ENZO

Santa Maria Novella

The Piazza, the Basilica, the Monumental Complex

Since the 14th century, Santa Maria Novella has given its name to one of the city's quarters. It had as its emblem the sun shooting out golden rays in an azure field and the banners of the Golden Lion, the Red Lion, the Viper and the Unicorn. This quarter encapsulated the Sestiere of San Pancrazio (from the name of the church protected by the Rucellai family), on the western edge of the city walls. Around 1219 some Dominican monks, who had previously resided within the walls at the Spedale di San Paolo, near San Pancrazio, came to live here. Very soon the monks began their battle against the Paterine heretics (the Cathars), who had many followers in Florence. Over the centuries, the spiritual and cultural commitment of the Dominican order made the monastery and church of Santa Maria Novella, at the opposite pole from the Franciscan Santa Croce, the reference point for the whole quarter. The vast square was not only a place where sermons were preached but also a theater for the "palio dei cocchi", a carriage race that turned around the two Seravezza marble obelisks resting on bronze turtles by Giambologna.

Opposite page:
The quarter of Santa Maria Novella around 1482, detail from the *Pianta della Catena,* water-color copy (1887) of the 15th century woodcut in the Berlin Museums. Museo di Firenze com'era.

HISTORY

At least from the 10th century, a little church called *Santa Maria inter vineas* (St. Mary's among the vineyards) existed in this area. The land, returned to cultivation near the end of the 11th century, and the construction of a new ecclesiastical building a short distance from the earlier one, determined the addition of the word "novella", new, to the original place name (from which also comes "Via della Vigna Nuova"). The church, consecrated in 1094, had its entrance facing east, opposite the place occupied today by the railway station. The Dominicans took possession of the building around 1219, and at the end of 1244 the Comune approved the request of Fra Pietro da Verona, come to Florence to defend othodoxy, to enlarge the space in front of the church. The first stone of the new building was blessed by Cardinal Latino in 1279. In 1287, with the façade not yet begun, plans were made for a new piazza, this time on the opposite side, toward the river. The church was however already in use, since in 1285 the Compagnia dei Laudesi founded by Pietro da Verona had commissioned for his chapel in Santa Maria Novella the famous *Maestà* by Duccio now in the Uffizi. In 1470 Giovanni Rucellai sealed with his own name the completion of the façade, harmoniously designed by Leon Battista Alberti who,

Opposite page:
Façade of Santa Maria Novella.

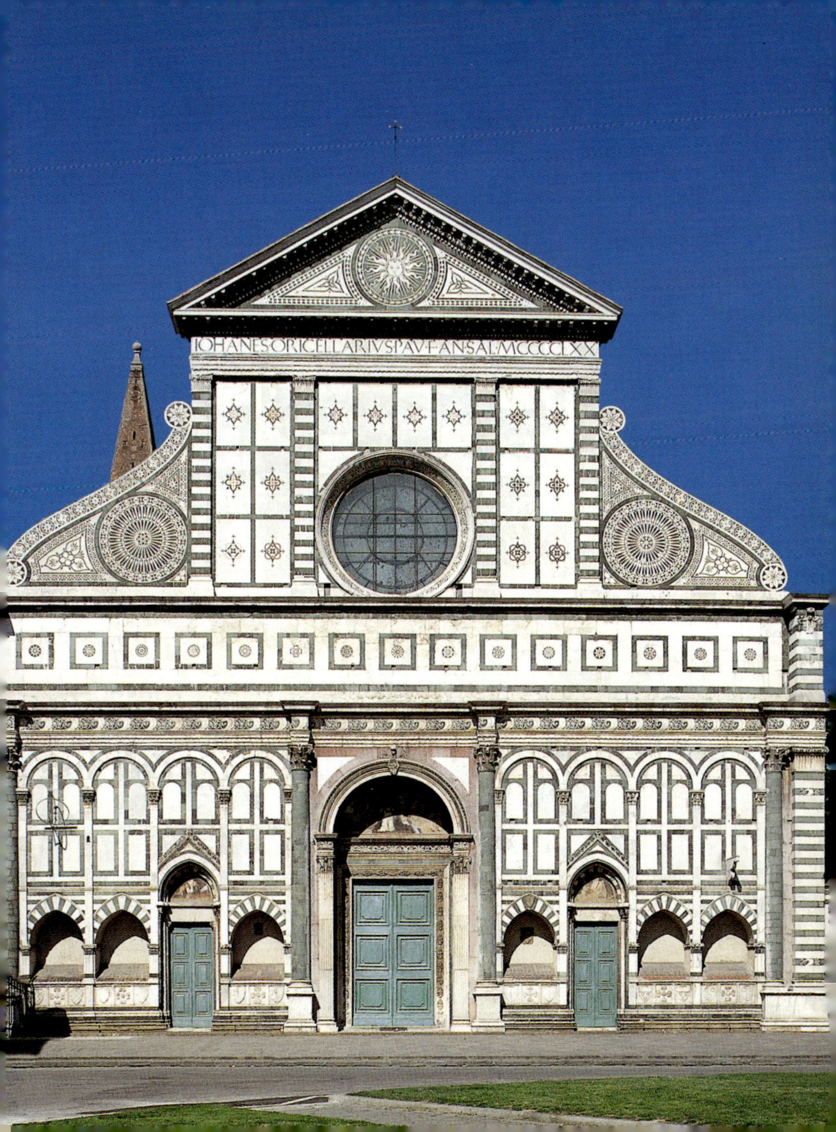
IOHANES·ORICELLARIVS·PAV·F·AN·SAL·MCCCCLXX

to reintegrate the existing Gothic structures, adopted proportions similar to those of the Romanesque façade of San Miniato al Monte: arranged on two levels, with the upper part crowned by a tympanum corresponding to the central nave. We know that Alberti at this time went up every day "to greet the temple of San Miniato, unless he were kept away by rain", as recalled by a Florentine chronicle writer. "Beauty is a concept of all of the parts arranged together with proportion", wrote the Florentine architect. In his façade, perfectly inscribable in a square, can be recognized the same sense of measure and proportion found in the tempietto of the Holy Sepulchre, also designed for the Rucellai. From the Florentine Romanesque style Alberti also took the inlaid white and green marble, and above all the preference for musical and geometric figures, inspired by the Neo-Platonic concept of heavenly music generated by the harmonious movement of the stars. The façade of Santa Maria Novella culminates, not by chance, in a tympanum decorated with the sun, "the greatest of the celestial gods and father of all things": a true figurative and architectural manifesto of the Neo-Platonic concepts promulgated by Marsilio Ficino.

The decoration of the church of Santa Maria Novella, consecrated by Pope Martin V in 1420, was financed not only by the Rucellai but also by many other powerful families residing in the quarter, among them the Guidalotti, the Minerbetti, the Strozzi, the Cavalcanti, the Gondi, the Tornaquinci, the Ubriachi, and the Ricci.

The interior of the building appears today in its 13th-14th century form: a Latin cross, marked by three naves divided by

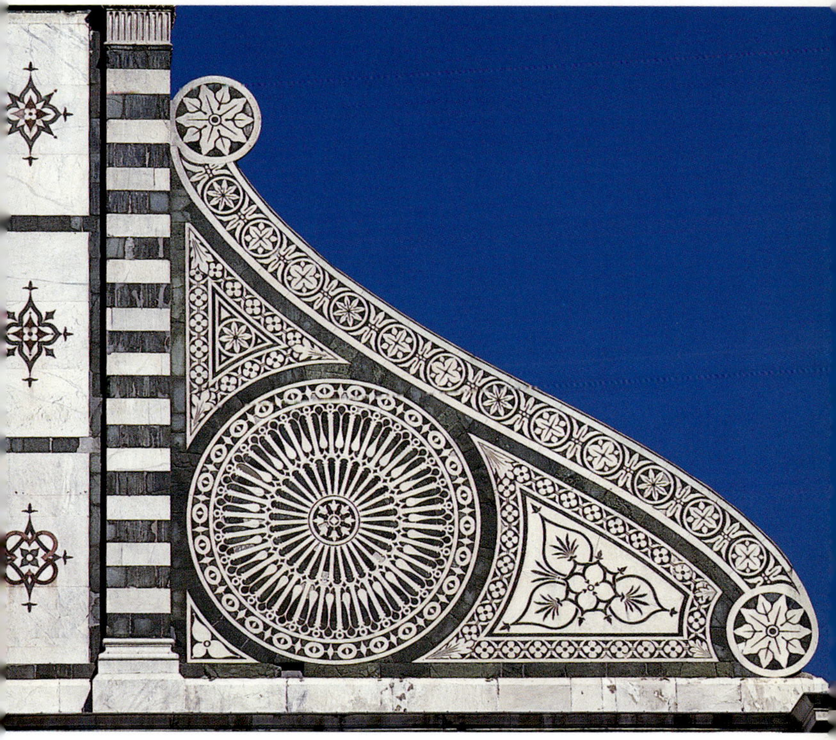

Above:
Façade of Santa Maria Novella, detail of the upper part designed by Leon Battista Alberti with marble friezes by Giovanni di Bertino.

bundle pillars supporting pointed arches faced with white and black marble. Like other monastery churches, Santa Maria Novella too originally had its walls entirely frescoed, and a rood-screen that separated the apse section reserved to the monks from that of the naves, where the faithful congregated. In the "remodernizing" carried out in the second half of the 16th century, the rood-screen and many of the frescoes were eliminated. Among these, the famous *Trinity* by Masaccio (1427), in the left nave, was covered with plaster, uncovered in 1861 and recently restored.

In the Cappella Maggiore are still found the great panels and lunettes frescoed between 1485 and 1490 by Domenico Ghirlandaio, who in his representation of the *Stories of the Virgin and St. John the Baptist* painted an extraordinary picture of life in late 15th century Florence. The various personages, some identified as members of the Tornabuoni family, are shown dressed in the costume of the times. Among them are Giovanna degli Albizi, wife of Lorenzo Tornabuoni, and Dianora Tornabuoni, wife of Soderini. Various views of the city and sumptuous domestic interiors can also be seen. The cycle was painted for Giovanni Tornabuoni, who had recently become patron of the chapel. It was instead Filippo Strozzi who commissioned Filippino Lippi, between 1494 and 1502, to fresco the *Stories of St. Philip and St. John the Evangelist* for his own chapel to the right of the Capella Maggiore.

Annexed to the monastry is the Spanish Chapel, originally the Charterhouse of the Dominican Order and later the private chapel of Eleonora di Toledo, the Spanish wife of Cosimo I (from whom comes the name given since then to the chapel).

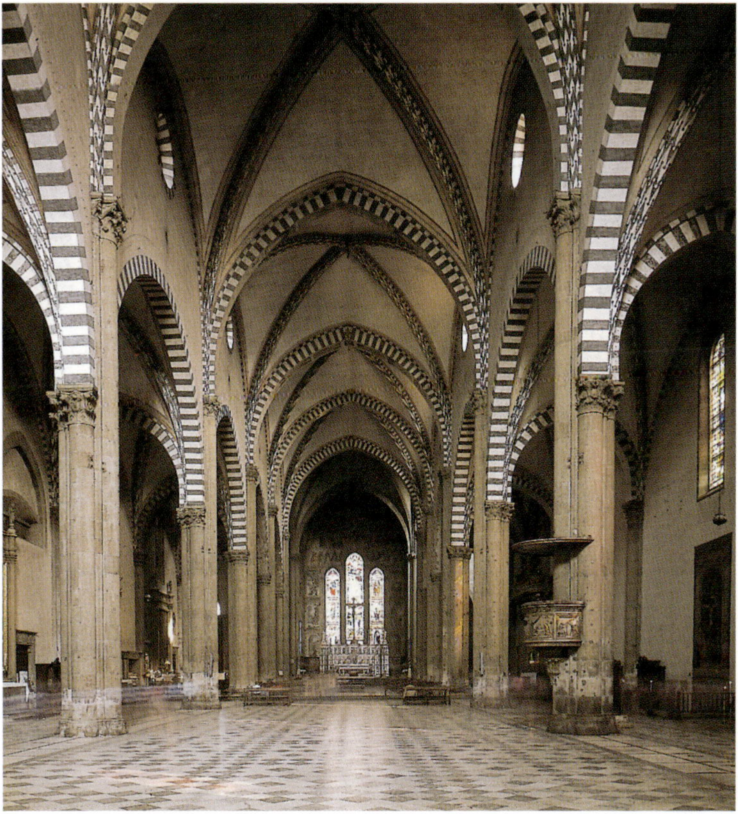

Opposite page:
The interior of the church
of Santa Maria Novella
looking toward the transept.

The Museum of Santa Maria Novella displays, among other things, important liturgical objects. It also includes the Cloister of the Dead, the refectory and the Green Cloister, where there remain fragments of Paolo Uccello's famous frescoes depicting *Stories of Noah*, painted with a special pigment called "terra verde" (green clay) from which comes the name of the cloister. Still today, with its cloisters, its museum, the church and the monastery (in part not accessible), the monumental building complex of Santa Maria Novella remains one of the city's most prestigious and rich in history. It was also famous for its studio, its library and an important *scriptorium*.

Opposite page:
Egnatio Danti, *Sun-dial*, 1572.
Santa Maria Novella,
façade.

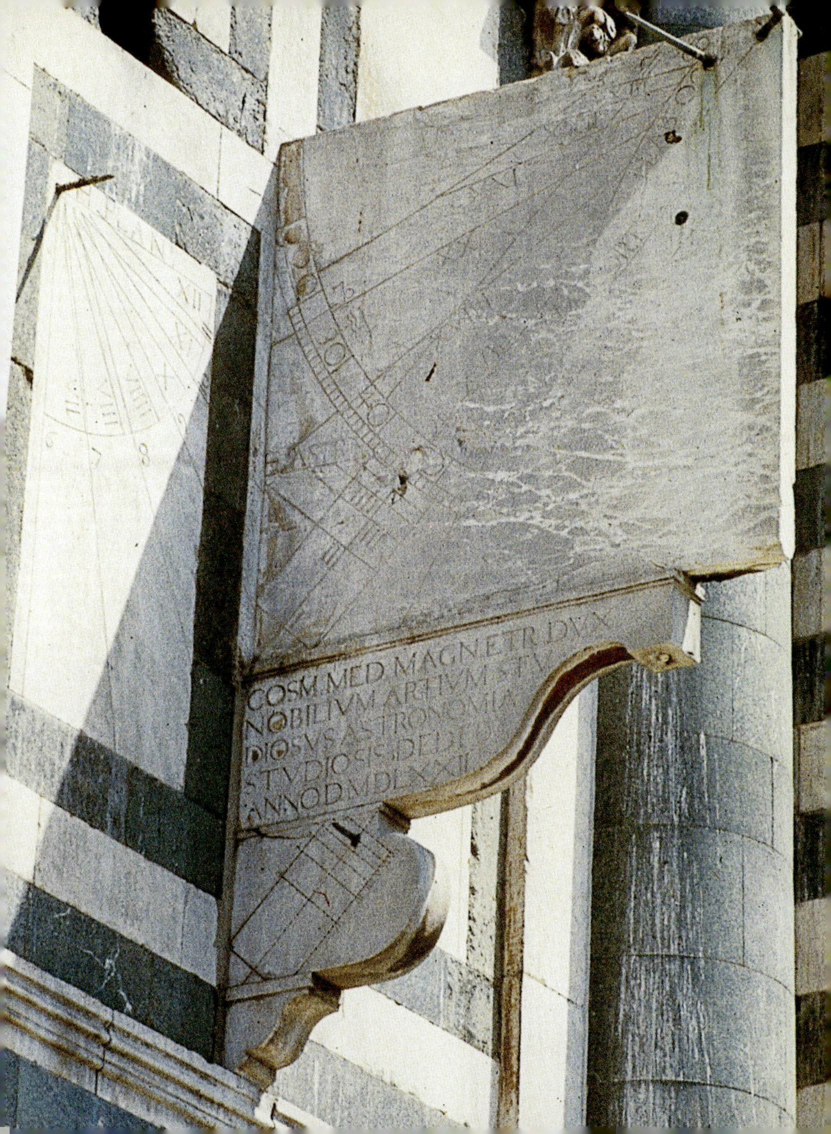
COSM. MED. MAGN. ETR. DVX
NOBILIVM ARTIVM STV
DIOSVS ASTRONOMIA
STVDIOSIS DEDIT
ANNO D. MDLXXII

Noteworthy are:

- the *Crucifix* by Giotto, a youthful work, recently restored and moved from the sacristy, where it long hung, to what must have been its original place, at the height of the rood-screen.
- the *Crucifix* (c. 1410-1415) by Filippo Brunelleschi.
- the *Trinity* (c. 1427) by Masaccio: the earliest exercise in perspective inspired by Brunelleschi's rules, with an illusionist chapel with barrel vault and coffered ceiling, and the two patrons kneeling at the foot of the holy scene (*Christ crucified, Mary and St. John*).
- the Cappella Maggiore (1485-1490), with frescoes by Domenico Ghirlandaio.
- the chapel of Filippo Strozzi, with frescoes (1497-1502) by Filippino Lippi.
- the frescoed decoration of the Pope's Chapel (1515) by Ridolfo del Ghirlandaio and Pontormo.
- the tomb of the Blessed Villana (1451) by Bernardo Rossellino.
- In the Museum, the remains of the frescoes and sinopites representing the *Stories of Noah* by Paolo Uccello (1430).

Opposite page:
Jacopo Pontormo, *Veronica*, detail, 1515, fresco. Santa Maria Novella, Pope's Chapel.

Following pages:
Giotto, *Crucifix*, c. 1300, tempera on wood. Santa Maria Novella, transept crossing.
Filippo Brunelleschi, *Crucifix*, c. 1410-1415, carved and painted wood.
Santa Maria Novella, Gondi Chapel.

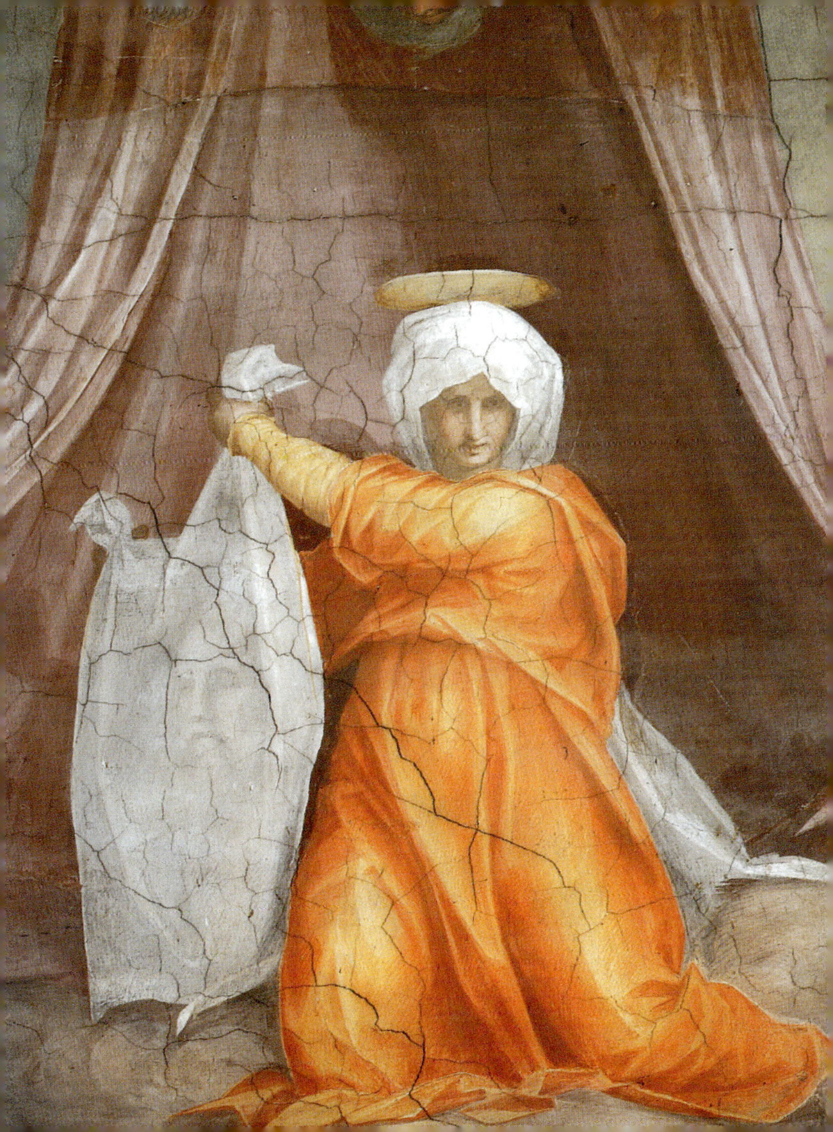

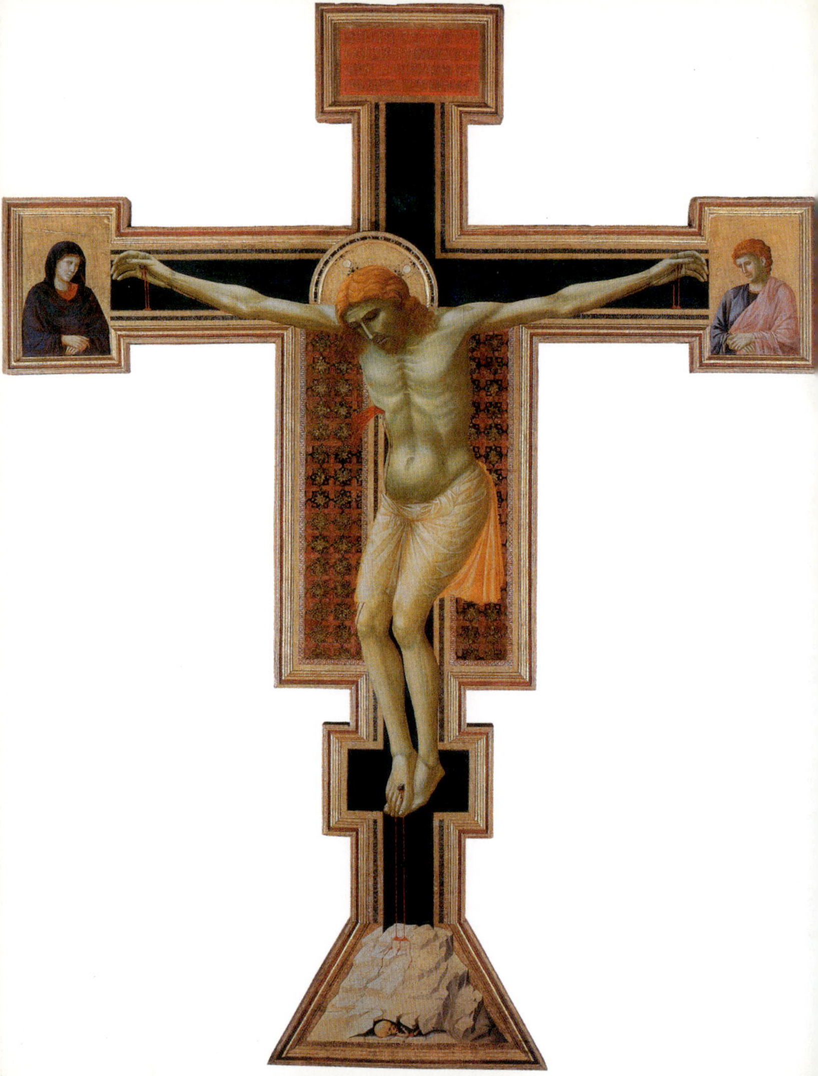

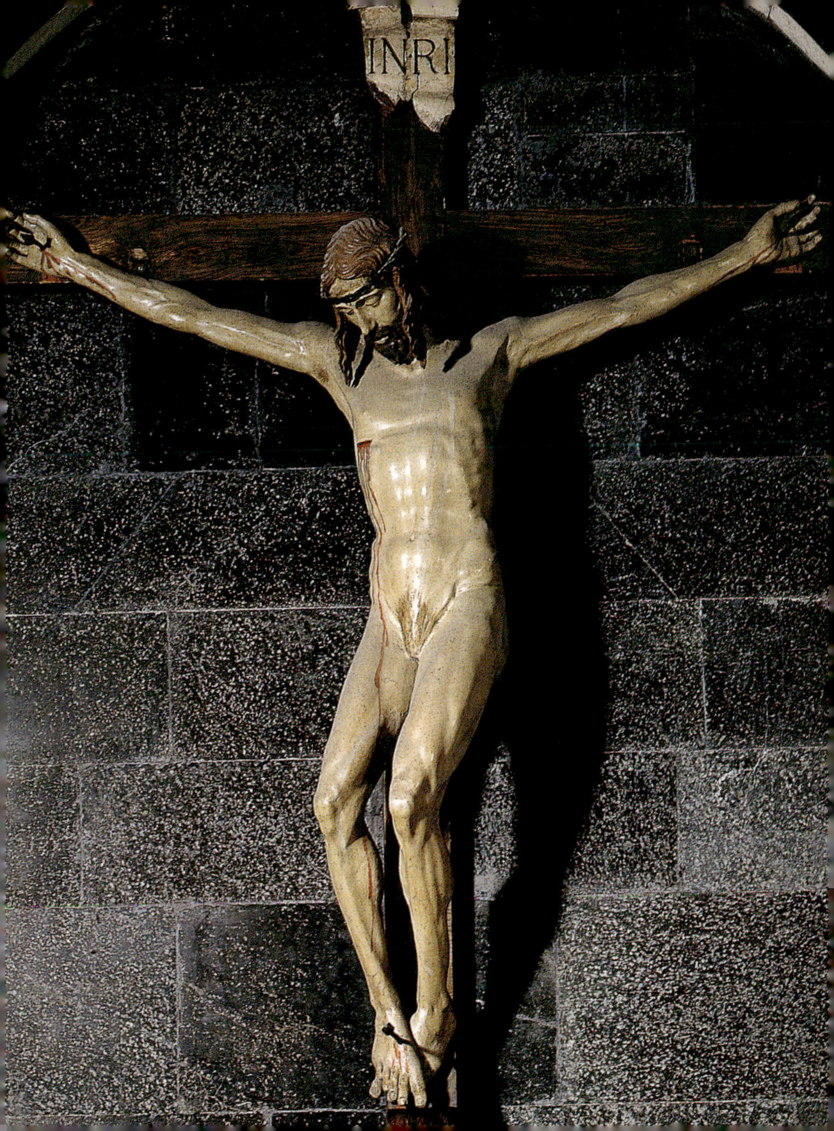
INRI

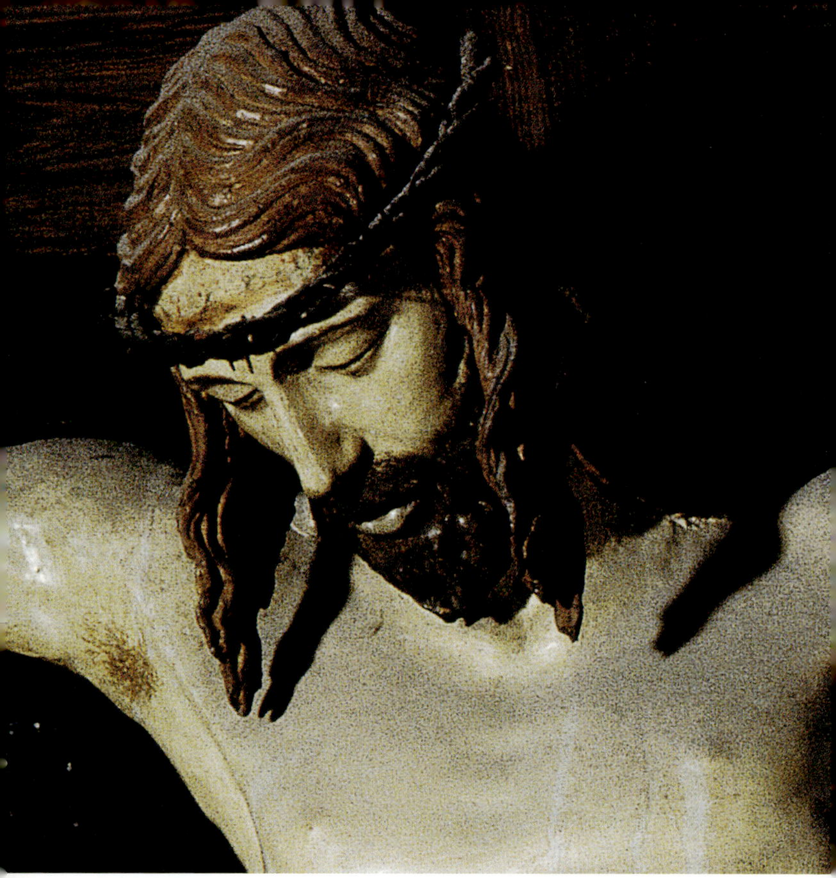

Above:
Filippo Brunelleschi, *Crucifix*, detail, c. 1410-1415, carved and painted wood. Santa Maria Novella, Gondi Chapel.

Opposite page:
Masaccio, *Trinity*, c. 1427, fresco. Santa Maria Novella.

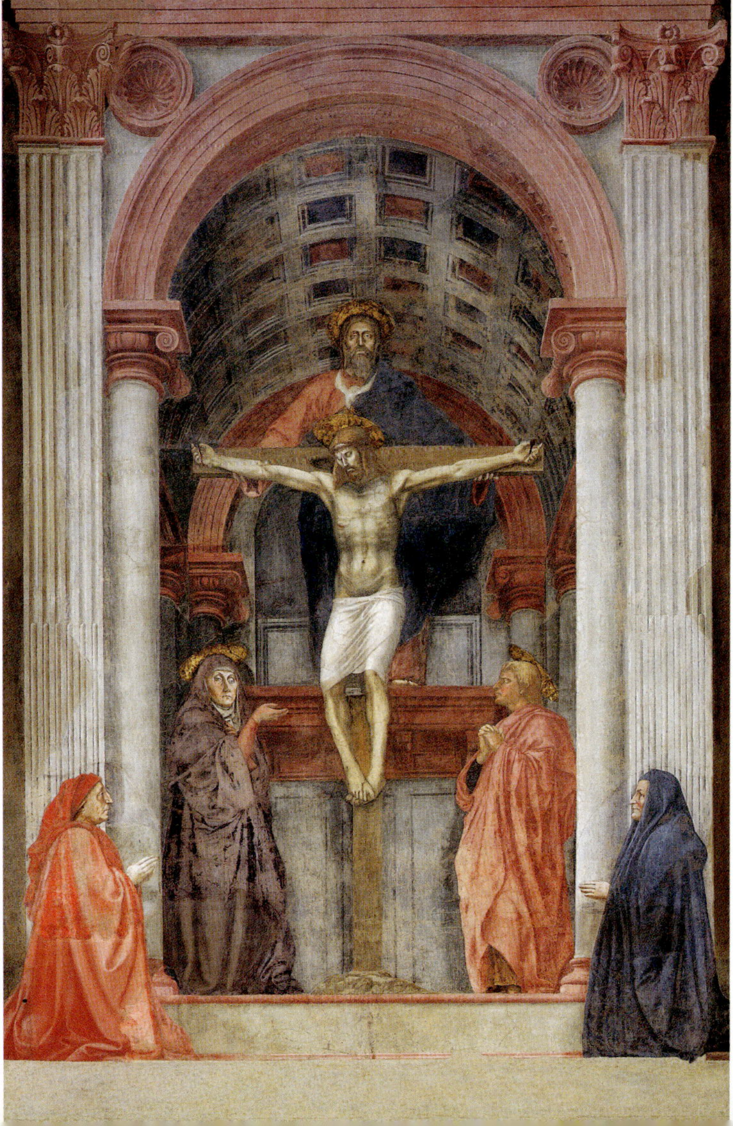

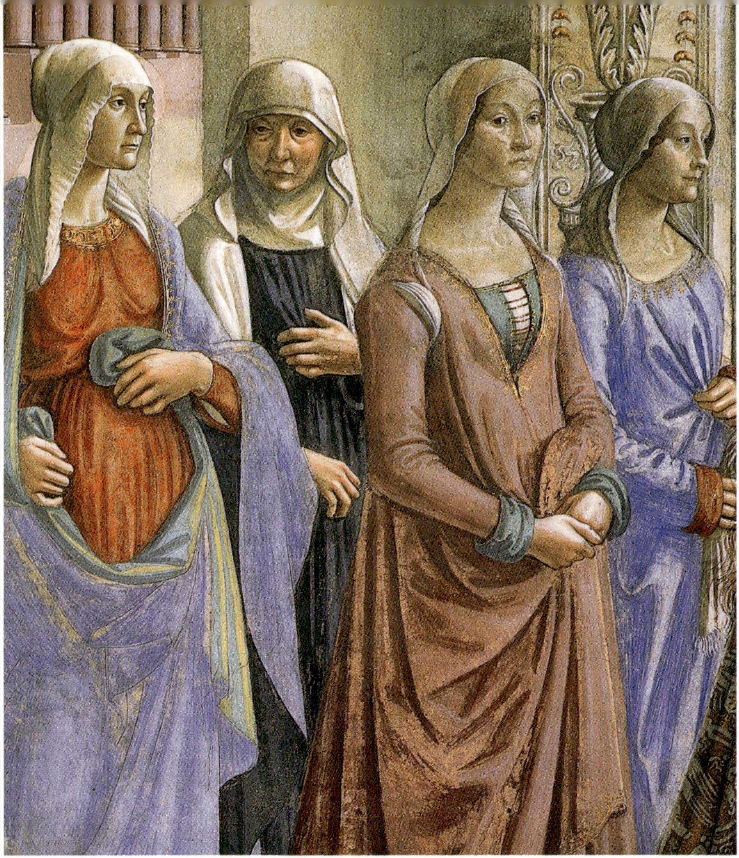

Above and opposite page:
Domenico Ghirlandaio, *Stories of the Virgin and St. John the Baptist*, details, c. 1485, fresco. Santa Maria Novella, Cappella Maggiore.

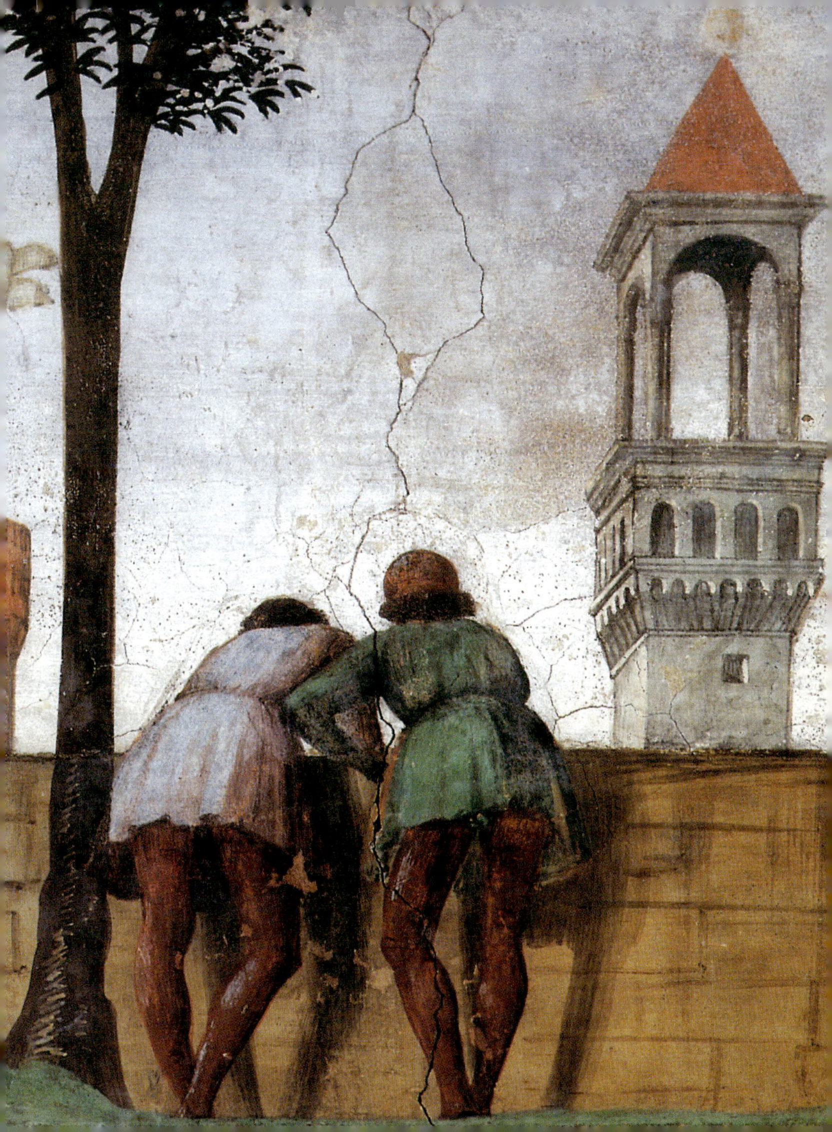

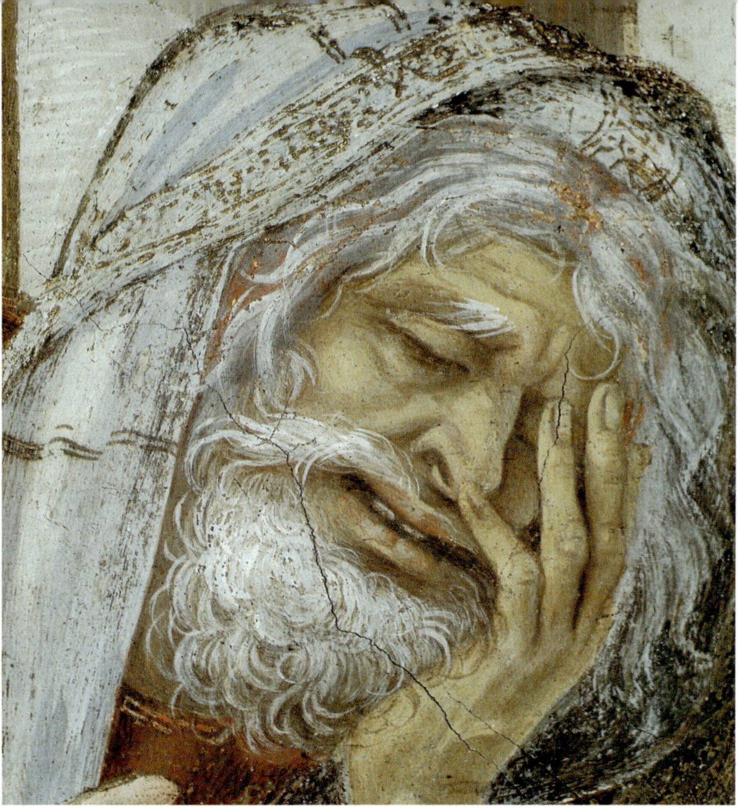

Above and opposite page:
Filippino Lippi,
Histories of Saint John the Evangelist, details,
c. 1485-1490, fresco.
Santa Maria Novella,
Strozzi Chapel.

Following pages:
Andrea Bonaiuti, known as Andrea da Firenze, *Triumph of St. Thomas Aquinas,* details from the *Stories of Christ and St. Dominic*, 1365-1367, fresco. Santa Maria Novella,
Spanish Chapel.

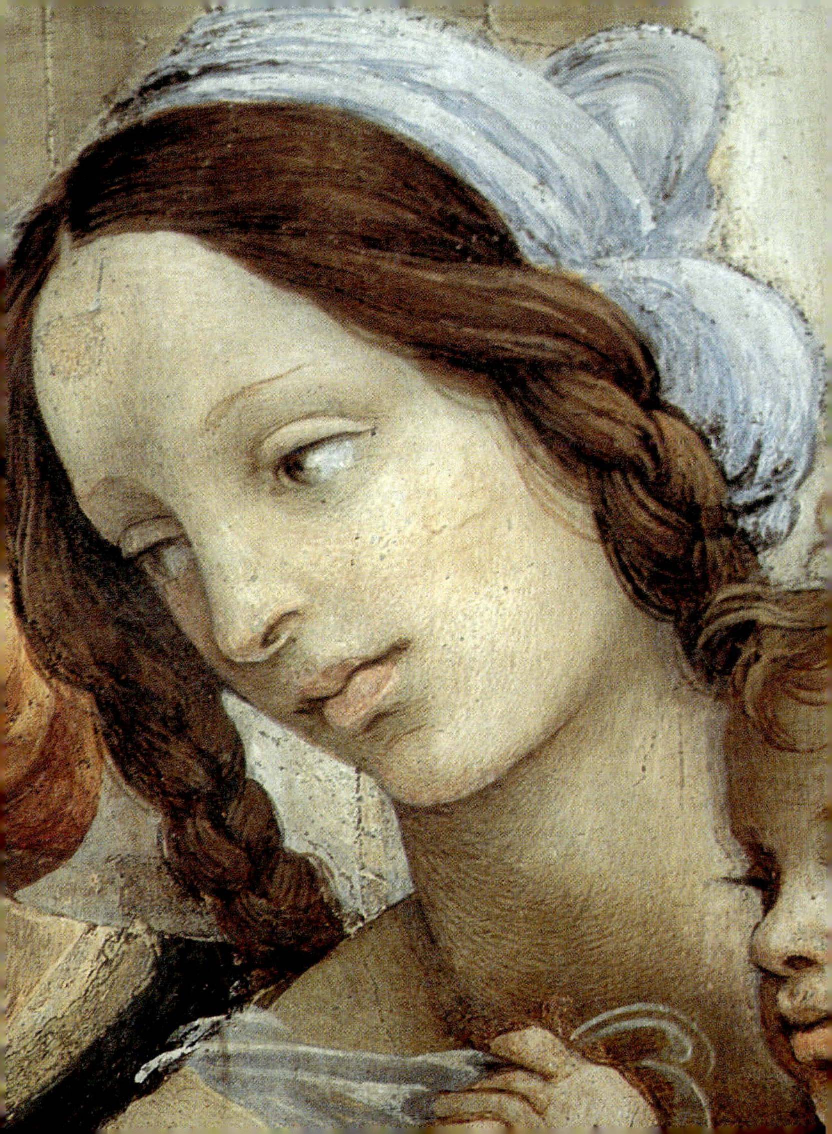

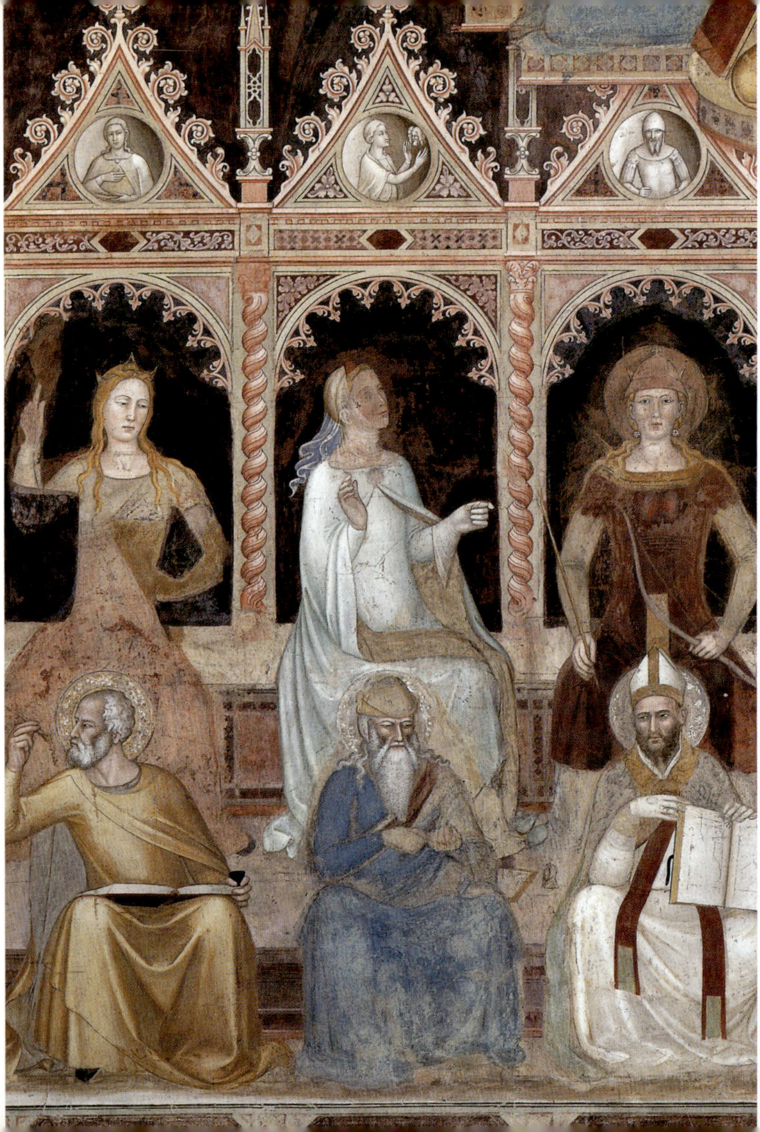

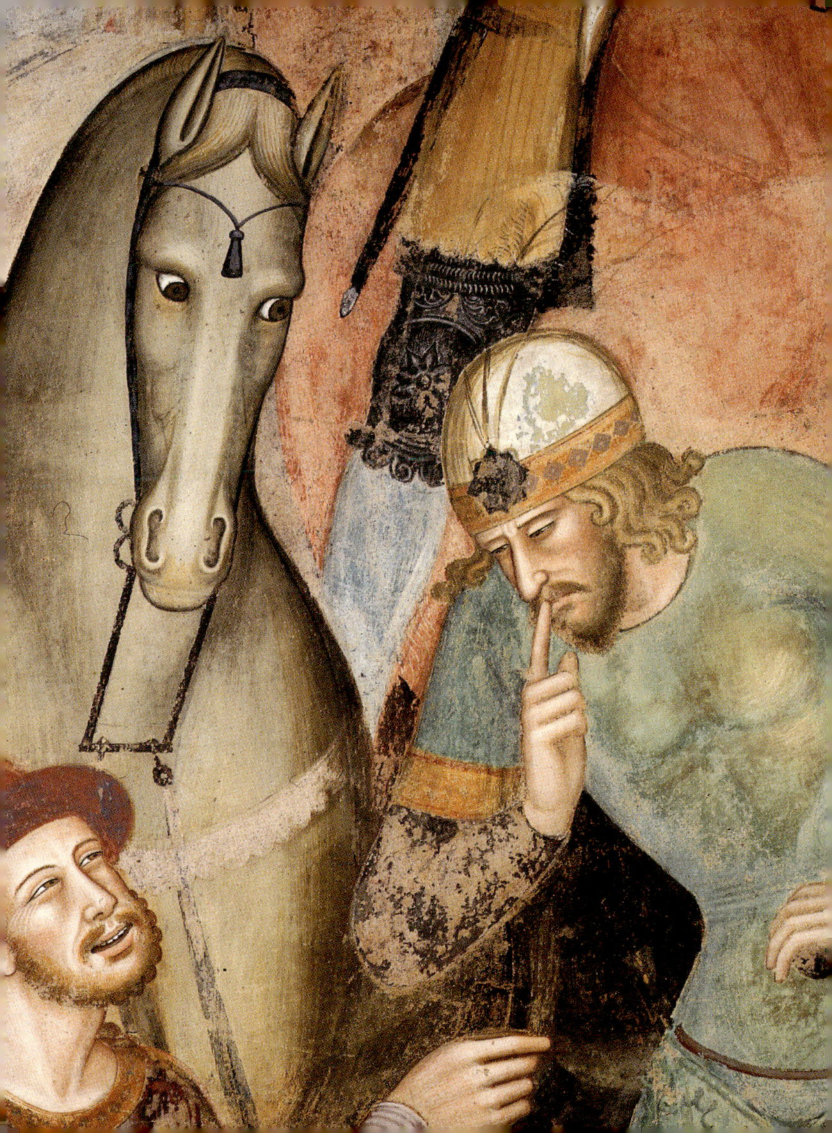

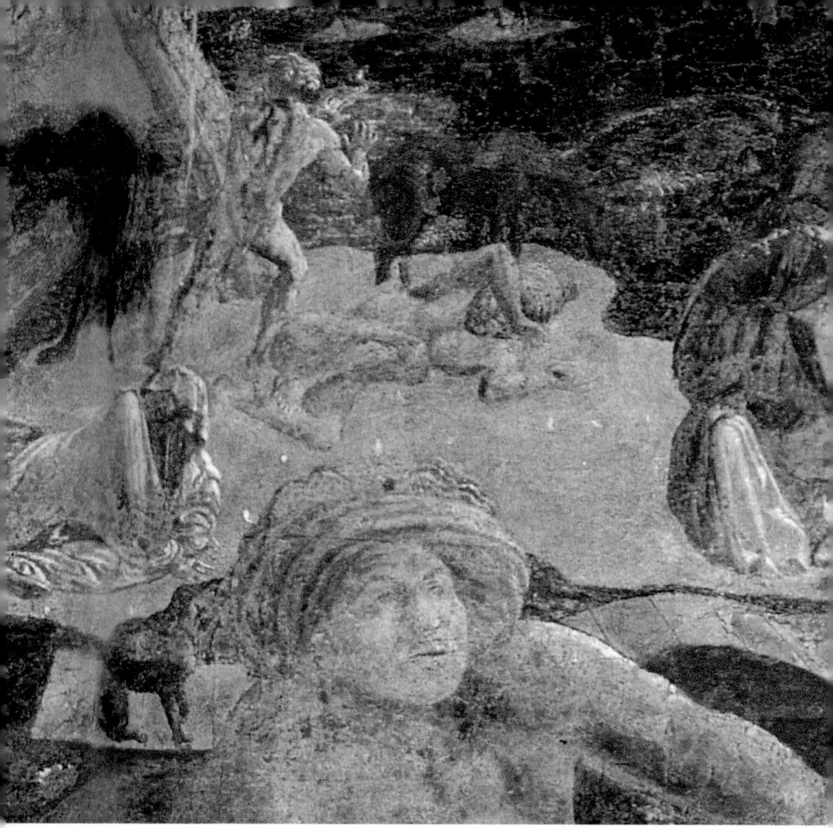

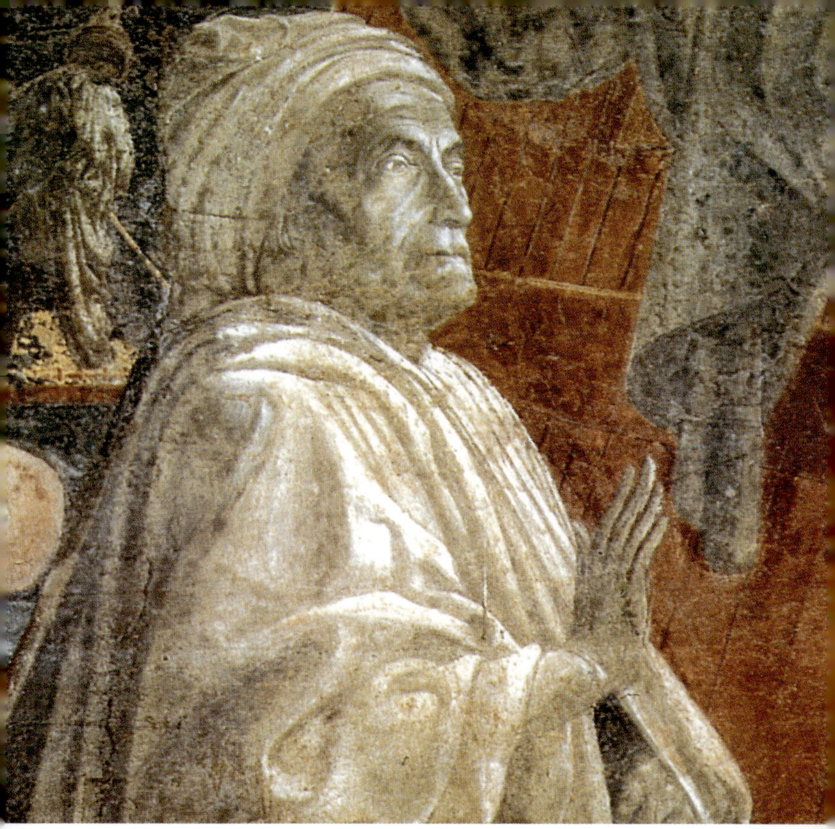

Above:
Paolo Uccello, *Stories of Noah*, detail, c. 1447, fresco in terra verde. Santa Maria Novella, Green Cloister.

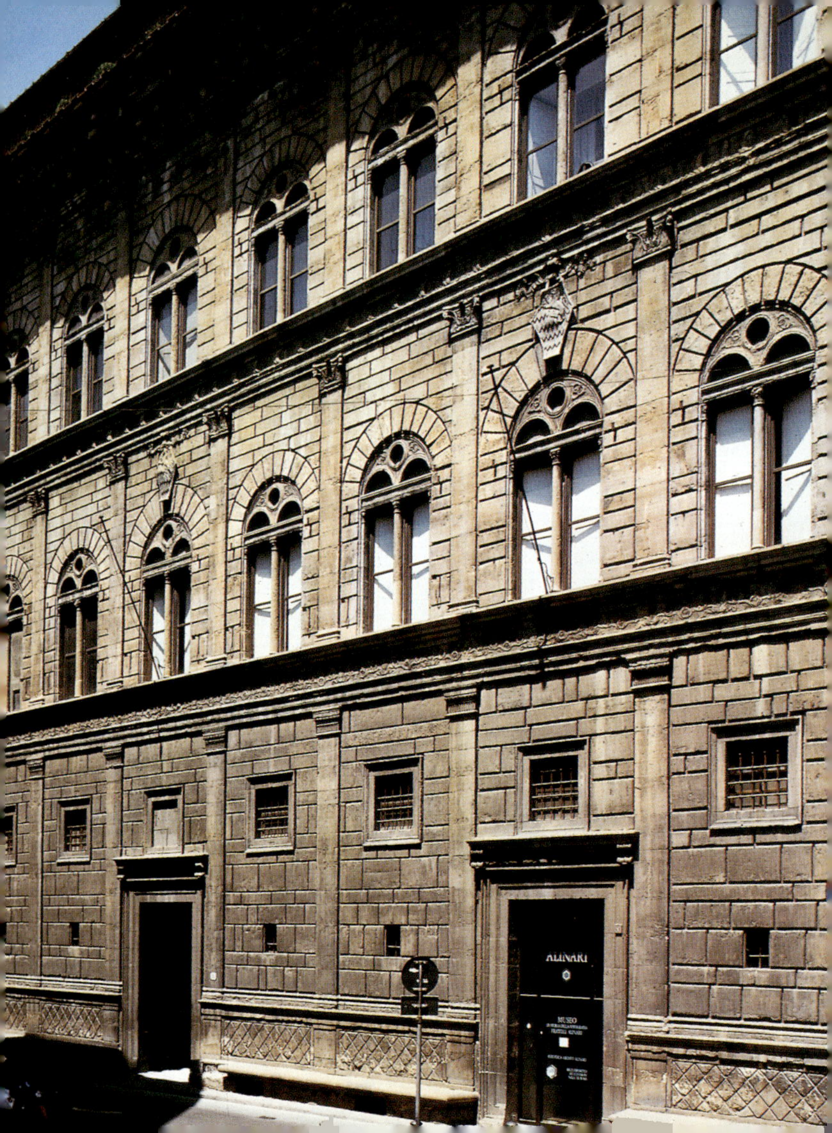
ALINARI
MUSEO

Palazzo Rucellai and its Loggia

"Of eight houses I have made one", Giovanni di Paolo Rucellai liked to say, boasting of his splendid palace facing on Via della Vigna Nuova. Leon Battista Alberti had designed it for him, on the area occupied by some family residences and other houses that Giovanni had bought between Via della Vigna and Via dei Palchetti. The elegant three-storey façade, later modified in width, is divided by pilaster strips and decorated by a frieze with the repetitive motif of full-blown sails, the emblem of the Rucellai that also appears on the façade of Santa Maria Novella. The windows are also decorated with the Medicean symbol of three interwoven diamonds (*deo amante*). Bernardo, a son of Giovanni Rucellai, had in fact married Nannina de' Medici, one of Piero's daughters, in 1466, and this marriage was a true act of dipolomacy. Giovanni was proud of it, so much so as to recall in his book of memoirs, the beautiful *Zibaldone*, that he had been "honored, esteemed and highly considered" expressly due to his kinship with Piero di Cosimo de' Medici. In the little square in front of the family palace, the refined Rucellai Loggia, with three arcades, occupied today by shops, had been the scene of the wedding ceremony that sealed the friendship between the Medici and the Rucellai. Giovanni described it, recalling that between

Opposite page:
Palazzo Rucellai, c. 1457-1466.

the loggia and the palace a stage had been erected, draped in tapestries and precious fabrics and covered with a "sky" of turquoise fabric as protection against the sun, "all adorned with garlands and roses and with shields bearing the arms of the Medici and the Rucellai". In addition, a sumptuous sideboard was furnished with "richly worked silver vessels", which contained food and wine.

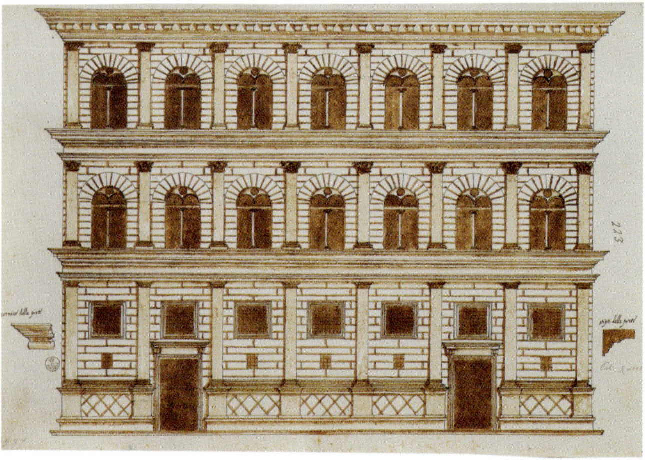

Following pages:
Giorgio Vasari the Younger, *Palazzo Rucellai*, c.1600, G.D.S.U, 4937.

Engraving portraying Giovanni Rucellai with the buildings he commissioned.

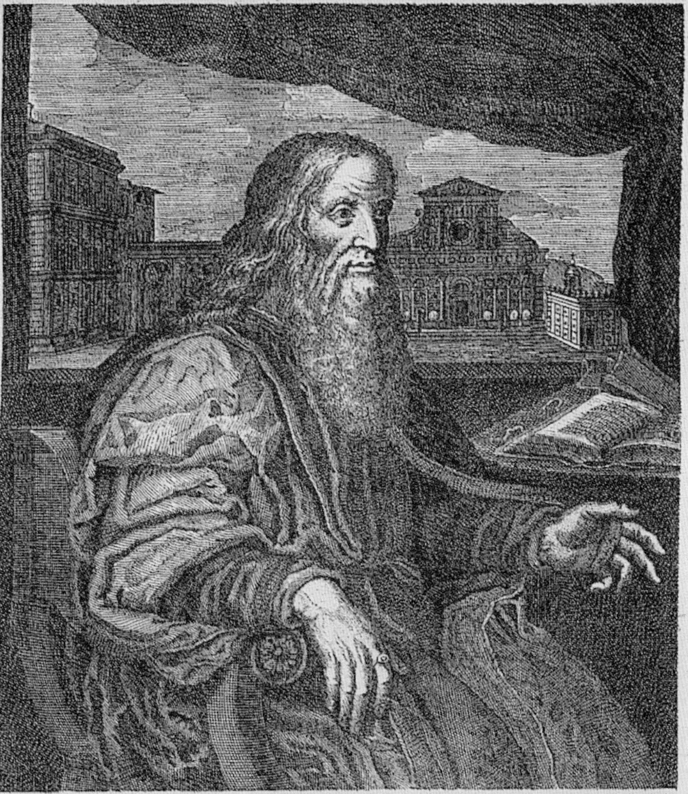

GIOVANNI DI PAOLO DI PAOLO RUCELLAI GONFALONIERE DELLA REPUBBLICA FIORENTINA, ED INSIGNE PER LA MUNIFICENZA CON CUI INALZÒ FABBRICHE PUBBLICHE, E PRIVATE.

nato il dì 26. 8bre MCCCCIII. morto il dì 18 9bre MCCCCLXXVII.

All' Illmo, e Clarmo Sigre Senatore, e Cavre Giulio Rucellai Segretario del Regio Diritto, ec. ec. ec.

Preso da un Quadro in Asse appo la sua Nobil Famiglia.

Giuseppe Zocchi del: F. Allegrini inci: 1764.

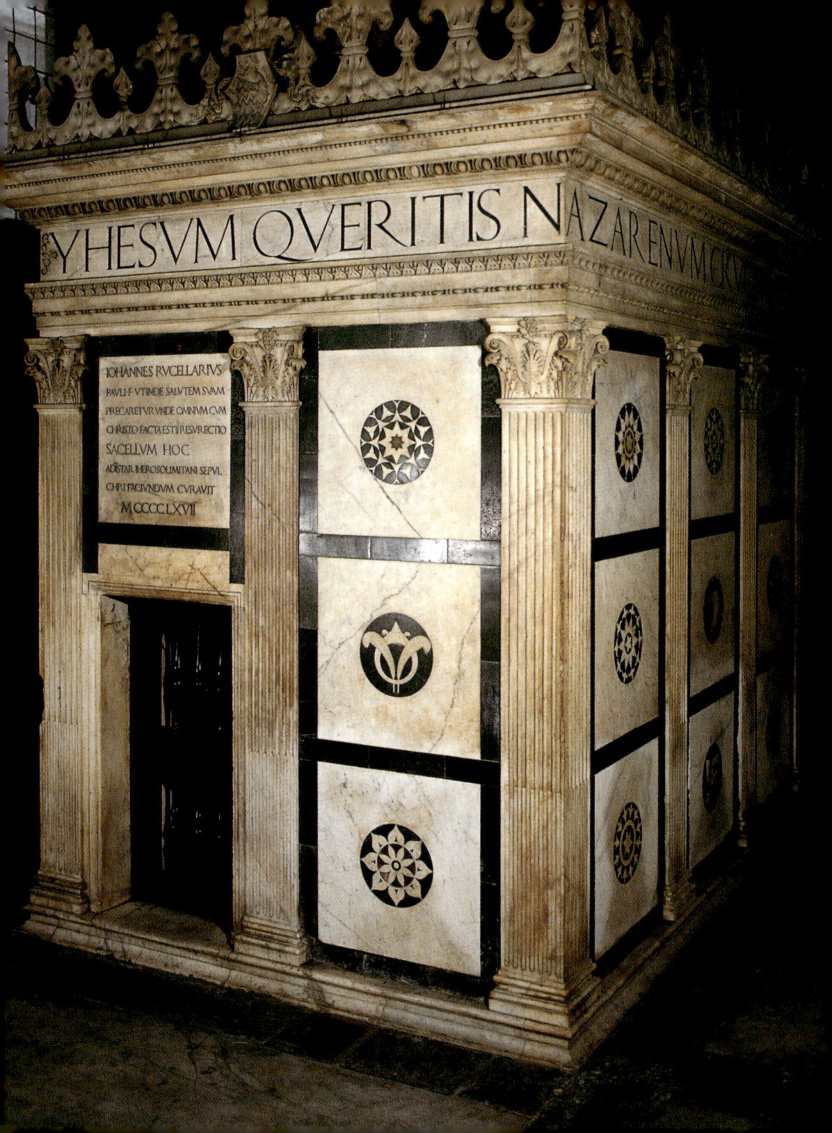
YHESVM QVERITIS NAZARENVM
IOHANNES RVCELLARIVS
PAVLI·F·VTINDE SALVTEM SVAM
PRECARETVR VNDE OMNIVM CVM
CHRISTO FACTA EST RESVRECTIO
SACELLVM HOC
ADISTAR IHEROSOLIMITANI SEPVL
CHRI FACIVNDVM CVRAVIT
MCCCCLXVII

SAN PANCRAZIO

The Rucellai Chapel and the Museo Marino Marini

The former church of San Pancrazio, one of the most ancient in Florence (today occupied by the Museo Marino Marini), was in the past, like the church of Santa Maria Novella, a religious site favored by the Rucellai family, who in the 15th century had exclusive jurisdiction over the Cappella Maggiore. On the outside of the church, modified in the 19th century, can be seen a humanistic architrave and a triforium attributed to Leon Battista Alberti. Not by chance, in an area adjacent to the church (entrance on Via della Spada), stands the Rucellai Chapel, with its elegant tempietto of the Holy Sepulchre. Designed between 1464 and 1467 by Leon Battista Alberti for Giovanni Rucellai, the sacellum, or votive chapel, replicates the Holy Sepulchre in Jerusalem. To provide adequate space for the work, Alberti transformed the existing room, which now appears with a barrel-vault ceiling, white plastered walls divided by a Corinthian order in *pietra serena*, tondoes and a frieze bearing the Rucellai coats-of-arms. The tempietto is faced with intarsia in white Apuan marble and green serpentine marble from Prato, in a pattern of geometric motifs alternating with the heraldic emblems of the Rucellai and Medici families, who were kinsmen. Like the

Opposite page:
Leon Battista Alberti,
Tempietto of the Holy Spirit,
1467, inlaid marble.
San Pancrazio, Rucellai Chapel.

façade of Santa Maria Novella, also designed by Alberti, the tempietto is clearly inspired by the classic, serene forms of the most typical monuments of the Florentine Romanesque style, in particular the Baptistery and San Miniato al Monte, which were in turn influenced by the most harmonious buildings of antiquity. The frieze on the sacellum bears a humanist inscription inlaid in marble. The text refers to a passage from the New Testament describing the announcement of Christ's resurrection to the three Marys.

THE MUSEO MARINO MARINI

Since 1988 the church of San Pancrazio, which has undergone various modifications and restorations over the centuries, has been the site of the Museo Marino Marini, exhibiting 176 important works donated to the city by the Tuscan sculptor (1901-1980) and his family. The fascinating spaces of the church deconsecrated in 1808, then used for various purposes, and lastly as a storeoom for the Manifattura Tabacchi, have been restored and reorganized on several levels for the exhibition, from the mezzanine to the crypt, of sculptures, plaster casts, paintings and drawings by one of the greatest Italian sculptors of the 20th century.

Opposite page:
The interior of the Museo Marino Marini.

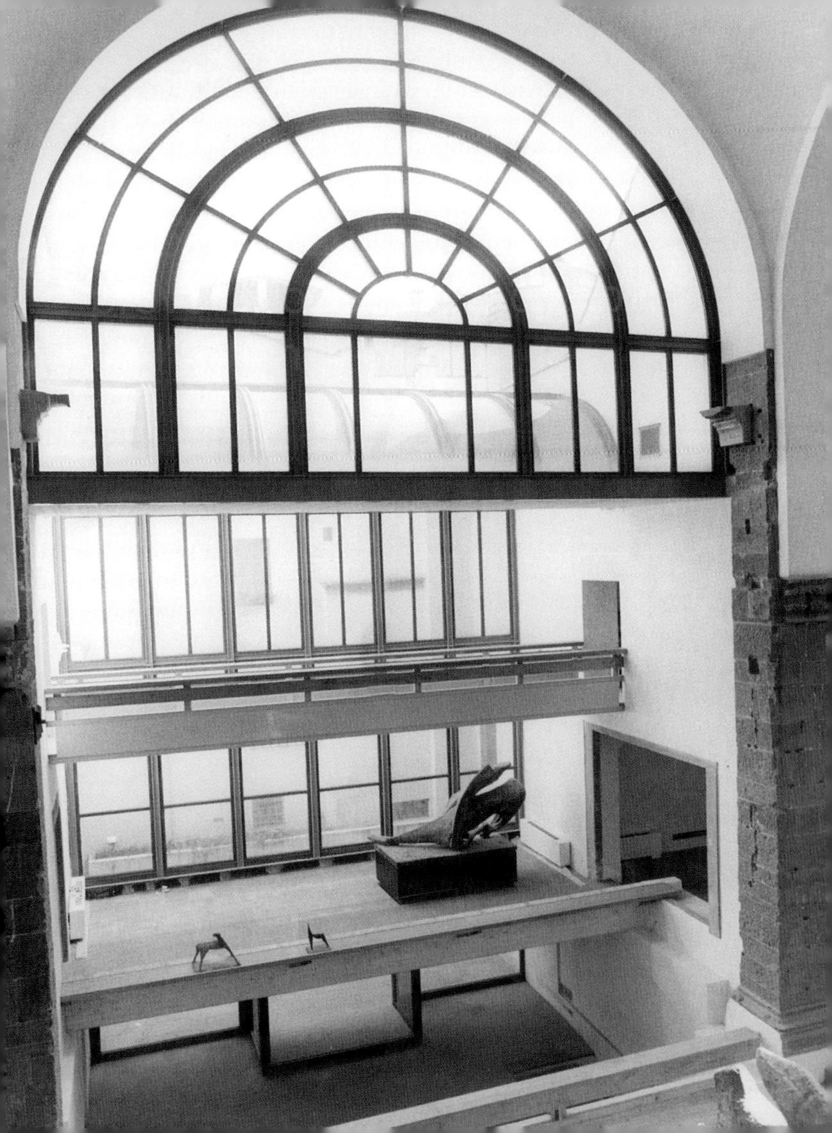

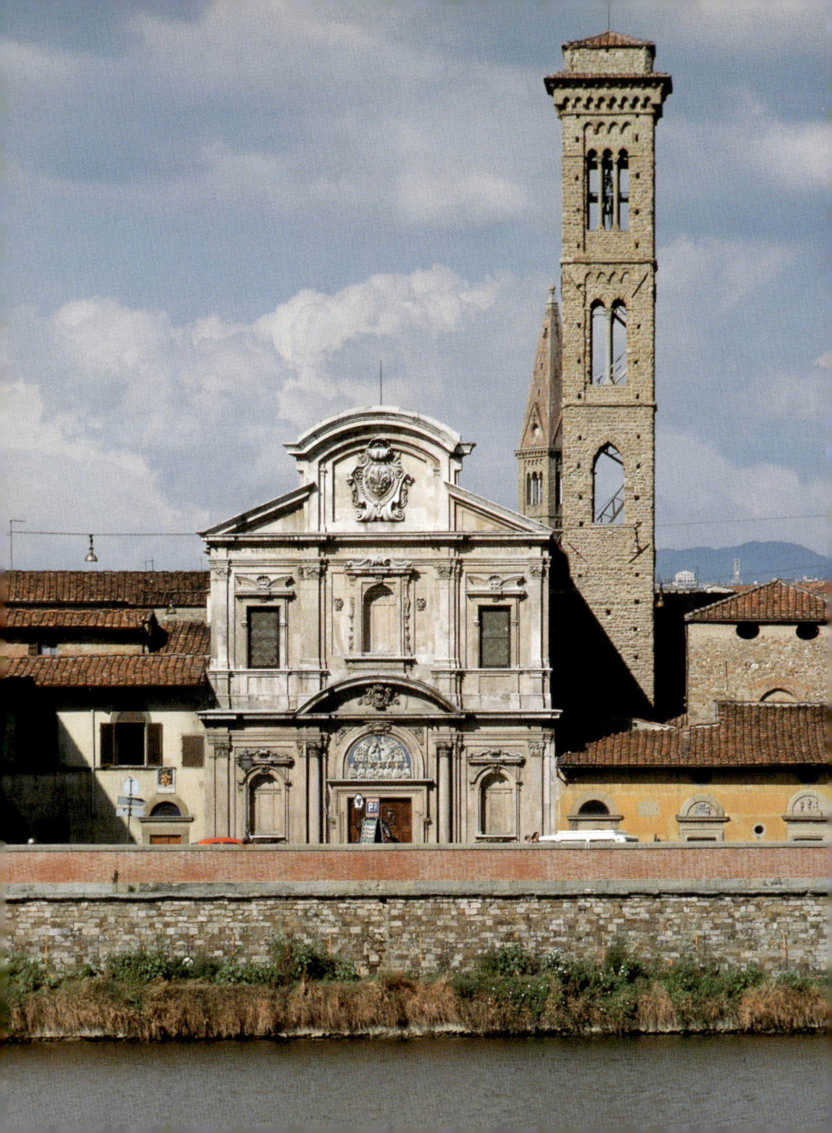

OGNISSANTI

The Borgo, the Piazza, the Church, the Refectory

In 13th-14th century Florence many industrial and commercial activities were concentrated along the two banks of the river, which was at the time navigable down to the sea. The area of Borgo Ognissanti, in the vicinity of the Arno, was particularly involved in this phenomenon. Here there had settled around the middle of the 13th century the Congregation of the Humiliati, who had come to Florence from Lombardy in 1239 to reorganize the industry of weaving and dying fabrics, extremely important for the city's future economy. The Order of the Humiliati, first a secular community and then a monastic order (their Rule was approved by Pope Honorius III), did not live by begging alms but by what they earned, and they were, in fact, skilled wool-workers and glass-workers. Their decision to settle near the banks of the Arno was thus not taken at random. It was here that, after having founded in 1256 the church and monastery dedicated to the Madonna and to All Saints (from which the name "Ognissanti") the Humiliati assumed control and the right to appoint the guardian of the Ponte Nuovo (new bridge) (built in 1218, later renamed Carraia). Their interest was evidently that of supervising their workers who resided in the area,

Opposite page:
The façade by Matteo Nigetti (1637) and the bell tower of the church of Ognissanti in a view from the other side of the Arno.

where the Mugnone, later deviated, flowed into the Arno. In the square, sloping slightly downward and connected directly to the banks of the river, were their washing troughs, and the site was highly suited to exploiting hydraulic power for processing wool. The Humiliati were also responsible for building the Pescaia di Santa Rosa weir, along with a complex system of canals, drying shops and fullers' shops. And it was just here, in the area known as the "Prato", or field, west of Borgo Ognissanti, that the Comune had planned since the early 14th century to build an artificial lake (a project never realized) and had already started work on a "public walk" along the walls, demolishing some houses in 1294 and moving a leper hospital elsewhere. Borgo Ognissanti was also the zone par excellence of the Vespucci, who resided here, not far from the house of Sandro Botticelli, in Via del Porcellana, who worked for them and was buried in the church. We also know that when, in the early 16th century, reports reached Florence of the discoveries made by Amerigo Vespucci, the Gonfaloniere Soderini had festive lanterns lit outside the Vespucci home to celebrate the event appropriately at the expense of the Signoria.

It is thus unsurprising that the history of the church is linked to the Vespucci family, who had their own chapel here, decorated

Opposite page:
Domenico Ghirlandaio, *Lament for Christ Dead,* detail with the presumed portraits of members of the Vespucci family, c. 1473, fresco. Ognissanti, Vespucci Chapel.

Following pages:
Inlaid marble tombstone of Sandro Botticelli, buried here in 1510. Ognissanti, first chapel in the right transept.

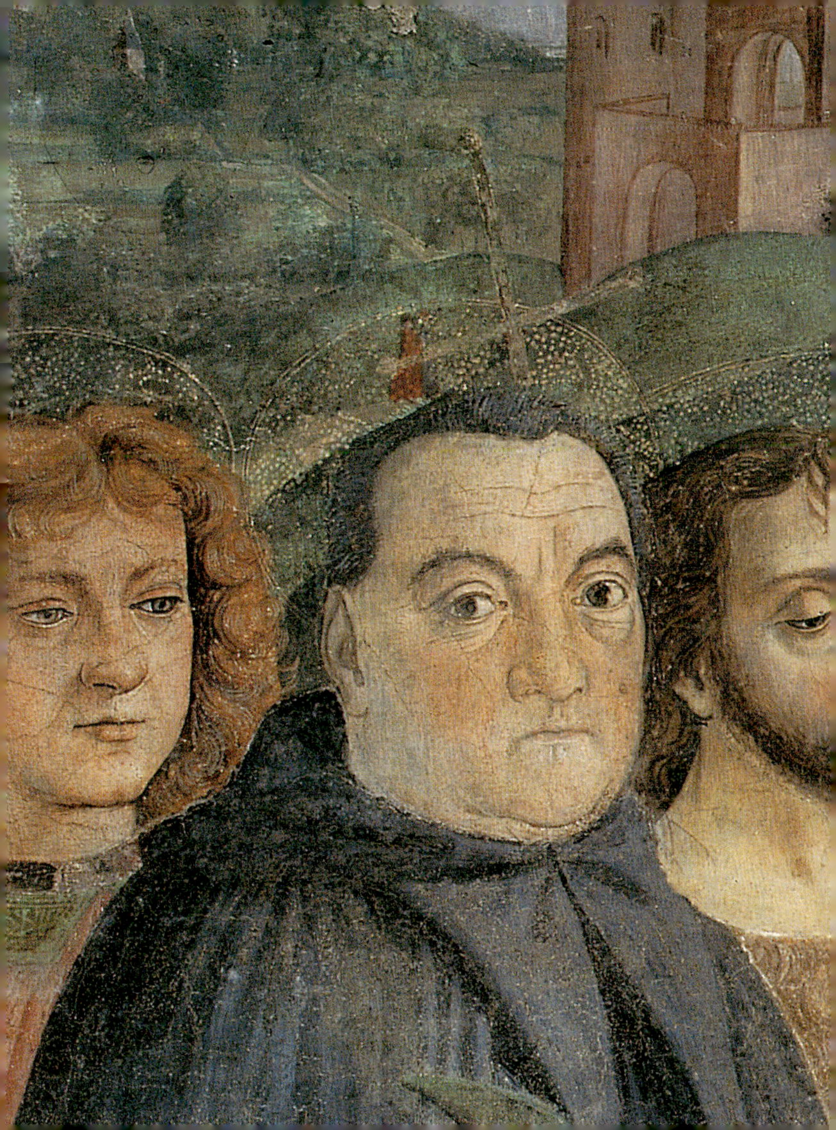

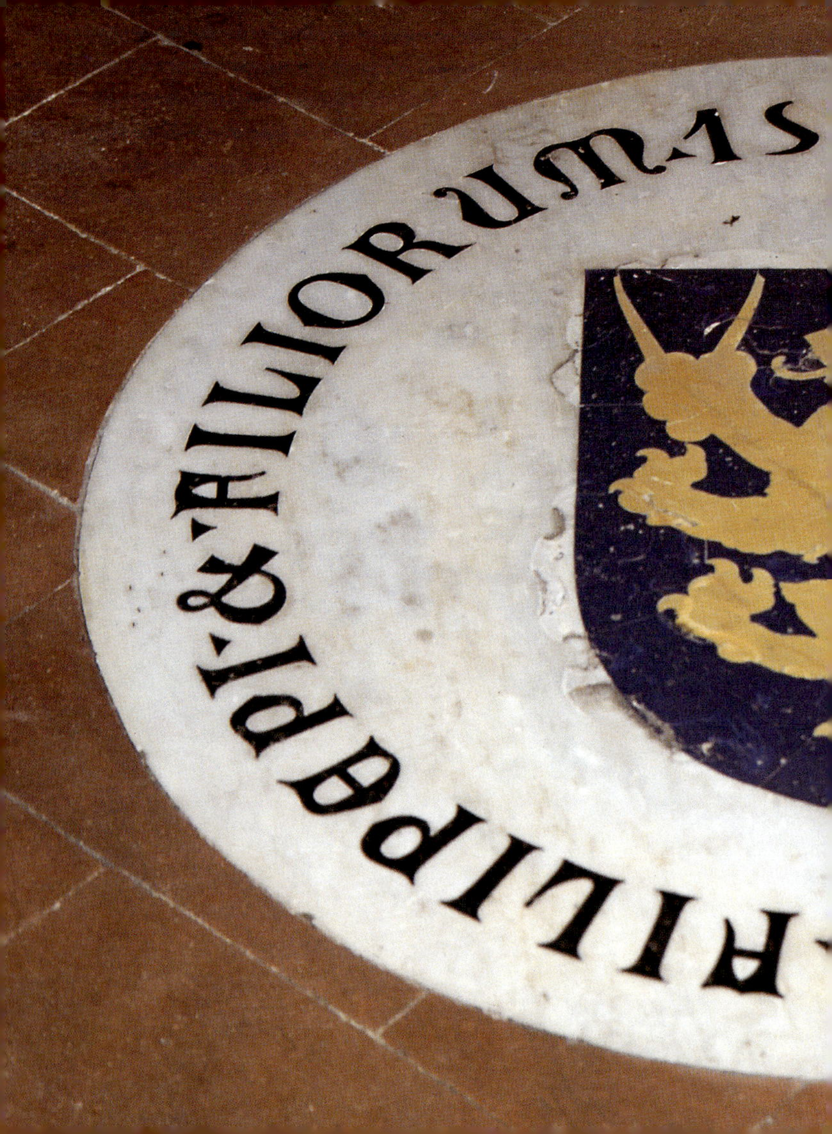

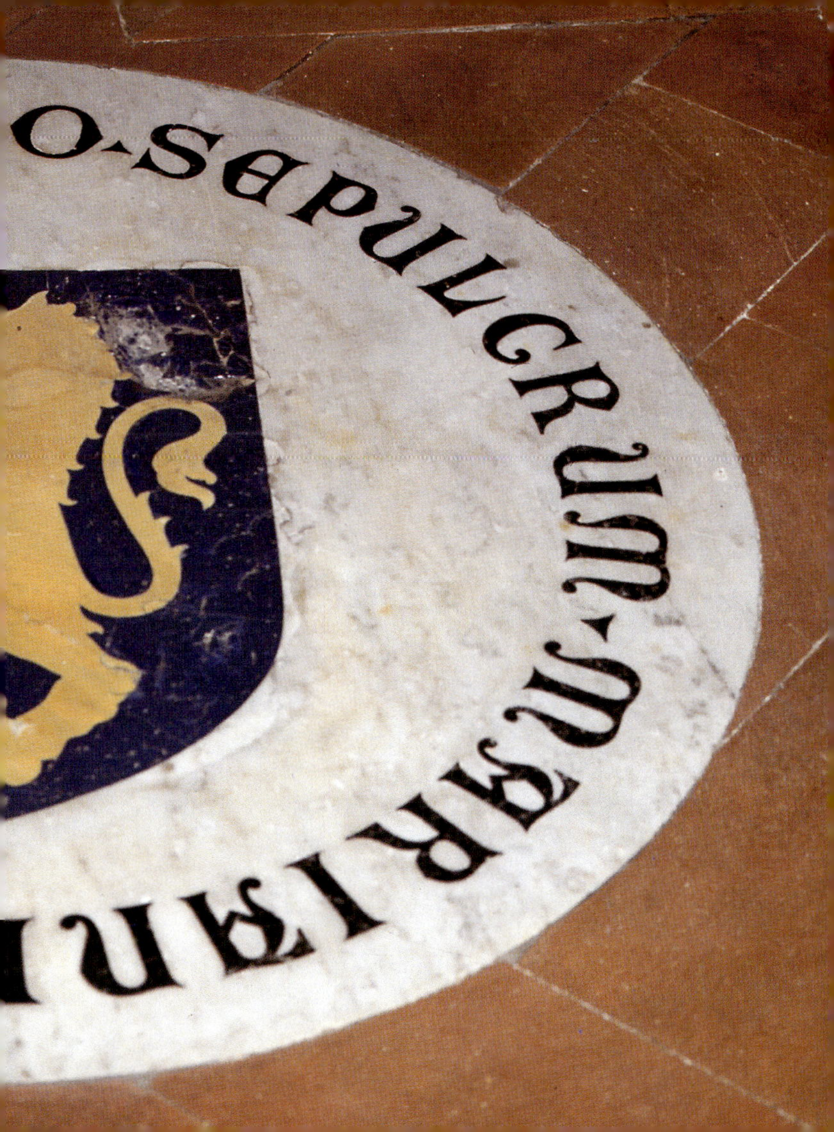
O·SEPULCRUM·MARIANI

by Ghirlandaio around 1472. In the frescoes representing the *Lamentation* and *Our Lady of Mercy protecting members of the Vespucci family*, several members of the family are portrayed, among them Giorgio Antonio, the learned mathematician who was tutor to the young Amerigo, the future explorer who was never to return to Florence after his wondrous exploits across the ocean.

HISTORY

The church, founded in the 13th century by the Humiliati, must have been at the time one of the city's richest in works of art. Giotto worked here for years, and perhaps Taddeo Gaddi; then slightly later, Giovanni da Milano. The great prestige of the Humiliati, increasing over the course of the 14th century, is confirmed by the precious works of art still remaining today in the church, as well as by those now in the Uffizi and other museums. It was for the Humiliati that, around 1310, Giotto painted his monumental *Maestà*, which must have been placed over the lintel of the rood-screen (later destroyed), a *Dormitio Virginis* now in Berlin and a series of frescoes in a side chapel (lost). For the high altar, forty years later, Giovanni da Milano painted a polyptych, later dismembered. In the 15th century too, important works were commissed: in addition to the Vespucci Chapel, the

Opposite page:
Sandro Botticelli,
St. Jerome in his Study,
detail, 1480,
detached fresco.
Church of Ognissanti.

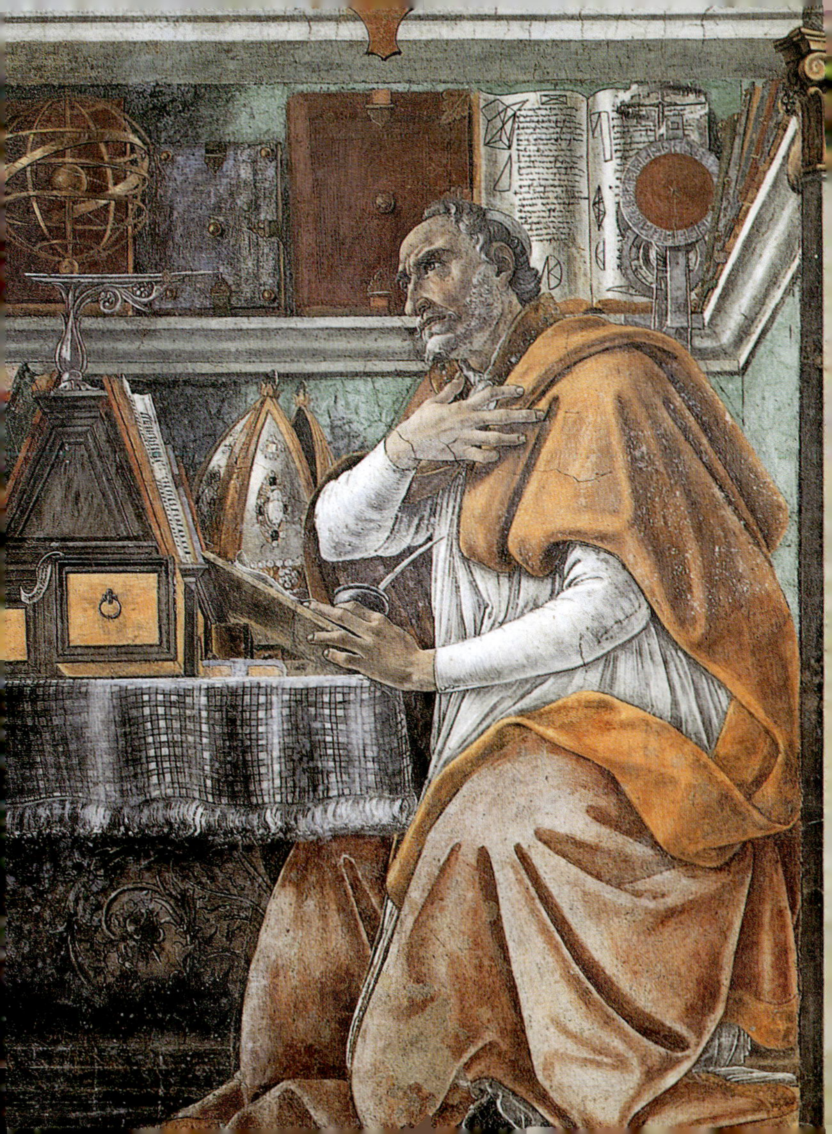

two frescoes of *St. Jerome and St. Augustine*, by Ghirlandaio and Botticelli respectively, which the two artist painted in 1480 as companion pieces for the two chapels at the sides of the choir (today on the walls of the nave). Ghirlandaio also painted a *Last Supper*, with a magnificent grove of citrus trees appearing beyond an espalier, commissioned of him by the Humiliati for the wall of the monastery's refectory. The order of the Humiliati declined however in the 16th century, and they were succeeded by the Observant Minorites (1571). The church too underwent large-scale renovation, and today its original layout has almost totally disappeared. The new façade, Baroque but still interpreted in the Mannerist style, was designed by Matteo Nigetti in 1637. In 1872 the City of Florence made drastic changes in the original design, replacing the stone floor with one in travertine by Rapolano.

Opposite page:
Domenico Ghirlandaio,
St. Augustine in his Study, detail,
1480, detached fresco.
Church of Ognissanti.

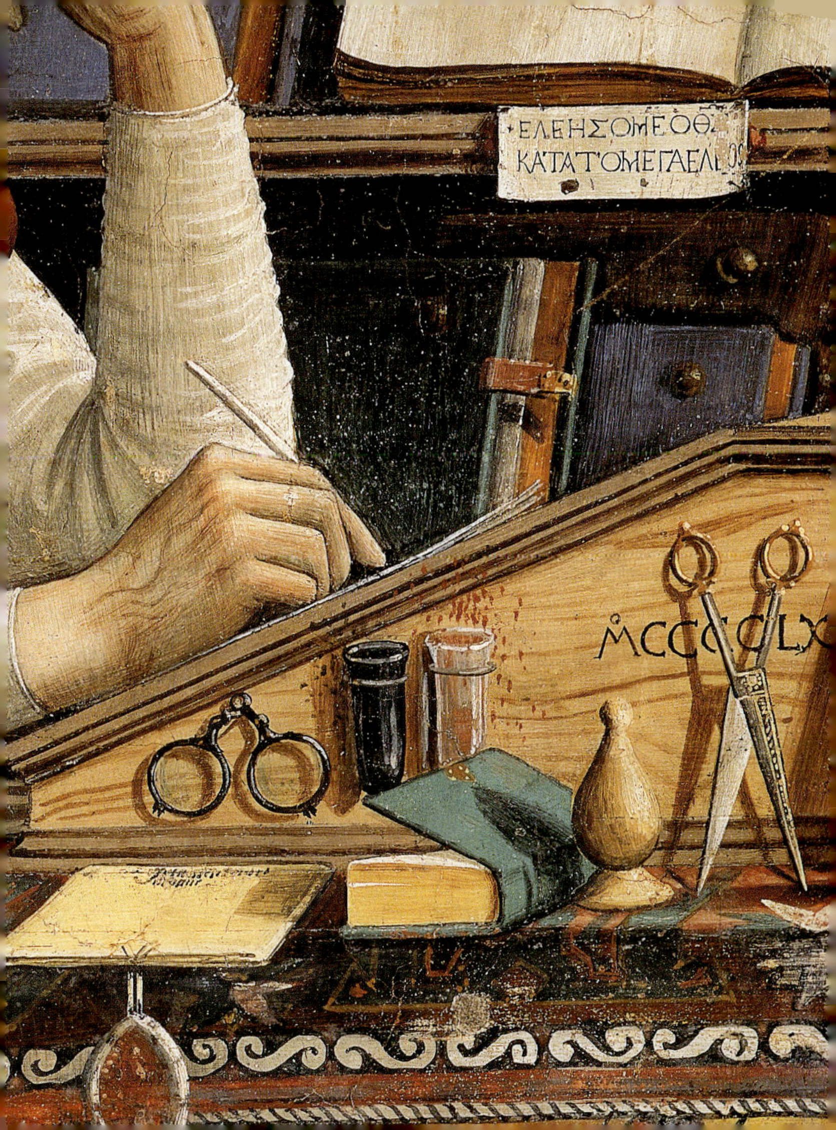
ΕΛΕΗΣΟΜΕΟΘ
ΚΑΤΑΤΟΜΕΓΑΕΛ
MCCCCLX

Noteworthy are:

- the Vespucci Chapel, with frescoes by Davide and Domenico Ghirlandaio portraying the Vespucci family.
- the *Crucifixion*, attributed to Taddeo Gaddi and his school,
- the two frescoes (1480) of *St. Augustine* and *St. Jerome in his Study*, by Ghirlandaio and Botticelli, detached from the choir.
- the Chapel of the Holy Name of Jesus (1722), in the right transept, with frescoes by Giovan Domenico Ferretti and Lorenzo del Moro.
- the little Chapel of San Pietro d'Alcantara (1727), with frescoes by Matteo Bonechi, also in the right transept.
- the fresco by Giuseppe Benucci and Giuseppe Romei depicting the *Glory of St. Francis and St. Pasquale Baylon* (1769-1779) in the great vault over the name.
- in the Refectory, *The Last Supper* (1480) by Domenico Ghirlandaio, a fresco considered the "twin" of the one painted in the same year by the same artist for the Refectory in the San Marco Monastery, set in an airy Renaissance interior, against a background of citrus trees and birds in flight.

Opposite page and following pages:
Domenico Ghirlandaio,
The Last Supper, detail (*this page*)) and whole (*following pages*),
1480, fresco.
Church of Ognissanti, Refectory.

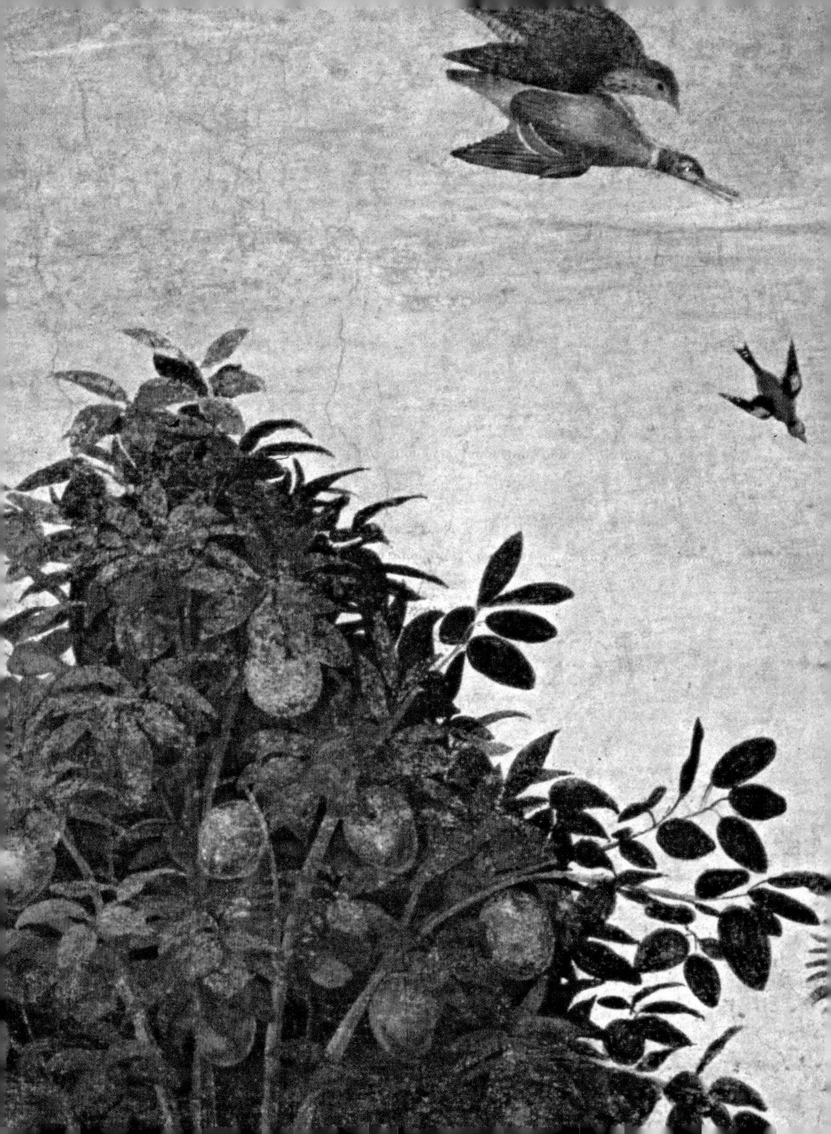

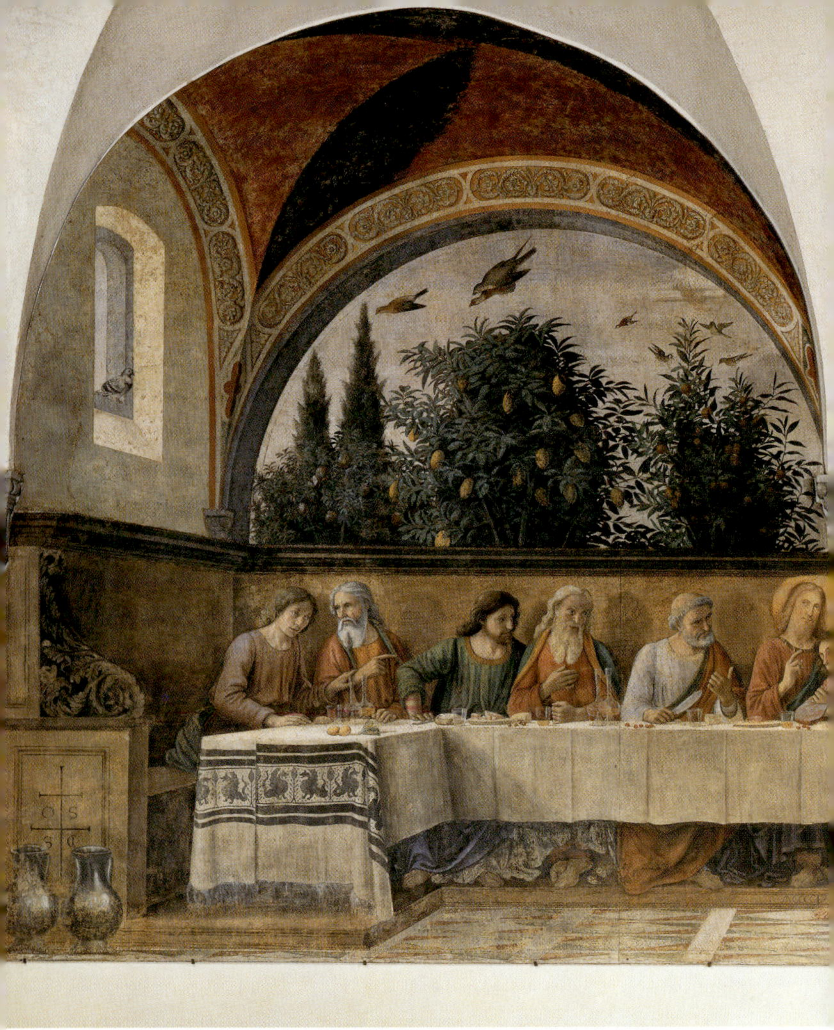

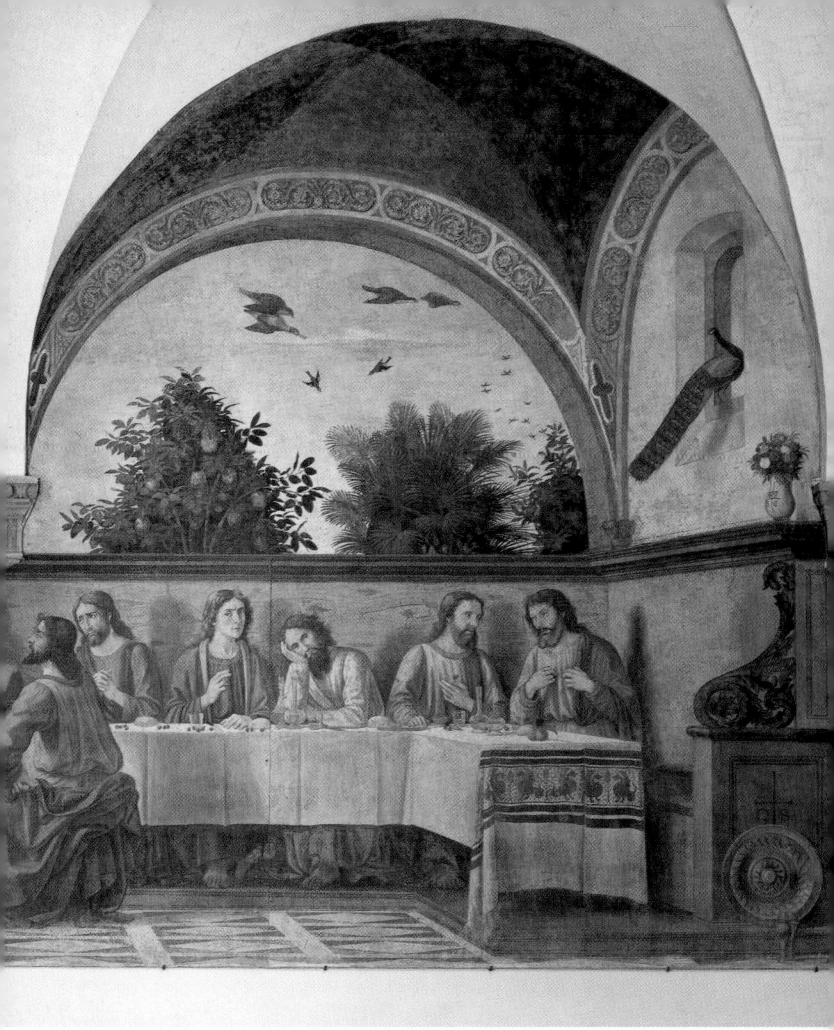

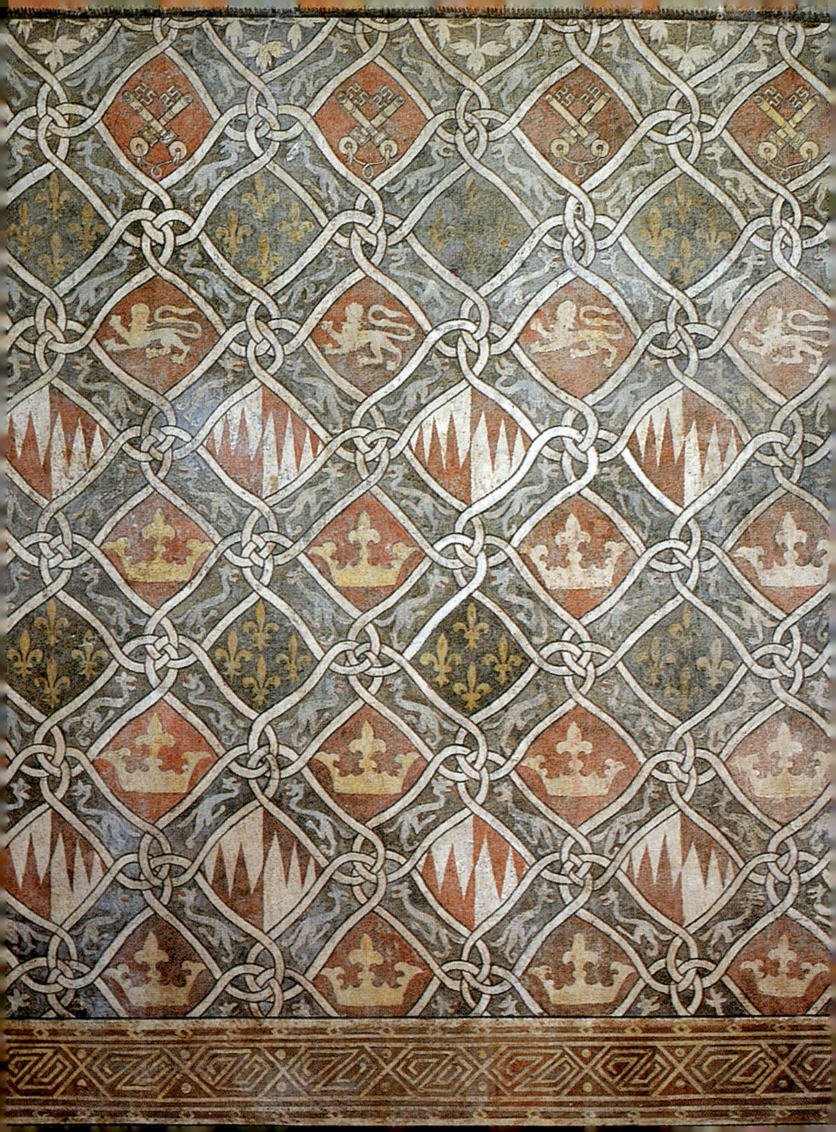

Museo di Palazzo Davanzati

The Museo di Palazzo Davanzati, also known as the Museum of the Ancient Florentine House, is situated in Via di Porta Rossa in a building whose oldest parts date from the 14th century, at which time it belonged to the Davizzi family. Acquired by the Bartolini in the 16th century, it was sold to Bartolomeo Davanzati in 1578. In the early years of the 20th century it was bought by the interprising antiquarian Elia Volpi, who restored it, partially altering the original structure to make it resemble as much as possible a medieval residence. The antiquarian furnished it with objects coming from various places. Purchased by the State in 1951, since 1956 the building, which has been undergoing restoration in the last few years, is the site of the museum that exhibits furnishings, fabrics, objects of domestic use and fragments of wall decorations coming from Florentine museums or purchased especially to document the typical aspect of a Florentine upper-class home in the Middle Ages and Renaissance period. In addition to furniture and chests, the museum displays a collection of lace and embroidery work, the famous tondo representing the *Gioco del Civettino* (game of the owl) (second half of the 15th century), a tapestry mounted as headboard with grotesque motifs against a yellow background and the allegory of *Charity* (1553), from a drawing by Bachiacca.

Opposite page:
Fragment of wall decoration with heraldic symbols, 14th century.
Museo di Palazzo Davanzati.

Above: Florentine workshop,
Painted chest with iron fittings,
late 14th century.
Museo di Palazzo Davanzati.

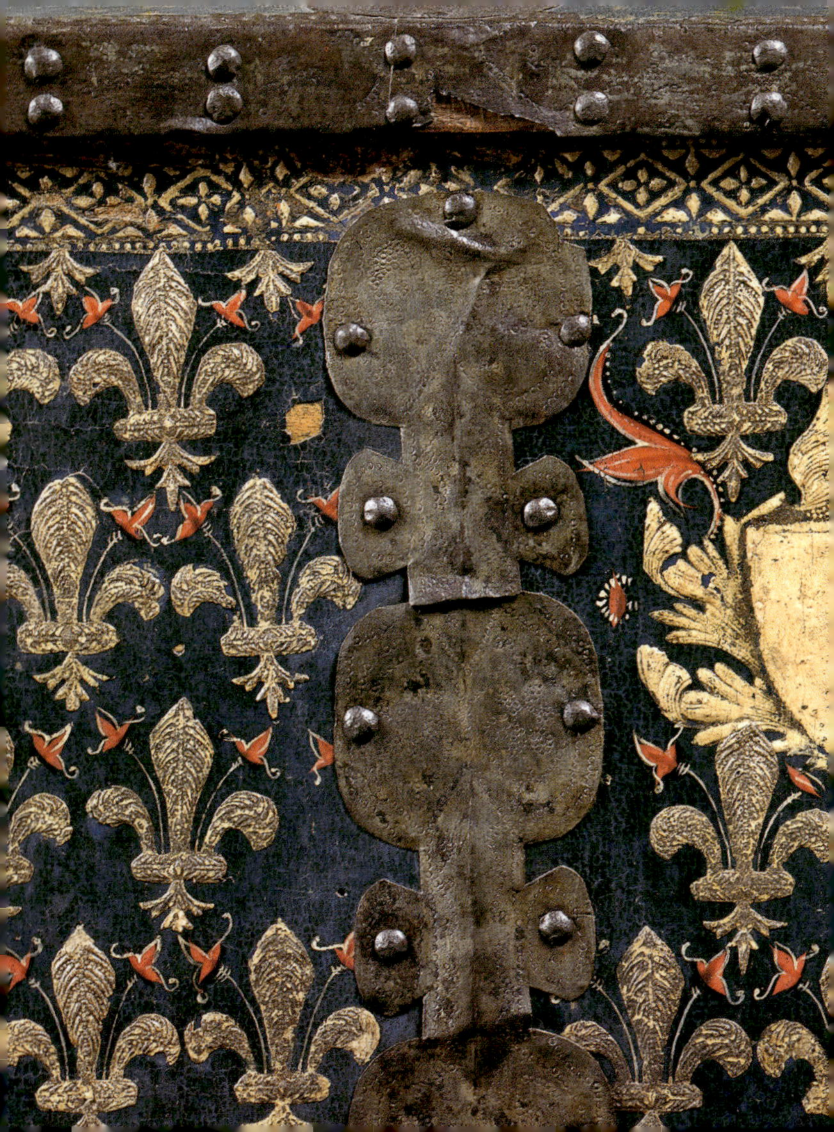

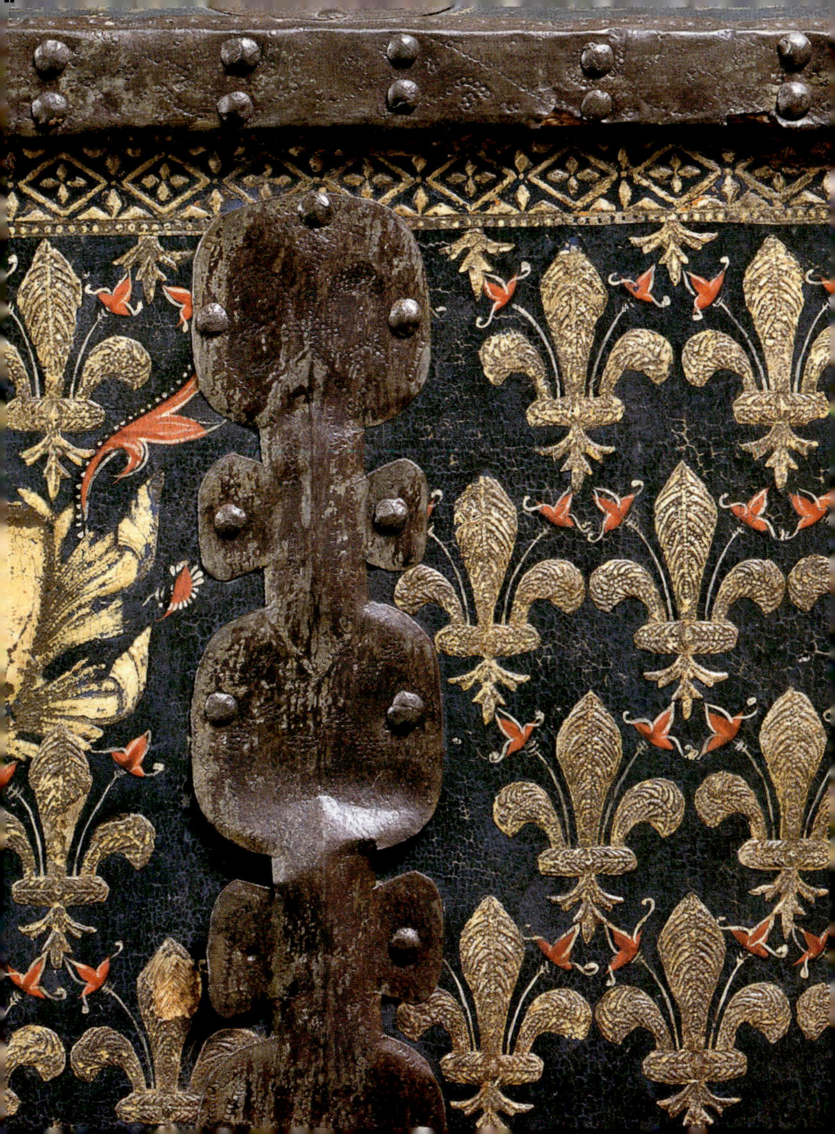

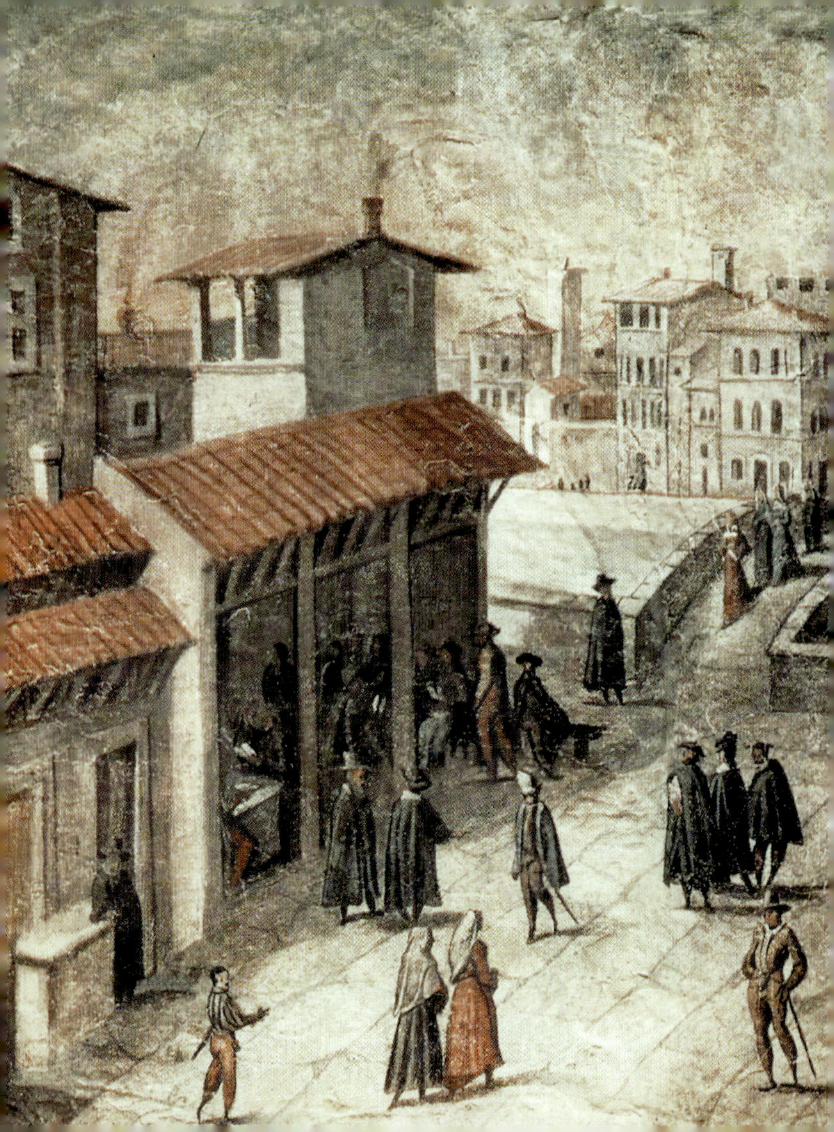

Santa Trinita

The Church, the Bridge, the Piazza

Situated in one of Florence's most scenographic settings, the Church of Santa Trinita, founded by the Vallombrosian monks in the 11th century along with the adjacent monastry, faces on a square cited by Stendhal for its typically 16th century aspect. Still today, if from the other side of the Arno we cross the bridge at Santa Trinita, it appears to us as a grandiose theatrical scene onto which open no less than five streets (Via del Parione, Via Tornabuoni, Porta Rossa, Via delle Terme and Borgo Santi Apostoli). From here passed all of the official processions in the time of the Grand Dukes. The itinerary, which started from the residence of Palazzo Pitti where Cosimo I de' Medici had moved, paraded down Via Maggio to arrive at the Loggia de' Frescobaldi, crossed the bridge and continued toward Piazza San Giovanni, surrounded by sumptuous temporary decorative structures, ephemeral but significant signs of grand-ducal power. In Via Tornabuoni there were, among other things, sculptures such as *Hercules and the Centaur* by Giambologna (now in Piazza Signoria under the Loggia dei Lanzi), and on the occasion of the most important processions, this vivacious sculptural monument in marble, placed in the Canto dei Carnesecchi, was transformed into a "fountain of Bacchus", flowing with

Opposite page: Giovanni Stradano, *The Santa Trinita Bridge seen from the Frescobaldi Loggia on the other side of the Arno*, 1562, fresco. Palazzo Vecchio.

Following pages: View from above of Piazza Santa Trinita, with Palazzo Spini Feroni, the column of Justice and the façade of the church.

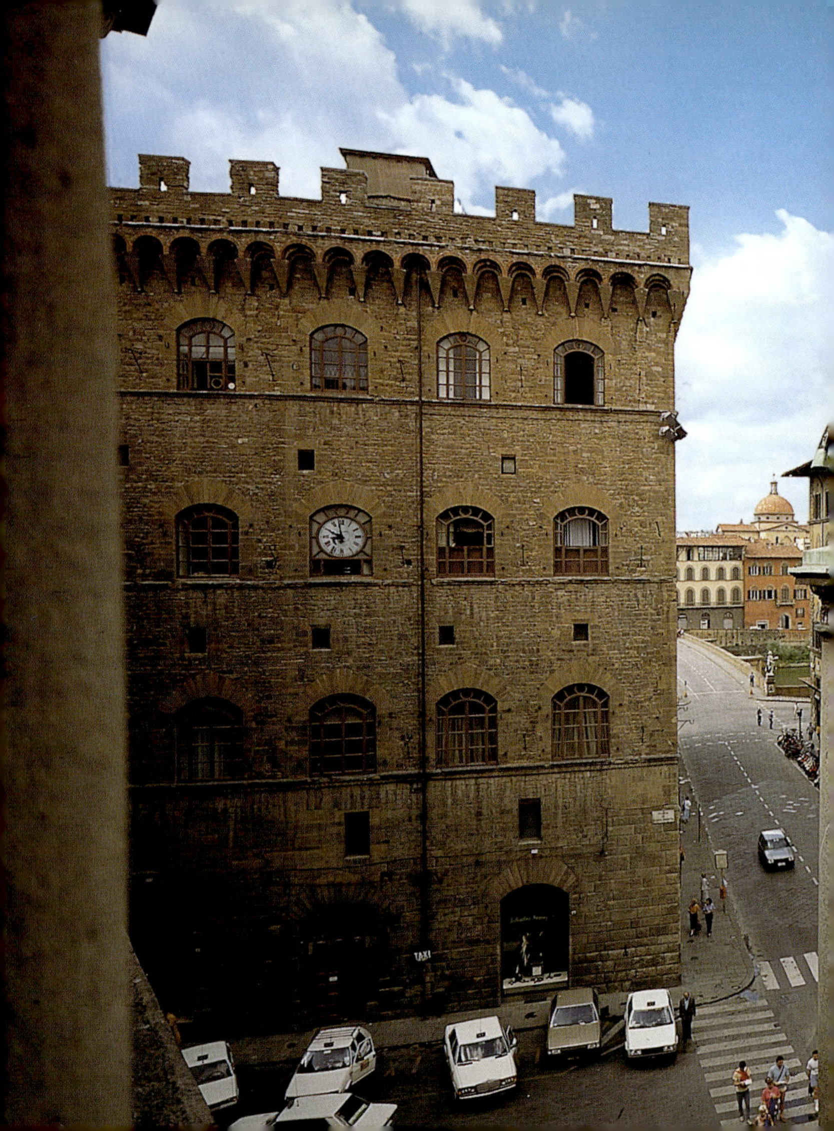
TAXI

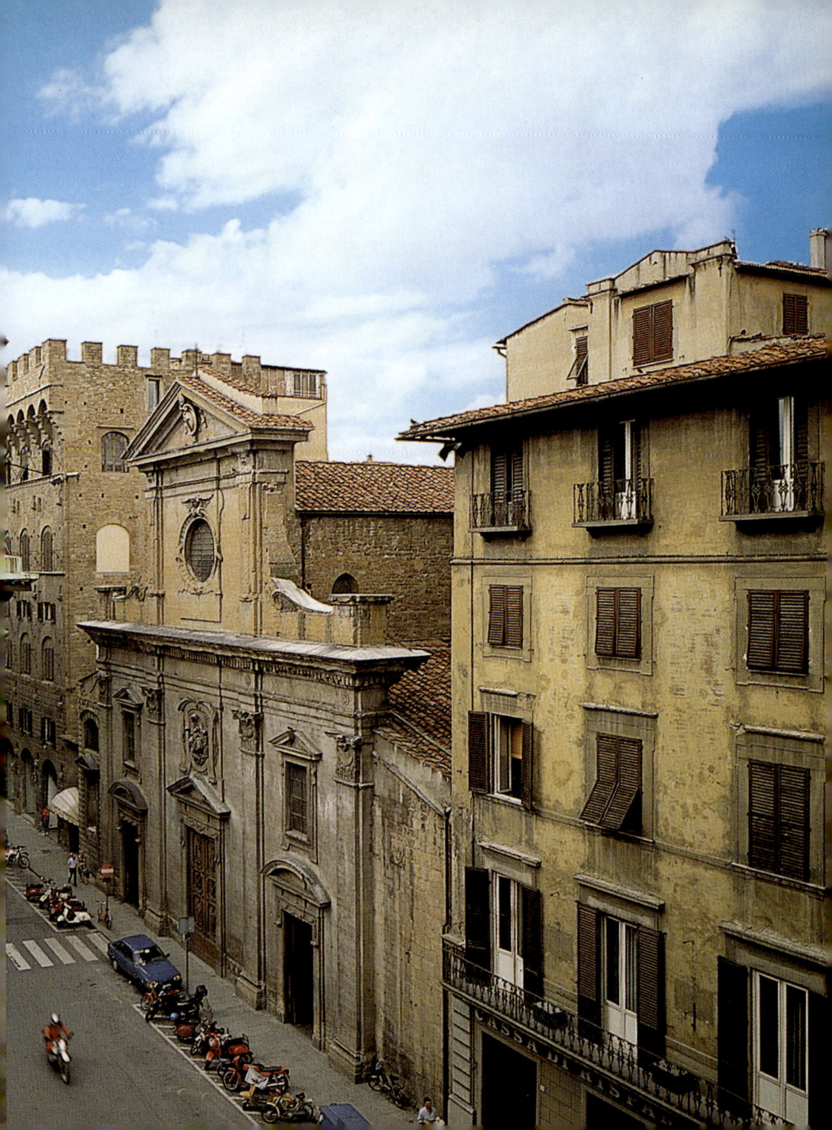

wine for the passersby. One of the most emblematic monuments of Medicean prestige still remains in the square: the ancient column in pink granite, coming from the baths of Rome. Donated by Pope Pius IV to Cosimo I de' Medici in 1565, the column is surmounted by a statue of *Justice,* carved in 1581 in such a precious material as porphyry by Francesco Ferrucci del Tadda. Symbol of grand-ducal power, the ancient column with its statue, which dominates the spectacular crossroads/piazza of Santa Trinita, must have reminded all citizens of the victorious Battle of Marciano fought against Siena (1554).

Already a century before, near the entry to the bridge, the Florentines used to converse seated on the stone "panconi" (benches) or "seggette da via" (street chairs) along the ground floor of Palazzo Spini and the Gianfigliazzi Tower (as shown by Ghirlandaio in a fresco illustrated on the following pages). The bench of the Gianfigliazzi palace was known as the "pancone dei Ragusei" because it was here that the merchants of Ragusa conducted their bargaining. The bridge of Santa Trinita also has a long and very troubled history. Built in wood in 1252, destroyed by the flood of 1333, rebuilt around 1346, perhaps to the project of Taddeo Gaddi, again swept away by a flood in 1557 and rebuilt by Ammannati, it was mined in 1944 and finally rebuilt after World War II. The statues of the four *Seasons* adorning the

Opposite page:
Francesco Ferrucci del Tadda, to the design of Bartolomeo Ammannati, *Justice*, 1565-1581, porphyry. Piazza Santa Trinita.

Following pages: Domenico Ghirlandaio, *Piazza Santa Trinita with the stone benches of Palazzo Spini*, detail from the *Miracle of the Boy*, c. 1485, fresco. Santa Trinita, Sassetti Chapel.

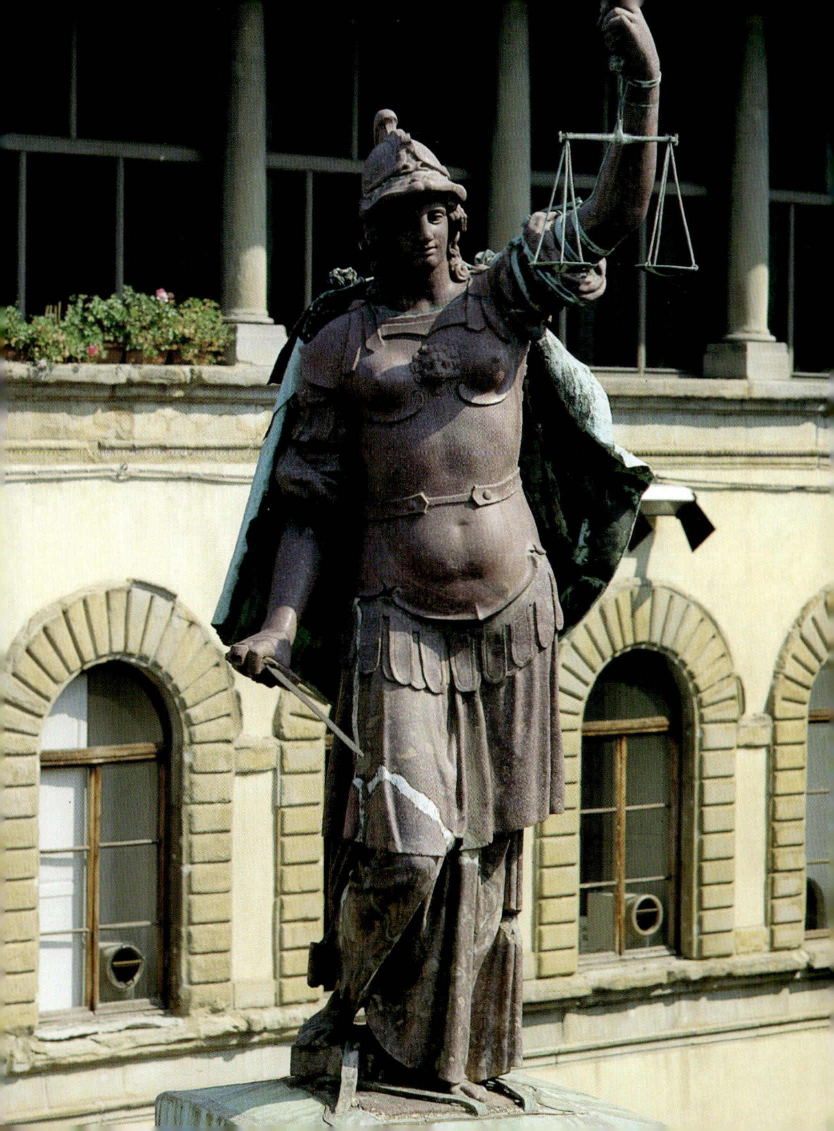

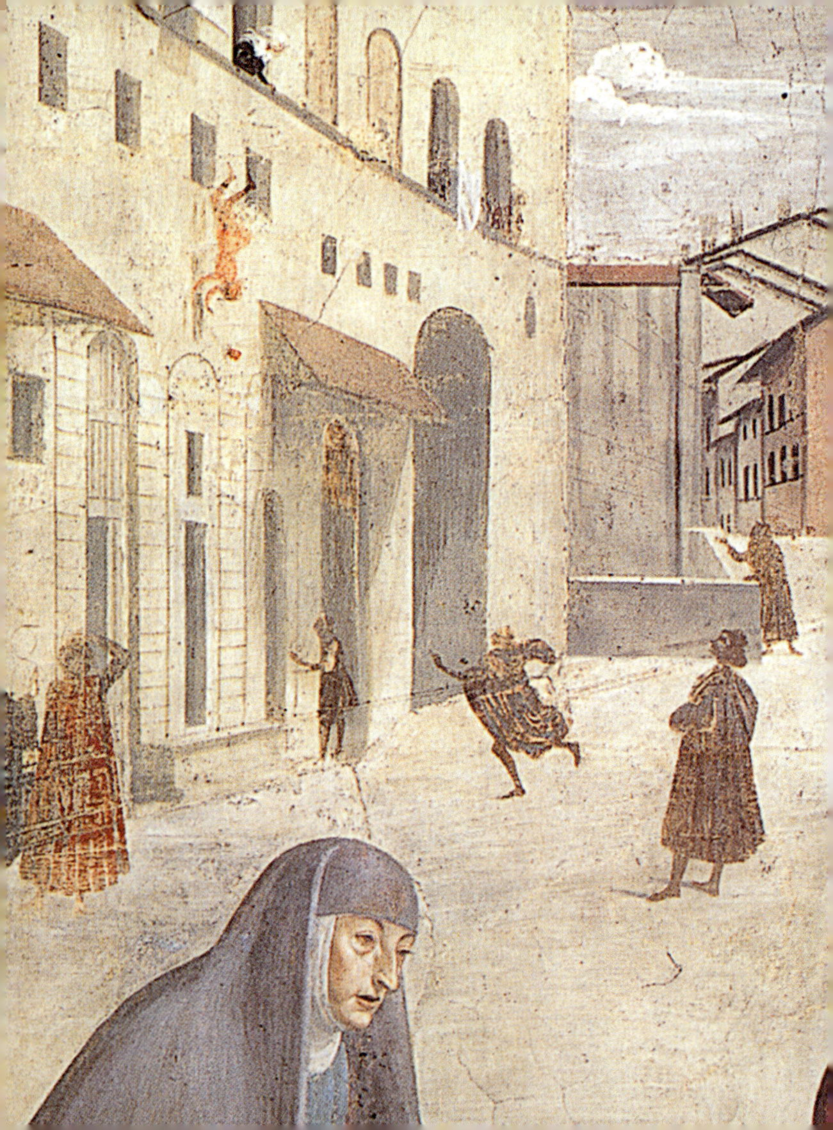

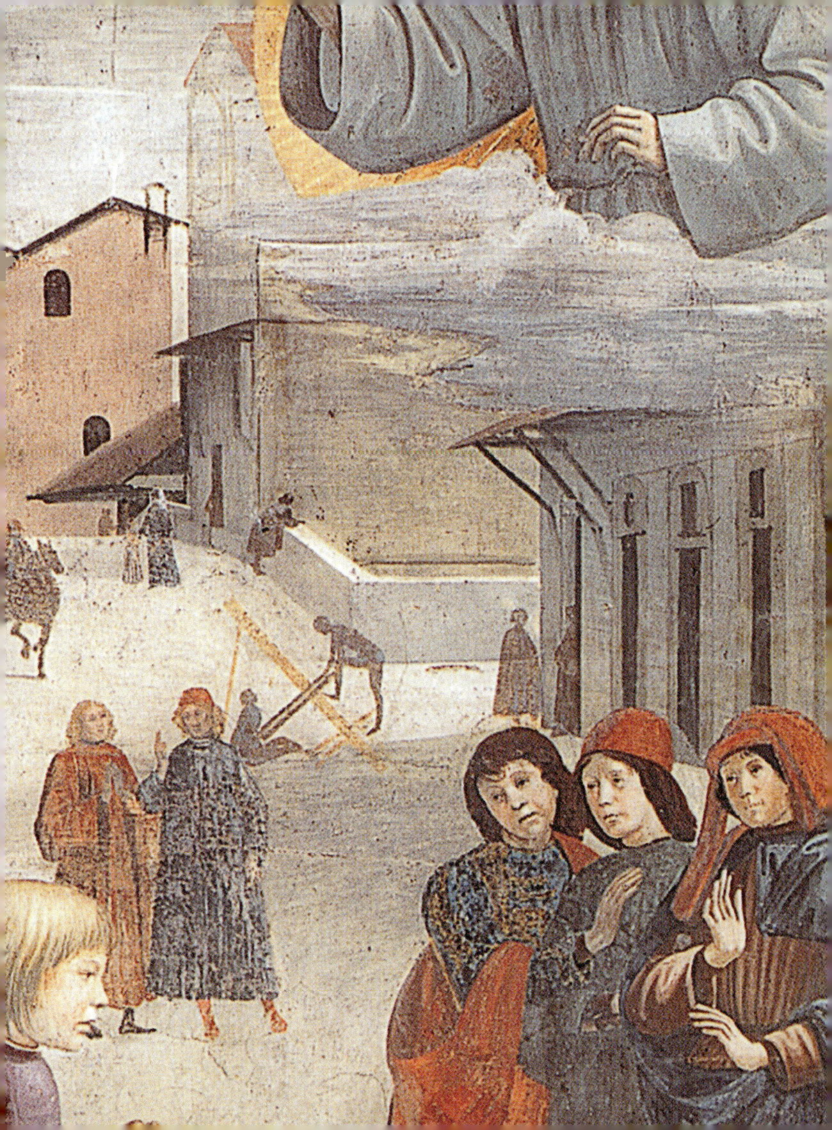

ends of the bridge were sculpted in 1608 by Pietro Francavilla, Giovanni Caccini and Taddeo Landini on the occasion of the wedding of Cosimo de' Medici, eldest child of Grand Duke Ferdinando II, and Maria Maddalena d'Austria. On October 28 of that year, in honor of the bridal couple, a memorable mock Battle of the Bridge was fought along this section of the river.

THE CHURCH AND ITS PATRONS

Founded around 1060 on the site of the ancient Chapel of the Madonna dello Spasimo, the Romanesque edifice of Santa Trinita, annexed in the 12th century to the new Vallombrosian monastery, was renovated and enlarged between the 13th and 14th centuries, and was later subjected to ulterior modifications. The façade of the church, which appears today in its 16th century aspect, was designed around 1593-1594 by Bernardo Buontalenti, who also designed a stupendous Mannerist stairway (1574), later moved to the Church of Santo Stefano al Ponte where it still stands today. The Gothic interior, designed in the second half of the 14th century, probably by Neri di Fioravante, was modified over the course of the next century by the construction of several chapels, and has been subjected to further changes as well as heavy restoration initiatives in the 19th and 20th centuries.

Opposite page:
The interior of the church of Santa Trinita seen from the transept.

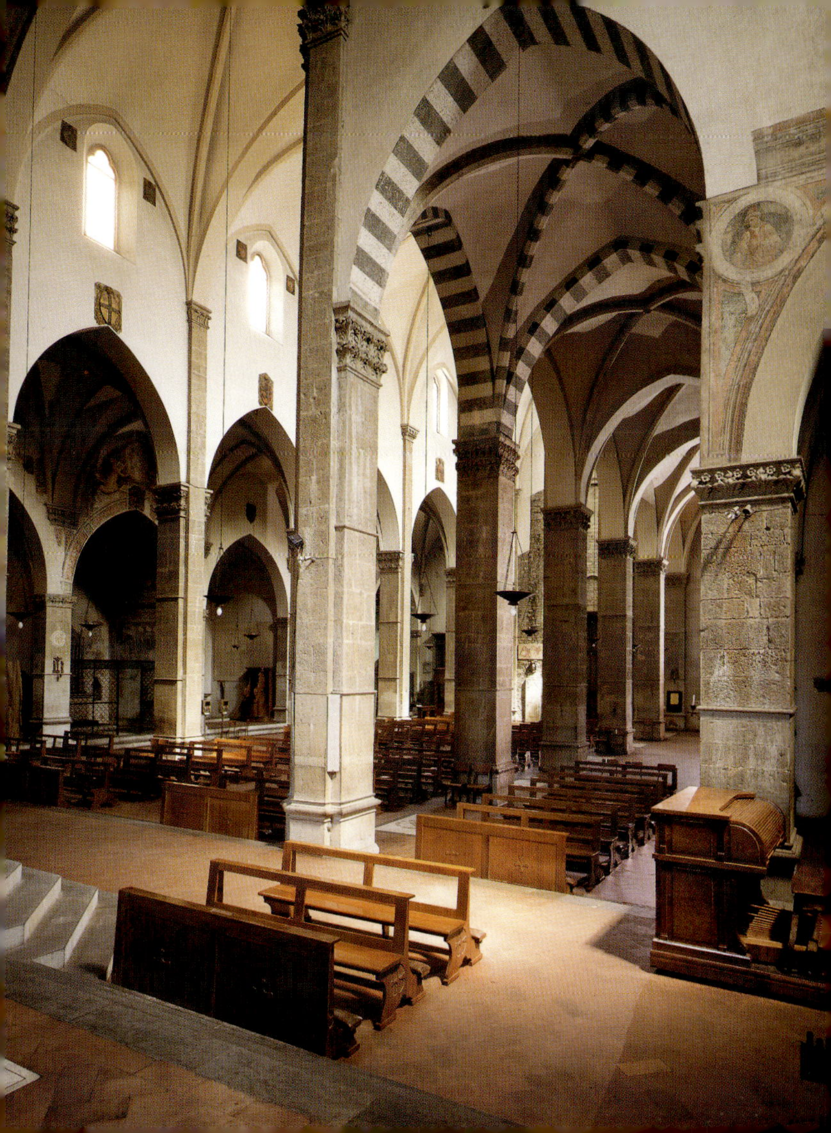

The rich decoration of the Church of Santa Trinita had been largely financed, since medieval times, by important patrons, members of the wealthy families who lived in the area: among them were the Strozzi, the Sassetti, the Gianfigliazzi, the Davanzati, the Bartolini Salimbeni, and the Ardinghelli.
Several of the works commissioned for this church have however long been moved to museums, or remain in the church only in part, reduced to fragments. Among these are the great *Maestà* by Cimabue (c. 1301, now in the Uffizi), formerly above the high altar; the frescoes of Spinello Aretino for the Bartolini Salimbeni Chapel, which were later covered by the new cycle painted by Lorenzo Monaco. The two precious altarpieces with the *Adoration of the Magi* by Gentile da Fabriano (1423, now in the Uffizi) and the *Deposition* (c. 1423-1433, now in the Museo di San Marco), begun by Lorenzo Monaco and finished by Fra Angelico, were instead destined to the sacristy of the church, which became in the 15th century the family chapel of the vastly rich and highly cultured merchant Palla di Noferi Strozzi, a rival of the Medici. The chapel, designed by Lorenzo Ghiberti who finished it in 1423, had been ordered by Palla Strozzi to house the sumptuous funerary monument to Noferi Strozzi, his father. Another of the works no longer in the church is the intense altarpiece portraying *The Deposition of Christ* by Agnolo Bronzino (1530, now in the Uffizi).

Opposite page:
Lorenzo Monaco, *Annunciation*, detail, c. 1425, tempera on wood. Santa Trinita.

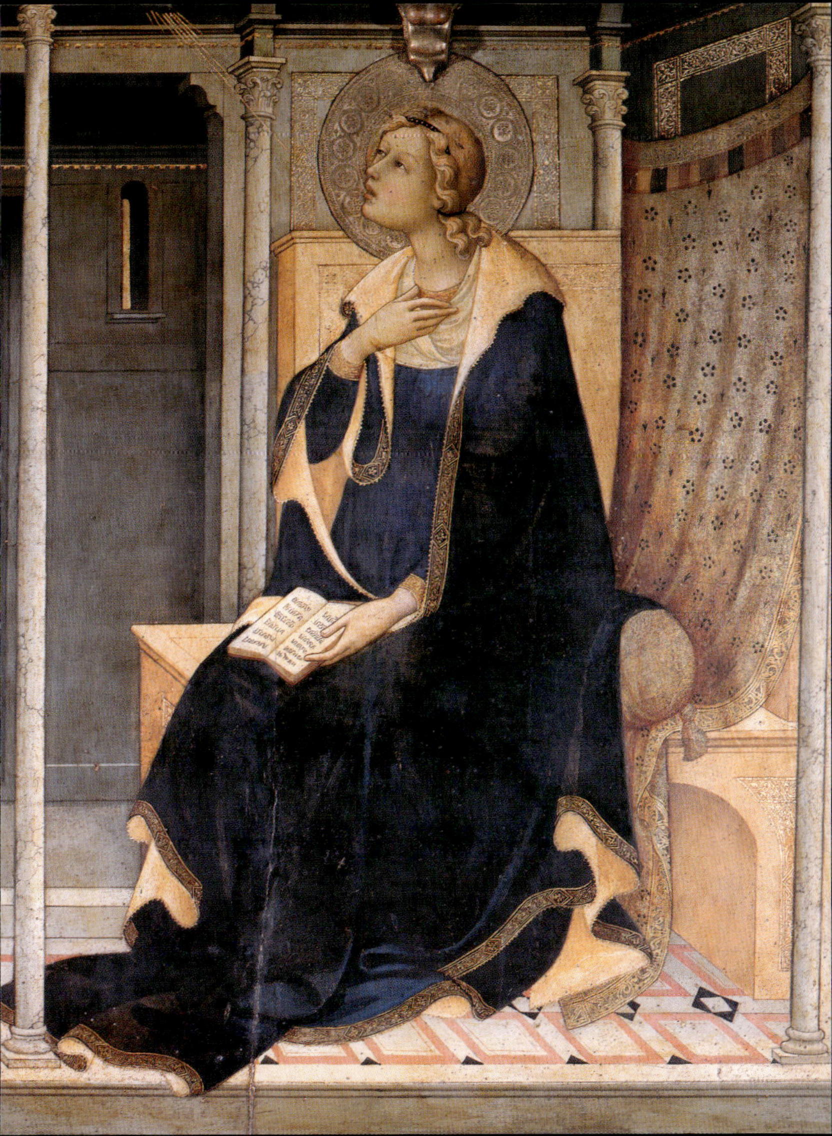

Inside the church we find:

- in the Bartolini Salimbeni Chapel (right nave), the *Stories of the Virgin, Saints and Prophets* (c. 1425) by Lorenzo Monaco.
- in the Sacristy, the *Tomb of Onofrio Strozzi* (1421) with a sarcophagus carved by Niccolò di Pietro Lamberti.
- in the Sassetti Chapel, the *Stories of St. Francis of Assisi* (1480-1485), frescoes by Domenico Ghirlandaio. The scene of the *Confirmation of the Rule*, with portraits of members of the Medici and Sassetti families, is also another precious 15th century documentation of Piazza della Signoria. The altarpiece with the *Adoration of the Shepherds* (1485) at the center of the chapel is flanked by a frescoed portrait of the two patrons, the banker Francesco Sassetti and his wife Nera. Francesco was always at the service of the Medici and in the frescoes he appears, not by chance, close to members of the Medicean entourage: from Lorenzo the Magnificent with his sons Giuliano, Piero and Giovanni, to the poet Agnolo Poliziano.
- the marble tomb of Bishop Benozzo Federighi (c. 1455, formerly in the Church of San Pancrazio) by Luca della Robbia, decorated with a refined naturalist frame made of polychrome glazed terracotta tiles.
- the Chapel of the Reliques of St. Giovanni Gualberto, bounded by polychrome marble, decorated in the 16th century with paintings by Domenico Cresti, known as Passignano.

Opposite page:
View of the Sassetti Chapel in the right transept of Santa Trinita.

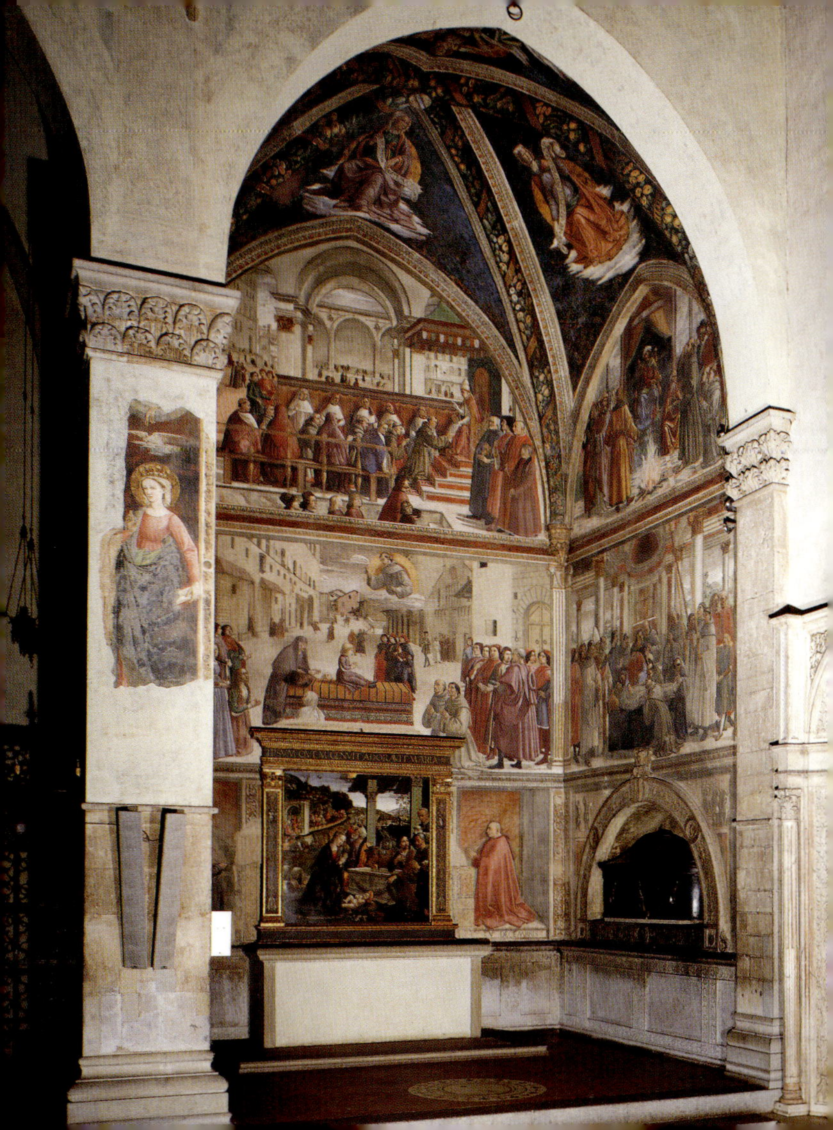

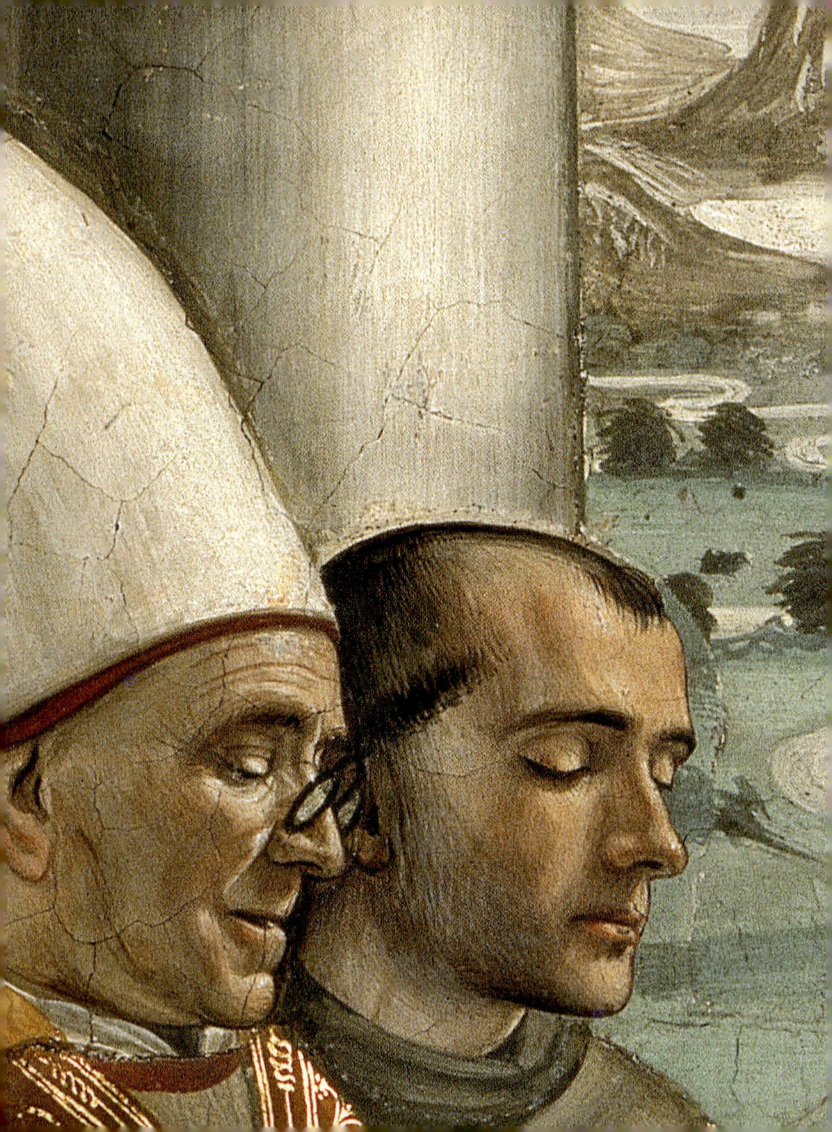

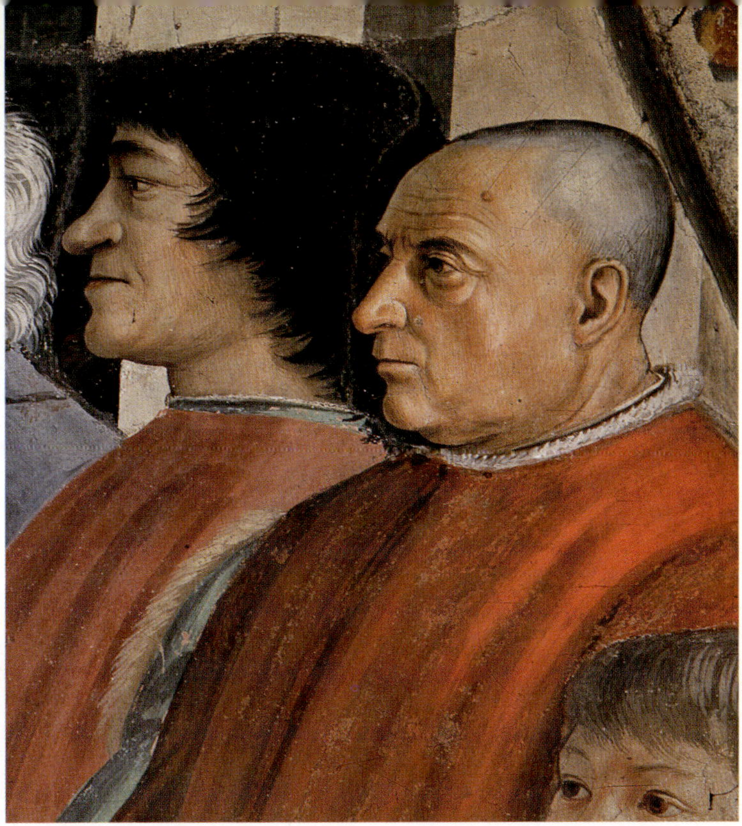

Opposite page:
Domenico Ghirlandaio,
Funeral of St. Francis,
detail, c. 1485,
fresco. Santa Trinita,
Sassetti Chapel.

Above: Domenico Ghirlandaio,
Confirmation of the Rule, detail
with Lorenzo the Magnificent
and the patron Francesco Sassetti,
c. 1485, fresco.
Santa Trinita, Sassetti Chapel.

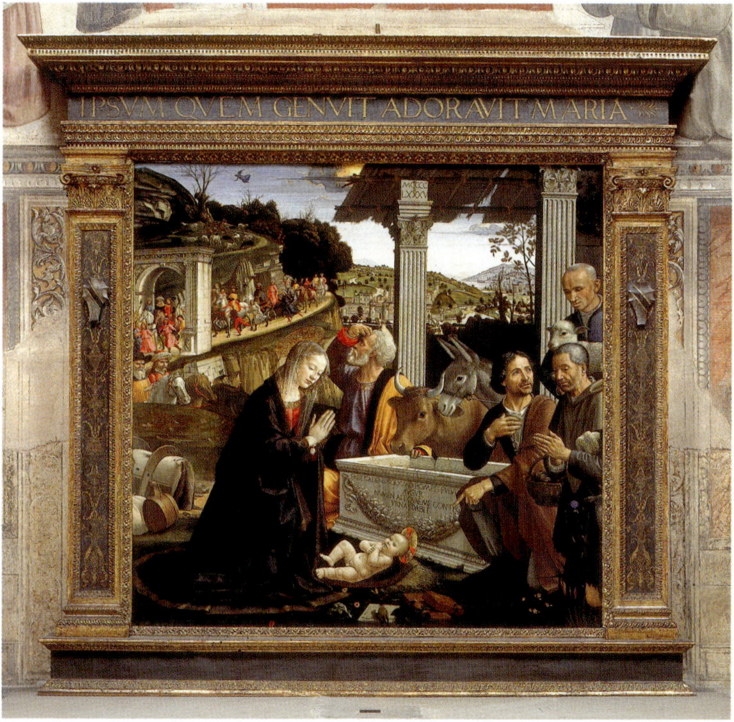

Above and this page:
Domenico Ghirlandaio,
Adoration of the Shepherds,
whole and detail,
c. 1485. Santa Trinita,
Sassetti Chapel, altarpiece.

Following pages: The Chapel of San Giovanni Gualberto,

Luca della Robbia, *Funerary Monument to Benozzo Federighi,*
c. 1456, marble and glazed
terracotta. Santa Trinita, formerly
in the church of San Pancrazio.

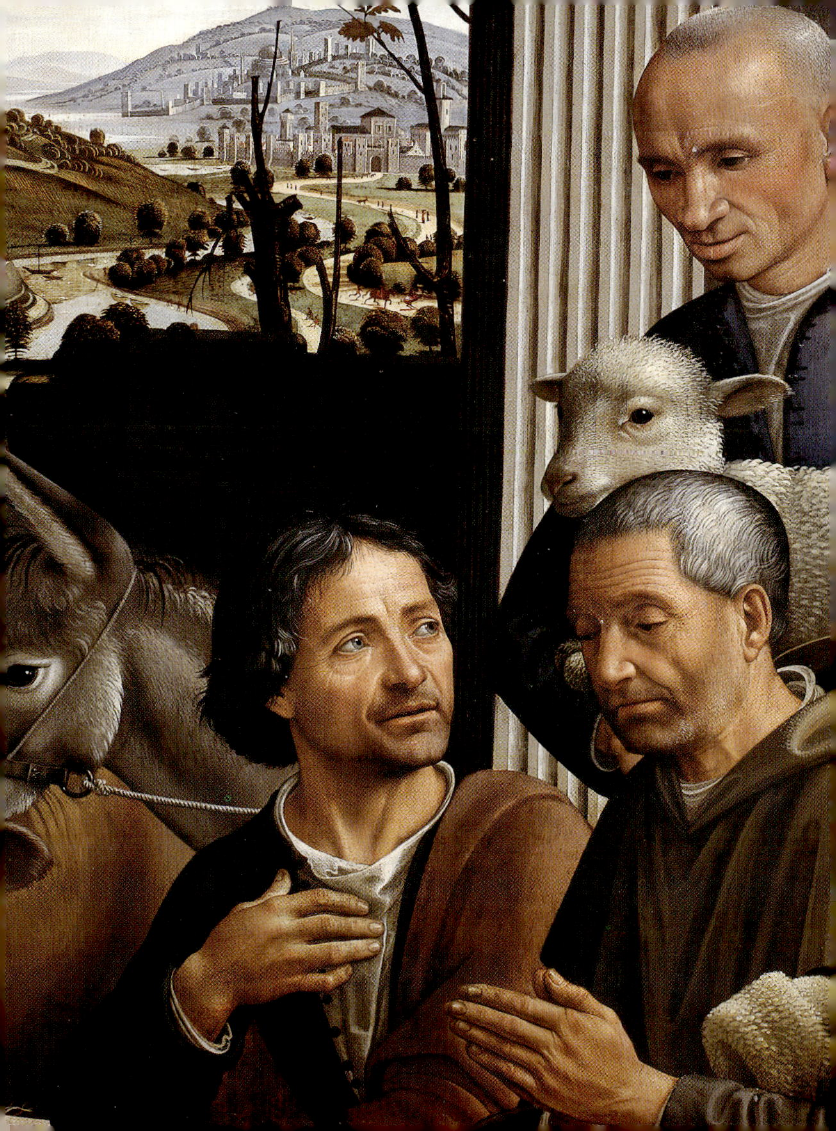

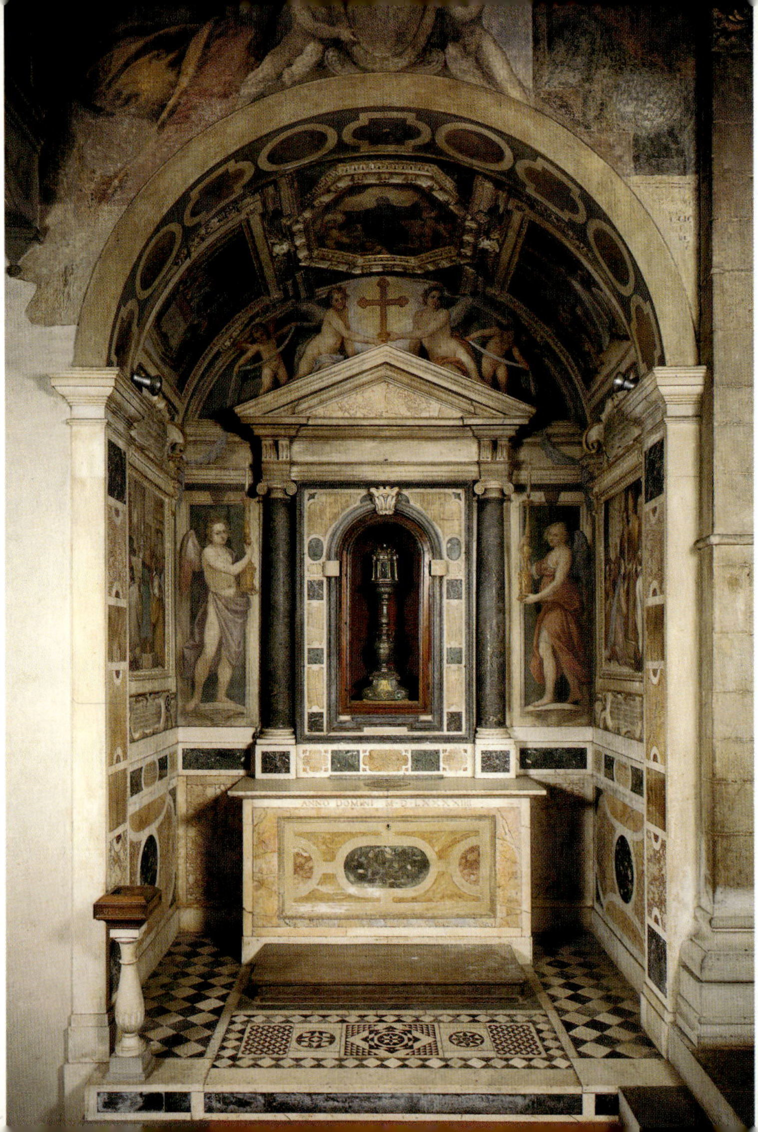
ANNO DOMINI M D LXXXXIII

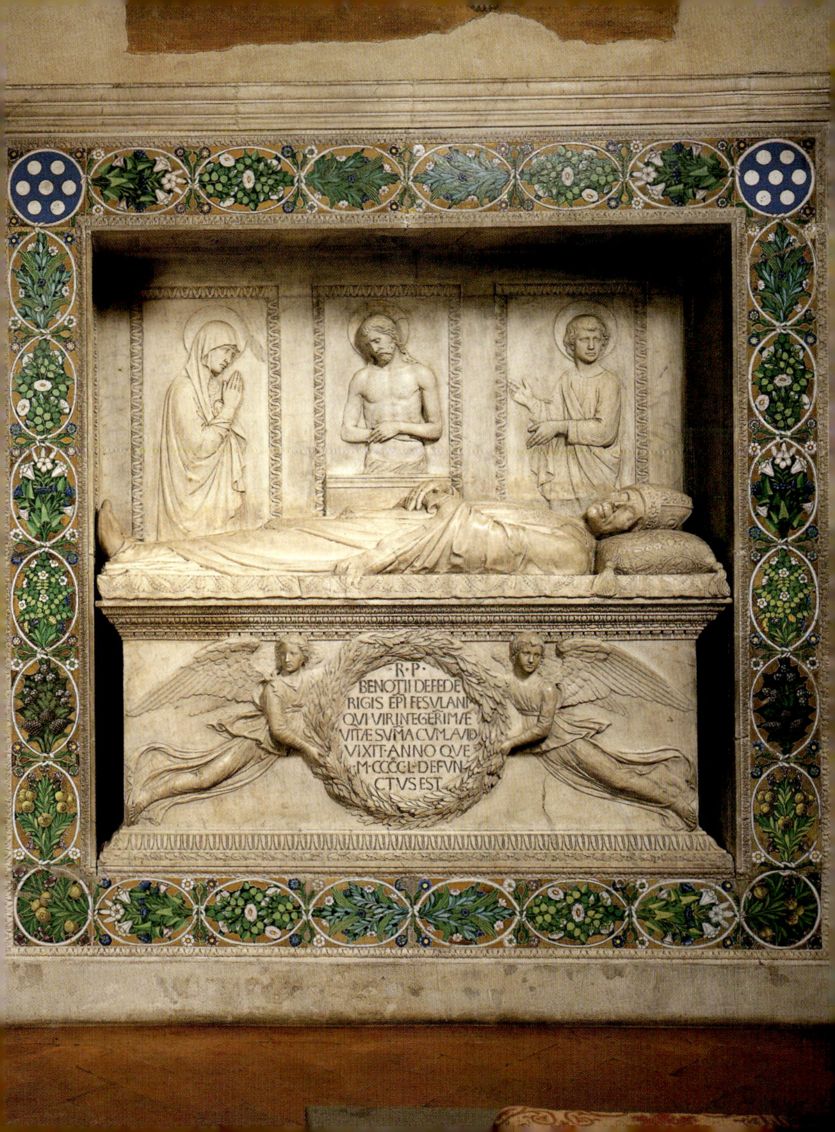
·R·P·
BENOTII DE FEDE
RIGIS EPI FESVLANI
QVI VIR INTEGERIMAE
VITAE SVMA CVM LAVD
VIXIT·ANNO QVE
M·CCCCL·DEFVN
CTVS EST

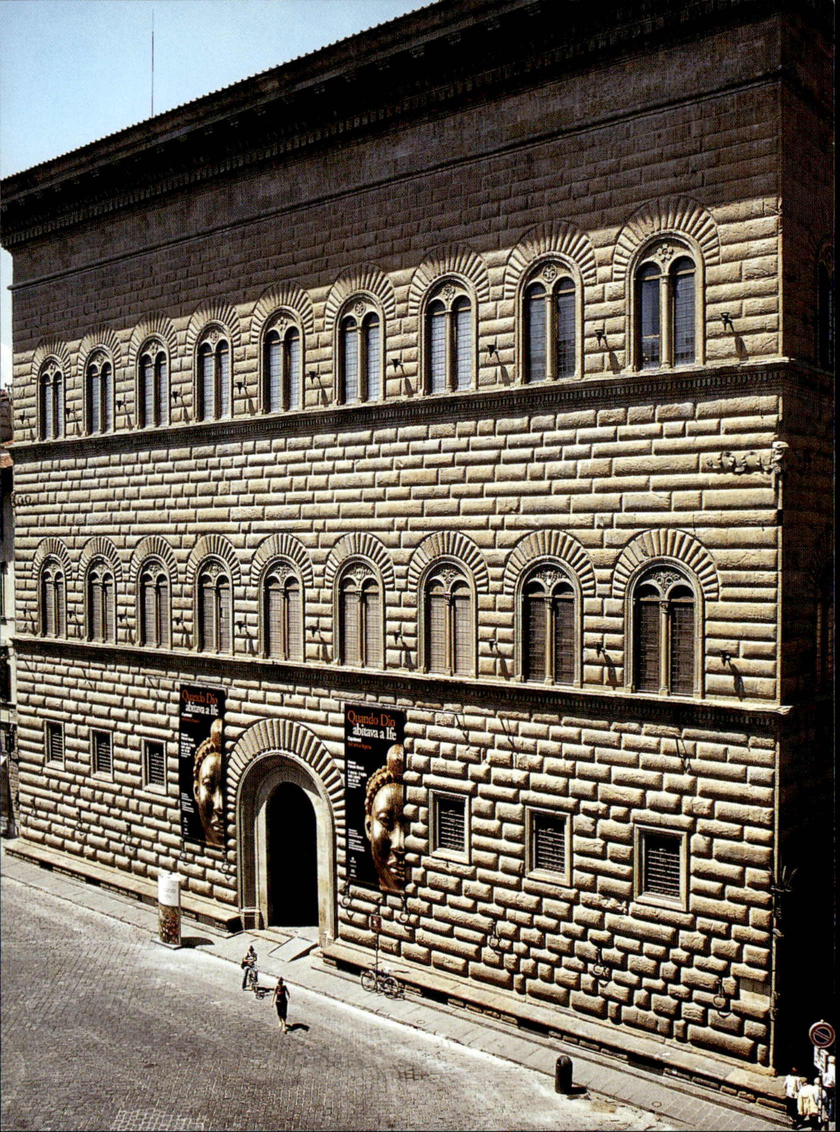
Quando Dio
abitava a Ife

Palazzo Strozzi

The Strozzi, one of the wealthiest families in Florence, began around 1489 to build their monumental residence at the heart of the city. In the original project designed with three façades, one on the square known as Piazza delle Cipolle (today's Piazza Strozzi) toward the Old Market, another, which remained unfinished, on today's Via Tornabuoni (then called Via Larga dei Legnaiuoli), and one to the north on today's Via Strozzi, the palace was begun at the time of Filippo di Matteo Strozzi. This was an exceptionally flourishing period for construction in the city, a time during which Florence was "remodeled" urbanistically, thanks especially to the buildings erected by the richest mercantile families. As Luca Landucci recalled in his diary, the urge to build was so strong that it led to a shortage of both labor and materials in the city. In the same year that the foundations of Palazzo Strozzi were laid, with a coin embedded in the walls for good luck, Lorenzo the Magnificent proposed to the Signoria that those who built new houses should be exempt from taxes for forty years. And while already to build Palazzo Medici, twenty houses had been torn down around Via Larga, to make space for the enormous Palazzo Strozzi

Opposite page:
Palazzo Strozzi, c. 1489-1537.

its owner had to commit himself for sixteen years, from 1473 to 1489, purchasing the houses of the Tornaquinci, the Popoleschi and the Rucellai that bordered on his land. The project for the building seems to have been commissioned of Benedetto da Maiano, who replicated, with larger and more elaborate dimensions, Michelozzo's model for Palazzo Medici, built thirty years earlier. The Florentine architect soon left for Naples however, and it seems that the construction site was then supervised, at various intervals, by Giuliano da Sangallo and later by Simone del Pollaiolo, known as Cronaca. In 1537 the palace, just finished after various modifications had been made in the original project (but already inhabited since 1504), was confiscated during one of the Strozzi family's many periods of exile, due to political discord with the Medici. As compared to the surviving wooden model (attributed to Benedetto da Maiano himself), the modifications made by Cronaca are apparent. Differing from the original project, the present-day building, higher and faced in rusticated stone (rough-hewn squared stones protruding from the wall) up to the second floor has now become a perfect cube.

The central inner courtyard is divided by columns, as was usual in Renaissance palaces. On the top floor is a loggia open on four sides. Today the palace houses several differ-

Opposite page:
Benedetto da Maiano (attr.), *Wooden model of Palazzo Strozzi*, details showing the façades on Piazza Strozzi and Via Strozzi, 1489.
Museo Nazionale del Bargello.

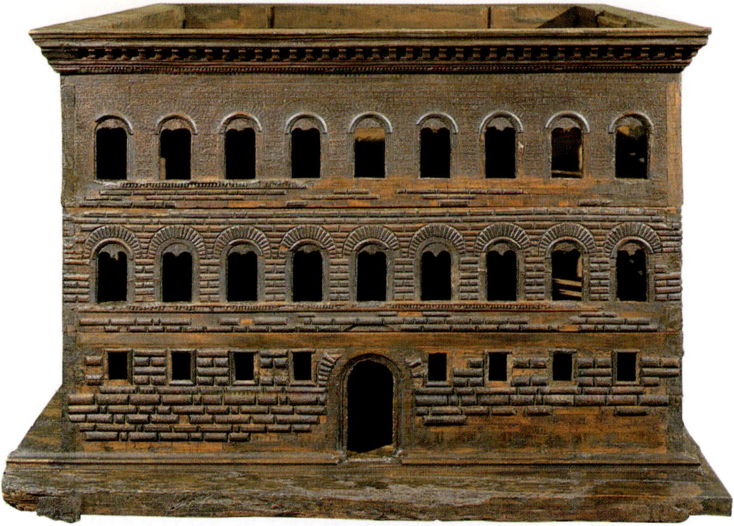

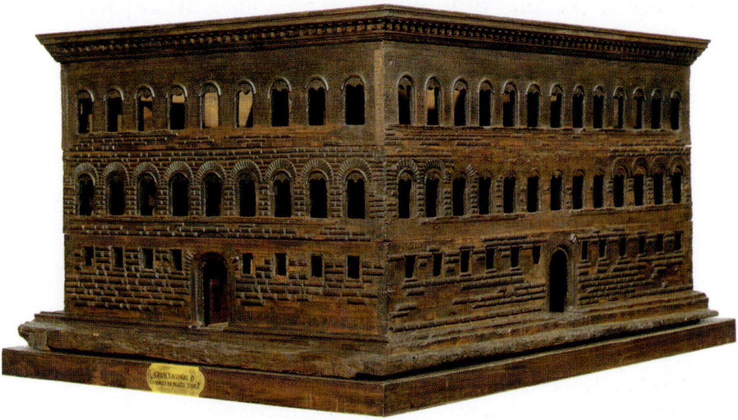

ent institutions, among them the Gabinetto Vieusseux, with its prestigious library, and the Istituto Italiano del Rinascimento. On the upper floor, important exhibitions are held.

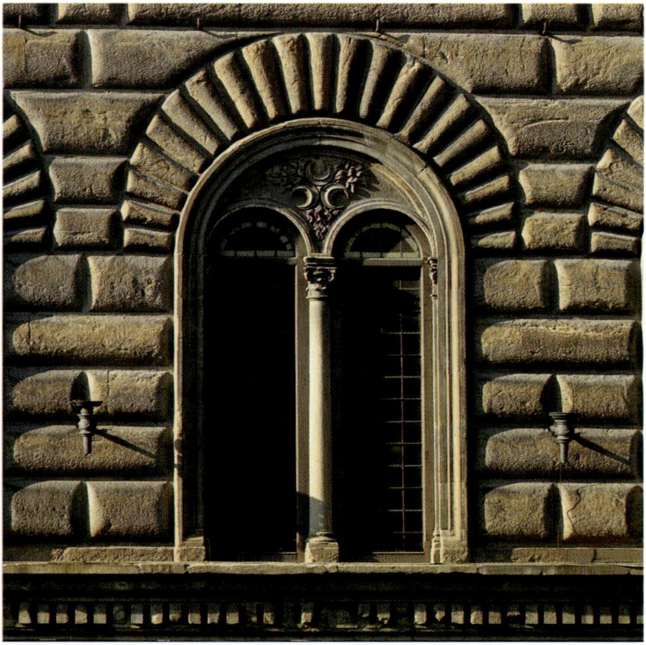

Above: A window in Palazzo Strozzi decorated with crescent moons, a family symbol.

Opposite page: The courtyard of Palazzo Strozzi.

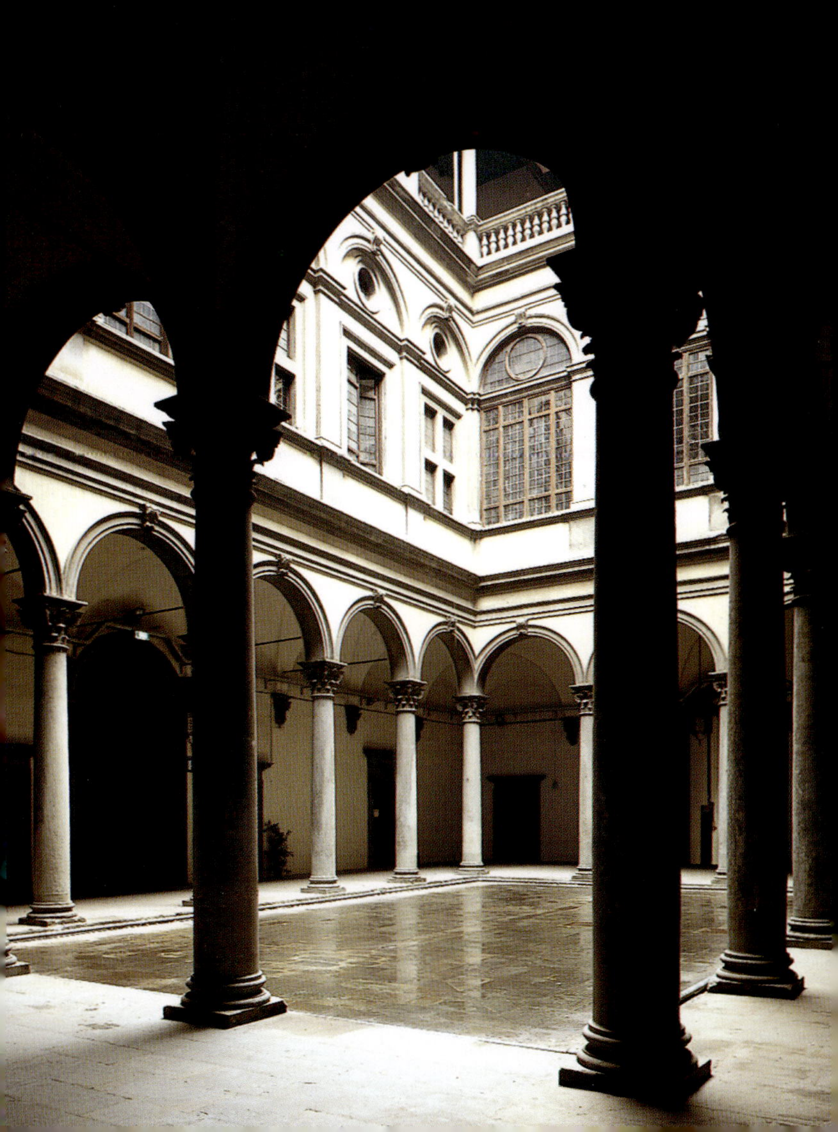

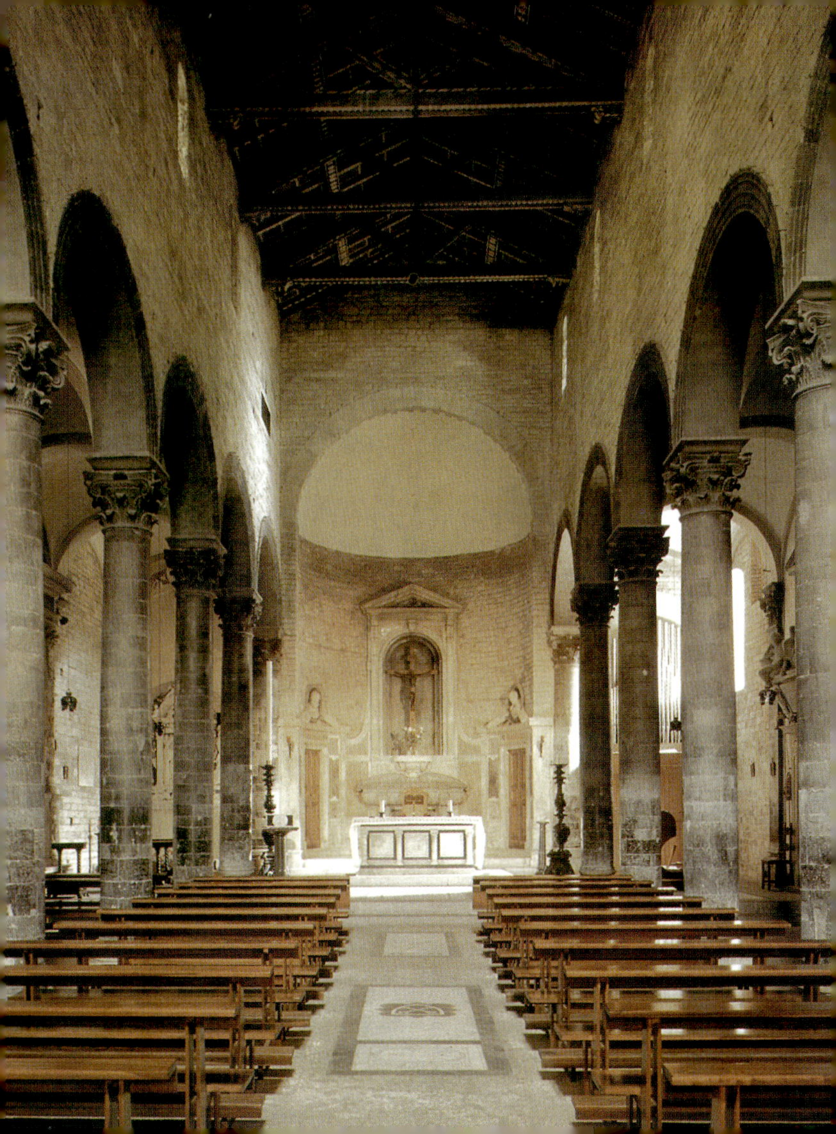

Santi Apostoli

This lovely, refined church hidden away near Borgo Santi Apostoli in the exquisite, secluded Piazza del Limbo, only a few steps from the river, dates from the late 11th century and was remodeled in the 15th-16th century. The name of the little square derives from the fact that, in medieval times, it was the site of a cemetery for babies who died before being baptized.
The simple stone facade of the church has a 16th century portal attributed to the sculptor Benedetto da Rovezzano, who also sculpted inside the building the Renaissance *Tomb of Oddo Altoviti* in marble (1507). The interior of the church is divided by columns made of green Prato marble, and the wooden ceiling still has its original polychrome decoration (13th-14th century). Outstanding among its works of art are the canvas representing *The Immaculate Conception* (1541) by Giorgio Vasari and the elaborate glazed terracotta tabernacle by Giovanni della Robbia. And it is here that there has been kept for centuries the refined *Portafuoco*, the flame-bearer made of copper and gilded silver still today used on Holy Saturday for the ceremony of the "Scoppio del Carro" in Piazza del Duomo.

Opposite page:
Interior of the Santi Apostoli Church.

Following pages:
Benedetto da Rovezzano, *Tomb of Oddo Altoviti*, 1507, marble. Santi Apostoli Church.

Portafuoco of Holy Saturday, 15th century, silver and gilded copper. Santi Apostoli Church.

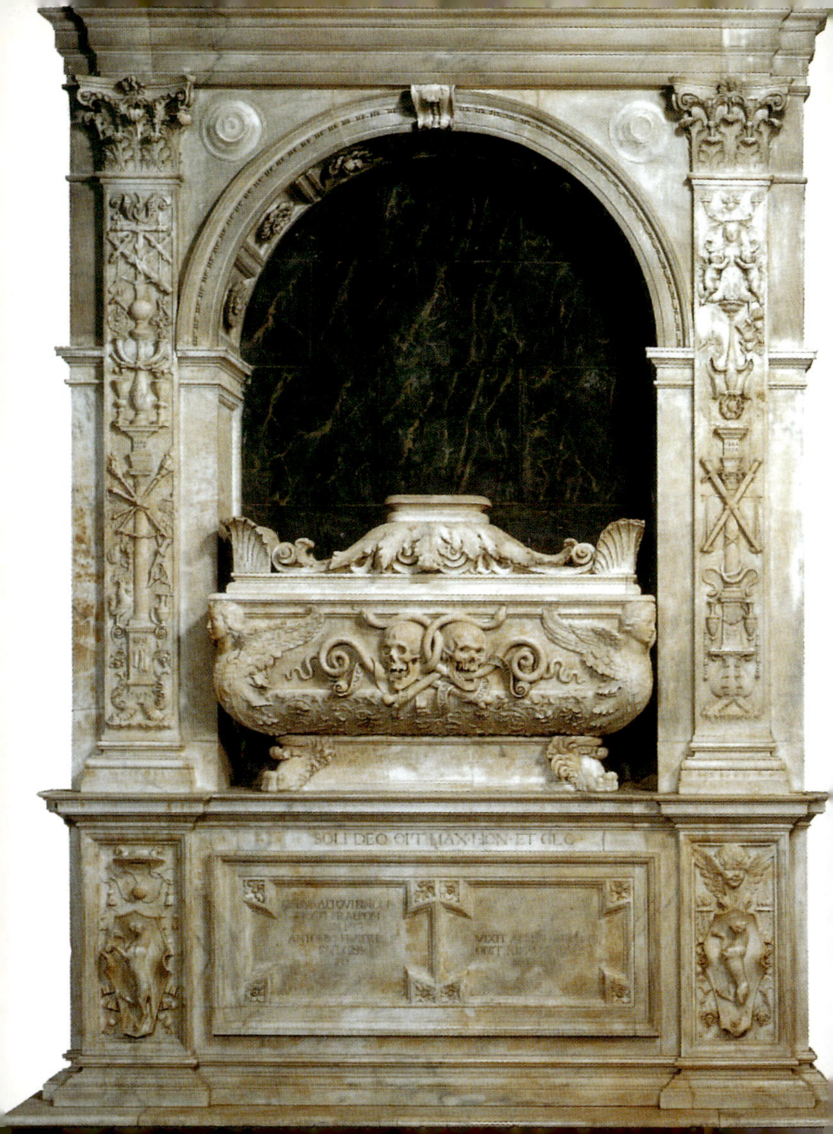
SOLI DEO OPT MAX HON ET GLO

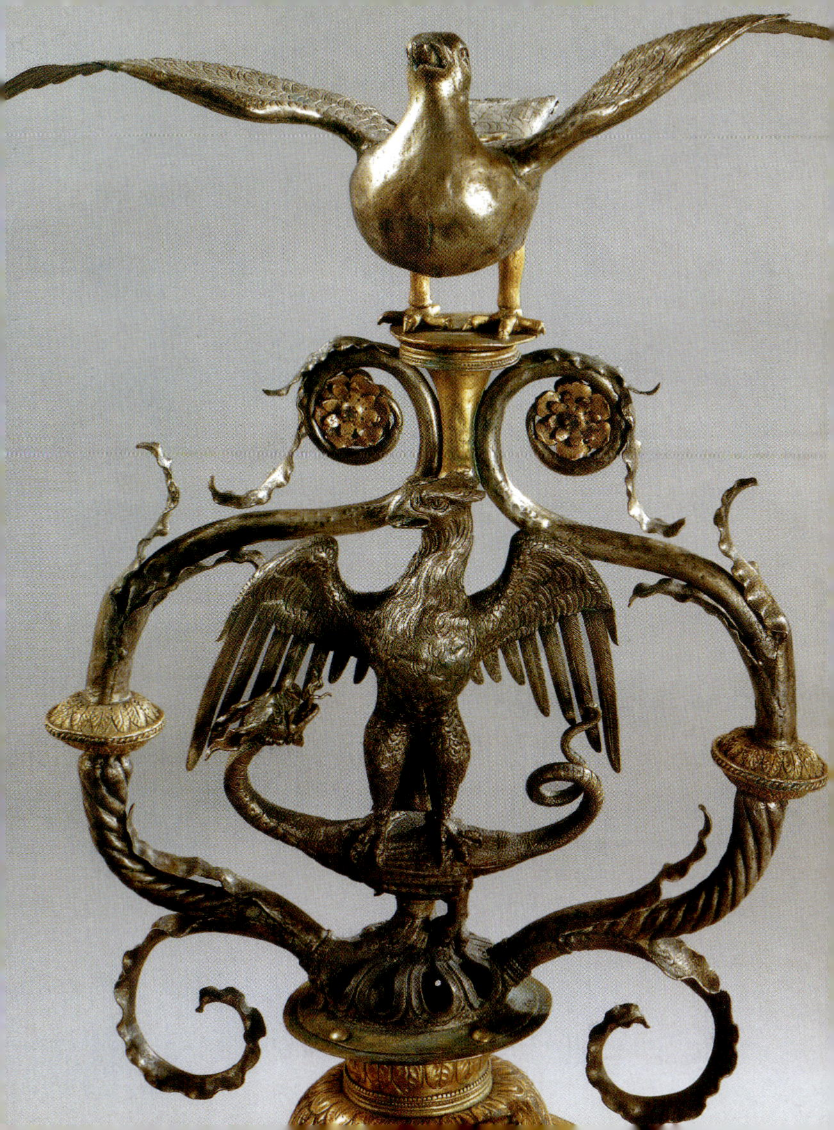

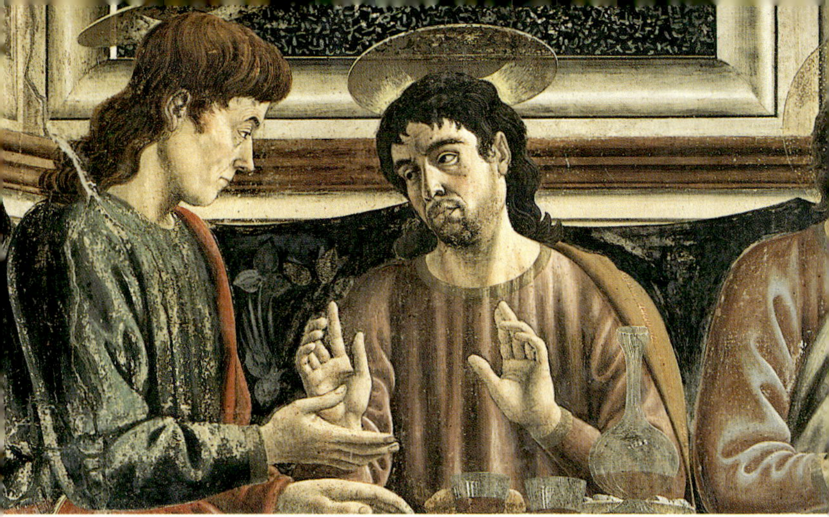

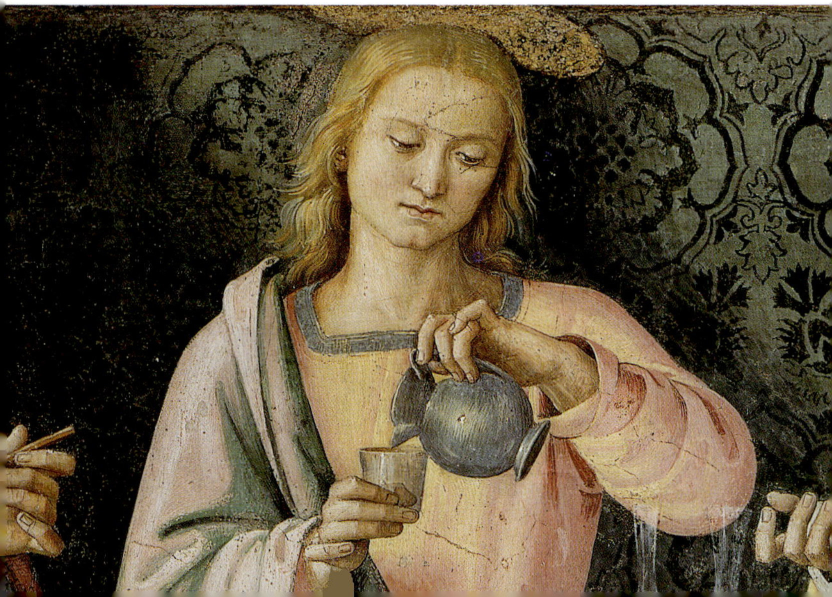

The "Cenacoli"

Hidden away in places that are some of the quietest, most reserved and perhaps least known and least visited in Florence, although of great historic and artistic importance, the Last Suppers are an invitation to a more tranquil visit than the *tour de force* of the traditional itineraries through churches and museums. In the spiritual customs of the monasteries, dining too was a ritual and it is for this reason that the refectory, the place where the monks or nuns took their meals, called for a special atmosphere of meditation. Accordingly, these airy halls were frescoed on one of the long walls, usually with a representation of the Last Supper (in Italian, "Cenacolo") or with scenes of dining in some way alluding to the truth of faith. In addition to the Last Suppers of Ognissanti and of San Marco (frescoed by Ghirlandaio) and to the one in Santa Croce (by Taddeo Gaddi), illustrated here on the relevant pages, are those frescoed, from the 15th to the 17th century, by Andrea del Castagno (in Sant'Apollonia), Perugino (Cenacolo di Fuligno), Franciabigio (della Calza), Andrea del Sarto (San Salvi), and Giovan Battista Vanni (at the Carmine).

Opposite page:
Andrea del Castagno, *Last Supper*, detail, 1450, fresco. Museo del Cenacolo di Sant'Apollonia.

Pietro Perugino, *Last Supper*, detail (*this page*), and whole (*following pages*), c. 1485-1490, fresco. Cenacolo delle Contesse di Sant'Onofrio, or "di Fuligno".

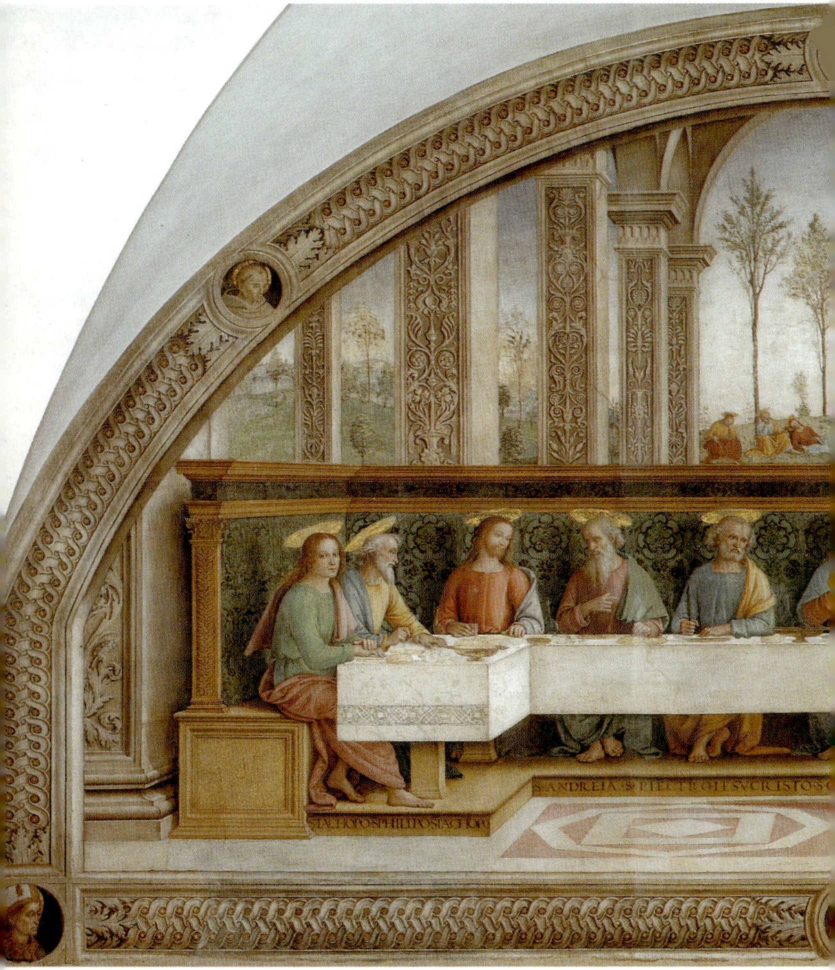

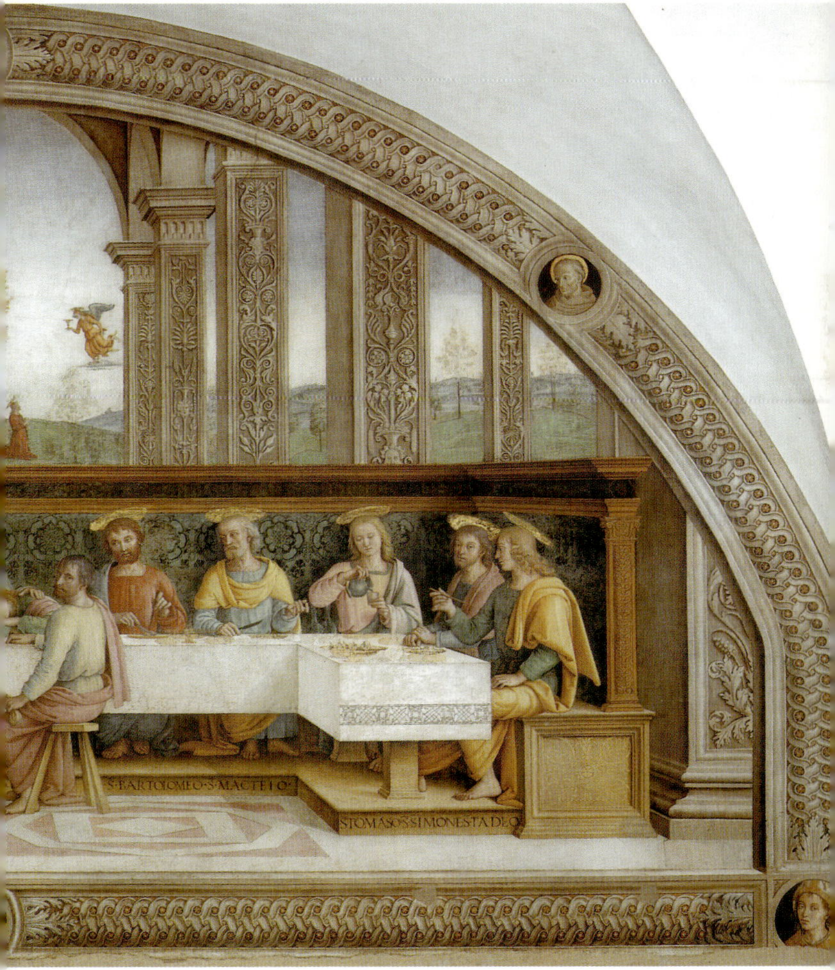
S·BARTOLOMEO·S·MACTEIO·
S·TOMASO·S·SIMONE·S·TADEO

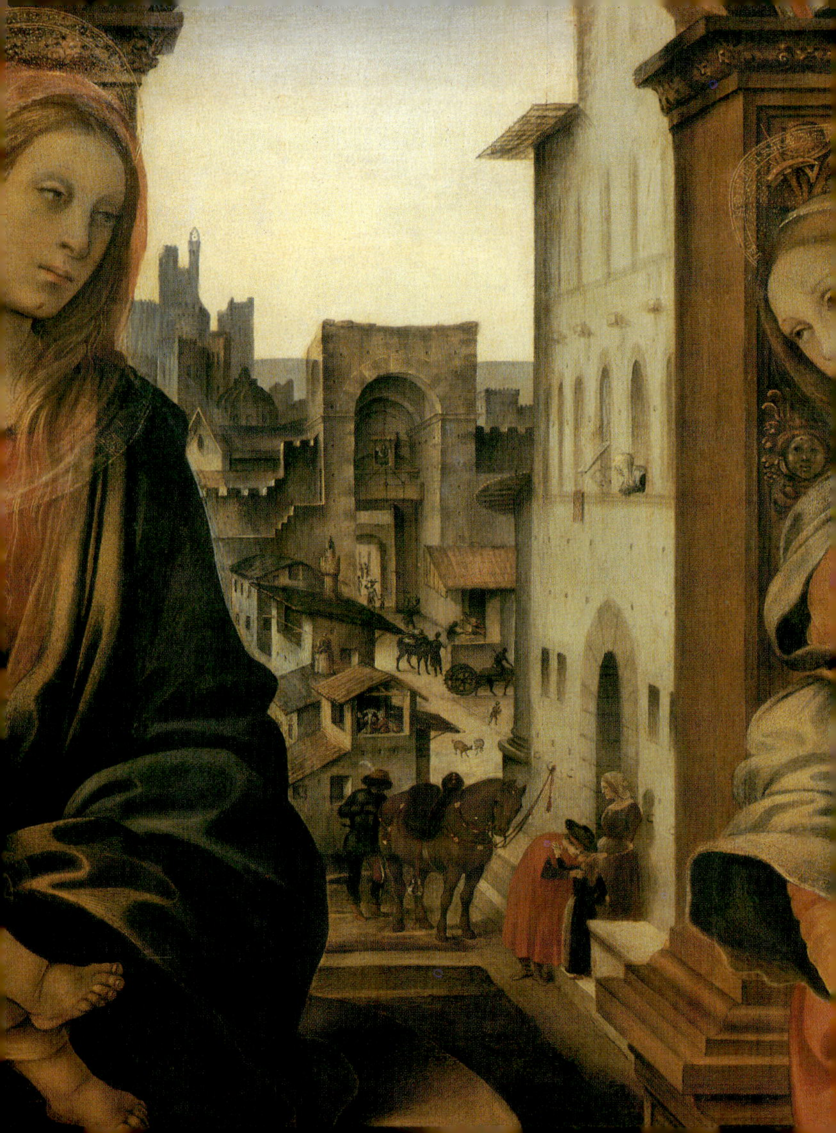

OLTRARNO

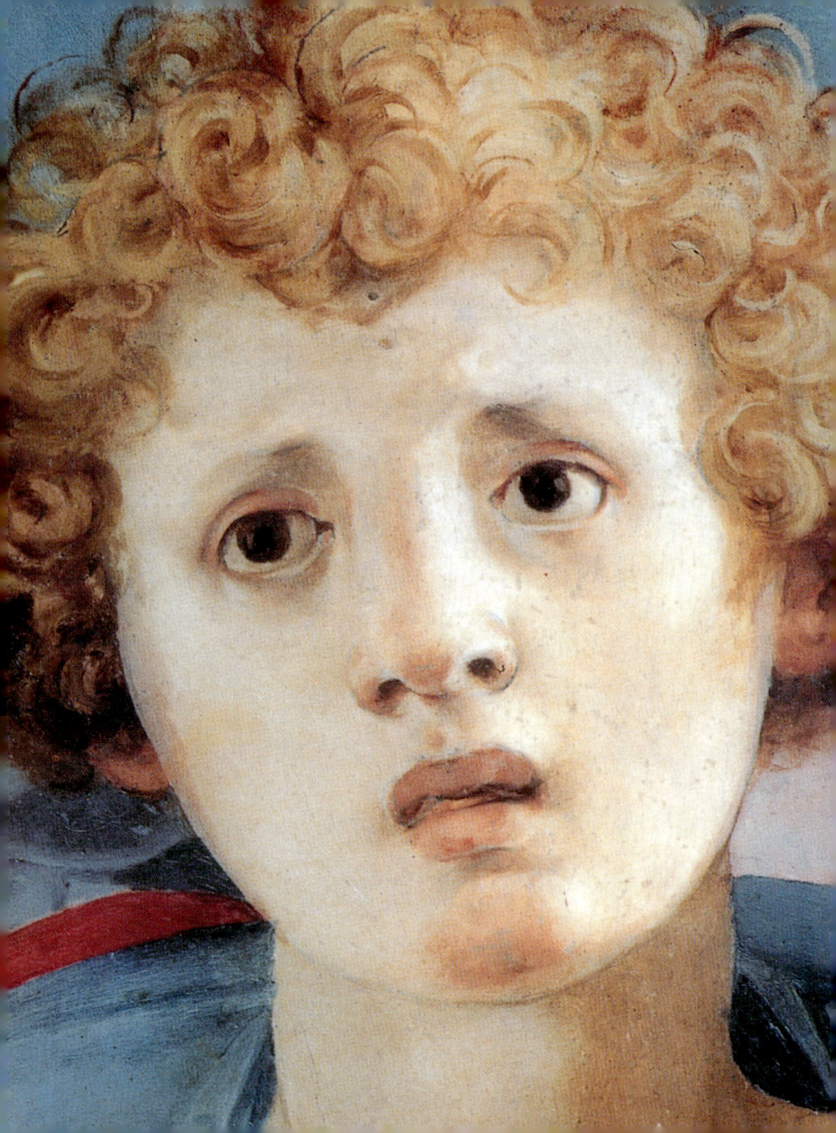

SANTA FELICITA

Just across the Old Bridge, in a little square opening off Via Guicciardini, the church of Santa Felicita marked the boundary, in the Middle Ages, of the "borgo" of Piazza, which extended as far as the church of San Felice in Piazza, at the San Pier Gattolini Gate. The church, one of the oldest in Florence, was included in 1565 in the overhead passage created by Giorgio Vasari to connect Palazzo Vecchio and the Galleria degli Uffizi to Palazzo Pitti. On a platform still visible on the inner facade, the Grand Dukes and court dignitaries who were traversing the Vasari Corridor could, without being seen, look out from above into the church (chosen as their parish church in the 18th century). Hidden away in this secluded church are some of the greatest masterpieces of Florentine art: the Barbadori Chapel, designed by Brunelleschi around 1420, on the walls of which, a century later, between 1525 and 1527, Pontormo left a stupendous series of frescoes in gelid colors, as accompaniment to his equally innovative altarpiece representing the *Deposition*. For three years the eccentric artist kept the chapel closed, allowing no one, not even its new owner Ludovico Capponi, to see it.

Opposite and following pages: Pontormo, *Deposition*, detail of an angel and whole (page 538), c. 1527, oil on wood. Santa Felicita, Capponi (formerly Barbadori) Chapel.
The Chapel designed by Brunelleschi for the Barbadori family and decoraded by Pontormo for the Capponi family.

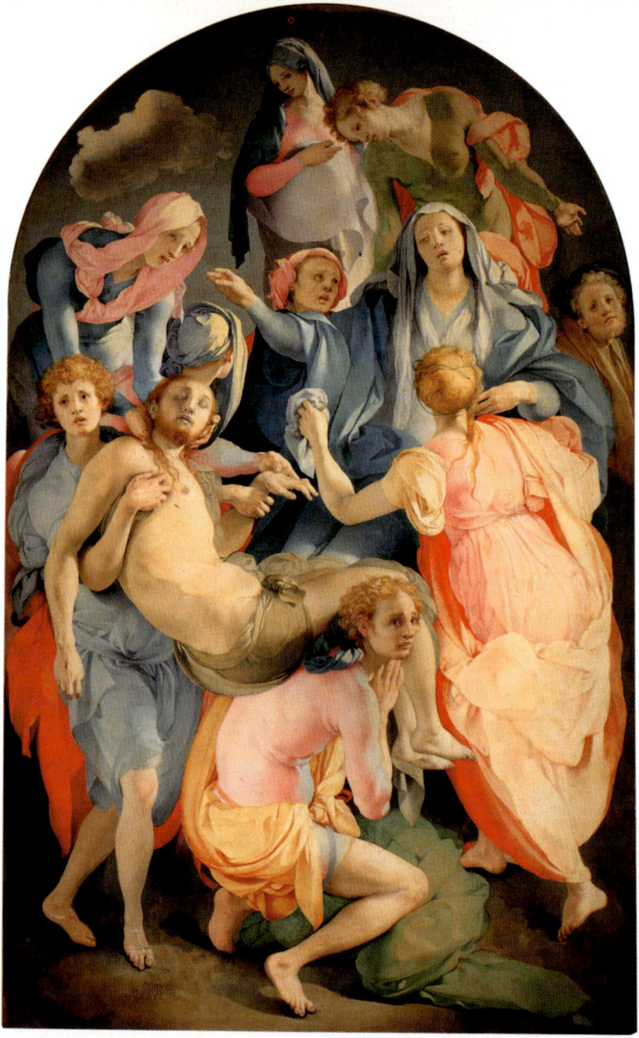

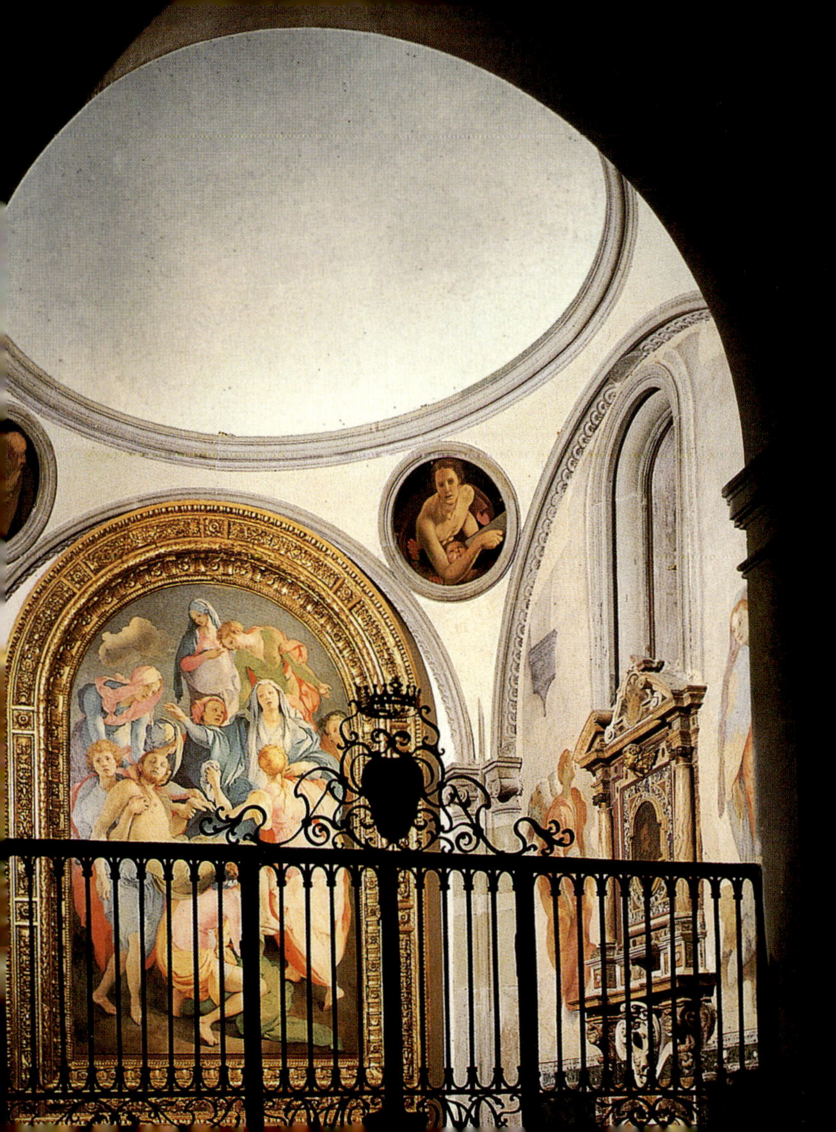

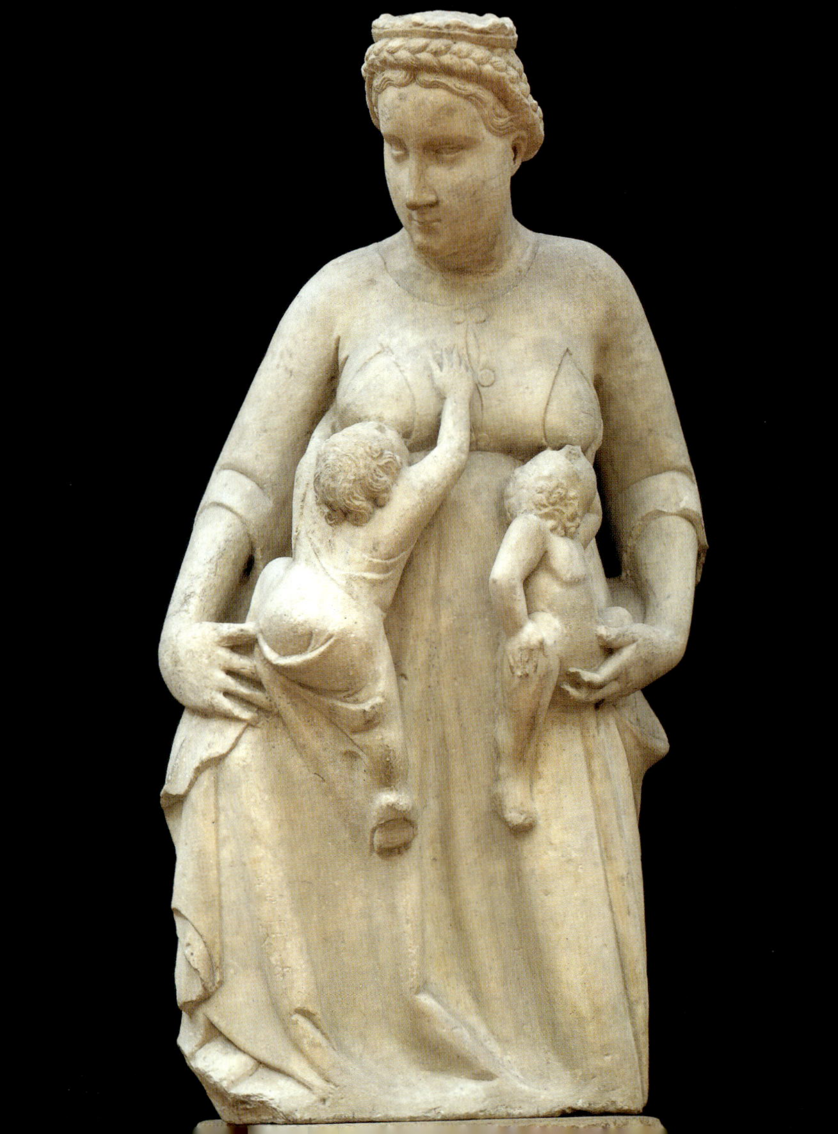

MUSEO BARDINI

In the zone of San Niccolò Oltrarno, in Piazza de' Mozzi, the Bardini Museum, donated to the City of Florence by Stefano Bardini in 1922, is a typical example of the intense activity of collecting and dealing in antiques for which Florence became, over the course of the 19th century, an international center. The 19th century palace was built for the antiquarian, collector, and connoisseur Stefano Bardini (1836-1923) to house his immense collection of works of art, furniture, classical marble statues, tapestries, arms, porcelain, chimneys, leather objects, musical instruments, carpets, and furnishings of every kind from antiquity to the Baroque age. In building the edifice in 1883, after demolishing the little church of San Gregorio della Pace (founded in 1273 in memory of Gregory X and the brief truce between Guelphs and Ghibellines) materials of various provenance were used, including the remains of the altars from San Lorenzo a Pistoia to frame the windows on the first floor of the façade and for the monumental staircase and the 16th century ceilings inside. The Museum's many works of art include the *Charity* by Tino di Camaino, the *Pavis with the Blessed Bonamici* attributed to Taddeo di Bartolo, the *Virgin of the Rope-makers* by Donatello and the *Archangel St. Michael* by Antonio del Pollaiolo.

Opposite page:
Tino di Camaino, *Charity*,
c. 1321-1323. Bardini Museum.

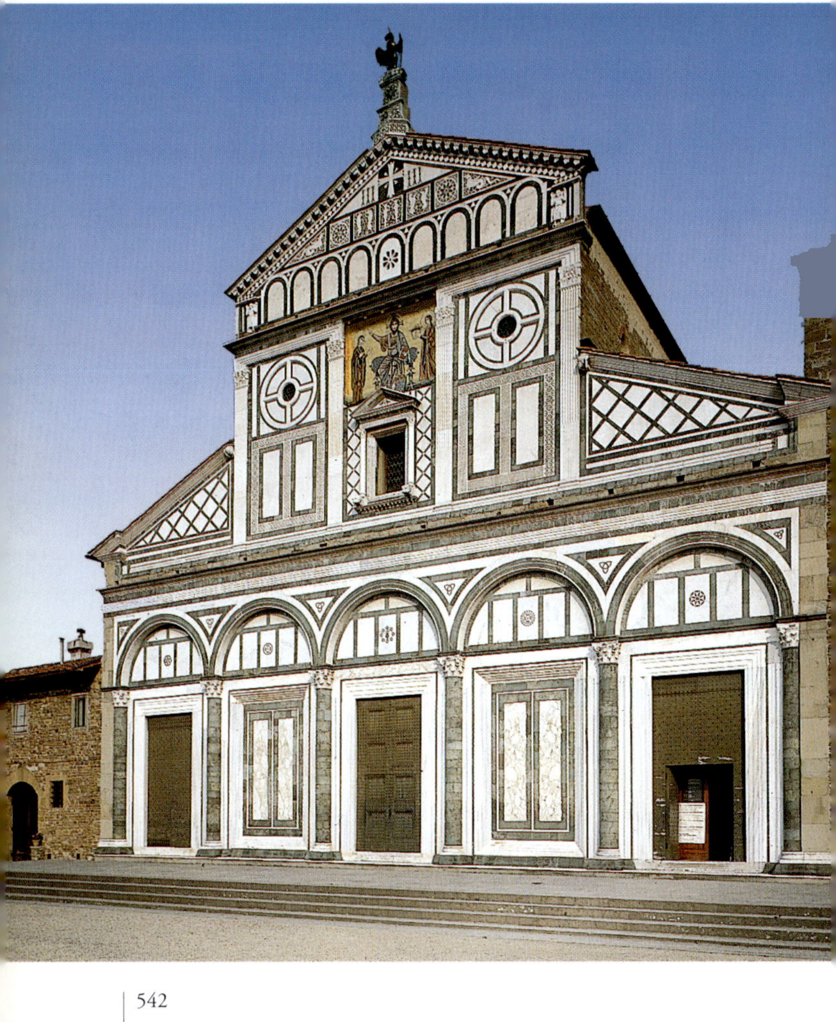

San Miniato al Monte

Among all the churches of Florence, San Miniato al Monte occupies a unique position, overlooking the city from its high hill. Its facade, with its abstract geometric motifs, does not perhaps communicate the maternal warmth of Brunelleschi's dome, which although soaring to the sky, as it was described by Leon Battista Alberti, is nonetheless placed at the center of the city, as if to keep watch over the tangled skein of streets and people. Seen by night, from the opposite hill of San Domenico, San Miniato seems almost an apparition; with that façade so perfect, that marble gleaming like a mirror, it stands against the sky like a prodigious quasi-celestial vision; a message that, although barely heeded today, must have been strikingly effective in the Middle Ages. Its anonymous builders were well aware of this, when in the 12th and 13th centuries they designed the geometric patterns that evoke silence and pauses, the musical rhythms of the heavenly spheres that were later to enthrall such an architect as Leon Battista Alberti who, inspired by this church, re-created something similar on the upper part of the façade of Santa Maria Novella and the walls of the Tempietto of the Holy Sepulchre in the Rucellai Chapel.

Opposite page:
The façade of San Miniato al Monte, faced in inlaid white and green marble, is surmounted by an eagle made of gilded copper, the emblem of the Arte di Calimala which protected the basilica. In the middle register, above the tympanum over the window, is a mosaic representing *Christ Enthroned* (13th century).

HISTORY

Protected in the Middle Ages by the Arte di Calimala, the Romanesque church is dedicated to the martyr saint who in the year 250, under Emperor Decius, was allegedly beheaded near where the stream called Affrico flowed into the Arno. Legend has it that Miniato picked up his head and, accompanied by a host of angels, walked up to the top of the *Mons florentinus*, on the other side of the river, just above today's church of San Salvatore and Piazzale Michelangelo. Here there rose the first oratory dedicated to him, which was renovated in the 11th century by Bishop Hildebrand, thanks to the support of Henry II of Saxony and his wife Cunegonda, with a church built over the course of many years. The interior of the church, divided by three naves, with a ceiling of wooden trusses (painted however in the 19th century), has a raised presbitery and a wealth of marble decoration. The columns, the mosaics in the apse, the signs of the Zodiac inlaid in the 13th century floor, are correlated with one another by a network of symbolic meanings related to the light entering through the windows. According to a precise astrological program, the sun lights up the Zodiac in the mosaic floor. It touches on the columns, gilds and warms the marble and, near the end of

Opposite page:
Anonymous sculptor, *Marble lion cub with eyes encrusted in lapis lazuli*, detail of the pulpit on the balustrade of the presbitery, early 13th century. San Miniato al Monte.

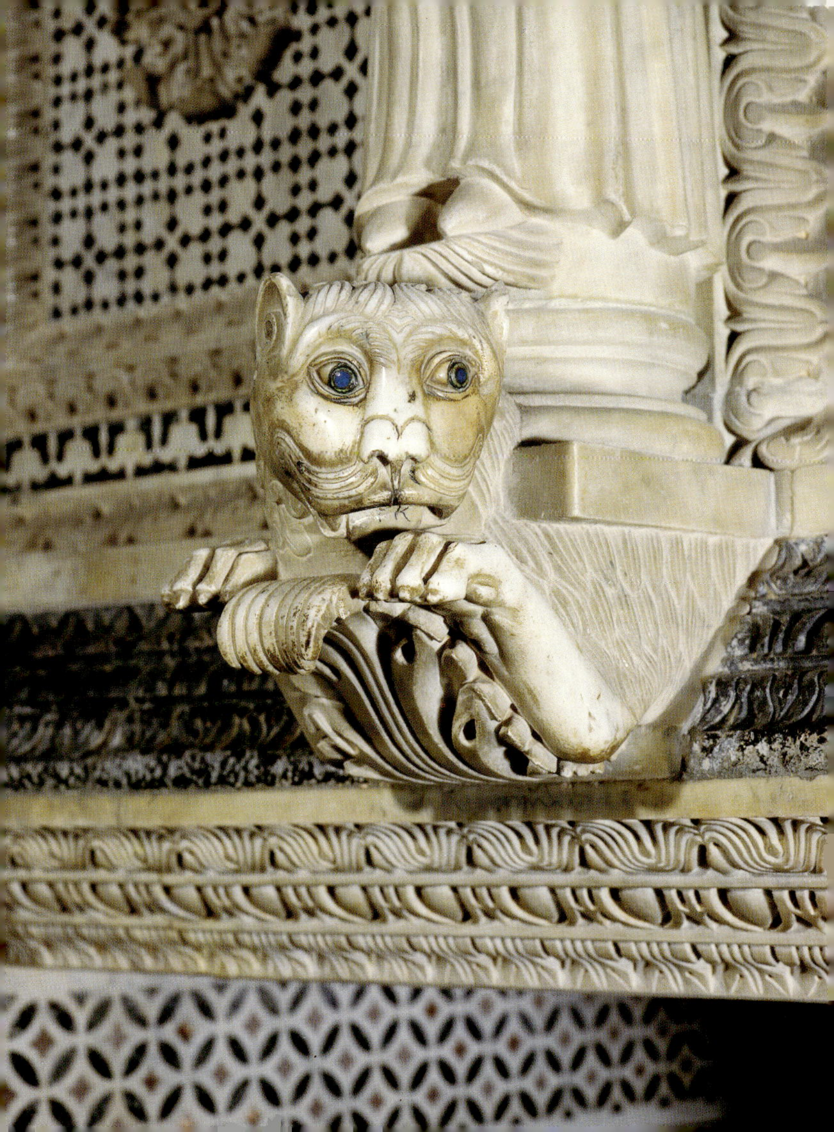

September, on only one day in the year, toward sunset it strikes the left foot of Christ, portrayed in the mosaics decorating the apse. The light comes from the easternmost window in the nave. First the sun casts its glimmer over the entire mosaic, then as it slowly sets, it pauses on Christ's foot. The illuminated point is reflected onto the mosaic, and that ball of fire becomes the symbol of the world, of the universe that lies under the foot of its Creator. Other churches, down in the city, also offer spectacles of this kind, specially studied, particularly in Medieval and Renaissance times. In Santa Maria Novella, for example, a beam of light strikes the top of the next-to-the-last pillar in the left nave, on the relief sculpture of *The Annunciation to the Virgin* in Buggiano's pulpit (1448), and this happens on March 25th, the day of the Annunciation and the last day of the year according to the Florentine calendar.

In the 14th century too, the church of San Miniato al Monte was enriched with works of art and cycles of frescoes, such as the one by Spinello Aretino in the sacristy, which represents *Stories of St. Benedict* (1387). It should be recalled, as was reported at the time by the "novelliere" Franco Sassetti, that it was here, around the middle of the century, that artists such as Orcagna and Taddeo Gaddi used to meet after dinner, to discuss who had been the greatest painter of the period just elapsed, prior to the disaster of the Black Plague of 1348 that had reaped so many lives and had brought the development of art to an abrupt halt.

During the course of the 15th century the church was enriched by other importants works, partially changing its lay-

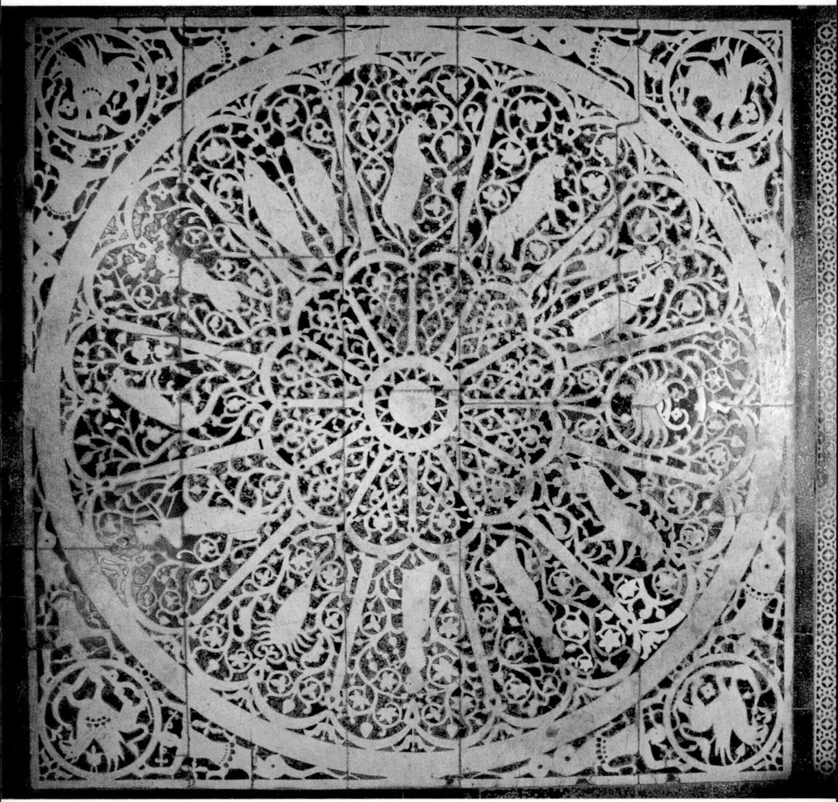

Above:
Marble inlaid floor with signs of the Zodiac,
13th century. San Miniato al Monte, central nave.

Following pages:
Christ Pantocrator with the Virgin and St. Miniato, 1297, mosaic. San Miniato al Monte, apsidal conque.

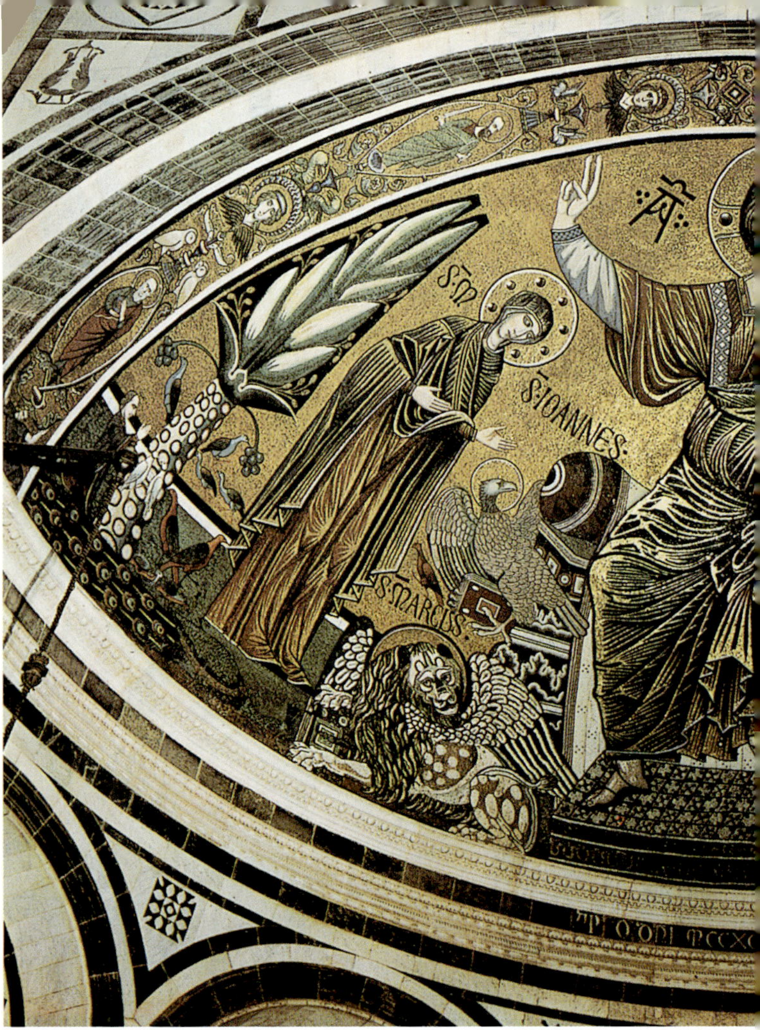
S·IOANNES·
S·MARCUS·

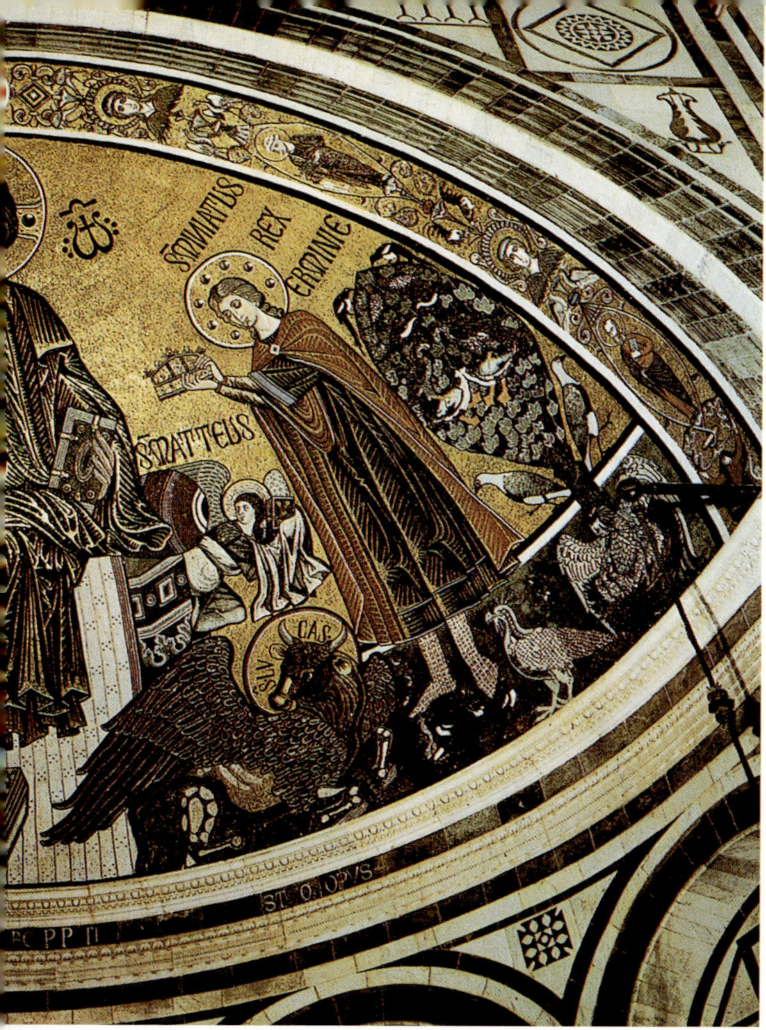
SMINIATUS
REX
ERMINIE
SMATTEUS
CAS.
SLV
ST. O. OPVS
EC PP II

out. In the 1447 the Arte di Calimala had allowed Piero de' Medici, at his request, to have a marble tabernacle built, designed, like the one in Santissima Annunziata, by Michelozzo. The tabernacle, with barrel vault decorated with glazed terracotta coffers by Luca della Robbia, faced on the outside with polychrome scales, also in glazed terracotta, is also known as the "Chapel of the Crucifix", since it was destined to house the *Crucifix of St. Giovanni Gualberto*, an image thought to have miraculous powers. The Arte di Calimala had agreed to the insertion of this tablernacle, which breaks the rhythm of the nave and confuses the plan of the medieval building, on condition that only the emblems of the guild would appear on it. But a year later it allowed Piero, the "great citizen", who had ordered the tempietto erected with "magnificence and vast expense", to add to it his own symbols, the diamond with three feathers. Around 1461 the Cardinal of Portugal's Chapel was built, dedicated to Jacopo di Lusitania, a cardinal from Lisbon who died in Florence in 1459. It was designed by Antonio Manetti and decorated with the collaboration of the greatest artists of the day.

Opposite page: The Cardinal of Portugal's Chapel, on the left nave of San Miniato al Monte. The altarpiece (c. 1466) by Antonio and Piero del Pollaiolo is a copy of the original, now in the Uffizi. Alesso Baldovinetti collaborated on the fresco above it. The marble funerary monument (1461) is by Antonio Rossellino.

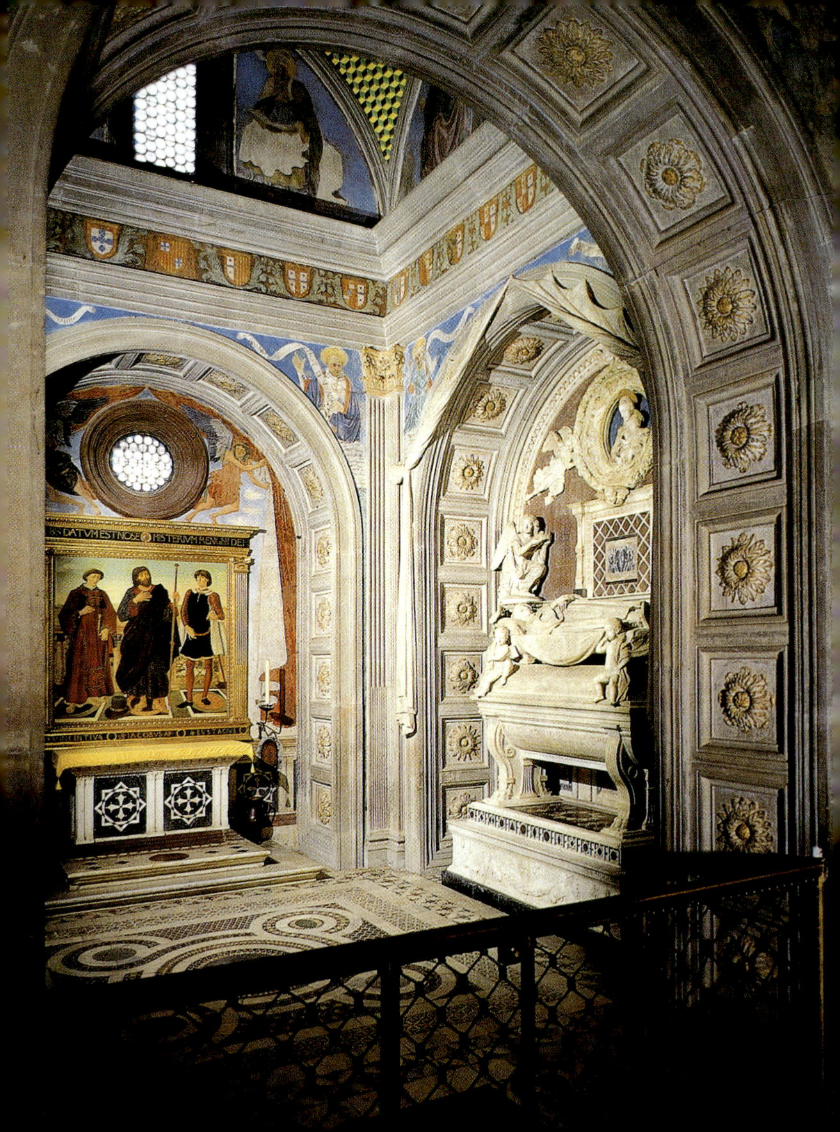
DATVM EST NOSE HISTERIVM REGNI DEI

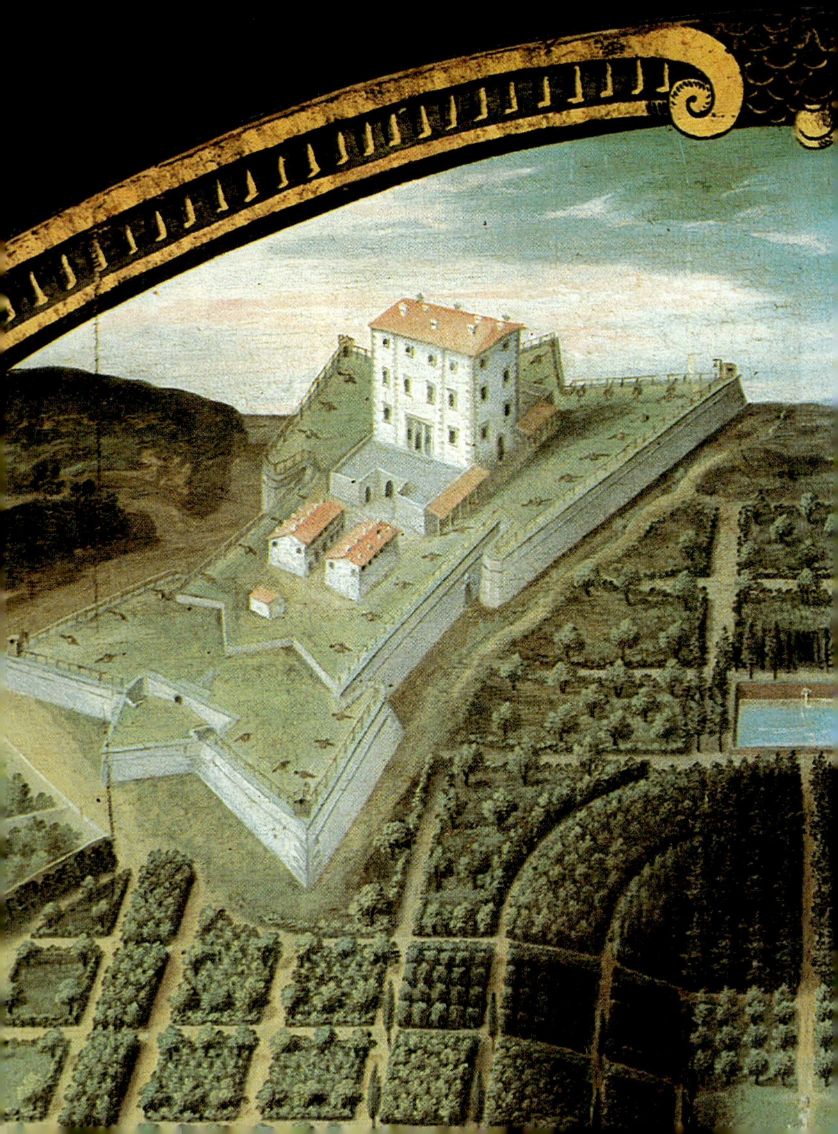

FORTE BELVEDERE

Near the end of the 16th century, on the top of the hill of San Giorgio, a new fortress was erected by order of Ferdinando I de' Medici. Consecrated to St. George, but already known as "Forte Belvedere", it was built several decades after the one that had already been constructed down in the city: the Forte di San Giovanni, later called "Fortezza da Basso" (lower fort) to distinguish it from the one on the hill. While Fortezza da Basso, a real fortified citadel, had been designed in the 1530s by Antonio da Sangallo, Forte Belvedere was, in all probability, designed by Bernardo Buontalenti, an eclectic artist who had also met with success as architect and military engineer to the Grand Duchy. The "new wall and marvelous fortress" as Agostino Lapini called it in his diary in 1590, seems to have been designed in accordance with some ideas of Prince Giovanni, brother of Ferdinando I and expert in the arts of war. Its function was mainly that of surveying the city rather than defending it against attack, an event which had become improbable, since the Medici now dominated a great part of Tuscany. The Medici family's strong-box was also kept here, hidden in an underground gallery fitted with ingenious trapdoors. The fortress is built to a star-shaped plan with four main bastions; the two overlooking the city flank a fifth buttress, called the "Diamantina". At present the Fort is used for art exhibitions and as a scenic spot from which to admire the city.

Above:
Forte Belvedere, in a view of the western bastions looking toward the building, now used for temporary exhibitions.

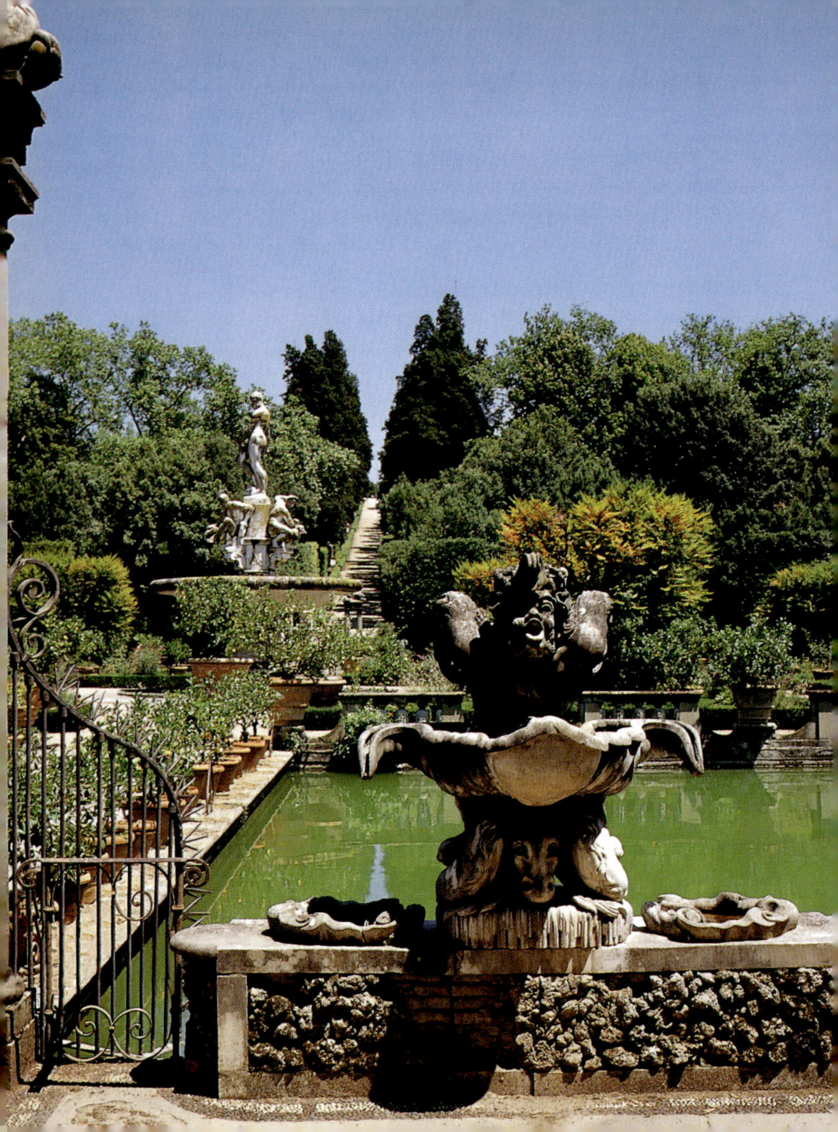

BOBOLI GARDENS

The immense Boboli Gardens, stretched out on the hill of Oltrarno between Forte Belvedere and Porta Romana, behind Palazzo Pitti, the only vast green area in Florence, is a sort of microcosm enclosing in itself the essential elements of Florentine urban development; it seems, in short, to be a "stylized version" of the urban image of Florence that has slowly grown up over the centuries.

Its origins date from the time when Palazzo Pitti was purchased by Eleonora di Toledo in 1549. Under the direction of Tribolo and later of Ammannati, the garden began to be laid out almost at once, on the Boboli hill behind the enormous edifice that had belonged to the Pitti family. No less than four generations of architects were to be engaged in carrying out the systematic, integrated project for the Boboli park, which was to become a little city within the city, reflecting the ample spaces occupied by gardens typical of country residences, filled with lawns, grottoes, woods, mazes, garden theaters, gazebos and summerhouses, numerous sculptures, fountains and lemon-houses. Bernardo Buontalenti worked on the first stage of laying out the gardens. In the first "chamber" of the big grotto, whose walls were decorated by Bernardino

Opposite page:
The garden on the Island
in the Boboli Gardens.

Poccetti with fascinating illusionist effects, Buontalenti invented for Francesco I, around 1583, a great glass ball on the ceiling, filled with water, in which swam fish of various kinds. It was an astounding overhead acquarium, which from above endlessly transformed the rays of light that filtered through the transparent glass. His vocation for the "capriccio", typically Mannerist, and his inventive genius had allowed Buontalenti to create still another masterpiece, dense in symbolic allusions. Within the context of this grotto, even Michelangelo's *Slaves* (now in the Galleria dell'Accademia) appeared to symbolize the forces of nature, in a metamorphic atmosphere of ambiguity suspended between reality and magic. In addition to Buontalenti's Grotto, recently restored, which also contains, in the intimate setting of the "third chamber", the *Venus emerging from her Bath* (1573) by Giambologna, Boboli boasts a 17th century amphitheater, remodeled at a later time, and a great number of statues and fountains, among them the *Fountain of the Ocean* (c. 1576) by Giambologna, with a Perseus emerging from the water on his horse, at the center of the *Fountain on the Islet* by Alfonso Parigi, as well as the *Fountain of the Monkeys* (late 16th century), attributed to Pietro Tacca.

Opposite page:
The innermost chamber
of the Large Grotto in Boboli,
with the *Venus* by Giambologna.

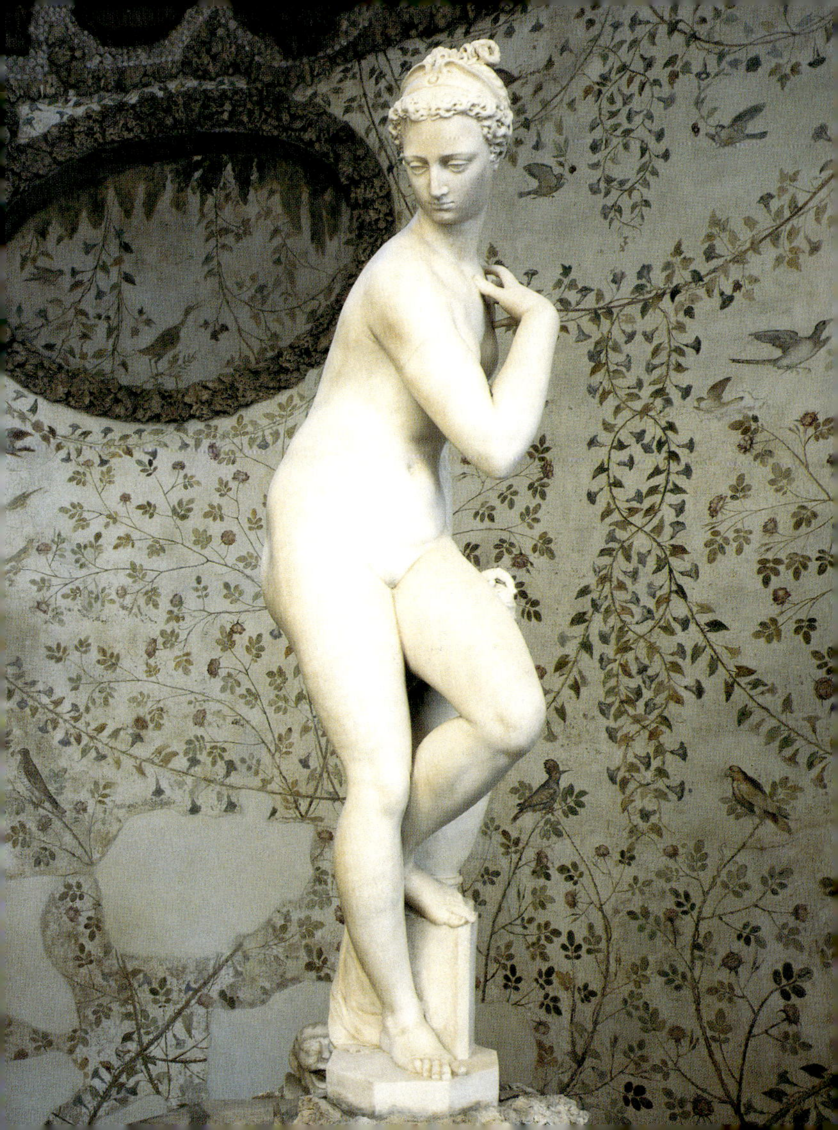

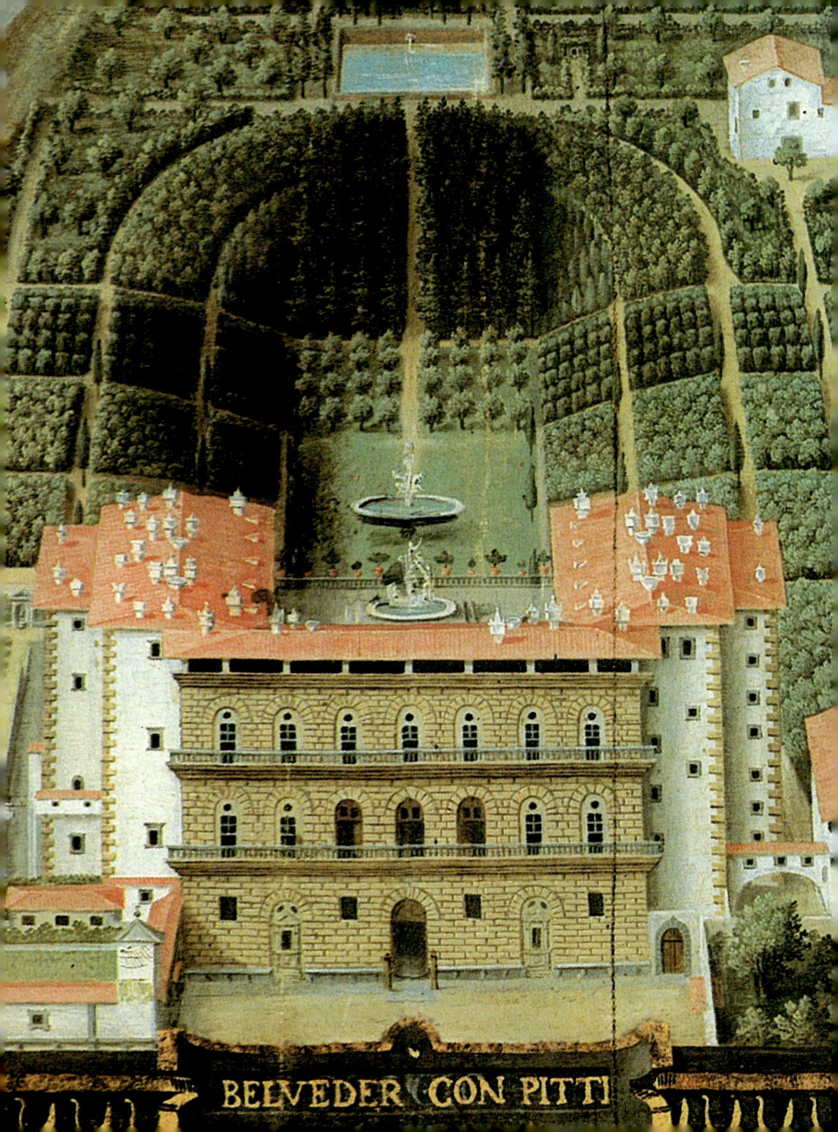
BELVEDER CON PITTI

Palazzo Pitti

The Palace and its Museums

Palazzo Pitti, which today houses the most varied museum complex in the city, containing no less than seven museums, is pre-eminent in many ways, considering also its Monumental Apartments. It is, in the first place, the most grandiose Florentine private residence of Renaissance origin, behind which stretches out a vast garden, the largest in the city. The building is still known by the name of its first owner, Luca Pitti, a wealthy banker and friend of Cosimo the Elder, who however never managed to live there, having fallen into disgrace in 1464 for having participated in the conspiracy against Piero de' Medici, at a time when the powerful dynasty had not yet come to an end.

Work on the original core of the palace was begun around 1458, in a zone of Oltrarno that was peripheral but strategically important, on the slopes of a hill and in the vicinity of a stone quarry, near cultivated fields which Luca transformed into "fruit-bearing orchards" that were to become in the 16th century, through the work of numerous craftsmen and artists, the immense Boboli Gardens. The palace of Luca Pitti was the first private one to be conceived in Florence according to an innovative design, which called for a vast plaza in front of it, closed off on three sides.

Opposite page:
Giusto Utens,
Belvedere with Pitti,
detail of the lunette
depicting Palazzo Pitti
and the Boboli Gardens,
c. 1559, tempera on canvas.
Museo di Firenze com'era.

Something similar had been planned earlier by Brunelleschi for Palazzo Medici in Via Larga, which was originally designed to face on Piazza San Lorenzo, a concept rejected by Cosimo the Elder on the grounds that it was "too princely", that is, too ostentatious. It seems highly probable that, as reported by Vasari, the architect then proposed a concept similar to that of Luca Pitti's palace, around 1440.

HISTORY

The palace was however begun many years after the death of its probable designer (who had died in 1446).
The plaza in front of Palazzo Pitti, created by demolishing several houses owned by Luca in the area, is the only one in Florence designed to allow the front of the building to be best seen from below. The façade, which in its 15th century structure consisted of the seven central windows, with three portals on the ground floor, is faced in huge rusticated ashlars taken from the nearby stone quarries. The great round-arch windows descend to the floor on each storey and are connected through a long, continuous outside terrace.
Starting from the middle of the 16th century, the palace was the residence of Duke Cosimo and his wife Eleonora; later it was inhabited by the Grand Dukes who succeeded him and lastly by the Lorraines. From 1865 to 1871, at the time when Florence was the capital of Italy, it was the residence of Vittorio Emanuele II di Savoia.

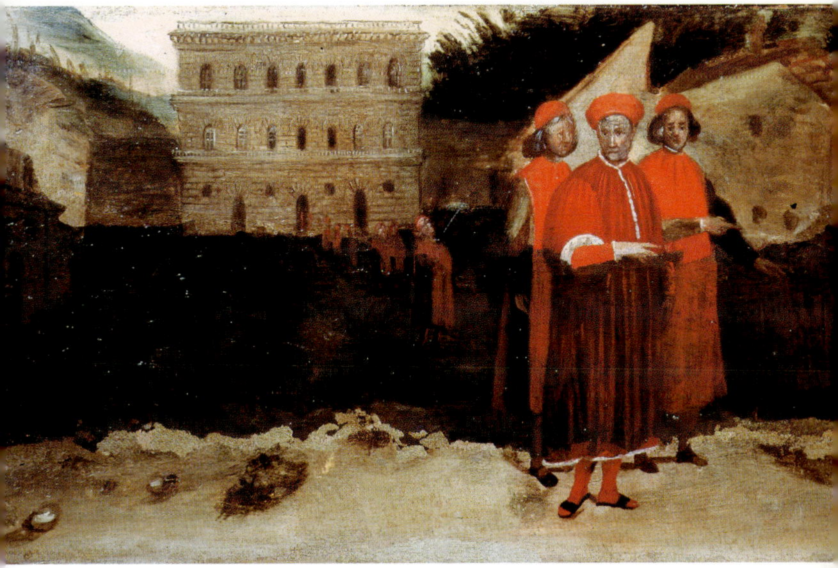

Above:
Alessandro Allori, *Predella of the Ten Thousand Martyrs of Ararat*, detail showing Palazzo Pitti in the 15th century and its owner Luca Pitti, 1574, oil on canvas.
Santo Spirito, Pitti Chapel.
Next to the palace, on the left, can be seen the *pietra forte* quarry whose stones were used over the centuries to enlarge the building.

Following pages:
Detail of the central part of Palazzo Pitti's façade.

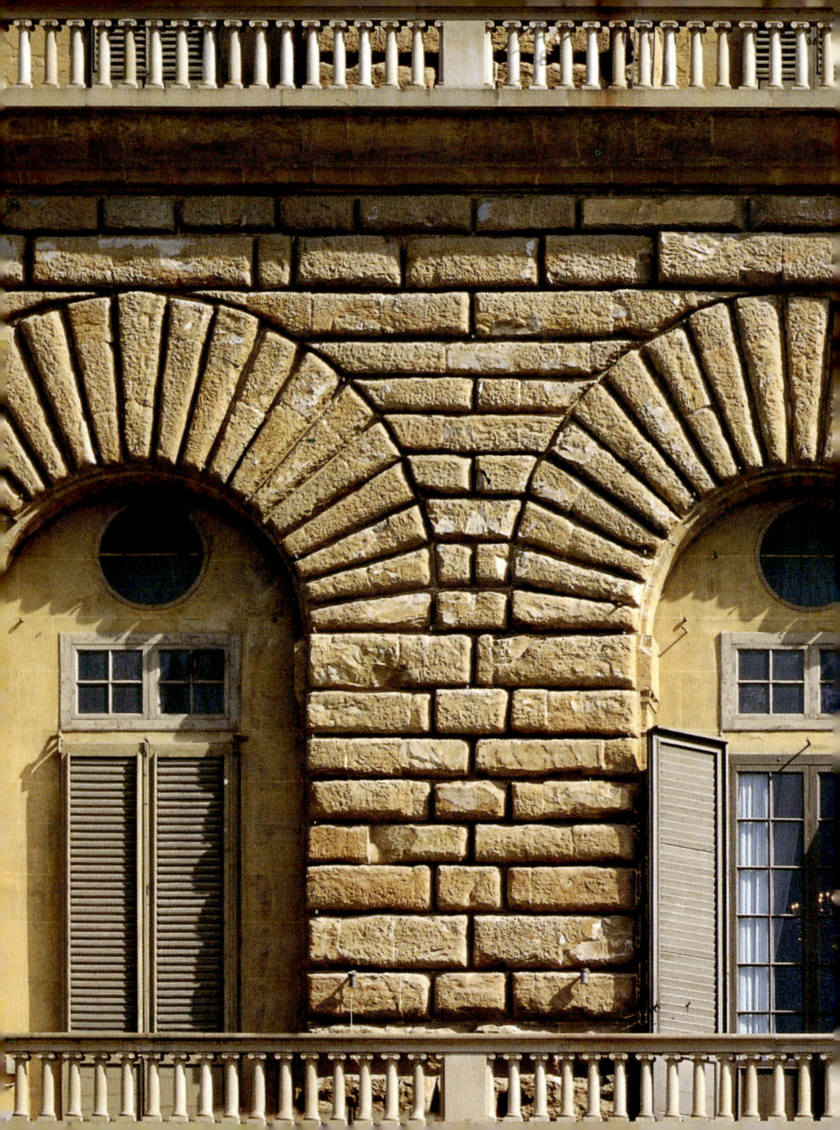

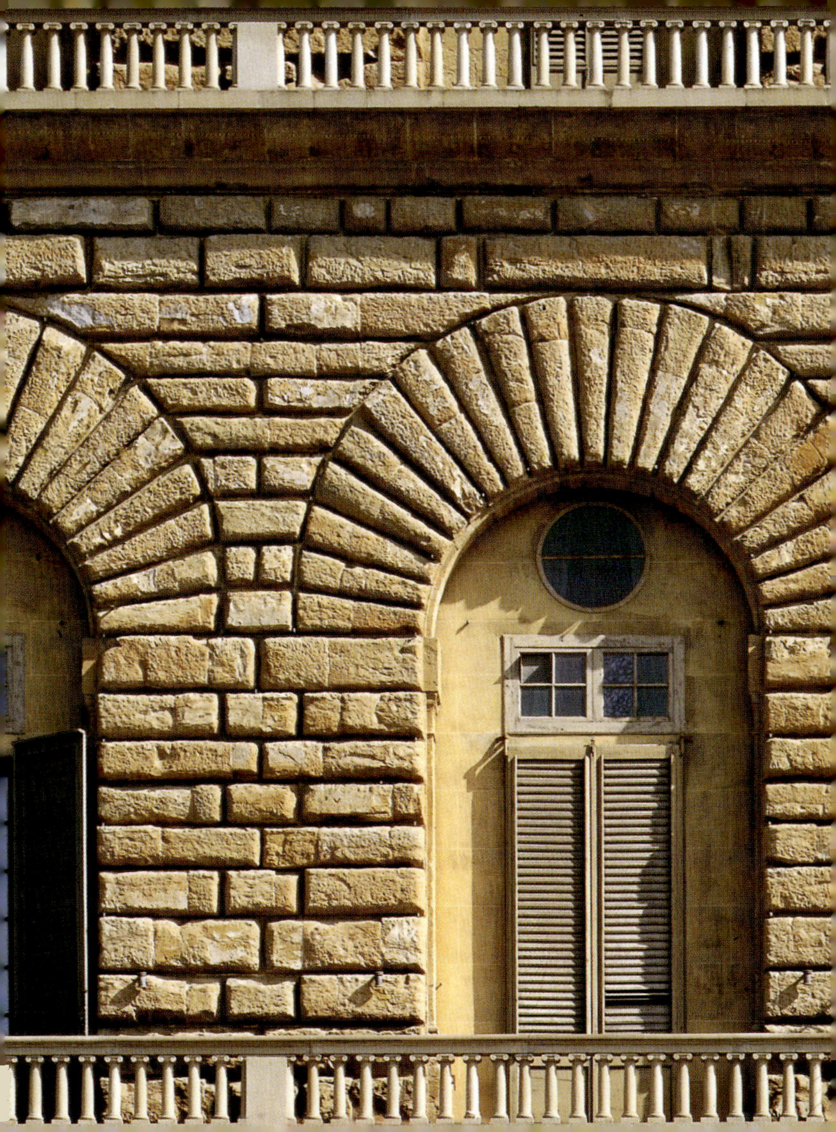

Over the centuries the palace has been substantially enlarged, on both the façade and the back. But its magnificence may be said to have begun at the time when Cosimo I and his wife came here to live. It is here, in the Palatine royal palace, that the historian Giorgio Spini has recognized the vertex of that ideal triangle "of power and its ideology", one side of which consisted, in grand-ducal Florence, of Piazza Signoria with its Medicean emblems (the palace, the loggia, the fountain and the statues), the other of the processional route that from Via Maggio crossed the Arno to arrive at Santa Trinita. The base of the triangle was instead delimited by the loggia of the New Market situated in today's Piazza Repubblica and Palagio di Parte Guelfa behind Orsanmichele, remodeled by Cosimo I in 1549 as the administrative seat of public works. It was Bartolomeo Ammannati who began the work of transforming Palazzo Pitti into a royal palace, around 1556. At the back, toward the Boboli hill, a vast quadrangular courtyard was created, and the laying out of the park was begun. That courtyard took on an evident scenographic aspect; Marco Chiarini has called it a kind of "optical channel" that runs in the direction of the garden sloping

Opposite page:
View of the part of Palazzo Pitti's façade corresponding to the original 15th century core.

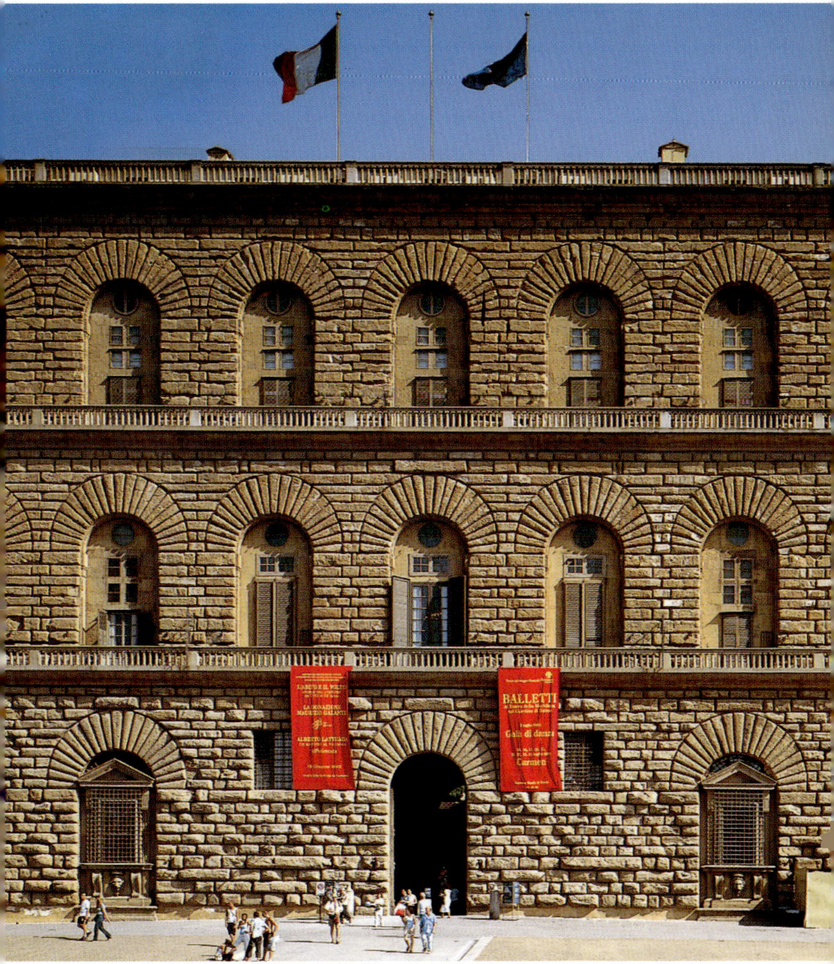
BALLETTI
Carmen

upward to cover the Boboli hill, where the open-air theater was placed. In 1589 the courtyard designed by Ammannati, frequented today by visitors to the Palazzo Pitti museums, was perfectly sealed so that it could be filled with water. There was then presented an amazing spectacle, a *Naumachia*, watched from the windows and balconies above by the guests invited to the festivities for the arrival in Florence of Cristine of Lorraine, the fiancée of Ferdinando I. At the time of Cosimo II, in the early 17th century, the palace was again enlarged on the facade, with an extension of six arcades designed by Giulio Parigi. Two lower wings were added between 1640 and 1650, the epoch in which the splendid Baroque decorations inside the palace were created, which was in the meantime being enriched, in the Grand Duke's private apartments, by precious art collections, thanks to the collector's passion and refined, discriminating taste of Cosimo II, Cosimo III and his son, Grand Prince Ferdinando. It was the latter who commissioned of Pietro da Cortona, in 1640, the frescoes for the rooms of the Planets in the magnificent apartments on the first floor, while already in 1634, for the wedding of Ferdinando II and Vittoria della Rovere, Giovanni da San Giovanni had decorated the walls and ceiling of the present-day Sala degli Argenti on the ground floor. In the

Opposite page:
Alessandro Allori and Assistants,
Frescoed Loggetta, 1588.
Palazzo Pitti.

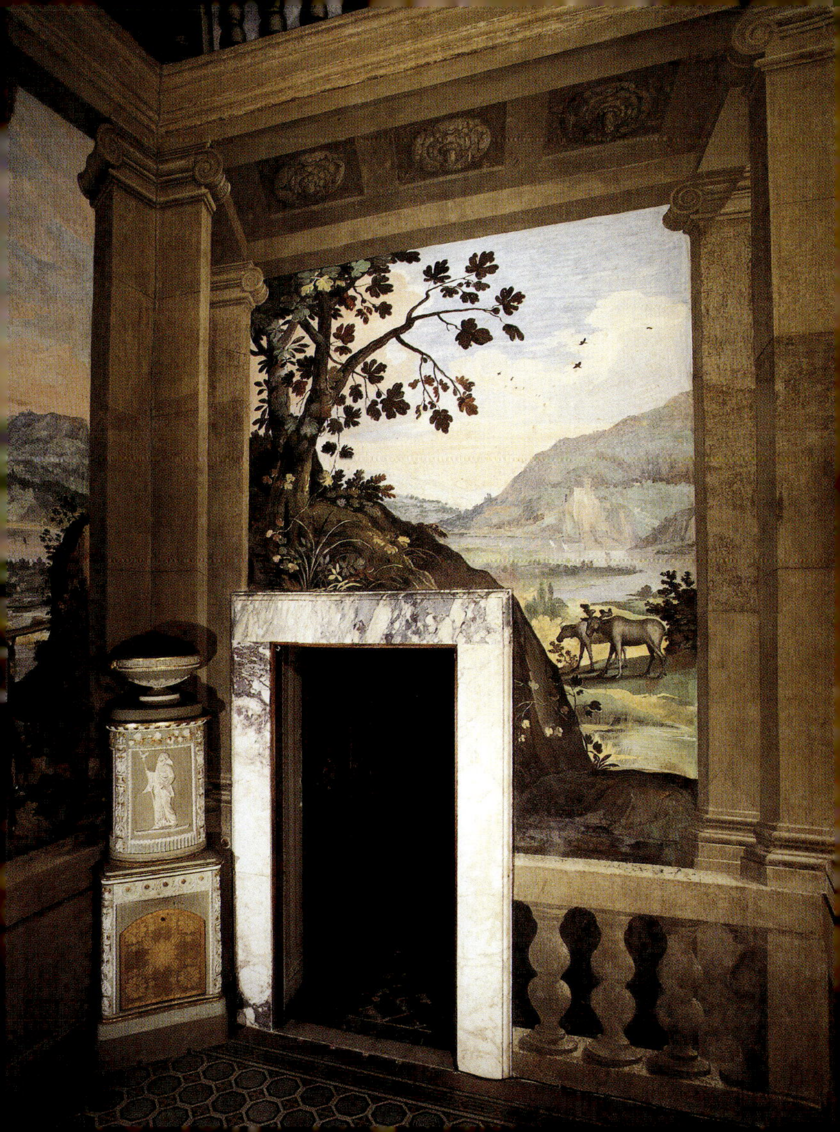

rooms that now house the Palatine Gallery, on the first floor, is the delightful Stanza della Stufa, decorated with a cycle dedicated by Pietro da Cortona to the Ages of Man: a masterpiece that aroused wonder for its viewpoint "from underneath upwards" and for "that almost celestial play of light" described a century later by Abbot Luigi Lanzi. Other rooms were decorated in the second half of the 17th century by Salvator Rosa, Anton Domenico Gabbiani and Sebastiano Ricci, while subsequently various apartments were transformed in keeping with neoclassic style. Dating from the Lorraine regency is the creation, on the outside of the palace, of two lateral projecting bodies which confer on the building its characteristic "pincers-like" structure: the Rondò delle Carrozze (or "di Mezzogiorno", finished by the architect Giuseppe Ruggeri in 1783, which now houses the Carriage Museum), and the Rondò di Bacco (or "di Settentrione", begun by Giuseppe Maria Paoletti in 1784 and finished by Pasquale Poccianti in 1815).
A visit to Palazzo Pitti offers a chance to admire the rooms of the palace, in which a great many of the works of art and furnishings displayed are closely related to the lives of their owners and to the history of Medicean and Lorrain collecting.

Opposite page:
Giuseppe Antonio Torricelli,
Bust of Vittoria della Rovere,
c. 1697, semiprecious stones.
Palazzo Pitti, Museo degli Argenti.

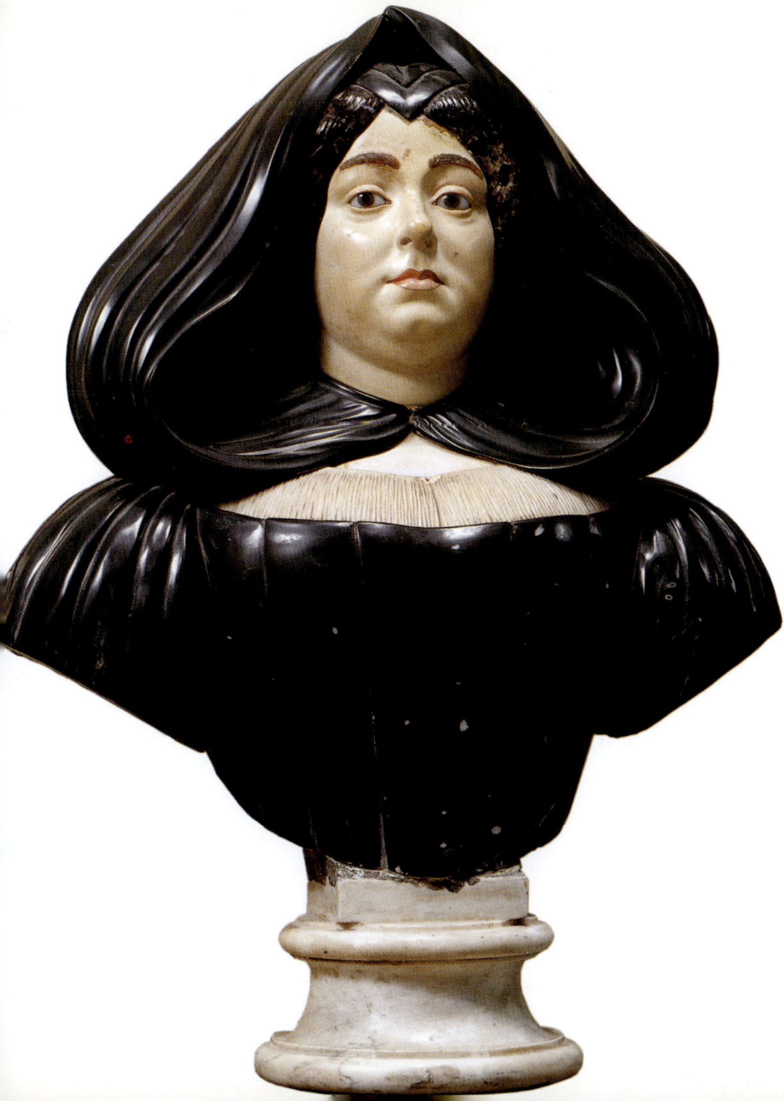

The museums that make up this complex unique the world over are:

• THE MUSEO DEGLI ARGENTI

A series of "wonder chambers" containing the objects coming from the ancient Gemstone Cabinet in the Uffizi, collections of ivory and amber carvings, the collection of glassware formerly exhibited at the Bargello, the jewels of the Palatine Electress Anna Maria Ludovica, last heiress to the Medici dynasty, and the treasure of the Princes of Salzburg, brought to Florence in 1814 by Ferdinando III of Lorraine. The museum, opened in the 1920s, took its name, in fact, from the wealth of silverware brought by Ferdinando III of Lorraine, formerly displayed in 1866 in the hall of Giovanni da San Giovanni, known for this reason as the Sala degli Argenti, or Silverware Room.

• THE PALATINE GALLERY

Reached from the 16th century monumental staircase to the right of the portico on the courtyard: an extraordinary pinacoteca, crowded with paintings like a typical Baroque picture gallery, hung in sumptuously furnished and decorated rooms: the halls of Venus, Apollo, Mars, Jove, of the Iliad, of the Education of Jove, of Ulysses, Prometheus, and then

Opposite page:
Alessandro Allori (and Andrea Commodi ?), *The little dog's bath*, c.1588, fresco. Palazzo Pitti, ceiling of the Loggetta.

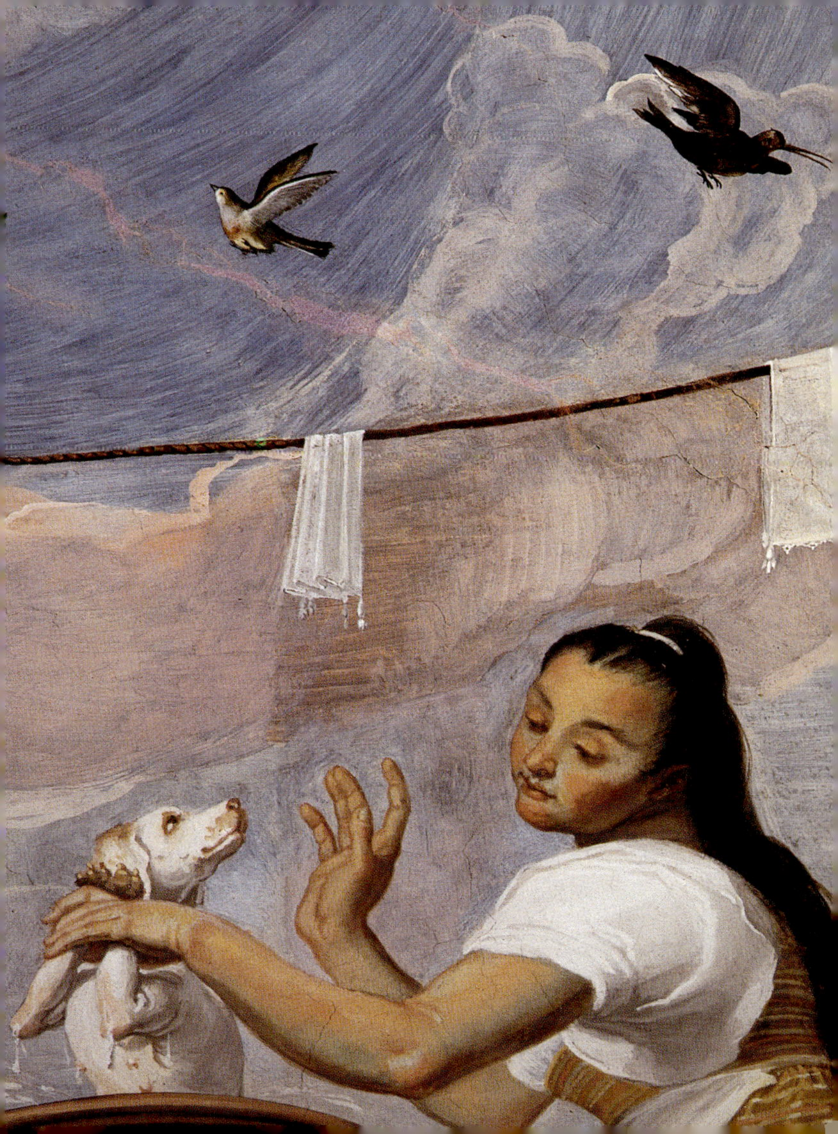

the Corridor of the Columns, the rooms of Flora, of Music, of "Castagnoli", of Allegories, of the Fine Arts, the Arc, Aurora, Psyche and Fame.

• THE MONUMENTAL APARTMENTS (OR ROYAL APARTMENTS) inhabited first by the Medici and Lorraine dynasties and then by the Savoia, filled with furnishings and paintings, entered from the room of Niches, where in the 16th century Cosimo I had arranged the first Florentine museum of ancient sculptures, some of which were later moved to the Uffizi.

• THE GALLERY OF MODERN ART
which displays paintings and sculptures from the Neoclassic, Romantic and Purist epochs, and the finest public collection of paintings by the Macchiaioli, a group of artists who raised Tuscan artistic culture, by now become marginal, to a movement of international importance thanks to their contacts with France and to an outstanding personage, Diego Martelli, a friend of Degas, from whose collection many important works are exhibited.

Opposite page:
Raphael, *"La Gravida"*,
c. 1506, oil on wood.
Palazzo Pitti, Palatine Gallery.

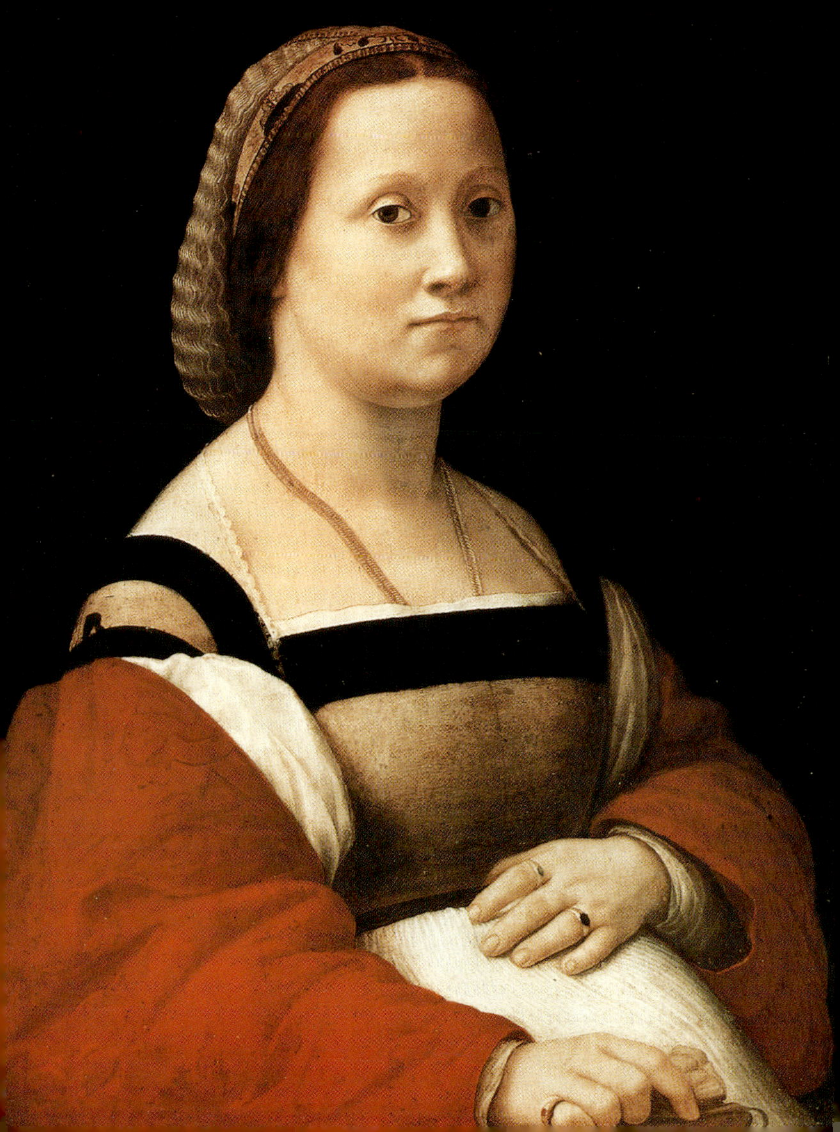

- the Carriage Museum, containing an exceptional collection of carriages dating from the 16th to the 19th century.
- the Porcelain Museum, exhibiting pieces of various provenance, to document the history of European porcelains, of the Italian and French manufacturies and those of Vienna, Meissen and Berlin.
- the Costume Gallery, inaugurated in 1983, which documents the evolution of fashion from Napoleonic times almost up to the present day, thanks to continuous donations (see illustration below).

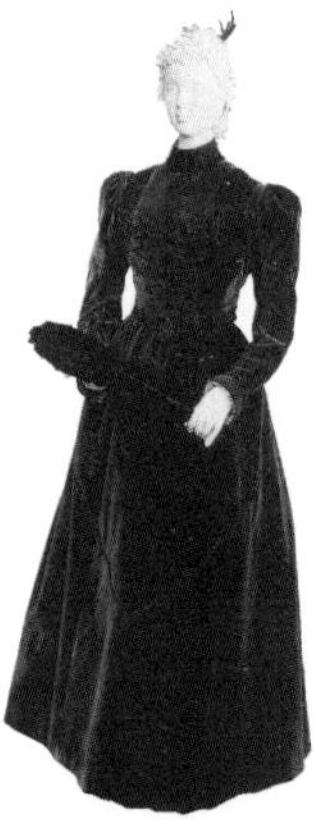

Opposite page:
Gottfried Schalcken,
Girl with a Candle,
late 17th century, oil on canvas.
Palazzo Pitti, Palatine Gallery.

Following pages: The Audience Chamber, frescoed by Angelo Michele Colonna and Agostino Mitelli between 1636 and 1644.
Palazzo Pitti, Museo degli Argenti.

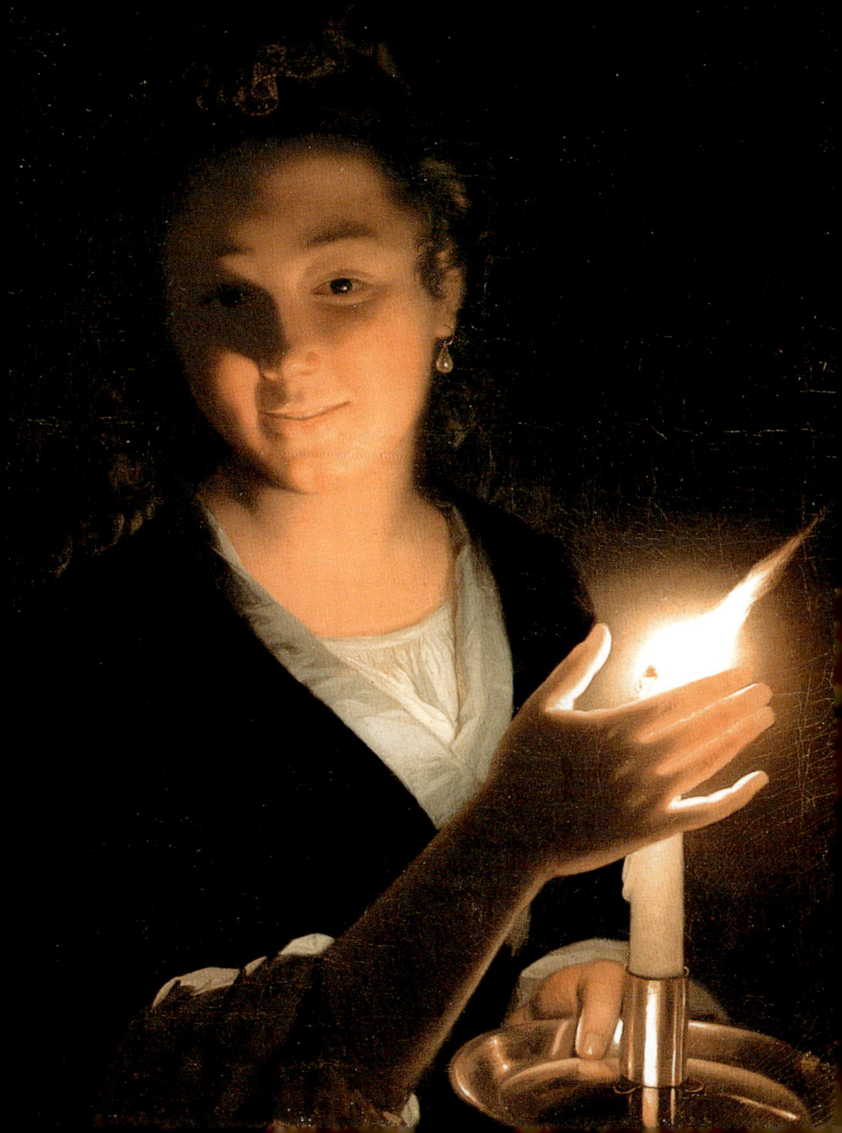

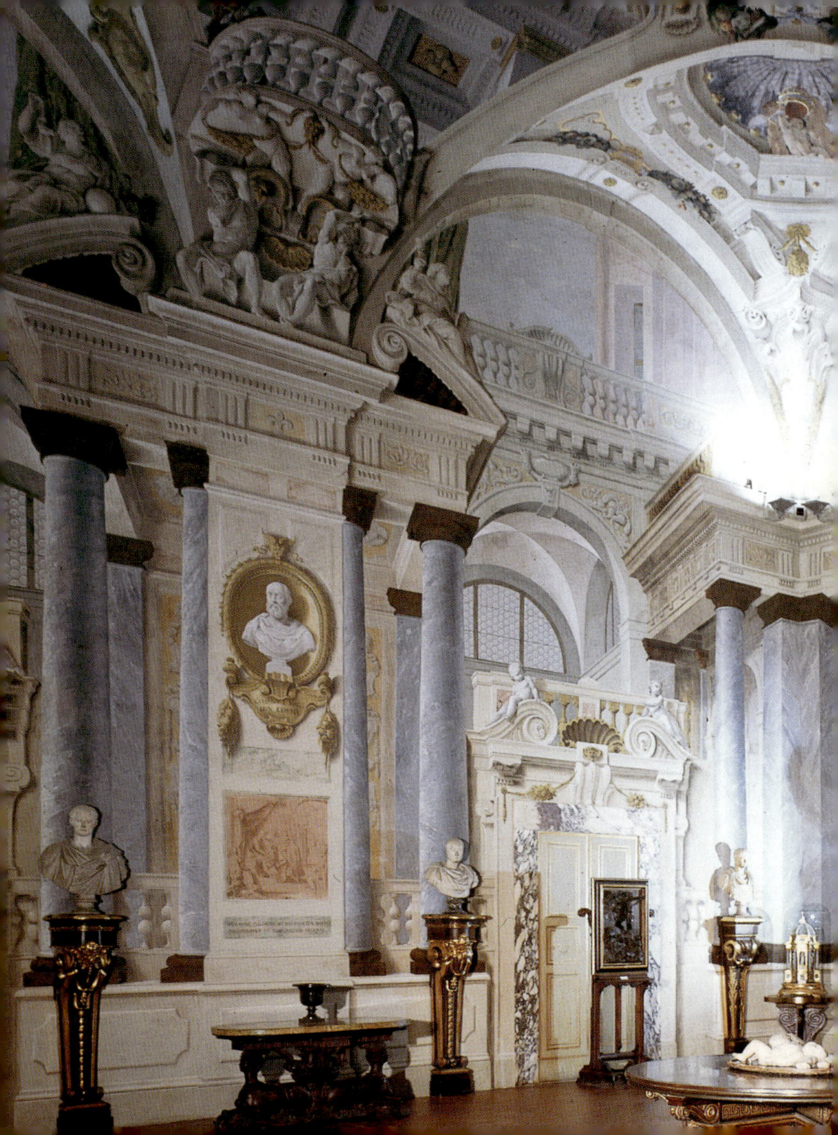

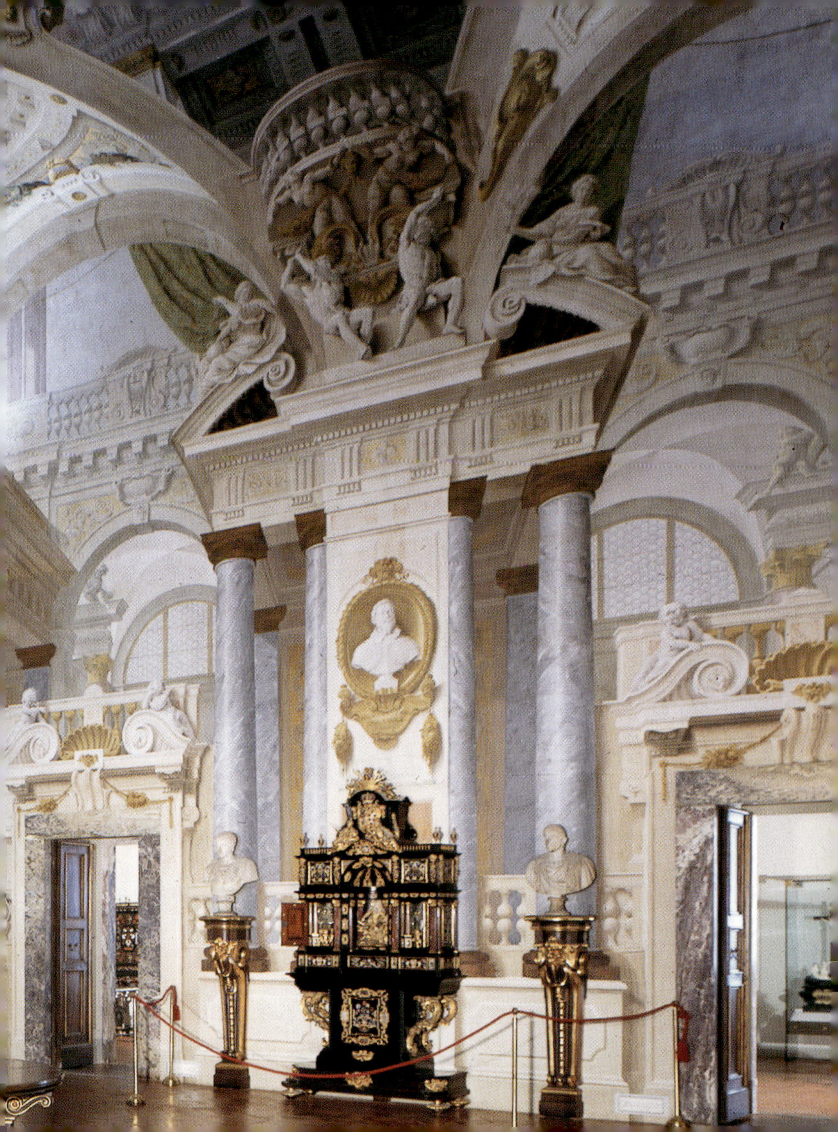

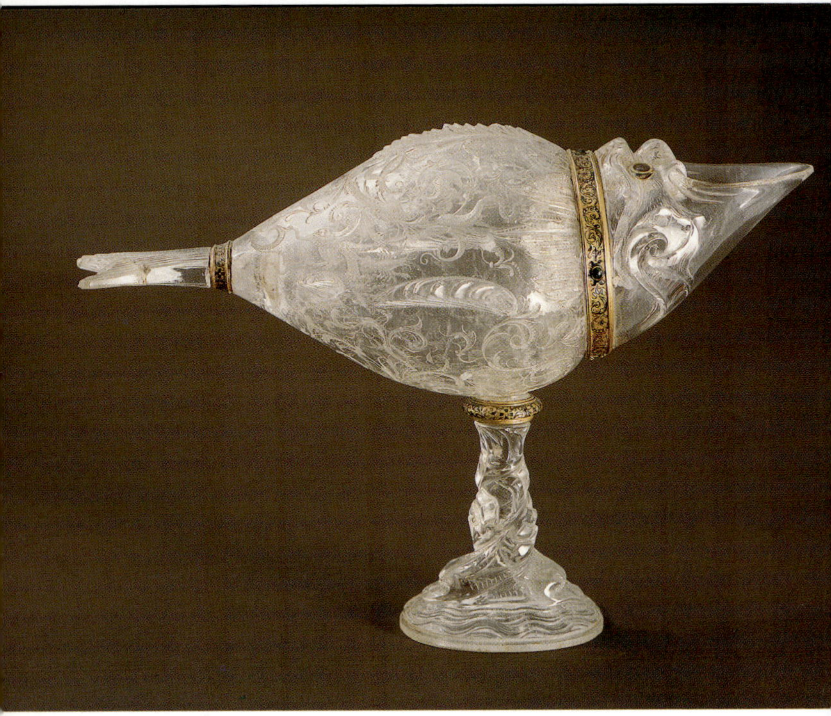

Above:
Florentine Manufactory,
Ewer in the shape of a fish,
16th century, rock crystal mounted in gold.
Palazzo Pitti,
Museo degli Argenti.

Following pages:
Grand-ducal workshops to the design of Giovan Battista Foggini,
Cabinet of the Palatine Elector, 1709,
ebony, gilded bronze, mother-of-pearl and semiprecious stones.
Palazzo Pitti, Museo degli Argenti,
Audience Hall.

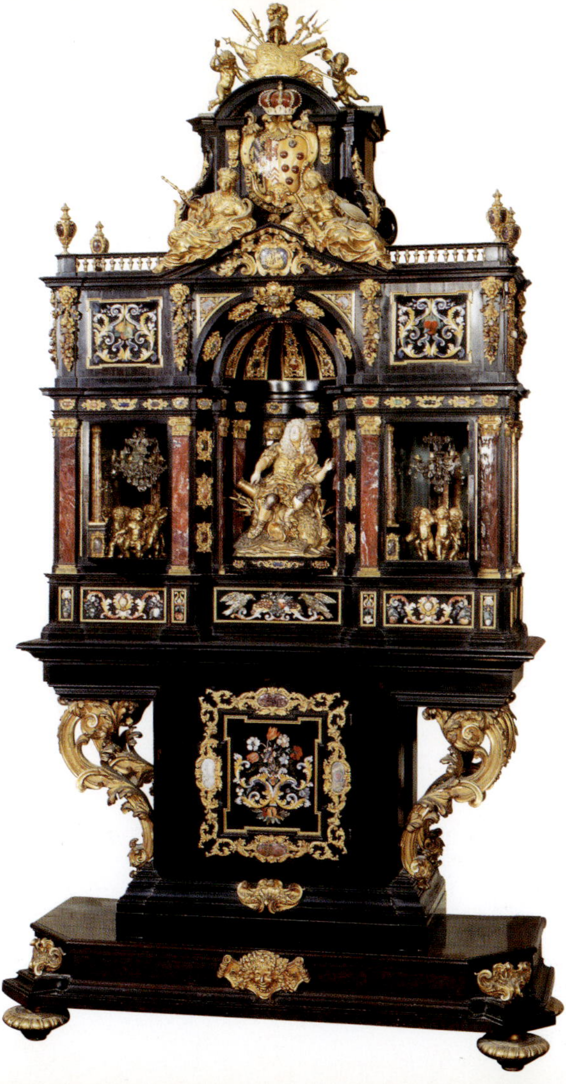

Opposite page:
Florentine Manufactory,
Late Roman double cup, mounted in gilded silver with Medici emblem on the top of the cover,
13th-15th century.
Palazzo Pitti, Museo degli Argenti.

Following pages:
Grand-ducal workshops,
Composite figure,
detail, late 17th century, seashells.
Palazzo Pitti,
Museo degli Argenti.

Roman stucco-workers and Cosimo Salvestrini (to the design of Pietro da Cortona, who painted the frescoes), *Portraits of Ferdinando II de' Medici and his son, Grand Prince Cosimo, the future Cosimo III* (the latter was a new-born baby at the time when this stucco decoration was created, but he is portrayed as already a young man, in sign of good omen), 1642.
Palazzo Pitti, Palatine Gallery.

Antonio Canova,
Italic Venus,
1810-1812, marble.
Palazzo Pitti, Palatine Gallery,
Hall of Venus.

The Apollo Room, with ceiling frescoed by Pietro da Cortona with allegorical subjects, as in the preceding Venus Room and the three subsequent rooms (the so-called Halls of the Planets).
On the walls are numerous paintings, among them some masterpieces by Titian, Andrea del Sarto, Rosso Fiorentino, Tintoretto, Guido Reni.
Palazzo Pitti, Palatine Gallery.

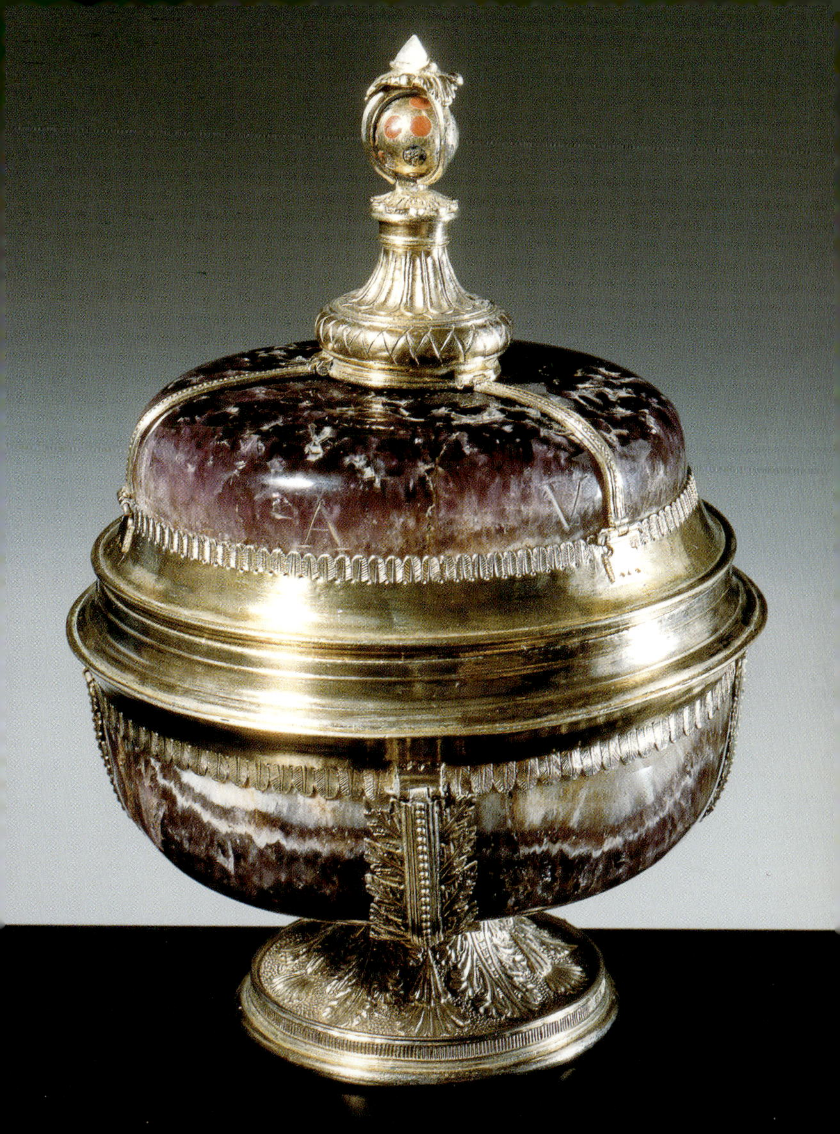

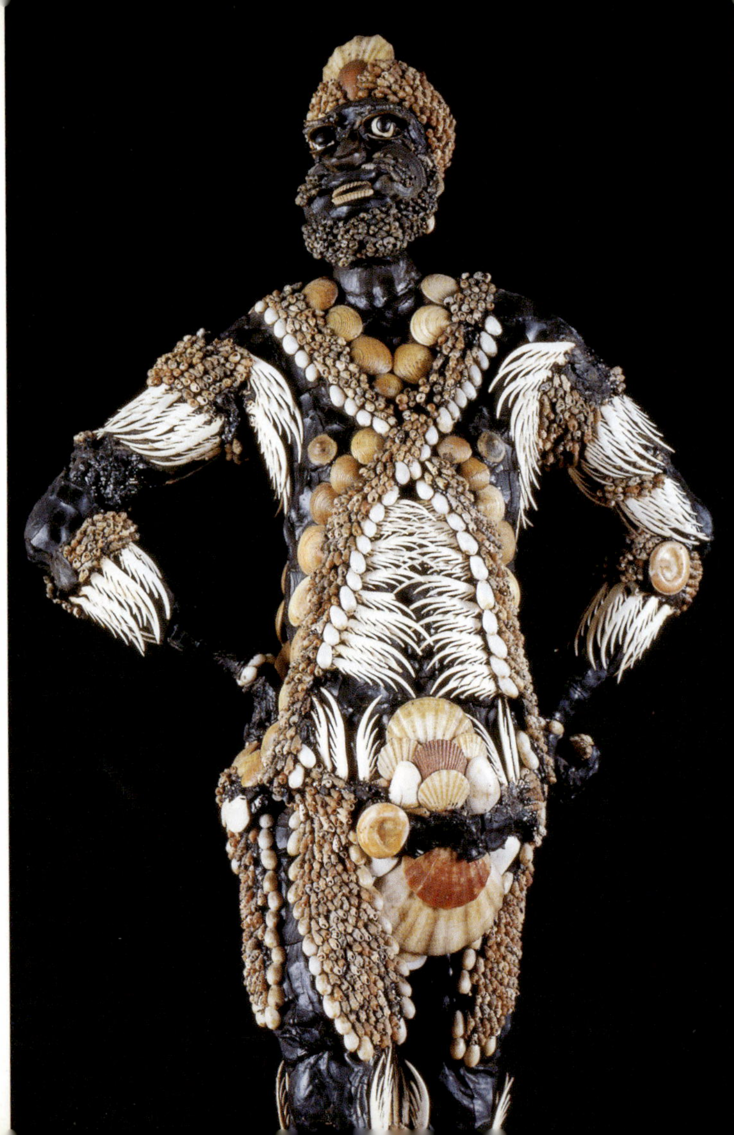

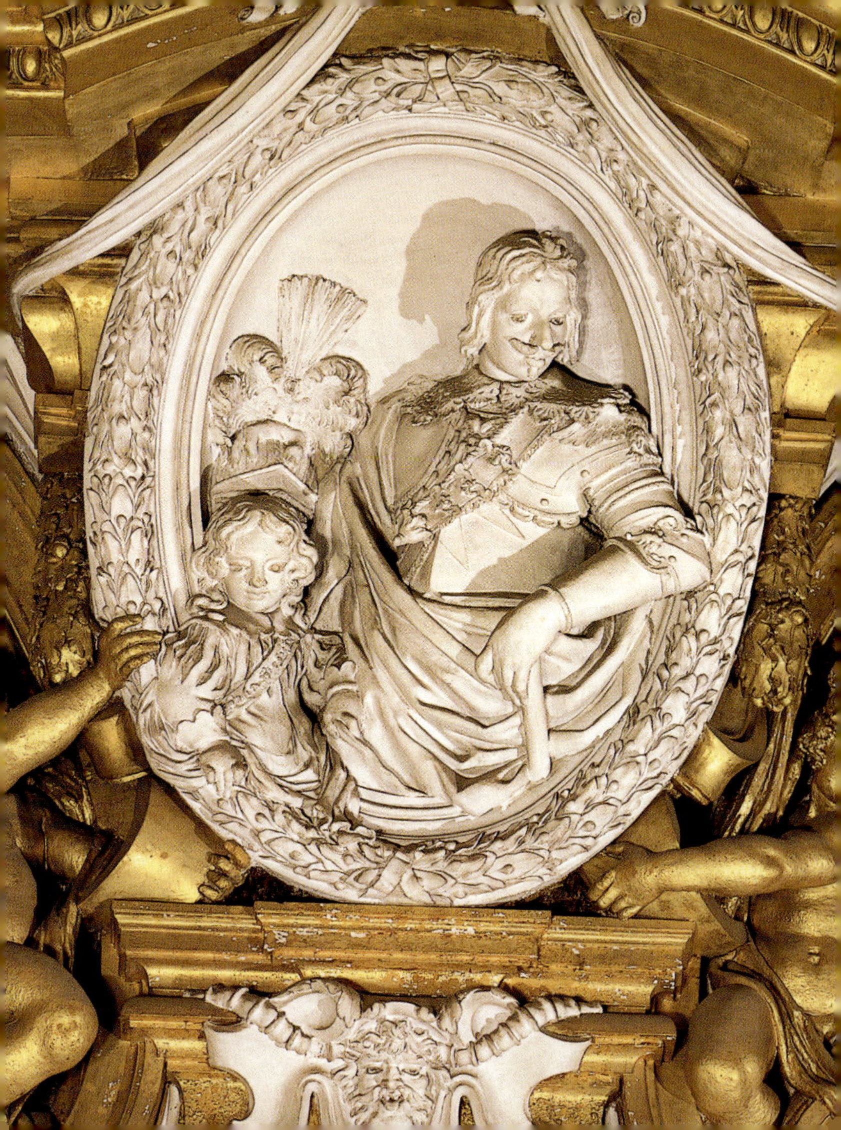

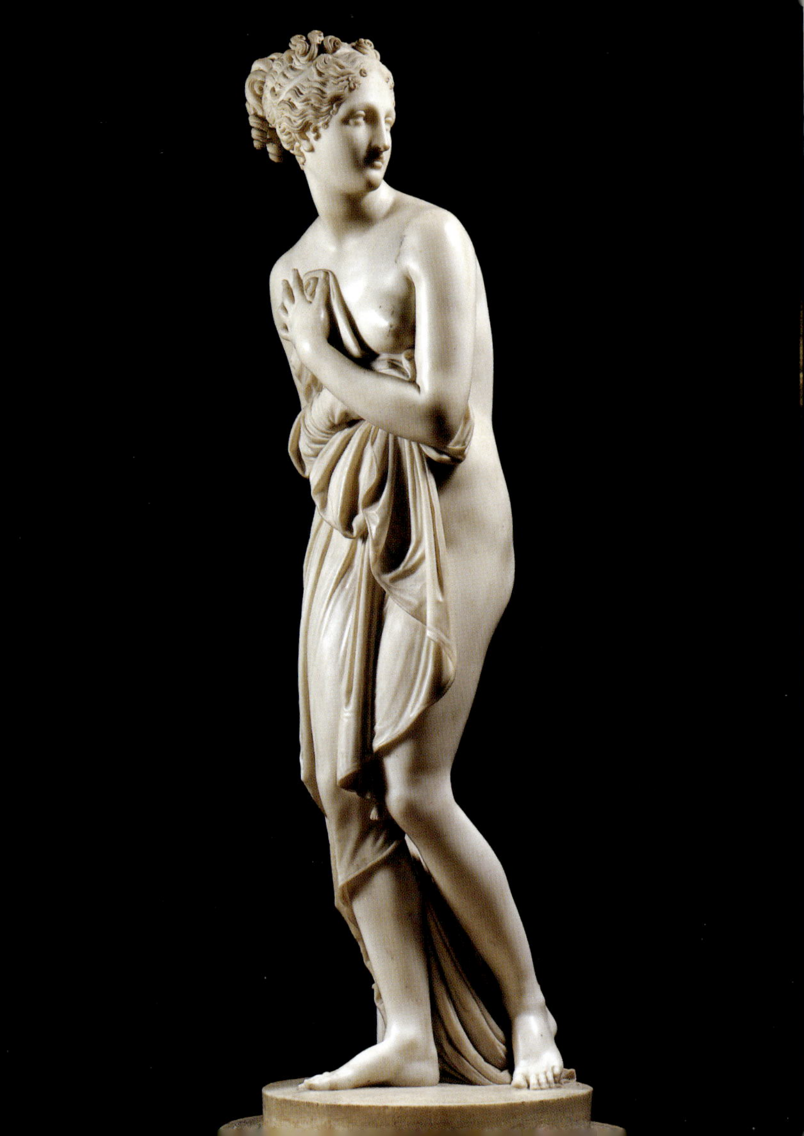

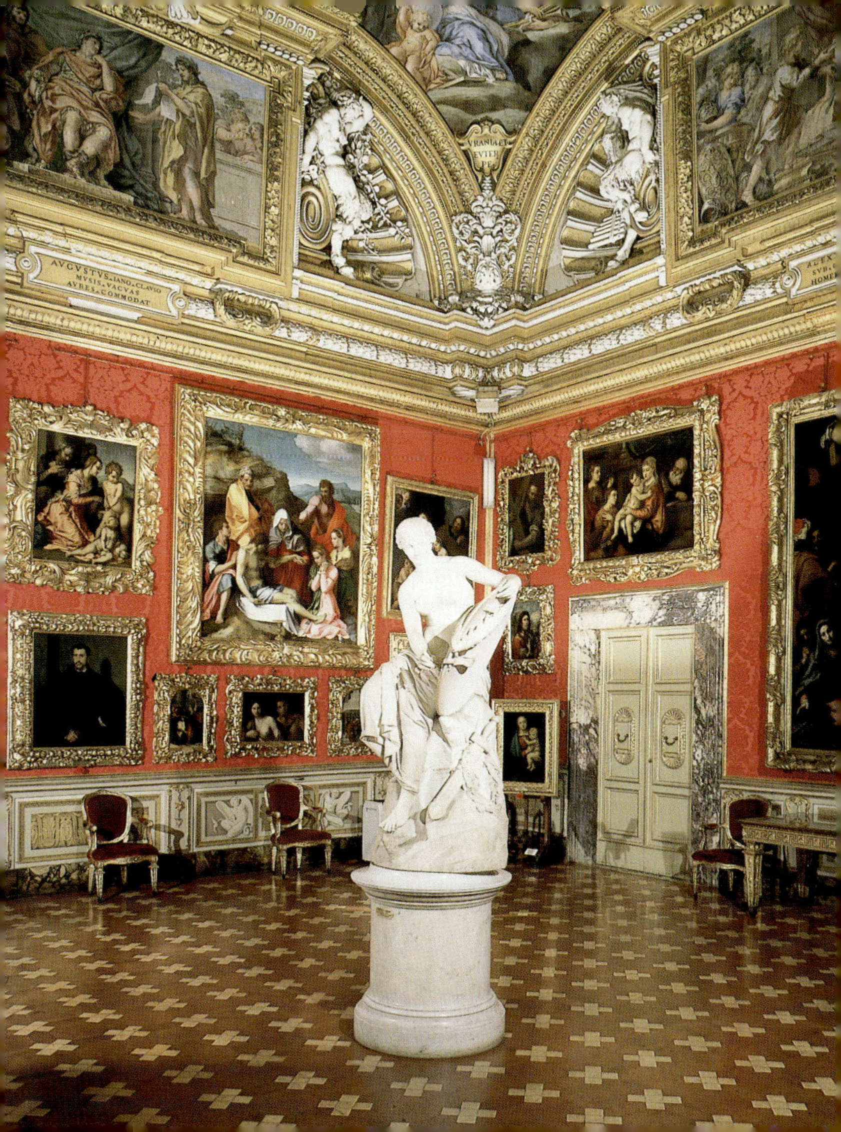
AVGVSTVS IANO CLAVSO
MVSIS VACVAS
AVRES COMMODAT

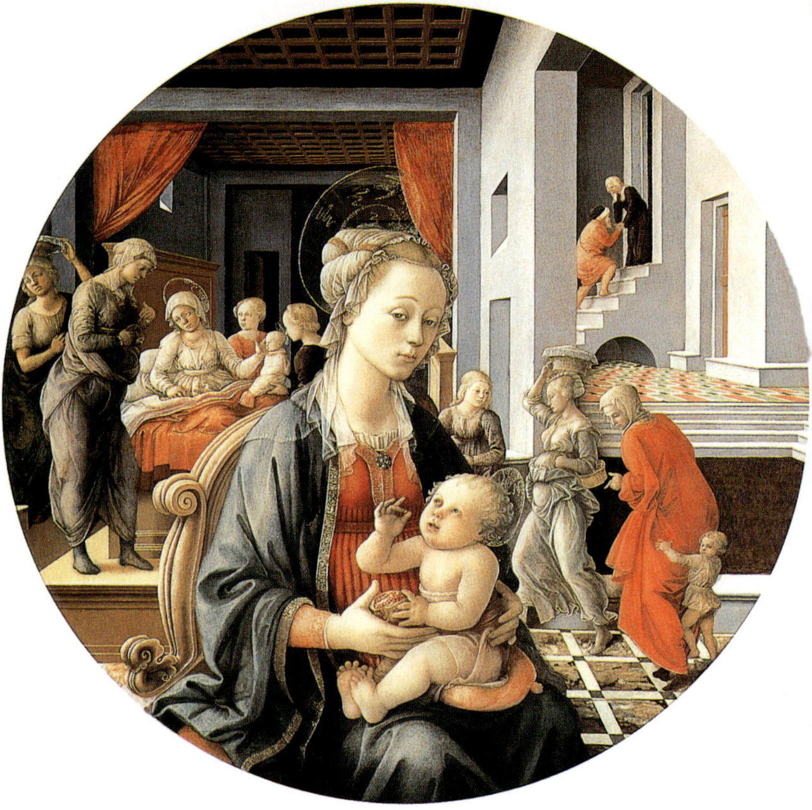

Filippo Lippi, *Virgin and Child and Stories of Saint Anne*, c. 1452, tempera on wood. Palazzo Pitti, Palatine Gallery.

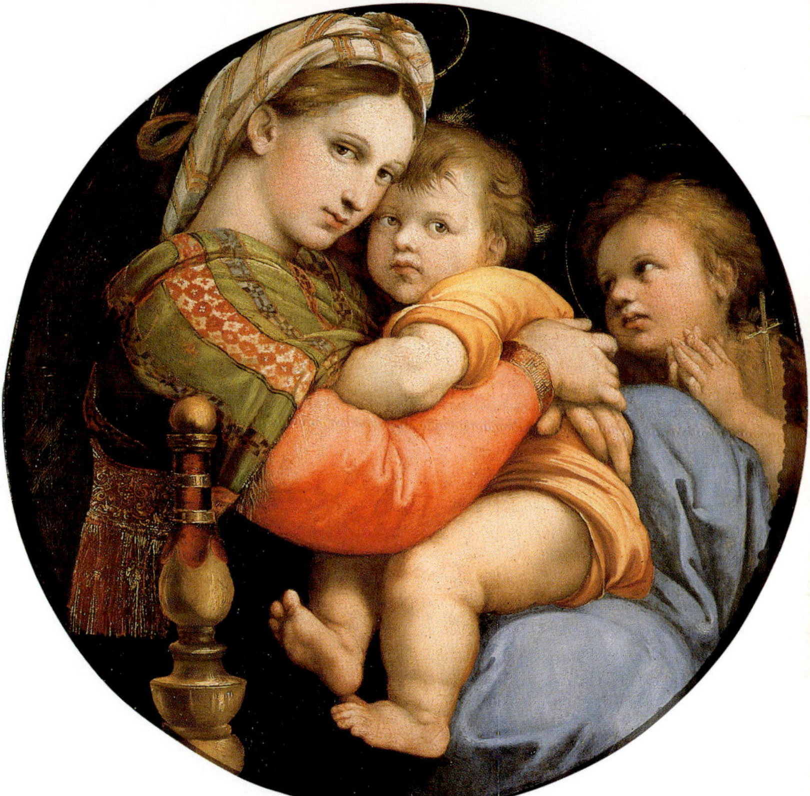

Raphael,
Madonna of the Chair,
c. 151, oil on wood.
Palazzo Pitti, Palatine Gallery.

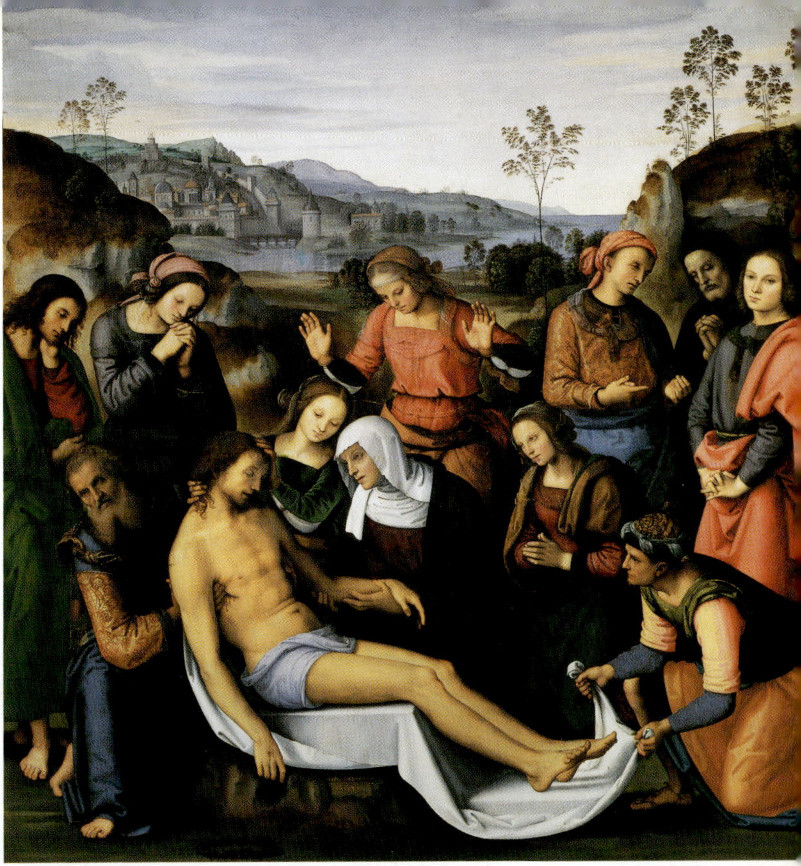

Opposite page:
Titian, *Portrait of a Gentleman ("The Young Englishman"),*
c. 1545, oil on canvas.
Palazzo Pitti, Palatine Gallery.

Above:
Pietro Perugino,
The Lamentation,
1495, oil on wood.
Palazzo Pitti, Palatine Gallery.

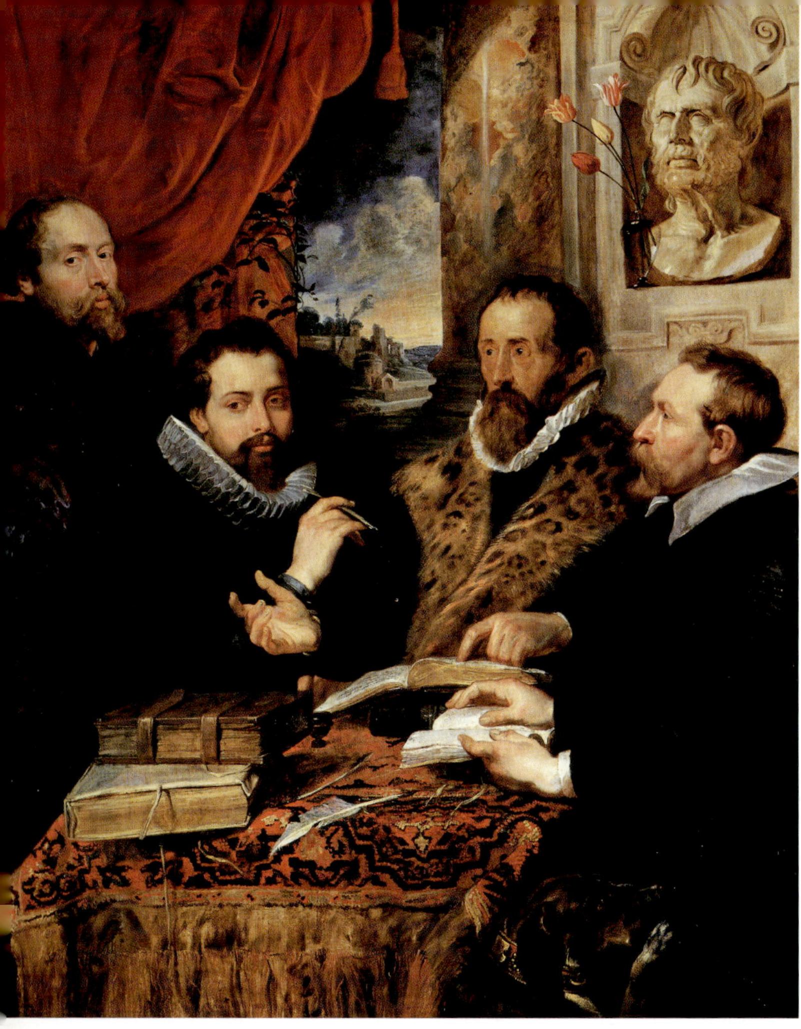

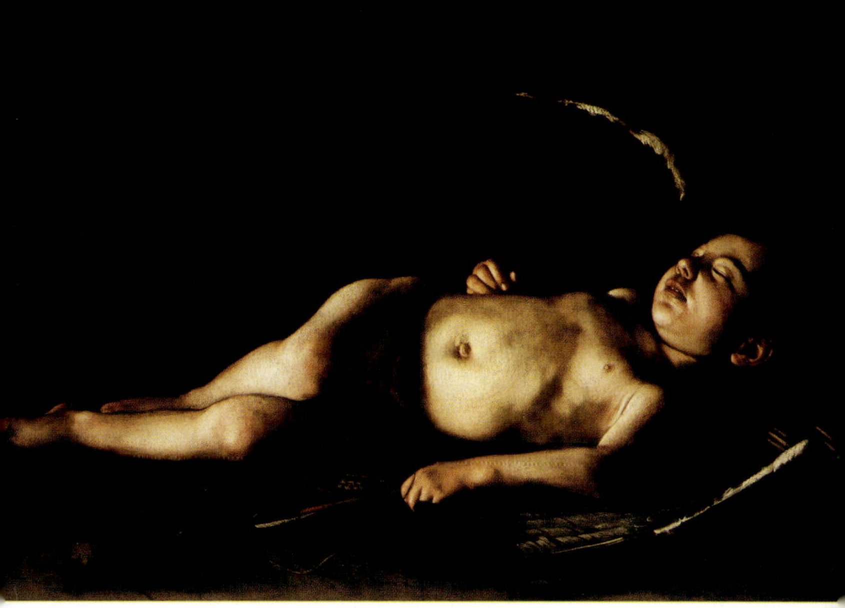

Opposite page:
Rubens, *The Four Philosophers*,
c. 1611, oil on wood.
Palazzo Pitti, Palatine Gallery.

Above: Caravaggio,
Sleeping Cupid,
1608, oil on canvas.
Palazzo Pitti, Palatine Gallery.

Following pages:
The Queen's Chamber.
Palazzo Pitti, Royal Apartments.

Giovanni Fattori,
The Italian Field at the Battle of Magenta, 1862,
oil on canvas. Palazzo Pitti,
Gallery of Modern Art.

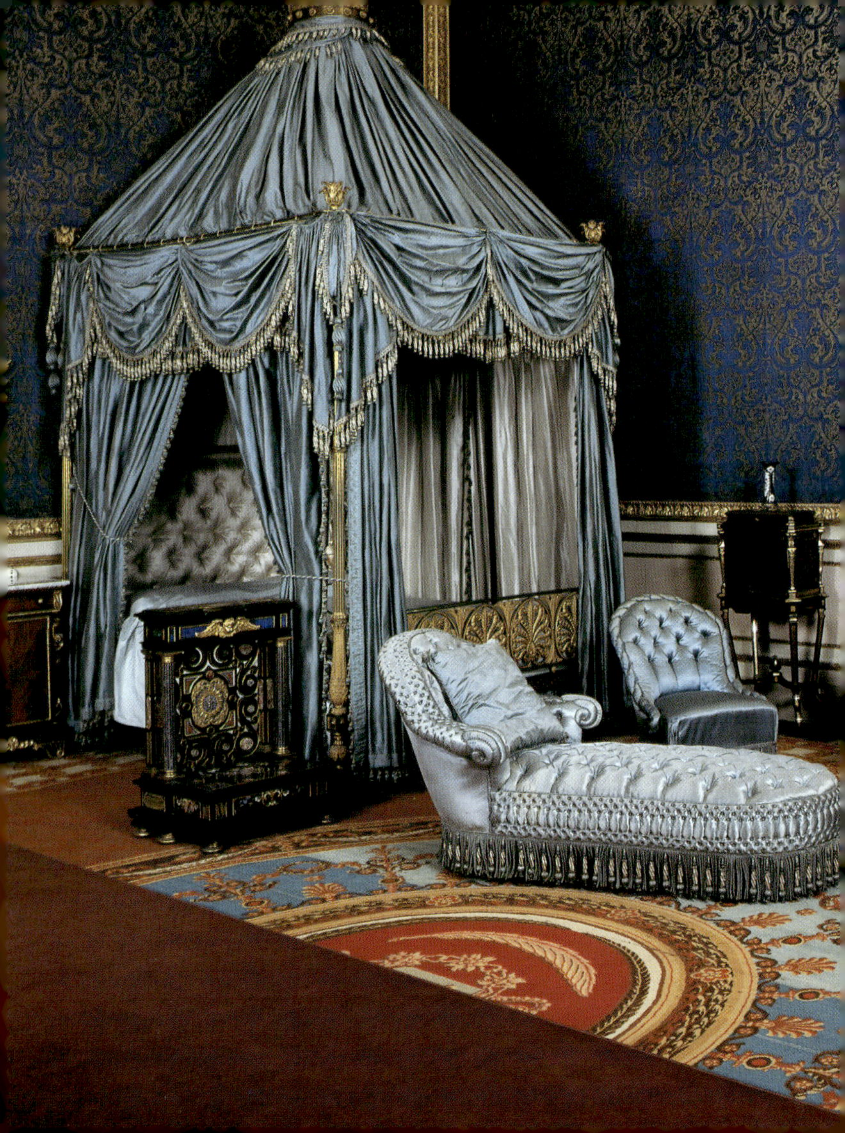

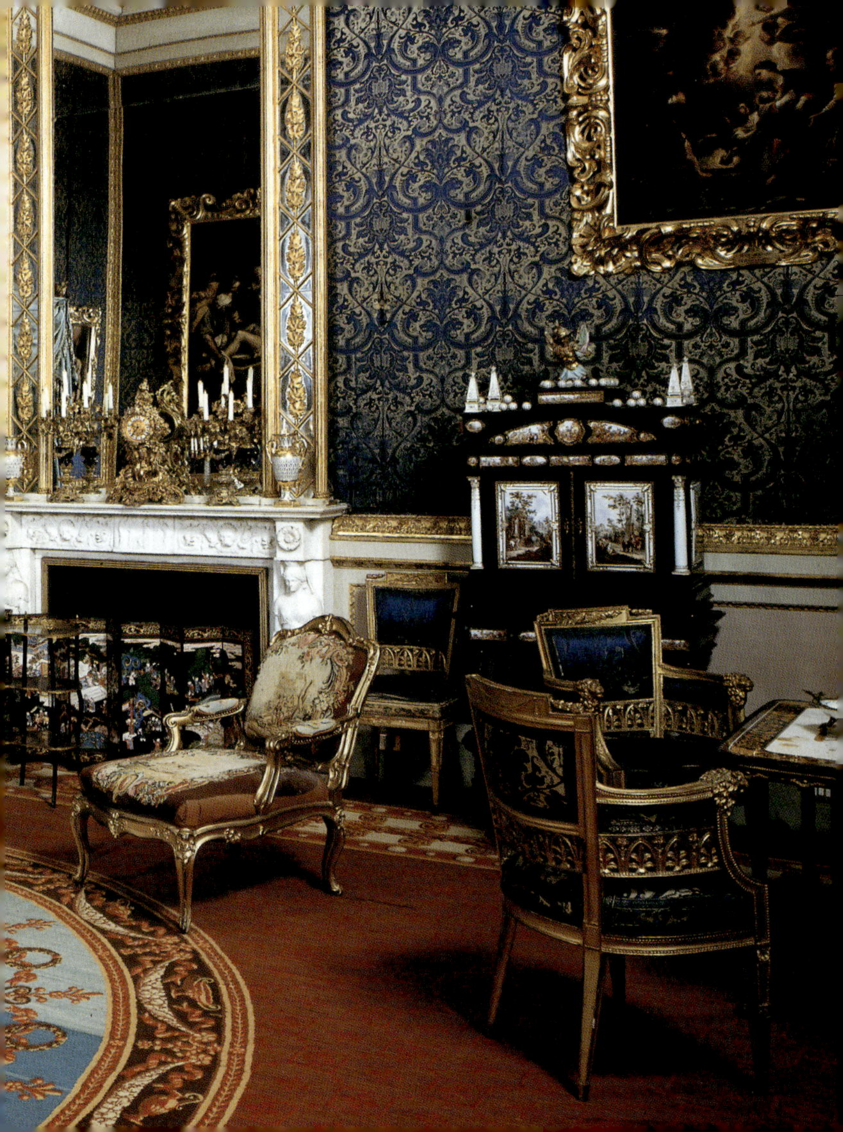

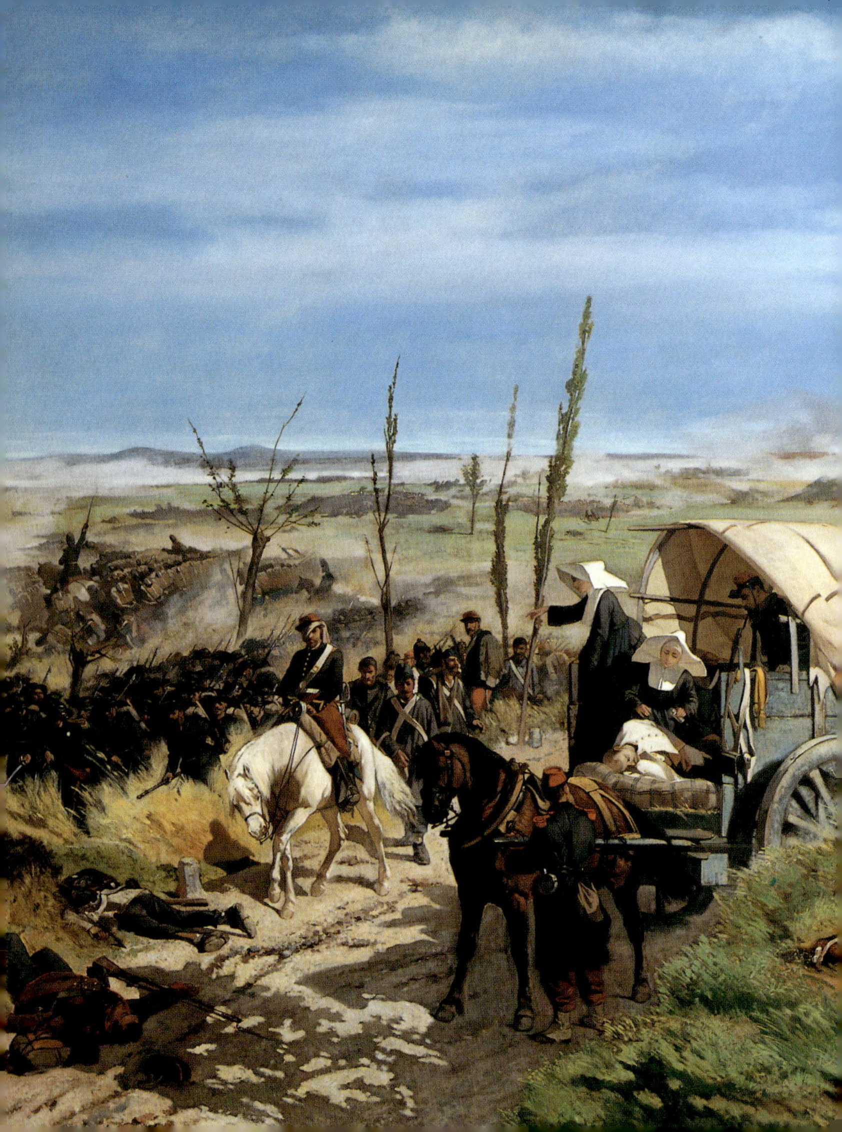

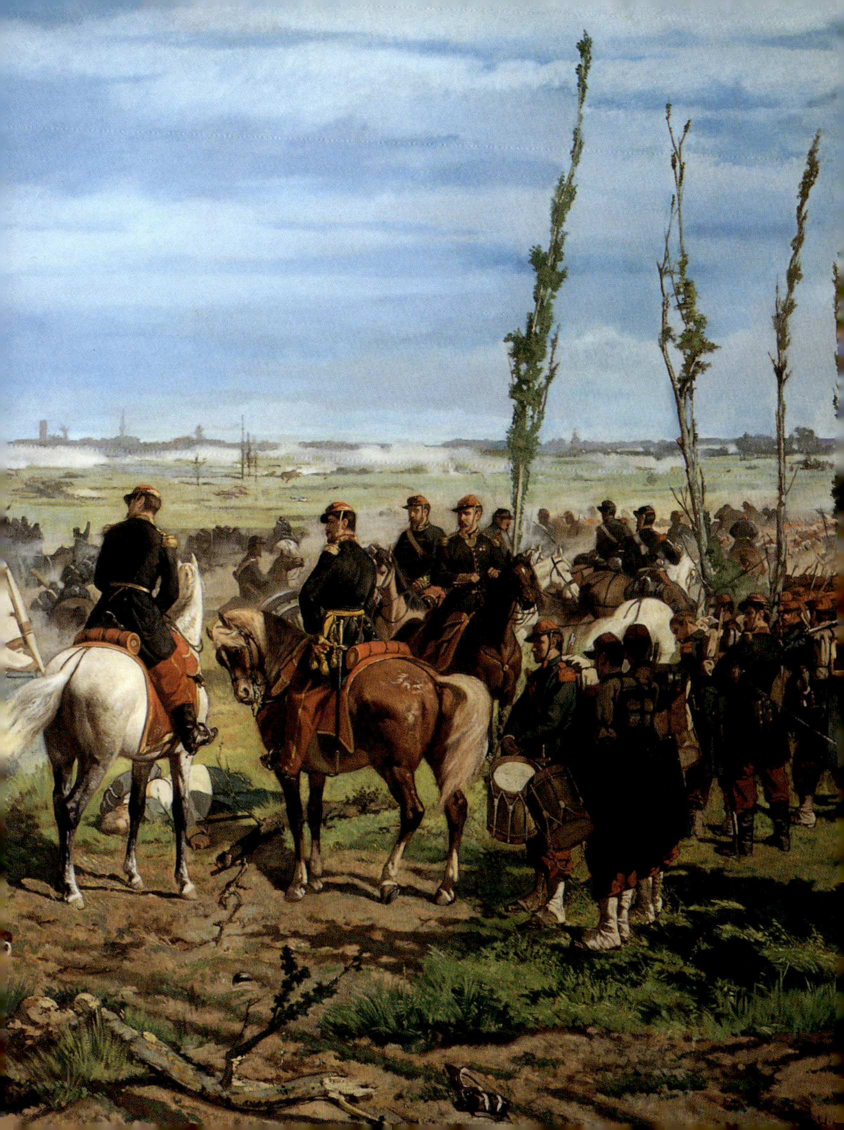

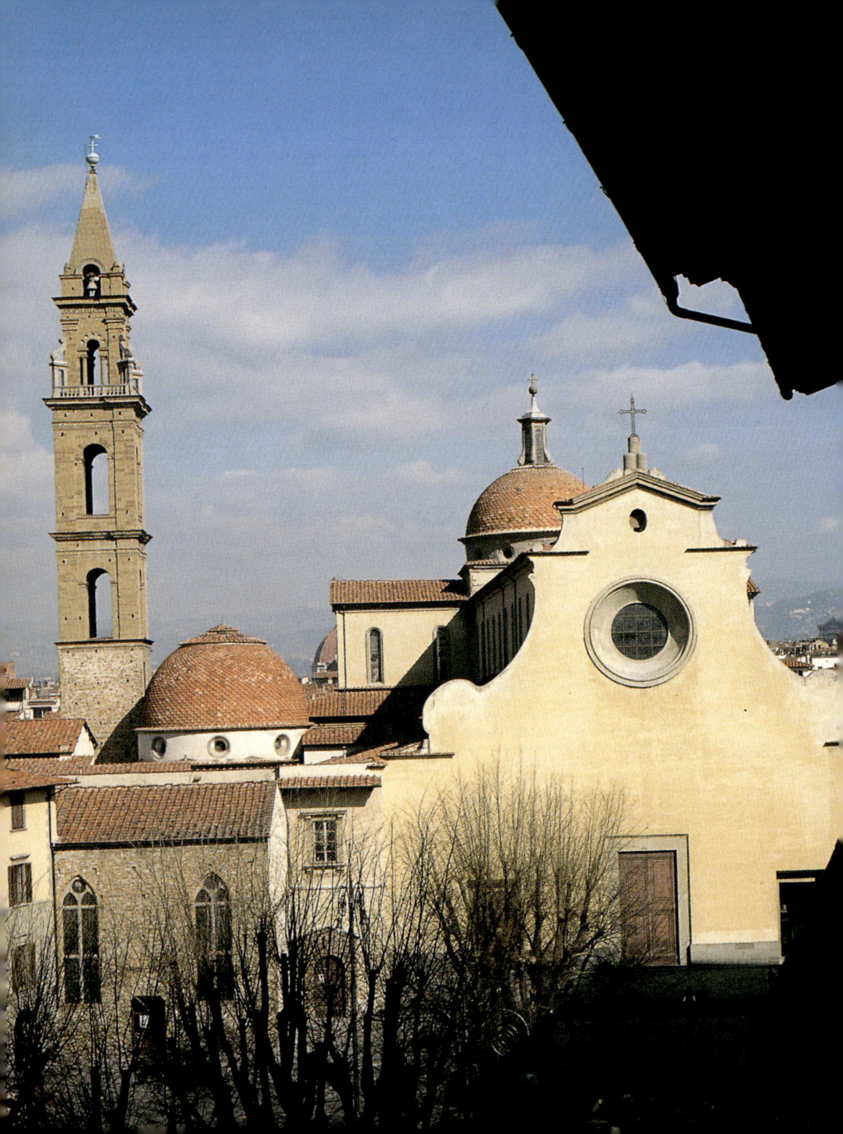

SANTO SPIRITO

The Quarter, the Piazza, the Church

An exceptionally vivacious zone on the other side of the river, still today the "citadel" of craftsmen's workshops, frequented in the evening by foreigners and Florentines, the young in particular, Santo Spirito formed part, from 1172, of the Sestiere d'Oltrarno, and became a quarter in 1343, subsequent to the division of the city into four zones after the expulsion of the Duke of Athens. It has as emblem a white dove with rays of gold in an azure field, and the standards of the Stairway, the Alcove, the Lash and the green Dragon on a red field. Before being encapsulated within the town walls, this populous area included three "borghi" branching off from the Old Bridge (Sant'Jacopo, Pitiglioso, di Piazza). In the 13th century, more or less at the same time in which, in the other three spiritual centers of the city – Santa Maria Novella, Santissima Annunziata and Santa Croce – the Dominican, Servite and Franciscan monks founded their respective monasteries, the Augustinians came down from their hermitage of San Matteo on the Arcetri hill to found the church of Santo Spirito, which gives its name to the quarter, and which soon became the chief reference point for all activity on the left bank of the river. That was the time when, a short distance away,

Opposite page:
The church of Santo Spirito.

the Carmelites were founding the monastery of Santa Maria del Carmine, while on the other side of the river the Vallombrosians were building the new church of Santa Trinita, and a little later the Silvestrines began to work on San Marco. Like the most important monastic organizations in the city, Santo Spirito too was a theological and cultural center of great vitality, already frequented by intellectuals such as Petrarch and Boccaccio (who contributed to the library by bequeathing it books) and then by humanists such as Leonardo Bruni, Niccolò Niccoli and Poggio Bracciolini.

HISTORY

The first Augustinian edifice dedicated to the Holy Spirit was built on the site of an ancient oratory called "Caselline". The new church was begun in 1269, enlarged in 1292 and again in the 14th century. Dating from 1428 is the rebuilding project commissioned of Brunelleschi, which however was not implemented in its revolutionary urbanist conception, nor was the one for Palazzo Medici approved. The architect had here planned to reverse the church's façade, turning it from the square toward the river; a solution that would have been more "convenient for all the rest of the city", as his biographer commented, and would have allowed persons arriving via river and from the sea to to see

Opposite page:
The cupola of the church of Santo Spirito, built by Salvi d'Andrea between 1479 and 1482.

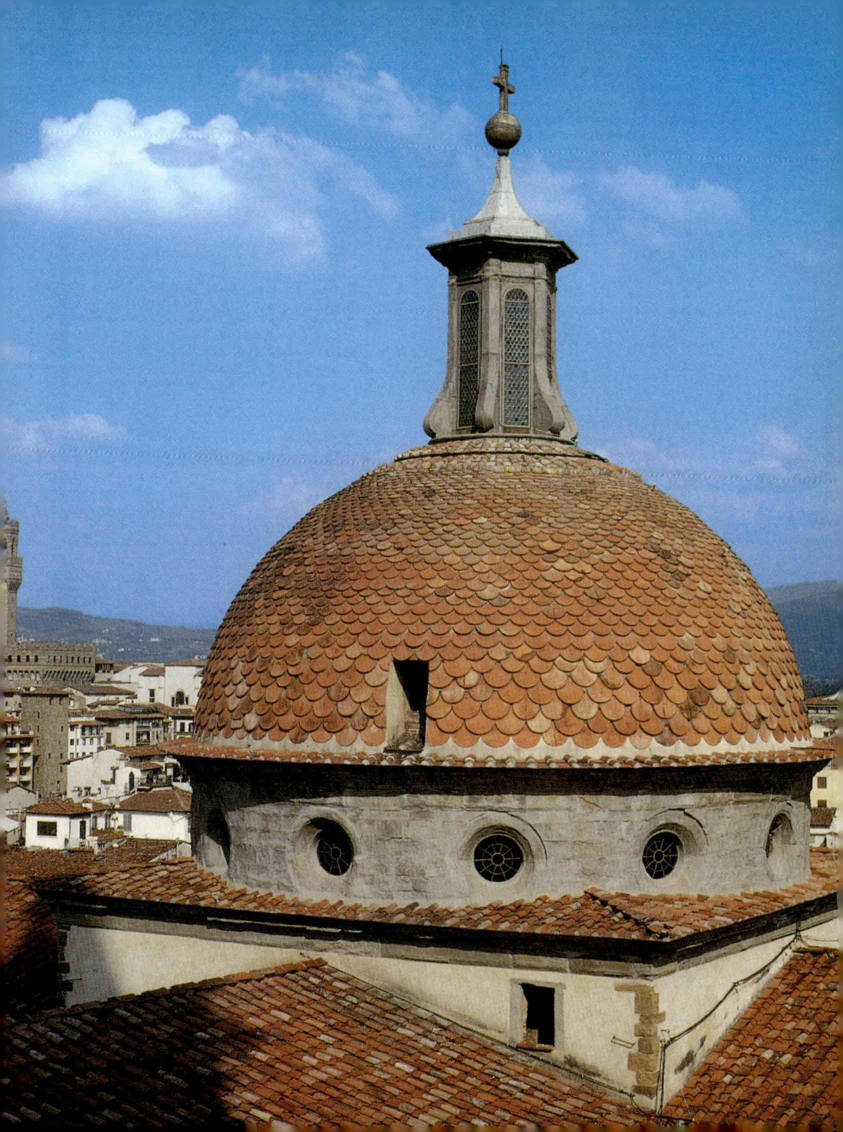

the façade. Nor does the interior of the church, in the shape of a Latin cross with a cupola over the crossing of the transept wings, and with three naves divided by Corinthian columns and rounded arches, entirely respect Brunelleschi's project. The chapels were designed as semicircular niches divided by columns, with windows toward the outside, and are as high as the side naves, creating a complex effect, more fragmented than the one the same architect had imagined beyond the river for the Basilica of San Lorenzo, with continuous changes in the vanishing points of the perspectives, which find their fulcrum toward the altar, and which would appear more accentuated today if Brunelleschi's plan had not been modified in the work done after the architect's death. The church was consecrated in 1481, but the construction site was open throughout the century. The beautiful cupola was added between 1479 and 1482, to the working design of Salvi d'Andrea, from a model by Brunelleschi, who had probably planned it of smaller size.
Between 1503 and 1517 the bell tower was built, to the project of Baccio d'Agnolo. Dating instead from the 18th century is the simple contoured façade, distinguished by a great central oculus. Many families contributed to the decoration of Santo Spirito, with an impressive number of altarpieces. Of the ancient Augustinian monastery there remains the Refectory, frescoed by Orcagna with a *Last Supper* and a *Crucifixion*. It is here

Opposite page:
The interior of Santo Spirito looking toward the transept.

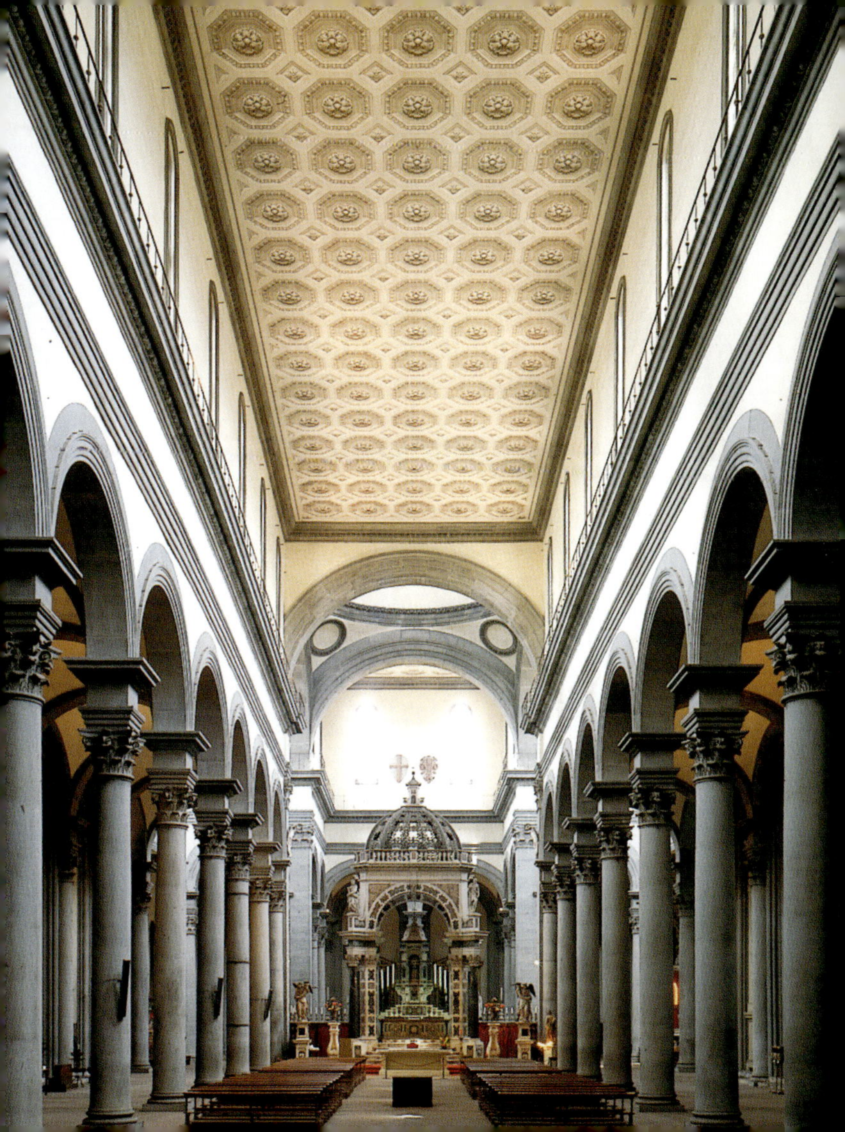

that the Romano Foundation Museum, with Medieval and Renaissance sculptures donated by the antiquarian Salvatore Romano in the last century, is located.

VISITORS' ITINERARY AND WORKS OF ART

Noteworthy are:

- the 15th century altarpieces, many of which have conserved their original aspect remarkably well: the painted panel proper is supported by a wooden apparatus resting on the stone mensa of the altar, covered by a wooden altar-frontal, it too painted with bright colors and figured scenes.
- the choir and the high altar (1559-1608) by Giovanni Caccini, Gherardo Silvani and Agostino Ubaldini.
- the Corbinelli Chapel (1492) by Andrea Sansovino.
- the sacristy (1488-1497) designed by Giuliano da Sangallo.

Opposite page:
View of the left transept in Santo Spirito.

Following pages:
The Corbinelli altar with the altarpiece by Cosimo Rosselli and the altar-frontal by Bernardo di Stefano Rosselli (1482).

Madonna del Soccorso (c. 1470) by Domenico di Zanobi in the Velluti Chapel.

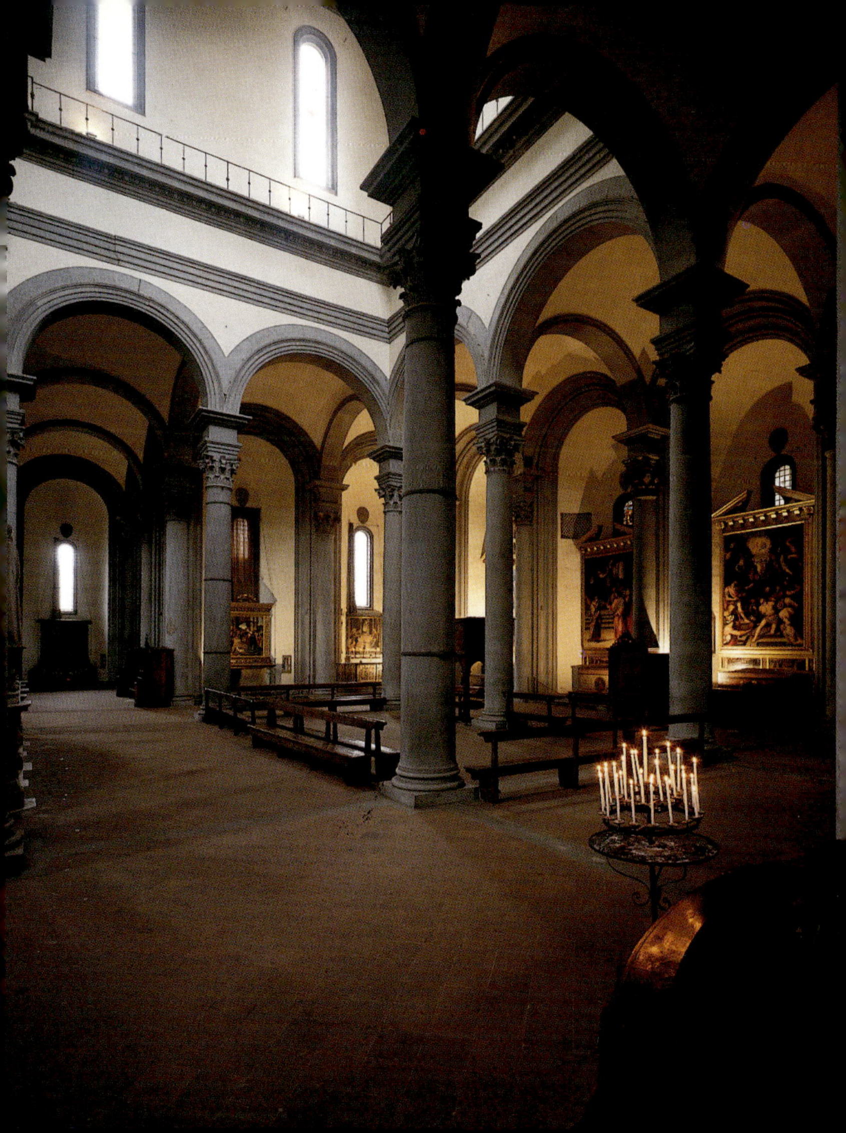

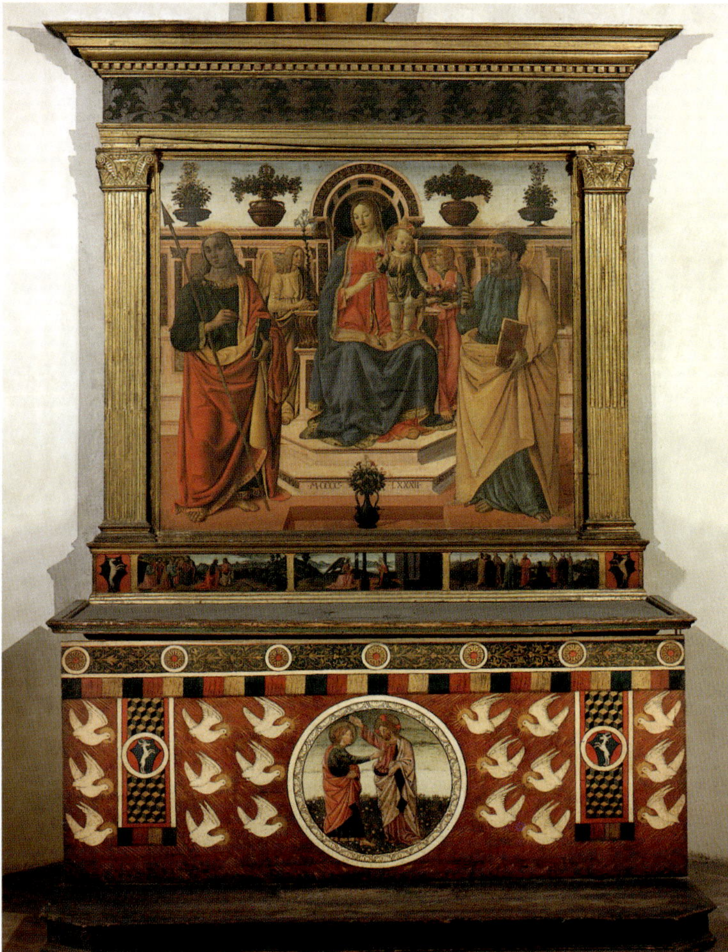

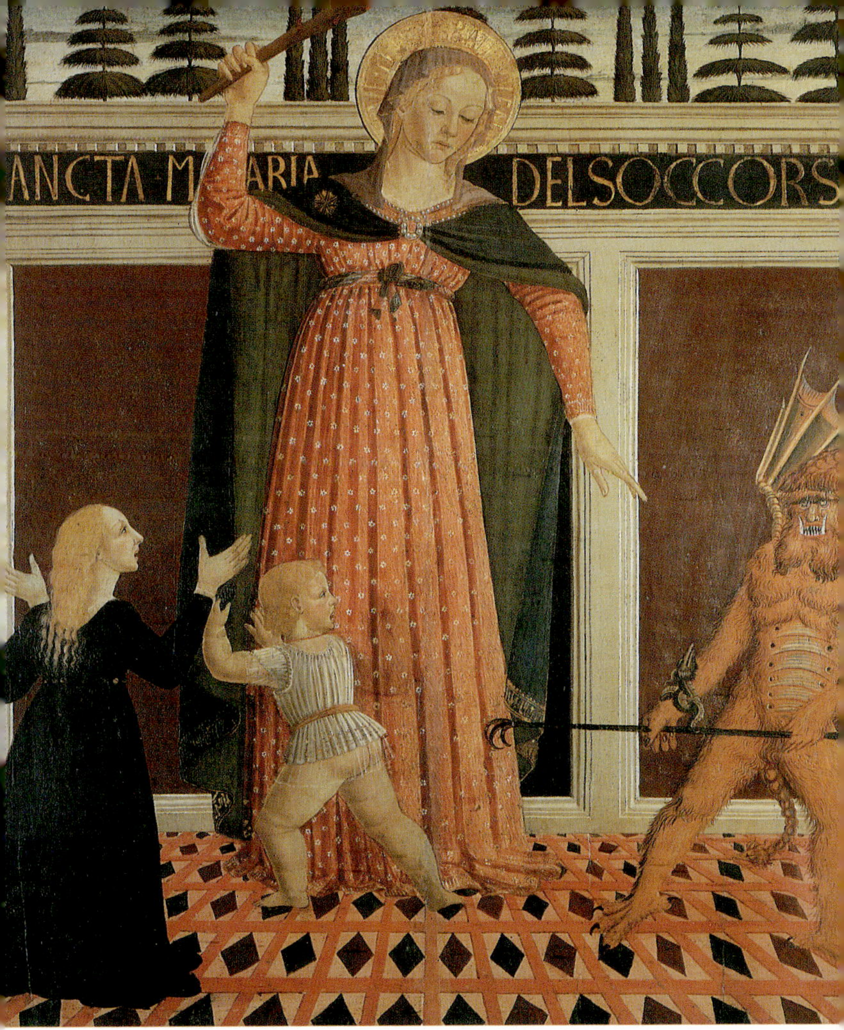
ANCTA·M ARIA DELSOCCORS

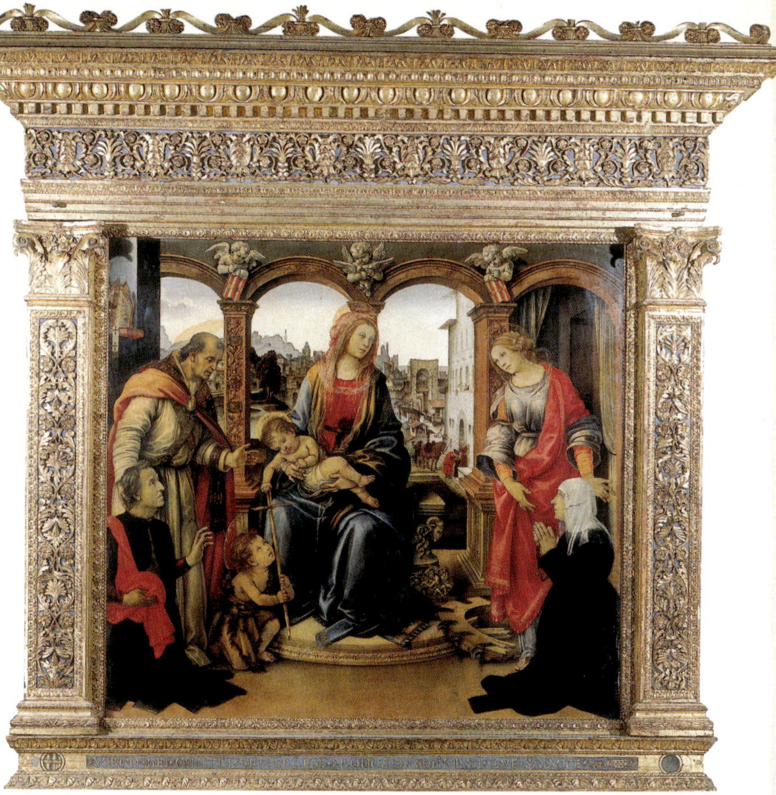

Above and right:
Filippino Lippi, *Madonna and Child, the Infant St. John, St. Catherine and St. Martin of Tours, and the spouses Tanai and Nanna Nerli in prayer*, whole and detail with a view of Porta San Frediano, 1494, tempera on wood, original frame.Santo Spirito, Nerli Chapel.

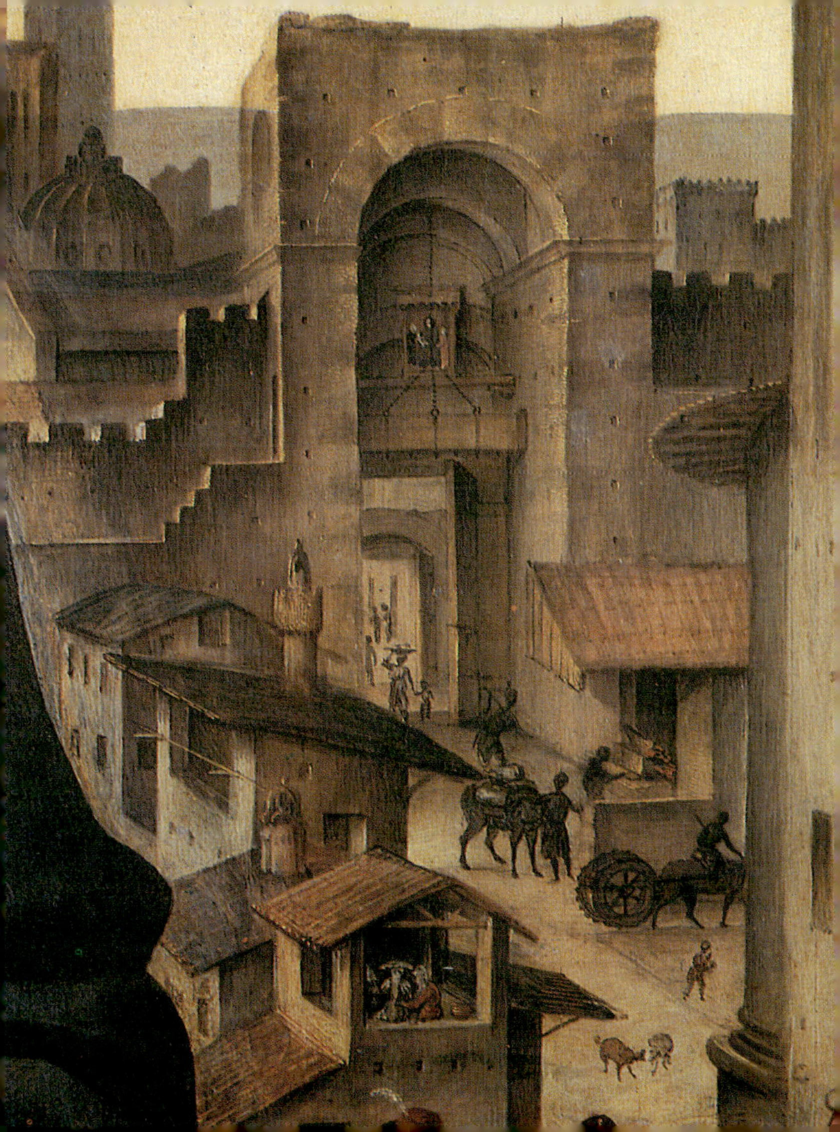

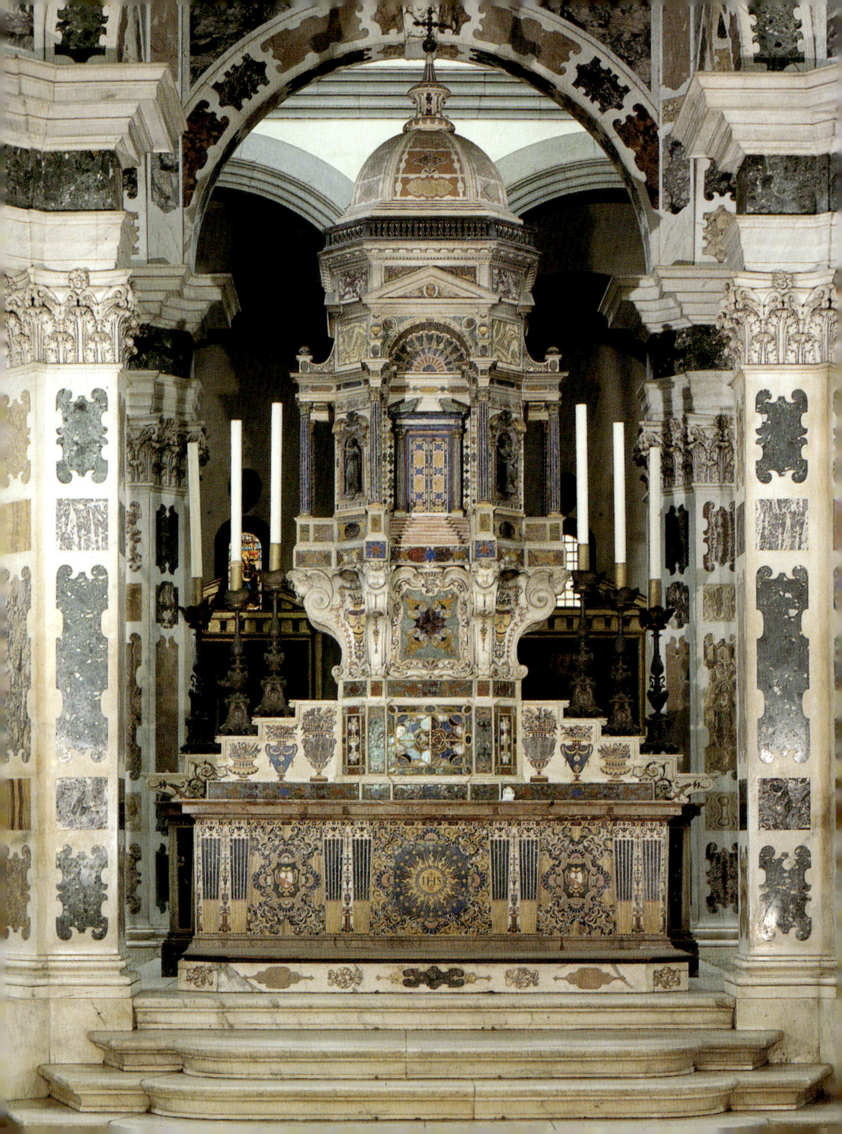

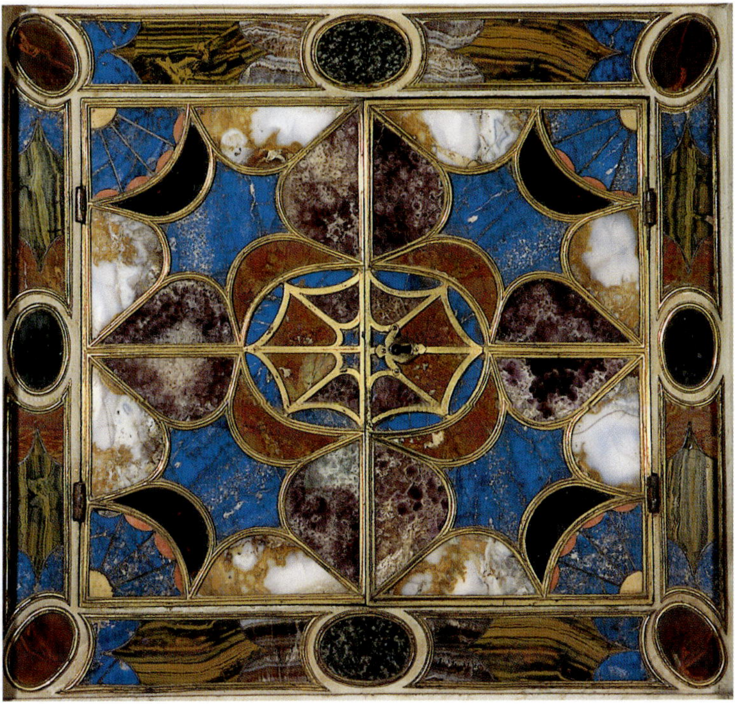

Above and opposite page:
Giovanni Caccini,
Altar and ciborium inlaid with marble and semiprecious stones, whole and detail,
1599-1607, Santo Spirito.

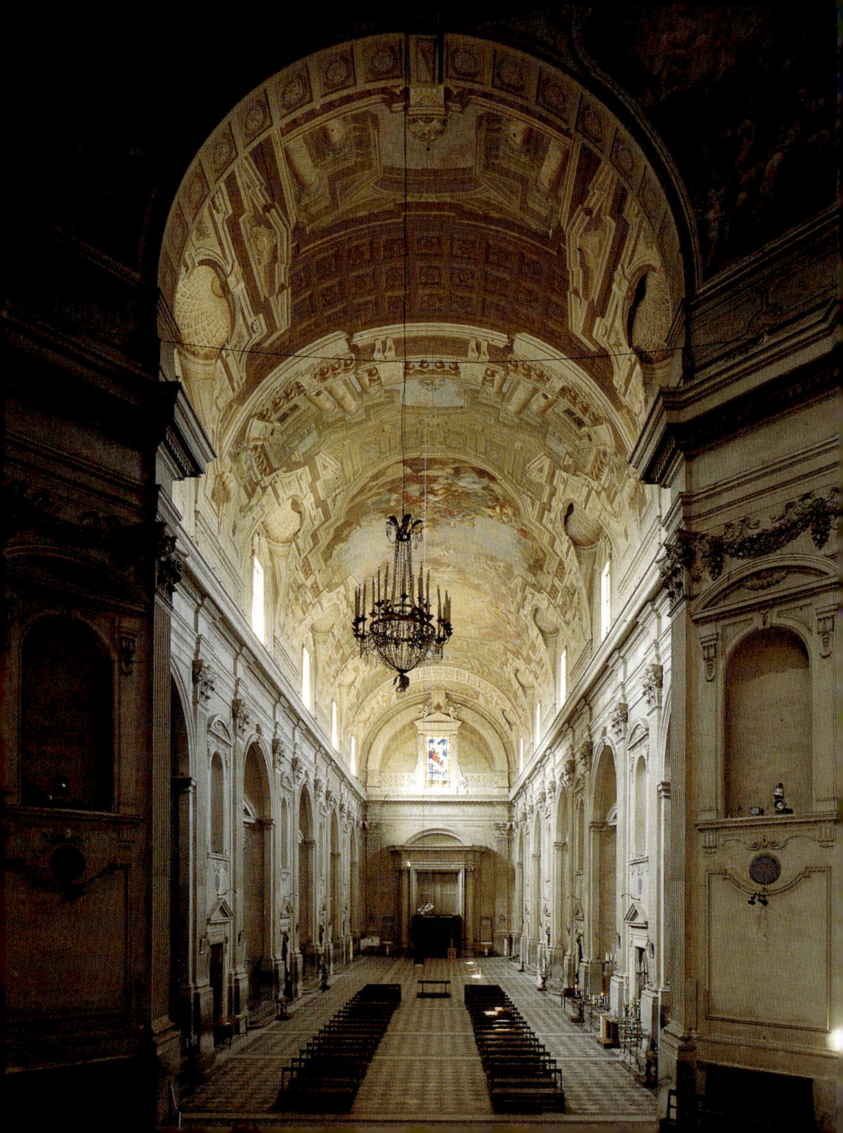

Santa Maria del Carmine

In a vast asymmetrical square looking toward Borgo San Frediano, today invaded by a big parking lot, the church of Santa Maria del Carmine almost risks passing unnoticed, although it is one of the most noteworthy in Florence. In the left wing of the transept, in the Brancacci Chapel, it houses the masterpiece of Masaccio, a cornerstone in the history of art from the early 15th century. It was here that Filippo Lippi (born not far away, in 1406) also painted some of his first works, of which only a few fragments of frescoes remain in the monastery. A recalcitrant monk, little inclined to follow monastic rules, Filippo spent his time, or so the biographers say, studying the frescoes of Masaccio. If we are to believe Vasari, the young monk became so totally absorbed in the work of his ideal master that the spirit of Masaccio seemed to have entered into his body. Also conserved in the Carmine is its famous Florentine Baroque decoration: the Corsini Chapel, designed by Gherardo Silvani (1675-1683), with the cupola frescoed by Luca Giordano, and three marble altarpieces by Giovan Battista Foggini (1683).

Opposite page:
View of the interior of the church
of Santa Maria del Carmine.

HISTORY

Santa Maria del Carmine, where the monks of the Carmelite Order resided, had been founded by Bishop Giovanni Mangiadori in 1268. The building was completed around 1476, and remodeled between the 16th and 17th centuries. In the past the church enjoyed great prestige, also in relation to the history of the quarter, but since it was devasted by fire in 1771, nothing remains of its 15th and 16th century magnificence, of its works of art, except historical testimony, which documents the patronage of dozens of family chapels of the nobility that have been lost (among them a refined *Silver Cross* by Pollaiuolo). The only thing saved from the flames, along with the sacristy and the splendid Baroque chapel of the Corsini family, is the Brancacci Chapel. The present-day church was rebuilt by Giuseppe Ruggieri and Giulio Mannaioni and completed in 1782.

The Carmine is also famous for the popular festivals and the spectacular performances presented by the Compagnia di Santa Maria delle Laudi, on the occasion of Ascension Day: spectacles on which, in the 15th century, it seems that Brunelleschi also collaborated, with ingenious theatrical machines.

Opposite page:
Masaccio, *St. Peter healing the lame,* detail, c. 1424-1425, fresco.
Santa Maria del Carmine,
Brancacci Chapel.

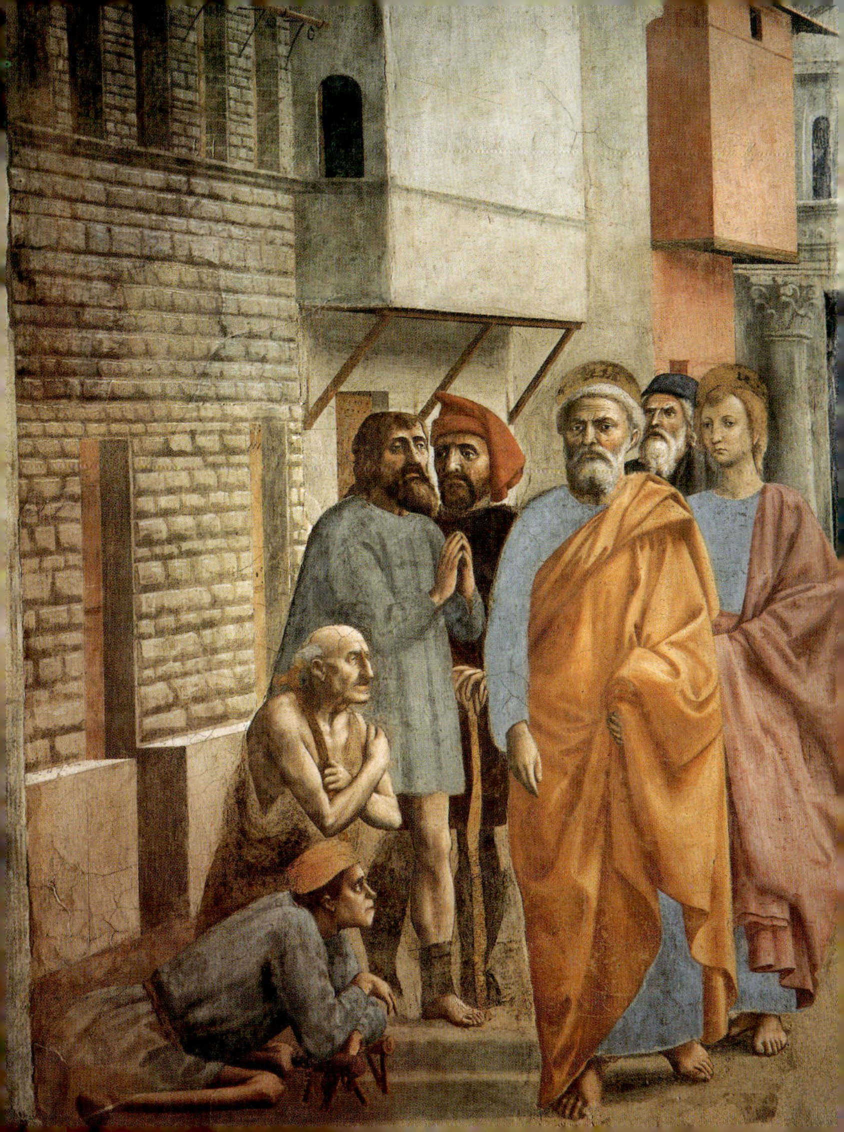

THE BRANCACCI CHAPEL

In the second decade of the 15th century, during the years in which Brunelleschi, a short distance away, was working on the project for the church of Santo Spirito, Masaccio must have been standing on the scaffolding in the Carmine, frescoing, in collaboration with Masolino da Panicale (the artist with whom he painted the *Saint Anne Metterza* now in the Uffizi) the chapel of Felice Brancacci: a vastly rich Florentine, ambassador of the Republic to Cairo, from where he had returned in 1423. Masaccio was perhaps the first among the Florentine artists to represent "the space" of the city: no longer an idealized place, but finally real, with laundry hung out of the windows to dry, a monkey on a leash walking along a cornice (illustrated here in the first pages of the book), passersby stopping to chat, lame men: a representation that even in its realistic approach is not analytical but rather essential. Like Brunelleschi and Donatello, Masaccio too had studied antiquity, and at times evoked in his figures the poses of ancient sculptures, but only partially. In his "trembling nude" appearing in the *Baptism of the Neophytes*, only the torso derives from an *Ares* of the Ludovisi type. Masaccio's neophyte does not appear anatomically perfect, because the posture of the body does not correspond to the original movement of the classical statue. And in the *Tribute* as well, it is only the head of St.

Opposite page:
Masaccio, *"Trembling" nude*, detail from the *Baptism of the neophytes*, c. 1425-1426, fresco. Santa Maria del Carmine, Brancacci Chapel.

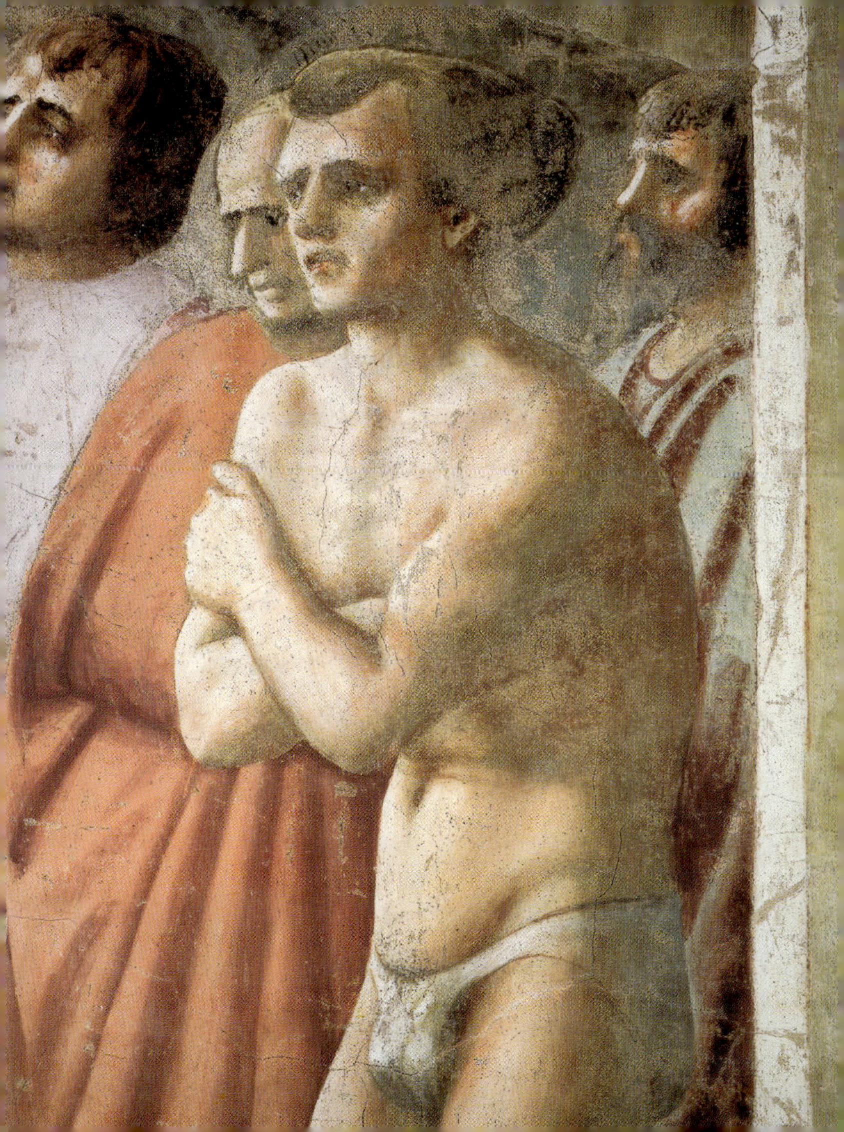

John that testifies to its derivation from antiquity, and not the rest of the body. If we compare the stiff, static progenitors of Masolino's *Original Sin* with the same figures painted as companion pieces by Masaccio on the pilasters of the chapel, in the *Expulsion from the Garden of Eden*, we immediately note Masaccio's revolutionary concept of space, already influenced by Brunelleschi's research, as well as by the new perspective effects achieved by Donatello in the bas-relief of *St. George and the Princess* in Orsanmichele (now in the Bargello). In the church Masaccio also painted a "Sagra" of illustrious men, destroyed in the fire, in which, among other Florentines, Giovanni di Bicci, father of Cosimo de'Medici the Elder, was also portrayed.
Only eight scenes out of the twelve appearing in the chapel were completed by Masaccio and Masolino, who had both left Florence, perhaps already by 1426. It was to be Filippino, between 1481 and 1485, to finish the work, when by now the Brancacci had fallen into disgrace due to their opposition to the Medici.

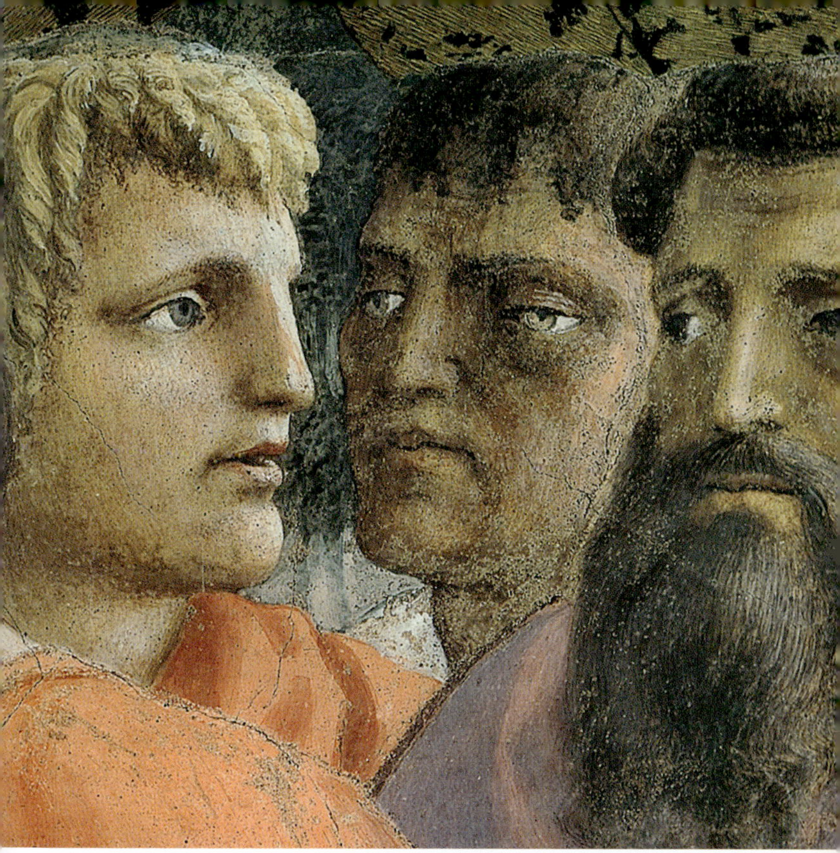

Masaccio, *Tribute*, detail, c. 1424-1425, fresco. Santa Maria del Carmine, Brancacci Chapel.
Following pages: Masolino, *Original Sin*, and Masaccio, *Expulsion from Paradise*, c. 1425-1426, frescoes. Santa Maria del Carmine, Brancacci Chapel.

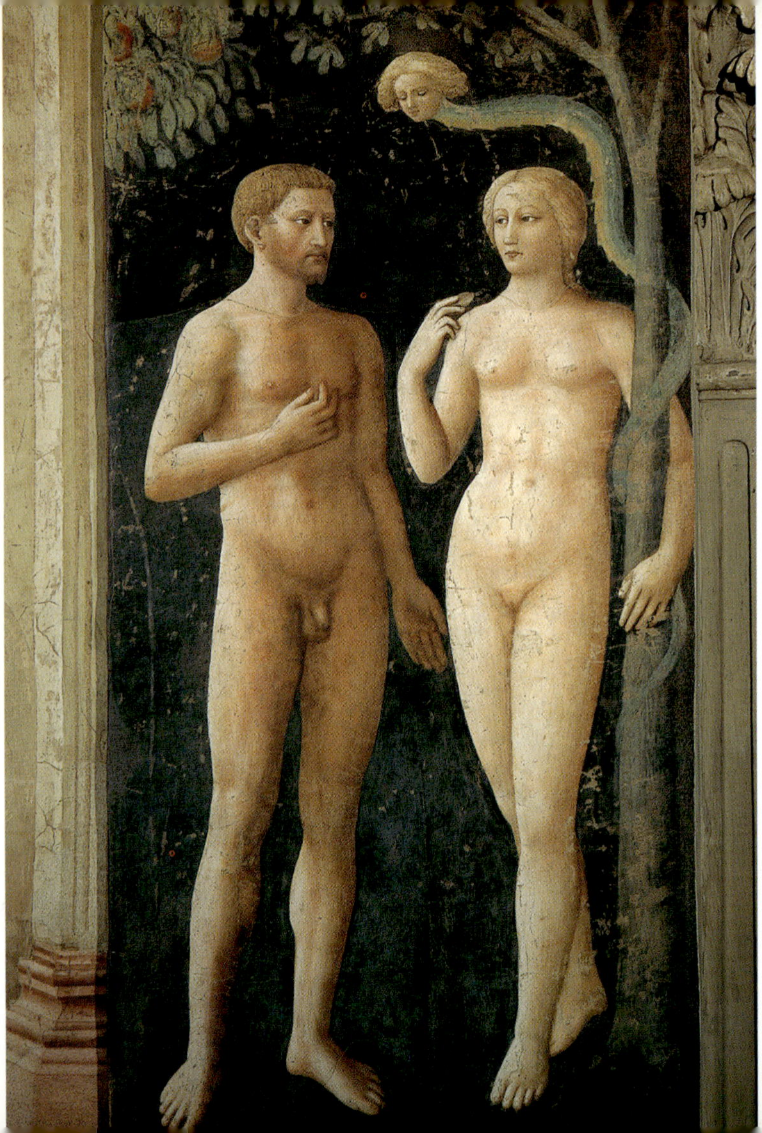

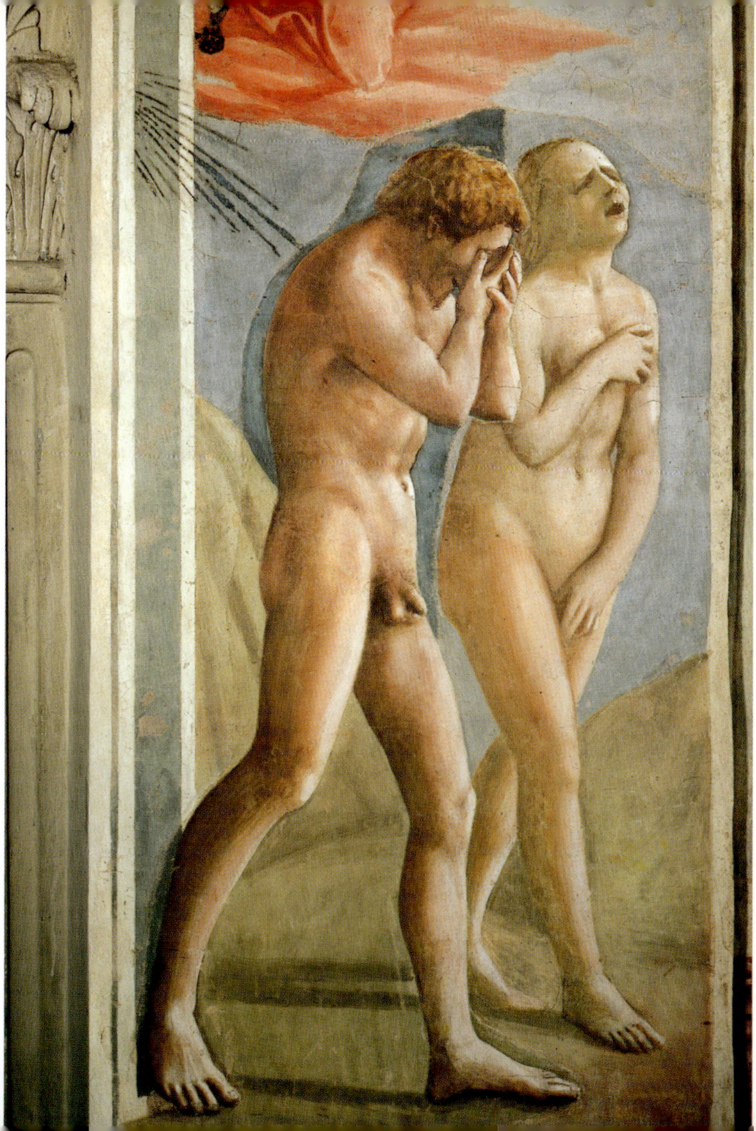

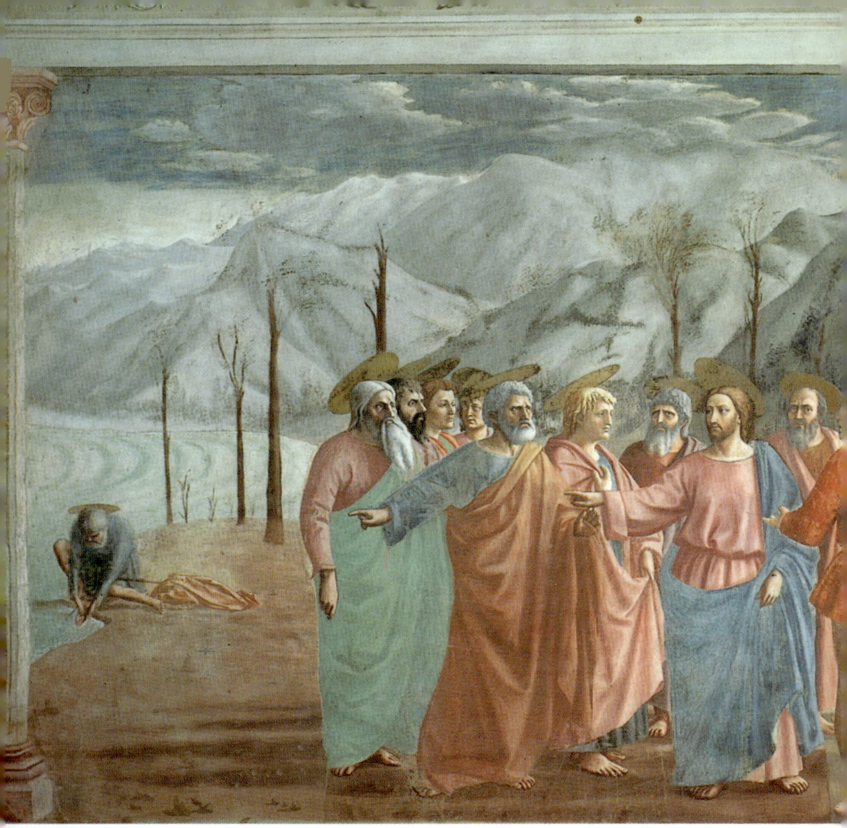

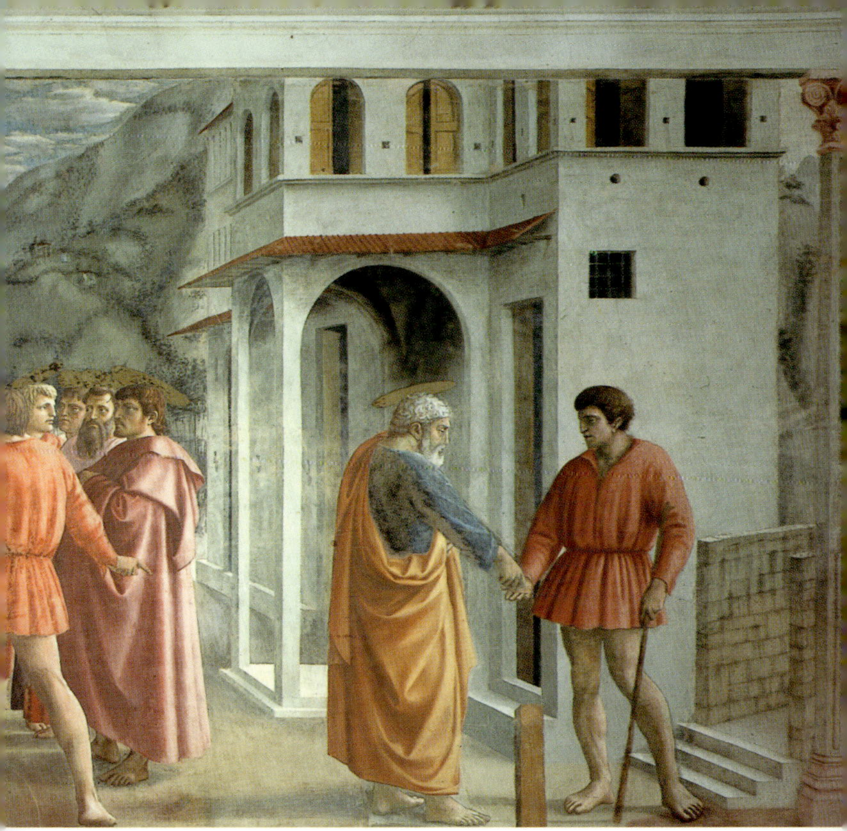

Above:
Masaccio, *Tribute*, c. 1424-1425, fresco.
Santa Maria del Carmine, Brancacci Chapel.

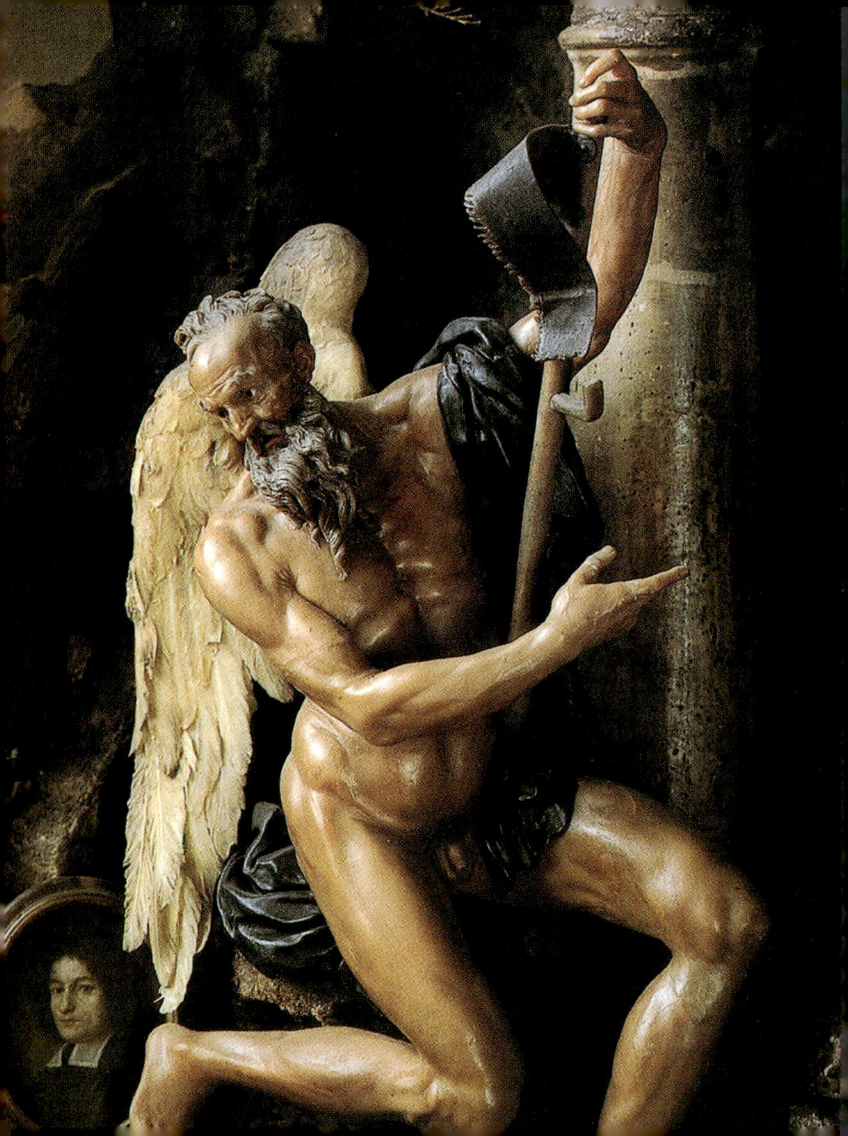

Museo della Specola

At the beginning of Porta Romana, in the ancient Palazzo Torrigiani remodeled by Gaspero Paoletti, the Museo Zoologico della Specola was founded in 1775 by Grand Duke Pietro Leopoldo di Lorena to house the observatory of astronomy and meteorology (the derivation of the name "specola meteorologica"). This was the origin of the Museo di Fisica e Storia Naturale, which was arranged by the scientist Felice Fontana. In 1841, to display Galilean instruments and mementos, Leopoldo II ordered built here the Tribune of Galileo, to the project of Giuseppe Martelli. Today's University Museum contains an exceptional zoological collection and is famous for its anatomical figures made of wax. From the 18th century to 1895, a renowned workshop of scientific ceroplastics was active here, in which worked, among others, Clemente Susini and Luigi Calamai. The museum today still exhibits the even older wax theaters created by the Sicilian Gaetano Zumbo, which evoke, with their crudely realistic details, the *vanitas* of all earthly things: they represent the *Triumph of Time* and the *Corruption of Bodies* (commissioned by Grand Prince Ferdinando), and the *Plague* (purchased by Cosimo III).

Opposite page:
Gaetano Zumbo,
Time, detail
from the *Plague*, last decade
of the 17th century, wax.
Museo della Specola.

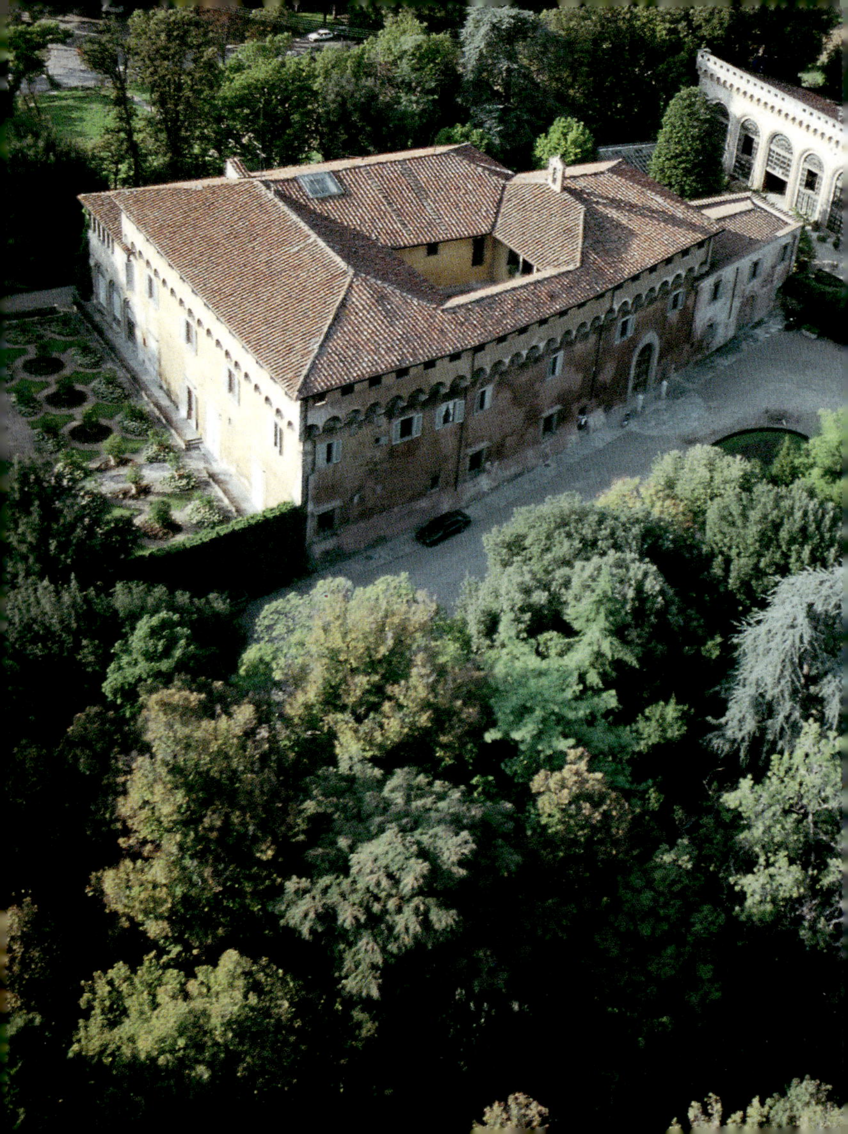

THE SURROUNDINGS

...tecc fono
po leradici eroo
iel bene ssi

e tubi si partissi
te nando ma
europa era dis
europa pello
cipta di fiesole
fond cipta poso
dopo la morte
liuoli E pta
do bele ss
a ma arcca
tato. Gurato
treccia pose
a disfatta.
amossi troya
a poso mo
istola
dadamo i sino
nto cusepio
a cqbella de

epp. secho
anni. Clx

nsono anni
olo pbuone
do.
corsono anni

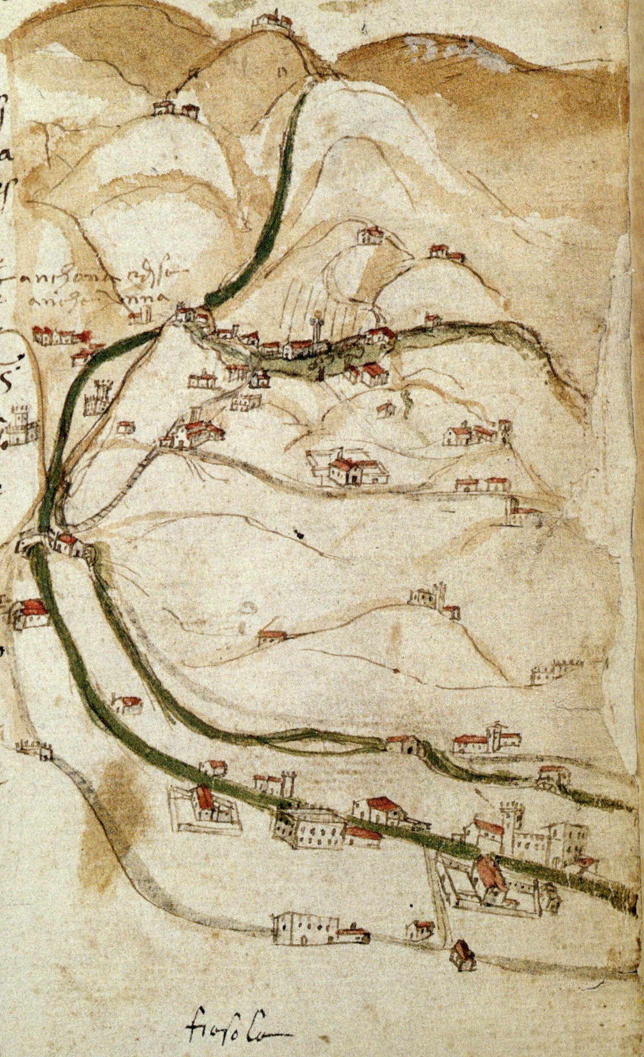

This brief appendix is dedicated to the main places of historic and artistic interest found in the immediate vicinity of Forence. It also includes a list, albeit minimal, of other monuments and museums located in the city which have not been previously mentioned due to lack of space.

The list includes:

- in the city: the Diocese Museum of Santo Stefano al Ponte, the Anthropological Museum, the Alberto della Ragione Museum of Contemporary Art, and the Stibbert Museum. The churches of Sant'Ambrogio, Sant'Egidio, San Felice in Piazza, San Frediano in Cestello, San Giovannino degli Scolopi, San Giovannino dei Cavalieri, Santa Maria Maddalena dei Pazzi, San Michele in Visdomini, Santa Maria Maggiore, Santi Michele e Gaetano, and Sant'Jacopo sopr'Arno.
- on the hill of Fiesole: the Badia Fiorentina and the monastery of San Domenico, the Roman theater and the Archaeological Museum, the Cathedral of San Romolo and the Bandini Museum.
- at Pratolino: the villa and Medicean park of Villa Demidoff.
- the Certosa del Galluzzo.
- the Medicean villas of Castello, Petraia and Poggio a Caiano.
- At Sesto Fiorentino: the Porcelain Museum of Doccia.

Opposite page:
The ancient road to Fiesole, from the *Codice* of Marco di Bartolomeo Rustici, 1475. San Frediano in Cestello, Biblioteca del Seminario Maggiore.

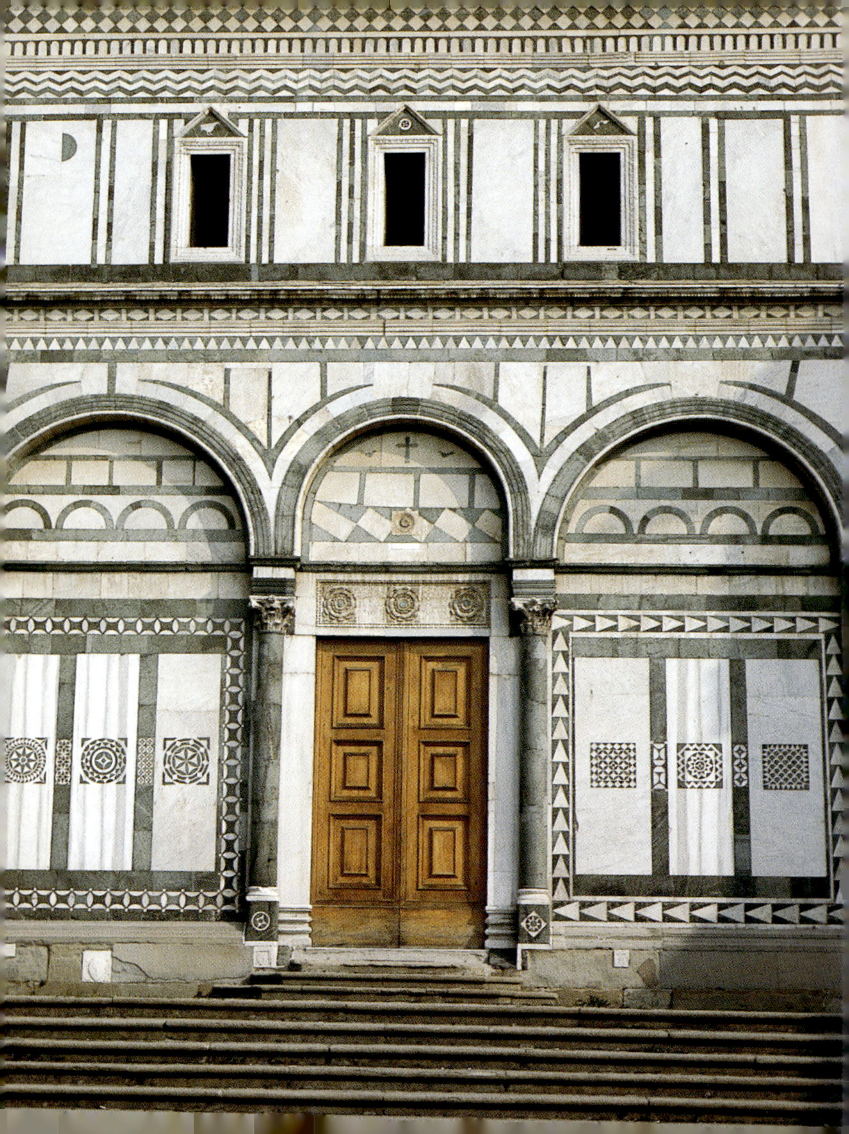

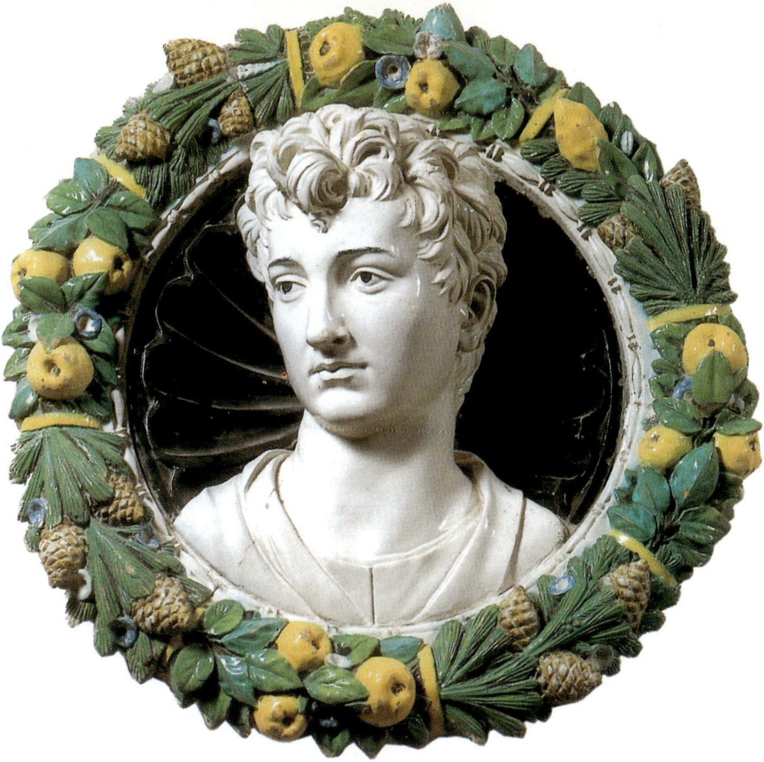

Opposite page:
Badia Fiesolana, façade.
San Domenico di Fiesole.

Above:
Andrea della Robbia, *Tondo*,
c. 1500. Fiesole, Museo Bandini.

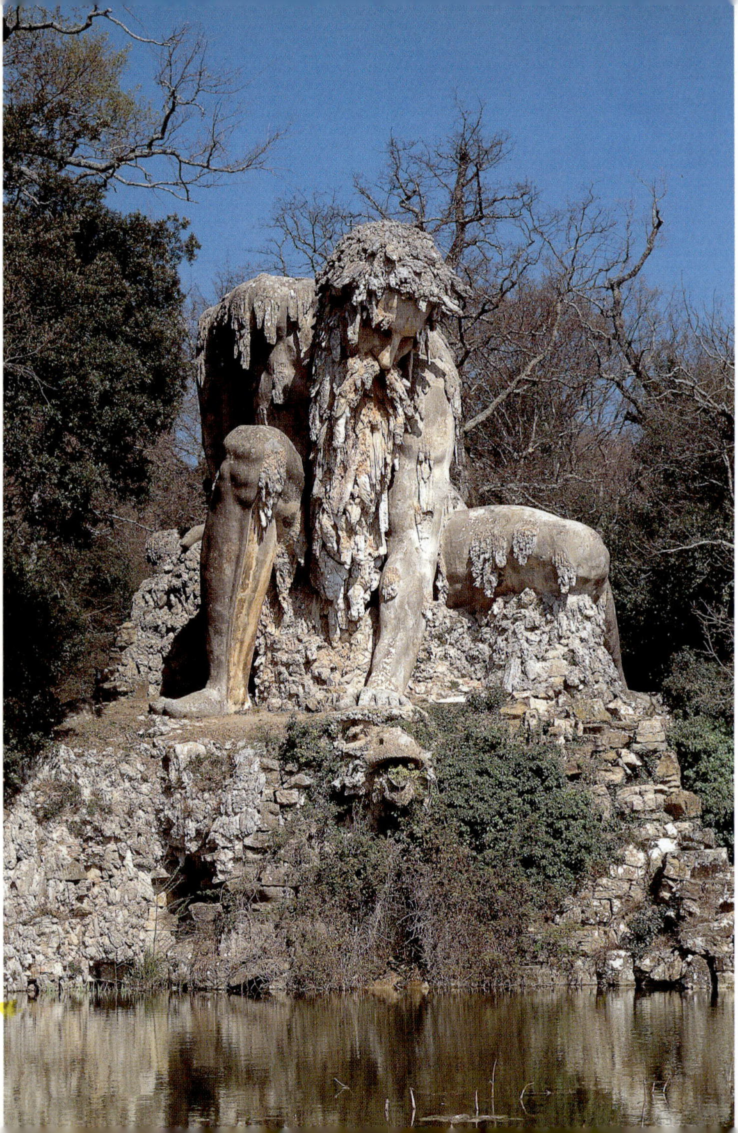

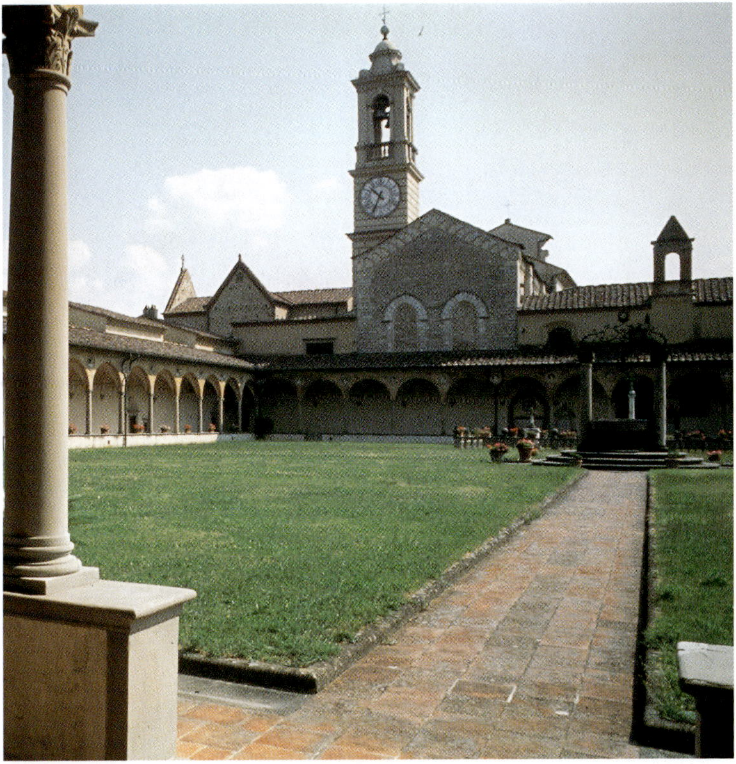

Opposite page:
Giambologna, *The Giant Appennino*, 1580. Pratolino (Florence), Villa Demidoff.

Above:
View of the Cloister and the Church. Galluzzo, Certosa.

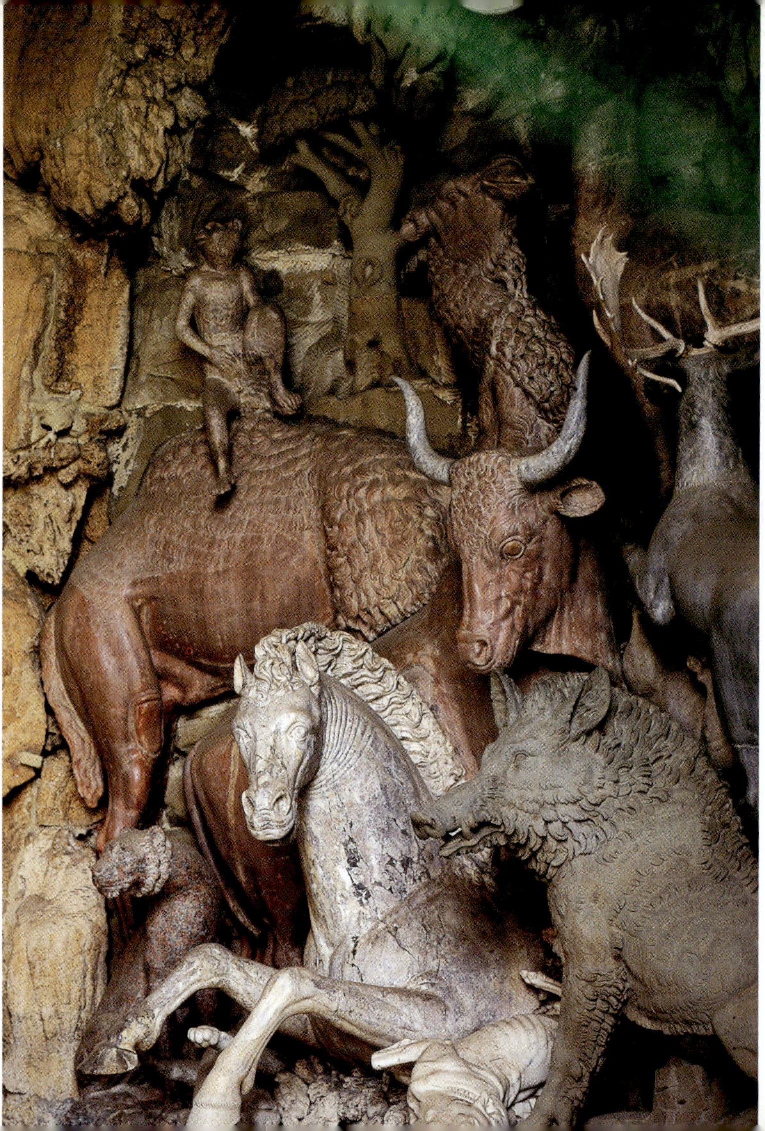

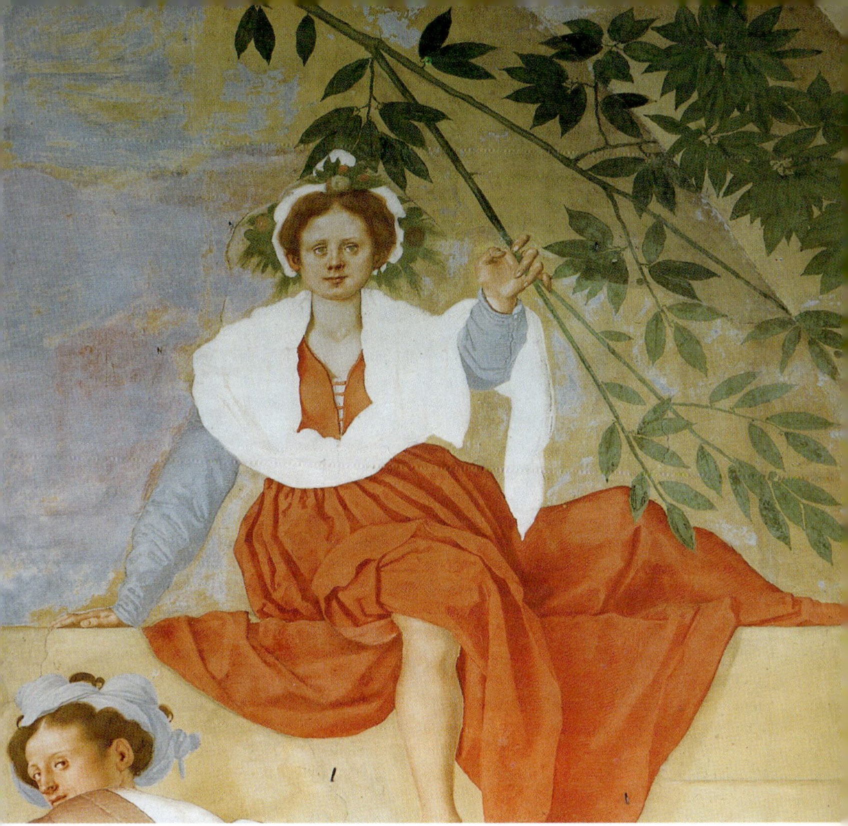

Opposite page:
Bernardo Buontalenti,
Grotto,
1580.
Castello, villa Medicea.

Above:
Pontormo, *Pomona*,
1519-1520, detail, fresco.
Poggio a Caiano (Prato),
villa Medicea.

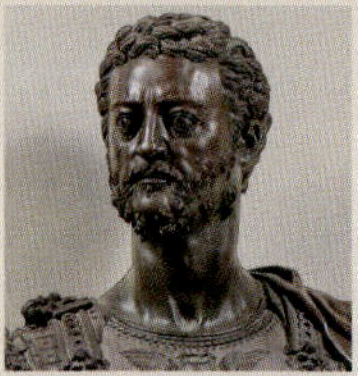

Cosimo I (1519-1574)

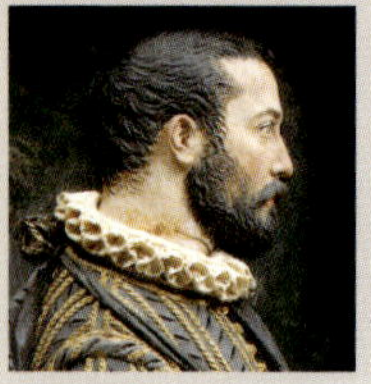

Francesco I (1541-1587)

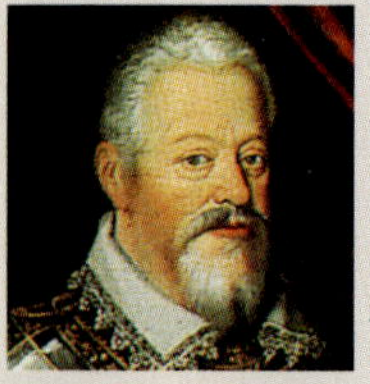

Ferdinando I (1549-1609)

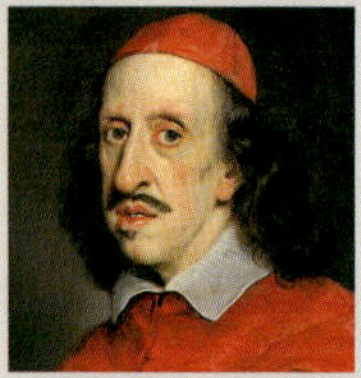

Leopoldo (1617-1675)

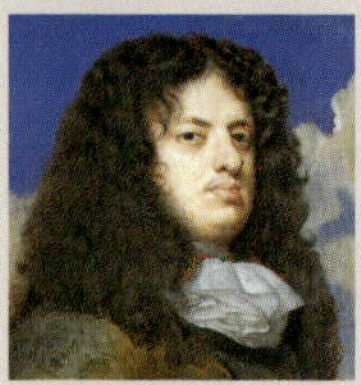

Cosimo III (1642-1723)

Cosimo il Vecchio (1389-1464) «Father of the Patria», m. Contessina dei Bardi († 1473)

Piero the Gouty (1416-1469), m. Lucrezia Tornabuoni (1425?-1482)

Filippo († 1464)

Lorenzo the Magnificent (1449-1492), m. Clarice Orsini (1451-1488)

Giuliano (1453-1478), murdered in the Pazzi conspiracy

Giulio (natural son; 1478-1534), from 1523 Pope Clement VII

Piero II (1471-1503), m. Alfonsina Orsini (1472-1520)

Giovanni (1475-1521), from 1513 Pope Leo X

Lorenzo II (1492-1519), Duke of Urbino, m. Maddalena de la Tour d'Auvergne (1501-1519)

Alessandro (1510-1537; officially natural son of Lorenzo II; in reality son of Giulio, future Pope Clement VII), first Duke of Florence from 1532, m. Margherita, natural daughter of Charles V

Caterina (1519-1589), m. Henri II King of France

Genealogy of the Medici Family

GIOVANNI DI AVERARDO
(1360-1429), m. di Piccarda
di Odoardo Bueri († 1432)

Lorenzo (1395-1440),
m. Ginevra Cavalcanti

Giovanni (1421 ca.-1463),
m. di Ginevra
degli Albizzi

Carlo
(natural son; 1428-1492)

Pier Francesco (1430-1475),
m. Laudomia Acciaiuoli of
the Dukes of Athens

Lorenzo (1463-1503),
Lord of Piombino,
m. Semiramide Appiani

Giovanni (1467-1498),
2nd hus. of Caterina Sforza

Pier Francesco (1487-1525),
m. Maria Soderini

Ludovico, known as Giovanni
delle Bande Nere (1498-1526),
m. Maria Salviati

Giuliano (1479-1516),
Duke of Nemours,
m. Filiberta of Savoia
(1498-1524)

Lorenzino (1514-1548),
murderer of Duke
Alessandro

Cosimo I (1519-1574),
Grand Duke of Tuscany from
1569, m. Eleonora di Toledo
and Camilla Martelli

Ippolito (natural son;
1511-1535), Cardinal

Francesco I
Grand Duke (1541-1587),
m. Joan of Austria
and Bianca Cappello

Giovanni
(1543-1562),
Cardinal from 1560

Ferdinando I
Grand Duke (1549-1609),
m. Christine
of Lorraine

Antonio
(1576-1621)

Maria (1573-1642),
m. Henri IV King
of France and Navarre

Carlo
(1596-1666)
Cardinal from 1615

Cosimo II Grand Duke
(1590-1621), m. Maria
Maddalena d'Austria

Giovan Carlo
(1611-1663)
dal 1645 cardinale

Ferdinando II Grand Duke
(1610-1670), m. Vittoria
della Rovere

Leopoldo (1617-1675),
Cardinal from 1667, founder
of the Accademia del Cimento

Cosimo III Grand Duke
(1642-1723) , m.
Marguerite Louise d'Orléans

Ferdinando (1663-1713),
Grand Prince,
m. Beatrice Violante
of Bavaria

Giangastone Grand Duke
(1671-1737), m. Anna
Maria of Julius, Duke
of Saxony Lauenburg

Anna Maria Luisa
(1667-1743),
m. Johann Wilhelm
Palatine Elector

INDEX OF ARTISTS

Photographs

All the photographs are from the Giunti Archives, taken by the following photographers: Stefano Giraldi, Nicola Grifoni, Antonio Quattrone, Marco Rabatti-Serge Domingie.
In addition: Corbis: 75; Foto Scala: 104, 178, 249, 278-279; 526, 528, 529; photo Rabatti & Domingie: 111, 261; Saulo Bambi, Museo della Specola: 112; Archivi Alinari: 183; photo Rabatti & Domingie: 111, 261; Maria Brunori: 257, 264; Franca Principe, Istituto e Museo di Storia della Scienza: 370, 372, 373; Archivio Giovanni Breschi: 554.

The works found in State Galleries and Museums have been reproduced by permission of the Ministry of Culture.